Mary Campbell

# The Microsoft Access Handbook

**Osborne McGraw-Hill**
Berkeley New York St. Louis San Francisco Auckland Bogotá Hamburg London Madrid Mexico City Milan Montreal New Delhi Panama City Paris São Paulo Singapore Sydney Tokyo Toronto

Osborne **McGraw-Hill**
2600 Tenth Street
Berkeley, California 94710
U.S.A.

For information on software, translations, or book distributors outside of the U.S.A., please write to Osborne **McGraw-Hill** at the above address.

**The Microsoft Access Handbook**



234567890 DOC 9987654

ISBN 0-07-882014-6

# Contents at a Glance

## IV Macros and Programming



## V Network and Administrative Topics



## VI Appendixes

# Contents

## 3 DEFINING PROPERTIES AND RELATIONSHIPS 61

## III Forms and Reports

## IV Macros and Programming

## VI Appendixes

**D NOTES FOR SQL USERS 701**



**E TOOLBAR REFERENCE 709**



**F LIMITS IN MICROSOFT ACCESS 731**

## About the Author ...

Renowned author Mary Campbell has written numerous best-selling books on computing, including **Access Inside and Out**, **1-2-3 Release 2.4 Made Easy**, **1-2-3 Release 3.4: The Complete Reference**, **Quicken 3 for Windows Made Easy**, **QuickBooks for Windows: Making the Numbers Work**, and several books on WordPerfect.

She is an experienced computer trainer who has taught computer skills to end users in both large corporations and small business. Respected throughout the industry for her wisdom and expertise, she is often among the first testers to receive beta versions of new computer software.

# Acknowledgments

I would like to thank Cedar Point Amusement Park/Resort in Sandusky, Ohio, for the pictures of the roller coasters in the book. I also appreciate the helpful information they supplied on the 100 years of roller coasters at the park and their construction and operation. Cedar Point has ten roller coasters, more than any amusement park in the world. Special thanks to Robin Innes of Cedar Point Amusement Park/Resort for his help in getting the material we needed during the park's busy summer season. For more information on park hours for the 1994 season, you can call (419) 628-0830.

I would like to thank Gabrielle Lawrence and Elizabeth Reinhardt for all their work on the project.

Special thanks to the many individuals at Microsoft who helped with this project, especially Tracy Van Hoof.

All of the staff at Osborne played an important role in completing this project. Jeff Pepper was a great help in securing the needed beta and making arrangements for the special photographs needed for the book. Vicki Van Ausdall and Edith Rex were also helpful in coordinating all the pieces of this large project as we worked against grave deadlines. Helena Worsley did a meticulous job typesetting this book and all the dedicated staff members in the production department at Osborne helped make this tightly scheduled project as painless as possible.

# Introduction

Microsoft is the industry leader in providing application software for the Windows environment. Since they are the developers of Windows itself and have many years of experience with this environment, their leadership position in application software for the Windows platform is not surprising. The new Access data management software has many innovative features that will help it to become the leading Windows data management program.

Access database management software has been many years in development. It is designed for users who want to take full advantage of the Windows environment for their database management tasks while remaining end users and leaving the programming to others. Access supports Object Linking and Embedding (OLE) and dynamic data exchange (DDE), the ability to incorporate text and graphics in a form or report. The product provides a graphical user interface (GUI) like one you would expect from any leading product in this market. Reports, forms, and queries are easy to design and execute. For individuals with a technical slant, you'll appreciate the macro and programming capabilities of this full-featured product. Access Basic is the programming language supported, which some users may have already mastered by using Quick Basic. Access version 2 introduces several new features that make data management easier as well as expand the programming features and the behind-the-scenes processing you can add to forms and reports.

## About This Book

*The Microsoft Access Handbook* is designed for every Access user. A new user will probably want to start at the beginning of the book and read the chapters in the first few parts before skipping to specific topics at the end. Intermediate and advanced users will probably want to skip to the exact information that they need to solve the problem at hand.

This book provides the essential information that you will need on each topic. It provides the necessary steps to duplicate complicated actions quickly. The examples are designed to be practical business applications with as much high-interest material as possible. This book has numerous examples that show creative screen and report designs.

## How This Book Is Organized

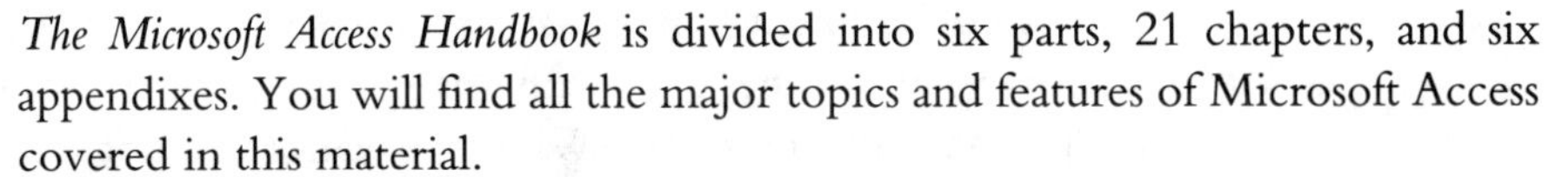

*The Microsoft Access Handbook* is divided into six parts, 21 chapters, and six appendixes. You will find all the major topics and features of Microsoft Access covered in this material.

Part I introduces you to basic features. In Chapter 1 you learn about the new terminology for Access and the database components, and you get an overview of what the product does. In Chapter 2 you learn how to design an Access database and its associated tables. You can use the Table Wizard or create the tables from scratch. You learn what field types to use for each type of information that you want to store. In Chapter 3 you learn how to customize the basic tables by changing field properties, relationships, and indexes. In Chapter 4 you learn how to enter and edit data. Chapter 5 shows you how to capitalize on any data entry investment you have already made as you import and export data, using the applications in the Microsoft Office suite as examples.

Part II focuses on queries, which are used to answer questions about the database data as you view a subset of the records. In Chapter 6 you learn how to design queries and filters that select data. In Chapter 7 you create more sophisticated queries that access multiple tables, compute query totals, and produce cross tabs.

Part III covers forms and reports. In Chapter 8 you learn how to create a custom form with AutoForm and the Form Wizards. In Chapter 9 you learn how to create, name, save, and print a basic report using AutoReport and the Report Wizards. Chapters 10 and 11 cover customizing forms and reports with controls and other settings. In Chapter 12 you learn how to use the Expression Builder to create expressions in reports and forms to compute a field on a form or report or compute totals across records. Chapter 13 focuses on using multiple tables in reports and forms. In Chapter 14 you learn how to use fonts, color, 3D, and special effects. Chapter 15 shows you how to use Object Linking and Embedding (OLE) to add pictures, charts, and objects that have been created in other programs, such as Microsoft Graph, to your forms and reports.

Part IV covers macros and modules, which allow you to automate tasks. Chapter 16 introduces you to basic macro concepts and options. Chapter 17 provides some examples of using macros in forms and reports. Chapter 18 shows you how to create a custom application as well as discusses Access add-ins you will want to use. Chapter 19 introduces programming with Access Basic.

Part V covers network and administrative topics. Chapter 20 covers editing data in a multiuser environment and other special considerations for network users. Chapter 21 is a network administrator's guide for Access covering security settings, customization settings, backup considerations, and recovery and compaction procedures.

Part VI contains all of the appendixes for this book.

## Conventions Used in This Book

Throughout the book, menu selections and dialog box options are shown with underlined letters to indicate which letter you type to activate a menu or make a selection from it.

Although this book is not a tutorial, there are some examples of how to complete data entry. The data to be entered is shown in bold.

When keys are to be pressed in combination, they are joined with a plus sign, as in CTRL+HOME. Keys to be pressed sequentially, one after the other, are joined with a comma (,), as in HOME, DOWN ARROW.

# I

# Creating Access Databases

# Chapter 1

What Is an Access Database?

Requirements for Using Access

Acquiring the Basic Skills

# Introduction to Access

MICROSOFT Access is a powerful, yet user-friendly database management system for Windows. It provides standard data management features for data storage and retrieval but uses graphical tools made possible by the Windows environment to make tasks easier to perform.

Microsoft Access' new terminology and wide array of features may seem a little overwhelming at first. This book is designed to put you at ease and explain the terminology and features that you need to be productive immediately, even if this is the first database that you have used. This chapter introduces the basic components of the package and provides general instructions that will work in any part of the package.

## What Is an Access Database?

Like other database management systems, Access provides a way to store and manage information. Microsoft refers to Access as a *relational database product* because Access allows you to relate data from different sources. Although the package may not meet some other components of a true relational database, we will consider it to be such for the purposes of this book. If you are interested in reading more rigorous descriptions of relational databases, look at one of the several college textbooks available on database management or consult C.J. Date's *Database: A Primer* or James Martin's *Principles of Database Management.*

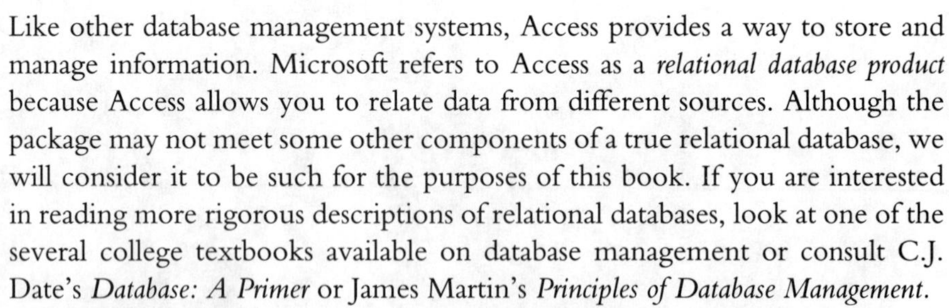

Access considers both the tables of data that store your information and the supplemental objects that present information and work with it to be part of the database. This differs from standard database system terminology, in which only the data itself is considered part of the database. For example, when you use a package such as dBASE IV, you might have an employee database, a client database, and a supplier database. Each of the databases are separate files. You would have additional files in your dBASE directory for reports and forms that work with the database. With Access you could have all three types of information in one database along with the accompanying reports and forms. All of the data and other database objects would be stored in one file in the same fashion as an R:Base database.

Access stores data in tables that are organized by rows and columns. A database can contain one table or many. Other objects such as reports, forms, queries, macros, and program modules are considered to be part of the database along with the tables. You can have these other objects in the database along with the tables—either including them from the beginning or adding them as you need them.

The basic requirement for a database is that you have at least one table. All other objects are optional. Storing the related objects in the same file as the table makes it easy to organize everything you need in one place with one filename, which expedites making the crucial backups needed to safeguard your data investments. While this approach means improved relational integrity between database components, it also has some drawbacks—such as lengthier and more difficult data recovery and database optimization.

Since an Access database can contain many tables and other objects, it is possible to create one database that will meet the information requirements for an entire company. You can build this database gradually, adding information and reports for various application areas as you have time. You can define relationships between pieces of information in tables.

You can have more than one database in Access. Each database has its own tables and other objects. You can use the move and copy features of this package to move and copy objects from one database to another, although you can only work with one database at a time.

As you build more sophisticated systems, you will use all of the objects that Access supports. For now, a quick look at each component will show you the building blocks that you can use as you create your own databases.

## Tables

Tables are tabular arrangements of information. *Columns* represent *fields* of information, or one particular piece of information that can be stored for each entity in the table. The *rows* of the table contain the records. A *record* contains one of each field in the database. Although a field can be left blank, each record in the database has the potential for storing information in each field in the table. Figure 1-1 shows some of the fields and records in an Access table.

Generally each major type of information in the database is represented by a table. You might have a Supplier table, a Client table, and an Employee table.

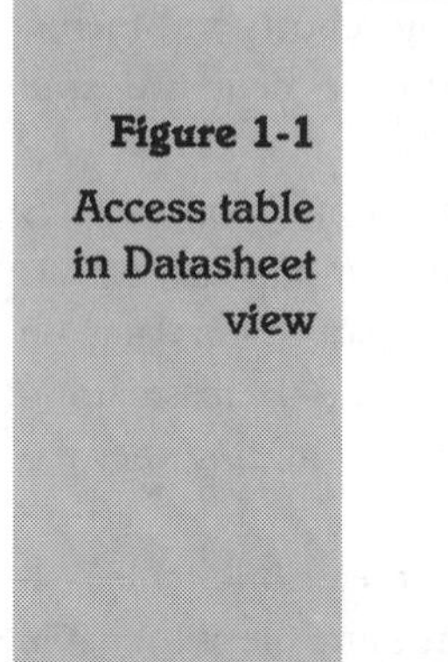

**Figure 1-1** Access table in Datasheet view

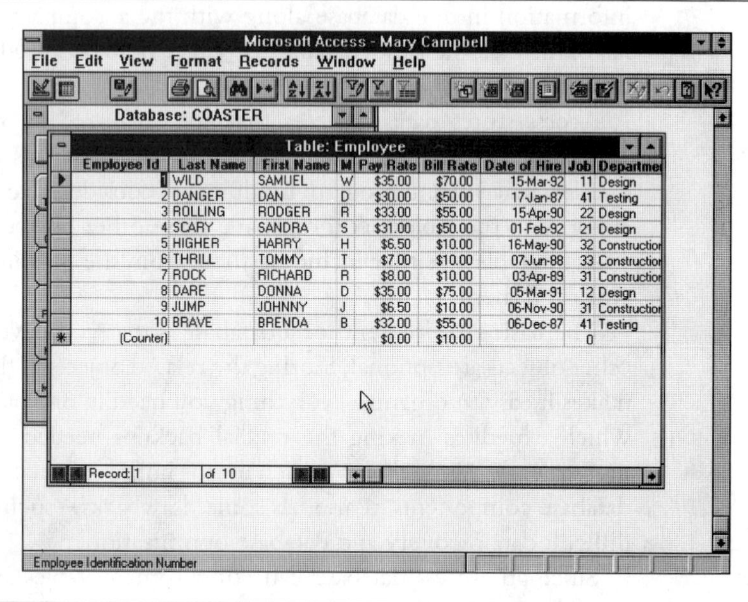


| Employee Id | Last Name | First Name | M | Pay Rate | Bill Rate | Date of Hire | Job | Departme |
|---|---|---|---|---|---|---|---|---|
| 1 | WILD | SAMUEL | W | $35.00 | $70.00 | 15-Mar-92 | 11 | Design |
| 2 | DANGER | DAN | D | $30.00 | $50.00 | 17-Jan-87 | 41 | Testing |
| 3 | ROLLING | RODGER | R | $33.00 | $55.00 | 15-Apr-90 | 22 | Design |
| 4 | SCARY | SANDRA | S | $31.00 | $50.00 | 01-Feb-92 | 21 | Design |
| 5 | HIGHER | HARRY | H | $6.50 | $10.00 | 16-May-90 | 32 | Constructio |
| 6 | THRILL | TOMMY | T | $7.00 | $10.00 | 07-Jun-88 | 33 | Constructio |
| 7 | ROCK | RICHARD | R | $8.00 | $10.00 | 03-Apr-89 | 31 | Constructio |
| 8 | DARE | DONNA | D | $35.00 | $75.00 | 05-Mar-91 | 12 | Design |
| 9 | JUMP | JOHNNY | J | $6.50 | $10.00 | 06-Nov-90 | 31 | Constructio |
| 10 | BRAVE | BRENDA | B | $32.00 | $55.00 | 06-Dec-87 | 41 | Testing |
| (Counter) | | | | $0.00 | $10.00 | | 0 | |

It is unlikely that such dissimilar information would be placed together in the same table, although this information is all part of the same database.

Other considerations determine how you group data into tables. For example, you try to eliminate any duplicate data (referred to as *data redundancy*). You would avoid a database design that requires the same information to be entered multiple times; for example, you should separate tables for client information and orders rather than maintaining only one table and duplicating client data in multiple order records.

Access version 2 has a new Table Wizard that makes table creation easy. When you use the Wizard to build a table, you can select fields from one or more sample tables. This feature can provide a starting point for table design that you can revise to meet your exact needs with a minimal investment of time.

Access allows you to define relationships between fields in various tables. With Access version 2, defining relationships is easier than ever, because you can visually connect data in the various tables by dragging fields between them. Using the associations you establish, you can show data from more than one table on the screen or in a report.

Access provides two different views for tables. The *Design view*, shown in Figure 1-2, is used when you are defining the fields that store the data in the table. For each field in the table you define the field name and data type. You can also set field properties to change the field format and caption (used for the fields on reports and forms), provide validation rules to check data validity, create index entries for the field, and provide a default value.

In the *Datasheet view,* you can enter data into fields or look at existing records in the table. Figures 1-1 and 1-2 show the same Employee table—Figure 1-1 presents the Datasheet view of it and Figure 1-2 shows the Design view.

## Queries

Access supports different kinds of queries: *select, crosstab,* and *action queries.* You can also create *parameters* that let you customize the query each time you use it. Select queries choose records from a table and display them in a temporary table called a *dynaset.* Crosstab queries provide a concise summary view of data in a spreadsheet format. The four types of action queries (described later in this chapter) let you perform actions using data in tables.

If you have defined relationships between tables, a query can recognize the relationships and combine data from multiple tables in the query's result, which is called a dynaset. If the relationships are not defined, you can still associate data in related tables by joining them when you design the query.

Queries can include *calculated fields.* These fields do not actually exist in any permanent table, but display the results of calculations that use the contents of one or more fields. Queries that use calculated fields let you derive more

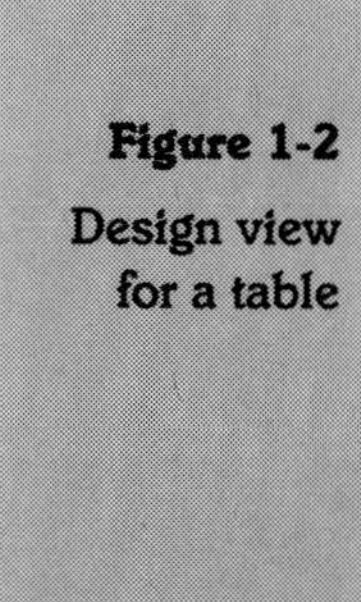

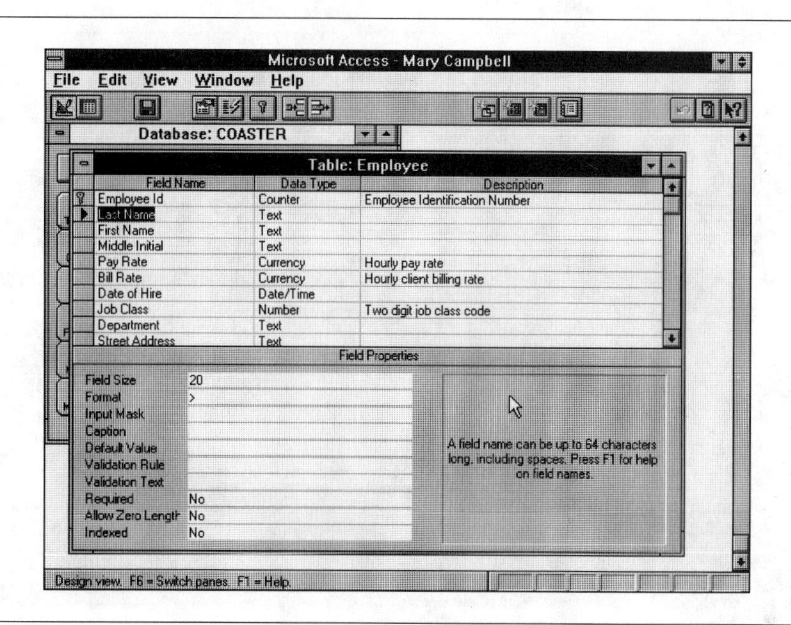


**Figure 1-2** Design view for a table

meaningful information from the data you record in your tables, such as year-end totals for sales and expenditures.

Access version 2 offers a new method for creating queries—the Query Wizards. The Query Wizards can guide you through the steps of creating some common, but more complicated, types of queries.

## SELECT QUERIES

Select queries are essentially questions that ask Access about the entries in tables. When most database users think of queries, select queries are the type that come to mind. You can create queries with a QBE (Query-by-Example) grid. The entries you make in this grid tell Access which fields and records you want to appear in a temporary table—the dynaset—that shows the query results. You can use complicated combinations of criteria to define your needs and see only the records that you need. Figure 1-3 shows the entries in the QBE grid that will select the records you want. This QBE grid includes a Sort row that allows you to specify the order of records in the resulting dynaset.

## CROSSTAB QUERIES

Crosstab queries let you display the data retrieved from tables in a format that is easier to understand, similar to a spreadsheet. When you use a crosstab query, you designate one field that provides column headings and another field that

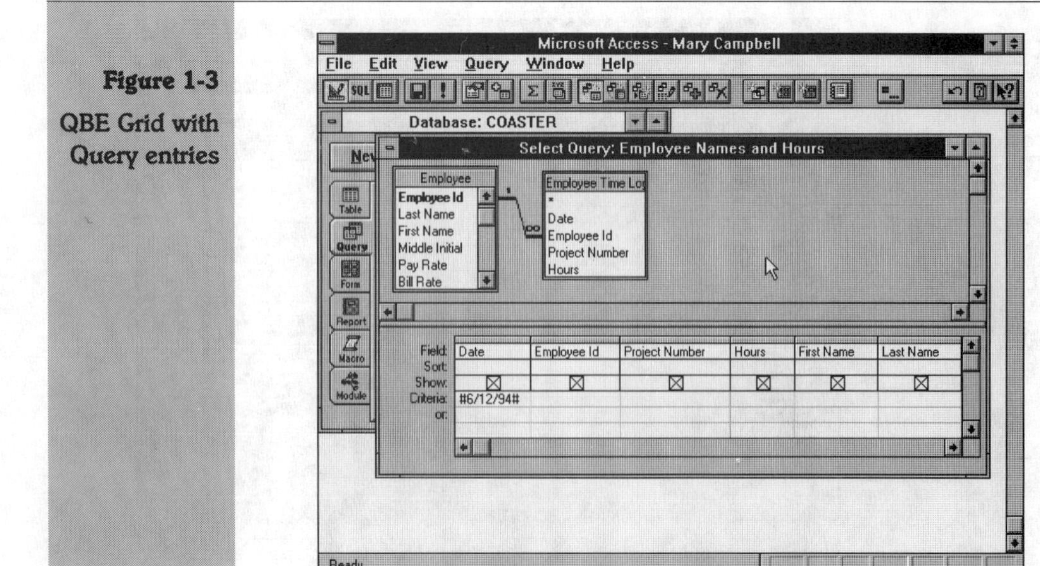


**Figure 1-3** QBE Grid with Query entries

provides row headings. The grid these fields create is filled in by the associated values from another field. You can use crosstab queries to summarize data in an easy-to-read fashion when you use functions or expressions to calculate totals, averages, or other statistical analyses of the data and then display them in this spreadsheet-like grid.

#### ACTION QUERIES

Access provides four types of action queries: make-table, delete, append, and update action queries. Each type of action query lets you perform a different operation using data from tables. For example, you can use a delete action query to remove records for former employees or an update action query to increase the salary field for a specific job code by 10 percent. Make-table action queries take information from one or more tables and create a new table, while append action queries take information and add it to an existing table. You must specify that you want an action query; Access displays the action queries with special icons to ensure that records are not deleted or fields altered inadvertently.

#### PARAMETERS

Parameters, which you can add to any type of query, allow you to change the criteria the query uses to select records with each use of the query. Access will prompt you for new criteria entries to use in the QBE grid. Parameters are a useful tool that you can create for end users who want to fill in a dialog box rather than a QBE grid.

#### SORTING AND GROUPING WITH FILTERS

Filters behave like select queries, but you can use them in table datasheets and forms. Just as water filters trap objects and do not let them flow through to the other side, filters in forms stop records from being available when they do not match the criteria established for the filter. They can also be used to sort the records in a table datasheet or form into a different order. Filters are like simple, temporary queries and can be saved as queries when you want to reuse them later.

## Reports

Reports are the tool of choice when you want to print information from a number of records. In reports, you can see the detail as you can with a form on the screen but you can also look at many records at the same time. Reports also let you look at summary information obtained after reading every record in the table, such as totals or averages. Reports can show the data from either a table or a query. Figure 1-4 shows a report created with Access. The drawing was created with CorelDRAW!; Access can use OLE and DDE which are Windows features that let you share data between applications.

For an easy approach to creating a report, use the Report Wizards that come with Access. By responding to a series of questions, you tell Access exactly what you want your report to look like. You can create a variety of different reports with the Report Wizards, including mailing labels that might be needed for a customer file. Access version 2 has an AutoReport feature that creates a report for a table or query without any prompting from you.

You do not have to use the Report Wizards to create a report. Instead, you can create reports entirely on your own, laying them out exactly the way you want. The report Design view shown in Figure 1-5 is divided into sections. The sections indicate whether the information prints at the beginning or end of a report, at the top or bottom of each page, or for each new record processed. The controls that you add to each section control the data that prints at these locations in the report.

Since reports can be used to show a summary of all the records, you can present a summary view rather than the detail. You can add a graph to a report

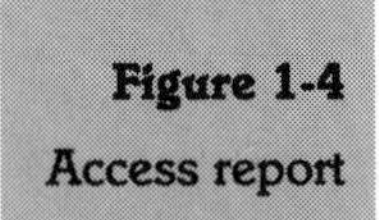

**Figure 1-4** Access report

**Figure 1-5**
**Report design**

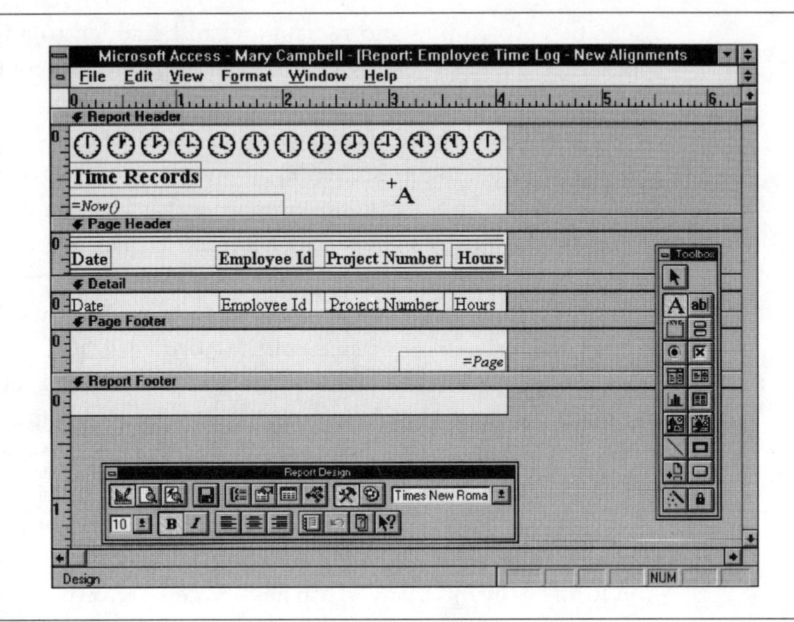


with Microsoft Graph. Graphs are frequently used to create a picture of the data using a few fields of a table or query.

## Forms

You can use forms to view the records in tables or to add new records. Unlike datasheets, which present many records on the screen at one time, forms have a narrower focus and usually present one record on the screen at a time (you can use subforms to display related records from another table at the same time). You can use either queries or tables as the input for a form.

You can create forms with Form Wizards and have Access help you with the creation process. A few quick choices enable you to create a form with little work. Your best bet may be to create a form with Form Wizards and then customize it to meet your needs. Access version 2 has an AutoForm feature that can automatically create a form for a table or query.

Controls are placed on a form to display fields or text. You can select these controls and move them to a new location or resize them to give your form the look you want. You can move the controls for fields and the text that describes that field separately. You can also add other text to the form. You can change the appearance of text on a form by changing the font or making the type boldface or italic. You also can show text as raised or sunken or use a specific color. Lines and rectangles can be added to a form to enhance its appearance. Figure 1-6 shows a form developed to present data in an appealing manner.

The controls on a form have properties, just like fields. You can change these properties to make a form function differently. Controls, sections of a form, and the form itself all offer different properties that you can change.

Forms allow you to show data from more than one table. You can build a query first to select the data from different tables to appear on a form or use subforms to handle the different tables you want to work with. A subform displays the records associated with a particular field on a form. Subforms provide the best solution when one record in a table relates to many records in another table. Subforms allow you to show the data from one record at the top of the form with the data from related records shown below it.

For example, Figure 1-7 shows a form that displays information from the Client table at the top of the form and information from the Employee Time Log table in the bottom half of the form, in a subform.

A form has events that you can have Access perform as different things occur. *Events* happen at particular points in time in the use of a form. Moving from one record to the next is an example of an event. You can have macros or procedures assigned to an event to tell Access what you want to happen when an event occurs. Other events that frequently have macros or procedures assigned to them include opening a form, changing the current record, changing

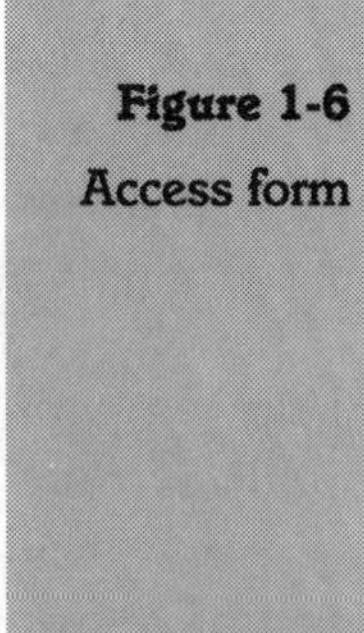

**Figure 1-6**
**Access form**

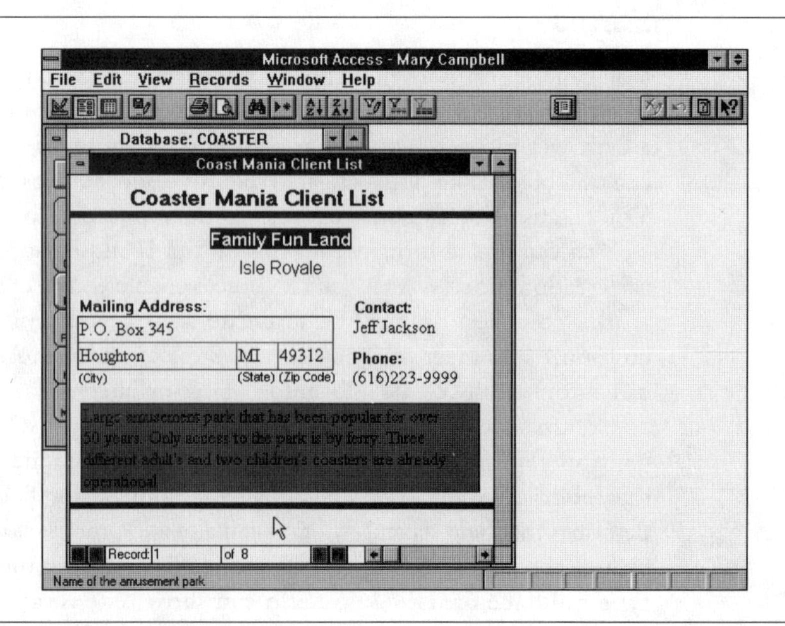

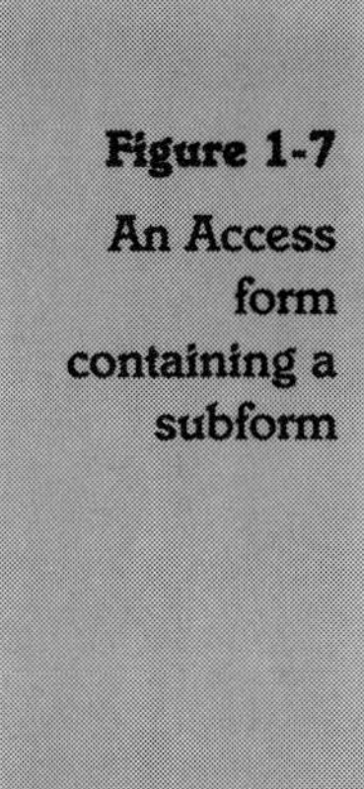

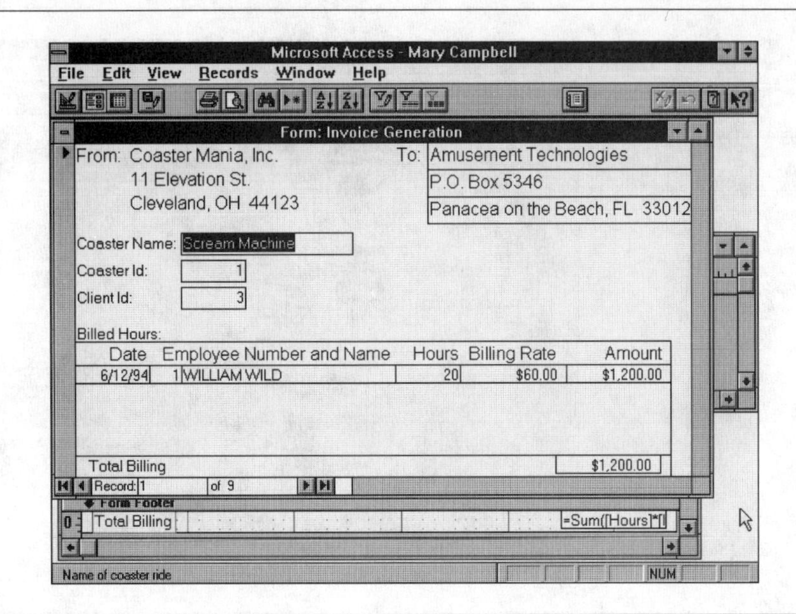


**Figure 1-7** An Access form containing a subform

data on a form, inserting a record, deleting a record, selecting a control, closing a form, pressing a command button, or double-clicking a control.

## Macros

Macros are a series of actions that describe what you want Access to do. Macros are an ideal solution for repetitive tasks. You can specify the exact steps for a macro to perform and the macro can repeat them whenever you need these steps executed again, without making a mistake. Macros are like having an unpaid assistant who's committed to precision.

Access macros are easy to work with because Access lets you select from a list of all the actions that you can use in a macro. Once you select an action, you use *arguments* to control the specific effect of the action. Arguments differ for each of the actions, since each action requires different information before it can perform a task. In Figure 1-8 you can see macro instructions entered in a Macro window. For many argument entries, Access provides its best guess at which entry you will want—you only need to change the entry if you want something different.

You can create macros for a command button in a form that will open another form and select the records that appear in the other form. Macros also allow other sophisticated options such as custom menus and pop-up forms for data

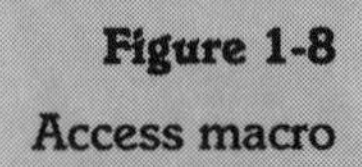

**Figure 1-8**
**Access macro**

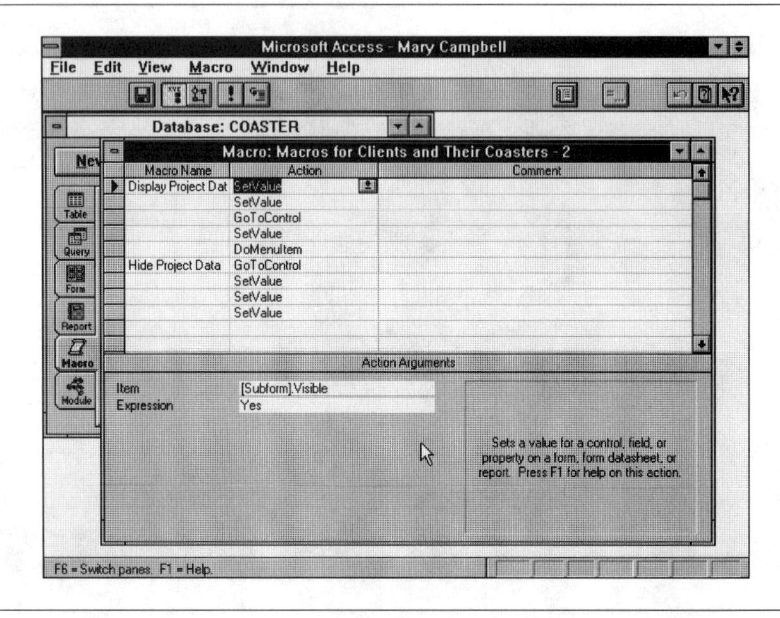


collection. Access version 2 offers a new and easier way to create custom menus to work with macros, called the Menu Builder.

You can execute macros from the Database window or other locations. Figure 1-9 shows a number of macros in the Database window. You can highlight a macro and then select Run to execute it.

## Modules

Modules are programs or sets of instructions designed to perform a specific task or series of tasks. Modules are slightly more complex than macros and should be avoided until you have mastered the basic Access features.

Modules consist of a number of procedures written in Access Basic, which is the programming language provided with the package. These procedures can be one of two types: function procedures, which return a value that can be used within an expression, and sub procedures, which cannot be used in expressions.

Module code can be viewed and edited in a Module window that looks like this:

```
Module: Custom Functions
Function Proper (OldText)
    Proper = UCase(Left(OldText, 1)) & LCase(Right(OldText, Len(OldText)
End Function
```

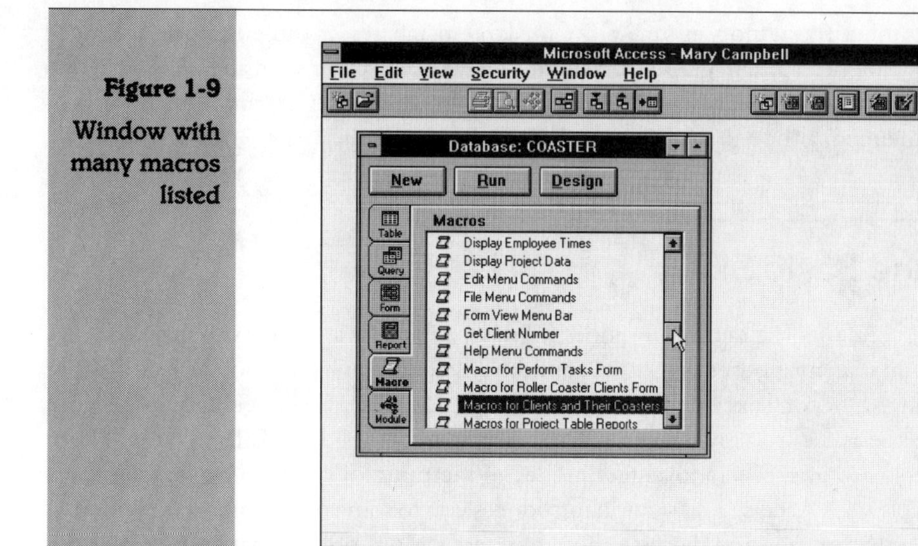


**Figure 1-9** Window with many macros listed

The Module window provides a text editor that works like the Windows Notepad accessory or a word processor, making it easy to enter and edit text.

## Requirements for Using Access

There are specific hardware requirements that must be met to use Access effectively. Although you might be able to start Access without it, if you are missing some of this required hardware, you will not be pleased with the system's performance. You must have specific operating system software and adequate hardware to install and use Access.

Microsoft Access is installed from within Windows; therefore, you must install the required operating system software first. Microsoft Access requires DOS 3.1 or later as well as Windows 3.1 or later for Access version 2. Access version 1 only needs Windows 3.0 or later.

Hardware requirements include approximately 20MB of free space on your hard disk (11MB for Access version 1) and at least 6MB of RAM (2MB for Access version 1), although performance will be much better with more. You will not want to run Access at minimum memory if you are creating more than a very simple database using few advanced features, because the performance at minimum memory is very slow for large databases or those that use advanced features or contain graphics. You must have a computer with an 80386 or 80486 processor and a Microsoft-compatible mouse. A VGA monitor is recommended, although an EGA display can be used.

# Acquiring the Basic Skills

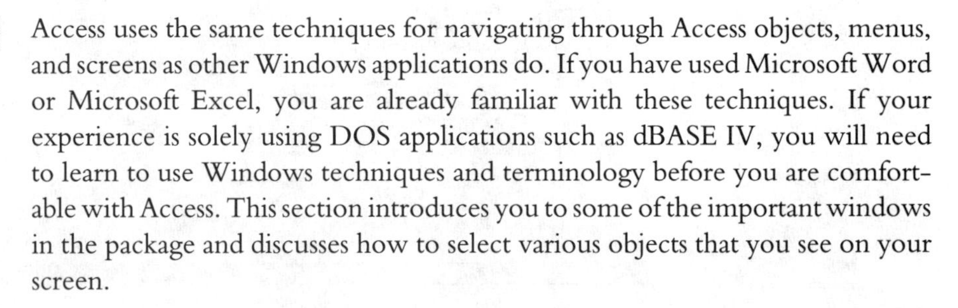

Access uses the same techniques for navigating through Access objects, menus, and screens as other Windows applications do. If you have used Microsoft Word or Microsoft Excel, you are already familiar with these techniques. If your experience is solely using DOS applications such as dBASE IV, you will need to learn to use Windows techniques and terminology before you are comfortable with Access. This section introduces you to some of the important windows in the package and discusses how to select various objects that you see on your screen.

## The Access Window

When you first start Access, the Access window shown in Figure 1-10 appears. No database is open and there are only two drop-down menu items. You will use this window to open a database or to perform other tasks that are not possible once a database is open. These tasks include compacting a database to save hard disk space and encrypting the database to ensure that unauthorized users cannot decipher anything useful from the database file.

When you are ready to create a new database, choose New Database from the File menu. You will then type a filename for the database and select OK. The Database window will appear. You could also open an existing database by choosing Open Database from the File menu, selecting the database you want, and selecting OK.

## The Database Window

Once you have opened a database, a window like the one in Figure 1-11 appears. This window allows you to access any object in the database with a quick selection of one of the object buttons. Initially the Table button is selected and all of the tables in the database are listed.

If you want to look at a list of all the objects of another type, click the button for that type of object and a complete list of all the named objects appears. This

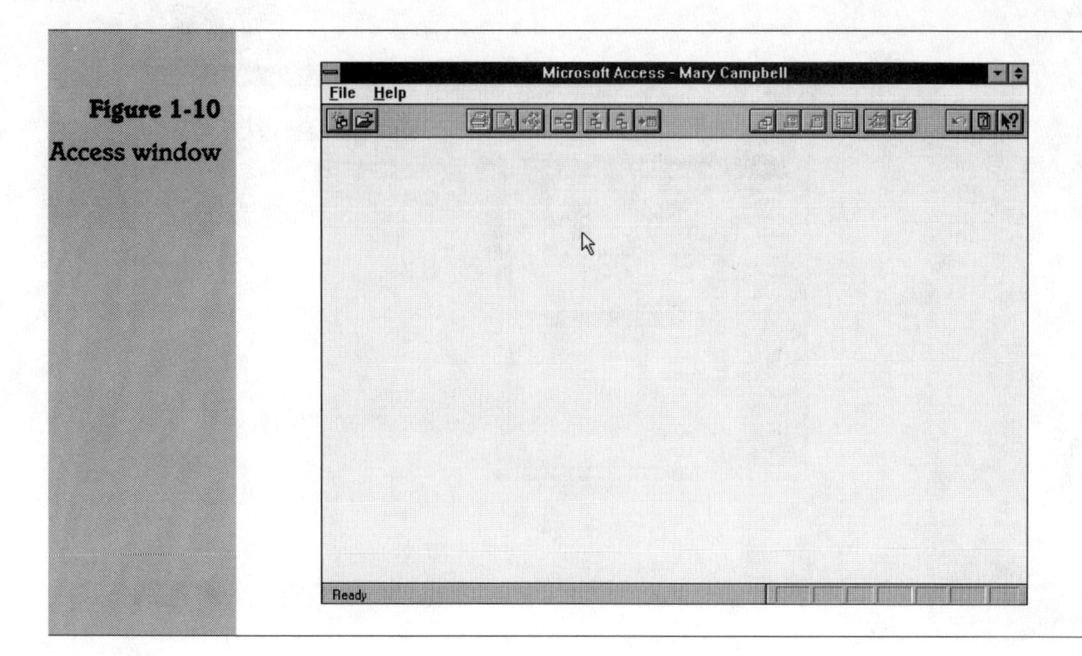


**Figure 1-10**
**Access window**

means that you can click the Macro button for a list of all the macros in the current database, or you can click the Query button to see if any queries have been created in the current database. The buttons that appear near the top of the window allow you to create a new object, use an existing one, or redesign the current one.

The menu bar that appears when the Database window is active is much more comprehensive than the initial Access menu bar, although some of the Access menu options are not listed. Some menu options are missing primarily because some tasks such as encryption and compaction cannot be done while a database is open. The basic menu options remain the same even though you change the type of object that provides the entries in the current list of object names.

## Using Menus

Menus offer choices within Access. You use them to select many different tasks as you work with the package.

As mentioned earlier, there are only two choices in the menu bar when you first start Access. After opening a database, the menu bar offers six different drop-down menu options.

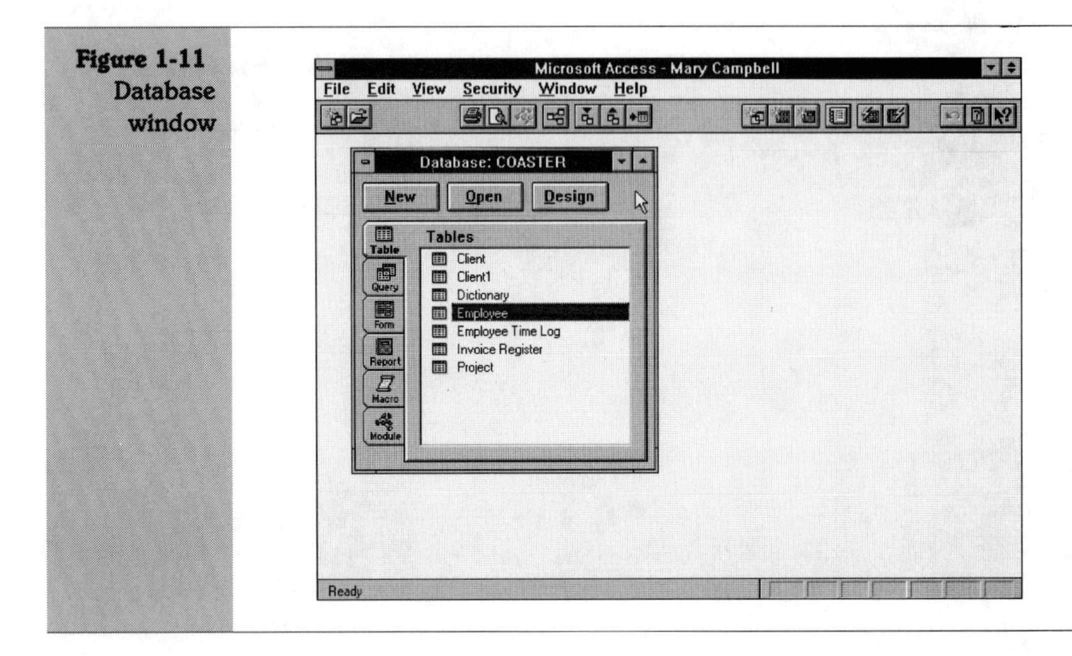


**Figure 1-11** Database window

You can drop down a menu in several ways. You can click the name of the menu in the menu bar. For instance, if you click File, you will see this menu:

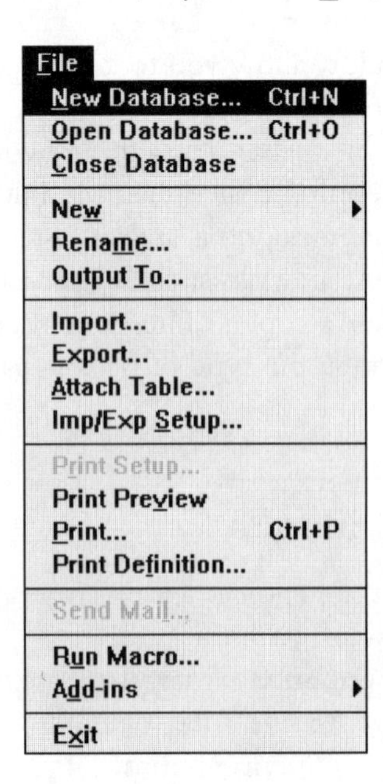

Another option is to press the ALT key and the underlined letter from the menu name. Once the menu is displayed, you can type the underlined letter in an option or click on it to select that option. Menu options that appear dimmed or in a different color are not available for you to select at the current time. They may only be appropriate with a different object or after another action. Menu options that are followed by an ellipsis (. . .) display a dialog box when selected. Menu options followed by a triangle display another menu to give you more options.

Access version 2 offers another type of a menu, the *shortcut menu*. You can open a shortcut menu by *right-clicking* on an object in the Access window. Right-clicking is the process of clicking an object using the right mouse button instead of the left. Shortcut menus present a limited selection of options related to that specific object that include the commands you will most frequently use. For example, Figure 1-12 shows a shortcut menu opened when a control in a form's Design view is right-clicked. You can perform a command from the shortcut menu by clicking the command. Some commands will display a dialog box just like commands you select from the regular menu. All of the options available on a shortcut menu are also available through the regular commands, so shortcut menus are not mentioned often in this book. You can right-click

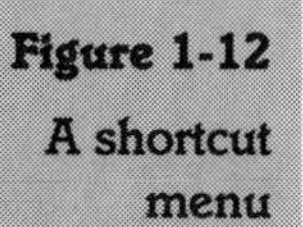

**Figure 1-12** A shortcut menu

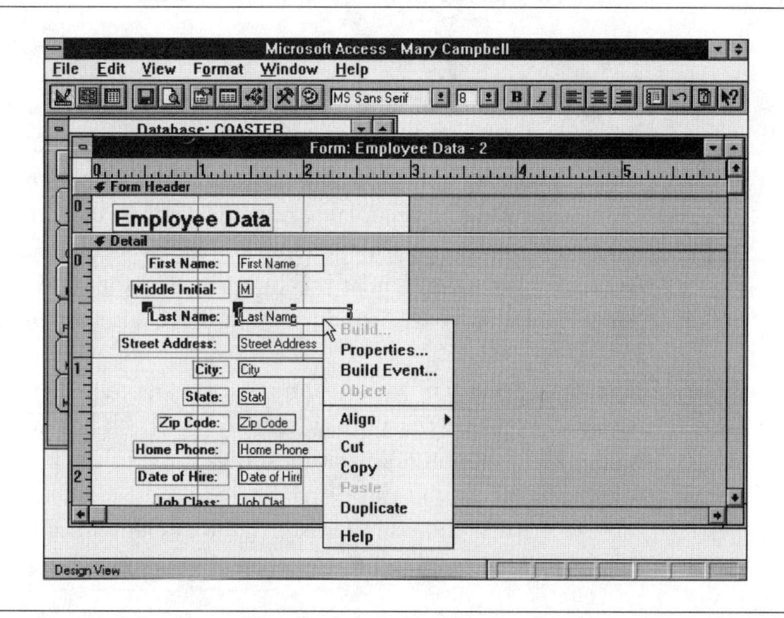

any object in the Access window to see the most frequently used commands that the object uses.

## Using the Toolbar

The toolbar initially appears beneath the menu bar. The buttons it contains will vary depending on the object that you are working with. You can click the desired button to make your selection. The toolbars in Access version 2 are more flexible and varied than those in Access version 1. In version 2, you can move the toolbar to make it appear on any side of the Access window, to have it *float,* like a dialog box, in the Access window. Access version 2 also lets you display more than one toolbar at a time, and even lets you edit existing toolbars or create new ones. See Appendix E for a complete list of the default toolbars and their buttons, and instructions on creating and using your own toolbars.

When you are working with a table, there are default toolbar options for choosing a Datasheet or Design view. When working with macros, there are buttons in the toolbar for single-step mode and for displaying conditions and macro names.

The toolbar choices have comparable menu selections. You can use either approach to accomplish the task, but since the toolbar only requires a click, it can be the quickest way to accomplish a task.

## Completing Dialog Boxes

An ellipsis after a menu option indicates that a dialog box will appear when you select the menu option. Unlike menus, there is no single method of making choices in dialog boxes. Dialog boxes present several different elements to elicit information from you, depending on the type of information being sought. Access employs the standard techniques used for all Windows applications, so you will know what to do if you have already used another Windows application.

If Windows is a new environment for you, you will need to learn how option buttons, drop-down list boxes, text boxes, check boxes, and command buttons work. The following illustration shows some of the possible components for a dialog box. You will notice names near most elements in dialog boxes. You can use the underlined letter to make that element of the dialog box active or simply click the mouse on the element you want.

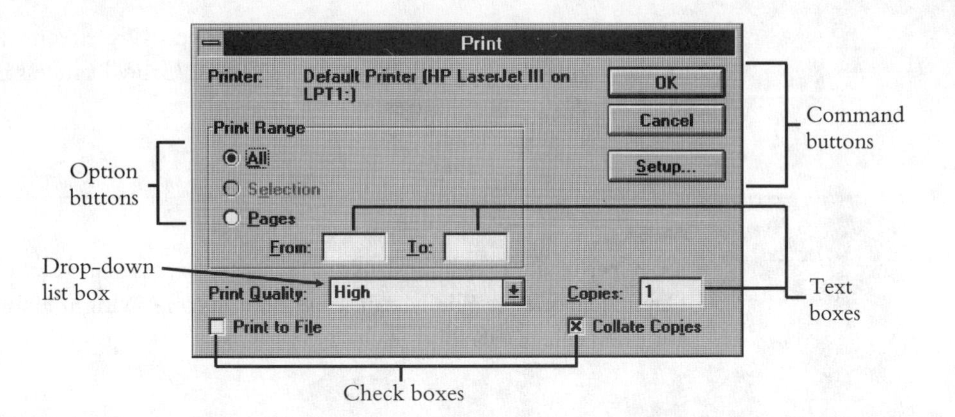


Text boxes offer the most flexibility for your entry. You can type whatever text you want into the box—within the limitations for the entry you are making. If you are attempting to look for a record that contains a specific entry, you will use a text box to specify the entry you are seeking. When you choose the Run Macro command from the File menu, you will enter the name of the macro to run in a text box.

Check boxes let you toggle features on or off. You select a check box by pressing ALT and the underlined letter of the check box's label or by clicking it. An X appears when the check box is selected or turned on. Clicking or selecting the check box again removes the selection, which turns the feature off and makes the X disappear. Check boxes are often grouped together. Unlike option buttons, discussed next, you can have more than one check box selected at a time.

Option buttons offer mutually exclusive choices for a feature. Selecting one option button unselects any other option button in the group that may be currently selected. You can select an option button by pressing ALT and its underlined letter or by clicking the button with your mouse.

A drop-down list box looks a lot like a text box with an entry already in it. A drop-down list box has an arrow to the right of the box that you can click to drop down a list of options. You can also activate the box with the ALT key and underlined letter and then use ALT and the DOWN ARROW key to display the list of options. An option in the list can be chosen by highlighting it using the arrow keys and pressing ENTER or by clicking it with the mouse.

Command buttons carry out some action from the dialog box. If you press ENTER with a command button highlighted or click on the button, that action is executed immediately. Command buttons can open other dialog boxes or finalize the settings in the current dialog box. Most command buttons close the current dialog box as they carry out the action. Most dialog boxes have command buttons representing OK and Cancel. OK executes the requested command with the current dialog box settings. Cancel cancels the request and ignores the dialog box entries.

## Quick Reference

**To Create a New Database** From the Access window, choose New Database from the File Menu, type a name (one to eight characters long), and then select OK.

**To Make a Selection from the Menu** Click the menu name and then click the desired menu option. If using the keyboard, press ALT and the underlined letter in the menu and then type the underlined letter of the desired menu option.

**To Move to a Different Element in a Dialog Box** Click the desired element, or press ALT and the underlined letter.

**To Use a Shortcut Menu** Right-click the object you want to work with for the shortcut menu. Click one of the commands in the menu. Access either performs the command then or after you complete the dialog box that Access displays when you select a command.

# Chapter 2

# Designing an Access Database

AN Access *database* is a collection of tabular information *and* the tools that you create to access the information. This terminology may differ from other databases in which each type of information is stored as a file and the entire collection of files is called a database; in those databases, information for creating reports and defining screens is kept in other types of files.

The tools included in an Access database are reports and forms. These integral components of the Access database unlock its power and usefulness, as you'll see throughout this book. Also, Access makes it easy to back up all of your important information since your data, reports, forms, queries, and indexes are all part of one database file.

All of the data within an Access database is stored in *tables*—rectangular arrangements of data that have a row and column orientation. An Access database can be as simple as a table containing the names and addresses of your clients or, if you are storing personal data, perhaps a table containing information about your CD collection. On the other hand, an Access database can be comprehensive tables of employees, suppliers, inventory, and billing information in addition to the table of clients. The Access database contains all the forms and reports that you designed to utilize the data tables just mentioned.

Microsoft refers to Access as a *relational database* because it allows you to define relationships between tables. For example, you can combine information from an employee table and a payroll table to put employee names and addresses on checks without recording them in both the employee and payroll tables.

Whether you want to create an Access database that consists of a single table or utilize its ability to handle data relationships, you start the process by analyzing your needs and designing the database to meet those needs. Access version 2 provides a Wizard that will help you create tables by supplying a list of suggested information for each table. Although you may be able to create simple applications without any change to what the Table Wizard provides, you will want to understand the process of analysis and data gathering necessary to build your own database tables. You will have an opportunity to see tables created with and without the help of the Access Table Wizard in the "Defining a New

Table" and "Using the Table Wizard to Create a Table" sections later in this chapter.

If you plan to do a detailed analysis before creating a database, you will find that an iterative approach to analysis and design will best serve your long-term goals. After making your best first attempt, take another look at both your analysis and design to see if you have forgotten any important data or if you can improve the organization and relationships that you initially defined. Time invested in these vital tasks can save you significant time later since you will build a database that provides good performance and meets both short-term and long-term needs. You might want to browse through Appendix B which lists the sample fields in the sample databases available with the Table Wizard. Many of these field lists provide fairly extensive coverage of potential fields for different categories of data. Looking at them may prompt you to think about data needs you have forgotten.

If you are an old hand at database design, you have already developed your own techniques for defining information needs and creating a workable database design. Your techniques will work with Microsoft Access just as they have for any other relational database package. Your database design may be complete, in which case you'll be eager to start setting up your own database rather than reading about the analysis phase of database creation. Skip to "Setting Up a Microsoft Access Database" later in this chapter, where you can apply your own design to creating a new Microsoft Access database.

## Performing the Required Analysis

The objective of your analysis is to create a database design that will meet your short-term and long-term needs. To do this you must define what data is needed, and then look at options for organizing it into tables. The best way for you to do this is to examine current work flows and information sources. Look at the information that flows into various departments in the business as orders or invoices are processed, and then look at the information outflows as data is sent to accounting or shipping departments.

One of the initial steps in the design process is to define the *fields* or the important pieces of information. A field can be a phone number, city, ZIP code, or part number. While designing your database, you will need to define each of the fields of information that you currently use. You will also need to list fields that you would like to use in the future to ensure that your design meets your needs for tomorrow as well as today. Figure 2-1 shows fields of information currently in use as well as new fields being compiled into a list.

## Defining Current Needs

Look at existing reports, computer applications, and all forms that you currently use. Approach one application area at a time if you are working with several. For example, explore all the information on employees before you address the projects that they might be assigned to or the clients they are assisting. As you address each new area, relevant data for other areas might come to light and can be added to the list for that area. You will do a more thorough job if you focus on one area at a time. Sometimes you will look at reports that actually bring together information from several different sources. Try to identify the basic categories of information and examine each in detail.

Jot down each field that you identify on a sheet of paper or, better yet, enter each field on a new line in a word processing document. This is the beginning of your *data dictionary* or list of relevant fields for your new database application. Later you can add information such as length, data types, definition, and database tables to your data dictionary as shown in Figure 2-2.

Jot down or enter every field you come up with, even if you are not certain that you want all of them. This is not the time to eliminate information but

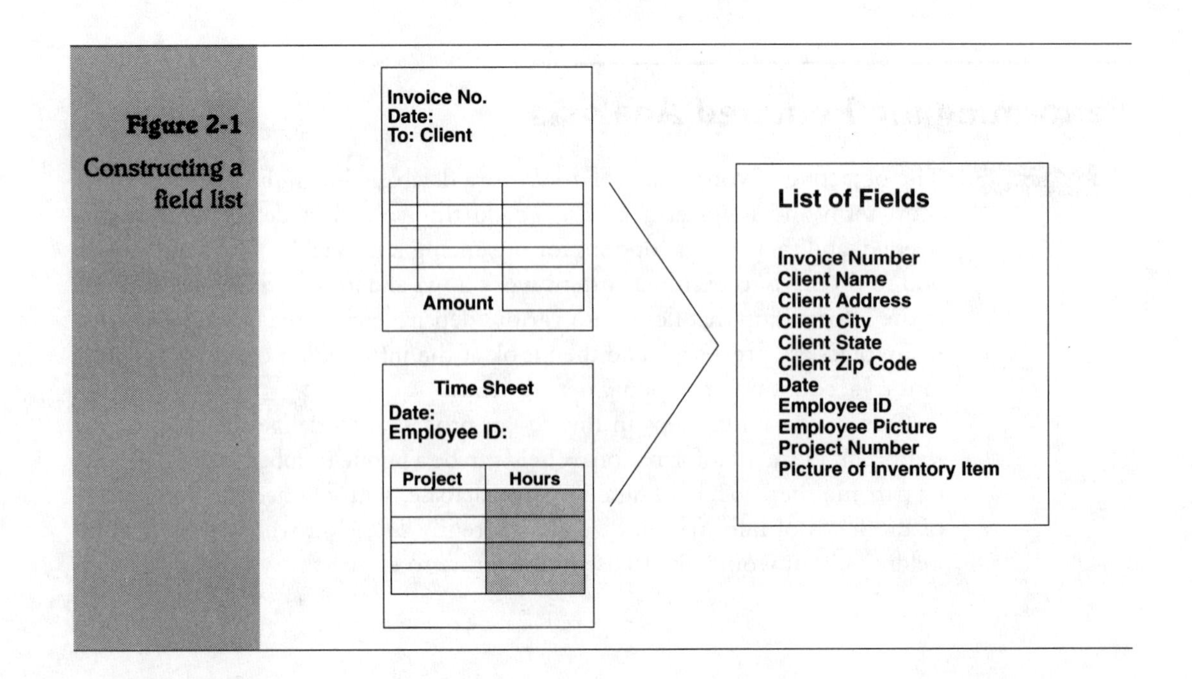


**Figure 2-1** Constructing a field list

**Figure 2-2** Data dictionary entries

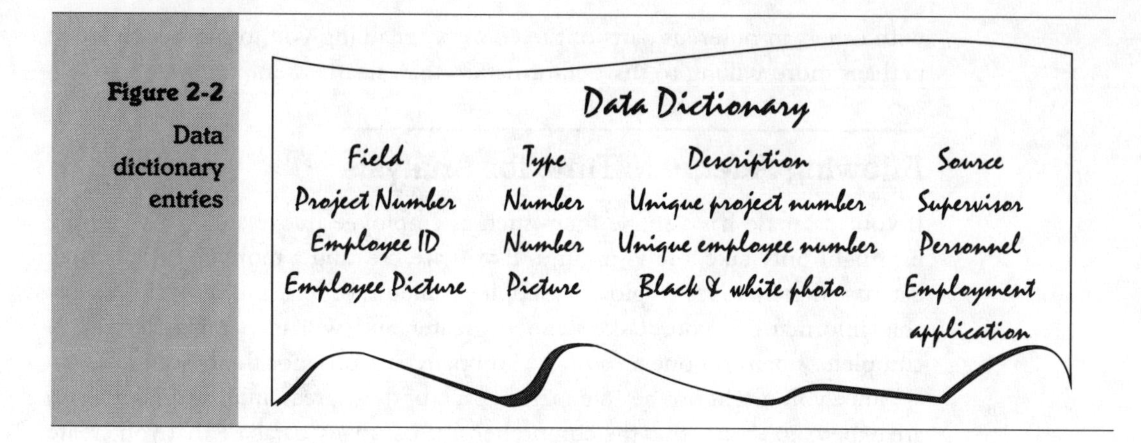


rather a chance to make an exhaustive list of every field you might possibly want to include. Before creating the database tables you can purge fields that you do not need.

## Defining Future Needs

After listing all of the known fields of information that you currently use, focus on what you wish you had available. For example, the current employee report may show the employee's name, social security number, and salary. You might wish you had the employee's supervisor and phone extension on the report. Add these two elements to your field list. If you are aware of planned changes that might necessitate additional fields of data later, add them to your list. Maybe your company intends to add an employee health plan and will eventually need a field that indicates whether the employee subscribes to the plan. Although the plan is not yet in effect, this future need should be covered by the addition of a new field now.

Maybe payroll is currently handled by an outside service bureau. If you want to continue with the service bureau arrangement, fields for exemptions and filing status will not be needed in the employee table. If you think your company will ever consider bringing payroll processing in house, you will most likely need a social security number field and fields for benefit withholding such as medical insurance.

Ask people who use the information to list currently unavailable fields that would enable them to make better business decisions. If possible, look at systems implemented by others in your industry group to see what types of information they capture that you currently ignore. Industry trade groups are often good sources for this type of information as well as a free exchange of information with others in different parts of the country, enabling you to meet individuals perhaps more willing to share information than nearby competitors.

## Allowing Adequate Time for Analysis

If your database has a single focus such as employee information, making the list might only take a few minutes. If you are creating a more comprehensive database that includes employees, suppliers, clients, orders, and accounts receivable information, your task is much greater and will take much longer to complete. Focus on one area of the company at a time for the best results.

Since you might not be an expert in each of these areas, interview users who are experts to ensure that the comprehensive company database that you create will meet their needs.

**tip:** *Have several users from each area look over the list of elements that you have created to ensure that you have not omitted vital fields that are only needed occasionally.*

Since a rushed design is often discarded for a new one at a later time, reports and forms must often be redone. To save yourself time, money, and frustration, do not rush through the design phase no matter how much you need the database application. If your time is limited or you are facing a deadline, your best strategy is to focus on one area and give it adequate time. You can add the other information later when you have sufficient time to explore your options more thoroughly.

## Looking at a Fictional Example

One of the advantages of a product such as Access is that you can customize the database to meet your exact needs. This is important since even two companies in the same business are unlikely to design the same database. This also means that no example in this book will match your needs exactly. However, you can learn a lot about how to construct your ideal system by looking at existing system designs and deciding which features you want to incorporate into your own design and which features don't work for you.

The examples in this book use a fictitious company, Coaster Mania, which constructs amusement park roller coasters. This type of company was chosen because its records show different types of data and a variety of tables. Although your company probably does not construct roller coasters, it likely requires employee and client data just like Coaster Mania's. Also, you probably need to send invoices or bills for products or services just like Coaster Mania does.

Other aspects of Coaster Mania's needs may be quite different. You probably are not concerned with the cost of a coaster car or its angle of ascent. Even so, the opportunity for an in-depth look at Coaster Mania's design dilemmas and the decisions made here will help you design a database to fit your needs. Although some of the fields of information vary greatly from yours, the opportunity to look at the formatting and validating for Coaster Mania will help you define your own data tables.

During the analysis for Coaster Mania, employees, coaster projects, clients, and invoicing were examined. Coaster Mania has many other information areas not currently addressed as Figure 2-3 shows.

Every area is studied separately to create the most thorough field list possible. Each of the following sections describe the considerations in listing the Coaster Mania fields. You may have some of the same types of information in your database.

Other business areas, such as payroll and inventory, were not included in this analysis. Although some companies attempt to perform a complete conversion to automation for all areas at one time through the creation of a very comprehensive database, this is often the wrong approach. It's often best to get some of the application areas up and running, while you plan the addition of other information tables to the database for a later time.

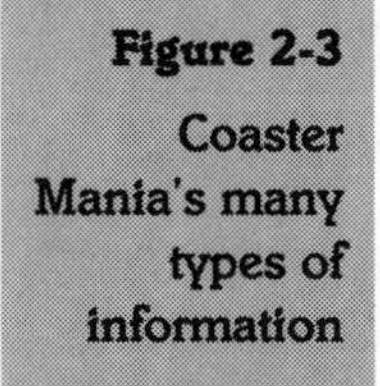
**Figure 2-3** Coaster Mania's many types of information

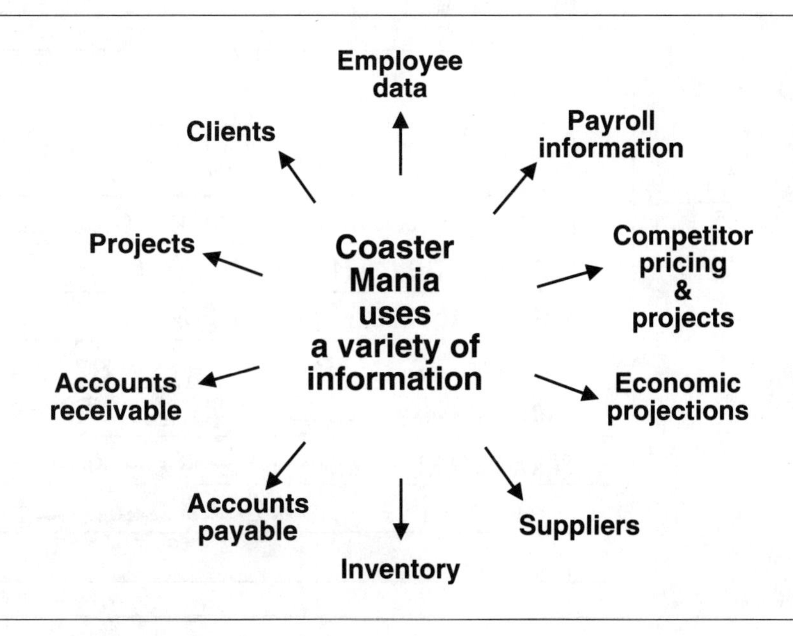

## CLIENT INFORMATION

Although Coaster Mania has only a small number of active clients at one time, they include prospective clients in their client list. If the firm's management visits a current construction site they will often visit nearby amusement parks to check on the completed projects and to explore the potential for new coaster projects.

Currently Coaster Mania stores basic information on the various parks on index cards like the one shown in Figure 2-4. The initial fields taken from their list of existing clients might include any of these fields:

Client Id
Client Name
Contact
Park Location
Mailing Address
City
State
ZIP Code
Phone
Park Description

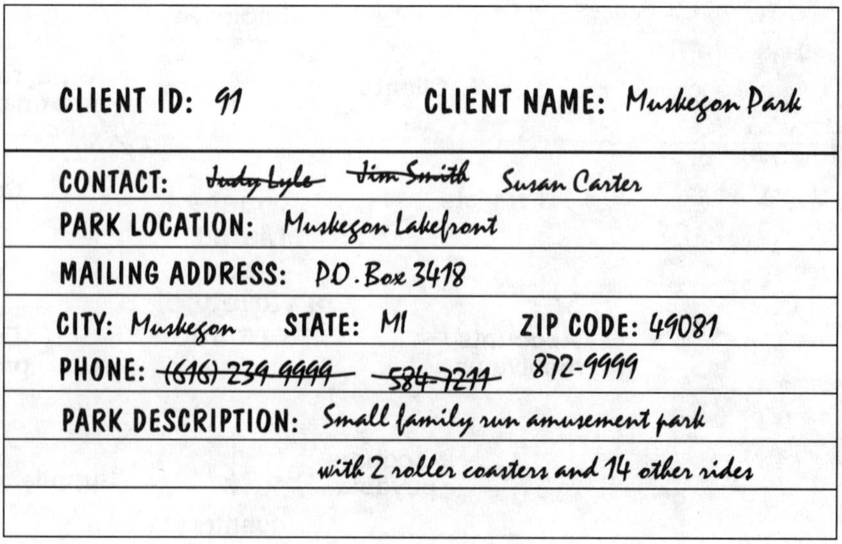

**Figure 2-4** Index card containing client information

CLIENT ID: 91 CLIENT NAME: Muskegon Park

CONTACT: ~~Judy Lyle~~ ~~Jim Smith~~ Susan Carter

PARK LOCATION: Muskegon Lakefront

MAILING ADDRESS: P.O. Box 3418

CITY: Muskegon STATE: MI ZIP CODE: 49081

PHONE: ~~(616) 239-9999~~ ~~584-7211~~ 872-9999

PARK DESCRIPTION: Small family run amusement park with 2 roller coasters and 14 other rides

In talking to the marketing people you find that they would like to include the year-to-date and total payments and invoices. These fields are added as a result of those discussions:

YTD Invoices
YTD Payments
Total Invoices
Total Payments

## EMPLOYEES

Currently, Coaster Mania does not have an electronic file containing employee information. All of the available information on employees is maintained in Personnel, and the file there is requested and updated periodically by the employee's supervisor. Since it is unlikely that Personnel will be dismantled, you don't need to add information such as emergency contact phone numbers to your database list. Also, because payroll is handled by an outside service bureau, there is no need to add payroll fields such as social security number and number of exemptions to the list.

Although there has been some discussion of creating a Skills database to help select the best employee for a project, the company feels that there won't be sufficient knowledge of the information that must be maintained to make a Skills database workable until they have an opportunity to study the data stored by other companies. Management would like to include each employee's picture in the database. Thus far, this is the list of fields for the employee database:

Employee Id
Name
Pay Rate
Bill Rate
Date of Hire
Job Class
Department
Street Address
City
State
ZIP Code
Picture
Home Phone
Extension

After examining the initial list it is decided to split the Name field into three components: first name, last name, and middle initial.

### COASTER PROJECTS

The roller coaster project files that Coaster Mania maintains include information on proposed coasters, active construction sites, and completed coasters. These files are not currently stored in one central place. A proposed project file is kept by the member of the management team that is handling the proposal and current project folders are kept by the project manager. Completed project files can be in one of many locations and often are located only after a lengthy search. A database containing the information would offer the advantage of being instantly accessible to everyone. The company is especially eager to be able to share sketches or pictures of the coaster with everyone, and is looking for a database solution that will allow the use of these pictures in addition to other data.

The total number of coasters is less than 100, including those being planned, those under construction, and those completed. Although some fields are only pertinent to active projects, management wants to be able to enter queries that would include active, completed, and inactive sites—so all 100 will be stored in one table. Since there is no single correct design for a database, it is possible to develop another equally feasible solution that would not have all three types of projects in the same table. The fields of information relating to coaster projects are as follows:

Coaster Id
Coaster Name
Client Id
Completed
Operational
Est Cost
Actual Cost
Track
Height
Drop
Angle
Time
Speed
Capacity
Vehicles
Picture
Features

Separate fields for the park and the location were considered but you can get this information from the table for the Client information using the Client ID. Getting the data from the Client table means you do not have to duplicate the information.

## TIME REPORTING

Employees might work on several different projects at any one time. This is especially true for projects in the design phase when employees might put the finishing touches on several different blueprints or models in a given week.

Employees log their hours on weekly time sheets, which give total hours spent on each project that week. Figure 2-5 shows one of these time sheets. Although management considered having the employees account for time by activity, they decided that this would not give them any better information and so abandoned the idea.

This is the data from the time logs:

Date
Employee Id
Project Id
Hours
Comments

**Figure 2-5** Weekly employee time sheet

**Time Sheet**

**Employee name:** Donna D. Dare
**Employee ID:** 8
**Week ending:** 7/24/94

| Client ID | Project | Hours | Comments |
|---|---|---|---|
| 3 | 3 | 8.2 | Meet with engineers |
| 3 | 1 | 24 | Complete project sketches |
| 3 | 19 | 8.5 | Site selection |
| | | | |
| | | | |
| | | | |
| | | | |
| Total | | 40.7 | |

Currently these sheets are processed monthly. Invoices are prepared manually to bill clients for hours on a cost plus basis. Time sheets are sorted by project, and the preparer then groups them by client. To automate this task, the Project number can be combined with the Project table to get the Client Id for a project. Then, the Client table can be used to return client information for the given Client Id.

## INVOICING AND ACCOUNTS RECEIVABLE

Coaster Mania charges clients a fixed up-front fee to cover the cost of all equipment, materials, and overhead. This payment is handled somewhat like a deposit on the project and is not part of the normal monthly time charges billing. Labor costs are billed monthly on a cost plus basis.

As shown in Figure 2-5, employees submit weekly time sheets showing the hours spent on each project. The individual who processes the time sheets verifies the project number and adds the Client ID to the record by looking up the Project Id. Later, costs are totaled by project and invoices are prepared.

An open invoice file contains invoices that have not yet been paid. When payments are processed, closed invoices are removed from this file, although these invoices would likely be stored in a history file for some time (for at least three to seven years to meet IRS tax record audit mandates). These closed invoice records aren't included in this database simply to keep the examples simple.

In addition to the employee time logs, these fields of information are needed to complete the invoicing and billing cycles:

Bill Rate
Invoice Number
Invoice Date
Invoice Amount
Payment Amount
Payment Date
Project Id
Hours
Employee Id

Some of this information is stored in fields in other tables. Year-to-date and total invoice and payment amounts are also needed but are grouped with the company information. Several different database tables probably will be used for this information in order to eliminate duplication between tables and to build the best relationships between tables.

## Completing Design Activities

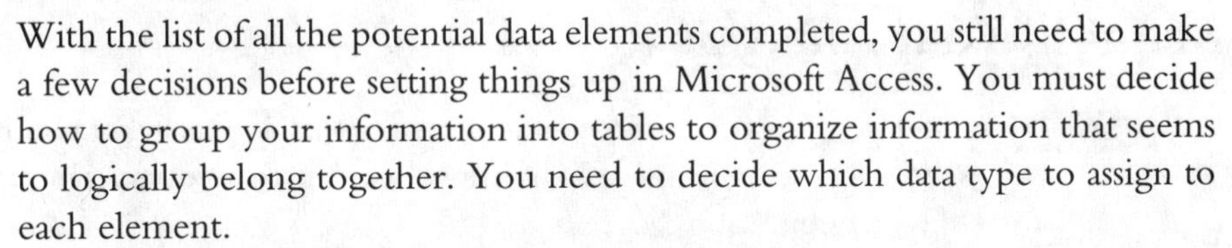

With the list of all the potential data elements completed, you still need to make a few decisions before setting things up in Microsoft Access. You must decide how to group your information into tables to organize information that seems to logically belong together. You need to decide which data type to assign to each element.

As you progress with your database definition, you will also need to set properties and define relationships between the various tables. This chapter looks at the various data types that you can select. The discussion of relationships and setting properties has been reserved for Chapter 3. These two topics allow you to customize your database design and provide for more efficient operation of your database system.

Let's first consider your remaining decisions and then look at how you make your decisions known to Access.

### Deciding How to Group Tables

After your analysis, usually you have a long list of data fields. There may seem to be some logical groupings in this list if you have explored one area at a time. Cut and paste from your list if need be; examine each of the areas that you explored and decide which information about an entity should comprise a table. You may have to move some fields to make this grouping possible. The Coaster Mania company will have an employee table, a project table, an employee time log table, an invoices table, and a client table.

Although we have eliminated some duplication by not storing time billing information with employee data and requiring multiple records for each employee, during the design phase this initial structure might still result in duplicate information in a number of records. Normally, creating a separate table will solve this problem. Check each of the tables that you initially propose to see if the design is likely to cause duplication. Eliminating duplication is easy at this point but much more difficult once you begin entering data.

Let's assume for a minute that Coaster Mania is handling purchases with this database. A table created for orders might have the same supplier information in many records. If it is necessary to process order information you might want two tables, one for orders and one for suppliers. This way you can put a supplier ID in each order record and only need to record each supplier once in the supplier table. Chapter 3 provides additional information about relationships between tables to eliminate duplicate data.

# Refining Your Analysis

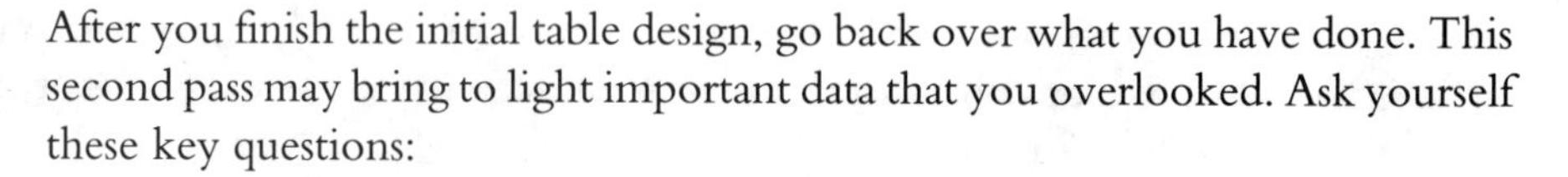

After you finish the initial table design, go back over what you have done. This second pass may bring to light important data that you overlooked. Ask yourself these key questions:

- Are there any missing fields?
- Are there fields in the database that can be calculated?
- Can any fields be eliminated?
- Should database fields be broken into several additional fields?

## Adding and Eliminating Elements

Now that you have an organized list it may be easier to see what you left out or what you can discard. Show your list to business associates that work with the data. They may have some ideas for additional fields, such as for year end or quarterly processing. They may also be aware of fields that you can calculate versus those that must be stored in the database. These same users may be able to tell you that certain fields are no longer needed. If you look at old personnel systems you may find information on religious preference or disabilities; neither of these fields can be retained under the current law.

## Splitting Fields

You might also decide that a field would be better broken into several different fields in order to allow each piece of information to be accessed separately. An example would be the contact name in the client database. If you want to be able to access first name, last name, and title separately, you will want to split the contact field into three fields.

Sometimes dividing a field makes sense for almost every database. For instance, the second line of an address contains city, state, and ZIP code. For these often-used entities, it is always better to use three fields since at one time or another you are likely to want to query the database by state or ZIP code. Figure 2-6 shows a report created by state and mailing labels for a bulk rate discount created in ZIP code sequence.

Dividing other fields can be more subjective. For example, a real estate management firm might need to be able to access street names separately from street numbers because they have more than one tenant on the same street. In this case, the database is designed with the street number and street name as two separate fields.

## Deciding What Type of Data a Field Will Contain

Unless you have Access version 2 and plan to let its Table Wizard set up your tables, you will need to decide what type of data you want to allow in each field. Do you want to allow the field to contain alphanumeric characters or just numbers? Will the field contain a date or time? If the field contains text, is it a short entry or a number of paragraphs? Can you represent the field contents by a Yes/No answer or a logical on or off state? Does the field contain an integer or a monetary amount? Should the field be incremented with the next sequential number in its record to provide a count of new records? If you think about these questions, you will be prepared to make the correct selection of a Microsoft Access data type for each field.

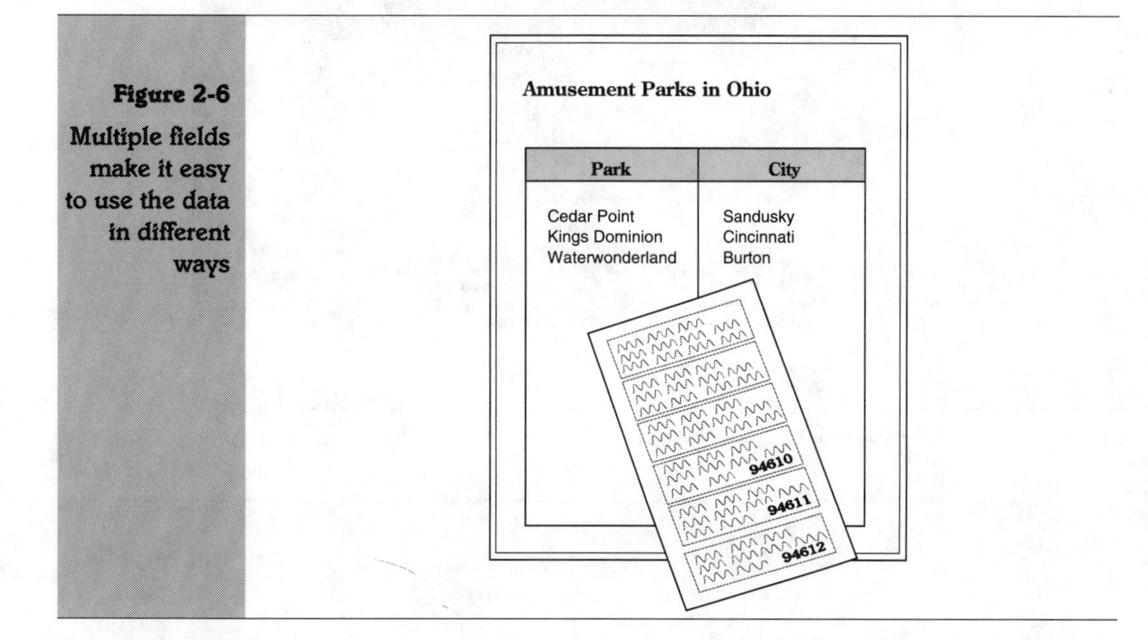


**Figure 2-6** Multiple fields make it easy to use the data in different ways

## Setting Up a Microsoft Access Database

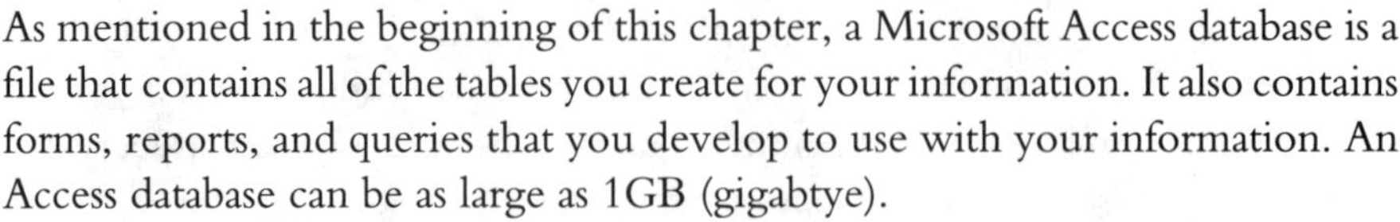

As mentioned in the beginning of this chapter, a Microsoft Access database is a file that contains all of the tables you create for your information. It also contains forms, reports, and queries that you develop to use with your information. An Access database can be as large as 1GB (gigabtye).

Because a database is a file, you must provide it with a unique filename, up to eight characters in length. Since Access allows only one open database at a time, you will want to close any open database before creating a new one, although Access will do it for you if you forget.

Any database that you create will begin from the Access window. Follow these steps to create a database:

1. Choose New Database from the File menu.

   You can also click the New Database button on the toolbar that looks like this:

2. Type a one- to eight-character filename in the File Name box as shown here:

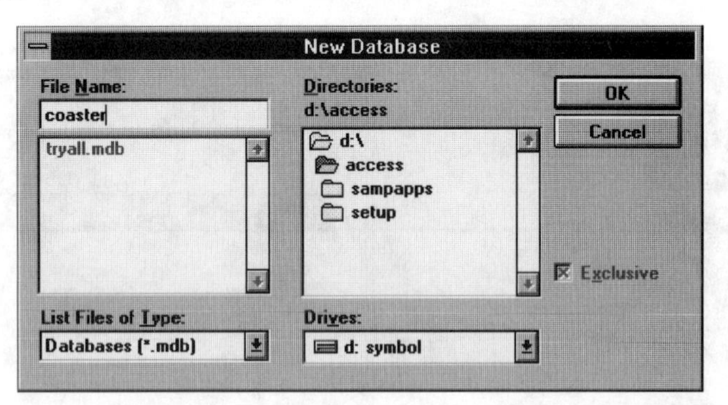


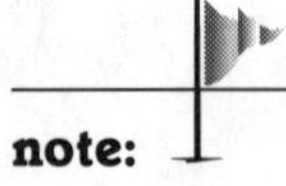

**note:** *The filename should only contain the characters A–Z, 0–9, and the underscore ( _ ). Although DOS will allow other characters, they do not add meaning to your name and should be avoided.*

3. Choose OK to have Access create the file on your disk with an .MDB extension.

When the Database window shown in Figure 2-7 appears, you can add objects such as tables, forms, and reports to it. Your only real limitation on database size is disk space since you can have up to 32,768 tables.

## Defining a New Table

A table is only one type of object that you can add to a Microsoft Access database. A table contains data about a specific topic or area. You can have as many as 255 fields in one table and as many as 32,768 tables in one database although you are limited to 254 open tables at one time.

A table is arranged in rows and columns much like a spreadsheet. Each column represents a field or individual piece of information and each row is a record or set of related fields.

A table must be defined before you can enter data in it. You will define each field you plan to store in the table. At a minimum each field must have both a field name and a data type. If you have Microsoft Access version 2 and use the Table Wizard you can pick field names from sample tables and a field type will be assigned automatically. You will want to learn how to create a table on your own as well as with the Table Wizard. First, you will look at what's involved when you do all your own work, and then when you see what the Table Wizard offers you will have a better appreciation of the time savings it affords.

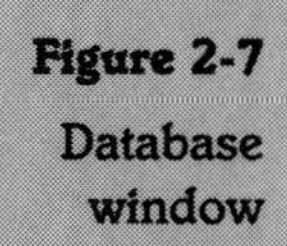

**Figure 2-7** Database window

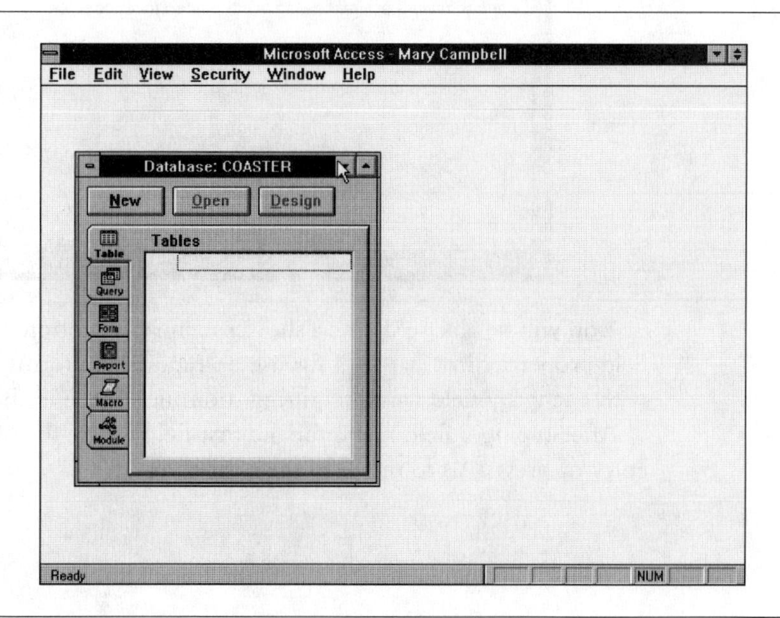

To create a new Access table without the Table Wizard, follow these steps:

1. Click the Table button on the left side of the Database window or choose Tables from the View menu.
2. Choose the New button at the top of the Database window.
3. Choose New Table in the New Table dialog box.

Access creates Table*n,* where *n* is the next sequential number. The table window appears in Design view as shown in Figure 2-8 to allow you to define the fields you want to store in the table.

### NAMING A FIELD

Each field within a table must have a unique name. Try to make this name as descriptive as possible. You can use as many as 64 characters including letters, numbers, and spaces within this limit. If you are using a long name you will find that the Field Name column will not display a full 64 characters. You can continue typing and have your entry scroll off the screen or press SHIFT+F2 to display a Zoom box where you can see the entire entry with the field name, as shown here:

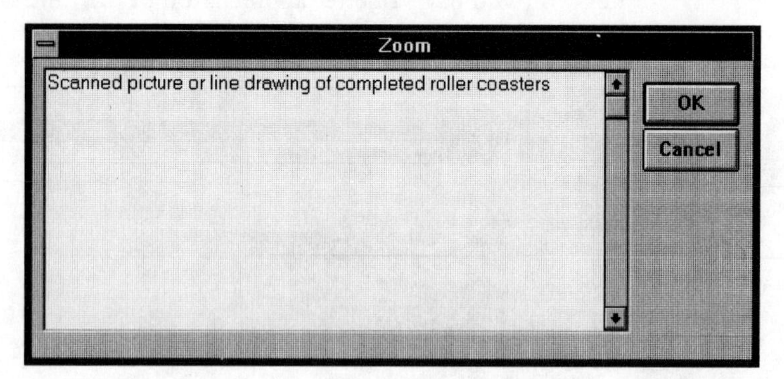


You will be able to define a shorter name as a caption when you learn about field properties in Chapter 3 for use on reports and forms if you are concerned with a lengthy field name requiring too much space in these other objects.

After typing a field name for the first field in the form click the Data Type entry or press TAB to move to the next column.

**tip:** *Access version 2 offers you a shortcut for adding some frequently used fields. Select the Build button in the toolbar while in the Field Name column, and Access opens the Field Builder. Select a sample table from the Sample Tables list box to display a different set of fields in the Sample Fields list box. Then select the field you want to use from the Sample Fields list box and select OK. Access inserts the design for the field, just as if you had created it yourself, into the Table window in Design view.*

## CHOOSING THE CORRECT MICROSOFT ACCESS DATA TYPE

Microsoft Access provides eight different data types to allow you to make this definition. You can use this drop-down list box to make your selection:

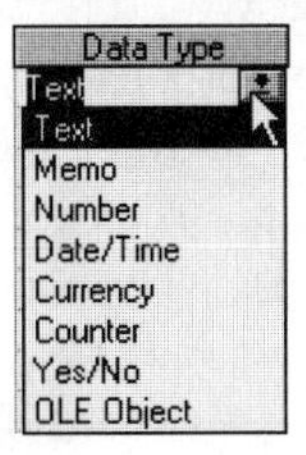


You must choose one of these data types for each field or Microsoft Access will use the default data type of Text, which allows as many as 255 alphanumeric characters in a field.

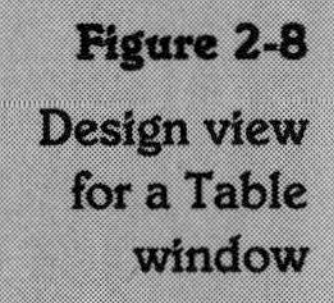

**Figure 2-8** Design view for a Table window

Table: Project

| Field Name | Data Type | Description |
|---|---|---|
| Coaster Id | Counter | Unique coaster identification number |
| Coaster Name | Text | Name of coaster ride |
| Client Id | Number | Number from client table |
| Completed | Yes/No | Completed project |
| Operational | Date/Time | Projected or actual operational date |
| Est Cost | Currency | Projected out of pocket cost for labor and material |
| Actual Cost | Currency | Actual labor and material costs |
| Track | Number | Length of ride track |
| Height | Number | Maximum height |
| Drop | Number | Maximum Drop |

Field Properties

| | |
|---|---|
| Format | |
| Caption | |
| Indexed | Yes (No Duplicates) |

A field name can be up to 64 characters long, including spaces. Press F1 for help on field names.

The eight data types offer variety. A Text field allows any alphanumeric character and a Yes/No field records only two different states for a field. A Memo data type is like a long text field that may contain paragraphs of information with a limit of 32,000 characters. A Number data type can contain an integer or decimal fraction. A Counter data type is automatically incremented by Access as you add each new record to a table. A Currency data type is designed to contain a monetary value. A Date/Time data type can contain only a valid date or time. An OLE Object data type is the most unique data type and can contain graphics, scanned pictures, binary data, or objects with a size limit of 1GB in Access version 2, or 128MB in Access version 1. OLE Object fields allow you to add such things as product sketches, employee pictures, and graphs to a database that would not otherwise be possible.

Your selection of a data type affects the amount of storage Access sets aside for your entries. Picking a data type that allows much more space than needed can be inefficient. An extreme example of a poor choice would be storing a Yes/No value in a Memo field rather than the much more efficient Yes/No data type.

The operations that you plan to perform with the data as you create reports and forms is another important factor. If you need to use a numeric entry to calculate a discount amount you must choose a Number or Currency field. Currency and Number fields are the only two logical options for calculations. You can store numbers in a Text field and still use them for calculations but the most common application of this would be for imported data since you would be more likely to choose a Currency or Number field type when setting up a new Access field for numbers. If you store a number in a Memo field data type you will not be able to use your data in a calculation.

Access allows you to sequence data in tables and reports by the values in a particular field. You cannot use Memo or OLE Object data type fields for sequencing your entries.

You can change data types before entering your data if you decide you've made the wrong choice. Look at Table 2-1 to see the size of each data type, what it contains, and any other limiting factors associated with the use of a particular data type. In Chapter 3, you will learn how to refine your selection with property settings and how to specify a field size.

## ADDING A FIELD DESCRIPTION

Although the description for a field is optional you will want to use it unless the field name is fully descriptive. You are limited to 64 characters in your description entry.

| Data Type | Size | Contains | Limitations |
|---|---|---|---|
| Counter | 4 bytes | An integer that is incremented by Access for each new record | Only 1 Counter in each table |
| Currency | 8 bytes | A number representing a sum of money | |
| Date/Time | 8 bytes | A date or time entry | |
| Memo | 32,000 bytes max | Text in the form of phrases, sentences, or paragraphs | Cannot be used to index a table |
| Number | 1 to 8 bytes | Numeric values | |
| OLE Object | 1 gigabyte or 128 megabytes max | Graphs, pictures, binary objects | Cannot be used to index a table |
| Text | 255 bytes maximum | Alphanumeric characters | |
| Yes/No | 1 bit | Boolean entries | Cannot be used to index a table |

**Table 2-1**
**Data Types**

For example, the Last Name field in the Employee table does not require further definition. The Angle field in the Projects table would require a definition to clarify which angle was being referred to. If you press ENTER or TAB, Access will move down to the next record.

### CREATING A PRIMARY KEY

A *primary key* uniquely identifies each database record. Although a primary key normally consists of a single field you can use more than one if you do not have a single field with unique entries.

You can use a multiple key field if a single field does not contain unique entries. Although Access allows as many as 32 fields to be combined, you will want to keep the entries shorter than this in most cases for efficiency. If you have a table of class offerings for a college, for example, you might want to use each faculty member's last name in combination with the day of the week and time of the course as a key to the table. None of these fields would be unique by themselves as faculty members typically teach several courses and multiple courses are offered on the same day and time. Together they must be unique as you would not want a faculty member to teach two different courses at the same time. Access even helps you ensure that faculty members are not double-scheduled as it rejects all attempts to create a duplicate primary key entry.

To create a primary key, click the selector to the left of the field name. If you need to select multiple fields to create a key with unique entries, hold down

CTRL as you click each field. Click the Set Primary Key button or choose Set Primary Key from the Edit menu. You can also right-click the field name and choose Set Primary Key from the shortcut menu.

Access indexes a table by the primary key and displays the records in this order on a form or datasheet. Access enforces the unique entries within an index when you enter new records into the table. Access will reject an entry for a new record if it has the same primary key as an existing record. If you save a table before designating a primary key, Access 2 displays this dialog box:

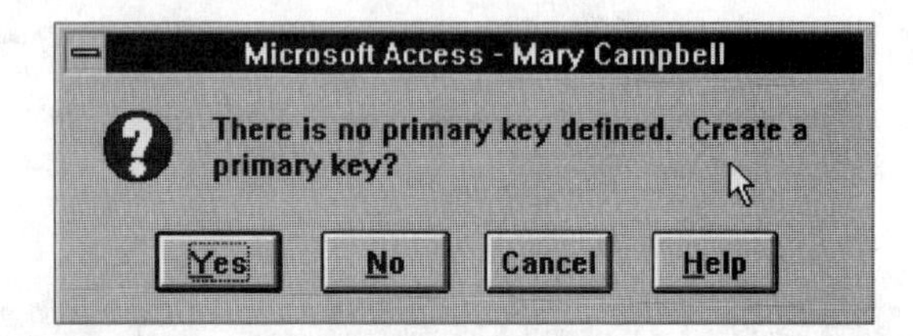


If you choose Yes and have a field with a data type of Counter, Access will use this field for a primary key. If the table does not have a Counter data type field, Access will add an ID field with a data type of Counter and automatically increment the value in the field for each new record. If you select No, the table is saved but no primary key is selected. If you choose Cancel, the save request is suspended and you can choose your own primary key.

## Using the Table Wizard to Create a Table

The Table Wizard can be a real time saver if you are creating tables for personal or business use. You can select whether you want a personal or a business option and then choose fields from a sample table in the list provided. Appendix B lists the sample fields in each sample table available from the Table Wizard. You can choose all the fields from one table type or just a few. You can even switch to a second table type before making additional selections if you want to construct your table from several sample tables. Any fields added in this way have a default name and data type defined automatically. Follow these steps to create a table from the Table Wizard:

1. Click the Table button on the left side of the Database window or choose Tables from the View menu.
2. Select the New button at the top of the Database window.
3. Select the Table Wizards button.

Access displays the dialog box shown in Figure 2-9. The Sample Tables list box lists possible predefined tables the Wizard can create. The Sample Fields list box contains the fields in a sample table. The Fields in My New Table list box contains all of the fields you add from any of the sample tables into the one you are creating.

4. Select either the Business or the Personal option button to determine which list of sample tables displays.
5. Select an entry from the Sample Tables list box.
6. Select an entry from the Sample Fields list box and then select the > button to add a single field to your table. You can add all of the fields to the list for your table by selecting the >> button to individually select fields to be added.
7. Select the Next button after making all of your selections.
8. Type the name you want to use for the table in the What do you want to name your table text box.
9. Select Let Microsoft Access set a primary key for me to have Access choose a primary key for you or select Set the primary key myself to choose your own. If you select Set the primary key myself, select Next and then select the field for the primary key from the What data will be unique for each record drop-down list box. You can select the type of data this primary field will contain from one of the three option buttons.
10. Select Next after setting the primary key.

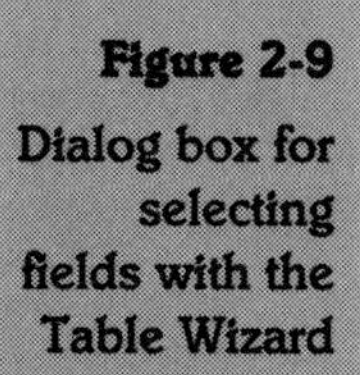

**Figure 2-9**
**Dialog box for selecting fields with the Table Wizard**

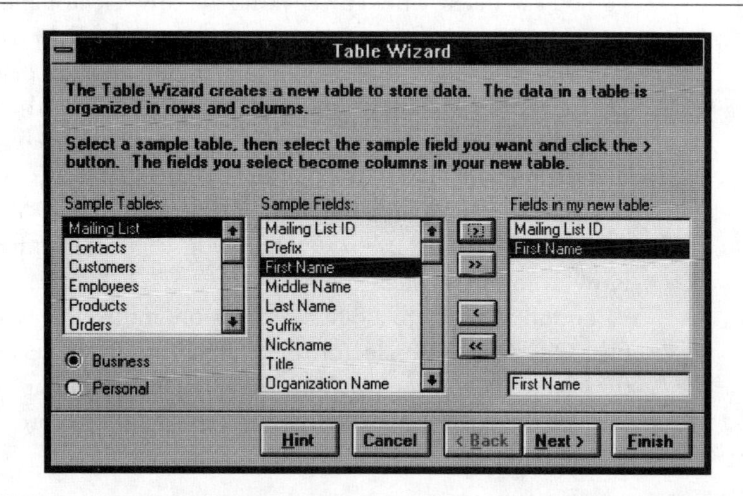

11. The next dialog box lets you set relationships between the table you are creating and other tables in the database. Relationships are explained in Chapter 3. For now, simply select Next without defining any relationships.
12. Select Modify the table design then Finish to view the table in Design view so you can modify the field names or data types.

If you are ready to enter data into the table at this time, you can select Enter data directly into the table and Finish instead.

**tip:** *Note that the sample tables in the Table Wizard are the same tables as appear in the Field Builder when you are creating a table without the Table Wizard.*

## Changing and Reorganizing Your Entries

You can use Design view to change any of your fields whether you entered them yourself or added them with the Table Wizard. You can also insert rows to add additional fields or delete a row to eliminate a field you no longer want.

If you create a table with the Table Wizard you might want to alter some of the field names to conform to the standards used in your company. To change a field name or a description press F2 to change from having the entire field selected to having an insertion point. Once the insertion point appears in the entry, you can use the arrow keys to move the insertion point to a different location. You can also type field names that were not added initially.

You can delete a field by clicking the row selector and then pressing the DEL key. The *row selector* is the box to the left of the field name. Clicking the row selector selects the entire row. If you prefer, you can delete a row by choosing Delete Row from the Edit menu or right-clicking the box to the left of the field name and selecting Delete Row from the shortcut menu.

To insert a field press the INS key or choose Insert Row from the Edit menu. A blank row is added above the current field name. You can also right-click the row selector for the row where you want the field added and select Insert Row from the shortcut menu.

To move a field to a different location in the table layout, you must select it first. Click the row selector. Next, drag the row selector to where you want the selected row to appear. You can either click another location on the window or press the RIGHT ARROW key to unselect the record.

## Saving Your Work

Once you start entering data, saving is no problem. In the Design view data is not saved until you specifically request it or close the Design view. When you are working in the Datasheet view, Microsoft Access saves a database record as soon as you move the *focus* to a new record. You can tell if the focus is on a record by the pointer to the left of the record in the table. You can also tell where the focus is by where the insertion point is located.

The design is not saved for you automatically. You must choose Save As from the File menu to save the current design settings. If the database design has been saved before, you only need to select OK to save it. If you choose Save from the File menu and have not saved the design before, the Save As window will appear anyway and prompt you for a table name.

Subsequent save requests can be made by choosing Save from the File menu unless you want to save the table under a new name. You must choose Save As to specify a new name.

If you have a table open and choose Close from the File menu, Access will close your table. If there are object changes that have not been saved, a dialog box displays the message "Save changes to Table *X*?" where *X* is the name of the table that has unsaved changes. You can decide whether or not to save and choose Yes, No, or Cancel. When the table is closed the Database window displays again unless there are other open tables.

If you choose Close Database from the File menu in the Database window, the database is closed and the Access menu appears again.

# Accessing Data in Existing Databases and Tables

You must open a database before you can use any of its tables. To open an existing database choose Open Database from the File menu. Once the database is open you can select the desired table and then select OK. If you choose Exit from the File menu, Access will close the database for you. If you are wondering why there is no Save option in the File menu, it is because Access saves database changes to records automatically. Your only real concern should be saving changes to objects such as tables in which you work in Design View for long periods of time. You can save every five minutes, save every hour, or in any increments in between; how often you save depends on how much work you can stand to redo in the event your machine crashes unexpectedly.

# Keeping a Copy of the Table Design

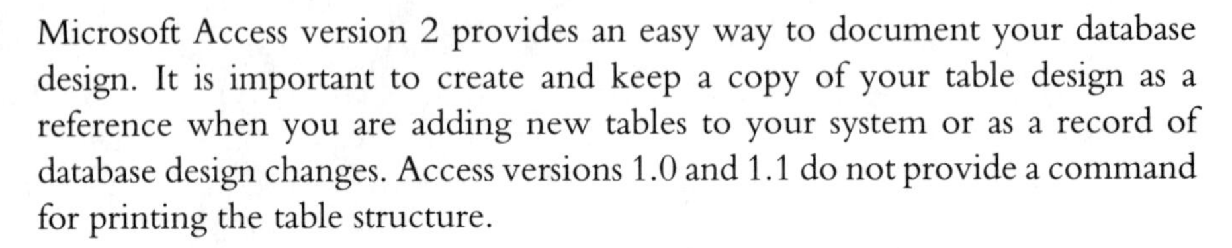

Microsoft Access version 2 provides an easy way to document your database design. It is important to create and keep a copy of your table design as a reference when you are adding new tables to your system or as a record of database design changes. Access versions 1.0 and 1.1 do not provide a command for printing the table structure.

## Printing Your Database Structure with Access Version 2

Access version 2 has two ways you can print information about the tables and other objects you have in a database. One way prints the information for one table or other object at a time. The second way prints the information for multiple tables or other objects at a time. When you print information about a table or another object, you can select the type of information to print.

To print the information for a single table or another object in a database, follow these steps:

1. Highlight the table in the Database window that you want to print information about.

   Later when you learn how to create other types of objects such as queries, forms, and reports, you can use these same steps to print information about those objects. Access will print information about the selected object.

2. Choose Print Definition from the File menu.
3. Select the information you want to print. Your choices include:

   - *Properties* to print table properties.
   - *Relationships* to print relationship information that describes how the records from one table are connected to another. You will learn more about relationships in Chapter 3.
   - *Permissions by User and Group* to print information about the users and groups that can use the selected table. You will learn about using permissions to limit accessibility to database objects in Chapter 20.
   - *Include for Fields* to select which information about the fields is printed.
   - *Include for Indexes* to select which information about the indexes is printed. You will learn about indexes in Chapter 3.

Later you can try these steps on other types of database objects, as you will learn about in Chapter 4 with tables, Chapter 6 with queries, Chapter 8 with forms, and Chapter 9 with reports. The choices you have in this step will vary to match the information that the object has available.

4. Select OK.

   Access opens a report window just like the one Access opens when you preview a report. From this window you can see how the printed information will appear. In Chapter 9, you will learn about many of the options you have for printing. These options are also available when you print the table information.

5. Click the Print button in the toolbar and choose OK to print the report.

   Figure 2-10 shows the information Access prints for the Client table. The logo is created using letterhead paper. In this example, in the By Print Table Definition dialog box, the Properties, Relationships, and Permissions by User and Group check boxes are cleared, the Data Names, types, and Sizes option button is selected under Include for Fields, and the Nothing option button is selected under Include for Indexes. The letterhead requires a top margin of 2 inches so you will use the print options described in Chapter 9 to increase the margin.

6. Press CTRL+F4 or click the Close Window button in the toolbar to close the report window.

The other method for printing table information lets you print information for multiple tables at once. To print the information for more than one table at a time, follow these steps:

1. Choose Add-Ins from the File menu and then Database Documentor.
2. Select the types of objects you want to print information about from the Object Type drop-down list box.
3. Double-click the names of the tables or the other objects to print information about. You can also highlight the name from the Objects list box and choose Select.
4. Select Options and choose the information to print as described in step 3 in the previous procedure.
5. Select OK twice to generate the report.

**Figure 2-10** Report of information on the Client table

Thursday, November 11, 1993 | **Table: Client** | Page: 1

**Columns**

| Name | Type | Size |
|---|---|---|
| Client Id | Number (Long) | 4 |
| Client Name | Text | 50 |
| Contact | Text | 50 |
| Park Location | Text | 50 |
| Mailing Address | Text | 50 |
| City | Text | 50 |
| State | Text | 50 |
| Zip Code | Text | 50 |
| Phone | Number (Double) | 8 |
| Park Desc | Memo | N/A |
| YTD Invoices | Currency | 8 |
| YTD Payments | Currency | 8 |
| Total Invoices | Currency | 8 |
| Total Payments | Currency | 8 |
| Comments | Memo | |

6. Click the Print button in the toolbar and choose OK to print the report.
7. Press CTRL+F4 or click the Close Window button in the toolbar to close the report window.

### Printing Your Database Structure with an Earlier Release

In versions 1.0 and 1.1 there are two different approaches that you can take to keep a hard copy record of each table design. One method is to capture pictures of the screen. You can use a screen capture application such as Collage or you can copy a picture to the Clipboard by pressing PRINT SCREEN that you can subsequently paste into a word processing document. The drawback to this method is that it may not show all of the fields at one time and you might need a number of screens to see everything.

Another method involves more work but it does not require another application and can give you a more complete perspective, including settings for field properties. To use this approach create another table as a data dictionary. The fields in this table will be database table, field name, type, description, size, format, decimal places, caption, default width, and so on. Each data element in your database system would have an entry in this dictionary database. You could index by database and field name to group all the elements for a single table in the same location. Your design for this table might look something like Figure 2-11.

You can create reports like the one in Figure 2-12 that show the fields in your tables.

## Creating the Database Tables for Coaster Mania

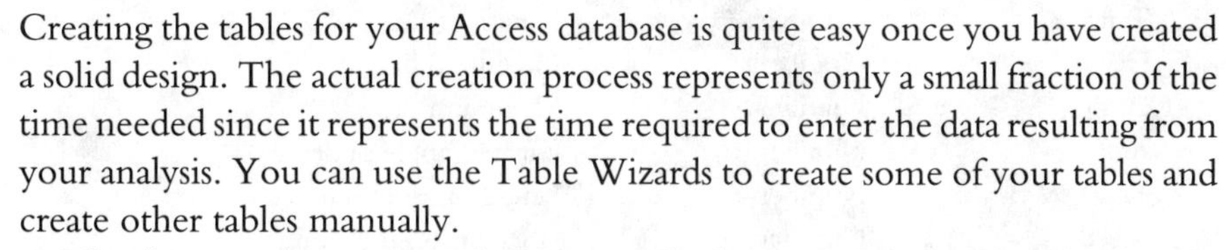

Creating the tables for your Access database is quite easy once you have created a solid design. The actual creation process represents only a small fraction of the time needed since it represents the time required to enter the data resulting from your analysis. You can use the Table Wizards to create some of your tables and create other tables manually.

The first step is to create the Coaster database. Next you create each table separately. You then establish field names and data types. Where needed, add descriptions to clarify the field contents. Chapter 3 discusses properties for these tables.

Table 2-2 shows the field names, data types, and descriptions used to establish the Project table. The data type choice for Coaster Id requires an explanation. A Counter data type field is automatically incremented for each new entry so this field handles numbering all of your new and old projects.

**Figure 2-11**
**Data dictionary**

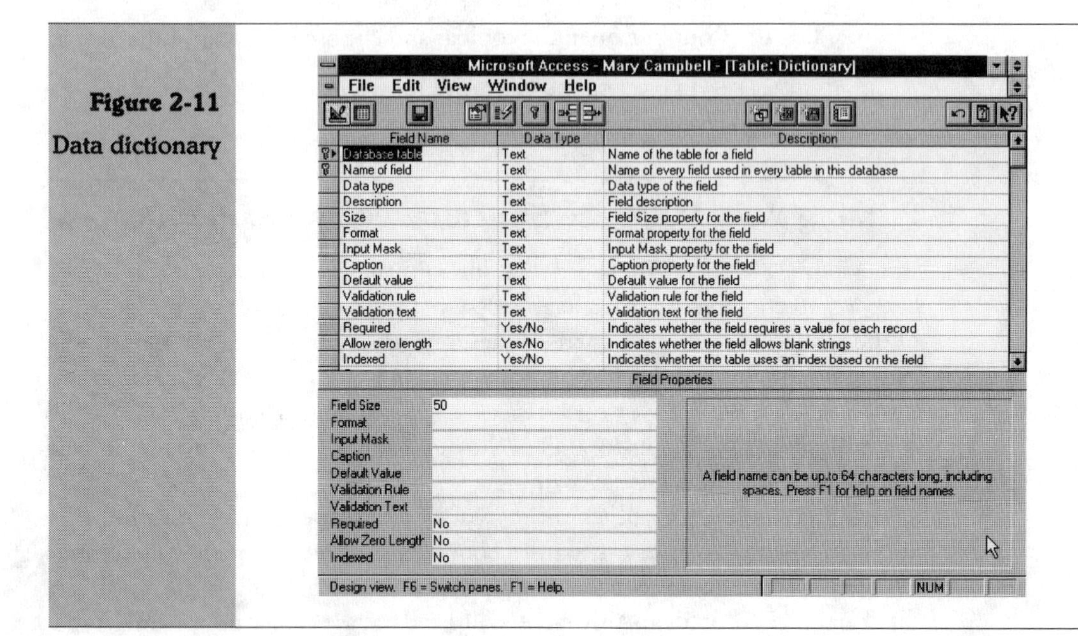


| Field Name | Data Type | Description |
|---|---|---|
| Coaster Id | Counter | Unique coaster identification number |
| Coaster Name | Text | Name of coaster ride |
| Client Id | Number | Number from client table |
| Completed | Yes/No | Completed project |
| Operational | Date/Time | Projected or actual operational date |
| Est Cost | Currency | Projected out-of-pocket cost for labor and material |
| Act Cost | Currency | Actual labor and material costs |
| Track | Number | Length of ride track |
| Height | Number | Maximum height |
| Drop | Number | Maximum drop |
| Angle | Number | Greatest angle of descent |
| Time | Number | Length of ride in minutes |
| Speed | Number | Greatest speed in mph |
| Capacity | Number | Maximum number of riders in 1 hour |
| Vehicles | Number | Total number of vehicles |
| Picture | OLE Object | Picture of model or operational ride |
| Features | Memo | Unique features of the ride |

**Table 2-2**
**Projects Table**

**Figure 2-12**
Report showing fields in different tables

## Dictionary of Fields Used in Coaster Database

| Table | Name of field | Data type | Description |
|---|---|---|---|
| Client | | | |
| | City | Text | |
| | Client Id | Counter | Unique client identification number |
| | Client Name | Text | Name of the amusement park |
| | Contact | Text | Contact individual |
| | Mailing Address | Text | P.O. Box or other mailing address |
| | Park Desc | Memo | Park description and information on other park coaster |
| | Park Location | Text | Location of park rather than mailing address |
| | Phone | Number | |
| | State | Text | |
| | Total Invoices | Currency | |
| | Total Payments | Currency | |
| | YTD Invoices | Currency | |
| | YTD Payments | Currency | |
| | Zip Code | Text | |
| Employee | | | |
| | Bill Rate | Currency | Hourly client billing rate |
| | City | Text | |
| | Date of Hire | Date/Time | |
| | Department | Text | |
| | Employee Id | Counter | Employee Identification Number |
| | Extension | Number | |
| | First Name | Text | |
| | Home Phone | Text | |
| | Job Class | Number | Two digit job class code |
| | Last Name | Text | |
| | Middle Initial | Text | |
| | Pay Rate | Currency | Hourly pay rate |
| | Picture | OLE Object | |
| | State | Text | |
| | Street Address | Text | |
| | Zip Code | Text | |
| Employee Time Log | | | |
| | Date | Date | First day of the week |

| Field Name | Data Type | Description |
|---|---|---|
| Client Id | Counter | Unique client identification number |
| Client Name | Text | Name of the amusement park |
| Contact | Text | Contact individual |
| Park Location | Text | Location of park rather than mailing address |
| Mailing Address | Text | P.O. Box or other mailing address |
| City | Text | |
| State | Text | |
| Zip Code | Text | |
| Phone | Number | |
| Park Desc | Memo | Park description and information on other park coasters and planned projects |
| YTD Invoices | Currency | |
| YTD Payments | Currency | |
| Total Invoices | Currency | |
| Total Payments | Currency | |

**Table 2-3**
**Client Table**

The Coaster Id field was set to be the primary key field before saving the table.

The decisions made for the Client table are recorded in Table 2-3. The Client Id field is a Counter data type field for the same reason that Coaster Id was established as a counter data type field. The Phone field was set up as a number although text would have been another possibility. It depends on whether you want to be able to list telephone numbers using letters (such as FO7-8999 or LIM-OS4U) or want to always use numbers (367-8999 or 546-6748).

The primary key is Client Id.

The Employee table fields are shown in Table 2-4. Employee Id was set up as a Counter data type primarily to show you how to use functions to link it with data in another table in Chapter 3. Although you would normally use the same data type for all phone number fields, the Home Phone field is a Text data type to allow you to see the different ways to handle formatting for this field depending on its data type. Employee Id is the primary key.

| Field Name | Data Type | Description |
|---|---|---|
| Employee Id | Counter | Employee Identification Number |
| Last Name | Text | |
| First Name | Text | |
| Middle Initial | Text | |
| Pay Rate | Currency | Hourly pay rate |
| Bill Rate | Currency | Hourly client billing rate |
| Date of Hire | Date/Time | |
| Job Class | Number | Two digit job class code |
| Department | Text | |
| Street Address | Text | |
| City | Text | |
| State | Text | |
| Zip Code | Text | |
| Picture | OLE Object | |
| Home Phone | Text | |
| Extension | Number | |

**Table 2-4**
**Employee Table**

The Employee Time Log table contains records for each project an employee worked on during the week. The definition of the table contains the elements shown in Table 2-5. The primary key consists of three fields to create unique entries: Date, Employee Id, and Project Id.

The tables for invoices and payments require only a few fields. For Coaster Mania, they are combined into a single table. Their primary key is the Invoice Number field. Table 2-6 contains the fields for Invoice Register.

| Field Name | Data Type | Description |
|---|---|---|
| Date | Date/Time | First day of the week |
| Employee Id | Number | Matches up with Employee Id in the Employee table |
| Project Number | Number | Matches up with Coaster Id in the Project table |
| Hours | Number | Number of hours spent on project |

**Table 2-5**
**Billing Table**

| Field Name | Data Type | Description |
|---|---|---|
| Invoice Number | Number | |
| Invoice Date | Date/Time | |
| Invoice Amount | Currency | |
| Payment Amount | Currency | |
| Payment Date | Date/Time | |
| Project Id | Number | Matches up with Coaster Id in the Project table |

**Table 2-6**
**Invoice Register Table**

## Quick Reference

**To Create a New Database** From the Access window choose New Database from the File menu. Type a filename in the File Name box (between one and eight characters long) and click OK.

**To Create a New Table** Click the Table button in the Database window, and then click New. If you have Access version 2 you can choose whether to create a table with the help of the Table Wizard or on your own.

**To Save the Table Design** Choose Save As from the File menu and type a name between 1 and 64 characters and spaces in length. You can also choose Save the first time you save but the Save As dialog box will be displayed anyway. With subsequent save requests choose Save unless you want to save the table with a new name.

**To Close a Table** Choose Close from the File menu. You will be prompted to save the table design if you have not already saved it.

**To Close a Database** Choose Close database from the File menu.

**Quick Reference**

**To Create a Primary Key for a Table** Click the selector to the left of the field name you want to use and then click the Primary Key button or choose Set Primary Key from the Edit menu. If you want a multiple field primary key, press the CTRL key while selecting fields.

**To Delete a Row of a Table Definition** Click the field selector to the left of the field name, and press the DEL key.

**To Add a Row of Table Definition** Click the field selector to the left of the field below where you want to add the new field, and then press INS.

**To Print a Copy of a Table Structure in Access Version 2** Highlight the table in the Database window that you want to print information about. Choose Print Definition from the File menu. Select the information you want to print. Select OK. Click the Print button in the toolbar and choose OK to print the report. Click the Close Window button in the toolbar to close the report window.

# Chapter 3

Defining Relationships

Defining Table and Field Properties

Creating Indexes for a Table

Changing Table Definition and Property Defaults

# Defining Properties and Relationships

**A**LTHOUGH you can skip to Chapter 4 and begin entering data as soon as you define the fields and data types for your initial table, you should first consider two issues: the relationships between tables in your database and the properties that customize those tables. This requires examining the relationships between all of your tables, which might lead you to create yet another table or revise the database design to eliminate redundancy and create usable relationships between tables. You also need to define properties for the various table fields. Changing properties after entering data can result in data loss. Not changing properties allows errors to be entered into tables; this can be prevented by using validity check properties. The properties that you set also affect the forms and reports that you create because these objects inherit the current property settings of a field when you design the report or form.

## Defining Relationships

Access lets you define connections called *relationships,* between fields in different tables, letting you use data from related tables together in reports, queries, and forms. In order to establish relationships between tables you first define a unique field or combination of fields for each table, called the *primary key*, which can identify a specific record.

When you relate two tables, you relate the primary key in the primary table to one of the fields in the related table. These fields must use the same data type, with one exception. A Counter field can be related to a Number field with a Field Size property set to Long Integer. (Field properties, including the Field Size property, are explained later in this chapter.) The fields in the two tables must contain the same types of entries to make the relationship meaningful. For example, when the Client table and the Project table are related, the Client Id field is used. This relationship associates data on specific projects with the data about the client for whom the project is being done.

## Planning for a Primary Key

Just as you use a Social Security number, serial number, or vehicle identification number to identify something uniquely, Access uses a key that identifies a record uniquely to bring together information from multiple tables. Access can locate records much faster when a table has a primary key field because Access builds an index of primary key values and the corresponding record numbers. This makes locating a record faster than if Access searched through the records themselves. Assigning a primary key is the essential first step if you plan to establish relationships between fields in different tables.

Entries in a primary key field must be unique. Nicknames, last names, and company names will not work since there can be duplicates in these fields (even if current data does not contain a duplicate, future entries may be duplicates). Make certain that future entries in a primary key field are not duplicates of current entries.

If you do not have one field that is unique you can use a combination of fields as a primary key. For instance, you might have a database of parcels of land located in various states. Each piece of land has a plat number recorded in the county where it is located. Although you will not have duplicate plat numbers within one county, as you cross county and state borders there could be duplicate plat numbers. But if you use a combination of the county, state, and plat number fields as the primary key, you can prevent any duplicates.

Figure 3-1 shows how several fields in a Properties table are designated as a primary key. The three fields at the top have a key in their row selector. You learned in Chapter 2 that you can select more than one field by holding down the CTRL key while clicking the row selector for each field you want to include in the primary key.

**caution:** *Do not include unnecessary fields in the primary key; long keys adversely affect database performance.*

If you do not have a unique field or if a unique combination would result in too lengthy a key, use a Counter field that simply assigns the next sequential number to each new record in the database. The advantage of using a Counter field is that its entries are short until you have many records, and having a short primary key makes Access operate more efficiently.

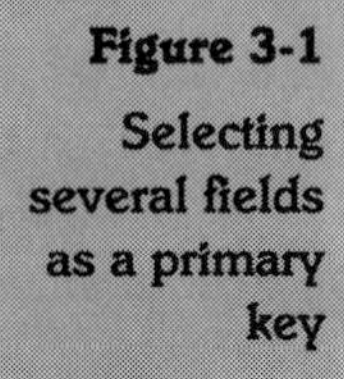

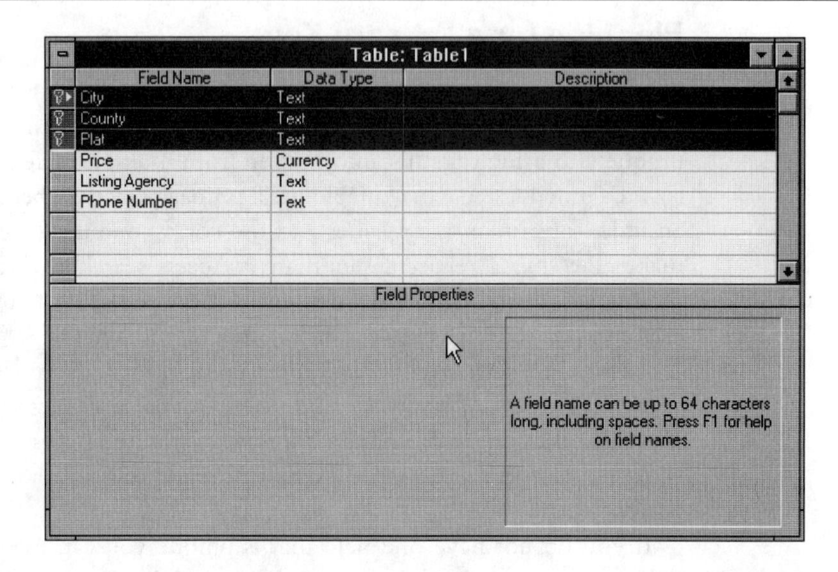


**Figure 3-1** Selecting several fields as a primary key

**tip:** *Boost performance by choosing a primary key that works along the lines of how you normally search the table for answers to specific questions. Do you search by product Id, a combination of first name, last name, and location, or employer Id? Whatever the answer, consider using that field or combination of fields as your primary key.*

## Understanding Possible Relationships Between Tables

You need to consider the relationship between the records in each table to achieve the best database design. The most important component of the relationship is how many records in the related table match entries in the primary table. For instance, if you look up the Supplier Id in the Inventory table, are there likely to be many records for a single Id or just one record?

Related tables may have one of three possible relationships: one-to-one, one-to-many, or many-to-many. Usually, a one-to-many relationship is the best design. A one-to-one relationship is appropriate in limited instances, such as when the data in one table is needed only temporarily. You cannot create a many-to-many relationship in Access. If you need to relate data in two tables this way you need to create a third table and relate the two tables to it, using one-to-many relationships. The following sections explore each of these types of relationships.

Before establishing relationships, you should diagram the relationship between your tables by drawing a line between related fields. This will make it easier for you to visualize how you want the data to be related. You can even write **One** and **Many** at the end points to remind you of the type of relationship the tables have. Figure 3-2 shows an example of such a diagram.

## A ONE-TO-MANY RELATIONSHIP

In a one-to-many relationship, a record in table 1 may have many matching records in table 2, but each record in table 2 can match only one record in table 1. It is important that you examine the relationship between tables from both tables.

Although the one-to-one relationship (explained next) is acceptable between some tables, a one-to-many relationship is usually the best design. All of the related tables in Coaster Mania's database use one-to-many relationships, as shown in Figure 3-3. One record in the Client table is associated with many records in the Project table, yet each project is for only one client. One record in the Employee table associates with many records in the Employee Time Log

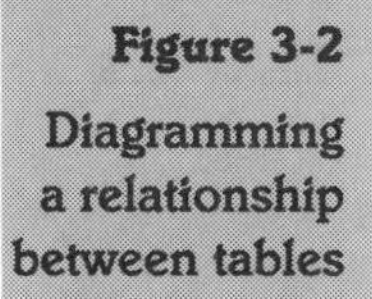
**Figure 3-2** Diagramming a relationship between tables

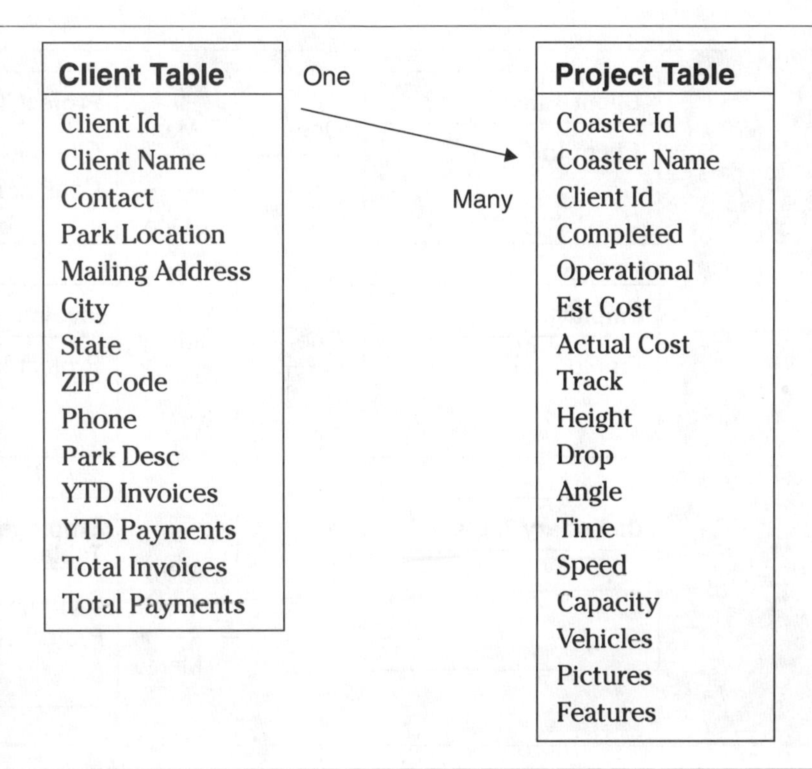

table, but each time record associates with a specific employee record. One client record associates with many invoices, yet there is only one client for each invoice.

Figure 3-4 shows how one client record might have several associated project records. Even though most clients have only one project going at a time, there are cases in which one client has more than one active project.

**tip:** *The text in Figure 3-4 may look larger than the text on your screen. Here, and on several other screens, the text is shown larger to make it easier for you to read.*

### A ONE-TO-ONE RELATIONSHIP

If two tables have a one-to-one relationship, each record in the primary table associates with only one record in the related table. For example, when relating the Employee table and the Payroll table (which contains the information necessary to process the payroll), each employee will have only one record in

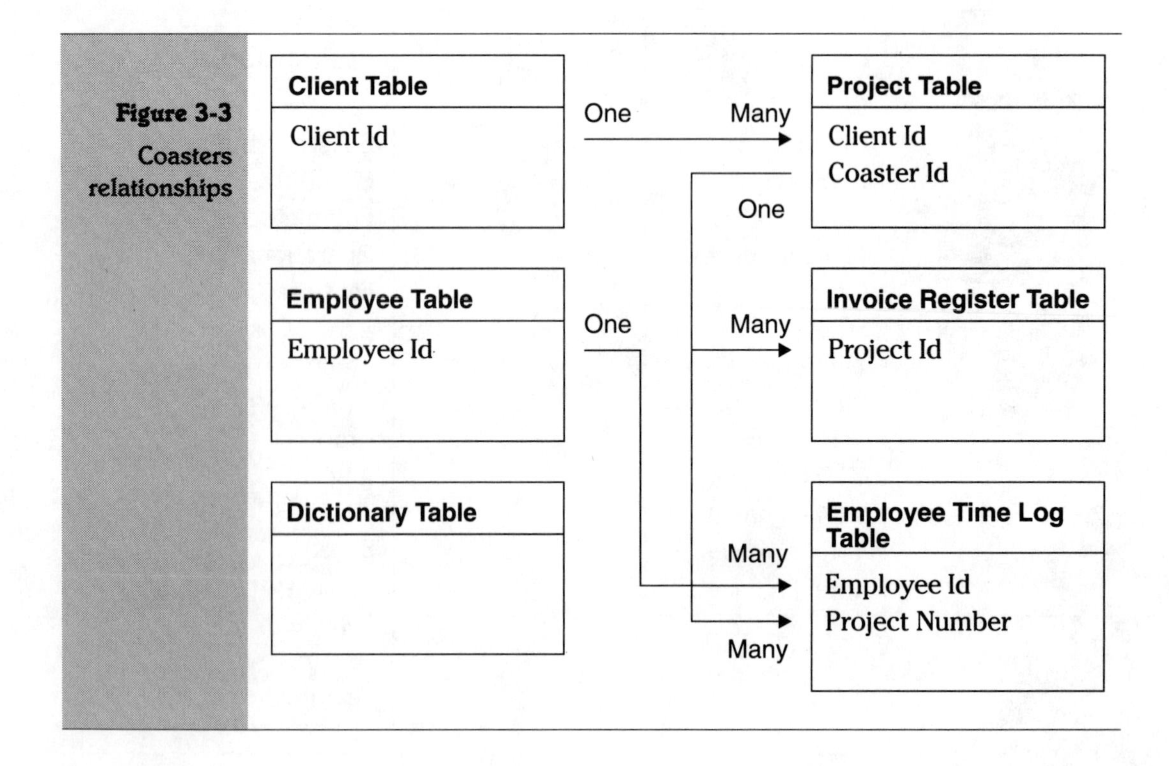


**Figure 3-3** Coasters relationships

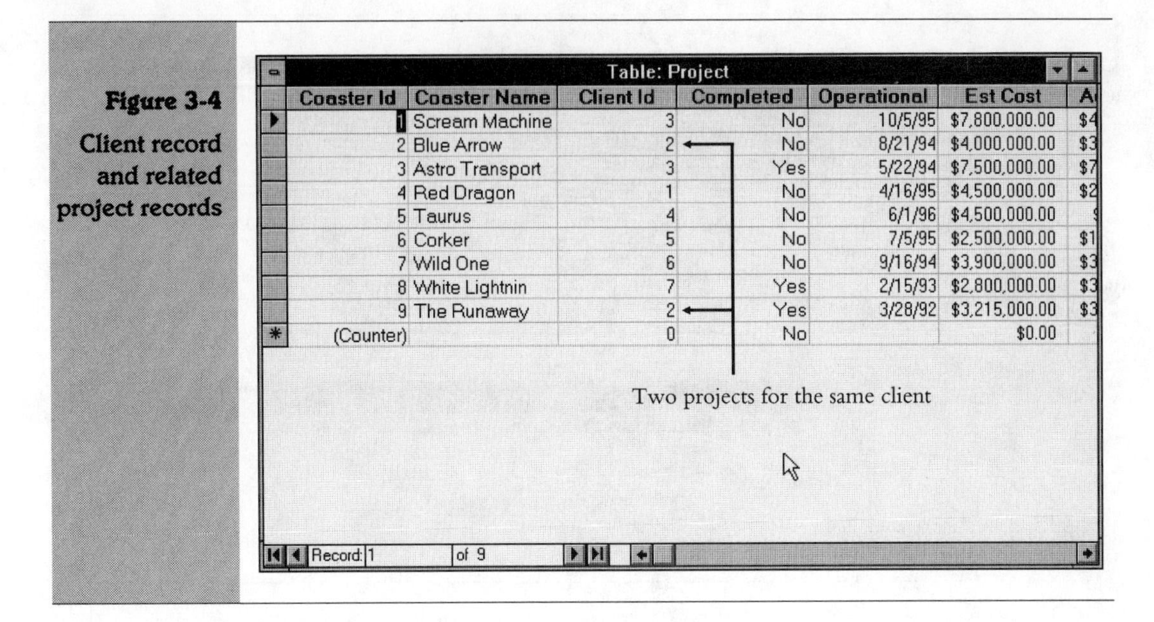

Table: Project

| Coaster Id | Coaster Name | Client Id | Completed | Operational | Est Cost | A |
|---|---|---|---|---|---|---|
| 1 | Scream Machine | 3 | No | 10/5/95 | $7,800,000.00 | $4 |
| 2 | Blue Arrow | 2 | No | 8/21/94 | $4,000,000.00 | $3 |
| 3 | Astro Transport | 3 | Yes | 5/22/94 | $7,500,000.00 | $7 |
| 4 | Red Dragon | 1 | No | 4/16/95 | $4,500,000.00 | $2 |
| 5 | Taurus | 4 | No | 6/1/96 | $4,500,000.00 | $ |
| 6 | Corker | 5 | No | 7/5/95 | $2,500,000.00 | $1 |
| 7 | Wild One | 6 | No | 9/16/94 | $3,900,000.00 | $3 |
| 8 | White Lightnin | 7 | Yes | 2/15/93 | $2,800,000.00 | $3 |
| 9 | The Runaway | 2 | Yes | 3/28/92 | $3,215,000.00 | $3 |
| (Counter) |  | 0 | No |  | $0.00 |  |

Record: 1 of 9



**Figure 3-4**

**Client record and related project records**

the Payroll table and each record in the Payroll table will match only one of the current employees.

When you have a one-to-one relationship between two tables, you can probably combine the fields into one table. No relationships are needed then because all of the data is in one location. You might not be able to combine these tables, however, if one table, such as the Payroll table, is created and maintained in another database, so that the relationship is to a table outside the current database. Another obstacle to combining tables would be if a table is locked so that only a few people can access it, because it contains confidential information.

Creating one combined table is the best approach unless the data is only needed for a short time—such as during the United Way campaign. Figure 3-5 shows one table for employee data and another table for the United Way campaign. Also, you probably wouldn't combine two one-to-one tables when only a few records in one table have associated records in the second table. For example, if you have to record school information on your minor employees, you would have this school information in a separate table, even though there is a one-to-one relationship between this table and the Employee table.

Examine the relationships between the database tables you have established. If you have any one-to-one relationships between tables, see if it makes more sense to combine the two tables.

**Figure 3-5**
**One-to-one relationship**

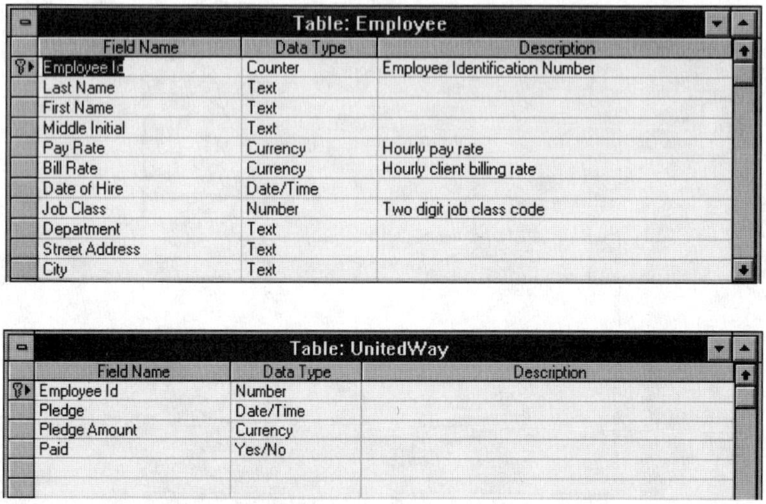

Table: Employee

| Field Name | Data Type | Description |
|---|---|---|
| Employee Id | Counter | Employee Identification Number |
| Last Name | Text | |
| First Name | Text | |
| Middle Initial | Text | |
| Pay Rate | Currency | Hourly pay rate |
| Bill Rate | Currency | Hourly client billing rate |
| Date of Hire | Date/Time | |
| Job Class | Number | Two digit job class code |
| Department | Text | |
| Street Address | Text | |
| City | Text | |

Table: UnitedWay

| Field Name | Data Type | Description |
|---|---|---|
| Employee Id | Number | |
| Pledge | Date/Time | |
| Pledge Amount | Currency | |
| Paid | Yes/No | |

## A MANY-TO-MANY RELATIONSHIP

In a many-to-many relationship you have many entries from table 1 that potentially match entries within table 2 and many entries in table 2 that match entries in table 1. This type of relationship—in which many records in both tables match a record in the other table—is not acceptable.

The data in two tables like this cannot be related directly because Access cannot create a many-to-many relationship. The data from the two tables can only be brought together through a third table, called a *junction table.*

The potential for a many-to-many relationship exists for the Coaster Mania database. For example, billing information could be entered directly into the Employee table, so that there would be several records for each employee—one for each billing period. Each record could reference several projects. An employee Id could be entered in the Project table, identifying project leaders. With one employee record containing references to several projects and one project record referencing many employee records, the many-to-many relationship would be built into the database design. Because this is not acceptable, a different approach was used.

To create invoices for Coaster Mania that list projects worked on and the employees that worked on each project, you need to establish a relationship between the Employee table and the Projects table. However, this would create a many-to-many relationship: Many different employees work on a single project while a given employee may work on many different projects. For this reason, no direct relationship can be established between these tables. However, the Employee Time Log table can serve as a junction table that has a one-to-many relationship with both the Employee table and the Project table. Using a third table eliminates a direct many-to-many relationship by letting you create two one-to-many relationships instead.

## Defining Default Relationships

You can wait until you create a form, report, or query to define the relationship between tables used in these objects. However, there are several advantages to defining default relationships when you create the tables involved in them.

One advantage is that Access will enforce the referential integrity when you add or delete records. *Referential integrity* is the set of rules that determines that the data you enter are considered valid, given the relationships between tables. This ensures that your tables continue to relate to each other as you originally defined. Part of maintaining referential integrity is making sure that records are added to the primary table before they are added to a related table. This means adding an employee's record to the Employee table before using that employee Id to record billing data. It also means not deleting an employee record when you still have billing records that reference that employee's Id.

Another advantage to setting default relationships is that Access can use them to perform tasks for you. Access uses the default relationships you define to create joins in queries as well as subforms and subreports that show related records.

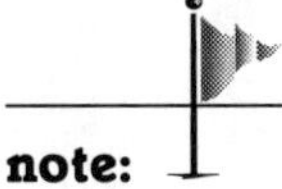

**note:** *You will learn about creating queries and joins in queries in Chapter 7. You will learn about creating forms and reports, including subforms and subreports, in Chapters 8, 9, and 13.*

You can have Access enforce referential integrity for you or take on the responsibility yourself. When Access enforces the referential integrity of a relationship, you cannot change records in the primary table if it would cause a mismatch with records in the related table. Also, you cannot add records to the related table that reference records not yet entered in the primary table. When Access does not enforce referential integrity, it is your responsibility to make sure the records in a related table match the records in a primary table.

Defining a relationship between two tables is easy once you have diagramed the relationship between your tables. Access version 2 also offers a new graphic method that makes defining relationships as easy as creating the diagram. Remember, in a one-to-many relationship, the table with one is the *primary table* and the table with many is the *related table*. In a one-to-one relationship, the main table, if there is one, is the primary table. For instance, if you have an Employee table and a table with employee table tennis scores from the company's tournament, the Employee table would be the primary table.

From the Database window in Access version 2, define the relationships between tables by following these steps:

1. Choose Relationships from the Edit menu to open the Relationships window.

If you have not defined relationships before, the Add Table dialog box also appears. If you have created relationships before, you can open this dialog box by selecting Add Table from the Relationships menu or clicking the Add Table button shown here.

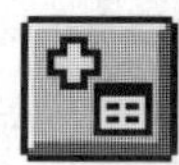

2. To add tables to the Relationships window so that you can use them to define relationships, highlight them in the Table/Query list box in the Add Table dialog box and select Add. After adding the tables for which you want to define relationships, select Close.

**tip:** *You can select several tables at once by pressing* CTRL *and clicking each table, or by dragging across all the tables.*

Your Relationships window now displays the tables you have added and the relationships between them, as shown in Figure 3-6.

The lines between tables indicate the relationships, just as the lines between tables in your diagram indicate relationships. When the relationship is one-to-many, 1 appears on the line at the table that is the one, and ∞ appears at the other end, by the table containing many associated records.

3. To create a relationship, drag the field in the primary table to the equivalent field in the related table. The primary key of each table is boldfaced.

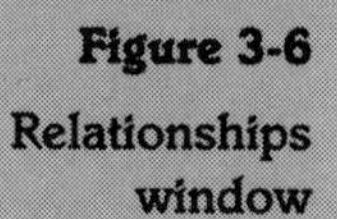

**Figure 3-6**
**Relationships window**

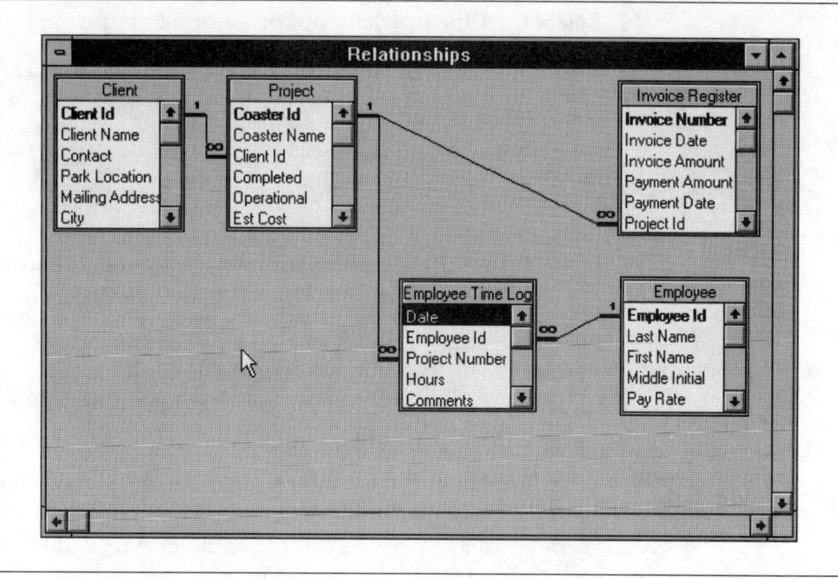


**note:** *Remember, use the primary key in the primary table to define relationships because Access can then find associated data more quickly. Also, the related fields must use the same data type. However, when the primary table's field is a Counter, the related table's field may be a Long Integer.*

4. A Relationships dialog box, shown here, is used for defining relationship options; the dialog box appears after you drag the field to the related table.

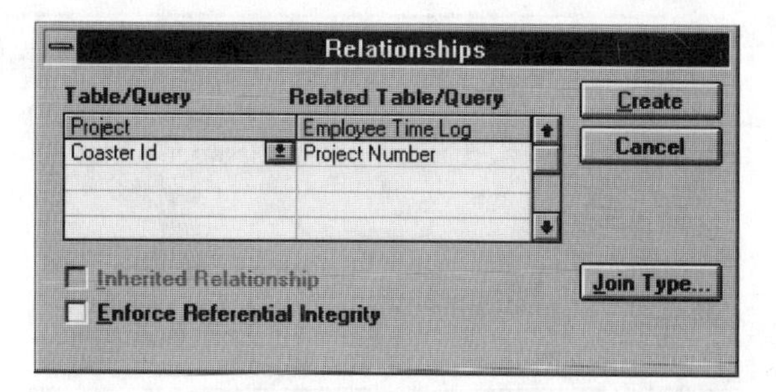


5. Check that the correct fields appear in the Table/Query and Related Table/Query list boxes.
6. Select the Enforce Referential Integrity check box to have Access maintain the relationship between these tables.

7. Select the One or Many option button to define the type of relationship.
8. Select Create to establish the relationship between the tables. The relationship is indicated by the line between the fields in the two tables.
9. Close the Relationships window by selecting Close from the File menu or by double-clicking the window's control box.

When you close the Relationships window, Access asks if you want to save the layout changes. No matter what you select, the relationships you create are saved. If you select Yes, Access saves how the tables are arranged in the window, but this arrangement is not saved if you select No.

In Access version 1, you define relationships differently. Start by selecting Relationships from the Edit menu. Then select the primary table from the Primary Table drop-down list box, and the related table from the Related Table drop-down list box. You are telling Access that you want to relate the primary key from the primary table to this other table. Access displays the primary key of the primary table beneath the list box.

Select the One button if this is a one-to-one relationship, or Many if it is a one-to-many relationship. Next, define which fields in the tables are related by selecting Suggest if the related fields have the same names in both tables or by selecting fields in the Select Matching Fields drop-down list box that match to the primary key in the primary table. To stop the referential integrity check, clear the Enforce Referential Integrity check box. Select the Add button to add this relationship to the database. Repeat these steps for all relationships before selecting the Close button.

### AN EXAMPLE OF DEFINING A RELATIONSHIP

Use the procedure that you just learned with the Client and Project tables. The Client table is the primary table in which the primary key is Client Id. This field name is used again in the Project table.

**tip:** *Since the two fields have the same name, you can choose Suggest in the Relationships dialog box in Access version 1 to have Access provide the correct field from the related table.*

If you wish, continue defining default relationships, using the Employee Time Log, Invoice Register, and Employee tables as related tables. The default relationships are easy to identify because the related tables use the same fields as the primary keys in the Employee and Project tables.

## Defining Table and Field Properties

You can change property settings for tables or for fields in a table. Properties let you customize settings such as the size of data entered in a field, default values, or criteria for valid entries. In Access version 2, you can even create an *input mask,* which makes entering some data easier, by providing characters such as parentheses and hyphens in phone numbers, for example.

Consider each of the property settings that you can make. Take special note of the different options available—these depend on the data type selected for the field. Changing the properties of some of the Coasters fields is discussed in this chapter. You can practice changing properties using these examples, or you can begin customizing the settings for your databases.

**note:** *Appendix C lists the fields and properties for the tables of the Coasters database used in this book.*

You need to be in the Design view of a table to change the property settings of the table or its fields. If you have already closed the table, reopen it in Datasheet view and then switch to the Design view by clicking the Design View button in the Database toolbar. You can also open the Design view directly by clicking the Design button in the Database window after highlighting the table name.

### Setting Properties

You set both field and table properties from the Design view of the table, using different steps. When you move to a field in the upper half of the Table window, that field's properties are displayed in the bottom half. To see or edit table properties, you must display the property sheet for the table.

To set field properties, switch to the Design view, highlight the field, and move to the field properties with the F6 key or the mouse. The exact steps that you need to perform are listed here:

1. In the top part of the Table window, highlight the field that you want to change.
2. Click the property in the lower half of the Table window, or press F6 to move to the Field Properties area.

   You change the property settings for the highlighted field in the bottom part of the table window in Design view.
3. When ready to work with another field, click the field in the top of the window or press F6 and move to the field.

Depending on the type of field selected, the available properties may include:

| Property | Sets |
|---|---|
| Field Size | Length of a text field or type of a number field |
| Format | How data is displayed using predefined or user-created formats |
| Decimal Places | How many places right of the decimal are displayed |
| Input Mask | How data is displayed while being entered using predefined or user-created masks |
| Caption | Label used for the field by default in a form or report |
| Default Value | Data entered in the field automatically when each record is created |
| Validation Rule | Data entry rules |
| Validation Text | Text displayed when invalid data is entered |
| Required | Requirement that data be entered in this field before the record is saved |
| Allow Zero Length | Whether zero-length strings are allowed |
| Indexed | Whether the field is used in an index |

To set properties for a table, you can do either of the following:

- Select Table Properties from the View menu.
- Click the Properties button from the toolbar, shown here:

Access displays a property sheet that lists the available properties you can set, as shown here:

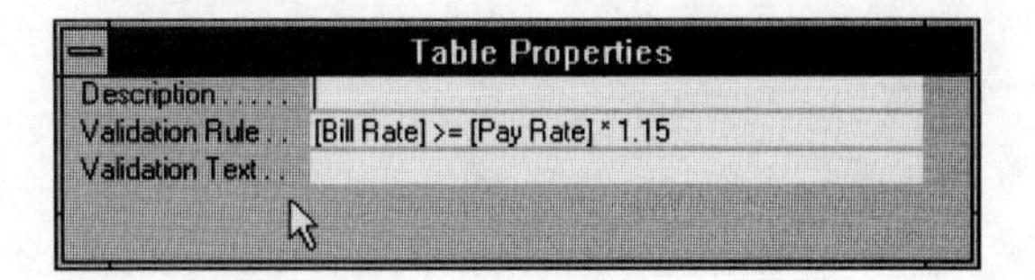


Access versions 1 and 2 have different table properties, because Access version 2 displays index entries in another location. The different table properties are shown in the following table.

| Version 1 | Version 2 |
|---|---|
| Description | Description |
| Primary Key | Validation Rule |
| Index1 - Index5 | Validation Text |

Setting the primary key of a table, in either version of Access, is described in the previous chapter. Setting indexes, which is done differently in each version, is described later in this chapter under "Creating Indexes for a Table." Setting table validation rules or validation text is described under "Performing Validity Checking" later in this chapter.

## Changing the Field Size

The default size established for each field depends on the data type that you selected for the field when you created the field. You can change the default size for Text and Number fields if your data requires a different size. The default size for a Text field is 50 and the default size for a Number field is Double, which allows the entry of any number from $-1.797 \times 10^{308}$ to $1.797 \times 10^{308}$.

### OPTIONS FOR TEXT FIELDS

If your table has a Text field for part numbers that cannot exceed 12 characters, you can change the field size to 12 to ensure that no user accidentally enters a longer part number. On the other hand, if you want to enter an account description that is longer than the 50-character default for Text fields, increase the field size to 75 or even 100 characters. In either case, as described earlier, all you need to do is highlight the field in the Design view, click the Field Size property, or press F6 and move to it, and enter a new field size.

## OPTIONS FOR NUMBER FIELDS

You can also alter the Field Size property when working with a Number field, but you need to know a little more about the option. Table 3-1 shows each of the options that you can select. Access uses the largest available size, Double, as the default, because Access wants to ensure that your field can automatically hold any number. You can make your database more efficient by reducing the size of Number fields that do not require Double.

One change you might make in the Project table is to set the Field Size property for the Time field to Byte. No Coaster project will ever be more than 255, the maximum this setting allows. You might change the Field Size setting for the Capacity field in the same table to Integer. This field size extends to 32,767, which should be adequate for any Coaster ride. Long Integer would be a suitable choice for the Invoice Number and Project Id fields in the Invoice Register table because this field size allows numbers up to 2,147,483,647. Single and Double Field Size settings are appropriate when the number entries are even larger. You must choose Single or Double when you want to store nonmonetary values with decimal fractions because they are the only Field Size settings that support decimals.

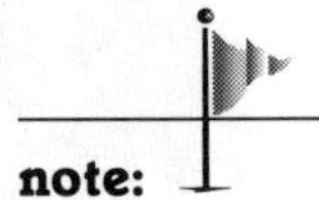

**note:** *Remember that if you want to relate a Counter field to a field in another table, that second field must be either a Counter or a Long Integer field.*

Even if you changed all the fields in the Coaster database to their smallest possible settings, you would not notice improved performance. This database contains too few records for an efficient choice of Field Size settings to have a significant impact. In a table with tens or hundreds of thousands of records, the

| Field Size | Max Decimal Places | Storage Range | Storage Bytes |
|---|---|---|---|
| Byte | 0 | 0—255 | 1 |
| Double | 15 | $-1.797 \times 10^{308}$ to $1.797 \times 10^{308}$ | 8 |
| Integer | 0 | –32,768 to 32,767 | 2 |
| Long Integer | 0 | –2,147,483,648 to 2,147,483,647 | 4 |
| Single | 7 | $-3.4 \times 10^{38}$ to $3.4 \times 10^{38}$ | 4 |

**Table 3-1**
**Field Size Property Options for Number Fields**

performance differences between a system with optimized settings and one without them are much more noticeable.

## Setting the Format

You can change the default Format settings for fields. Access provides a number of predefined Format settings for each data type or lets you create custom formats. Access provides predefined formats for Counter, Currency, Date/Time, Number, and Yes/No fields, but you can create custom formats for every field type except OLE Object.

To change the Format setting for a field from the default General setting, highlight the field, move to the field properties using F6 or the mouse, and then use the drop-down list box to select the format you want. If you prefer a custom format, enter the custom format using symbols in the Format property field. Once you save the table design, this format is used to display the field in the table datasheet, forms, reports, and query dynasets.

Format changes can make a significant difference in the appearance of data. You can display a field such as the phone number from the Client or Employee table as 7998769876 or change the format and display it as (799)876-9876. Formatting makes the number much more readable, which makes it easier to catch data entry errors.

Table 3-2 shows how the default General format displays each of the data types with the Windows Control Panel International setting as the United States. You can change the Country setting to change how data with the General format appears. You can also change to a format other than the General format.

| Data Type | Entry | Appearance with the General Format |
|---|---|---|
| Text | Abc | Abc |
| Number | 2378.6 | 2378.6 |
| Currency | 2378.6 | $2,378.60 |
| Date/Time | 1/22/94 | 1/22/94 |
| Yes/No | Yes | Yes |

**Table 3-2**
**Appearance of the General Format with the United States Country Setting in the Windows Control Panel**

**note:** *If you change the International setting in the Windows Control Panel, Access uses the appropriate monetary symbol, thousands separator, and decimal separator.*

### SELECTING A FORMAT FOR NUMBER, COUNTER, AND CURRENCY DATA TYPES

Access provides six different formats for fields with a Number, Counter, or Currency data type. In addition to General Number you can choose Currency, Fixed, Standard, Percent, and Scientific. These formats work with the Decimal Places property (discussed later) to let you adjust the number of decimal places displayed. If you leave the Decimal Places property at its default, Auto, all formats except General Number and Fixed display two decimal places. The General Number format always displays the number of decimal places you actually enter, while Fixed displays no decimal places unless you change the Decimal Places property. Table 3-3 shows the effect of each of the predefined Format options.

**caution:** *You do not get the same calculation results with a Number field using a Currency format as with the Currency data type. Use the Currency data type to work with numbers having one to four decimal places. If you use a Number field with the Currency format property, the numbers are not rounded correctly because Number field calculations use floating-point arithmetic, usually reserved for scientific calculations.*

| Format | Effect | Entry | Displays As |
|---|---|---|---|
| Standard | Adds thousand separator. Displays 2 decimal places. | 45667.8 | 45,667.80 |
| Currency | Adds monetary symbol for the country. Adds thousands separator. Displays 2 decimal places. | 45667.8 | $45,667.80 |
| Fixed | Rounds to the nearest whole number unless you specify Decimal Places. | 45667.8 | 45668 |
| Percent | Multiplies number by 100. Adds a percent symbol (%). Displays 2 decimal places. | .456 | 45.60% |
| Scientific | Displays number as a power of 10. | 4566.7 | 4.57E+03 |

**Table 3-3**
**Format Options for Number, Counter, and Currency Data Types**

You can improve the display of the Capacity field in the Project table of the Coasters database by using the Standard format. Try other options if you like. Since a format change affects the display of your data but not the entries stored in the table, you cannot change your data by changing the format.

### SELECTING A DATE/TIME FORMAT

The default format for dates when the Windows Control Panel International setting is United States looks like this:

7/15/94

Times display like this:

3:15:00 PM

This default setting is called General Date, though it applies to both date and time entries. If you change the International setting in the Windows Control Panel, this same format option looks very different, because the most common date and time formats for the selected country are used.

Each of the other time and date formats correspond to either a date or a time entry. Like the General Date option, these other formats will look different when the International setting in the Control Panel is changed. The effects of the other predefined date and time formats are shown here:

| Format | Effect |
|---|---|
| Long Date | Wednesday, July 15, 1994 |
| Medium Date | 15-Jul-94 |
| Short Date | 7/15/94 |
| Long Time | 3:15:00 PM |
| Medium Time | 3:15 PM |
| Short Time | 15:15 |

In the Coasters database, the Invoice Date, Payment Date, Completion Date, and Date of Hire fields from the Invoice, Register, Project, and Employee tables can all use any of the default formats. The examples you see in this book use the Medium Date format for Date of Hire in the Employee table and leave this property empty for other date fields.

### SELECTING A YES/NO FORMAT

The default format for a Yes/No field is to display Yes or No. If you delete the format setting, –1 appears for No and 0 appears for Yes. You can also change the format to True/False or On/Off. The first option in each format corresponds to Yes.

In the Coasters Project table, Yes/No is probably the best format choice for the Completed field. True/False is often the best selection for fields in a database that contains survey responses. If you were to record a series of switch settings for a machine's control panel or printer switch in different database fields, On/Off might be a more appropriate format choice.

### CREATING A CUSTOM FORMAT

After looking at the standard formats you might wonder why custom formats are even needed. Later, as you begin to create reports and screens for other users, you are likely to find that users request changes to the appearance of their data to match the way it looked in the system used before Access or to match handwritten documents. You will find that the custom format provides a significant number of new options, each of which are suitable in specific situations.

You can add fixed text to entries with custom formats. You can provide different formats for fields that are empty or that contain negative numbers. You create your custom format by making entries in the Format property field using symbols valid for the data type. All custom formats cause data to be right-aligned unless an exclamation point (!) is used to left-align the entries.

The Number, Text, and Date/Time data types each have their own symbols used in creating formats. Most symbols are valid with only one data type, although there are six symbols or words that can be used with any data type: ! for left alignment, [*color*] to specify a color for the data, \ to display the next character as a literal, * to fill the field with the next character, a space to insert a space, and quotation marks to enclose literal text. These universal symbols are discussed in more detail in the section on entering custom number formats. Other than these six options, you cannot mix symbols for multiple data types in one format.

***Defining a Custom Format for a Number Field*** When you construct a custom format for a field with a Number data type, you can have four different parts positive number and the second part when the field is negative. The third part of the format is used when the entry contains a zero and the fourth part is used only if the field is empty or null. Semicolons are used to separate the different parts of the format when you use multiple parts.

The symbols that you can use and their effect on the data are as follows:

| Symbol | Effect |
|---|---|
| "*xxx*" | Displays the characters between the quotation marks. |
| \ | Displays the character after the backslash as a literal: "N/A" and \N\/\A are equivalent entries. |
| 0 | Displays a digit or a zero if no digit is provided. |
| # | Displays a digit or a blank if no digit is provided. |
| . | Marks the decimal location. |
| % | Multiplies the entry by 100 and displays a percent symbol after it. |
| , | Inserts a thousands separator. |
| E– e– | Displays the number using scientific format with a – for negative exponents. |
| E+ e+ | Displays the number using scientific format with a – for negative exponents and a + for positive exponents. |
| – | Displays the – as a literal. |
| + | Displays the + as a literal. |
| $ | Displays the $ as a literal. |
| ( ) | Displays the ( ) as a literal. |
| [*color*] | Displays the number in the color specified. Useful for showing negative numbers as red. Colors supported are black, blue, cyan, green, magenta, red, yellow, and white. |
| * | Fills the field with the character that follows. |

You could use the following formats for some of the Coasters database fields:

| | |
|---|---|
| Client->Client Id | 000000 |
| Client->Phone | (000) 000-0000 |
| Client->Total Invoices | $##,###,###.##[Blue];–$##,###,###.##[Red] |
| Client->Total Payments | $##,###,###.##[Green];–$##,###,###.##[Red] |
| Employee->Job Class | 00;"Temporary Employee";"Management"; "Management" |
| Project->Angle | ##" Degrees" |
| Project->Capacity | #,###" rph" |

The format for the Client Id adds zeros when a number with fewer than six digits is entered so that you always display a six-digit Client Id. The Phone format adds parentheses and a dash to make the phone number more readable.

The Total Invoices and Total Payments fields display in different colors depending on whether the values are positive or negative. The Job Class field displays in different ways depending on the number entered. Constants are added after Angle and Capacity.

The following example shows the effect of changing some of the default formats for fields in the Project table:

Table: Project

| Height | Drop | Angle | Time | Speed | Capacity |
|---|---|---|---|---|---|
| 168 ft | 160 ft | 54 degrees | 3 min | 70 mph | 1,800 rph |
| 205 ft | 182 ft | 60 degrees | 2 min | 73 mph | 2,300 rph |
| 68 ft | 30 ft | 58 degrees | 2 min | 50 mph | 1,900 rph |
| 78 ft | 60 ft | 48 degrees | 2 min | 42 mph | 2,000 rph |
| 135 ft | 119 ft | 56 degrees | 3 min | 65 mph | 3,500 rph |
| 100 ft | 85 ft | 54 degrees | 2 min | 50 mph | 1,800 rph |
| 100 ft | 87 ft | 52 degrees | 2 min | 50 mph | 1,000 rph |
| 68 ft | 60 ft | 48 degrees | 3 min | 50 mph | 2,500 rph |
| 120 ft | 100 ft | 53 degrees | 2 min | 46 mph | 1,350 rph |
| ft | ft | degrees | min | mph | rph |

**tip:** *Try to use consistent formats for all fields that contain similar information. For example, to provide a consistent appearance, all phone numbers should have the same format whether they are in the Employee table or the Client table. Consistency is also important for other properties such as validation rules, although there are instances in the Coasters database where a consistent format has not been followed in order to show you the greatest number of options.*

***Defining a Custom Format for a Text Field*** There are two types of symbols that you can use to format text fields. One type affects only a single character and the other type affects all the characters in the string. A *string* is all the characters entered in a text field.

The format options offered are to use a space or a null when a character is not supplied in a position, to change the display from uppercase or lowercase, and to change the alignment of characters in the field.

Format expressions can consist of up to three sections in Access version 2, or one or two sections in Access version 1. When only one section is defined, it applies to all strings. If a second section is defined, it applies to zero-length strings in Access version 2, or to both zero-length and empty strings in Access version 1. In Access version 2, the third section applies to empty strings. The sections are separated by semicolons.

The following table lists the characters that you can use and the effect of each:

| | |
|---|---|
| < | Displays all characters in the field as lowercase |
| > | Displays all characters in the field as uppercase |
| ! | Uses the characters in the field to fill from left to right rather than right to left |
| @ | Displays a character if one is entered; otherwise, uses a space for a placeholder |
| & | Displays a character if one is entered; otherwise, leaves the position empty |

You can enter symbols and text within a string by entering them in the format expression; for example, use @@@-@@-@@@@ to provide dashes for Social Security number entries.

You can combine the symbols that affect the entire string with ones that affect only a single character, as in !&&&&&. In this format, alignment is from left to right due to the exclamation point (!). The placeholder directions for characters that are not supplied are given by the ampersands (&).

The following table lists string formats that you can use for the Coasters database:

| | |
|---|---|
| Employee->First Name | > |
| Employee->Last Name | >;"***Missing Information***“ |
| Employee->Home Phone | (@@@)@@@-@@@@ |

The first format displays First Name in all capital letters although it does not change the storage of the data from the way that it was entered. The second format displays Last Name in all capital letters if a name is supplied and displays ***Missing Information*** if the field is left blank. If Home Phone is a Text data type, this format displays the parentheses for the area code and the hyphen separator.

***Defining a Custom Format for a Date/Time Field*** Date and time serial numbers are stored in database tables as numbers, which means you can use the Number format options for them. However, you probably want to use a more traditional date or time format. Since date and time formats have multiple components—month, day, and year and hour, minute, and second—the options are somewhat overwhelming. Keep in mind that the more abbreviated displays are represented with fewer symbols. This list shows each symbol and its effect:

| | |
|---|---|
| c | Displays both the date and time using *ddddd ttttt* if the number has both an integer and a decimal portion |
| a/p | Uses a 12-hour clock and displays a lowercase *a* with hours before noon and a lowercase *p* with the noon hour and later |
| A/P | Uses a 12-hour clock and displays an uppercase *A* with hours before noon and an uppercase *P* with the noon hour and later |
| am/pm | Uses a 12-hour clock and displays *am* with hours before noon and *pm* with the noon hour and later |
| AM/PM | Uses a 12-hour clock and displays *AM* with hours before noon and *PM* with the noon hour and later |
| AMPM | Uses a 12-hour clock and uses the WIN.INI file's 1159 string with hours before noon and the WIN.INI file's 2359 string with hours after noon |
| h | Displays an hour between 0 and 23 with no leading zero |
| hh | Displays an hour between 00 and 23 with a leading zero if the hour is one digit |
| n | Displays a minute number between 0 and 59 without a leading zero |
| nn | Displays a minute number between 00 and 59 with a leading zero if the minute number is one digit |
| s | Displays a second number between 0 and 59 without a leading zero |
| ss | Displays a second number between 00 and 59 with a leading zero if the second number is one digit |
| ttttt | Uses the default time format h:mm:ss with the time separator defined in the Control Panel International setting |
| d | Displays the day number without a leading zero |
| dd | Displays the day number with a leading zero if the day number is one digit |
| ddd | Displays a three-character abbreviation for the day of the week (Sun–Sat) |
| dddd | Displays the full word for the day of the week (Sunday– Saturday) |
| ddddd | Displays the date using the Short Date setting in the Control Panel International setting. The default format is m/d/yy |
| dddddd | Displays the date using the Long Date option in the Control Panel International setting. The default format is dddd mmmm, yyyy |
| m | Displays a month number without a leading zero |
| mm | Displays a month number with a leading zero for a one-digit month number |
| mmm | Displays a three-character abbreviation for the month (Jan–Dec) |
| mmmm | Displays the full month name (January – December) |
| q | Displays the quarter of the year (1–4) |
| w | Displays the day of the week as a number (1 for Sunday) |
| ww | Displays the week of the year as a number (1–53) |
| y | Displays the day of the year as a number (1–366) |
| yy | Displays the year as a two-digit number (00–99) |
| yyyy | Displays the year as a four-digit number (100–9999) |

The Date of Hire field in the Employee table could be customized to present the date in another format. As you construct an entry with the special symbols and finalize it, Access checks for a match with predefined formats and displays the name of the predefined format instead of the symbols if there is a match. For example, if you type **c** and press ENTER, General Date displays. If you are only interested in showing the month and year the employee was hired, you could enter a format of **mm/yy** to display 01/91.

## Establishing Decimal Places for Currency and Number Fields

You can set the decimal places to Auto or a specific number of decimal places. Choosing the default of Auto causes Access to display no decimal places for a Fixed Format field and two decimal places for other formats.

You can set decimal places for a Number, Counter, or Currency field no matter which format you have chosen. If you set Decimal Places to more than zero for a field with a Byte, Integer, or Long Integer field size, the decimal places always display zeros because no decimal places are stored with the entries. If you type a number such as **5.5** in an Integer field set with two Decimal Places, the number would display as 6.00. Consider this when setting properties for these fields, since the numbers you display could appear to contain decimal accuracy that does not exist.

**caution:** *Choose carefully between Number and Currency data types. Setting the accuracy with the Decimal Places property will not solve the problem of accuracy with monetary calculations if you accidentally choose the Number data type.*

In the Coasters database you might set the decimal places for some of the fields in the Project table. Try one, two, or three decimal places for the Speed measurement. The Time field should probably have one or two decimal places. Track could have one or two decimal places. Vehicles should definitely be set as no decimal places since it is not possible to have a partial vehicle.

## Creating Data Masks for Entering Data

Access version 2 has a new field property, Input Mask, to help enter correct data. An input mask displays a template for data entry in blank fields, and displays it entered in that form, as shown here:

| | | | | | |
|---|---|---|---|---|---|
| | OH | 42124 | | 777-2222 | 1098 |
| ▶ | OH | 44040 | | 999-9999 | 1230 |
| * | OH | ##### | | ###-#### | #### |

You can use the Input Mask Builder to help you create input masks for Text and Date/Time fields. You can also create an input mask by directly entering the special formatting and mask characters. The Input Mask Builder is a much quicker solution if you are creating a fairly common input mask.

To use the Input Mask Builder, click the Build button to the right of the Input Mask field. You can then select from a list of predefined input masks and make further selections to customize the mask you've chosen.

To enter the input mask directly, move to the Input Mask property for the field you want to work with and enter the special characters to create a mask, which are shown in Table 3-4. Some characters are used to reserve spaces in the mask for entries, some are used to set how the mask displays, and others are used to add extra characters, making the entries easier to read.

## Using a Different Field Name on Reports and Forms

When you create tabular forms and reports to show your data, the space a field uses depends on field size and the heading used for the field. You don't want a field three or four characters long consuming 30 or 40 characters of the report width due to a long field name. The solution is to provide a Caption property for fields that have a small field size yet have a long name. You can also use the

| Character | Purpose |
|---|---|
| 0 | Requires a digit, +, or – |
| 9 | Allows a digit, or converts blank positions to spaces |
| # | Allows a digit, +, or –, or converts blank positions to spaces |
| L | Requires a letter |
| ? | Allows a letter |
| A | Requires a letter or digit |
| a | Allows a letter or digit |
| & | Requires a character or space |
| C | Allows a character or space |
| .,:;-/ | Allows entry of a decimal point, thousands separator, or date and time separator |
| < | Converts following characters to lowercase |
| > | Converts following characters to uppercase |
| ! | Right-aligns entry (default is left-aligned) |
| \ | Causes following character to be shown as a literal character |

**Table 3-4**
**Characters for Creating an Input Mask**

Caption property when you want to use text other than the field name to identify a field in reports, forms, and queries.

You might decide that Job Class should be shortened in reports and forms since the data itself only requires two digits. Shorten the entry to Class by typing **Class** in the Caption field property. The new caption will be used in all reports and forms created from that point on. You can also include & in front of a letter that you want to be underlined in forms. When the text for a field in a form has an underlined letter, you can move the insertion point to that field by pressing ALT and the underlined letter.

**tip:** *In addition to using the Caption property to shorten a field name, you can also change the caption when you are designing a report or form for a specialized need. For example, you might have a field named Uncollectible Accounts that you want to call Bad Debts when you create several reports. You can add Bad Debts as a Caption, create the reports, and then delete the caption so that other new reports will use the field name.*

## Establishing a Default Value

Default values provide an entry for a field automatically when a new record is created. Any field with a Number data type is automatically assigned a default value of 0. Fields with a Yes/No data type have a default value of No. If you make no changes to these fields they retain the default setting. You can delete the default to have a null entry in each new record or you can enter another value.

In the Employee table, you might want to use OH automatically for the State field of new employees if most of them live in Ohio. You would highlight State in the Design view, move to Default Value in the Field Properties area, and type **OH**. If you want to make the default Pay Rate $6.00 an hour, move to the Pay Rate field to display its properties, move to the Default Value property, and type **6**. Each new employee record will have a Pay Rate of $6.00 unless you change the record.

You can also use expressions to establish default values. (Chapter 12 fully covers the use of expressions.) Use the Date function to supply the current date for the Date of Hire field in the Employee table if employee records are typically entered on their date of hire. The entry would look like Figure 3-7. This same expression could be used for the Invoice Date field in the Invoice Register table.

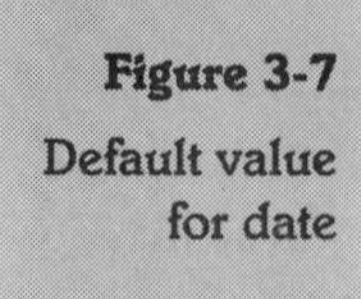

**Figure 3-7** Default value for date

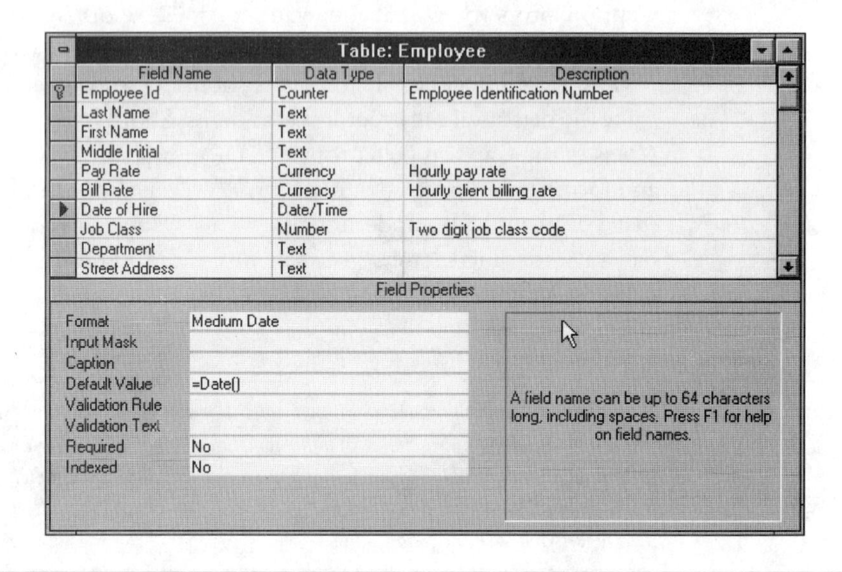


## Performing Validity Checking

Validity checking screens your entries rather than supplying an entry for you. Even if you leave the Validation Rule property blank on all of your fields, some validity checking is still performed to see that your entry is valid for the data type that you have selected. Although Access accepts any entry for a Text or Memo field, it ensures that Number and Currency fields do not contain text. It also ensures that Date/Time and Yes/No fields have acceptable entries. Likewise, OLE Object fields cannot contain a number or text.

Validation rules are entered as expressions. These expressions can include constants and functions. In Access version 1, the expression can include references to other fields. However, to create a validation rule that refers to another field in Access version 2, you must create the validation rule as a table property rather than a field property. This is because validation rules can verify a single field or an entire record. Validation rules that reference another field are being used to verify a record, and are therefore table validation rules.

Validation rules can be as long as 255 characters, although in most cases you can express more succinctly the type of checking you want to perform. Your validation rules apply to data you enter using forms that are created after you add the validation rule. Existing forms must be modified to perform the same check that you just defined. Even if you alter the controls for an existing form, existing data is not checked to see if it conforms to the validation rule. Data that does not meet the rule that you establish is rejected.

If you are going to reject users' entries, ease their frustration by using the Validation Text property to explain exactly what is wrong with an entry. For example, if the expected entry for Pay Rate in the Employee table lies between $4.25 and $35.00, your Validation Text entry might be "Pay Rate must be between $4.25 and $35.00. Please enter a valid Pay Rate." Another possible entry for the same example could be "Pay Rate must be between minimum wage and $35.00."

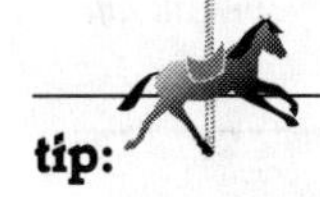

**tip:** *If you want your message to appear on more than one line, press* SHIFT+ENTER *to create line breaks when entering the text.*

## VALIDATING NUMBER AND CURRENCY FIELDS

It is easy for data entry operators to transpose digits when entering numbers. You can sometimes trap errors by using validation rules with numeric fields. You might have an upper or lower limit for the value entered in a field, find any number except zero an acceptable entry, or only allow one of four numeric codes. In Access version 1, you can even reference the value in another field within the table if you enclose the field name in square brackets. In Access version 2, you can only use a second field to verify the first field if you are creating a table validation rule. Any of these conditions can be checked by adding an appropriate rule and accompanying text.

The following are examples of some rules and text that might be appropriate for fields in the Coasters database:

Project->Vehicles

| | |
|---|---|
| Validation Rule | >0 |
| Validation Text | Each coaster ride must have at least one vehicle |

Employee->Job Class

| | |
|---|---|
| Validation Rule | 10 Or 20 Or 30 |
| Validation Text | 10, 20, and 30 are the only valid job class codes |

or

| | |
|---|---|
| Validation Rule | >=10 And <=70 |
| Validation Text | Job Code must be between 10 and 70 |

Employee->Bill Rate (Access version 1 only)

| | |
|---|---|
| Validation Rule | >=[Pay Rate]*1.15 |
| Validation Text | Billing Rate must be at least 15% higher than the Pay Rate |

Access version 2 applies the validation rules set for a single field to that field's entry as soon as you leave that field. However, it does not apply table validation rules until you move to the next record. This means that if your data does not pass a table validation rule, you will not know it when you leave the relevant field, but only when you start to move to the next record.

**tip:** *If you establish default values for your fields, make sure that they can pass the validation rules. Otherwise, you will receive a message indicating that the newly created record has failed the validation rules before you even enter any data. One way around this is to alter your validation rule so that entries either pass the rule or equal "Is Null".*

### VALIDATING TEXT FIELDS

Text fields must sometimes follow a set pattern. For example, valid part numbers may always begin with AT followed by a dash and four characters. You can ensure that the entries match the defined pattern. The Validation Rule property would read **Like AT-????** and an appropriate message would be placed in the Validation Text property. You can also check for a set of valid codes, such as states where your company delivers or has retail stores at the time of entry.

In the Coasters database, you might set this Validation Rule property for the State field in the Employee table:

"OH" Or "PA" Or "MI"

The Validation Text property would read "Employee state code must be OH, PA, or MI."

### VALIDATING DATE FIELDS

Access automatically validates a date entry to ensure that it is a valid date. Access does not let a user enter a date such as 2/31/93 because February never has 31 days. You can perform other validations on date and time fields to ensure that they meet your needs. You may only want dates within the current calendar year entered in a field, or you might want to ensure that the date entered is before or after the current date.

For the Coasters database you might consider these validation settings:

| Employee->Date of Hire | |
|---|---|
| Validation Rule | >=#1/1/93# |
| Validation Text | Date must be on or later than 1/1/93 |

| Invoice->Invoice Date | |
|---|---|
| Validation Rule | >=#1/1/92# |
| Validation Text | Date must be on or later than 1/1/92 |

### VALIDATING FIELDS BASED ON OTHER FIELDS

One change between Access version 1 and Access version 2 affects how you enter certain validation rules. In Access version 1, all validation rules were entered as properties for fields. If the validation rule you wanted to use referenced another field in the record, you would enter this validation rule as a field property. In Access version 2, however, validation rules that reference another field in the record are not field properties. Instead they are table properties. For example, in the "Validating Number and Currency Fields" section, you entered a validation rule to check that the bill rate for an employee was correct by comparing it to the Pay Rate field entry. To validate the field in Access version 2, you would enter the same rule as part of the table Validation Rule property, as shown here:

| Employee (table property) | |
|---|---|
| Validation Rule | [Bill Rate]>=[Pay Rate]*1.15 |
| Validation Text | Billing Rate must be at least 15% higher than the Pay Rate |

**tip:** *You can combine multiple rules using the AND logical operator.*

## Creating Indexes for a Table

You can create indexes for tables beyond the primary key that you learned about in Chapter 2. Additional indexes are useful when you need to search frequently for specific values in a field. Indexes can also speed up a request to display records in a sorted sequence if you already have an index in the desired order.

You can create indexes that require unique entries for a field or allow duplicates. If you have only a few values for a field that occurs many times, an index may not be efficient since the same index entry points to many different database records.

You can create an index for one field or use multiple fields when building the index entries. Indexes that use multiple fields are created differently in Access versions 1 and 2, but the indexes work the same way.

**caution:** *You cannot create an index using a Memo or OLE Object field.*

## Indexing with One Field

Create an index for any individual field with the Indexed property. Options for this property are No, Yes (Duplicates OK), and Yes (No Duplicates). Changing a setting from Yes to No deletes an existing index on the field. Figure 3-8 shows the property setting for the Indexed property of the Job Class field in the Employee table set to Yes (Duplicates OK). The index that is created can have duplicate entries because a number of employees have the same job class.

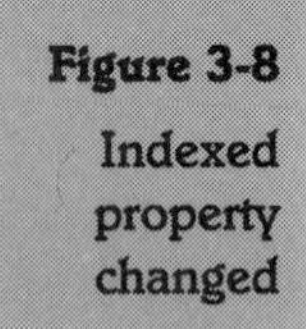

**Figure 3-8** Indexed property changed

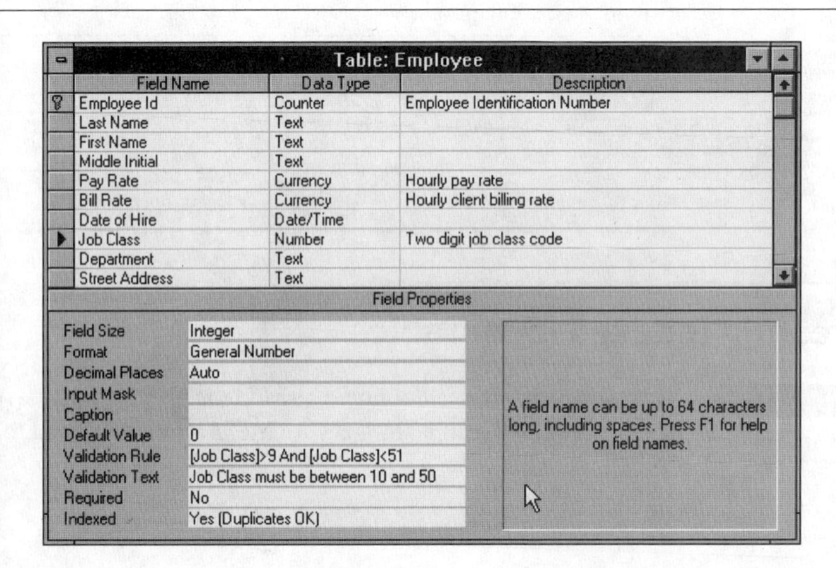

## Indexing Multiple Fields

Although you could create a multiple field primary key from the Table window in Design view, you need to use another window to create the multiple field indexes. Access version 2 does not have a limit on the number of multiple field indexes you can create, but in Access version 1, you can only create up to five.

### IN ACCESS VERSION 2

To create a multiple field index in Access version 2, follow these steps:

1. From the Table window in Design view, select Indexes from the View menu or click the Indexes button in the toolbar, opening the Indexes window.

This window shows all indexes for the table, including the primary key, if it is defined. The index definition displays the name of the index, the fields it uses, and the order in which it is searched. The bottom half of the window displays the properties of the index, which includes whether it is the primary key, whether each entry in that field must be unique, and whether that field may contain null strings.

2. Enter the index name in the first column of a row.
3. Enter the field names for other fields used in the index in the second column, starting in the row with the index name.

When Access uses a multiple field index, it sorts the records according to the first field listed and then sorts records that had duplicates in the first field using the second field, and so on. For each of the fields, you can select whether the values are arranged in ascending or descending order.

Access treats all rows as part of the previous index name until it encounters a new index name. If you want to make an existing index into a multiple field index, right-click the row selector where you want the row added and select Insert Row from the shortcut menu, or press INS. Then enter the field name and sort order in the new row.

4. Put the Indexes window away by selecting Indexes from the View menu, clicking the Indexes button in the toolbar, or double-clicking its control box.

The following shows multiple field indexes for the Employee table on Last Name, First Name, and Middle Initial as well as on Department and Job Class.

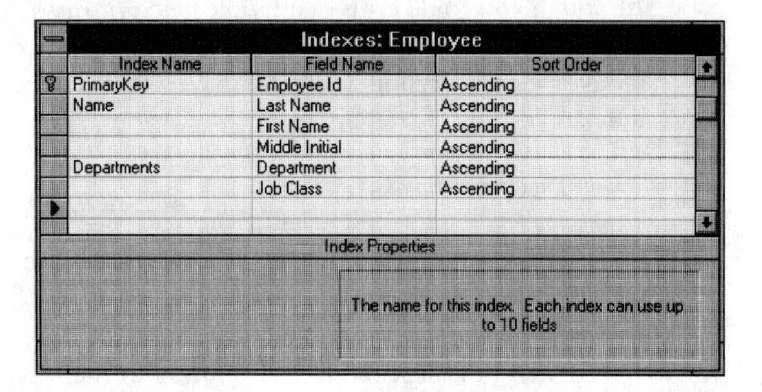


#### IN ACCESS VERSION 1

To create a multiple field index from the Design view of the Table window, follow these steps:

1. Click the Properties button or choose Table Properties in the View menu.
2. Click the next unused index.
3. Type the fields to be used in the index, separating them with semicolons.

The fields should be listed in order of priority, with later fields in the list serving only as tiebreakers when there are duplicate entries in earlier fields.

4. Choose Save from the File menu to save these changes.

## Changing Table Definition and Property Defaults

In Chapter 4 you will begin entering data into tables. Although you can change any table and field settings before data is entered, you will encounter some problems if you try doing so after data is entered. This does not mean that you cannot change your tables after entering data; it does mean that you should be fully aware of the consequences of certain types of changes.

The changes that you need to be concerned with are new and deleted fields, changes to an incompatible data type, and changes to a Field Size property. Access displays a warning when you save the new table design if data will be lost in the conversion process. Watch closely for these messages and take appropriate action to avoid losing data.

**tip:** *Create a backup of your database before making significant changes. If you do lose data, you can always use the copy.*

## Adding and Deleting Fields

You can add a new field to a table at any time. You can enter new values for this field at any time by using the Datasheet view. If you want to add the data using an existing form, you need to modify the form design first to include the new field. Likewise, you need to modify existing report designs to see the data for the new field on the reports.

If you delete a field from a table you lose all the data stored in this field. Deleting the field from the table does not remove this field from forms, reports, and queries, which you will need to revise.

In addition to deleting fields, you sometimes need to rename them. Although you do not lose data when you rename fields, the data is not available on existing forms and reports until you revise them to use the field's new name. If a form cannot find the field it is looking for, the field's contents may display as **#Name?** or be empty. If a report cannot find the field it is looking for, you will see a prompt for a parameter value.

## Changing Data Types

Before changing a field's data type, think about whether the new data type is more or less restrictive than the original. For example, changing a Number data type to a Text data type is no problem since the new field type accepts anything that might be in the field. Changing a Text data type to a Number might not work as well; if the entries in the Text data type are not numbers, they are changed to null values. Your original data is lost and indexes for the data no longer exist.

When you convert from other data types to Text, all of the formatting characters—such as currency symbols and thousands separators—are lost. When you convert from Text to another format these characters are recognized and handled correctly.

If you change a field's data type from Text to Memo, none of the data is lost, but any index you created with the field no longer exists because Memo fields cannot be indexed. If you change a field's data type from Memo to Text, the integrity of your data depends on the length of the Memo field entries. A maximum of 255 characters can be converted, although the Field Size default setting is 50 and may need to be changed.

## Changing Properties

If you change the Default Value or Validation Rule properties, the existing data is not altered. These new properties only apply to new entries. Format, Caption, and Decimal Places property changes do not have potentially damaging effects either. It is the Field Size setting for Number fields that you need to be concerned about.

If you change the Field Size property to a smaller size, you can lose data from the field if your data uses larger numbers than the new size permits. For instance, if 124578.8976 is stored in a field as Double and you change the Field Size to Byte or Integer, you can lose data. If the only difference is that the new Field Size setting does not support decimal places, the number is rounded and the decimal accuracy is lost forever.

## Quick Reference

**To Set Default Relationships Between Tables** Open the database for which you want to establish relationships, choose Relationships from the Edit menu, and then:

- *In Access version 1,* select the main table from the Primary Table drop-down list box and then select the table containing related data from the Related Table drop-down list box. Select One to relate tables by their primary keys or select the field containing related data in the Select Matching Fields drop-down list box. Choose Add.
- *In Access version 2,* select the tables to add to the Relationships window and choose Add. Select Close. Drag the field to relate from the primary table to the related table. Select Enforce Relational Integrity to have Access reject invalid entries, and choose One or Many to set how the tables relate. Choose Create.

**To Define an Index for One Field** In Design view for the table, highlight the field, and move to the Indexed property by clicking it or pressing F6 and using the arrow keys. Change the Indexed property to Yes (Duplicates OK) or Yes (No Duplicates).

**To Define a Multiple Field Index** From Design view for the table:

- *In Access version 1,* click the Properties button and then add the names of the fields in one of the Index properties, using semicolons (;) as separators.
- *In Access version 2,* click the Indexes button, then add the index name and the first field in one row, and the following field names in the following rows.

**To Change Field Properties** In Design view for the table, highlight the field, click the bottom half of the window or press F6, and then make the desired changes.

# Chapter 4

Adding Records

Editing Records

Customizing the Datasheet Layout

Printing a Table

Copying a Table

# Entering and Editing Data

WITH the design of your database complete, you are ready to enter data into tables. You can enter data directly in the Datasheet view or create a more sophisticated form to handle data entry. This chapter shows how to enter data in the datasheet; Chapter 8 shows how to use forms for data entry. This chapter teaches you to recognize the special indicators for the status of records, to cut and paste data on a datasheet, and to make customizing changes to the layout of a datasheet. You also will learn how to print entries made in the datasheet and how to create another table by copying an existing table.

## Adding Records

You must open a table to add records to it. If the database containing the table is not open, you must open it first. You can quickly open one of the last four databases you used by selecting the database name from the bottom of the File menu. You can open any database by choosing Open Database from the File menu and selecting the database you want from the File Name list box. With the database open, select any existing table and then choose Open from the Database window. Another way to open the table is by double-clicking the name of the table in the Database window.

You use the blank record at the bottom of the datasheet to enter new records into a table. A new table displays nothing other than this blank record until you have entered data. Access uses an asterisk to mark this blank record when it is not the current record. When it is the current record, the regular current record indicator (which looks like an arrowhead) points to it. Figure 4-1 shows some data in the Client table with an asterisk marking the blank record and the current record indicator pointing to the record before it. To move to the blank record, you can choose Go To from the Records menu and then choose New or you can click the New button in Access version 2's toolbar, shown here:

You can also press CTRL+END to move to the last field in the last record and then press HOME to move to the first field in the record quickly.

As you enter data in new records, Access applies all the knowledge it has about your table definition to check that the entries you make match the data type and properties you set for each field.

**tip:** *Later, in Chapter 8, you will learn about creating and using forms. Forms provide another method of looking at or entering your data. You can quickly create a basic form for entering new records by clicking the AutoForm button. When you finish entering your new records, close the window with the form and select No when prompted to avoid saving it unless you decide to use the form again.*

## Entering the Data

To enter data into a blank record, first click the first field in the blank record to make it the current record. An insertion point marks your place in this field. By default, you can begin making entries immediately. If Access rejects your attempt, a setting has been changed. Choose Allow Editing (Editing Allowed in Access version 1) from the Records menu to allow the table records to be added or edited.

You normally start entries with the leftmost field and move to the right, completing each field. There are two exceptions to this pattern: you skip

**Figure 4-1** An asterisk marks the blank record

Table: Client

| | Client Id | Client Name | Contact | Park Location | Mailing Address | Ci |
|---|---|---|---|---|---|---|
| | 1 | Family Fun Land | Jeff Jackson | Isle Royale | P.O. Box 345 | Houghtor |
| | 2 | Teen Land | Mary Morris | Ashtabula Park | P.O. Box 786 | Ashtabula |
| | 3 | Amusement Techn | Mark Williams | Panacea on the Be | P.O. Box 5346 | Panacea |
| | 4 | Arden Entertainmer | Jerry McCellars | Indianapolis | 100 Federal Avenu | Indianapo |
| | 5 | Family Amusements | Shelly Rogers | Stanton | P.O. Box 123548 | Stanton |
| | 6 | Playland Consortiur | Jim Mattison | Wheeling | P.O. Box 5839 | Wheeling |
| | 7 | Island Waterplay In | Andrea Jacobx | Raleigh | 1 Waterplay Lane | Raleigh |
| ▶ | 8 | Entertainment Plus | Charles WInter | Jersey City | P.O. Box 4892368 | Jersey Cit |
| * | (Counter) | | | | | |

Record: 8 of 8

counter fields because Access supplies the next sequential number automatically, and you skip fields where data is unavailable.

After you type the value for each field, press TAB to move to the next field. Access scrolls data off the left side of the screen as you move to the right. Later in this chapter, you will learn how to freeze the display to keep critical identifying data visible at the left side of the window as you type in fields to the right.

Table 4-1 shows some of the messages that Access might display if you enter data that does not match the definition you have supplied for a field. The last error message will be either a field's Validation Rule (Access version 1) or a table validation rule (Access version 2). Access checks both the data type and the Validation Rule property that you establish for the field and table.

You must close the error message dialog box by selecting OK before the error can be corrected. The exception is when you attempt to type an entry in a Counter field. Although no dialog box appears, an error message is shown in the status bar. Press TAB to move to the next field and the message disappears. The following illustration shows the message that appears in the dialog box when you attempt to enter text into a field with a Number data type:

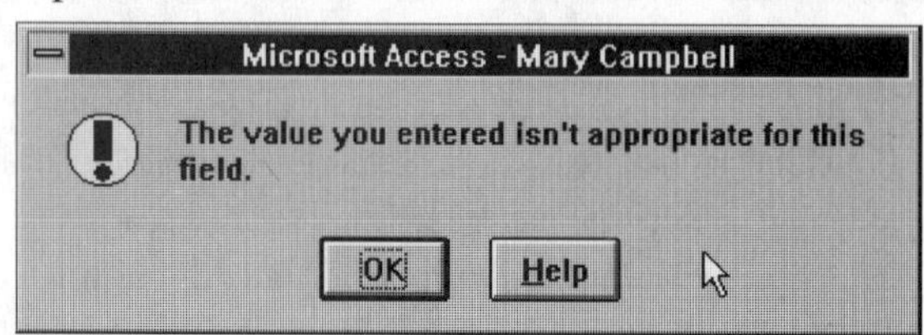


After selecting OK, you can press ESC or click the Undo button in the toolbar to undo the change in the record that caused the problem, or you can edit the entry to correct it.

| Error Message | Reason for Error |
|---|---|
| The value you entered isn't appropriate for this field | Data type does not match. |
| Can't have Null value in index | Index field was left blank and is not a Counter data type. |
| Can't have duplicate key; index changes were unsuccessful | You attempted to reuse an existing index entry with the Indexed property set to No Duplicates. |
| To make a profit, the billing rate must be at least 10% more than the pay rate | Validation Text that matches a user-defined Validation Rule. Since the entry does not fulfill the rule, the text is displayed. |

**Table 4-1**
**Sample of Data Entry Messages**

## Entering Client Records

Try the data entry process for one of your tables. Appendix C lists the records entered in each table in the Coasters database. For now, try a few records in the Client table. All you need to do is open the Client table and begin entering the data shown here:

**Record 1**

| Field | Entry |
|---|---|
| Client Id | *None needed - Counter data type* |
| Client Name | Family Fun Land |
| Contact | Jeff Jackson |
| Park Location | Isle Royale |
| Mailing Address | P.O. Box 345 |
| City | Houghton |
| State | MI |
| Zip Code | 49312 |
| Phone | 6162239999 |
| Park Desc | Large amusement park that has been popular for over 50 years. Only access to the park is by ferry. Three different adult's and two children's coasters are already operational |
| YTD Invoices | 2500000.00 |
| YTD Payments | 2300000.00 |
| Total Invoices | 2500000.00 |
| Total Payments | 2300000.00 |

**Record 2**

| Field | Entry |
|---|---|
| Client Id | *None needed - Counter data type* |
| Client Name | Teen Land |
| Contact | Mary Morris |
| Park Location | Ashtabula Park |
| Mailing Address | P.O. Box 786 |
| City | Ashtabula |
| State | OH |
| Zip Code | 44321 |
| Phone | 2169999090 |
| Park Desc | Turn of the century amusement park with many family rides and some superb coasters |
| YTD Invoices | 3900000.00 |
| YTD Payments | 1900000.00 |
| Total Invoices | 7100900.00 |
| Total Payments | 5100900.00 |

After you finish the entry of the last field in the second record, you can choose Save Record from the File menu or simply move to another record.

## Skipping Fields

Most of the time you move across the row in the table placing an entry in each field and then using the TAB key to move to the next field. You can also use SHIFT+TAB to move left and complete an entry. Move to the first field in the record by pressing HOME; move to the last field by pressing END. To display a field that is not currently showing, click the horizontal scroll bar or drag the scroll box, shown below:

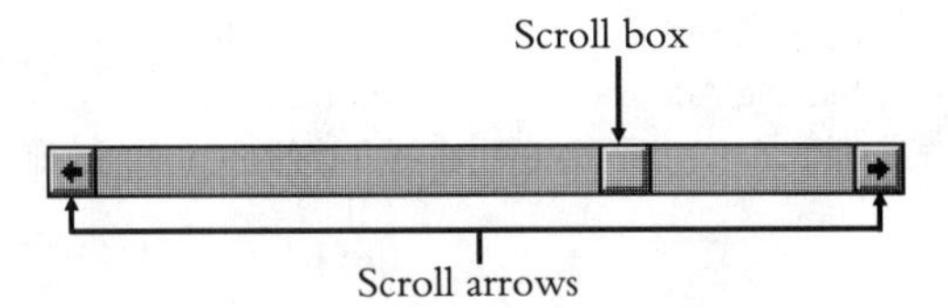


Then click the field to move the insertion point to it. In Access version 1, you can move to a specific field by selecting the field from the Field list box on the toolbar.

## Adding an OLE Object to a Record

When a field's data type is OLE Object, you will add its data differently than you would fields with other data types. A data type of OLE Object lets you add graphs, worksheets, drawings, and scanned pictures or art to a database table. Any objects created with applications that support object linking and embedding (OLE) can be included. You can insert an existing object as an OLE object or create the OLE object from within Access. In Access version 2, you can do in-place editing, a new feature offered through OLE version 2. In-place editing replaces the Access menu with the menus of the other application so that you can use the other application to create and edit the OLE object within Access.

Existing objects must be created by an application that supports OLE. The Microsoft Paintbrush application provided with Windows can create OLE objects. You might also have a picture or drawing scanned by a service bureau and stored in a format such as .BMP or .PCX. After moving to the field where you want to place this object, follow these steps:

1. Choose Insert Object from the Edit menu to display the dialog box shown here:

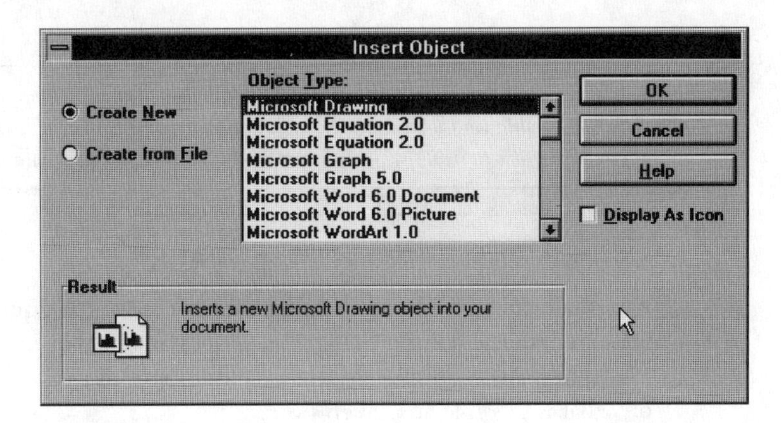


2. Select Create from File (in Access version 1, select the File button).
3. Type the name of the file containing the data that you want to use.

   In Access version 2, you can use the Browse button to select the file using the same dialog box options available when you open a database. In Access version 1, these options are available automatically.

To create an object and insert it, choose Insert Object from the Edit menu and then select the application that you want from the Object Type list box. (In Access version 2, you may first need to select the Create New option button.) When you select the object type and OK, the application opens ready for you to create the OLE object to add to the table. Next create the data you want stored as the OLE object in your Access table. If you want to use an existing file as the basis for the object you are creating, the application will probably have an option for importing its own files. Choose Exit or Return from the File menu in the application to continue with your entries in the Access table.

In Access version 2, the Insert Object dialog box has a Link check box that you can see when you are creating an OLE object from an existing file. When this check box is selected, Access does not keep the data from the file in the Access database. Instead, the field has a link to the file. When the contents of the file change, the OLE object that appears in the field also changes. With linking you can use the most current version of a file as an OLE object. Of

course, the format of the file you select must be one which the applications that can work with OLE objects will use.

**tip:** *You might want to create all of your OLE objects in a separate session rather than trying to create them while doing your data entry. In most applications, it is more efficient to work in the drawing or graph program to create all the pictures or graphs that you need and then complete data entry.*

## Using Undo to Remove a Change

Access allows you to undo editing changes as well as your last action. Because the extent of the editing changes can affect one field or many and the last action may differ, Access displays different Undo options in the Edit menu depending on what is possible at a given time.

Access allows you to undo one editing change to a field or to undo all the changes you make to a record. You must request that Access undo your changes *before* you start editing another record or switch to a different window. If you change the current field and want to undo the change, choose Undo Current Field from the Edit menu. If you have made other changes to this record and want to eliminate them, choose Undo Current Record from the Edit menu. You can also use the Undo Current Field/Record button, shown here, in the toolbar to undo all changes in the current record.

You can also undo the last action taken in a datasheet. Perhaps you deleted records, typed some data, or saved a record and want to eliminate the change. For example, if you edit the ZIP code in a client record and then realize that you have changed the wrong record, choose Undo Typing from the Edit menu. You can also select the Undo button, shown below, from the toolbar to undo your last action.

**tip:** *Press CTRL+Z to quickly undo your last action.*

## Editing Records

Although Access saves changes to a record as soon as you move to another record, you can always make further changes to the record if you wish to. When you start making changes to a record, the pencil icon appears to the left of the current record, indicating that you are modifying the record. Choose Save Record from the File menu to save your changes, or simply move to another record.

### Moving to the Record You Want to Change

To move to the record that you want to change, you can click the record, use the navigation buttons, or use the keyboard. The navigation buttons, which appear at the bottom of the Table window, can move you to the first or last record, to the previous or next record, or to a specific record, as shown below.

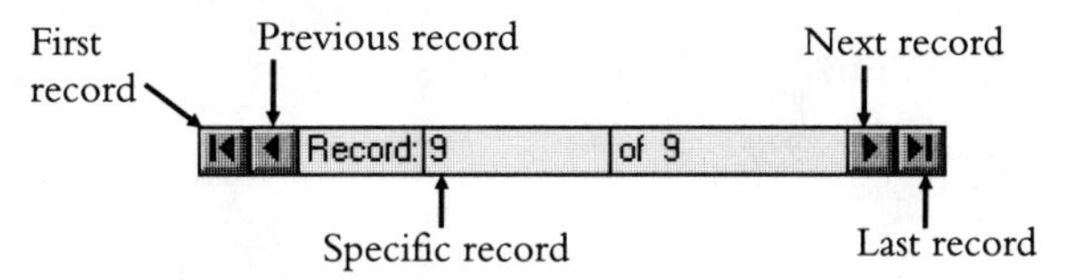


To use the navigation buttons, just click them. You can also enter the number of the specific record you want to move to in the center box and press ENTER to move to it.

Here are some more key combinations that can help you get where you are going quickly:

| | |
|---|---|
| CTRL+PAGE DOWN | Move to the right one window |
| CTRL+PAGE UP | Move to the left one window |
| CTRL+HOME | Move to the first field in the first record |
| CTRL+END | Move to the last field in the last record |
| F5 | Move to the specified record number |

You can move between records by choosing Go To from the Records menu. You can choose First, Last, Next, Previous, or New. These Records menu options are much like using the navigation buttons. Choosing New moves you to a blank record.

### Moving to the Field You Want to Change

When you want to edit a record, you may only want to change one field. Moving across the record one field at a time with TAB, LEFT ARROW, or

RIGHT ARROW may be too slow. Use END to move to the last field and then use SHIFT+TAB to move one field to the left or HOME to move to the first field. A more precise approach is to select the field by clicking it or, in Access version 1, to use the Field list box in the toolbar to move to a field that is not visible. You learned to use this technique when adding data in the "Adding Records" section earlier in this chapter.

## Access Record Indicators

Access provides symbols that appear to the left of the current record and indicate its status. Access refers to the current record as the record that has the focus, meaning that it contains the insertion point and it is the record you are working with, and marks it with this symbol:

As you make changes to this record, Access marks the current record with this symbol:

If a record is marked with this Pencil icon, you know it still has the focus and is being edited. These editing changes are not saved until you change the focus to another record or choose Save Record from the File menu.

Until the current record is saved, you can change your mind and eliminate all of your changes by choosing Undo Current Record from the Edit menu or by pressing ESC twice: Remember that this only works if you haven't yet moved to another record.

When a record is locked by another user, you cannot make changes to it. Locking is designed to prevent two overlapping sets of changes, which could result in losing one user's changes. This symbol marks a locked record:

## Selecting Data

You need to master the techniques for selecting data in fields and records to work effectively with the data in your datasheet. You use these techniques to edit data in existing records. You also use these techniques when you copy, move, and delete data in fields or records. You can use either the keyboard or the mouse for most options.

Using the keyboard can be convenient in some situations—it is quicker to press F2 to select an entire field than it is to move the mouse to the correct location before clicking, for example; however, in other situations using F2 requires extra steps. When selecting part of a field using the keyboard, move the insertion point to the location where you want to start. When using the keyboard to select an entire record, first move to the record that you want to select.

You can choose from the selection options in the table below. Both keyboard and mouse alternatives are provided where possible to allow you to choose the approach that seems easiest for each activity. Both options highlight the selected data.

| Option | Device | Action |
|---|---|---|
| Select part of a field | Mouse | Drag across the text to select |
| | Keyboard | Move the insertion point to the desired start location, press SHIFT+LEFT ARROW or SHIFT+RIGHT ARROW to complete your selection |
| Select the entire field | Mouse | Click the left edge of the field (the mouse pointer will appear as an arrow rather than an I-beam) |
| | Keyboard | Press F2 |
| Extend the selection within a field | Mouse | Press SHIFT and click the new ending position |
| | Keyboard | Press SHIFT+LEFT ARROW or SHIFT+RIGHT ARROW |
| Cancel the selection for a field | Mouse | Click another location |
| | Keyboard | Press F2 again |
| Select a record | Mouse | Click the record selector to the left of the record |
| | Keyboard | Move to the desired record and press SHIFT+SPACEBAR |
| Select multiple records | Mouse | Click the selector of the first record and drag to the selector of the last record |
| | Keyboard | Press SHIFT+SPACEBAR and then SHIFT+UP ARROW or SHIFT+SPACEBAR and then SHIFT+UP ARROW |
| Select all records | Mouse | Click the selector in the upper-left area of the datasheet |

## Editing Options

When editing a field, you can replace the entire contents of a field or make a minor change. You can move or copy data between fields.

To replace the entire contents of the field, select the field using the techniques described in the previous section and begin typing your new entry. The previous entry is replaced by what you type.

To eliminate an entry in a field, select the field and then choose Delete from the Edit menu. To delete part of a field, select the portion of the field that you want to eliminate before taking this action.

You can insert missing letters, digits, or words in a field by moving the insertion point to the desired location and typing the new data. The data is inserted at the insertion point. The distinction between inserting and replacing is that the entire field is not selected before you insert, so it is not overwritten. To make working with a field's entry easier, you can press SHIFT+F2 to display the entry in a Zoom window, which gives you a closer view of the field's entry, as shown here:

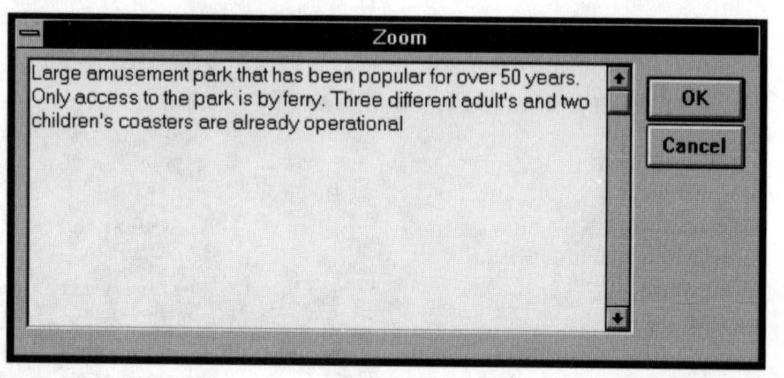


When you move or copy data from a field, you can use that data to fill an empty field, replace the contents of a field, or add to another field entry. Regardless of which approach you choose, these steps will work for you:

1. Select the data to be moved or copied, as shown in Figure 4-2.
2. Choose Copy or Cut from the Edit menu, depending on whether you want to copy or move the data.
3. Select the destination field or place the insertion point where you want to add the data.
4. Choose Paste from the Edit menu. The data you cut or copied replaces the selected data in the destination field or appears at the insertion point.

## Finding Records

You can let Access find records for you by specifying a field entry to search for. Rather than looking through a large table to find the last name you want, you can have Access find a matching record for you. When you are searching for an entry, follow these steps:

1. Move the insertion point to the field that contains the entry you want to find.
2. Choose Find from the Edit menu, press CTRL+F, press F7, or click the Find button, which looks like this:

Here is a sample of the dialog box that will open, with some entries:

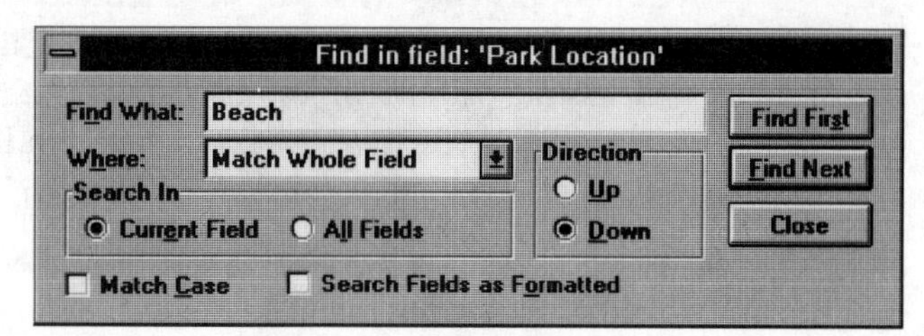


3. Type the entry to find in the Find What text box.
4. Select from the following options:

- *Search In* Select Current field to only search the current field for the entry in the Find What text box or select All Fields to search all fields in the table.
- *Direction* Select Up to search from the current record to the top of the table or Down to search from the current record to the bottom of the table.
- *Where* Select from the Where drop-down list box the part of the field entry that must match the entry in the Find What text box. You can choose Match Whole Field to require that the contents of the Find What text box match an entire field entry, Start of Field to search for the entry at the beginning of the field, or Any Part of Field to match any part of the field entry.

**Figure 4-2** Data selected for copying

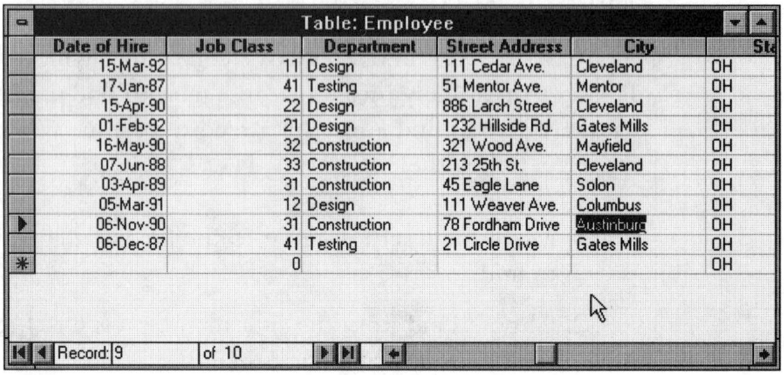

Table: Employee

| Date of Hire | Job Class | Department | Street Address | City | St |
|---|---|---|---|---|---|
| 15-Mar-92 | 11 | Design | 111 Cedar Ave. | Cleveland | OH |
| 17-Jan-87 | 41 | Testing | 51 Mentor Ave. | Mentor | OH |
| 15-Apr-90 | 22 | Design | 886 Larch Street | Cleveland | OH |
| 01-Feb-92 | 21 | Design | 1232 Hillside Rd. | Gates Mills | OH |
| 16-May-90 | 32 | Construction | 321 Wood Ave. | Mayfield | OH |
| 07-Jun-88 | 33 | Construction | 213 25th St. | Cleveland | OH |
| 03-Apr-89 | 31 | Construction | 45 Eagle Lane | Solon | OH |
| 05-Mar-91 | 12 | Design | 111 Weaver Ave. | Columbus | OH |
| 06-Nov-90 | 31 | Construction | 78 Fordham Drive | Austinburg | OH |
| 06-Dec-87 | 41 | Testing | 21 Circle Drive | Gates Mills | OH |
| | 0 | | | | OH |

Record: 9 of 10

- *Match Case* Select this check box to find only text whose case exactly matches what you have entered in Find What. When this check box is selected, Access only finds instances of the word with the same pattern of capitalization as the one you entered. For example, if you type **Beach** in the Find What text box and then select Match Case, Word will find Beach but not beach or BEACH.
- *Search Fields as Formatted* Select this check box when you want to restrict the search to entries that have the same format as the specific Find What text box entry. When this check box is cleared, Access searches for the entry regardless of the format.

5. Select Find First to find the first example of the entry you are searching for or select Find Next to find the next record that has the entry you are searching for.

The Find dialog box remains available so you can continue to select Find First or select Find Next. When you want to leave the dialog box and return to editing your records, select Close.

Besides finding entries in a table, you can also replace the entries that you find with other entries. This is done using the Replace command in the Edit menu. You can also perform this command by pressing CTRL+H or SHIFT+F7. The only difference in replacing and finding is that you must supply a replacement entry in the Replace With text box. The Replace dialog box's only difference from the Find dialog box is the Replace With text box. Selecting Find moves to the record that matches the entry in the Find What text box.

You can make a replacement by selecting Replace. Selecting Replace also moves you to the next instance of the entry in the Find What text box. You can also select Replace All when you want every instance of the entry in the Find What text box replaced by the contents of the Replace With text box.

## Moving or Copying Records

You can move or copy records from one Access table to another. This is useful if, for example, you keep prospective client information and current client information in separate tables. You could move a record from the Prospects table to the Client table as soon as you had an active project for that client. You might also want to move records between tables for Coaster Mania's employees. If you choose to maintain only current employees in the Employee table, you could move a record for a terminated employee to a table containing information on former employees, as shown here:

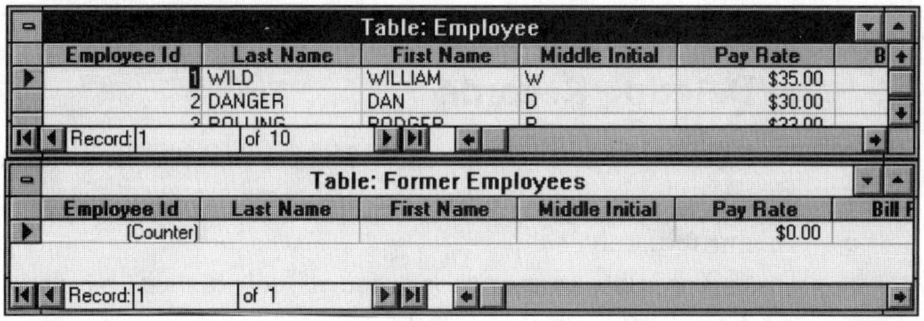

Table: Employee

| Employee Id | Last Name | First Name | Middle Initial | Pay Rate |
|---|---|---|---|---|
| 1 | WILD | WILLIAM | W | $35.00 |
| 2 | DANGER | DAN | D | $30.00 |

Record: 1 of 10

Table: Former Employees

| Employee Id | Last Name | First Name | Middle Initial | Pay Rate |
|---|---|---|---|---|
| (Counter) | | | | $0.00 |

Record: 1 of 1

To move or copy a record into another table, the fields in both tables must have the same data types, although the field names may be different. The fields in the two tables must be in the same order, and the field sizes in the destination table must be sufficient to contain the data. If the data is being placed in the primary key or in a field that is indexed and allows no duplicates, you need to check that none of the copied values match existing values in the destination table. Also, you cannot paste a record if any field entries violate a Validation Rule property in the destination table. Records that cannot be pasted for these reasons are written to a special table called Paste Errors for your review. You can change the source data as needed and attempt to move the records to the destination table again.

To move or copy a record to another table, follow these steps:

1. Select the records to be copied.
2. Choose Cut or Copy from the Edit menu.

Selecting Cut removes the record from the current table as it copies the record to the Clipboard. Selecting Copy keeps the record in the current table as it copies the record to the Clipboard.

3. Open the table that you want to move or copy the records to.
4. Rearrange the fields to match the order of the source records, if necessary.
5. Select the records to be replaced and then choose Paste from the Edit menu, or append the records at the end of the table by choosing Paste Append from the Edit menu.

**tip:** *In Chapter 7, you will learn about append queries that you can use to copy and move records between tables. Append queries let you have your fields in a different order and can handle fields that are in one table but not in the other.*

## Deleting Records

Removing records is easy. If you make a mistake and delete the wrong records, you can undo your mistake as long as you take the corrective action immediately.

To delete one or more records, select them by clicking the record selector. To select multiple records, select the first record selector and drag to the last record. Choose Delete from the Edit menu or press the DEL key. The dialog box that appears indicates the number of records about to be deleted and lets you decide whether or not to proceed with the deletion.

## Sorting Records in Access Version 2

In Access version 2, sorting the records in a table is very easy. Resequencing the records makes it easier to find the records you want to move, copy, or delete. For example, you might want to move records of employees at a separate plant or site to another table. The easiest way to select these records would be to sort the Employee table according to a Site field, so that all of the records you wanted were together in the table.

Start by moving the insertion point to the field you want to sort the table by. Then choose Quick Sort from the Records menu and select Ascending or

Descending. You can also sort the table by a field's values by clicking the Sort Ascending or Sort Descending buttons shown here:

**tip:** *The fields you sort by do not have to be indexed in order to use the Sort Ascending or Sort Descending buttons.*

## Customizing the Datasheet Layout

You can use the layout that appears when you open a table or you can make some significant changes to its appearance. You may find that changing the layout speeds up your work or makes the data you need to work with more accessible or attractive. While the Datasheet view is ideal for looking at many records at the same time, limiting the data that is displayed can make it easier to spot any changes you have to make. You can use each layout technique singly or combine them to achieve the best possible display. To make your changes a permanent part of the datasheet layout, choose Save Table from the File menu. If you want the changes to be temporary, just close the table without choosing Save Table from the File menu.

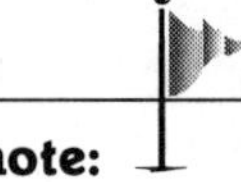

**note:** *Access will ask you if you want to save the layout changes if you attempt to close the table without having done so. You can select Yes to save the layout changes or No to abandon them.*

### Freezing the Display

Identifying fields, such as employee or client names, often appear at the left side of the datasheet. As you move to the right, these fields scroll off the display, which can make it difficult to tell which record you are working with. You can freeze fields at the left of the display so that they remain in view as you move to the right.

To freeze a field in the datasheet, click the field selector at the top of the column and then choose Freeze Columns from the Format menu (the Layout menu in Access version 1). Select multiple columns by pressing the SHIFT key as you click the field selectors at the top of the columns. Figure 4-3 shows the Client Name and Contact fields frozen at the left of the window while other fields from the right side of the display are viewed.

To unfreeze the columns when you no longer need them frozen, choose Unfreeze All Columns from the Format menu (Layout menu in Access version 1). The columns that were frozen now appear at the far left of the datasheet, no matter where they were before you froze them. To put them back where they were originally, move them using the instructions in the next section or close the table without saving the layout. Closing the table without saving the layout means column position and other settings are not saved. Whether or not you save the table layout has no effect on the table design or data.

## Reordering the Column Display

Initially the order of the columns in a datasheet corresponds to the order of the fields in the table design. If you need to enter only a few fields or check the values in several fields, your task would be much easier if the fields appeared in adjacent columns on the datasheet. Also, you may have frozen columns and found when you unfroze them that they were on the far left of your datasheet even if they were originally in a different location.

To move a column to a new location, select the field selector for the column. You can select several adjacent columns if you wish. Next, drag the selected columns to the new location. After freezing the Client Name and Contact fields from the Client table and then unfreezing the display, these fields appear to the left of the Client Id in the Client table. You can select these columns as shown in Figure 4-4 and then drag the field selectors to the right of the Client Id.

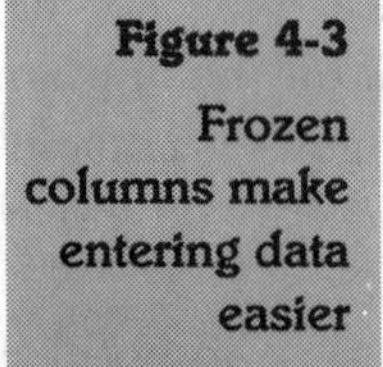
**Figure 4-3** Frozen columns make entering data easier

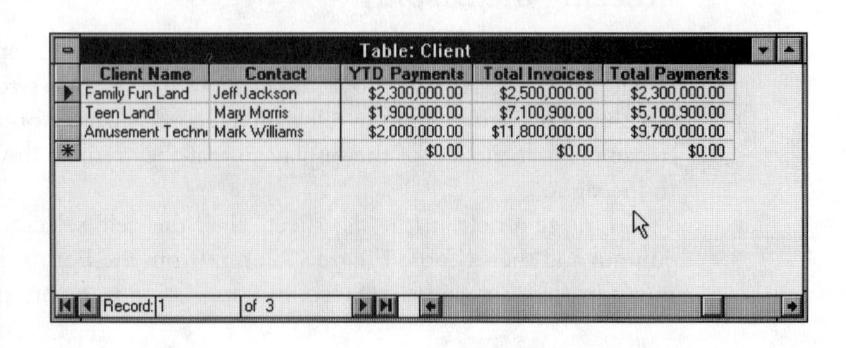


| Client Name | Contact | YTD Payments | Total Invoices | Total Payments |
|---|---|---|---|---|
| Family Fun Land | Jeff Jackson | $2,300,000.00 | $2,500,000.00 | $2,300,000.00 |
| Teen Land | Mary Morris | $1,900,000.00 | $7,100,900.00 | $5,100,900.00 |
| Amusement Techn | Mark Williams | $2,000,000.00 | $11,800,000.00 | $9,700,000.00 |
| | | $0.00 | $0.00 | $0.00 |

**Figure 4-4** Two columns need to be moved to the right of Client Id

Table: Client

| | Client Name | Contact | Client Id | Park Location | Mailing Address | Ci |
|---|---|---|---|---|---|---|
| ▶ | Family Fun Land | Jeff Jackson | 1 | Isle Royale | P.O. Box 345 | Houghtor |
| | Teen Land | Mary Morris | 2 | Ashtabula Park | P.O. Box 786 | Ashtabula |
| | Amusement Techn | Mark Williams | 3 | Panacea on the Be | P.O. Box 5346 | Panacea |
| * | | | (Counter) | | | |

Record: 1 of 3

## Hiding Columns

If your datasheet has more than a few fields you may not be able to see all of the fields in the window or print them all on one sheet of paper. When you only need to work with a few columns, you may find that hiding the unneeded columns can make this easier. Hidden columns do not appear on the screen or when you print.

**tip:** *Printing a table from the Datasheet view is described later in this chapter under "Printing a Table."*

To hide one or more columns, select the columns and choose Hide Columns from the Format menu (Layout menu in Access version 1). To select multiple columns, hold down the SHIFT key as you click the field selectors.

For example, if you are working with the Client table and do not need to see Mailing Address, City, State, and ZIP Code, select those fields and then choose Hide Columns from the Format menu (Layout menu in Access version 1). Although the columns are not permanently deleted, there is no evidence of their existence on the screen or on paper when the table is printed.

**tip:** *Since you cannot hide nonadjacent columns without making several selections, you might find it easier to use the Show Columns command from the Format menu (Layout menu in Access version 1) when hiding a large number of columns. After choosing this command, choose the fields to be hidden from the list of field names and click the Hide button. When you are finished marking which fields to hide, select Close.*

To redisplay columns that you have hidden, choose Show Columns from the Format menu (Layout menu in Access version 1). The Show Columns dialog box appears. Choose the field that you want to display again and then select Show. Continue selecting until all of the columns you need have been selected. Columns that will be shown have a check mark before their name in the list, while hidden ones do not. Select a column and choose Hide if there are columns that you want to conceal. When you are finished making changes, choose Close. Figure 4-5 shows how the Client table appears with many of its columns hidden.

## Changing the Column Width

Access establishes the column width based on the default column width setting, which is approximately one screen inch. If you do not need all that space to display a meaningful amount of data, you can shrink the column width, letting you show more columns on the screen. You can widen a column if you need to see more of its contents. Changing the column width does not change the length of the entries that you can place in the field, only how much of the entry appears.

Currency fields for small prices and other numeric data often do not fill the space allocated. Counter fields are often too large if you have a limited number of records. These are fields which are frequently narrowed because they take up so much excess space. With a Text data type you may want to widen the field so that you can see more of the entry.

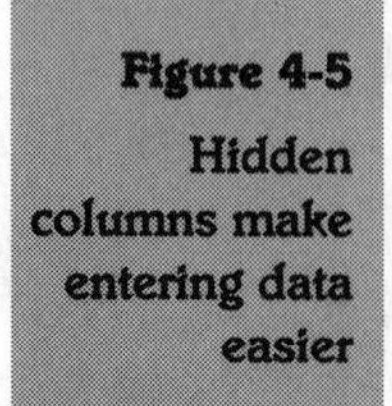

**Figure 4-5** Hidden columns make entering data easier

Table: Client

| Client Id | Client Name | YTD Invoices | YTD Payments | Total Invoices | Total Pa |
|---|---|---|---|---|---|
| 1 | Family Fun Land | $2,500,000.00 | $2,300,000.00 | $2,500,000.00 | $2,300 |
| 2 | Teen Land | $3,900,000.00 | $1,900,000.00 | $7,100,900.00 | $5,100 |
| 3 | Amusement Techn | $4,100,000.00 | $2,000,000.00 | $11,800,000.00 | $9,700 |
| (Counter) | | $0.00 | $0.00 | $0.00 | |

Record: 1 of 3

**tip:** *Sometimes you want to see the entire contents of several fields at once. Narrowing the columns hides some text, while widening them means you can't see all of the fields. One solution is to narrow the columns and then increase the row height, as described in the next section, so that more text can appear in each field. On the other hand, doing this means that you can't see as many records at once.*

To change the width of a column, simply drag the right side of the field selector for that column right or left to achieve the desired size. When the mouse is positioned correctly, the mouse pointer is a double-line with two arrows pointing left and right. Figure 4-6 shows the Park Desc field widened to show more text onscreen. You can also change a column's width with the Column Width command in the Format menu (Layout menu in Access version 1). In the Column Width text box, you can type the width you want for the column. You can also select Standard Width to return to the default column size. In Access version 2, you can select Best Fit to let Access size the column based on the field's contents. You can quickly change a column's width to Access's best fit by double-clicking the column's right boundary.

## Changing the Font or Row Height

You can change the font used to display a datasheet to any available screen font. You can let Access automatically adjust the row height to match the new font height or you can customize the row height to display multiple rows of data for a field.

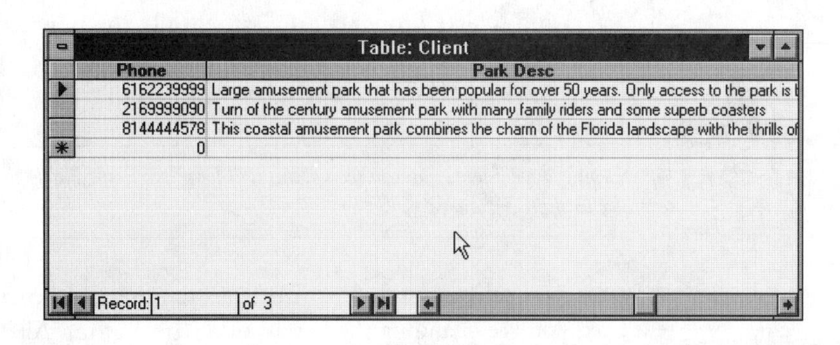


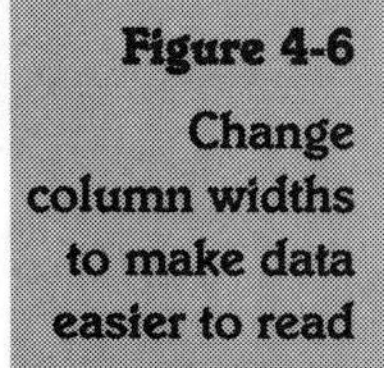

**Figure 4-6** Change column widths to make data easier to read

**tip:** *To make sure that the printed datasheet matches the appearance of your screen after you choose a new font, choose a TrueType font or another type of font that looks the same on the screen and when printed. If the font you choose is a screen font only, Access will select the closest possible match when printing your data depending on what printer options you have available.*

## CHANGING THE FONT

When you change the font for a table, you are changing the design of the characters. You can also change the style, size, and special effects. You may change a font to make your datasheet more readable or to conform to a particular company style for documents. All font changes are made by choosing Font from the Format menu (Layout menu in Access version 1) to display the dialog box shown here:

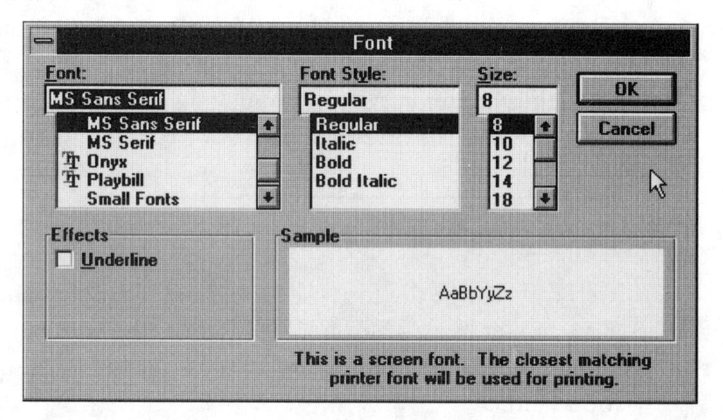


You can select a new font to use from the Font list box, which displays all the available fonts. TrueType fonts have a double T icon in front of them. Font Style options include Bold and Italic. When you change the font style, the characters and selected font stay the same; only the new style option is added for all the table entries.

**tip:** *When you change a font, you can see what it will look like immediately by looking at the Sample text box in the Font dialog box.*

When you select a new font size from the Size list box or type one in the text box, you are changing the height of the given font. All TrueType fonts are *scalable,* which means that they can be set to nearly any size. Other fonts can only use specific sizes, which will appear in the Size list box. The height of characters is measured in points. A point is equal to 1/72 of an inch (1/28 of a centimeter).

When you change the point size, the row height is automatically adjusted unless you have set a specific height, as described in the next section. Remember that the row height should be a little more than the height of the font, so that there is enough space at the top and bottom of the row. For example, when the font size is changed from 8 (the default) to 18, the row height is automatically adjusted from 10.5 to 22.5.

Figure 4-7 shows one of the Coaster tables displayed in a serif font with a larger point size.

**tip:** *Remember, you have already seen the font and row height adjusted; several figures in Chapters 2 and 3 were adjusted to make them easier for you to read.*

## CHANGING THE ROW HEIGHT

By default, Access automatically resizes the height of the rows in a table when you change the font. You can also set a specific row height. Row heights are measured in points just as the fonts are.

When you increase the row height without changing the font or font size, Access displays more than one line of the text in a row. To do this, select Row

**Figure 4-7**
**A datasheet displayed using a larger serif font**

Table: Employee

| Employee Id | Last Name | First Name | Middle Initial | Pay Rate | Bill |
|---|---|---|---|---|---|
| 1 | WILD | WILLIAM | W | $35.00 | |
| 2 | DANGER | DAN | D | $30.00 | |
| 3 | ROLLING | RODGER | R | $33.00 | |
| 4 | SCARY | SANDRA | S | $31.00 | |
| 5 | HIGHER | HARRY | H | $6.50 | |
| 6 | THRILL | TOMMY | T | $7.00 | |
| 7 | ROCK | RICHARD | R | $8.00 | |
| 8 | DARE | DONNA | D | $35.00 | |
| 9 | JUMP | JOHNNY | J | $6.50 | |
| 10 | BRAVE | BRENDA | B | $32.00 | |
| (Counter) | | | | $0.00 | |

Record: 1 of 10

Height from the Format menu (Layout menu in Access version 1). Enter a row height in points in the Row Height text box. Notice that the Standard Height check box is cleared when you enter a specific height. As long as this check box is selected, Access automatically sets your row height, based on the font used in the datasheet. If you leave the font size at 8 points—the default—and change the row height to 33 points, you can see three lines of field entry in one row, as shown in Figure 4-8.

## Printing a Table

Although the reports that you will learn about in Chapter 9 give you more sophisticated options, you can also print your data directly from the datasheet. Hidden columns will not appear, allowing you to limit the amount of data printed. Other customizing options such as font and height changes also affect the printout. You can retain the gridlines or remove them by choosing Gridlines in the Format menu (Layout menu in Access version 1).

Preview the appearance of the printout by choosing Print Preview from the File menu. If you need to select another printer, change the configuration of the current printer, or print to a file, choose Print Setup from the File menu.

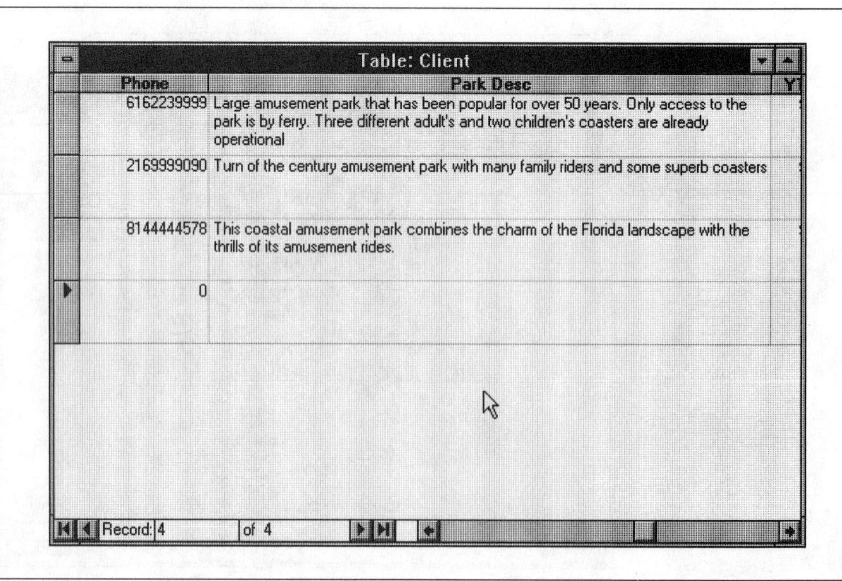


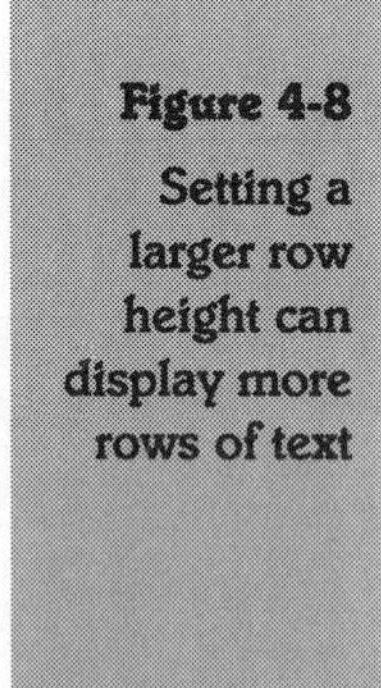

**Figure 4-8** Setting a larger row height can display more rows of text

If you want to print selected records, choose them and then select Print from the File menu. You can select All, Selection, or Pages to control the amount of data that prints.

## Copying a Table

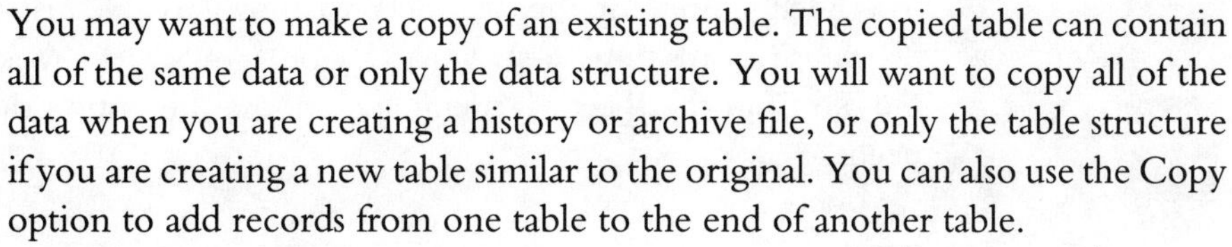

You may want to make a copy of an existing table. The copied table can contain all of the same data or only the data structure. You will want to copy all of the data when you are creating a history or archive file, or only the table structure if you are creating a new table similar to the original. You can also use the Copy option to add records from one table to the end of another table.

Follow these steps to copy a table:

1. Open the database containing the table that you want to copy.
2. From the Database window, select the table that you want to copy and then choose Copy from the Edit menu.
3. Choose Paste from the Edit menu to copy the table to the current database and supply a new name.

   You must open the destination database first if the new table is not needed in the current database.
4. Complete the Paste Table As dialog box.

   You need to provide a new table name in the Table Name text box, and to select a paste option. These are your paste options:

   - *Structure Only* creates a new table with the same fields and properties, but without the data.
   - *Structure And Data* creates a new table with the same fields, properties, and data.
   - *Append Data To Existing Table* adds the data in the copied table to the highlighted table, but without copying any of the field settings.
5. Select OK.

## Quick Reference

**To Move to Another Field** Use TAB or SHIFT+TAB to move to the next or previous field. You can also click the field. Use the horizontal scroll bar to display a field that does not currently appear in the window.

**To Move to Another Record** Click the navigation buttons at the lower-left corner of the datasheet to move to the first, last, next, or previous records. Use the UP ARROW or DOWN ARROW keys or choose Go To from the Records menu and choose the option that meets your needs.

**To Undo a Change** Choose Undo, Undo Current Field, or Undo Current Record from the Edit menu, or click the Undo or Undo Current Field/Record buttons.

**To Delete a Record** Select the record and then select Delete from the Edit menu or press DEL.

**To Copy a Field or Record** Select the data to be copied and then choose Copy from the Edit menu. Move the insertion point to where you want to copy the data, selecting data that you want to replace. Choose Paste or Paste Append from the Edit menu. Use Paste Append to add the copied records to the end of the destination table.

**To Move a Field or Record** Select the data to move and choose Cut from the Edit menu. Move the insertion point to where you want to move the data, selecting data that you want to replace. Choose Paste or Paste Append from the Edit menu. Use Paste Append to add the copied records to the end of the destination table.

**To Freeze the Display** Select the field selector for the columns to freeze and then choose Freeze Columns from the Format menu (Layout in Access version 1). To unfreeze columns, choose Unfreeze All Columns from the Format menu (Layout menu in Access version 1).

## Quick Reference

**To Move a Column** Click the field selector for the column to be moved. Drag the highlighted field selector to its new location.

**To Hide a Column** Click the field selector for the column you want to hide. Choose Hide Columns from the Format menu (Layout menu in Access version 1).

**To Show a Hidden Column** Choose Show Columns from the Format menu (Layout in Access version 1) and then select the columns you want to display and select Show. Choose Close after selecting all of the columns to be displayed.

**To Change the Column Width** Drag the right edge of the field selector for the column to the left or right.

**To Change the Font** Choose Font from the Format menu (Layout menu in Access version 1) and then select Font, Font Style, Size, or Underline. Select OK when you are finished making changes.

**To Change the Row Height** Drag up or down with the pointer between two record selectors, or choose Row Height from the Format menu (Layout menu in Access version 1) and specify the row height in points.

**To Print a Table** Select Print from the File menu and then select OK.

**To Copy a Table** From the Database window, select the table to be copied. Choose Copy from the Edit menu. Choose Paste from the Edit menu immediately to place the copy in the current database, or after opening another database to place the copy in that database. You can choose to copy both the structure and the data, the structure only, or just the records. Specify a name for the table and select OK.

# Chapter 5

Sharing Data Between Access and Other Suite Products

Accessing Data in Other Database Applications

Exporting Access Data

Using the Clipboard to Share Data Between Applications

# Interchanging Data with Microsoft Office and Other Products

IF you use a personal computer regularly, you may already be acquainted with other applications. You may have data from these applications that you would like to use with Access. Also, you may want to use some of your new Access data in these other applications. If you are using Microsoft Office's suite of products, you have several applications that are designed to be used together.

Because Access is a Windows application, you can easily share data with other Windows applications. You can copy one or more Access objects to the Clipboard and then paste them into another application. This allows you to transfer data from Access to products such as Word for Windows or Excel for Windows and also allows you to transfer data from one Access database to another. The steps for sharing data between Microsoft Office and Access illustrates many of Access' data-sharing capabilities.

You can use data from Access in other database applications or import data into Access. Access can work with FoxPro, dBASE, Paradox, Btrieve, and SQL. You can create an Access database from data stored in a spreadsheet or word-processing programs, or use your Access data in the other programs. For example, you can use your Access database for the data you need to run a mail merge in Word for Windows.

If you want to share the tables you created with other applications, read this chapter to find out how Access will share data with other applications such as Microsoft Mail, Excel, and Word for Windows. Once you learn about Access' data-sharing capabilities using these applications for examples, you can try exporting your data to other applications. Exporting takes your Access data and puts it in a file with a format that other applications can use. If you have data in these other formats, you should take the time to explore using the data with Access now, since you can build a database table with minimal work this way. If you are new to database management, skip this chapter and focus on other Access topics in the chapters that follow this one. You can return to importing and exporting when it applies to your work.

## Sharing Data Between Access and Other Suite Products

Access can work with many other applications, including Word for Windows, Excel, PowerPoint, and Microsoft Mail. These applications are included in Microsoft's Office package. Although they are not the only applications you can share data with, you may have purchased Access with the Office product and thus already have these applications. Also, sharing data between these applications will show off Access' data-sharing capabilities, which you may use with another application that is not part of the Office package.

### Mailing Access Data

Access version 2 will work with Microsoft Mail to send database data to other Microsoft Mail users. If Microsoft Mail is installed when you install Access, your File menu, as well as the shortcut menu in the Database window, will include a Send option. When you learn how to display reports you create, your toolbar will have a button that performs the same menu command and looks like this:

When you select this option or toolbar button, you are sending the output of the table, query dynaset, form, or report to another user. You can select records in a datasheet for a table or query as well as records in a form, and you will have the choice of sending either only the selected records or all of them. After selecting Send, you must choose the format of how the information is sent. Your options include Excel, Rich Text Format (RTF), or MS-DOS Text. RTF is accepted by most Microsoft applications. Once you select one of the formats and OK, Microsoft Mail starts and you are ready to provide the information in the To, Cc, and Subject text boxes. The data that will be sent appears as an attached file. Figure 5-1 shows a message about to be sent using Microsoft Mail.

### Exporting Access Data to an Excel File

Access has three ways to put your data from an Access table into an Excel file you can use with Excel. You can create an Excel worksheet file using the Export command in the File menu. In Access version 2, you can also choose the Output To command in the File menu, which also appears in several shortcut menus.

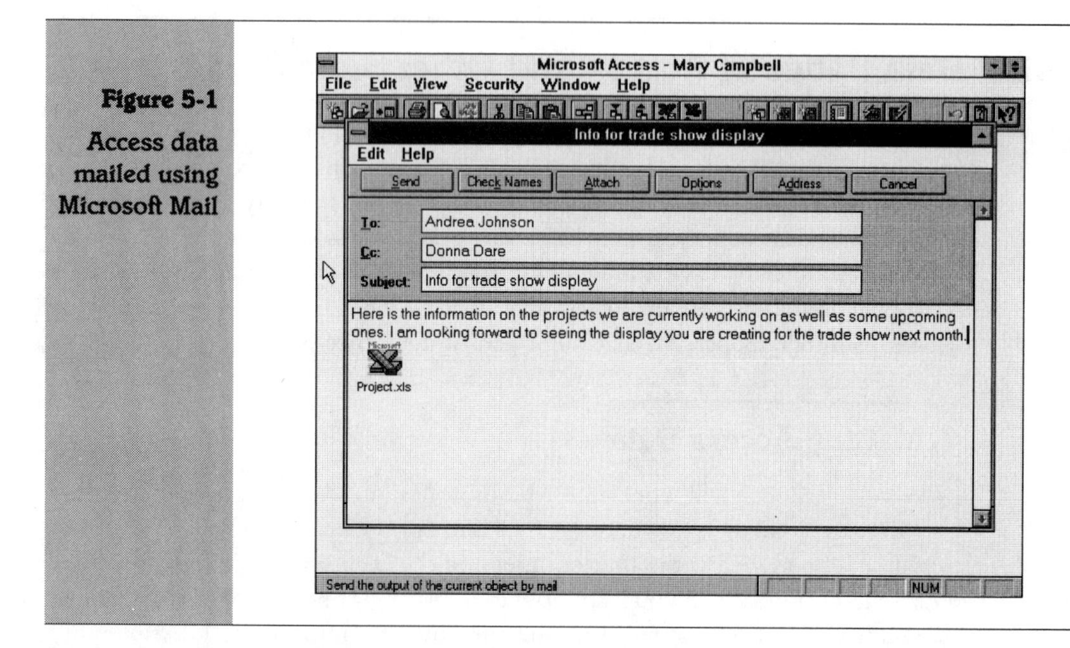


**Figure 5-1** Access data mailed using Microsoft Mail

The third option is to click this button in the toolbar, available in the Database window:

If you choose the Export command in the File menu, you will need to select Excel as the format and OK. Then select the database table to export and OK. If you choose Output To in the File menu, select Output To from the shortcut menu, or click the toolbar button shown above, select Excel as the format and OK. Then, for either command, type the name for the Excel file and select OK. If you use the Output To option, in the dialog box where you entered the filename, you can select AutoStart and Access will open Excel for you and open the worksheet file that Access just created.

You do not need to supply an extension because Access will add .XLS, which is the appropriate extension for Excel worksheets. Figure 5-2 shows an Access table and the same data that Access has saved to an Excel file.

## Exporting Access Data to Word for Windows

Access has two ways to put your data from an Access table into a Word for Windows document. You can create a Word for Windows document in Access

**Figure 5-2**

**Access table saved as an Excel worksheet**

version 2 by choosing Output To in the File menu. After choosing this command, select Rich Text Format (RTF) as the format of the file you are creating and select OK. Then type the name for the document to create and select OK. Access creates an RTF file. If you selected the AutoStart check box in the dialog box where you entered the filename, Access will open Word for Windows for you and open the file that Access just created. You can open this RTF file in Word for Windows as well as in most other Microsoft applications.

There is another way you can take your data from Access and put it into a new Word for Windows document that is available just for reports. When you display a report, the Print Preview toolbar that appears has a button that looks like this:

Clicking this button takes the current report and saves it in an RTF file. When the file is completed and saved, Access opens Word for Windows and opens the RTF file it just created.

**tip:** *When you save Access data using Output To in the File menu, the format you select chooses the information Access places in the file. When you save it using an Excel or RTF format, the formatting, layout, and fonts are saved in the file. Reports saved in .XLS format include the outline information, which you can use with Excel's outlining features. RTF and text files include both the text boxes and the adjacent text, while .XLS files only include the contents of text boxes without the adjacent text labels. OLE objects and the contents of check boxes are not included in these files.*

## Using Access Data in a Word for Windows Mail Merge Document

Access provides an easy way to store data you want to use for creating form letters. Access has several features that prepare its data to use with Word for Windows. These features include a Report Wizard and the ability to export data to a Word for Windows document. Another possibility with Word for Windows 6 is to create a link to the Access database.

### SETTING UP A MAIL MERGE BETWEEN ACCESS AND WORD FOR WINDOWS 6

If you have Word for Windows 6, Access has another way to set up a Word for Windows document to use the data you have in an Access table. This feature sets up a link between a Word for Windows document and the Access table. The advantage of this method is that, when the Access table data changes, the data that the Word document uses also changes. When you have a table whose data you want to use in a Word for Windows mail merge, follow these steps:

1. Select the table containing the data you want to use for the mail merge.

   When you learn how to create queries, you can use queries for the mail merge data by selecting a query instead of a table.

2. Click this button in the toolbar, available from the Database window:

   You can also select New from the File menu and then select Report or click the New Report button in the toolbar. From the next dialog box, select the Report Wizards button, then select MS Word Mail Merge and OK.

3. Make a selection based on whether you have already created the document that will use the data in the table during the mail merge process.

    - If you have already created the document, select the first option and OK. From the next dialog box, select the Access file whose data you want to use in the mail merge process. When you select OK, Access opens the document and sets it to use the selected table as the source of the data in a mail merge process.
    - If you have not yet created the document, select the second option and OK. Access will open Word for Windows for you and set up a new document to use the selected table for its variable data. The Mail Merge toolbar in Word for Windows will appear so you can choose where you want fields from the Access table placed in the document.

    Figure 5-3 shows a document set up in Word for Windows to use the data in the Employee Access table.

4. When you are ready to perform the mail merge, switch to Word for Windows and select Mail Merge from the Tools menu and select Merge twice.

## EXPORTING ACCESS DATA TO A WORD FOR WINDOWS MAIL MERGE DOCUMENT

You can tell Access that you want to export data from a table and put it into a document that you can use with Word for Windows mail merge features. Once you do this, you can create mail merge main documents that use the file created with Access to supply the variable information in the form letter. Many of the steps for creating the file are the same steps for exporting Access data that are detailed later. To take a table you have in Access and create a document to use with Word for Windows' mail merge features, you will follow these steps:

1. Choose Export from the File menu.
2. Select Word for Windows Merge in the Data Destination list box and OK.
3. Select the table containing the data you want to use in the Word for Windows mail merge and OK.

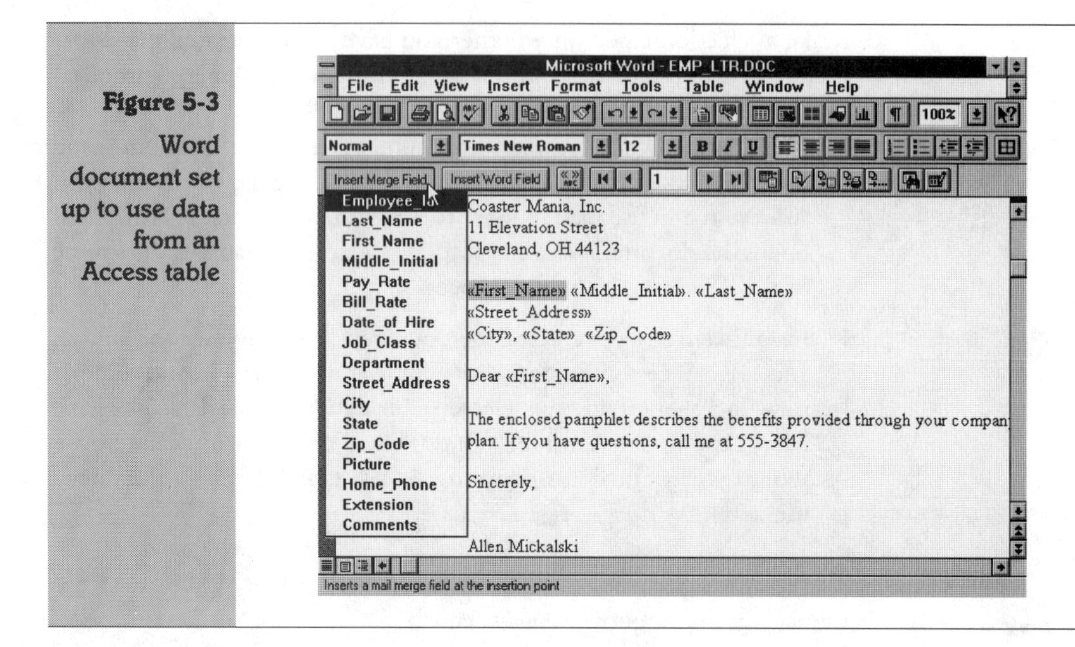


**Figure 5-3** Word document set up to use data from an Access table

In the next chapter, you will learn how to create select queries that can choose a subset of records in a table. You can create a mail merge data document using a query by selecting the query to use instead of the table. When you display the database's queries or both the tables and queries, you may not see all queries in the database. Action queries, which perform an action rather than selecting a subset of records from one or more tables, are not included in the list.

4. Type a name for the file you will create and select OK.

   Access displays a dialog box for how dates and times are put into the file Access will create. By making selections in this dialog box, you can choose the characters that separate parts of the date and time, the order of the parts of the date, and whether years use four digits or two.

5. Select OK after changing any options for dates and times.

At this point, Access creates the file. In Word for Windows you can select the file you just created as the source of data for a mail merge. Figure 5-4 shows a table from the file Access created to use for a Word for Windows mail merge. The tab stops are set so you can see where each field starts.

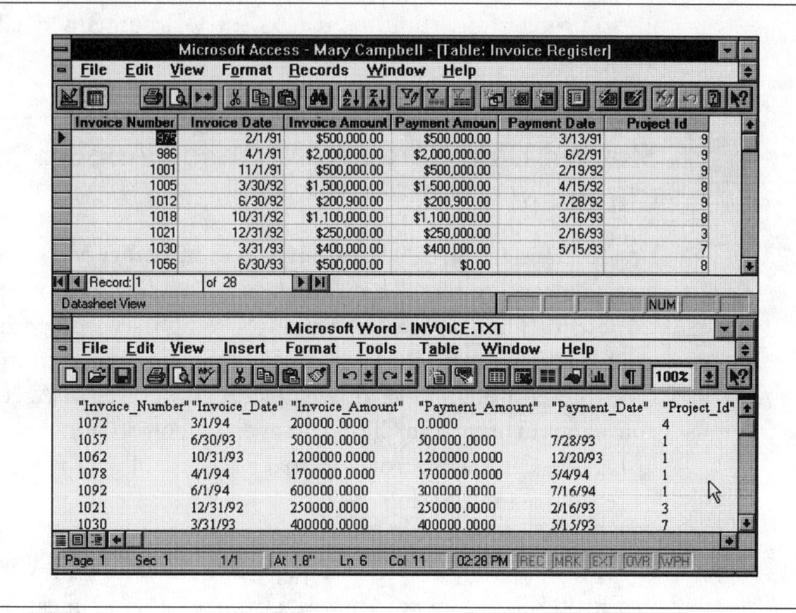


**Figure 5-4** Word for Windows mail merge data created from an Access table

## PUTTING AN ACCESS TABLE INTO A WORD FOR WINDOWS DOCUMENT

You can put an entire table from Access into a Word for Windows document. This feature lets you incorporate your tables into documents you have in Word for Windows. When you do this, you add the Access data as a table in Word. To add the table, choose Database from the Insert menu of Word for Windows and then select Get Data. From the next dialog box, select the Access database file. Then select whether you want to use DDE or ODBC (Open Database Connectivity) to handle bringing the data into the Word document. Then select the table from the database you want to insert and select OK. When you return to the Database dialog box, you can select Query Options or Table AutoFormat to select a subset of the records and fields or to add formatting to the table that this command will create. When you select Insert Data and OK, Word inserts the Access table into the Word document. Between selecting Insert Data and OK, you can select the Insert Data as Field check box to insert a Word field that represents the data from the table. The difference between inserting a field and inserting the data is that you can update the field to update the data in Word to match the version of the data in Access. When this check box is cleared, you can edit the data in Word without updating it from Access. If you run into a problem inserting the database, try closing any database you have open in Access.

## Sharing Data Between Microsoft Applications Using the Clipboard

Besides transferring data between Access and other Microsoft applications using files, you can also transfer information between Microsoft applications using the Clipboard. The *Clipboard* is Windows' temporary storage area where Windows can place information from any application designed to use it. The Clipboard can store entire tables or other objects you create in Access. The Clipboard's contents remain on the Clipboard even when you switch to another application. Using the Clipboard, you can make a copy of data from one application and paste it into another.

When copying data from Access to another application, you are usually copying data from a table or a query like the ones you will learn how to create in Chapter 6. When copying data from another application to Access, you are copying data to use as the data for an OLE Object data type field or you are copying something to include as part of a form or report's design. This method of using the Clipboard to copy data into Access is described in Chapter 15 along with other features that you use in forms and reports.

You can copy Access tables to other Microsoft applications when you want a copy of the data you have in a table in another application such as Word for Windows or Excel. When you select the data to copy, you can select part of a table or all of it. When you select the table from the Database window, you are selecting the entire table. You can also select an entire table when you are looking at it by choosing Select All Records from the Edit menu or by clicking the upper-left corner of the table's datasheet. To select a section of a table, drag the mouse over the record selectors of the records you want to choose. To put the selected records on the Clipboard, either choose Copy from the Edit menu, choose Copy from the shortcut menu, press CTRL+INS, or press CTRL+C. You can also choose Cut from the Edit menu or press CTRL+X or SHIFT+DEL to put the selected object on the Clipboard while removing the object from the current database. Once the data is on the Clipboard, you are ready to paste it into the other application. Most Microsoft applications have a Paste command in the Edit menu, with keyboard shortcuts of SHIFT+INS and CTRL+V. Figure 5-5 shows some of the Employee data after it is pasted from the Clipboard into

Word for Windows and into Excel. As you can see in this example, Word separates the fields with tabs and Excel puts each field in separate columns.

When you want to put data from another Microsoft application into Access, the steps are similar. In the other application, select the data you want to see in Access. Then copy it to the Clipboard with the Copy command in the Edit menu. Next, switch to Access and move to the field and record where you want the copied data. Choose Paste in the Edit menu. Access pastes the data and displays some description of the pasted data in the datasheet. Figure 5-6 shows a range in an Excel worksheet that has been copied to the Clipboard and then pasted as the field contents for the Projected Costs field. This field has an OLE Object field type. At this point, all that appears in the datasheet is **Microsoft Excel Worksheet**. However, you can double-click **Microsoft Excel Worksheet** to open Excel with the worksheet you see in Figure 5-6. When you use the table in a form or report, the form or report will display the Excel data rather than the words **Microsoft Excel Worksheet**.

When you paste data between Microsoft applications, if you do not like how the pasted data appears, try the Paste Special command in the Edit menu. This command lets you choose from the available data formats on the Clipboard that Access can use to put the data in the current object. For example, when you are pasting an Excel worksheet, some of your choices include Microsoft Excel Worksheet and Picture. When you are pasting a Word for Windows document,

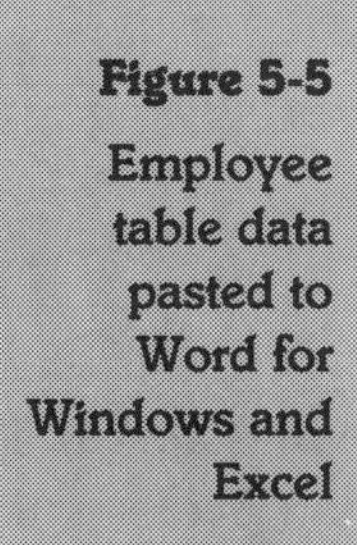

**Figure 5-5** Employee table data pasted to Word for Windows and Excel

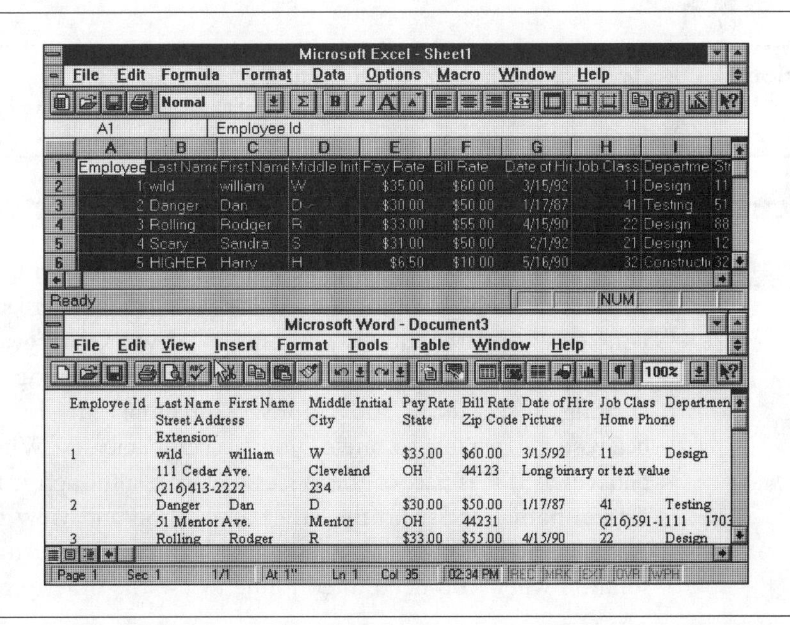

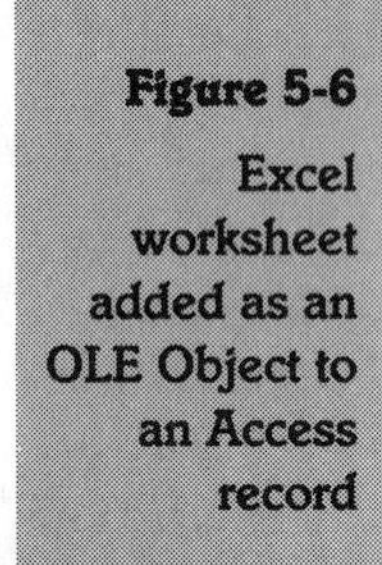

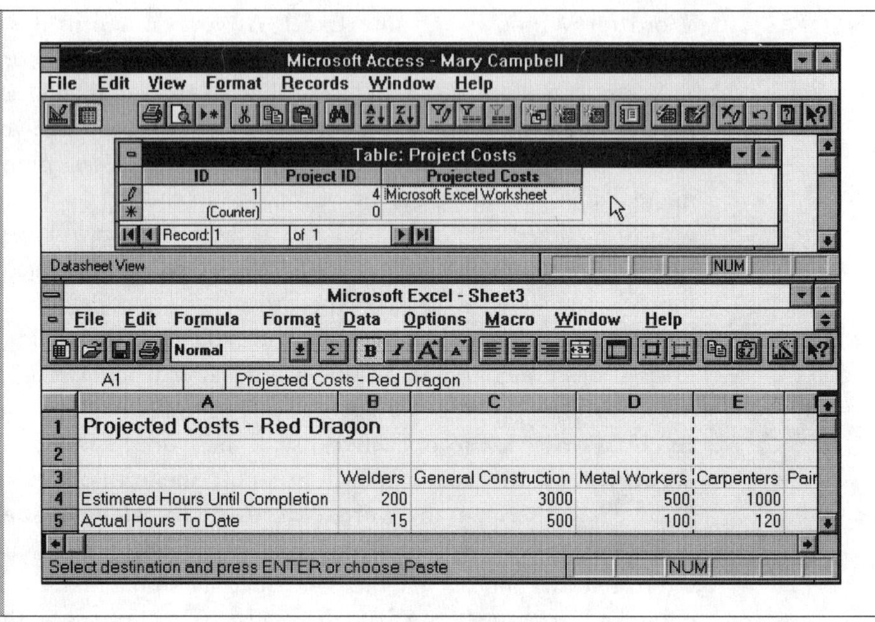


**Figure 5-6** Excel worksheet added as an OLE Object to an Access record

your choices include Microsoft Word 6.0 Document and Picture. The Paste Special command in the Edit menu lets you choose how the data is pasted rather than using the default.

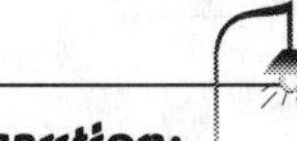

**caution:** *Access data does not work as OLE data in other applications.*

## Accessing Data in Other Database Applications

The investment you have made in building a base of information is not lost if you decide to begin using Access for your database tasks. Using Access with your existing data requires a minimum of work. Access is so flexible that it allows you to continue maintaining the data in the original file format while creating Access forms and reports. You simply attach the data in the other database file or table to one of your Access databases. When you *attach* data, it behaves as if it is part of the Access database although it is not. You can edit data in both Access and the other application and view the data as if it is an Access table although an Access table is not created. Attaching is the perfect solution when you need to continue to use the other program with the data.

Access can attach tables from other Access databases, dBASE, Paradox, FoxPro, Btrieve, and SQL.

When you no longer need to use your existing data with the program that created it, you can import the data into Access. *Importing* converts the data from its original format into an Access table. Access version 2 supports importing with dBASE, Paradox, FoxPro, text files, Excel, Lotus 1-2-3, Btrieve, and SQL. Access version 1 cannot import all of these formats. If you want to add data from an existing application to an Access table, you can append the data to an Access table as long as its format matches the existing table entries.

The difference between importing and attaching data is where the data is stored when you use it in Access. When you import data, you are taking a copy of the data and placing it in a table in an Access database, as illustrated in Figure 5-7. When you use data in an attached table in Access, you are using the data that is stored in a file in another application's format. The data is *not* in your Access database although you use your Access database to look at and use the data.

## General Guidelines for Importing and Attaching

When you want to use data stored in another application's format, you must decide whether to import or attach the data. The decision hinges on this question: Do you want to use the data in the other application again? When

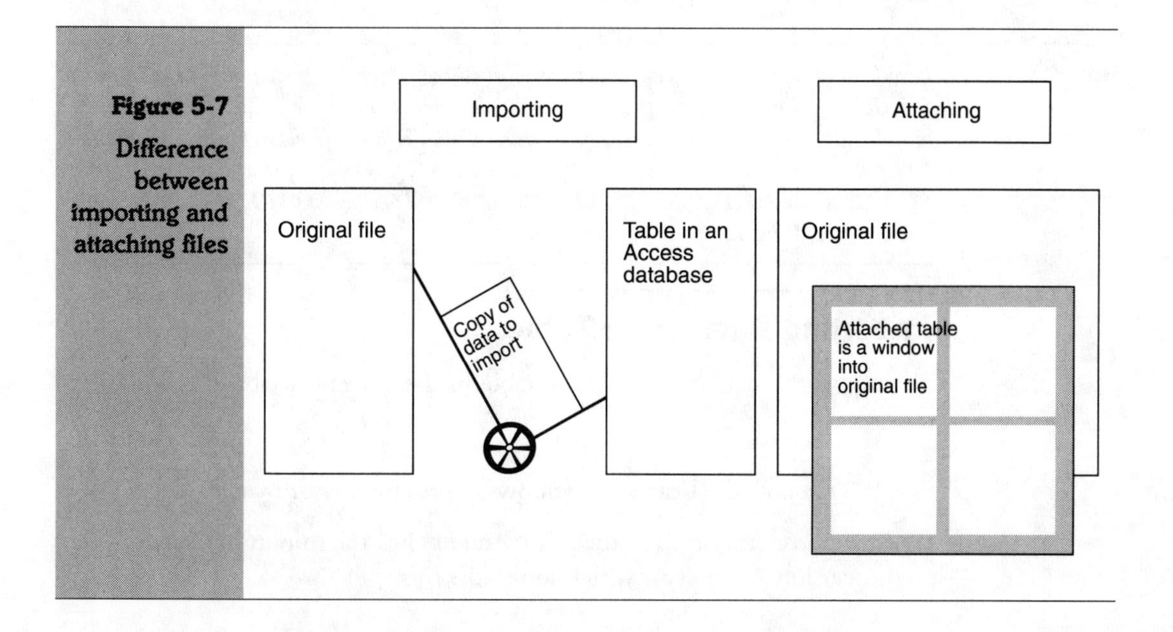


**Figure 5-7** **Difference between importing and attaching files**

the answer is yes (you want to create an Access report using dBASE and you will continue to use your other dBASE reports with the data, for example), attach the data to an Access database table. When the answer is no (you are upgrading to Access from your old software, for instance), import the data.

Either attach the data from the other format or import the data. Don't do both, because then you'll have more than one copy of the data. With more than one copy, you can't always be sure which copy is the most recent.

**tip:** *Make the original table your only copy, and attach it to the databases that require the information whenever necessary; this way you'll know that the original table always contains the most up-to-date information. When you change the data in the original tables or in one of the attached tables, the data is updated both in the original table and in all databases that use the data as an attached table.*

The steps for importing a file are summarized in the next section, "Importing Data into a Table." The steps for attaching a table into an Access database are summarized in the section after that, "Attaching a Table." Sections throughout this chapter will refer you to these two sections whenever you need to import into a table or attach a table in Access. When you either attach or import data into a table, you are creating a new table that has the same name as the file that contains the imported or attached data.

**tip:** *If you run into a problem with importing or attaching, check to see that SHARE is loaded. SHARE is a DOS program that allows multiple applications to use a file. You may want to include this command in your AUTOEXEC.BAT file by having a line containing C:\DOS\SHARE (assuming that DOS is installed in C:\DOS\). If you do not want to include SHARE in your AUTOEXEC.BAT file, you will need to enter* ***SHARE*** *at the DOS prompt before starting Windows.*

## Importing Data into a Table

To import the data in a file into a table in the current database, follow these steps:

1. Switch to the Database window by pressing F11 or by clicking it.
2. Choose Import from the File menu or click the Import button in Access version 2's toolbar, which looks like this:

3. Select the format of the data you want to import from the Data Source list box in the Import dialog box and OK.
4. Select the filename of the file you want to import and select the Import button. You may need to change the drive and directory of the listed files by selecting the directory from the Directories list box and the drive from the Drives drop-down list box.

   Access imports the file you have selected. When Access is finished, it displays a message that it has successfully imported the file.
5. Select the OK button.
6. Repeat steps 4 and 5 for each file of the selected file type that you want to import.
7. Select the Close button.

If the Database window is displaying the database's tables, you can see the newly imported tables in the list of tables. If you are prompted for a password when the file you select is password-protected, you must enter the same password you would enter in the other application to use the password-protected data.

## Attaching a Table

To attach data stored in another file as a table in the current database, follow these steps:

1. Switch to the Database window by pressing F11 or by clicking it.
2. Choose Attach Table from the File menu or click the Attach Tables button in Access version 2's toolbar, which looks like this:

3. Select the format of the data you want to attach from the Data Source list box in the Attach dialog box and select OK.

4. Select the filename of the file you want to attach and select OK. You can also change the drive and directory just as you can when you import a table.

   Access attaches the file you have selected. Once the table is attached, Access displays a message saying that attachment of the file is complete.

5. Select the OK button to return to the Attach Tables dialog box.
6. Repeat steps 4 and 5 for each file you want to attach.
7. Select the Close button after attaching all the files you want of the type you selected in step 3.

## DIFFERENCES BETWEEN ATTACHING AND IMPORTING

The tables that you import differ in several ways from tables that you attach. These differences include the icon, what happens to the table's data when you delete a table from the database, and whether the data you are adding to a database can be added as a new table or appended. The following sections cover these differences.

***The Icon*** Imported tables and attached tables use different icons in the Database window. Imported tables use the same icon as the tables you create in Access. Attached tables use slightly different icons, as shown here:

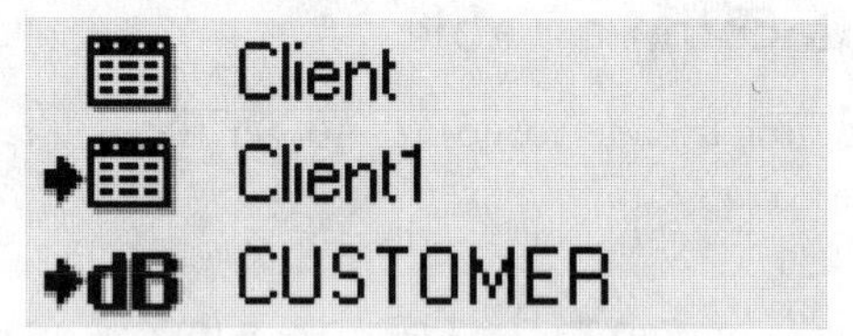


In Access version 1, all attached tables use the same icon. In Access version 2, the icon for attached tables indicates the application that created the table's data.

***Deleting a Table*** When you delete an imported table, the table's contents are removed from the Database window just as they are when you delete a table that you have created in Access. However, when you delete an attached table, you are only breaking the link from the current database to the external table. The data continues to be available in the original database as well as in all other databases that use the table as an attached table.

***Selecting the Table for the Data*** When you import a table, the data can be placed in a new table or added to an existing table. For example, when you import several files containing different parts of your customer list into an Access table, you'll want all of the files to be imported into the same table. Appending the data into the table means the data you are importing must have the same field definitions and order as the table to which you are appending the data. When you attach a table, the table is separate from the other tables in the database and cannot be combined with any of them.

**tip:** *You can rename the tables you import and attach. Most of the tables you import and attach use the same eight-character limitation imposed by DOS for filenames. You can rename the imported and attached tables to provide better descriptions of the table's contents. Rename the new tables with the Rename command in the File menu. In Access version 2, you can also right-click the table name and select Rename from the shortcut menu.*

## WORKING WITH ATTACHED TABLES

When you use an attached table in an Access database, you will notice that it differs in several ways from a table stored in the database. Attached tables in Access are not as fast as the tables stored in Access files because the data from the attached table must be constantly read from the original file. Also, while you can change the data in the table, you are more limited in the changes you can make to the table's design.

***Table Design*** One difference with attached tables is how the table behaves when you display the table's design. First, when you switch to the table's design, Access displays a message reminding you that the table is attached and not all table properties can be modified. After you select OK, you will notice that you cannot change the field names or data types. You also cannot rearrange or add fields in the table or delete any fields. However, you can change the field description as well as several of the field's properties. When you change the properties for the attached table, the property settings only affect the table within Access. If you look at the table's properties, you will see that the Description table property describes where the attached data comes from.

***Increasing Speed*** You can make attached tables work faster just by changing how you use them. With dBASE attached database files, you can improve performance by including an index file when you attach the database file (you'll learn how later in this chapter). The difference in speed when doing other operations on an attached table may not be noticed when you are using an attached table that is not shared. But if you are using an attached SQL table or a file stored on a network, you will want to use these suggestions to speed your work on attached tables. The more you move between the records in the table, the more Access must reread data from the disk. By only moving to the records you need, you make the attached table perform faster.

Also, if you only need to work with a select group of records from the attached table, you can create a query that selects only the records you want. When you create queries that use attached tables, avoid functions—especially aggregate functions such as DSUM. If you want to add records to the attached table, add them faster by creating a form that has the Default Editing property set to Data Entry (you will learn how in Chapter 10). When finished using the data in the attached tables, close the table window.

**tip:** *If you need to bring in data that is not already in one of the acceptable formats, you probably can convert the data by saving the data in the original application using one of the acceptable formats. For example, import data stored in a Quattro Pro format (which is not an acceptable Access format) by saving the file in Quattro Pro with an .XLS extension, thus changing the file to an Excel (.XLS) format, which is supported.*

## Sharing Data Between Access Databases

The tables and other objects you create for an Access database can be used by more than one database. You can import tables and other objects from an Access database. You can also attach a table from one Access database into another. You will import tables from other Access databases when you want to copy a table to a different database. You will import other objects into an Access database when you want to create a separate copy of the object for the current database. However, you will want to attach a table rather than importing when you have a table that you want to share between databases.

For example, you can import a form or report that you have created in another database to use as a model for a form or report you want to use in the current database. When you import queries, forms, or reports from one Access database to another, you are importing the design rather than the data that the query, form, or report displays. You'll see yet another option for sharing data between databases later in this chapter in the "Exporting Access Data" section. When exporting a table or other object from one Access database to another, the results are the same as when you import the object from the first database into the second one.

## IMPORTING OBJECTS FROM ANOTHER ACCESS DATABASE

When you import an object, you are placing a copy of it in your current database, where it will perform just as if you had originally created it in the current database. Most of this chapter focuses on importing tables, but when you import from another Access database, you can import other database objects as well. For example, you can create a report in one Access database and import it into another Access database to use with one of the tables in the second database.

To import an object from an Access database into the current database, follow the same steps described above for when you import data files. The difference is that there is more to step 4. After you select the Microsoft database to use for importing data, select OK to display this dialog box:

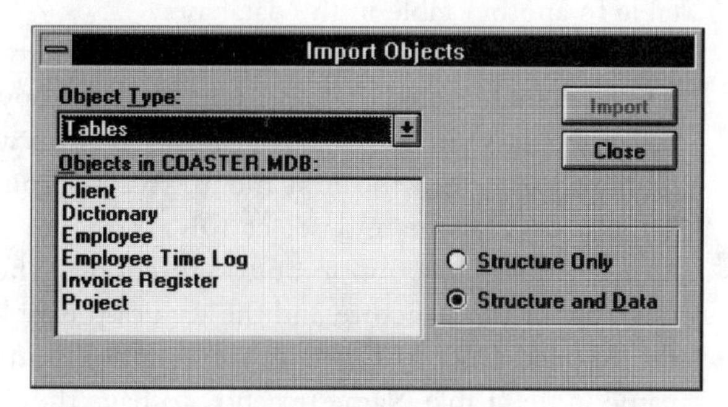


From this dialog box, select the type of object you want to import from the Object Type drop-down list box. You have Tables, Queries, Forms, Reports, Macros, and Modules as choices for the different types of objects listed in the Database window. Notice that when you select Tables from the Object Type drop-down list box, you can select the Structure Only or Structure and Data option button. These option buttons select whether you are importing only the table's structure or importing both the data and the table's structure. Finally, select the object you want to import from the Objects in the Database list box, then the Import button.

## ATTACHING TABLES FROM ANOTHER ACCESS DATABASE

Rather than importing a table from another Access database when you need to use it in the current one, you can attach it. Attaching a table lets you share the data in the table between more than one Access database. For example, you can have an employee table that you share between the personnel database and the payroll database. To attach a table from another Access database as a table in the current database, you will generally follow the steps given in the "Attaching a Table" section earlier in this chapter. In step 4, after you select the database and OK, you must select the table to attach before you select the Attach button. You cannot attach other types of objects, nor can you only attach a table's structure.

## PASTING OBJECTS FROM ANOTHER ACCESS DATABASE

You can also use the Clipboard to transfer tables between databases. This is the same Clipboard used to transfer data between applications. When you copy tables with the Clipboard, you can put the copied data in a new table or in one of the existing ones. You can also use the Clipboard to copy the data from one table to another table in the database.

To copy a table with the Clipboard, switch to the Database window. When you have highlighted the table you want to copy, choose Copy from the Edit menu. Next, switch to the database where you want to place the copied table. Choose Paste from the Edit menu. Access prompts for a name for the table. Type a table name and select OK. You can select the Structure Only or Structure and Data option button to choose whether to copy the structure of the table or the structure and the data of the table. Another option is to select the Append Data to Existing Table option button and type an existing table name in the Table Name text box to have the data in the Clipboard added to the end of the selected table.

**note:** *While this example only focuses on copying a table, you also can copy the other types of Access objects you will learn about in later chapters, such as forms, reports, and queries.*

You can paste the Clipboard's contents into the same database from which you cut or copied them; this means that you can have two similar reports in the same database by creating the first report, copying it to the same database, and then editing it and saving it under a different name.

**tip:** *If you want to append data to an existing table but are unsure if the format of the existing table and the data you want to import are the same, import the data as a new table. You can then check to see if the tables are similarly organized. If they are, copy the new table and paste it to the existing one. Another option is to create an append query, which you will learn to do in Chapter 7.*

## Using dBASE and FoxPro Data with Access

dBASE and FoxPro are popular database programs. If you have your data stored in dBASE III or IV, or FoxPro 2.0 or 2.5 files, you can import or attach these files. You use the same steps to attach and import data from dBASE or FoxPro; the only difference is the data source selection you make in step 3.

In dBASE and FoxPro, the tables of data are stored in database files. When you use dBASE data in Access, the dBASE Character fields are set to Text, the Numeric and Float fields are set to Number with a double width, the Logical fields are set to Yes/No, the Date fields are set to Date/Time, and the Memo fields remain Memo fields. In an attached table, the table continues to have the original field types that it had in dBASE or FoxPro, since the different field types only affect how they are treated in Access.

### IMPORTING TABLES FROM dBASE AND FOXPRO DATA

When you no longer need to keep dBASE and FoxPro data in the original file and you want to use the data in an Access database, import it to the current database. Once you import a dBASE or FoxPro data file, you can use the data in Access just as if you had originally created the table in Access. To import a dBASE or FoxPro database into the current database, follow the same steps that you use to import other data files. Figure 5-8 shows the dBASE data in dBASE and the same data imported into an Access table. After you import a table from a dBASE or FoxPro file, you will want to set a primary key for the table.

### ATTACHING TABLES FROM dBASE OR FOXPRO DATA

When you need to keep dBASE or FoxPro data in its original file, attach it to the current database. Once you attach a dBASE or FoxPro data file, you can use the data in dBASE or FoxPro as well as in the current Access database. To attach a dBASE or FoxPro database as a table in the current database, follow the steps described earlier in this chapter in the "Attaching a Table" section.

The only special feature in attaching a dBASE or FoxPro table is that you can select the indexes the attached table uses. After you select the dBASE or

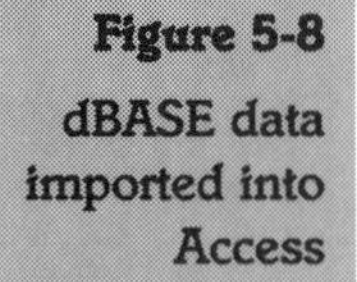

**Figure 5-8** dBASE data imported into Access

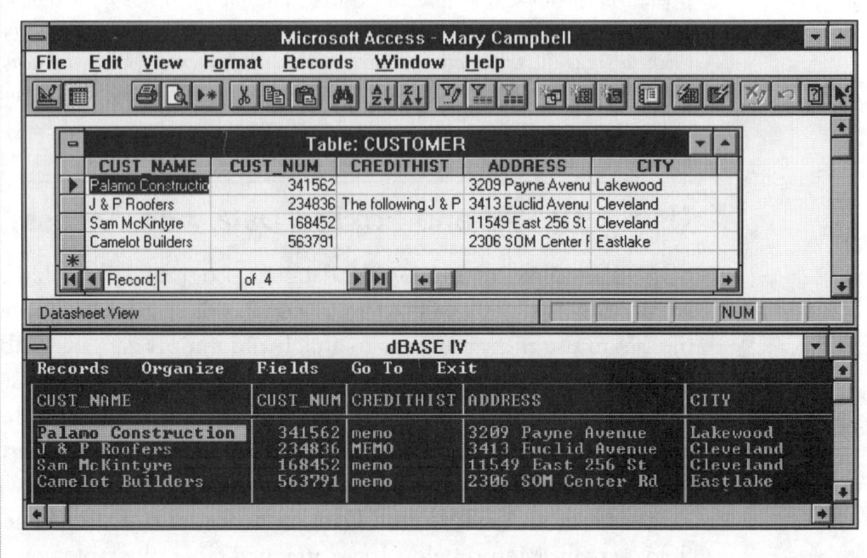


FoxPro file you want to attach, you can select the index files this dBASE or FoxPro data will use in Access. The .NDX, .MDX, .IDX, and .CDX index files organize the data in the dBASE or FoxPro file and improve how Access performs with the dBASE or FoxPro data.

Select each index file and then the Select button. When you select all of the indexes you want, choose the Close button. In Access version 2, if you selected the Allow updates in joins check box, you are prompted for an index that uniquely identifies each record in the table, just as a primary key does for many of the Access tables you create. Select one of the indexes and OK. A prompt tells you that Access has attached the selected dBASE or FoxPro database. Assuming you have selected index files when you attached a database, Access creates an index information file in the same location as the dBASE data and marks index files with an .INF extension. Be sure to keep the indexes you have selected current, because Access cannot open the attached table if the index files are out of sync with the information in the table.

**tip:** *Some products that work with dBASE data are not designed to work as part of attached dBASE files. For example, Access does not support Clipper .NTX files. This is not an issue if you use dBASE solely to access dBASE data. When you work with dBASE data in an application that is not dBASE, you may want to try attaching a test table to see how attaching the table works both with Access and with the non-dBASE application.*

## Using Paradox Data in Access

Paradox is another popular database management program. You can use your Paradox 3.0, 3.5, and 4.0 tables in Access. Like other database management files, you can either import or attach these files. In Access, the Paradox Alphanumeric fields are set to Text, the Number fields are set to Number, the Logical fields are set to Yes/No, the Date fields are set to Date/Time, and the Memo fields remain Memo fields. In an attached table, the table continues to have the original field types in Paradox, since the different field types affect only how they are treated in Access.

### IMPORTING PARADOX DATA

When you want to use Access in place of Paradox for your data management needs, import your Paradox tables into Access databases. Once you import your Paradox data, you can use the tables in Access just as if you had originally created the table in Access. To import a Paradox table into the current database, follow the same steps that you use to import other data files.

### ATTACHING TABLES FROM PARADOX

If you plan to continue using data in Paradox, you can still use the same data in Access by attaching the table to a database. Once you attach a Paradox table, you can use the data in Paradox as well as Access. To attach a Paradox table as a table in the current database, follow the steps described earlier in this chapter for attaching a table.

If the Paradox table has an index file with a .PX extension, Access uses this file to keep track of the table's primary key. You want to keep this index file with the Paradox data file, since you cannot open the attached table if Access cannot find the file. If the Paradox table does not have a primary key, you cannot update the Paradox information in Access.

## Using Btrieve Data in Access

Importing and attaching Btrieve tables is done differently than importing and attaching data from packages such as dBASE and Paradox. Btrieve has an Xtrieve dictionary file containing information about the database that holds the Btrieve tables. You use the Xtrieve dictionary file to select the files you want to import or attach. You will need the WBTRCALL.DLL file on your system to use the

Btrieve data. This file is installed as part of another application that uses the Btrieve data rather than by Access.

In Access, the Btrieve String, Lstring, and Zstring fields become Text fields; the Integer, Float, and Bfloat fields become Number fields; the Money fields become Currency fields; the Logical fields become Yes/No fields; the Date and Time fields are set to Date/Time; the Note fields become Memo fields; and the Lvar fields become OLE Object fields. In an attached table, the table continues to have the original field types in Btrieve, since the different field types affect only how they will be treated in Access.

### IMPORTING BTRIEVE DATA

When you want to use Access in place of Btrieve for database tables, import your Btrieve tables into an Access database. Once the data is in Access, the field is just as if you entered it in Access originally. To import a Btrieve table into the current database, follow the same steps you use to import other data files, except instead of selecting the file of data to import, you select the Xtrieve data dictionary file (FILE.DDF) and then select each table to import before you select the Import button.

### ATTACHING TABLES FROM BTRIEVE

When you plan to continue using Btrieve tables with Btrieve, you can share the data in the table between Btrieve and Access by attaching the table to the current database. After attaching a Btrieve table, you can use the data both in Btrieve and in Access. To attach a Btrieve table into the current database, follow the same steps you use to attach other data files, except instead of selecting the file of data to attach, select the Xtrieve dictionary and the table listed in the Xtrieve data dictionary file (FILE.DDF). Then select each table to import before you select the Import button.

## Using SQL Tables with Access

You can import and attach SQL tables with Access, but you must use the Open Database Connectivity (ODBC) drivers to do so. SQL tables are often used for large databases over a network. Attaching and importing SQL tables lets you work with the data from the SQL database in Access. Access includes the ODBC drivers for Microsoft SQL server and Sybase SQL Server. If you need an ODBC driver for another SQL database server such as ORACLE, contact Microsoft. You must have an installed ODBC driver for your SQL database server to import and attach tables in Access. You can use the ODBC Setup program provided with Access to add the ODBC drivers. The ODBC will be added to the Control Panel if it is not already there. When you select this icon, you can set up the link to the SQL database. The combination of information needed to get to the SQL database is called a *data source*. A data source must be set up for each SQL database you want to work with. Once the ODBC is set up, you have the same import and attach capabilities for SQL tables that you have with the other supported databases.

To install the required ODBC drivers, start Windows and then choose Run from the File menu in the Program Manager and enter **A:SETUP** in the text box to run the setup program. Be sure to put the ODBC disk that accompanies Access into drive A. Follow the directions in the dialog box to select the check boxes for the options that you want to install. Selecting the ODBC Control Panel option (ODBC Administration Utility in Windows 3.0) lets you work with the data sources, create new ones, and install ODBC drivers.

## IMPORTING SQL DATABASE TABLES

Importing an SQL table copies the SQL data into Access. For example, you may want to use Access when you no longer need to keep the SQL tables on the network or SQL server. When you import an SQL table, instead of selecting the filename of the data to import, select the SQL data source. Next, log on to the SQL server by entering the user name and password in the two text boxes of the dialog box Access presents. Once the connection is made, you can select which SQL table you want to import and then click the Import button. If you encounter any problems, check to be sure you can use the SQL table from the SQL server.

## ATTACHING SQL DATABASE TABLES

Attaching an SQL table lets you use Access rather than the SQL server to manage the data in the SQL table. You can use Access instead of the SQL server while other SQL users use a different interface. When you attach an SQL table, instead of selecting the filename of the data to attach, select the SQL data source. Next, log on to the SQL server by entering the user name and password in the two text boxes in the dialog box Access presents. Once the connection is made, select which SQL table you want to attach and then select the Attach button. If you encounter any problems, check to be sure that you can use the SQL table from the SQL server.

## Importing Text

Access can also import text files. Text files are files that contain only the data you would see in a table and the extra characters separating them. Text files usually do not include the unprintable characters other types of files contain that are instructions for a program you are running or indicate how you want data in a data file formatted. In a text file, each record is on a separate line. Each of the fields within a line is either separated by specific characters or starts in a specific column. Figure 5-9 shows two text files in different Notepad accessory windows.

Access can work with two types of text files. The DELIMIT.TXT file shown in the bottom of Figure 5-9 has the fields separated by colons and the text enclosed in quotes. This is a *delimited text file*. The FIXWIDTH.TXT file shown in the top of Figure 5-9 has the fields separated by spaces so that each of the fields starts in a specific column. This is a *fixed-width text file*. You have a lot of freedom in formatting text files you will import because you set up how the data is imported. When you import a text file, each column or section of delimited data should contain the same type of information. For example, if you had the following two lines, you would not want to import them because they do not follow a pattern.

```
Joe Smith,Vice President,ABC Company
23192 Main Road,Akron,OH
```

When you import a text file, you set up a pattern of how each line in the file is broken into different fields. The first step of importing a text file is to create this pattern and then use the pattern setup to import the file.

**tip:** *To create a text file you can import into Access, enter the data in your word processor and save the file in an ASCII text format. The exact steps to do this depend on your word processor.*

### IMPORTING A FIXED-WIDTH TEXT FILE

When you import a fixed-width text file, you must tell Access how to break each line into fields in a separate step before importing the text file. To set up the pattern for a fixed-width text file, choose Imp/Exp Setup from the File menu. The first step is to type a name for the specification in the Specification Name drop-down list box. Later, when you want to modify a specification,

**Figure 5-9** Fixed-width and delimited text files

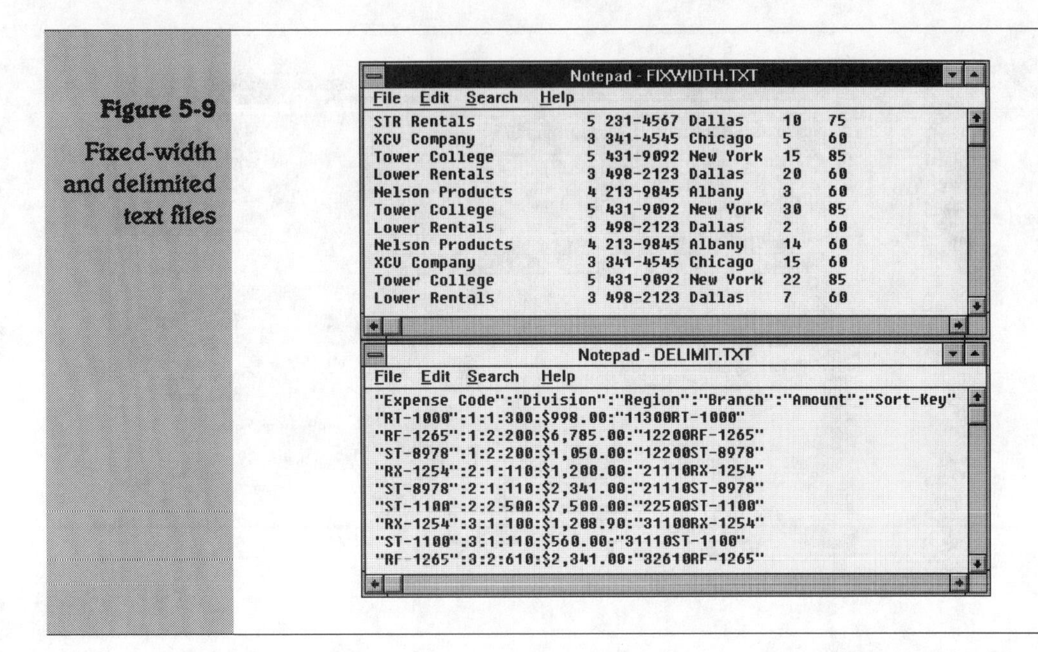
Notepad - FIXWIDTH.TXT
File Edit Search Help

```
STR Rentals              5 231-4567 Dallas     10   75
XCU Company              3 341-4545 Chicago    5    60
Tower College            5 431-9092 New York   15   85
Lower Rentals            3 498-2123 Dallas     20   60
Nelson Products          4 213-9845 Albany     3    60
Tower College            5 431-9092 New York   30   85
Lower Rentals            3 498-2123 Dallas     2    60
Nelson Products          4 213-9845 Albany     14   60
XCU Company              3 341-4545 Chicago    15   60
Tower College            5 431-9092 New York   22   85
Lower Rentals            3 498-2123 Dallas     7    60
```

Notepad - DELIMIT.TXT
File Edit Search Help

```
"Expense Code":"Division":"Region":"Branch":"Amount":"Sort-Key"
"RT-1000":1:1:300:$998.00:"11300RT-1000"
"RF-1265":1:2:200:$6,785.00:"12200RF-1265"
"ST-8978":1:2:200:$1,050.00:"12200ST-8978"
"RX-1254":2:1:110:$1,200.00:"21110RX-1254"
"ST-8978":2:1:110:$2,341.00:"21110ST-8978"
"ST-1100":2:2:500:$7,500.00:"22500ST-1100"
"RX-1254":3:1:100:$1,208.90:"31100RX-1254"
"ST-1100":3:1:110:$560.00:"31110ST-1100"
"RF-1265":3:2:610:$2,341.00:"32610RF-1265"
```

select an existing name using the drop-down list box. If you do not supply a name, you are prompted for one after you select OK. When you finish entering the setup for how to import a text file, select OK and your setup is ready to use to import a text file.

In the File Type drop-down list box, select Windows (ANSI), DOS, or OS/2 (PC-8) to tell Access whether the text file you are importing was created with Windows or with a DOS or OS/2 application. Under Dates, Times, and Numbers, you may want to select the order of the information in a date, how the parts of dates and times are separated, whether dates have a leading 0 for single digit months and days, and whether years use four or two digits.

The important part of setting up the import specification for a fixed-width text file is telling Access the names for the fields, the field types, the column each field starts at, and the width of each field. The Field Name, Data Type, and Width columns are just like the same columns for a table's design. The Start column counts the number of columns from the left of where the field starts. In Access version 2, you can create the starting columns using one of the database's tables as the basis by selecting Fill Specification Grid from Table and then selecting the database table. Figure 5-10 shows the Import/Export Setup dialog box used to import the FIXWIDTH.TXT file.

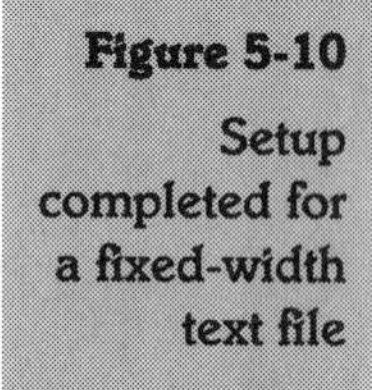

**Figure 5-10** Setup completed for a fixed-width text file

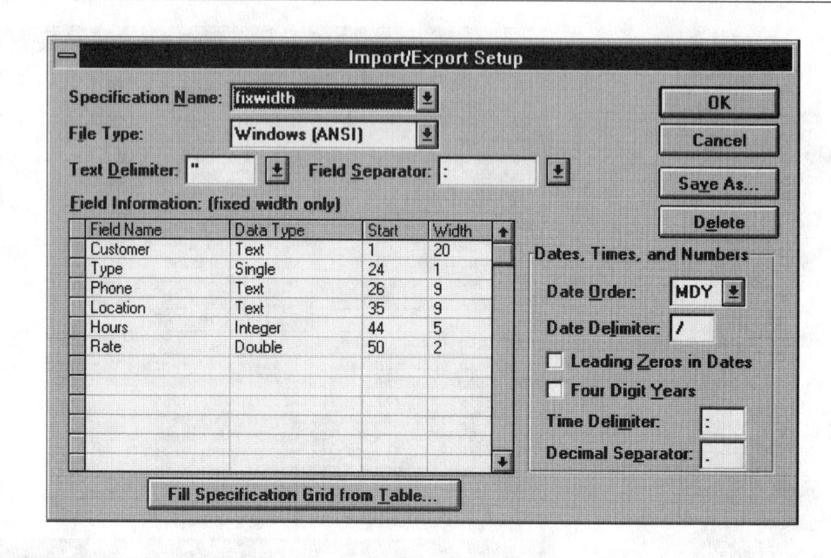

**tip:** *To see how the data is arranged in a text file to set up the import, open the text file using the Notepad accessory. The Notepad lets you see how the text file is organized. You may also want to use DOS' EDIT utility to look at the text file since this text editor, available in DOS 5 and 6, will show the column number as you move through the file.*

When the setup is complete, you are ready to import the text file. Choose Import from the File menu and then choose Text (Fixed Width) from the Import dialog box. Select the name of the file to import (for example, FIXWIDTH.TXT is the filename in Figure 5-10).

Next, select whether you are creating a new table or appending the data to an existing one, and choose the import specification you will use. Select the Create New Table option button if you want the text file imported as a new table or the Append to Existing Table option button if you want the text file added to an existing table. If you select the Append to Existing Table option button, select one of the existing table names from the adjoining drop-down list box. In the Specification Name drop-down list box, select a specification name that contains the pattern you want to use. When the specification name is selected, select OK to import the file. When you see the message about Access importing the data, select OK and Close.

**tip:** *If you want to add imported data to an existing table, copy the table's structure to a new table (selecting the Structure Only option button). Import the data to the new table and then use an append query to add the data from the new table to the existing table.*

Open the table you have just created and check that the data is correctly imported. Since you might miscount the columns, you can easily have the data off by a column and incorrectly imported. Figure 5-11 shows the FIXWIDTH.TXT file imported into a table.

**tip:** *Since you can easily enter the wrong starting column for importing a fixed-width text file, import the data to a new table. Later, when you are sure you have correctly imported the text file, you can copy it to an existing table.*

### IMPORTING A DELIMITED TEXT FILE

The text file pattern you use when you import a delimited text file tells Access how the different fields in each line are separated. To set up this pattern for a delimited file, choose Import from the File menu, Text (Delimited) from the Import dialog box, and the file you want to import. At this point, you can select between the Create New Table option button to import the delimited text file into a new table or the Append to Existing Table option button to import the delimited text file to an existing table. If you select the Append to Existing Table option button, select one of the existing table names from the adjoining drop-down list box.

An option for delimited files is the First Row Contains Field Names check box. Select this check box if the first row of the delimited file has text you want to use as the field names in the table.

**Figure 5-11** **Fixed-width text file imported into Access**

Table: FIXWIDTH

| Customer | Type | Phone | Location | Hours | Rate |
|---|---|---|---|---|---|
| STR Rentals | 5 | 231-4567 | Dallas | 10 | 75 |
| XCV Company | 3 | 341-4545 | Chicago | 5 | 60 |
| Tower College | 5 | 431-9092 | New York | 15 | 85 |
| Lower Rentals | 3 | 498-2123 | Dallas | 20 | 60 |
| Nelson Products | 4 | 213-9845 | Albany | 3 | 60 |
| Tower College | 5 | 431-9092 | New York | 30 | 85 |
| Lower Rentals | 3 | 498-2123 | Dallas | 2 | 60 |
| Nelson Products | 4 | 213-9845 | Albany | 14 | 60 |
| XCV Company | 3 | 341-4545 | Chicago | 15 | 60 |
| Tower College | 5 | 431-9092 | New York | 22 | 85 |
| Lower Rentals | 3 | 498-2123 | Dallas | 7 | 60 |

Record: 1 of 11

If you want to change how the delimited file is imported, select the Options button. You only need to make changes if you want to use settings different from the defaults. When you import a delimited file, Access must know which characters separate the fields and whether any special characters enclose text data. These characters are selected in the Text Delimiter and Field Separator drop-down list boxes. For example, to import the DELIMIT.TXT file as shown in Figure 5-9, type " and : for the text delimiter and field separator characters. The remaining options in the dialog box match the options for fixed-width text files. You can save the specification at this point by selecting the Save As button, typing a specification name, and selecting OK.

When the choices are set to your satisfaction and you are ready to import the file, select OK. When you see the message about Access importing the data, select OK and Close. Look at the table you have just created to check that the data is imported correctly. When you import the delimited file shown in Figure 5-9 into Access, the resulting table looks like this:

Table: DELIMIT

| Expense Code | Division | Region | Branch | Amount | Sort-Key |
|---|---|---|---|---|---|
| RT-1000 | 1 | 1 | 300 | $998.00 | 11300RT-1000 |
| RF-1265 | 1 | 2 | 200 | $6,785.00 | 12200RF-1265 |
| ST-8978 | 1 | 2 | 200 | $1,050.00 | 12200ST-8978 |
| RX-1254 | 2 | 1 | 110 | $1,200.00 | 21110RX-1254 |
| ST-8978 | 2 | 1 | 110 | $2,341.00 | 21110ST-8978 |
| ST-1100 | 2 | 2 | 500 | $7,500.00 | 22500ST-1100 |
| RX-1254 | 3 | 1 | 100 | $1,208.90 | 31100RX-1254 |
| ST-1100 | 3 | 1 | 110 | $560.00 | 31110ST-1100 |
| RF-1265 | 3 | 2 | 610 | $2,341.00 | 32610RF-1265 |

Record: 1 of 9

You can also create a specification name that represents the settings you want for importing delimited data with the Imp/Exp Setup command in the File menu. When you do this, you must provide a specification name but can ignore the Field Information section.

## Importing Spreadsheet Data

Besides using data management programs to store your data, you can import data from spreadsheets into an Access table. For instance, perhaps you have used Excel or Lotus 1-2-3 for data management and you want to use this data in Access now. As an example, you may want to import the spreadsheet data shown in Figure 5-12. You have several possibilities for importing spreadsheet data into an Access table. When importing spreadsheet data you have several more options, so you will want to follow these steps:

1. Switch to the Database window by pressing F11 or by clicking it.
2. Choose Import from the File menu or click the Import button in Access version 2's toolbar.
3. Select one of the Excel or Lotus options as the format of the data you want to import from the Data Source list box in the Import dialog box and select OK.
4. Select the name of the spreadsheet you want to import and then select Import.

   Access displays an Import Spreadsheet Options dialog box containing selections that apply solely to importing spreadsheets.
5. Select the First Row Contains Field Names check box if the spreadsheet range you are importing has labels in the first row that you want to use as the field names in the table.

   Figure 5-12 is a good example for which you would select the check box. In this spreadsheet, the entries in A1..G1 contain labels you want to use as field names. If you select the check box, Access uses the labels in A1..G1 as the field names for the table and imports data records starting with row 2.

A1: [W10] "Date

READY

| | A | B | C | D | E | F | G |
|---|---|---|---|---|---|---|---|
| 1 | Date | Days | Location | Meals | Lodging | Airfare | Misc. |
| 2 | 02-Jul-93 | 12 | Dallas | $350.04 | $2,067.25 | $350.46 | $211.40 |
| 3 | 02-Jul-93 | 2 | Akron | $58.34 | $123.29 | $474.34 | $14.02 |
| 4 | 03-Jul-93 | 3 | Chicago | $87.51 | $526.36 | $490.22 | $51.87 |
| 5 | 06-Jul-93 | 12 | Denver | $350.04 | $2,130.42 | $462.29 | $161.12 |
| 6 | 07-Jul-93 | 5 | Phoenix | $145.85 | $551.08 | $353.75 | $44.57 |
| 7 | 08-Jul-93 | 4 | Atlanta | $116.68 | $280.65 | $361.29 | $53.46 |
| 8 | 10-Jul-93 | 6 | New York | $175.02 | $787.16 | $439.04 | $70.65 |
| 9 | 12-Jul-93 | 3 | Portland | $87.51 | $257.18 | $420.02 | $43.89 |
| 10 | 12-Jul-93 | 5 | Cleveland | $145.85 | $818.31 | $456.53 | $56.86 |
| 11 | 14-Jul-93 | 8 | Seattle | $233.36 | $1,361.24 | $499.69 | $110.93 |
| 12 | 15-Jul-93 | 1 | Atlanta | $29.17 | $129.04 | $391.61 | $13.60 |
| 13 | 17-Jul-93 | 6 | New York | $175.02 | $441.86 | $433.51 | $13.31 |
| 14 | 19-Jul-93 | 3 | Washington D.C. | $87.51 | $356.61 | $463.60 | $9.54 |
| 15 | 19-Jul-93 | 7 | San Diego | $204.19 | $696.79 | $433.53 | $57.28 |
| 16 | 23-Jul-93 | 6 | Houston | $175.02 | $659.89 | $402.64 | $63.77 |
| 17 | 23-Jul-93 | 7 | Miami | $204.19 | $656.68 | $420.70 | $134.31 |
| 18 | 24-Jul-93 | 4 | Los Angeles | $116.68 | $535.76 | $352.65 | $18.70 |
| 19 | 26-Jul-93 | 2 | Charlotte | $58.34 | $336.57 | $338.55 | $23.91 |
| 20 | 28-Jul-93 | 4 | New York | $175.24 | $876.58 | $475.04 | $47.63 |

05-Jan-94 03:54 PM

**Figure 5-12** Spreadsheet to import into Access

6. Select the Create New Table option button if you want the spreadsheet data imported as a new table or the Append to Existing Table option button if you want the spreadsheet data added to an existing table. If you select the Append to Existing Table option button, select one of the existing table names from the adjoining drop-down list box.
7. Type the range name or range address that contains the data you want to import in the Spreadsheet Range text box. You can select a range name from the worksheet by clicking the down arrow and selecting a range name from the list.

   The spreadsheet range tells Access the data you want to import. When you do not make an entry in the text box, Access imports the entire spreadsheet. As an example, for the data in Figure 5-12, you can import only A1..G65, which is the range containing the database data. If the spreadsheet contains other information, this additional information outside the selected range will not be imported.

   If you are importing data from a spreadsheet that uses multiple sheets in a single file, you have additional options. You can select the Sheet Name option button, select the sheet name from the drop-down list box, and then enter the range in the Range text box. You can also select the Named Range option button, and then select the range name from the drop-down list box.
8. Select the OK button.

   When Access finishes importing the spreadsheet, it displays a message that indicates whether Access found any errors while importing the spreadsheet. If the first row in the spreadsheet contains entries that do not make valid field names when you have selected the First Row Contains Field Names check box, you cannot import the data as is. You must either modify the spreadsheet data so the first row contains valid field names or clear the First Row Contains Field Names check box.
9. Select the OK button again.
10. Repeat steps 4 through 9 for each spreadsheet you want to import.
11. Select the Close button.

Figure 5-13 shows the spreadsheet data from Figure 5-12 imported as an Access table.

**Figure 5-13** Spreadsheet data imported as an Access table

Table: EXPENSES

| Date | Days | Location | Meals | Lodging | Airf |
|---|---|---|---|---|---|
| 7/2/93 | 12 | Dallas | $350.04 | $2,067.25 | |
| 7/2/93 | 2 | Akron | $58.34 | $123.29 | |
| 7/3/93 | 3 | Chicago | $87.51 | $526.36 | |
| 7/6/93 | 12 | Denver | $350.04 | $2,130.42 | |
| 7/7/93 | 5 | Phoenix | $145.85 | $551.08 | |
| 7/8/93 | 4 | Atlanta | $116.68 | $280.65 | |
| 7/10/93 | 6 | New York | $175.02 | $787.16 | |
| 7/12/93 | 3 | Portland | $87.51 | $257.18 | |
| 7/12/93 | 5 | Cleveland | $145.85 | $818.31 | |
| 7/14/93 | 8 | Seattle | $233.36 | $1,361.24 | |
| 7/15/93 | 1 | Atlanta | $29.17 | $129.04 | |
| 7/17/93 | 6 | New York | $175.02 | $441.86 | |
| 7/19/93 | 3 | Washington D.C. | $87.51 | $356.61 | |
| 7/19/93 | 7 | San Diego | $204.19 | $696.79 | |
| 7/23/93 | 6 | Houston | $175.02 | $659.89 | |
| 7/23/93 | 7 | Miami | $204.19 | $656.68 | |
| 7/24/93 | 4 | Los Angeles | $116.68 | $535.76 | |
| 7/26/93 | 2 | Charlotte | $58.34 | $336.57 | |
| 7/28/93 | 4 | New York | $175.24 | $876.58 | |

Record: 1 of 19

**tip:** *Name the range in the spreadsheet you want to import. You can probably remember the range name more readily than the range address of the cells you want to import.*

## Import Problems

When you import spreadsheets and text files, if Access encounters data that it cannot properly import, Access creates a table that lists the problems. This table is called Import Errors followed by your name. When you import data and you get a message that Access found errors, immediately check to see what the errors are before importing more data. For each error Access finds, it creates a record in this table that lists the row number, field, and error description, as shown here:

Table: Import Errors - Mary Campbell

| Error | Field | Row |
|---|---|---|
| Type Conversion Failure | Date | 11 |
| Type Conversion Failure | Lodging | 11 |
| Type Conversion Failure | Days | 15 |

Record: 1 of 3

The following is a list of some of the reasons you may have errors.

- Access tried putting data into a field that is inappropriate for the field's type. For example, if you import a spreadsheet that contains a column of values except for where the label "N/A" indicates missing data, each occurrence of "N/A" in the column is reported as an error.

- Access made a bad guess about the contents of a field. When you import to a new table instead of appending to an existing one, Access looks at the first row of data (or second if the first row is used for field names) to decide the best field type. While Access makes the best possible guess, sometimes it picks the wrong type.
- Access found a row in the original file that contains more fields than it has set up in the new table or in the table to which you are appending the data. For example, if you have entries in A1..G16 and A17..I20 of a spreadsheet you import to a new table, Access creates a table that has seven columns for the entries in columns A through G of the spreadsheet. For rows 17 through 20, Access will find errors since the new table does not have room for the entries in columns H and I.
- Access found an entry that is wider than the field's size. If you are appending your customer address database into a table that has two spaces reserved for the field for the state, Access finds errors with the state names that you spelled out.
- Access tried importing the contents of a field that matches another record's entry for that field when the field has an index property set to Yes (No Duplicates).

To see the errors, open the Import Errors table just as you would open other tables in the database.

## Exporting Access Data

Besides exporting data to other Microsoft applications, you can also export your Access tables to other popular applications. These other applications include another Access database, fixed-width and delimited text files, Word for Windows mail merge, Excel, Lotus 1-2-3, Btrieve, dBASE, FoxPro, and SQL. You learned how you can export an Access table to Word for Windows and Excel earlier in the chapter. When you export an Access table, your data continues to be in your Access table. The steps for exporting a table are summarized in the next section.

## Exporting a Table

To export the data in a table to a file in a format other applications can use, follow these steps:

1. Switch to the Database window by pressing F11 or by clicking it.
2. Choose Export from the File menu or click the Export button in Access version 2's toolbar, which looks like this:

3. Select the format of the data you want to export from the Data Destination list box in the Export dialog box and select OK.
4. Select the table you want to export and select OK.

   As you create queries like the ones you will learn about in the next chapter, you can export the results of the queries by selecting a query name in place of a table.

5. Select the name of the file where you want the data exported and select OK.
6. Select any information Access needs to export the table. The exact information you are prompted for depends on the format you select in step 3. The Access, delimited text, fixed-width text, Word for Windows, Btrieve, and SQL formats prompt for additional information.

## Exporting to Another Access Database

When you export an Access table or another object, Access places a copy of it from the current database into the other database, where it works just as if you had originally created it in the other database. You can obtain the same results by importing the table from another database into the current database. You import when the current database is the database where you need a copy of the table or other object, and you export when you are in the database that contains the object or data you want copied to another database.

To export an object from the current database, follow the same steps you use to export data files, except that in the fourth and fifth steps, you have more to do. After selecting Microsoft Access as the format for the exported data in the third step, Access displays the dialog box for selecting the database object to export. This is the same dialog box you used when importing a database object to select the database object to import. In this dialog box, select the type of object to export from the Object Type drop-down list box. When you select Tables from the Object Type drop-down list box, you can select the Structure Only or Structure and Data option button. These option buttons set whether you are exporting only the table's structure or both the data and the table's structure. Finally, select the object you want to export from the Objects in the database list box and OK.

Next, for the fifth step, select the database that you want the exported object copied to. After selecting the name of the database to which you want the object exported, you have an additional prompt for the new name of the object in the database you have just chosen. Use the default, which is the name that the object uses in the current database, or type a new one. After exporting the table or other object, the table or other object is in both the current database and the database you selected while exporting the file.

Exporting a table or other object is different from attaching a file. After you export a table, for example, any changes you make to the table in the current database do not affect in the database to which you exported the table.

## Putting Access Data in a Fixed-Width Text File

Earlier you learned about fixed-width text files that Access, like other applications, can use to accept data. You can also create fixed-width text files from your Access tables. Before you export a table to a fixed-width text file, you must set up the pattern that you want the exported data to follow. For example, each field should start at a different column. This is just like the pattern you established for importing fixed-width text files, described earlier. You can even use the same setup specification you used for importing a fixed-width text file if you already have one that is appropriate. Once you have the setup specification, you can export the file. To export a table to a fixed-width text file, follow the steps for exporting a table. After you select the name for the file you are creating, select the setup specification name in the Specification Name drop-down box.

## Putting Access Data in a Delimited Text File

Besides exporting a table to create a fixed-width text file, you can also export a table to create a delimited file. For example, you may want to use the Employee table from the Coasters database as the data for a mail merge document in your word processor. When you want to export a table to a delimited text file, follow the steps for exporting a table. After selecting the filename for the delimited text file you are creating, select export options. Select the First Row Contains Field Names check box when you want the first row of the delimited file to contain the field names from the table. To change the characters used to separate the fields and enclose text as well as change the options used by dates, times, and numbers, select the Options button. Selecting the Options button expands the dialog box to include the same delimited setup settings you see when importing a delimited file.

## Putting an Access Table in a Spreadsheet

While you can use Access for all of your data management needs, you may want to use your Access data in a spreadsheet package such as Excel or Lotus 1-2-3. For example, you may want to perform regression analysis on data in a table. When you want to export a table to a spreadsheet format, follow the steps for exporting a table and choose the appropriate spreadsheet format in the Export dialog box. When Access finishes exporting the table, you can retrieve the file you just created in your favorite spreadsheet program. As an example, if you export the Employee table from the Coasters database to a Lotus WK1 spreadsheet, your data in Lotus 1-2-3 Release 2.4 will look like Figure 5-14.

## Exporting dBASE, FoxPro, or Paradox Data

You can put your Access data into dBASE, FoxPro, and Paradox formats. Once you have the dBASE, FoxPro, or Paradox files, you can use them in these applications to take advantage of reports or other product features you have already designed. To export a table to a dBASE, FoxPro, or Paradox format, follow the steps for exporting a table and choose the appropriate database format in the Export dialog box. When Access finishes exporting the table, open the file you have just created in dBASE, FoxPro, or Paradox.

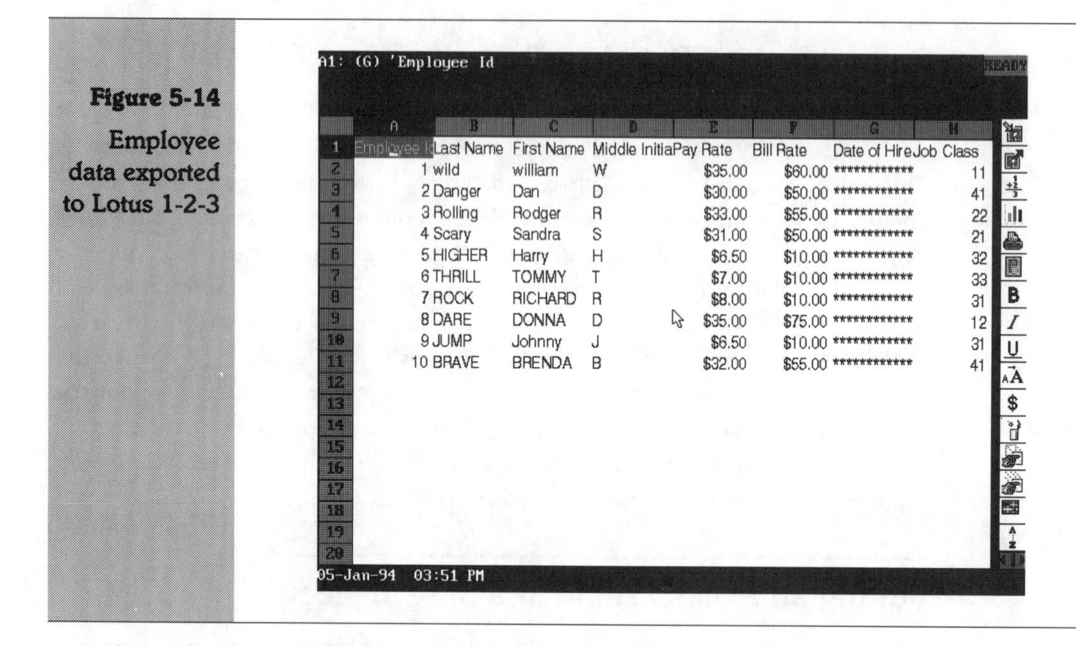


| | A | B | C | D | E | F | G | H |
|---|---|---|---|---|---|---|---|---|
| 1 | Employee Id | Last Name | First Name | Middle Initia | Pay Rate | Bill Rate | Date of Hire | Job Class |
| 2 | 1 | wild | william | W | $35.00 | $60.00 | ************ | 11 |
| 3 | 2 | Danger | Dan | D | $30.00 | $50.00 | ************ | 41 |
| 4 | 3 | Rolling | Rodger | R | $33.00 | $55.00 | ************ | 22 |
| 5 | 4 | Scary | Sandra | S | $31.00 | $50.00 | ************ | 21 |
| 6 | 5 | HIGHER | Harry | H | $6.50 | $10.00 | ************ | 32 |
| 7 | 6 | THRILL | TOMMY | T | $7.00 | $10.00 | ************ | 33 |
| 8 | 7 | ROCK | RICHARD | R | $8.00 | $10.00 | ************ | 31 |
| 9 | 8 | DARE | DONNA | D | $35.00 | $75.00 | ************ | 12 |
| 10 | 9 | JUMP | Johnny | J | $6.50 | $10.00 | ************ | 31 |
| 11 | 10 | BRAVE | BRENDA | B | $32.00 | $55.00 | ************ | 41 |
| 12 | | | | | | | | |
| 13 | | | | | | | | |
| 14 | | | | | | | | |
| 15 | | | | | | | | |
| 16 | | | | | | | | |
| 17 | | | | | | | | |
| 18 | | | | | | | | |
| 19 | | | | | | | | |
| 20 | | | | | | | | |

**Figure 5-14** Employee data exported to Lotus 1-2-3

## Putting Access Data in a Btrieve Table

You export your Access tables to Btrieve tables using the Xtrieve data dictionary file just as you do when importing. To export a table to a Btrieve format, follow the steps for exporting a table. Instead of entering the name of the file to contain the Btrieve table, select the name of the Xtrieve data dictionary file. This file is usually called FILE.DDF. Once the dictionary file is chosen, you are prompted for the name of the table in Btrieve; enter the table name and select OK.

## Putting Access Data in an SQL Table

Exporting to an SQL table lets you copy an Access table onto your SQL server. You may want to do this when you need to share the database's data with other users. If you export an Access table to an SQL table, you can later attach the SQL table to the current database and continue using Access for the interface between you and your data. When you export an SQL table, instead of typing the name for the file to which you want the data exported, first enter a name for the table in the SQL database. After selecting OK, select the SQL data source to which you want the table exported. After selecting OK again, log in to the SQL server by entering the user name and password in the two text boxes of the dialog box Access presents. Once the connection is made, Access exports the table and places it on the SQL server.

## Using the Clipboard to Share Data Between Applications

Besides using the Clipboard to transfer data between Microsoft applications, you can use the Clipboard to transfer data between Access and non-Microsoft applications. This is in addition to the options for sharing data by importing, attaching, and exporting data. You can also use the Clipboard to copy different database objects between Access databases.

When you select the data to copy from Access, you can select part of a table or all of it, as described earlier for copying data between Microsoft applications. Then copy it to the Clipboard. Once the data is on the Clipboard, you are ready to paste it.

### Transferring Access Objects Between Databases

When you copy between Access databases, you can copy entire tables as well as other database objects such as queries, forms, reports, macros, and modules. Copying objects between databases with the Clipboard has the same effect as importing or exporting. After you copy the database object to the Clipboard, switch to the database you want the object copied to and choose Paste from the Edit menu. You can even paste the selected object to the same database; for example, if you are creating two similar reports, you might use one as the basis for the other.

### Transferring Access Data to Another Application

When you need your Access data in other applications that can use the Windows Clipboard, you might find it easier to copy the data to them using the Clipboard instead of exporting the table's data to a file and then importing it to the application. You need to use the Clipboard to transfer data to another application when the other application cannot import any of the formats that Access can use to export data. For example, you may want to put records from the Employee table in the Coasters database into CorelDRAW!. After you copy the records to the Clipboard in Access, you can switch to CorelDRAW! and choose that application's Paste command in the Edit menu to paste the data

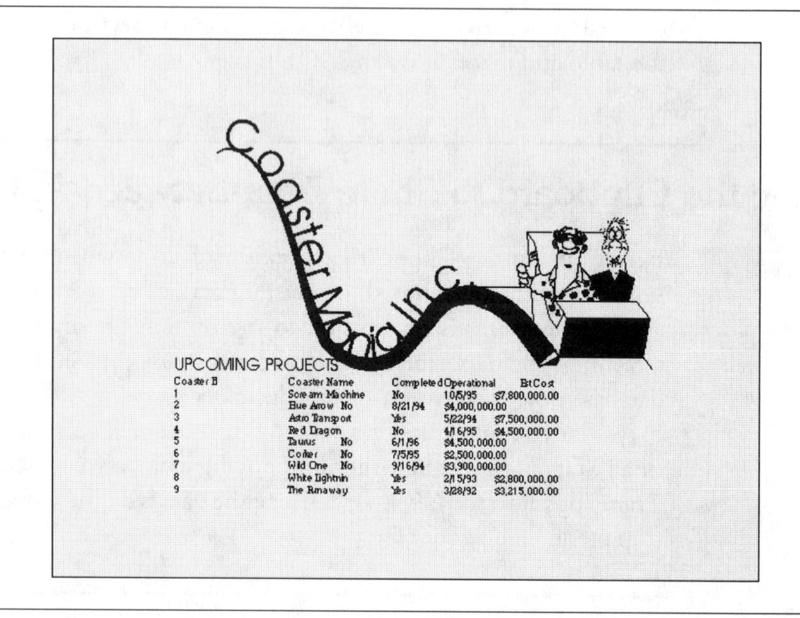


**Figure 5-15** Access data pasted into CorelDRAW!

into it. Figure 5-15 shows several records from the Employee table of the Coasters database pasted into a CorelDRAW! graphic.

## Transferring Data from Other Applications to Access

You also can copy data between applications when you want to take data from another application and use it in Access. For example, you may have a text file that you want to use as the contents for a record's Memo data type field. After you copy the data from the other application to the Clipboard, you can switch to Access and move to where you want the data inserted. Choose Paste from the Edit menu. This command will not be available when you try pasting the data into an inappropriate location.

## Quick Reference

**To Import a File** Choose Import from the File menu or click the Import button on the toolbar in the Database window. Select the application that created the data you want to import and OK. Select the file to import and the Import button. Select the OK button and then the Close button.

**To Attach a Table** Choose Attach Table from the File menu or click the Attach Table button on the toolbar in the Database window. Select the application that created the file containing the data you want to attach and OK. Select the file to attach and select Attach. Select the OK button and the Close button.

**To Export a File** Choose Export from the File menu or click the Export button on the toolbar in the Database window. Select the application you want to export the data to and then OK. Select the table you want to export and OK. Select the name of the file where you want the data exported and then OK.

**To Copy Access Data to the Clipboard** Select the table from the Database window or drag the mouse to cover the records on the datasheet that you want to copy. Choose Copy from the Edit menu. If you are copying into Access, move to where you want the data copied and choose Paste from the Edit menu.

**To Output Access Data** Choose Output To in the File menu. Select the format of the file to create and OK. Type the name for the document to create and select OK.

# II

# Queries

# Chapter 6

Creating a Query or Filter

Viewing a Query or Filter

Saving a Query or a Filter as a Query

Printing a Query

Additional Query and Filter Design Features

Creating Criteria to Select Records

Calculated Fields in a Query or Filter

# Using Queries and Filters to Select Data

AT times, you may want to see a subset of records in a table. For example, you may want to see only records for clients who have been billed over a million dollars in the last year, or records for employees paid over a certain amount. You can use queries and filters to choose which records to display. Queries and filters let you set specifications and see only the records that meet those specifications.

Queries are separate database objects and they are always available. You do not have to reenter the description of the data every time you want to look at the same subset of the table's data. Also, a query always uses the most up-to-date data you have stored in your tables. Changing a table's data also changes the data shown by a query that uses that table.

Filters, on the other hand, are like simple, temporary queries. They are not saved, so you have to recreate filters each time you use one. Filters do not have all the features of queries. However, they are simpler to create and may be useful when you need to look at a set of records just once and don't want to save the specifications for use again. The important difference is that filters are not separate database objects; they simply limit or sort which records are displayed in a table or form.

Queries and filters offer many features to select and sort the data presented. In a query, you can add, remove, and rearrange the fields presented. You enter *criteria* in both queries and filters that select the records from the table. Other options for queries let you hide fields and calculate values. When you finish the query or filter design, you can view the records that match the criteria you select. This data is the query's *dynaset*.

A dynaset is a temporary presentation of data in a table format, but it is not a table. The data is real, but the presentation is not. As you edit data that appears in a dynaset, you are changing the data in the table that the query uses to create that dynaset. You can print the dynaset as well as save the query's design for later use.

The most common query is a *select query*. Access also has other types of queries. These types of queries summarize groups of records, delete specific records, add records to another table, and create new tables containing specific records. You will learn about these additional types of queries in Chapter 7. You can use these select queries as the basis of the data you present in forms and reports. You will learn how to create forms and reports starting in Chapter 8.

Access version 2 offers new Query Wizards to help you create common but more advanced queries. These Query Wizards are discussed in Chapter 7, along with the more advanced queries they can help you create. In this chapter, you will learn to create a select query without a Query Wizard.

In Access version 1, you can only create filters for forms and not for tables. When you learn how to create your own forms starting in Chapter 8, you can apply the query and filter features you learn here to select which records a form displays.

## Creating a Query or Filter

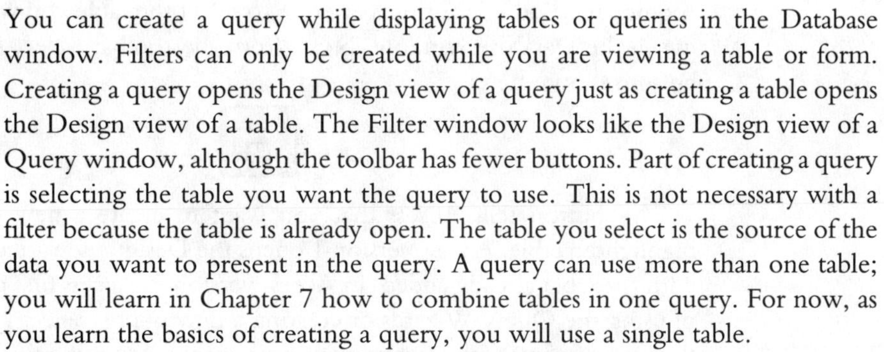

You can create a query while displaying tables or queries in the Database window. Filters can only be created while you are viewing a table or form. Creating a query opens the Design view of a query just as creating a table opens the Design view of a table. The Filter window looks like the Design view of a Query window, although the toolbar has fewer buttons. Part of creating a query is selecting the table you want the query to use. This is not necessary with a filter because the table is already open. The table you select is the source of the data you want to present in the query. A query can use more than one table; you will learn in Chapter 7 how to combine tables in one query. For now, as you learn the basics of creating a query, you will use a single table.

Follow these steps to create a query:

1. Add the table you want the query to use.
2. Add the fields from the table you want to use in the query.
3. Add any criteria that select the records to appear in the dynaset.
4. Add any sorting selections you want to organize your data in the dynaset.
5. Display the selected data.

Initially you can skip Step 3 to include all of the records. As you create queries with more and more query features, the basics of selecting the table, the fields, and displaying the dynaset remain the same. Several features, such as saving queries, printing queries, and organizing the output of the dynaset, are so easy that you'll want to put them to use quickly. Later in the chapter, you will learn about the wide assortment of criteria entries you can make to select which records appear in the dynaset.

When you create a filter, you use the same steps as you do when creating a query, with two exceptions. You do not need to select a table to work with, since the filter only works with the active table or form. Second, you cannot select which fields are displayed with a filter. All the fields in the table or form are displayed after the filter is used, but these fields only show the selected records. However, you can select which fields appear in a table's datasheet through the Format menu and which fields appear in a form through the form's design. With queries, you can control which fields appear in the dynaset.

## Opening the Query or Filter Window

A quick method of creating a query is to select the table you want the query to use in the Database window. Next, from the toolbar, select the New Query button, shown here:

This button tells Access that you want to create a new query using the highlighted table. Access version 1 opens the Design view of a Query window with the table already added. In Access version 2, Access first presents a choice of using the Query Wizards or creating a new query. Select New Query, and the Design view of the Query window appears. Assuming that the Client table is highlighted when you create a new query, the Query window will look like Figure 6-1.

You could also create a new query from the Database window by choosing New from the File menu and then choosing Query with the table selected. Another way to create a new query is by displaying queries in the Database window. First, switch to the Database window and choose Queries from the View menu or click the Query button. Next, choose the New button at the top of the Database window. You can also choose New from the File menu and then choose Query. Since you do not have a table selected for the query

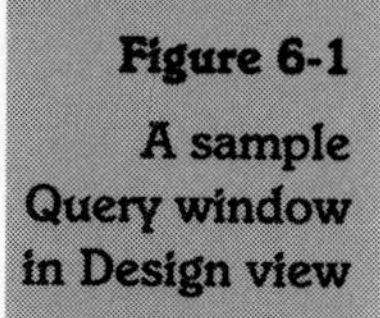

**Figure 6-1** A sample Query window in Design view

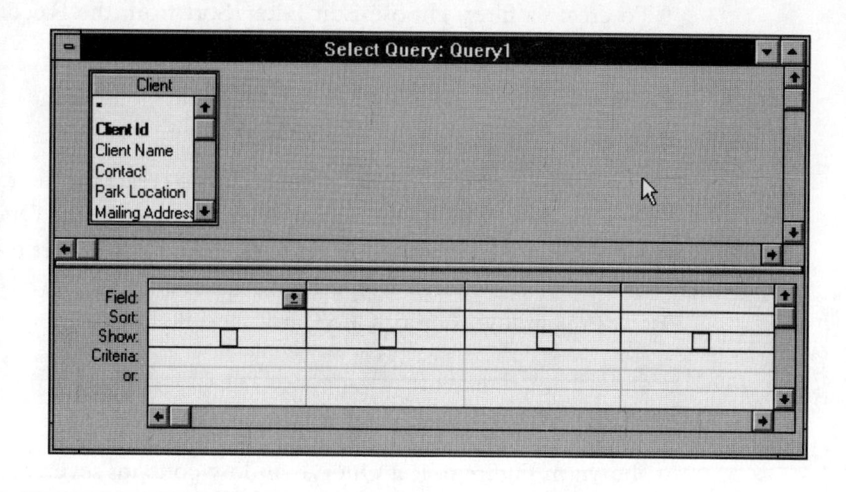


to use, you need to tell Access which table you want to use. Access displays the Add Table dialog box, shown here:

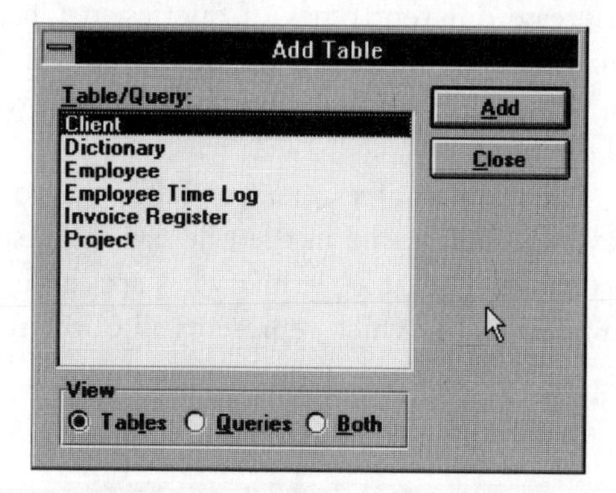


Select the table you want to base the query on from the list. After selecting the table, double-click it or select Add to add it to the query. Once the table is added, select Close to close the dialog box. With the table added, the Design view of the Query window looks like Figure 6-1. Now that you have a query design, look more closely at the various sections of this window.

**tip:** *You can create a query that uses the data from another query. Simply select the query name when you create the new query. This technique lets you make further changes to the second query without changing the original query design.*

To create a filter, choose Edit Filter/Sort from the Records menu or click the Edit Filter/Sort button, shown here:

This opens the Filter window in which you create the filter. Figure 6-2 shows a Filter window, which you can see is very much like the Query window. This window looks like the one in Figure 6-1. The Filter/Sort toolbar that appears when the Filter window is opened contains only the Save, Apply Filter/Sort, Database Window, Undo, Cue Cards, and Help buttons.

## Looking at a Query or Filter Window

As shown in Figure 6-1, a Query window contains several parts that you want to be familiar with as you create queries and filters. First, the title bar for a query shows *Select Query:* followed by the name of the query. The default name for a query is Query followed by the next unused number. When you learn how to create different types of queries in Chapter 7, you will see *Select Query:* replaced with other text to describe the type of query you are designing or viewing. Filter windows display *Filter:* followed by the name Access has assigned to the filter.

The top half of a Query or Filter window contains the field lists. Field lists have the table name in the title bar and display all of the fields from the table in the lists. The table's primary key appears in bold. The list of fields also includes an asterisk (*), which represents all of the fields in the table.

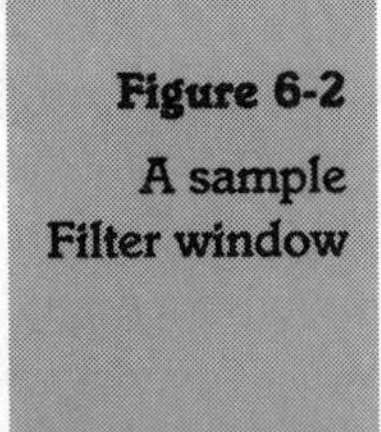

**Figure 6-2** **A sample Filter window**

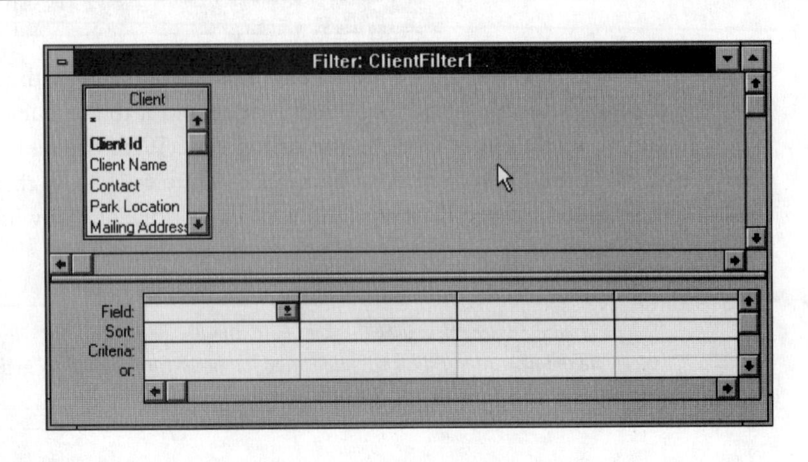

Notice the bar below the horizontal scroll bar that divides the top half from the bottom. You can change the proportion of the top and bottom of the window by dragging this bar up or down. You can switch between the top and bottom halves by clicking the half you want to work on or by pressing F6.

The bottom half of a Query or Filter window contains the QBE grid. QBE stands for *query by example*—you select records you want to see in the query by providing examples. This grid contains the field names a query uses, whether they appear in the query's datasheet, how they are sorted, and the criteria that select which records appear. Notice that there are fewer rows in the QBE grid in the Filter window than there are in the Query window. This is because queries offer features that filters do not.

The QBE grid contains separate columns for each of the fields used. Just as with a datasheet, you can make the columns wider or narrower by dragging the right side of the column selector right or left. The rows of the grid contain the data the field uses in the query. Most of your entries go into this area. The first entries you make in this area are the fields the query or filter uses.

**tip:** *You can temporarily enlarge the area you have to make an entry in the QBE grid by displaying the Zoom window. Pressing SHIFT+F2 to open the Zoom window gives you a larger area to make an entry.*

## Adding Fields to a Query or Filter

Once in a Filter window or Design view of the Query window, the first step is to select the fields the query or filter uses from the field list. You can add fields one at a time, or you can add all of them simultaneously. In queries, the order in which you add fields sets the order of the fields in the dynaset. The fields you add include all of the fields you want to see in the dynaset as well as the fields that select the data you see in the dynaset. In filters, you are only adding the fields you need to use to select the records you want to appear in the table or form, since you will see all of the fields in the table or form.

**tip:** *In Access version 1, fields that you use to sort the records the query selects do not appear in the same place they appear in the dynaset. When you save the query, Access version 1 moves fields used in sorting to the left side of the QBE grid, but displays the fields in the dynaset in the order that you originally entered them.*

You can add these field names in one of three ways. The simplest method is to double-click the field in the field list; Access adds that field to the next empty column in the QBE grid. Another way is to drag the field name from the field list for the table to one of the empty cells in the top row of the QBE grid. When you release the mouse in the QBE grid, the field name is added to the top of the selected column. Figure 6-3 shows a query design after several fields have been selected.

The third method for adding a field is to move to the cell in the Field row of the QBE grid where you want to add the field. You can see the down arrow that is part of all drop-down list boxes. Select one of the listed fields or type the field name. When you add a field name to the QBE grid for a query, the Show check box below the field name becomes selected. Filter windows don't have this check box, because you cannot hide fields with a filter.

You can also add the table name, a period, and an asterisk, as in **Client.***, which adds all of the table's fields to the grid. Even though the asterisk column only uses one column, when you display the datasheet for this query, all of the fields are shown. One advantage of using the asterisk rather than adding all of the fields separately is that new fields added to the table design automatically appear in the query dynaset.

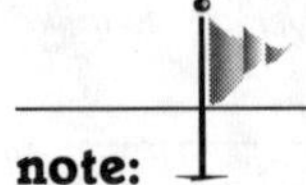

**note:** *You can also drag the asterisk from the field list.*

Unless you use the asterisk to add fields to queries, when you add a new field to a table, you must also add the new field to queries if you want the field to

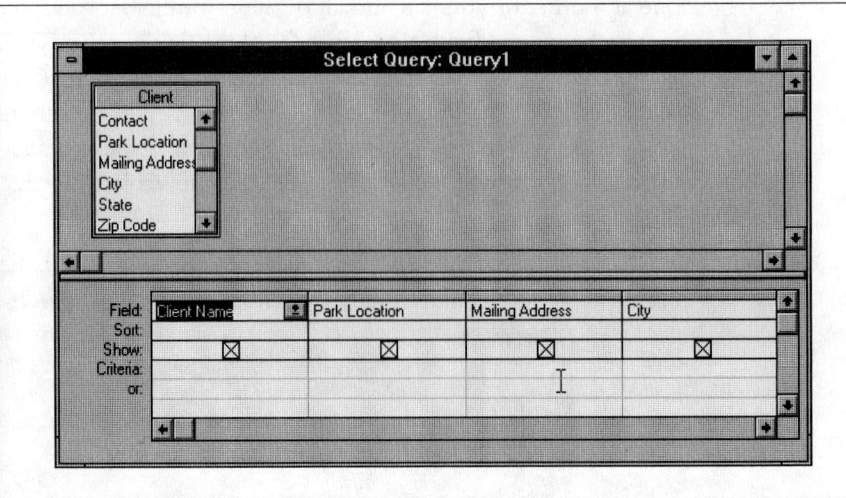


**Figure 6-3** A Query window in Design view after fields are added

appear in the query dynaset. You cannot use the asterisk as a field name for sorting or selecting the records that will appear in the query. When you want to use the asterisk along with sorting and criteria, you must have more than one copy of the field in the QBE grid. You can hide the extra copy of the field by clearing the Show check box.

You can also add all of the fields by using the field list. If you double-click the table name in the field list, all of the fields become highlighted except for the *. With all of these fields selected, drag any one of them to the QBE grid. You have thus added all of the fields from the table to the QBE grid just as if you had added each one individually.

**tip:** *If creating a query for a form or report, include all of the fields that you plan to use in the form or report.*

## Deleting, Inserting, and Moving Fields in a QBE Grid

As you add fields to the QBE grid, you can rearrange them as you change your mind about how you want the information displayed or filtered. You can add, delete, and rearrange the fields.

Before you make any of these changes, decide whether you want to change one or more columns in the QBE grid. If you only want to change one column, select the column by clicking the column selector, which is the gray box above the Field row of a column. When a column in the QBE grid is selected, the column becomes black. If you want to change more than one adjoining column, drag the mouse right or left across the column selectors for the columns you want to select. Once the column or columns are selected, you can insert, delete, and move the columns. When you delete, insert, or move the columns, you are moving the field and all of the settings the field has. To rearrange non-adjoining columns, adjust each column separately.

To delete the selected columns, press DEL or select Delete from the Edit menu. You can also use the Delete Column command in the Edit menu to get the same results. The remaining columns of the query are shifted to the left. To insert as many blank columns as you have selected, press INS or select Insert Column from the Edit menu.

To move the selected columns to the left or right, drag the column selectors to where you want the columns after selecting the columns. As you drag, you will see a line between columns indicating where Access will place the selected columns when you release the mouse. You can drag the mouse right or left; when the line is where you want the selected columns added, release the mouse.

## Viewing a Query or Filter

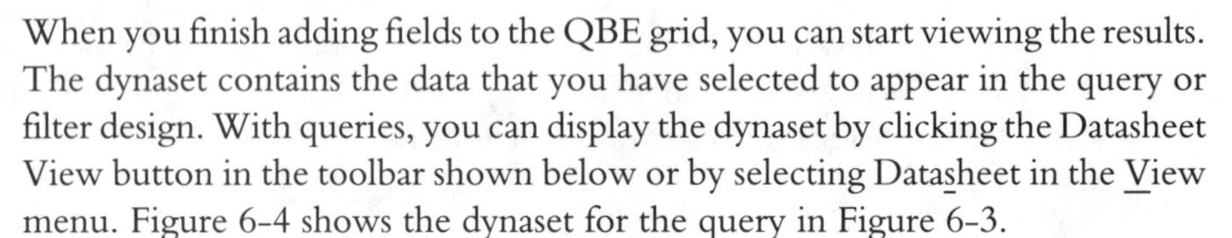

When you finish adding fields to the QBE grid, you can start viewing the results. The dynaset contains the data that you have selected to appear in the query or filter design. With queries, you can display the dynaset by clicking the Datasheet View button in the toolbar shown below or by selecting Datasheet in the View menu. Figure 6-4 shows the dynaset for the query in Figure 6-3.

To display the dynaset selected by a filter, you want to select Apply Filter/Sort from the Records menu or the Apply Filter/Sort button in the toolbar, shown here:

Access closes the Filter window and displays only those records the filter selects. You will see FLTR in the status bar to remind you that the displayed records are filtered. To display all of the records again, you select Show All Records from the Records menu, or the Show All Records button shown here:

The datasheet that displays the query's dynaset looks just like the datasheet you use to display a table. The only visible difference is the title bar, which displays *Select Query:* followed by the query name. Because the query selects which fields appear, which records appear, and the order of the fields and records, the fields and records appearing may differ from what you see in the query's underlying table. If the query design contains two copies of a field, the second copy of the field in the datasheet will be labeled Field and the next unused number. You will learn how to change the name of the fields later in the chapter.

The datasheet or form displaying the results of a filter is actually the table, rather than a separate database object like a query. All the filter does is control which records are displayed and how they are sorted. To return to the normal display, you simply select Show All Records from the Records menu or click

**Figure 6-4** The dynaset created by the query in Figure 6-3

Select Query: Query1

| Client Name | Park Location | Mailing Address | City | State | Zip C |
|---|---|---|---|---|---|
| Family Fun Land | Isle Royale | P.O. Box 345 | Houghton | MI | 49312 |
| Teen Land | Ashtabula Park | P.O. Box 786 | Ashtabula | OH | 44321 |
| Amusement Techn | Panacea on the Be | P.O. Box 5346 | Panacea on the Be | FL | 33012 |
| Arden Entertainmer | Indianapolis | 100 Federal Avenu | Indianapolis | IN | 67821 |
| Family Amusements | Stanton | P.O. Box 123548 | Stanton | PA | 78378 |
| Playland Consortiur | Wheeling | P.O. Box 5839 | Wheeling | WV | 45678 |
| Island Waterplay In | Raleigh | 1 Waterplay Lane | Raleigh | NC | 12378 |
| Entertainment Plus | Jersey City | P.O. Box 4892368 | Jersey City | NJ | 08767 |

Record: 1 of 8

the Show All Records button. To show all the records for a query, you must remove the criteria yourself.

While looking at the datasheet for the query's dynaset or the filtered table data, you can edit the data just as you would edit the data in a datasheet for a table. The filter's datasheet is the table's datasheet even though you do not see all of the records. The query's dynaset creates a pathway from the query's datasheet to the table the query uses to create the dynaset. When you edit an entry in the dynaset's datasheet, you are changing the data in the table that the data originally came from. Also, any table properties that affect data entry in the table's datasheet still affect data entry in the query's datasheet or in the filtered version of the table's data. The commands you learned about in previous chapters to change the appearance of a datasheet—hiding columns or changing fonts, row heights, column widths, and gridlines—also apply to a dynaset's datasheet.

If the query shows the data you want, you are ready to save and print the dynaset. If not, switch back to the query's design by clicking the Design View button in the toolbar or choosing Query Design in the View menu. Once back at the query's design, modify it and continue switching between the Design and Datasheet views until you have created the query you want. If you are working with filters, you may also need to go back and edit the filter to refine or change the selection of records by selecting Edit Filter/Sort from the Records menu or by clicking the Edit Filter/Sort button.

## Saving a Query or a Filter as a Query

When you have a query you want to keep for future use, save it. Saving a query means saving the settings of the query—not the dynaset. This means that each time you use the query, Access reapplies the same query settings to the current table data. Saving just the query's design means that every time you use the query, you are using the most current version of the data in the table the query uses.

Although a filter can't be saved as a filter, you can overcome this limitation. If you have a filter you think you might want to reuse, simply save it as a query.

Saving a query is just like saving other objects in a database. You can save a query with the Save command or the Save Query command (depending on which view you are in) in the File menu or by clicking the Save button on the toolbar. You can save a filter as a query by selecting Save As Query from the File menu or by clicking the Save button on the toolbar.

When saving a query for the first time, you must supply the query name. In the Query Name text box, type the name that you want for the query and select OK. You can have up to 64 characters in the name (the rule for naming all Access objects). You cannot name a query with the same name as a table or another query in the database. When you select a table or query as a source of data for another object in Access, Access does not distinguish between tables and queries. You are also prompted to save the query when you close its window. When you save a query after the first time, the query is saved under the name you gave it previously.

If you want to change the name of the query you are saving, choose Save As or Save Query As (depending on the view you are in) in the File menu and type a new name for the query before you select OK. For example, you may have one query that you want to use as the basis for another. In this case, save the original query with a new name and modify the new query to fit your changing needs.

Once you have saved the query, you can return to it at a later point. To open a query that is no longer displayed, select the query in the list of queries from the Database window. You can double-click the query name or select the Open button to open the query and show the datasheet containing the query's dynaset. In Access version 1, you also can use the right mouse button to double-click the query's name or select the Design button to open the query and show it in Design view.

## Renaming a Query

Just as with other objects in the database, you can rename queries. You may decide that an existing query could be more aptly named. To give it a new name, select the query from the Database window and choose Rename from the File menu or select Rename from the query's shortcut menu. In the Query

Name text box, type the new name for the query and select OK. Before you rename a query, close any window the query design or its dynaset datasheet appears in.

## Printing a Query

Later, starting with Chapter 8, you will learn about creating forms and reports that give you more sophisticated options, but you will also want to print your data directly from the datasheet. Printing a query's datasheet is just like printing a table's datasheet. Figure 6-5 shows a printed query using the query design shown in Figure 6-3. You can also preview the appearance of the printed datasheet before you print it by choosing Print Preview in the File menu. Remember that since a filter is applied to a table, you can simply print the table with the filter applied, as described in Chapter 4.

**tip:** *If your query has more fields than can fit across the page, you may want to hide some columns in the datasheet. Hidden columns are not printed, so you can limit the data printed to just the information that you need to see for a particular use. Hide columns by selecting them and choosing Hide Columns from the Format menu (the Layout menu in Access version 1) when you are looking at the query's dynaset. You can also hide fields from the query's design by clearing the Show check box below the fields to hide in the QBE grid.*

### Printing Options

When you print a datasheet, you have several choices for how to print the data. These options are available through either the Print dialog box or the Print Setup dialog box. To see the Print dialog box, choose Print in the File menu or click the Print button in the toolbar, shown here:

To display the Print Setup dialog box, choose Print Setup from the File menu or select the Setup button in the Print dialog box. All of these printing options apply when printing either tables or queries. When you learn about forms and reports starting in Chapter 8, you can use the same printing options to change how the forms and reports are printed.

**Figure 6-5** A printed copy of the dynaset created by the query

| Client Name | Park Location | Mailing Address | City | State | Zip Code |
|---|---|---|---|---|---|
| Family Fun Land | Isle Royale | P.O. Box 345 | Houghton | MI | 49312 |
| Teen Land | Ashtabula Park | P.O. Box 786 | Ashtabula | OH | 44321 |
| Amusement Technologies | Panacea on the Beach | P.O. Box 5346 | Panacea on the Beach | FL | 33012 |
| Arden Entertainment Group | Indianapolis | 100 Federal Avenue | Indianapolis | IN | 67821 |
| Family Amusements | Stanton | P.O. Box 123548 | Stanton | PA | 78378 |
| Playland Consortium | Wheeling | P.O. Box 5839 | Wheeling | WV | 45678 |
| Island Waterplay Inc. | Raleigh | 1 Waterplay Lane | Raleigh | NC | 12378 |
| Entertainment Plus | Jersey City | P.O. Box 4892368 | Jersey City | NJ | 08767 |

In the Print dialog box, the printing options let you select which data is printed and the quality of the print. The three option buttons under Print Range set the data Access will print. All prints the entire datasheet. Selection, which is only available when you have selected some of the records or fields in the query, prints only the highlighted data, as if only this data appeared in the datasheet. Pages prints only the range of pages you enter in the From and To text boxes after Access decides the data that would appear on each page if you printed all of the datasheet.

From the Print Quality drop-down box, select High, Medium, or Low. The higher the print quality, the longer it takes to print and the better the output looks. With some printers, changing the print quality has no effect.

Finally, set the number of copies to print by entering a number in the Copies text box and pressing OK. This number is reset to the default of 1 every time you print. The Print to File and the Collate Copies check boxes are described in Chapter 9.

In the Print Setup dialog box, shown next, you can set the printer, page orientation, paper size, and margins.

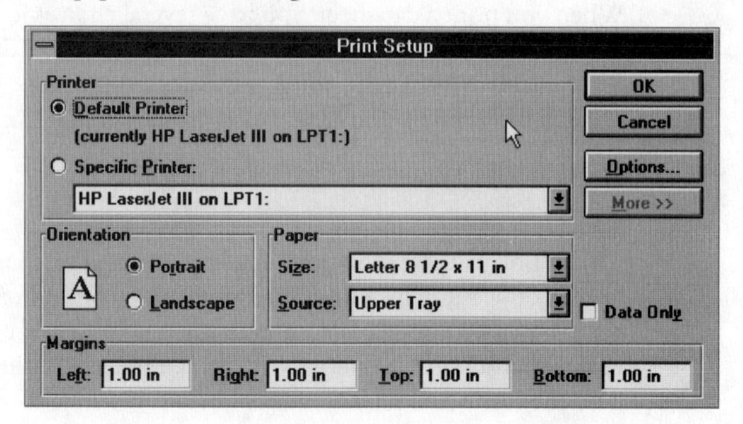

The printer is selected by leaving the Default Printer option button selected or by selecting the Specific Printer option button and choosing one of the available printers, installed through the Windows Control Panel program, from the adjacent drop-down list box.

You can select whether the data is printed on the page normally or rotated to print sideways by selecting the Portrait or Landscape option buttons. With the Size drop-down list box, select one of the listed paper sizes that you know your printer supports. After Source, select one of the paper feeding choices your printer has available. Select the Data Only check box if you do not want to print the datasheet with the borders and gridlines, and your data will be printed faster. In the Margins text boxes, type the new margins you want the printed copy to use. Use inches or centimeters as the current setting shows, or type **in** or **cm** after the new margin to indicate which measurement system you want to use.

Finally, select the Options command button to display the Windows settings for the selected printer. (You see the same settings when you select Configure and then Setup in Windows 3.0 or Setup and then Options in Windows 3.1 from the Printers dialog box in the Control Panel.) The changes you make from the Options dialog box affect all Windows applications.

The More button in the Print Setup dialog box is not available in the example shown, since this button is used to provide options applicable only to forms and reports.

## Additional Query and Filter Design Features

Your queries can use other features that change how the data appears in the dynaset. These features include renaming fields in a query, sorting the dynaset's data, and hiding fields. Filters cannot rename fields or hide them, although filters can sort the records.

### Renaming Fields in a Query

By default a query uses the same field names in its dynaset as the table the data comes from does. You can change the name for a field in a dynaset to another acceptable field name. For example, you might want to rename fields in a query when the table the query uses has abbreviations in the field names. Later, when you learn about calculated fields in a query, you can rename these fields so you have more descriptive names than the default names. Also, if you have multiple copies of a field, especially when one of the copies is hidden, you may want to rename both copies.

To rename a field, move the insertion point to the beginning of the field name you want to rename in the QBE grid of the query's design. Type the name you want to use for the field, followed by a colon. When the column previously contained a field name, leave the field name after the colon, as in **Estimated Cost:Est Cost**. The field name after the colon tells Access the source of the data in that field. When you view the dynaset in a Datasheet view, the column uses the new field name, Estimated Cost, as shown here.

Select Query: Coaster Cost

| Coaster Id | Coaster Name | Completed | Client Id | Actual Cost | Estimated Cost |
|---|---|---|---|---|---|
| 1 | Scream Machine | No | 3 | $4,000,000.00 | $7,800,000.00 |
| 2 | Blue Arrow | No | 2 | $3,900,000.00 | $4,000,000.00 |
| 3 | Astro Transport | Yes | 3 | $7,800,000.00 | $7,500,000.00 |
| 4 | Red Dragon | No | 1 | $2,500,000.00 | $4,500,000.00 |
| 5 | Taurus | No | 4 | $198,000.00 | $4,500,000.00 |
| 6 | Corker | No | 5 | $1,500,000.00 | $2,500,000.00 |
| 7 | Wild One | No | 6 | $3,200,000.00 | $3,900,000.00 |
| 8 | White Lightnin | Yes | 7 | $3,100,000.00 | $2,800,000.00 |
| 9 | The Runaway | Yes | 2 | $3,200,900.00 | $3,215,000.00 |
| (Counter) | | No | 0 | $0.00 | $0.00 |

Record: 1 of 9

If the new field name includes a colon as part of the name, enclose the field name in brackets, as in **[Cost: Estimated]:Est Cost**. When the field name for the column replaces the field name Access gives to a calculated field, remove the previous field name. Like field names in a table, each field name in a dynaset must be unique.

## Sorting the Records

You can use the query or filter to rearrange your data. Sorting the data organizes the records presented according to the values of one or more fields. You can use any field type except Memo and OLE Object for sorting. Sorting does not permanently change the order of the records in the table that the data comes from; it only changes the order in which records are presented. Sorting done with a filter is removed from the table as soon as the filter is removed.

Sorting records is done from the Filter window or the Query window in Design view. First, in the QBE grid, move to the column of the first field you want to use for sorting. This is the field in which all records are sorted according to their values. Then, in the Sort row, select Ascending, Descending, or (not sorted). Ascending sorts the records using the values for that field in increasing order. Descending sorts the records using the values for that field in decreasing order. The third choice, (not sorted), gives the same results as deleting

Ascending or Descending—that is, it stops the use of that field for organizing records. As soon as you select Ascending or Descending, Access uses the chosen field to sort the records.

If the field you select for the first sort field has the same value for two or more records, you may want to use another field's value to order those records having the same value for the first field. To organize the dynaset's records using a second field as a tiebreaker, click the Sort row of the field you want to use as the second field to organize the dynaset's records, and select Ascending or Descending from the drop-down list box. To tell Access that you want to use this field as the second field to sort the records, place the field to the right of the field you want to use as the first field.

Access sorts the dynaset's records by the fields that have Ascending or Descending in the Sort row of the QBE grid. Access starts with the field in the left side of the grid and continues to the right. When two or more records have the same values for the first and second fields, you can use a third field to order the records by selecting Ascending or Descending in the Sort row of the QBE grid and placing the field to the right of the fields you are using for the first and second fields. You can repeat this procedure for as many as ten fields.

Figure 6-6 shows a dynaset using two fields to organize its records. The first field is Project Id, which sorts records according to their project number. The records that have the same Project Id field values are sorted by the Invoice Date field, which is the second sort field. The query design for this dynaset is shown in Figure 6-7. You can see by the order of the fields that the query's records are sorted by Project Id first and Invoice Date second. For each field used for sorting, the Sort row indicates Ascending or Descending.

**Figure 6-6** The sorted dynaset

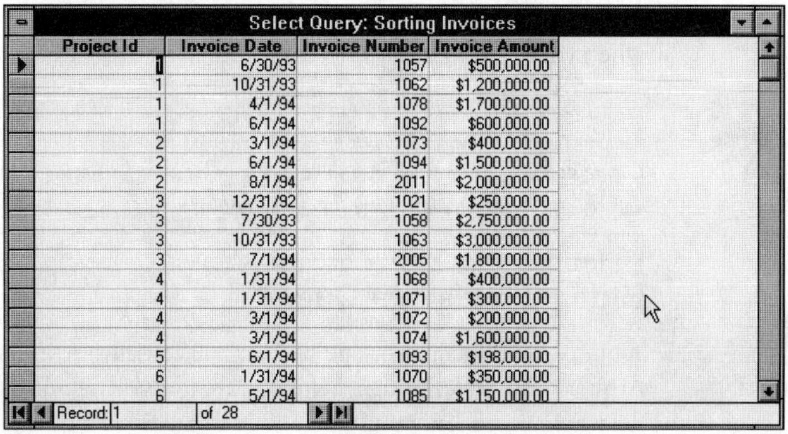

Select Query: Sorting Invoices

| Project Id | Invoice Date | Invoice Number | Invoice Amount |
|---|---|---|---|
| 1 | 6/30/93 | 1057 | $500,000.00 |
| 1 | 10/31/93 | 1062 | $1,200,000.00 |
| 1 | 4/1/94 | 1078 | $1,700,000.00 |
| 1 | 6/1/94 | 1092 | $600,000.00 |
| 2 | 3/1/94 | 1073 | $400,000.00 |
| 2 | 6/1/94 | 1094 | $1,500,000.00 |
| 2 | 8/1/94 | 2011 | $2,000,000.00 |
| 3 | 12/31/92 | 1021 | $250,000.00 |
| 3 | 7/30/93 | 1058 | $2,750,000.00 |
| 3 | 10/31/93 | 1063 | $3,000,000.00 |
| 3 | 7/1/94 | 2005 | $1,800,000.00 |
| 4 | 1/31/94 | 1068 | $400,000.00 |
| 4 | 1/31/94 | 1071 | $300,000.00 |
| 4 | 3/1/94 | 1072 | $200,000.00 |
| 4 | 3/1/94 | 1074 | $1,600,000.00 |
| 5 | 6/1/94 | 1093 | $198,000.00 |
| 6 | 1/31/94 | 1070 | $350,000.00 |
| 6 | 5/1/94 | 1085 | $1,150,000.00 |

Record: 1 of 28

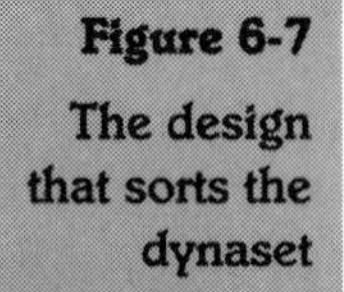
**Figure 6-7** The design that sorts the dynaset

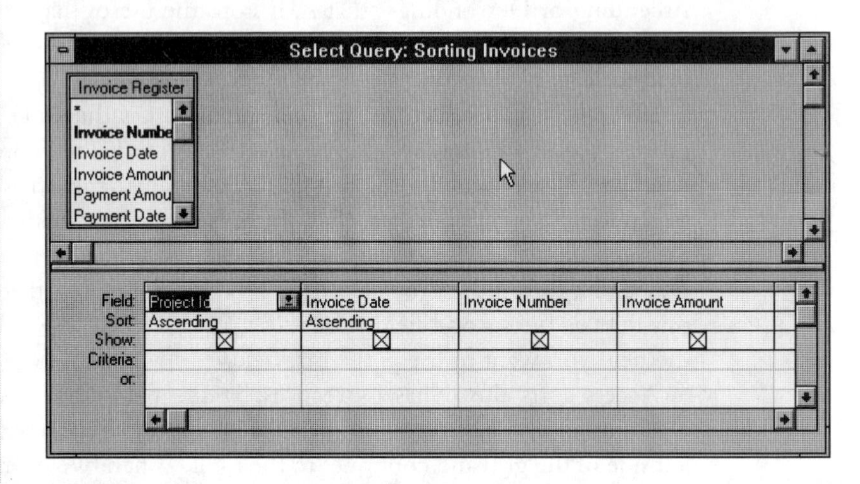


Prior to Access version 2, when you saved a query that used sorting, the sort fields were shifted to the left side of the QBE grid. If you are using an earlier release and want the fields used for sorting to appear in different locations than at the beginning of the dynaset, place two copies of the field in the query's design and hide the copy used for sorting (you'll learn how in the next section). Also, you may need more than two copies of a field when one of the columns in the QBE grid contains the table name followed by an asterisk, as in **Client.***, and you want to use one of the table's fields to sort the records.

In Access version 2, the fields used for sorting are not shifted to the left when you save the query, so that you do not need to enter a field in two columns, one for display and one for sorting. However, you may still wish to do so, since sorting starts with the first sorting column on the left and works to the right, when you want to display fields in a different order than you want them sorted.

**tip:** *Create indexes for the fields in a table that a query uses for sorting. Having indexes for the fields a query uses to sort makes using the query faster.*

## Hiding Fields in a Query

A query can contain more fields than you actually see in the dynaset's datasheet. A query can have hidden fields for a variety of reasons. You can use hidden fields when you have multiple copies of a field in a query. You also use hidden fields when the QBE grid contains an entire table added with an asterisk and you want to use some of the table's fields for sorting and adding criteria.

**note:** *Do not hide fields that you want to include when you use the query in a form or report. You can, however, tell Access to include all fields from a query's table in forms or reports by changing the Output All Fields property to Yes, as described in Chapter 7.*

Hiding fields in a query is easy—just clear the Show check box under the field in the QBE grid. For example, in the query design shown in Figure 6-8, the first three fields in the query's dynaset are First Name, Last Name, and Date of Hire, because they have checked boxes and the other fields do not.

You hide fields when you want to use fields to perform multiple functions in a query. For example, to use the Last Name field to sort the records for the query in Figure 6-8, you can have two copies of the field—one copy containing Ascending or Descending in the Sort row to organize the data, and another copy with the field shown in the datasheet. In the first copy the field is hidden, while in the second copy it is not. When you include an asterisk in the QBE grid as well as adding a field separately to sort or select the data, the field may appear in the table twice.

When you close and save a query, Access rearranges the fields in the QBE grid so that the hidden fields are shifted to the right. At the same time, sorting fields are shifted to the left. When a field is both hidden and used to sort,

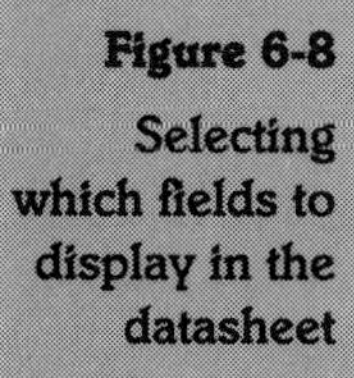

**Figure 6-8**
**Selecting which fields to display in the datasheet**

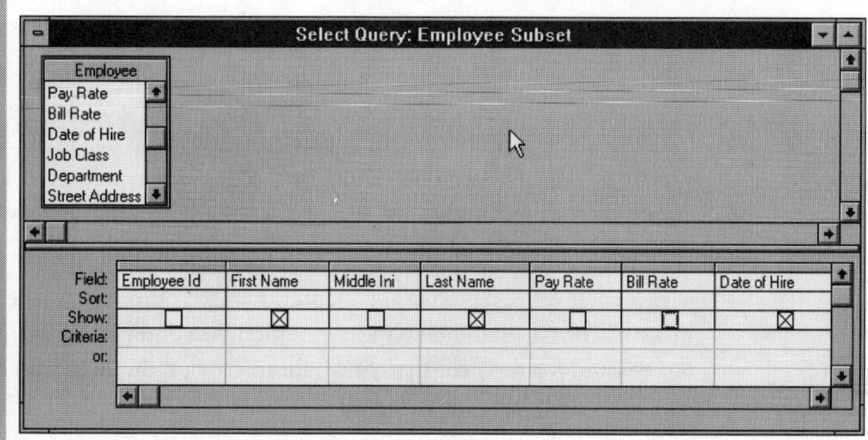

the field is placed on the left side. If you hide a field that is not used for selecting or sorting records, it is simply removed from the QBE grid when you save the query.

## Creating Criteria to Select Records

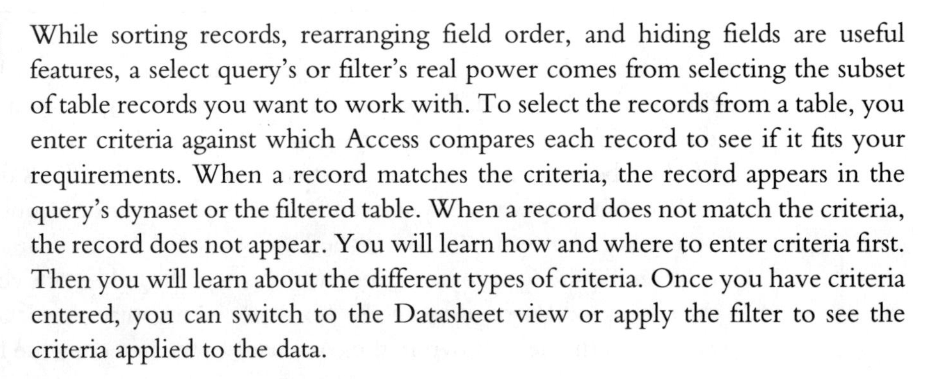

While sorting records, rearranging field order, and hiding fields are useful features, a select query's or filter's real power comes from selecting the subset of table records you want to work with. To select the records from a table, you enter criteria against which Access compares each record to see if it fits your requirements. When a record matches the criteria, the record appears in the query's dynaset or the filtered table. When a record does not match the criteria, the record does not appear. You will learn how and where to enter criteria first. Then you will learn about the different types of criteria. Once you have criteria entered, you can switch to the Datasheet view or apply the filter to see the criteria applied to the data.

### Entering Criteria

Criteria are entered in the criteria rows in the QBE grid of queries or filters. The criteria rows start with the row labeled Criteria and continue downward for as many rows as necessary. You can have one line of criteria or multiple lines. Each line can have one or more criteria that must be met. Where you place the criteria tells Access how the criteria are used. In this section, all of the criteria in the examples given are exact matches that look for specific entries in a field (for example, State equaling OH). Later you will learn about different types of criteria you can create.

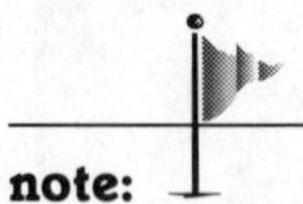

**note:** *Criteria are entered the same way in the QBE grids of queries and filters. This section primarily describes working with queries, but all of the steps can be used with both features.*

To enter exact match criteria, enter the text, number, or date you want to find in a particular field. The column in which you enter this text, number, or date is the column for the field that you want to contain the text, number, or date.

To enter the simplest of criteria, enter a single criterion under a single field. As an example, say you want to find the records for Design department employees using the Employee table. The QBE grid for the query looks like this:

| Field: | First Name | Last Name | Department | Job Class |
|---|---|---|---|---|
| Sort: | | | | |
| Show: | ☒ | ☒ | ☒ | ☒ |
| Criteria: | | | Design | |
| or: | | | | |

To enter this criterion, move the insertion point to the first criteria row under the Department field and type **Design**. When you move to another cell in the QBE grid, Access adds quotes around the text. When you display this query's datasheet, Access checks each record to see whether the value for the Department field equals Design. If it does, the record is part of the dynaset; if it does not, the record is ignored by the query. The query's datasheet looks like this:

Select Query: Query1

| First Name | Last Name | Department | Job Class |
|---|---|---|---|
| WILLIAM | WILD | Design | 11 |
| RODGER | ROLLING | Design | 22 |
| SANDRA | SCARY | Design | 21 |
| DONNA | DARE | Design | 12 |
| | | | 0 |

Record: 1 of 4

Another type of criteria is used when you want to find records that have one of two or more values for the same field. For example, you might want to know which employees are working on projects 2 and 7. To find this out using a query based on the Employee Time Log table, type **2** in the first criteria row underneath Project Number and **7** in the row below it, as shown here:

| Field: | Date | Employee Id | Project Number | Hours |
|---|---|---|---|---|
| Sort: | | | | |
| Show: | ☒ | ☒ | ☒ | ☒ |
| Criteria: | | | 2 | |
| or: | | | 7 | |

When Access evaluates this criteria, it checks each record to see whether the Project Number field equals 2. If it does, the record is included in the dynaset. If the record's Project Number field does not equal 2, Access then checks whether this field equals 7. If it does, the record is included in the dynaset. If the record's Project Number field does not equal either 2 or 7, the record is omitted from the dynaset. Figure 6-9 shows the dynaset's datasheet, which includes only records containing 2 or 7 in the Project Number field.

When you use multiple criteria lines in a QBE grid, the criteria do not have to apply to the same field. For example, you may have criteria that look like this:

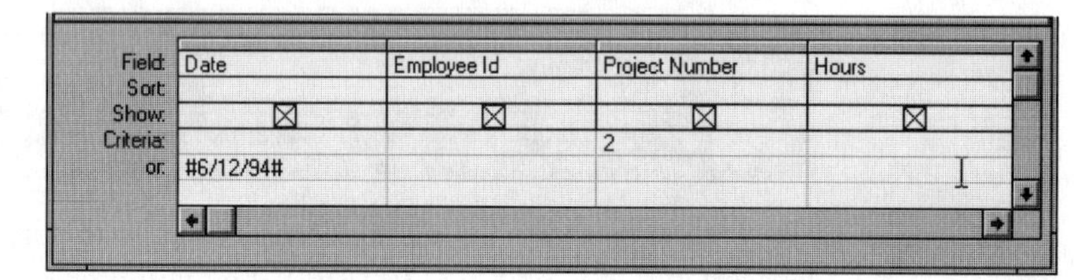

| | | | | |
|---|---|---|---|---|
| Field: | Date | Employee Id | Project Number | Hours |
| Sort: | | | | |
| Show: | ☒ | ☒ | ☒ | ☒ |
| Criteria: | | | 2 | |
| or: | #6/12/94# | | | |

For the date, you can type **6/12/94** and let Access add the # signs to enclose the date when you leave the cell. The criteria in this illustration match records from the Employee Time Log table that have a value of 2 for the Project Number field or a value of 6/12/94 for the Date field. A record must meet just one of these conditions to be included in the dynaset.

Think of different lines of criteria in the QBE grid as similar to tracks in a race course that include hurdles, as shown in Figure 6-10. Each record must run the length of the track to get to the finish line, or be included in the dynaset. Each track has separate hurdles that may be at different locations than the hurdles in other tracks. When a record cannot pass one of the hurdles in the track, it tries the hurdles in the next track. When a record cannot make it through any of the tracks, it is not included in the dynaset. Access does not care which track the record uses to get through the hurdles.

**Figure 6-9** The dynaset of records for projects 2 and 7

Select Query: Query1

| Date | Employee Id | Project Number | Hours |
|---|---|---|---|
| 6/12/94 | 1 | 7 | 8 |
| 6/12/94 | 2 | 2 | 35 |
| 6/12/94 | 7 | 2 | 40 |
| 6/12/94 | 9 | 2 | 40 |
| 6/12/94 | 10 | 2 | 40 |
| 6/19/94 | 2 | 2 | 28 |
| 6/19/94 | 2 | 7 | 12 |
| 6/19/94 | 5 | 2 | 30 |
| 6/19/94 | 7 | 2 | 40 |
| 6/19/94 | 9 | 2 | 40 |
| 6/19/94 | 10 | 2 | 40 |
| | 0 | 0 | 0 |

Record: 1 of 11

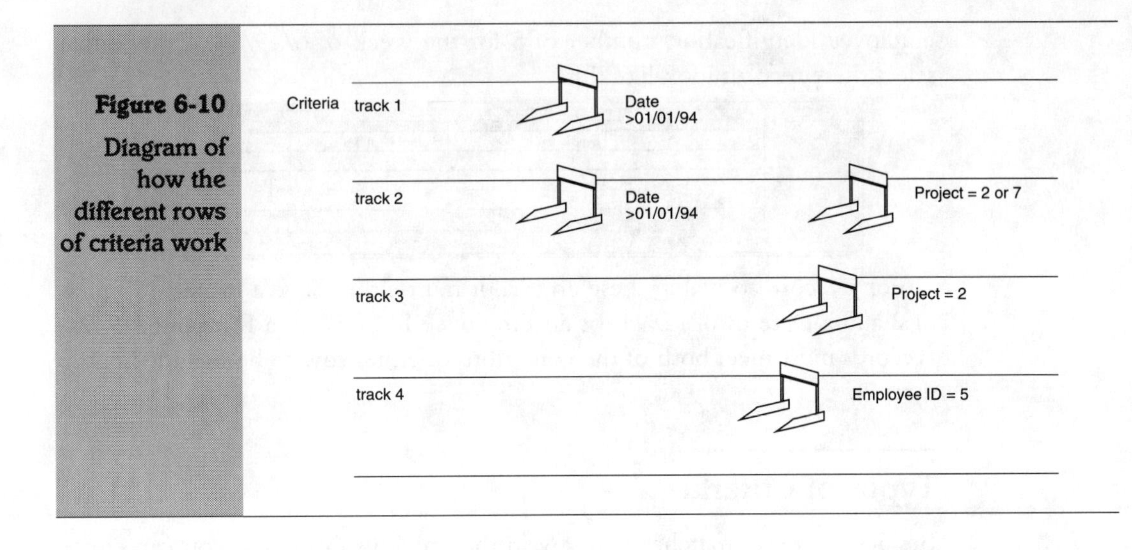


**Figure 6-10** Diagram of how the different rows of criteria work

Another way to enter criteria is to have more than one criterion in the same row. For example, you can select records from the Employee Time Log table whose Date field equals 6/12/94 and Project Number field equals 2. When you create criteria like this, each criterion a record must match is entered in a separate column on the same row, as shown here:

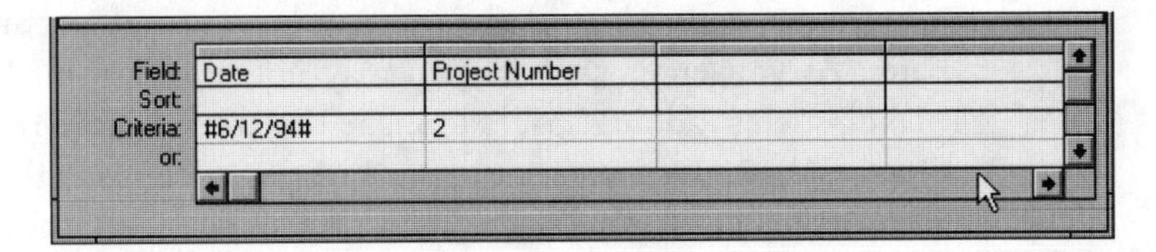


**note:** *Notice that this is a filter rather than a query (you can tell because you do not see a Showcheck box). Criteria are entered the same way in both.*

For a record to match this criteria, the Date field must equal 6/12/94 *and* the Project Number field must equal 2. Records that equal 6/12/94 for the Date field but do not equal 2 for the Project Number field are not included. Only records matching both criteria are displayed.

You can also combine both multiple lines and multiple criteria on the same lines. For example, you may want records from the Employee Time Log table for project 2 for the week of 6/12/94 and records for the employee with the employee identification number of 5 for the week of 6/19/94. Criteria that select these records look like this:

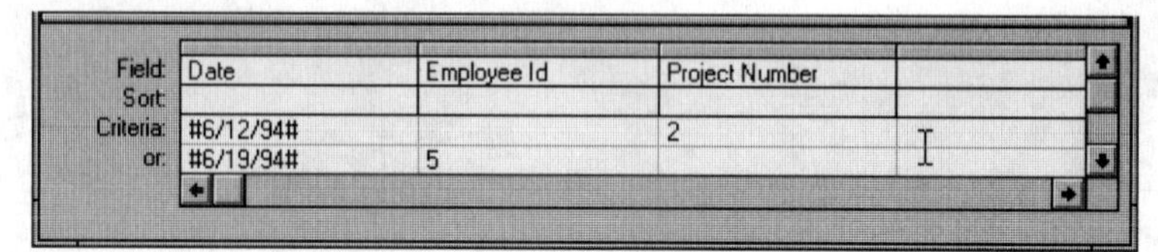


For a record to match these criteria, it must either have a Project Number of 2 and a Date of 6/12/94, or an Employee Id of 5 and a Date of 6/19/94. Records must meet both of the conditions of either row to be included in the dynaset.

## Types of Criteria

Besides the exact matches you saw in the previous examples, you can create additional types of criteria. These other types of criteria let you test for more than just whether a specific field matches a specific value. Some of the types of criteria you can use include using patterns of text, comparisons, and arithmetic. Several of the types of criteria you can create take advantage of *operators*. These operators tell Access to perform some operation such as math or a comparison.

All of the criteria you enter are converted to Access's syntax. For example, you learned earlier how Access adds quotes around text and # symbols around dates. As you enter criteria, you may notice other small changes that Access makes, such as adding spaces to make the criteria more readable. When Access changes the criteria you enter, it is creating statements that it uses to select the records. Access prefaces each cell in the criteria section of the QBE grid with the field name and an equal sign, as in State="OH". You will not see the field names or equal sign added, but Access provides them itself behind the scenes.

Access version 2 offers another way to create criteria that use operators, the Expression Builder. Using this feature, you can make selections to enter expressions, rather than having to remember the correct operators and type them in directly. You can start the Expression Builder by clicking the Build button in the toolbar, shown below, or by selecting Build from the shortcut menu while the insertion point is in one of the criteria rows. The following sections discuss the different types of criteria, all of which can be created using the Expression Builder or by typing your own entries. Chapter 12 gives more information on using the Expression Builder to create expressions.

## USING WILDCARD CHARACTERS IN CRITERIA

Sometimes you will want criteria that match a pattern of characters. For example, you may want a list of all the roller coaster names that start with W, or you might want a list of all clients that include Entertainment in their name. When an entry must match a certain pattern, you can use *wildcard characters* to create a pattern. When a field's value matches the pattern, that record matches that criterion. To screen for this type of criteria, enter the pattern the matching entry must follow.

When you move to another cell in the QBE grid, you will see the pattern enclosed in quotes and the term "Like" preceding the pattern. Like is an operator that tells Access you want to match a pattern with a field's value. If you use a range in the pattern (described later in this chapter), you must enter **Like** and the quotes yourself.

The pattern can contain four entries. The first type of entry a pattern contains is the specific characters that you want to appear in the matching entries. A pattern can contain one or more question marks, the second type of entry, when you want Access to fill in for the question marks any possible character that results in matches with your data. An example of using question marks in a pattern is **C??st??**, for which Access finds the matches Coaster, Caustic, Crested, and Crystal.

A pattern can contain an asterisk when you want the field's entries to contain zero or more characters in that location. An example of an asterisk in a pattern is ***the***, for which Access finds the matches other, theory, and lithe.

The fourth entry you can use in a pattern is a *range,* which allows one of a set of characters in the range's location. A range contains the available characters in brackets, as in [ABCDE] or [A-E]. The hyphen in the second range indicates that all of the characters between the characters on either side of the hyphen are included in the range. Access distinguishes between uppercase and lowercase characters in the brackets, so [A-E] will not yield the same results as [a-e]. The characters in ranges must be in ascending order; you can use [A-E] but not [E-A]. You can also use brackets to exclude characters by putting an exclamation point after the opening bracket, as in [!A-E], to *not* match an A, B, C, D, or E. An example of a range is [123][ABC]*, which matches 1A, 3B, and 2Coaster.

Let's return to our example of finding every coaster that starts with W. To do so using wildcard characters, just enter **W*** under the Coaster Name field in the Criteria row of a QBE grid. When you display the dynaset, the datasheet includes the records for Wild One and White Lightnin, whose names both match the pattern.

The In operator is an alternative to the Like operator. The In operator also determines whether a value matches a pattern. An In operator tests whether a value is part of a group. You can use this in place of multiple logical operators. For example, you can use the In operator for criteria to match records from the Employee table that have Design or Testing in the Department field. To use the In operator for these two departments, enter **In ("Design","Testing")**. Usually, you will type the different entries you want for a field into separate lines rather than using this operator unless you are combining this criteria with other criteria.

## COMPARISON CRITERIA

Instead of looking for specific entries with criteria, you may want to use criteria to match records that are more or less than another value. You can use comparison operators to create criteria that match records based on their relative value to one another.

The comparison operators you can include in criteria are less than, equal to, greater than, and a combination of these. These are the comparison operators:

| Operator | Meaning |
|---|---|
| < | less than |
| <= | less than or equal to |
| > | greater than |
| >= | greater than or equal to |
| = | equal to |
| <> | does not equal |

When a criterion containing the comparison operator is true, the record matches it. Otherwise, the record does not match that criterion. When you compare text, relative values are decided by the character's position in the alphabet. When you compare numbers, relative values are determined by which number is larger or smaller. When you compare dates, relative values depend on which date occurred before or after the other.

For example, you can use comparison operators to select invoices for 1994 by finding invoices with dates of 1/1/94 or later. The filtered table looks like Figure 6-11. To create this criterion, enter **>=1/1/94** under Invoice Date, as shown here, after moving to another cell in the QBE grid:

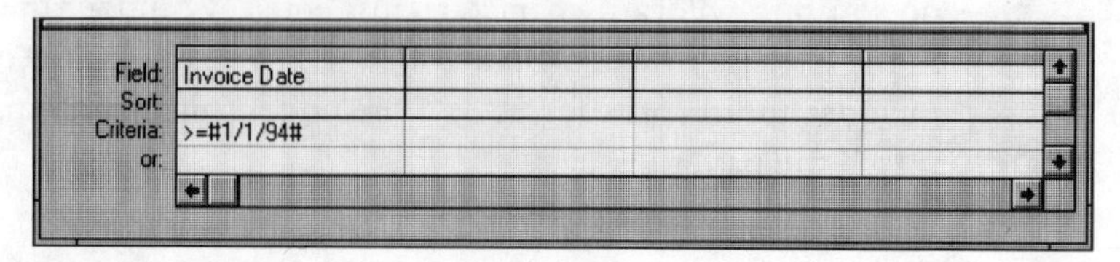

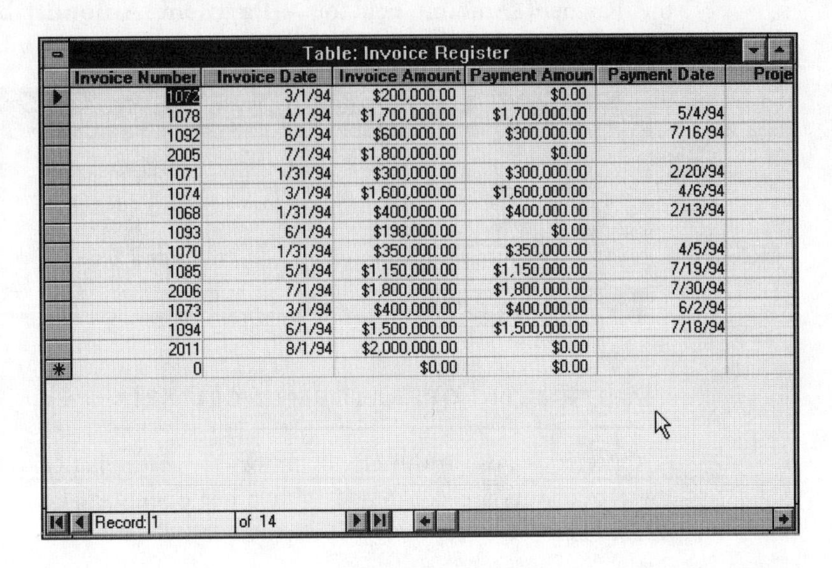

Table: Invoice Register

| Invoice Number | Invoice Date | Invoice Amount | Payment Amoun | Payment Date | Proje |
|---|---|---|---|---|---|
| 1072 | 3/1/94 | $200,000.00 | $0.00 | | |
| 1078 | 4/1/94 | $1,700,000.00 | $1,700,000.00 | 5/4/94 | |
| 1092 | 6/1/94 | $600,000.00 | $300,000.00 | 7/16/94 | |
| 2005 | 7/1/94 | $1,800,000.00 | $0.00 | | |
| 1071 | 1/31/94 | $300,000.00 | $300,000.00 | 2/20/94 | |
| 1074 | 3/1/94 | $1,600,000.00 | $1,600,000.00 | 4/6/94 | |
| 1068 | 1/31/94 | $400,000.00 | $400,000.00 | 2/13/94 | |
| 1093 | 6/1/94 | $198,000.00 | $0.00 | | |
| 1070 | 1/31/94 | $350,000.00 | $350,000.00 | 4/5/94 | |
| 1085 | 5/1/94 | $1,150,000.00 | $1,150,000.00 | 7/19/94 | |
| 2006 | 7/1/94 | $1,800,000.00 | $1,800,000.00 | 7/30/94 | |
| 1073 | 3/1/94 | $400,000.00 | $400,000.00 | 6/2/94 | |
| 1094 | 6/1/94 | $1,500,000.00 | $1,500,000.00 | 7/18/94 | |
| 2011 | 8/1/94 | $2,000,000.00 | $0.00 | | |
| 0 | | $0.00 | $0.00 | | |

Record: 1 of 14

**Figure 6-11** A filtered table using a comparison operator in the criteria

If you need to test whether an entry falls inside or outside of a range, you can combine the comparison and the logical operators (as described later in this chapter) or you can use the Between ... And operator. A record matches criteria containing this operator when the field's value is within the range set by the entries before and after the And. As an example, you can have a criterion of Between 1000000 And 2000000 under the Invoice Amount field in a query based on the Invoice Register table. To create the same criterion with a comparison operator, enter > 1000000 And < 2000000.

## USING FIELD NAMES AS PARTS OF CRITERIA

Sometimes you need criteria that compares the value of one field with the value of another. For example, when looking at the Invoice Register table, you might want to show records in which invoices have not been fully paid. In this case, compare the Invoice Amount and the Payment Amount fields. You can do this using comparison operators, but you need to include one of the field names in the QBE grid when you enter the criterion. To make sure Access understands where each field name begins and ends when you enter criteria, enclose field names with brackets, as in [Invoice Amount]. Access knows to use the field value for the current record in the criteria. For example, to find records for unpaid invoices, you can type a criterion of **<[Invoice Amount]** below the Payment Amount field or **>[Payment Amount]** below the Invoice Amount field. Either criterion provides the same results, which look like this:

Select Query: Query1

| Invoice Number | Invoice Date | Invoice Amount | Payment Amoun | Payment Date | Project Id |
|---|---|---|---|---|---|
| 1072 | 3/1/94 | $200,000.00 | $0.00 | | 4 |
| 1092 | 6/1/94 | $600,000.00 | $300,000.00 | 7/16/94 | 1 |
| 2005 | 7/1/94 | $1,800,000.00 | $0.00 | | 3 |
| 1093 | 6/1/94 | $198,000.00 | $0.00 | | 5 |
| 1056 | 6/30/93 | $500,000.00 | $0.00 | | 8 |
| 2011 | 8/1/94 | $2,000,000.00 | $0.00 | | 2 |
| 0 | | $0.00 | $0.00 | | 0 |

Record: 1 of 6

## ARITHMETIC OPERATORS IN CRITERIA

Criteria can use arithmetic operators for mathematical calculations. Usually these operators are combined with other operators. Here are the arithmetic operators:

| | |
|---|---|
| + | addition |
| – | subtraction |
| * | multiplication |
| \ and / | division (\ when both numbers are integers and / for other cases) |
| ^ | exponentiation |
| mod | calculating the modulus |

Exponentiation raises a number to another power, as in 3 to the fourth power (3*3*3*3, which you would enter as 3^4). The modulus is the remainder after the division of two numbers; for example, when you divide 11 by 5, the result is 2 with a remainder, or modulus, of 1.

An example of an arithmetic operator in a criterion is the query using the Client table in Figure 6-12. This figure shows two copies of the same query, so you can look at the query design and the results at the same time. The criterion is **[Total Invoices]–[Total Payments]>1000000**. The query only lists the client records when the difference between total invoices and total payments is more than one million. When you later look at this query, you will find that Access has created a hidden calculated field that subtracts the total invoices from the total payments and uses the calculated field for the query. You will learn about calculated fields later in this chapter.

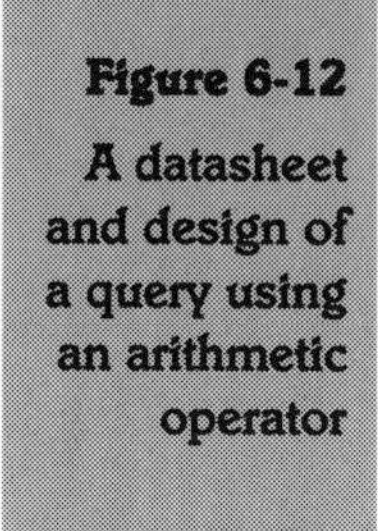

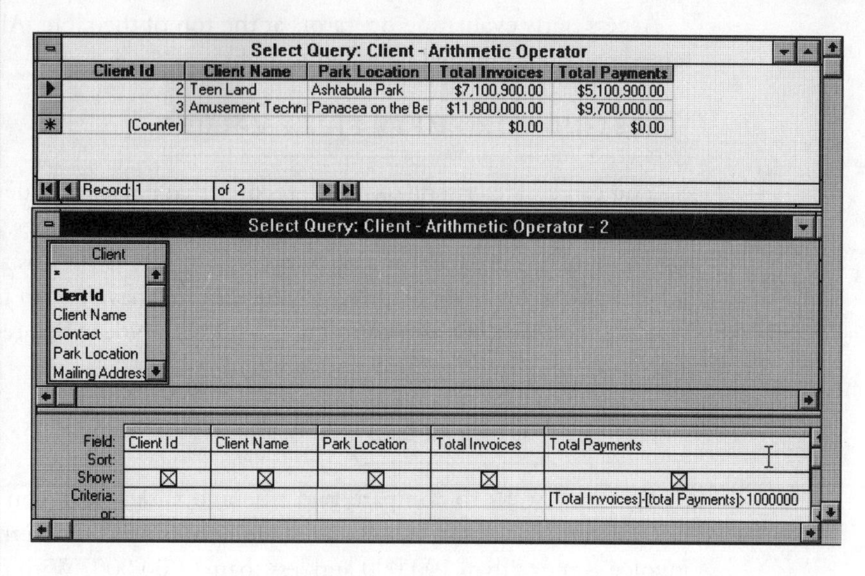


**Figure 6-12** A datasheet and design of a query using an arithmetic operator

## OPERATOR PRECEDENCE

When you have several operators in the same criterion, Access makes decisions about the order in which it evaluates them. Access has a *precedence order* that selects which operators are evaluated before others (see the following table). If you have both a comparison and an arithmetic operator in the criterion, Access performs the arithmetic before the comparison. You can always include parentheses to tell Access to evaluate one part of a criterion before the other. When you have several sets of parentheses, Access works from the inside out.

Access evaluates operators in this order:

| | |
|---|---|
| ( ) | parentheses |
| ^ | for exponentiation |
| – | to indicate negative numbers |
| * and / | for multiplication and division |
| \ | for integer division |
| mod | for the modulus |
| + and – | for addition and subtraction |
| & | for concatenation (described later) |
| And, Eqv, Or, Xor, Not, <, <=, >, >=, =, <>, Like | comparison operators, logical operators and the Like operator |

Access starts evaluating operators at the top of the table. All operators at the same level are evaluated from left to right.

## TESTING FOR EMPTY FIELD VALUES

You can create criteria to match records that have no value for a field. Using Is Null as a criterion finds fields with empty or null values. For example, to check your Client table for any empty values, use Is Null as a criterion for the different fields on separate lines; only records that have one or more empty fields will be listed. You can also combine Is Null with Not so that records only match that criterion when the field does contain a value.

## LOGICAL OPERATORS

You may want to compare two true and false values you have from other calculations. For example, you can have a criterion that determines whether an invoice is more than 100,000 and less than 1,000,000. With this example, you may want records to match the criterion when both conditions are true and not to match the criterion when either or both of the conditions are false. To make this type of evaluation, you use the *logical operators*.

Most of the logical operators compare two true or false results such as the ones created by comparison operators. Only the Not uses a single condition. Access has the following logical operators:

| | |
|---|---|
| And | Both conditions are true |
| Eqv | Conditions are either both true or both false |
| Or | One or both conditions are true |
| Xor | One condition is true, the other false |
| Not | Reverses the result of the condition |

You will use the Not operator most frequently in criteria. Use the Not operator to flip the result of a criterion by putting the Not logical operator at the beginning of a criterion so that records that would otherwise match the criterion no longer do and records that do not match the criterion now match the criterion. For example, changing a criterion from Is Null to Not Is Null or Is Not Null means that the criterion now matches records with an entry for that field instead of matching records that do not have entries for that field.

## USING FUNCTIONS IN CRITERIA

You can use functions to provide ready-made formulas and return information that is not readily available. While Access includes functions that are most often used in forms, reports, macros, and programming, you can use some of the functions in your criteria.

Functions have the format of the function name followed by its arguments, which are within parentheses. The function's arguments are the information you must supply for the function. Which arguments a function uses depends on the function, since various functions need different information. Function arguments are often field names or literals, such as a number, date, or string.

**tip:** *Functions are much easier to enter using the Expression Builder because you do not have to remember which functions are available and what arguments they require.*

An example of when you might use a function as a criterion is when you want to compare a field's date to the current date. For example, you can compare the current date to the dates in the Invoice Date field to see if they are less than 180 days overdue by creating a criterion that looks like this:

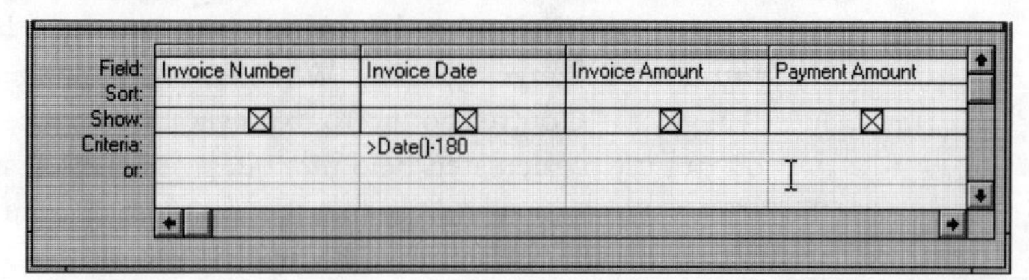


In this example, the Date function returns the current date. This function does not require arguments. The criterion subtracts 180 days from the current date and compares this value to the value of the Invoice Date field. Records with an invoice date that come later than 180 days ago match this criterion.

## Calculated Fields in a Query or Filter

When designing your database in Chapter 2, you learned that you do not want to include fields in a table containing values that can be calculated. Instead, you can create a query that contains calculated fields that are updated every time you use the query and do not occupy data storage space. For example, if you want to calculate the difference between invoices paid and invoices sent, you can create a calculated field in the query that computes this amount for you. This is the calculated field Access created for you when you entered the example arithmetic operators used in criteria earlier in this chapter. In a filter, you can create a calculated field to sort or select records, although you cannot display the results of this field in the table.

To create a calculated field in a query, move to the Field row in the QBE grid where you want to add the calculated field (you may need to insert a column first). Next, type the formula you want calculated for each field. The formula often uses names of other fields, which you can enter by enclosing the field names in brackets. When you move to another cell, the formula changes to include Expr followed by the next unused number and a colon, as in the example Expr1:[Total Invoices]–[Total Payments]. As mentioned earlier, you can replace the Expr# field name with another name.

**tip:** *Remember, you can also use the Expression Builder to create expressions such as this. To start the Expression Builder, select the Build button in the toolbar.*

When you display the datasheet for the query's dynaset containing the calculated field, the calculated field looks just like the others. The difference is that you cannot change the entry. When you try making a new entry, the status line changes to "Control bound to expression colum 'field name'".

You can use a calculated field in a query much the same way you do with the other fields, for example hiding it or using it to organize data. Figure 6-13 shows two copies of the same Invoice Register table query, which has the calculated field renamed to Total Still Due and uses this field to sort the data in descending order. Only the records with amounts still due are displayed because the criterion entered in the criteria row below this calculated field is >0.

## Joining Characters in a Calculated Field

One operator you did not see for criteria but that you might use in a calculated field is the concatenation operator, the ampersand (&). The ampersand joins two entries as if they are one and removes extra spaces at the end of either entry. For example, you can create a calculated field that combines the city, state, and ZIP code. A calculated field that performs this function is [City] & ", " & [State] & "  " & [Zip Code]. The concatenation operator is placed between the two entries you want to combine. The following shows a query's datasheet that uses

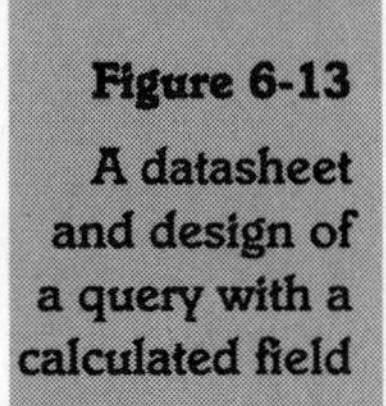

**Figure 6-13**

**A datasheet and design of a query with a calculated field**

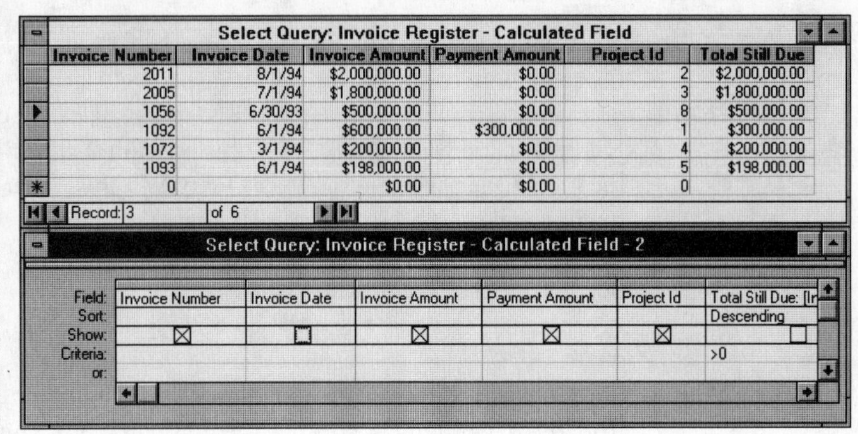

Select Query: Invoice Register - Calculated Field

| Invoice Number | Invoice Date | Invoice Amount | Payment Amount | Project Id | Total Still Due |
|---|---|---|---|---|---|
| 2011 | 8/1/94 | $2,000,000.00 | $0.00 | 2 | $2,000,000.00 |
| 2005 | 7/1/94 | $1,800,000.00 | $0.00 | 3 | $1,800,000.00 |
| 1056 | 6/30/93 | $500,000.00 | $0.00 | 8 | $500,000.00 |
| 1092 | 6/1/94 | $600,000.00 | $300,000.00 | 1 | $300,000.00 |
| 1072 | 3/1/94 | $200,000.00 | $0.00 | 4 | $200,000.00 |
| 1093 | 6/1/94 | $198,000.00 | $0.00 | 5 | $198,000.00 |
| 0 | | $0.00 | $0.00 | 0 | |

Record: 3 of 6

Select Query: Invoice Register - Calculated Field - 2

| | | | | | | |
|---|---|---|---|---|---|---|
| Field: | Invoice Number | Invoice Date | Invoice Amount | Payment Amount | Project Id | Total Still Due: [Ir |
| Sort: | | | | | | Descending |
| Show: | ⊠ | ☐ | ⊠ | ⊠ | ⊠ | ☐ |
| Criteria: | | | | | | >0 |
| or: | | | | | | |

the calculated field created with Second Line: [City] & ", " & [State] & " " & [Zip Code] entered in the Field row:

Select Query: Employee - Combined Address

| First Name | Middle Initial | Last Name | Street Address | Second Line |
|---|---|---|---|---|
| WILLIAM | W | WILD | 111 Cedar Ave. | Cleveland, OH 44123 |
| DAN | D | DANGER | 51 Mentor Ave. | Mentor, OH 44231 |
| RODGER | R | ROLLING | 886 Larch Street | Cleveland, OH 43212 |
| SANDRA | S | SCARY | 1232 Hillside Rd. | Gates Mills, OH 44040 |
| HARRY | H | HIGHER | 321 Wood Ave. | Mayfield, OH 44120 |
| TOMMY | T | THRILL | 213 25th St. | Cleveland, OH 44037 |
| RICHARD | R | ROCK | 45 Eagle Lane | Solon, OH 44019 |
| DONNA | D | DARE | 111 Weaver Ave. | Columbus, OH 43514 |
| JOHNNY | J | JUMP | 78 Fordham Drive | Austinburg, OH 42124 |
| BRENDA | B | BRAVE | 21 Circle Drive | Gates Mills, OH 44040 |

Record: 1 of 10

## Quick Reference

**To Create a New Query** Click the New button at the top of the Database window while displaying queries, click the New Query button on the toolbar while looking at a table or query, or choose New from the File menu and then Query. In Access version 2, you next need to select the New Query button, or select Query Wizards if you plan to create the query using the Query Wizards. If a table or query is not selected when you create the query, select a table or query from the Add Table dialog box and then select Add and Close.

**To Create a Filter** From a table or form, select the Edit Filter/Sort from the Records menu, or click the Edit Filter/Sort button in the toolbar.

**To Add a Field** Double-click the field name in the field list, drag the field name from the field list to the Field row in a column on the QBE grid, or select the field name from the drop-down list box available in the Field row of the QBE grid.

**To Display a Query** Click the Datasheet View button in the toolbar or choose Datasheet from the View menu. You can return to the design by clicking the Design View button in the toolbar or by choosing Query Design from the View menu.

**To Apply or Remove a Filter** Select Apply Filter/Sort from the Records menu, or click the Apply Filter/Sort button in the toolbar, closing the Filter window and displaying the table with the filter applied. To remove the filter, select Show All Records from the Records menu or click the Show All Records button in the toolbar.

## Quick Reference

**To Print a Query** Choose Print from the File menu and select OK. You have all the same printing options available for printing tables.

**To Rename a Field in a Query** Type the name you want to appear on the datasheet and a colon before the field name you are renaming in the Field row of the QBE grid. To rename a calculated field, replace the existing field name in front of the colon with a different field name.

**To Sort Records** Select between Ascending and Descending in the Sort row of the QBE grid below the field you want to use to sort. The fields for sorting must be in the order you want them sorted.

**To Hide Fields in a Query** Clear the check box below the field you want to hide in the Show row of the QBE grid.

**To Add Criteria** Move to one of the criteria rows below the field you want to use as the basis for deciding whether a record is included in the dynaset. Type the criteria you want tested for each record.

**To Add a Calculate Field to a Query** Move to an empty cell in the Field row where you want the calculated field and type the name for the field, a colon, and the calculation whose values you want to appear as the calculated field. If you omit the field name and colon, Access supplies the default field name. Other field names you include in the calculation must be enclosed in brackets ([]).

# Chapter 7

Using Multiple Tables in a Query

Editing a Query

Changing a Query Through Properties

Adding Summary Calculations to a Query

Parameter Queries

Crosstab Queries

Creating Action Queries

# Creating Sophisticated Queries for Selections, Actions, and Parameters

YOU can do much more with queries than just selecting data, as you did in Chapter 6. You can combine data from several tables, treating the combined data as a single record. You can change how a query works or appears by setting properties for the query or for fields in the query. You can add summary calculations to a query, in order to group or summarize data.

You can also create several different types of queries that work with the data in your source table differently than select queries. You can create parameter queries that are dynamic, meaning that they change how records are selected every time you use them. Access has a special crosstab query that creates a compact summary of data selected by a query. Finally, you can create action queries that perform actions on the data in the query's underlying tables, such as deleting records, adding records, creating a table, and updating values.

## Using Multiple Tables in a Query

One of the advantages of using a query instead of just tables is that you can include data from more than one table in a query. With more than one table in a query, you can show how the data in one table relates to the data in another. You can also use a query as the data source in another query. The steps for using tables or queries are the same, since the Add Table dialog box you have already used to add tables to a query displays both tables and queries. When you use multiple tables in a query, you must add the additional tables to the query and join the tables to show how the records in the different tables are related. You use multiple tables in a query design just as you use a single table, although Access has a few special options that change which of the records from the tables are displayed.

When you use multiple tables in a query, you create relationships called *joins*. You can create either a one-to-one relationship or a one-to-many relationship between the tables. In a one-to-one relationship, one record from one table combines with one record from the second table to create a single record in the query. In a one-to-many relationship, one record from table one combines with several records from the second table to create as many records in the query as there are records from the second table. These types of relationships should seem familiar, since you learned about establishing relationships between tables in Chapter 3.

When creating queries that use multiple tables, you may find it easier to work with the query when the table names are displayed in the QBE grid. To display the table names, choose Table Names from the View menu. This adds a Table row to the QBE grid, as shown in Figure 7-1. You can remove this row by selecting the command again. The Table row only appears when the Table Names command in the View menu has a check mark by it.

The table name never appears as part of the query's datasheet. When a table is selected in the Table row, the Field row's drop-down list box only contains the field names from that table.

## Adding Tables

To use additional tables in a query, you need to add the tables to the query in Design view. You can add these tables in one of two ways. When you first create a query and Access is displaying the Add Table dialog box, you can add more than one table either by double-clicking each one or by selecting them all and clicking the Add button. You can add all the tables you want to use in the query at this point.

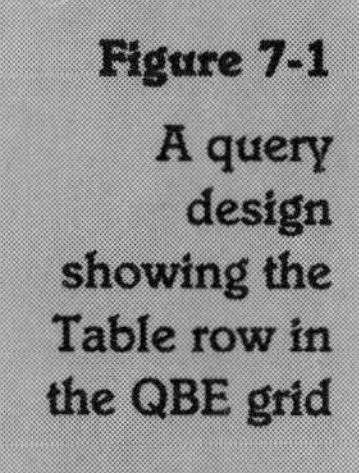

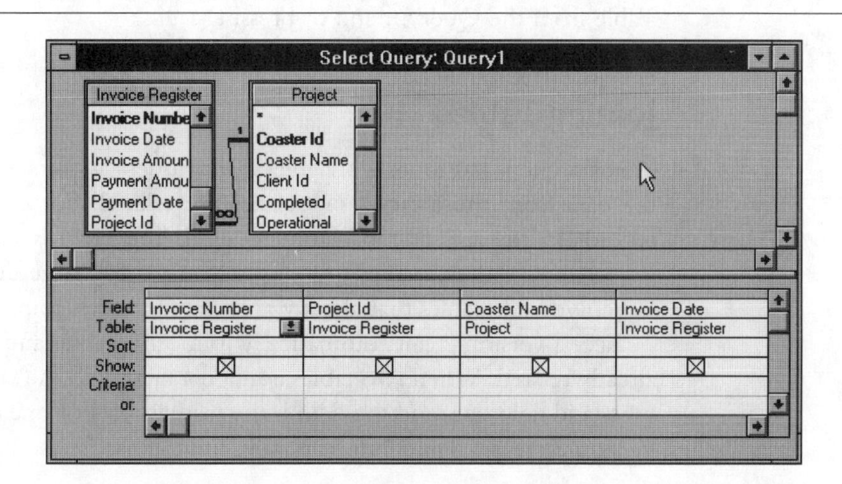


**Figure 7-1** A query design showing the Table row in the QBE grid

The other way to add tables to the query is by choosing Add Table from the Query menu or by clicking the Add Table button in the toolbar, shown in the following illustration. This opens the same Add Table dialog box you see when you first create a query, which you can use in the same way to add tables to the current query.

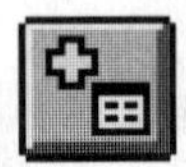

A shortcut for adding tables or queries is available when the Database window and the Query window are both visible. You can select the table or query you want to add from the Database window and then drag it to the top half of the Query window. Notice that the pointer changes to the shape of a table or query icon while you are dragging. When you release the mouse, Access adds a field list for that table or query.

No matter which method you use, when you add tables to a query, you are adding field lists to the Query window in Design view. If you have created relationships between tables, you will see a line between the field lists connecting the fields that contain common data, as shown in Figure 7-1. This line looks just like the one you see in the Relationships window in Access version 2.

## Deleting Tables

If you accidentally add tables you do not want to the Query window, you can remove them. You may also need to remove tables and queries from a query design as you change the information you want in the query. Remove tables by clicking the field list of the table you want to remove and choosing Remove Table from the Query menu or pressing DEL.

## Joining Tables

When a query has more than one table or query, you need to tell Access how the data from those tables or queries are related. For example, how do the records in the Client table connect with the records in the Project table? Fortunately, Access makes this easy if you already have defined relationships. When you add tables that already are related, Access joins the tables for you.

Access version 2 can automatically join other tables and queries that are not already related. When two tables contain a field with the same field name, data type, and field size, and the field is the primary key of one of the tables, Access version 2 creates a join automatically, using these fields.

Joined tables are marked by lines that connect the field from one table with a field in another table that contains the same value. Figure 7-2 shows an example of this type of line, in this case connecting the Employee and Employee Time Log tables. If one of the sources of data for a query is another query, or if you do not have relationships between the tables defined, you must join the tables or queries yourself unless Access version 2 does it for you on the basis of field name, data type, and field size.

To join tables and queries, first check that the fields you will use to join the tables or queries appear in the field lists. Then select the field from one of the field lists and drag it to the field you want to link with in the other field list. For example, in Figure 7-2, you would drag Employee Id from the Employee table's field list to the Employee Id field in the Employee Time Log table's field list.

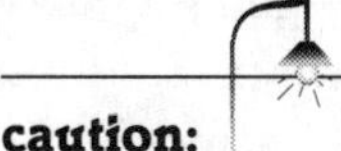

**caution:** *When you join tables, make sure that both fields used in the join are the same type, with the same field size. The only exception is if you are using a Counter field, in which case you can join it to a Long Integer size Number field.*

If you do not join tables but add more than one table to the query, Access joins every record in one table or query with every record in the other. For example, if you include the Project and Client tables in a query and the tables are not joined, the query will have 72 records because every one of the nine

**Figure 7-2** **A query design combining Employee and Employee Time Log tables**

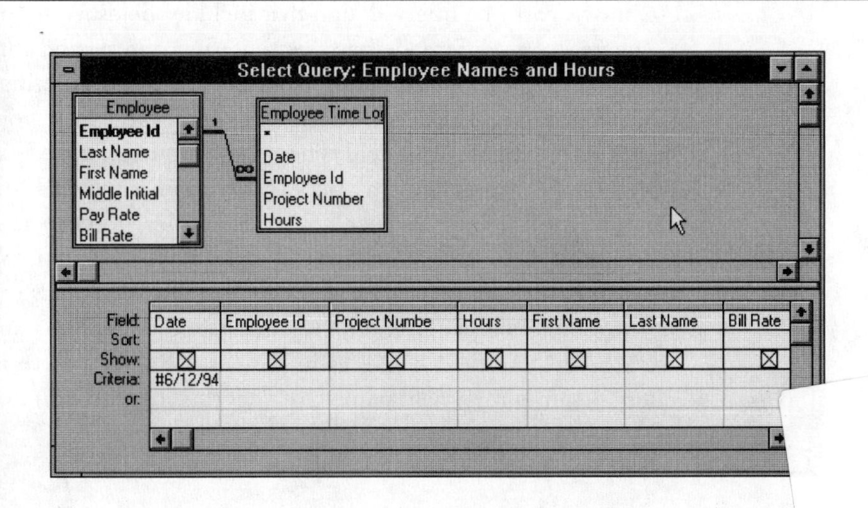

records in the Project table matches up with every one of the eight records in the Client table. When you do not join tables on larger queries, the dynaset will be huge and slow. Also, the records displayed in the dynaset are probably meaningless, because there is no reason for the data to be displaying together.

If you need to delete joins—for example, when you drag one field on top of the wrong field in another table or query—click the join line. When the join line is selected, it appears heavier. To delete the selected join, press DEL. Adding and deleting joins only affects the query—not the database. If you create a join between tables in a query, only the query uses that join; every time you want a join between the tables you must re-create it.

## Using Multiple Tables in a Query

Designing a query using several tables and queries is just like designing a query that uses a single table or query. Add fields by dragging the field names from the different field lists to the QBE grid or by selecting the field names in the drop-down list box in the Field row of the QBE grid.

You can intermingle the fields from each of the tables and queries. The drop-down list box in the Field row contains all of the fields from all of the tables and queries in the order that the tables or queries are displayed in the field lists. Another way to make sure that the field from the correct table is used is to display the table names in the QBE grid and select the correct table before selecting the field. If you display the table or query names in the QBE grid with the Table Names command in the View menu, the drop-down list box in the Fields row only contains the fields of the table selected in the Table row. Figure 7-2 shows part of a query design that includes fields from both tables.

There is one difference between entering criteria and calculated fields in a query based on more than one table or query and entering them in a query based on only one table or query; with multiple tables, you must tell Access which table contains the field when the same field name is used in more than one table. For example, in a query that combines the data from the Employee, Employee Time Log, Project, and Client tables, you can add a calculated field that combines the city, state, and ZIP code from the Client table. To tell Access to use the fields from the Client table rather than the fields with the same name in the Employee table, enter the table name in brackets and an exclamation mark before the field name, as in [Client Id]![City]. Here is an example of a query design with a field name that uses this method of indicating the table:

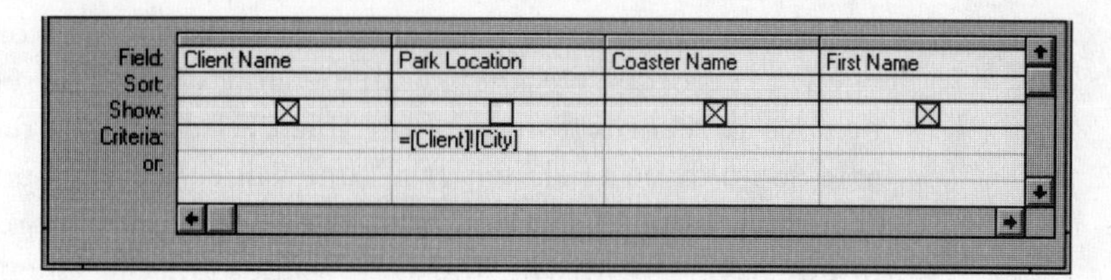


In this query design, the query selects only the records for clients where their city is the same as the park location. [Client]![City] describes which table provides the City field used for the comparison. You also have to include a query name if the data comes from a query and the field name is used by another of the tables or queries you are using to build this query.

## Editing the Join

Access has three ways to create records for the query based on the join established between the tables. The default is for the query to only include records from both tables that share a common value in the field used to create the join. This means in a query that combines the Client and Project tables, the query only uses data from the Client table that is joined to a record in the Project table and only uses data from the Project table that is joined to a record in the Client table. This type of join is often called an *equi-join.*

The second type of join includes all records from the first table, whether or not they match records in the second table. This is called a *left outer join.* Using a left outer join means that the query can include all the Client records, whether or not any of them match records in the Project table.

The third option is for the query to include all the records in the second table (the Project table), whether or not they match records in the first table (the Client table). This is a *right outer join.*

To change the type of join, double-click the line joining the two tables. Access displays the Join Properties dialog box shown here:

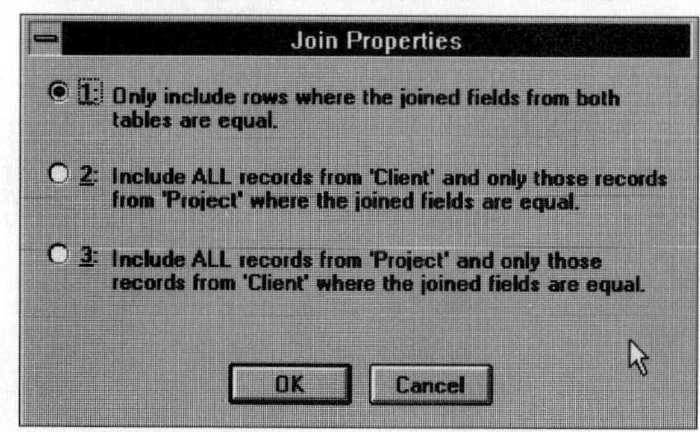

The top option button, the default, only includes records from both tables when the records have a field with the same value. The second option button includes all records from the first table even when the records in the second table do not have a field with the same value. The last option button includes all records from the second table even when the records for the first table do not have a field with the same value. For the Client and Project table example, if you select the middle option button, the query's results will include the eight Client records although no roller coasters have been built yet for the eighth customer.

## Editing a Query

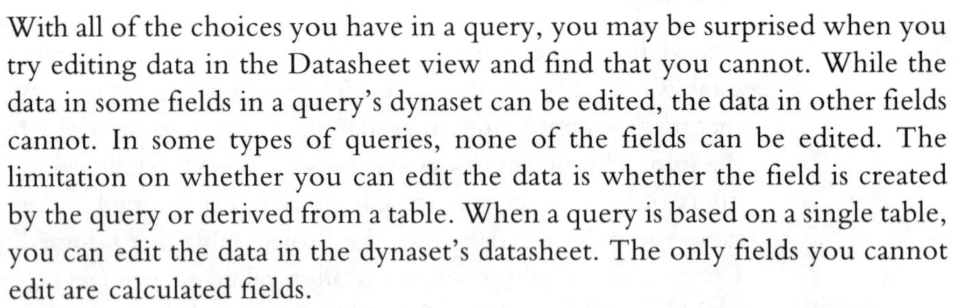

With all of the choices you have in a query, you may be surprised when you try editing data in the Datasheet view and find that you cannot. While the data in some fields in a query's dynaset can be edited, the data in other fields cannot. In some types of queries, none of the fields can be edited. The limitation on whether you can edit the data is whether the field is created by the query or derived from a table. When a query is based on a single table, you can edit the data in the dynaset's datasheet. The only fields you cannot edit are calculated fields.

Access versions 1 and 2 differ as to which fields can be edited in a query that uses multiple tables. In Access version 2, when the tables in the query have a one-to-one join you can edit all fields. In Access version 1, however, when the tables in the query have a one-to-one join, you can edit all of the fields except the field that creates the join because you might violate referential integrity if you changed the join field for the tables. For example, in Access version 1, if you had another table containing personal information about your client's contact people that was joined to the Client table by the Contact field, you could edit any other field in the query's datasheet except the Contact field. Since Access version 2 lets you edit the joined field, you will find that the value you enter in this field in the query appears in both tables that use that field.

When a query uses multiple tables with one-to-many relationships, which fields you can edit depends on which version of Access you are using. In Access version 1, you can edit all of the fields from the table on the many side of the join except for the field that creates the link to the other table. You will be unable to edit any fields from the table on the one side of the join. In Access version 2, however, you can edit all of the fields, including the one used to create the join.

When you edit the field used to join the records in an Access version 2 query, how the field is updated in both tables depends on the relationship for the link. When you join the underlying tables with the Relationships command in the Edit menu, if the Cascade Update Related Fields check box is selected, changing a joined field in a query using more than one table changes the joined field value in both of the tables. If this check box is not selected, or if you have created the join within the query, you may not be able to edit the field used to join the records.

**tip:** *Remember that you cannot edit Counter fields, whether or not they are the field used to create the join.*

The only exception to this rule in Access version 1 is when the query does not display any fields from the many side of the join. When this is true, you can edit the fields from the one side of the join. An example of this is when you use fields from the Invoice Register table to select which records from the Project table appear in the query's dynaset, and none of the fields from the Invoice Register table appear in the dynaset. In this example, you can edit all of the fields, including the field that links the two tables. In Chapters 8 and 13, you will learn to create forms that contain more than one query. Using a main/subform form, which you will also learn about in those chapters, you can edit the data from both queries.

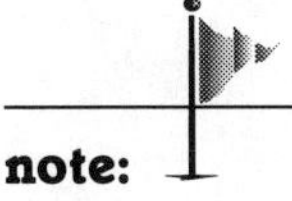

**note:** *You will learn about some advanced query features later in this chapter; when a query contains these features—which include displaying only unique values, including a Total row in the query design, and being a crosstab query—none of the data in the query can be edited.*

When a query is based on another query, the limitations created by the current query are added to the previous query. If the data from a previous query can be edited, you may still be able to edit the data when you use the query in another query. Any restrictions that the previous query places on editing the data in the dynaset will also apply to the current query.

## Changing a Query Through Properties

A query has several properties that you can modify to change the data presented. These changes include only selecting unique records and selecting which fields appear in a field list when you use a query as the basis for another object. These changes are made by displaying the query's properties. You can display these properties by choosing Properties from the View menu (Query Properties in Access version 1) or by clicking the Properties button in the toolbar, which looks like this:

**tip:** *In Access version 2, you can also change the properties of fields in the query, or those of field lists, by displaying the property sheet and then clicking on a field or a field list.*

The query properties you set apply only to the current query, not to any other tables or queries in the database. Access version 2 offers an expanded selection of query properties. The property sheet for a query in Access version 2 looks like this:

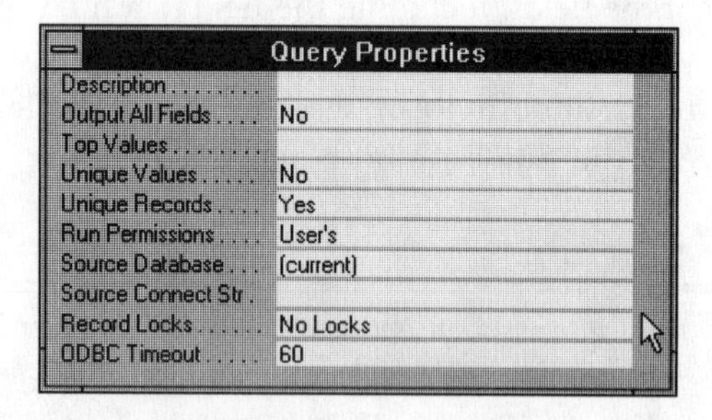


Access version 1 only offers three query properties in the Query Properties dialog box, as shown here:

Later, when you create other types of queries, the dialog box in Access version 1 will include additional properties. These match several of the properties shown previously in the Access version 2 property sheet. These additional properties are described with the types of queries that use the properties.

The Run Permissions property (Run With Owner's Permission in Access version 1) is set automatically, depending on whether the underlying tables need permission from the owner or the user to be used. This property is used with multiuser applications such as networks when you go through the process of assigning ownership to the parts of a database. You will learn how to do this in Chapter 20.

## Displaying Unique Records

When you display only some of the fields available in a query, some of the records displayed in the Datasheet view of the query may look identical. For example, if you are displaying the Bill Rate and Department fields from the Employee table, you will see four records that contain 10 for the Bill Rate field and Construction for the Department field, since all of the employees in the Construction department have the same values for these two fields. Rather than displaying every record, you may want to show only unique combinations of values.

You can limit your display to unique combinations by setting the Unique Values property to Yes in Access version 2 or by selecting the Unique Values Only check box in Access version 1. When this property is set, only the records with unique displays appear. When the property is not set, all records that match the criteria appear. Uniqueness is determined using only the fields that you include in the QBE grid. For example, you can create a query that shows a table of the unique combinations of the Bill Rate and Department fields for the Employee table records, which looks like this:

Select Query: Query1

| Bill Rate | Department |
|---|---|
| $10.00 | Construction |
| $50.00 | Design |
| $50.00 | Testing |
| $55.00 | Design |
| $55.00 | Testing |
| $70.00 | Design |
| $75.00 | Design |

Record: 1 of 7

The dynaset only shows the unique combinations of the Bill Rate and Department fields in the table. Also, notice that you do not have an extra line at the bottom of the data. The data in the datasheet is read-only, so you cannot edit the data or add new records. If you want to limit which records are included, simply include criteria in the QBE grid. You also can clear the Show check box for fields that you add to the QBE grid for the criteria, which means that their field values do not appear in the query's dynaset and therefore they are not considered when determining which records are unique. When a query displays only unique values, every field in the query's QBE grid must either select the fields that appear in the query or select the records that are in the query.

**tip:** *You can use uniqueness to create queries that list the unique values of a field. Chapter 10 shows you how to use a query like this for a form to provide the selections that appear in the list box.*

Access version 2 also offers another property called Unique Records, which is related to the Unique Values property but is not the same. The Unique Values property keeps you from displaying more than one record in a query dynaset that appears to be identical. However, when the Unique Values property checks to see if two records are the same, it only checks the contents of the displayed fields, not hidden fields that select the records to display. The Unique Records property checks the entire record created in the query, including all of the fields used for selecting. Therefore, when the Unique Records property is set to Yes, you may display two records that appear to be the same but are not, because a hidden field is different in those two records. The Unique Records property is set to Yes by default, while the Unique Values property is set to No by default. You cannot set these two properties to Yes at the same time, though you can set them both to No. The Unique Records property only affects a query when the query uses fields from more than one table and at least one field is hidden.

## Displaying All Query Fields

When you use a query as the basis for another object, the query only contains the fields that appear as part of the query's dynaset in Datasheet View. At this point, you will use queries only to create other queries, but in Chapters 8 and 9 you will learn about forms and reports that can use queries as the source of the data they present.

When you add a query to another query's design, the field list in Access version 2 only includes the fields that appear in the query's QBE grid with the Show check box selected. In Access version 1, all of the fields in the QBE grid are displayed, whether or not the Show check box is selected. However, you also can display all of the fields from the tables or queries that the query uses as the source of its data. Show all of these fields by setting the Output All fields property in Access version 2 to Yes or by clearing the Restrict Available Fields check box in the Query Properties dialog box in Access version 1.

**tip:** *If you set the Output All Fields property to Yes and then look at the Datasheet view for the query, you will find that all of the fields in the tables used to create the query are displayed, not just those in the QBE grid.*

For example, if you use the query shown in Figure 7-3 as the basis for another query with the Output All Fields property set to No or the Restrict Available Fields check box selected, the field list includes only the Coaster Name, Features, Client Name, and Park Desc fields. If the Output All fields property is set to Yes or the Restrict Available Fields check box is cleared, when you use the query as the basis for another query, the field list includes the 17 fields from the Project table and the 14 fields from the Client table. As this example indicates, changing this property for a query affects the objects that subsequently use the query. Changing this property does not change the fields included in the field lists of the current query.

## Limiting the Records Shown

Access version 2 offers a new query property, Top Values, that lets you control how many records appear in the dynaset. For example, you could use the Top

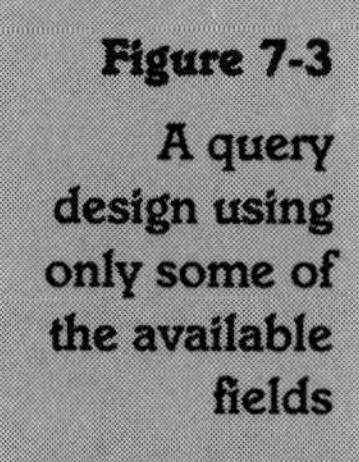

**Figure 7-3**
**A query design using only some of the available fields**

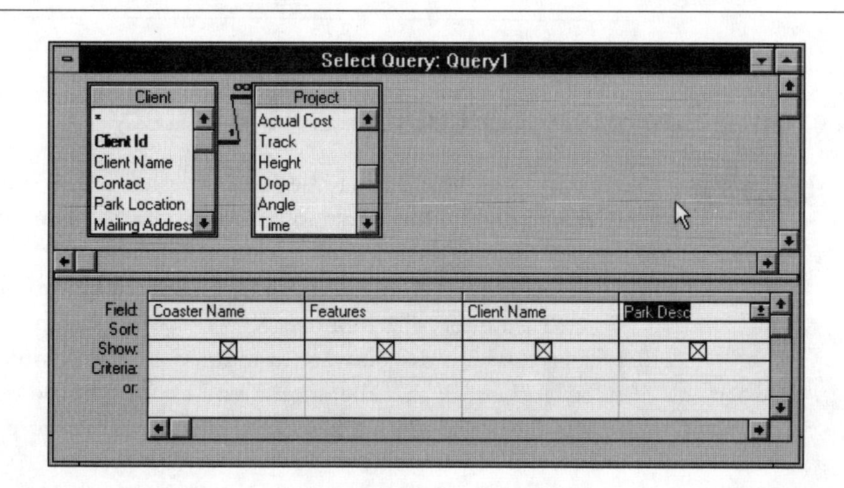

Values query property to create a query that returns your ten best or worst salespeople.

When you use the Top Values property, you must enter a number or percentage. A number tells Access the minimum number of entries you want from the top of the dynaset. A percentage tells Access the percentage of values from the top you want to see. For example, typing **5** displays at least five entries starting from the top and typing **5%** displays at least 5 percent of all entries, starting with the ones at the top of the dynaset. You will set the entry in the Sort row to select how you want to order the records. The sorted order of the dynaset records selects which records the Top Values property causes the query to display. Access limits the dynaset to the first records in the sorted field, using the number or percentage you entered in the Top Values property. For example, you could create a query as shown in Figure 7-4. This query's dynaset will display the five employees with the highest billing rates. Sometimes this type of query will return more records than you expect. For example, if the query in Figure 7-4 was set to only show the top pay rate, when you look at the query's dynaset, you will see two records. When the last record to be selected can be more than one record because several records have the same value, the dynaset shows all of them. As an example, suppose you create a query to display the top five records, but according to the current sorting order there are four records that could be the fifth record. Access will show eight records—the first four records and the four that tie as the fifth record.

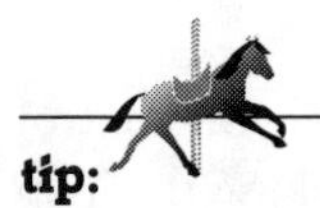

**tip:** *Set the Sort field to Descending when you want the largest values and to Ascending when you want the smallest values.*

## Adding Summary Calculations to a Query

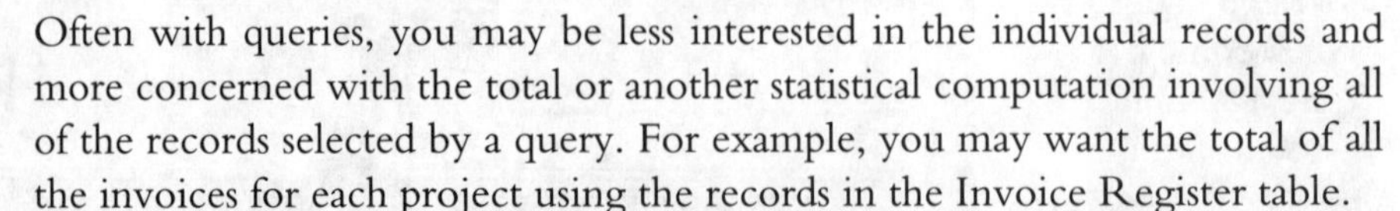

Often with queries, you may be less interested in the individual records and more concerned with the total or another statistical computation involving all of the records selected by a query. For example, you may want the total of all the invoices for each project using the records in the Invoice Register table.

To create a query that summarizes its records, start by creating a *select query* that selects the records you want to summarize, then switch to Datasheet view. This lets you check that the criteria you entered in the query select only the records you want to summarize. Once the criteria are correct, remove the fields

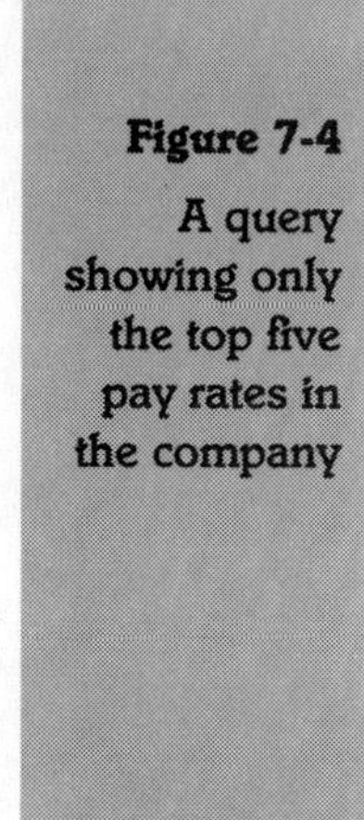

**Figure 7-4** A query showing only the top five pay rates in the company

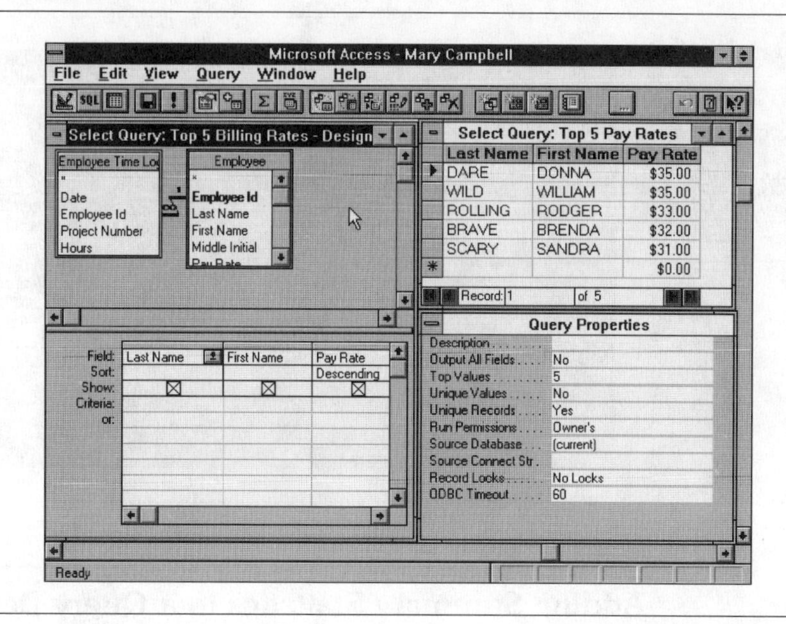


that will not be included in the summary statistics. The fields that remain are those you need to select records, to summarize, and to use in grouping the records. When only these fields remain, add the summary calculations to the query's design.

Figure 7-5 shows a query that has had these steps applied. Originally, the query included all of the records and fields in the Invoice Register table. Then the criterion >=1/1/94 was added in the Invoice Date column. The datasheet was displayed and only the invoices for 1994 appeared. Next, the Invoice Number and Payment Date fields were removed from the QBE grid. The remaining fields are the ones used to summarize and select the data. The Invoice Amount and Payment Amount fields will be totaled, the Invoice Date will be used for criteria, and the Project Id field will be used to group the records to be summed by their project number, as described in the next section.

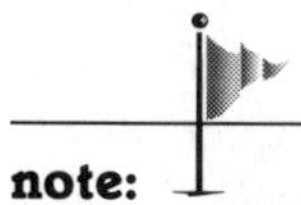

**note:** *Remember that when you tab out of a criteria field that contains a date, Access automatically adds the #s before and after the date. These #s are required for Access to understand the date, but you won't ever have to bother entering them.*

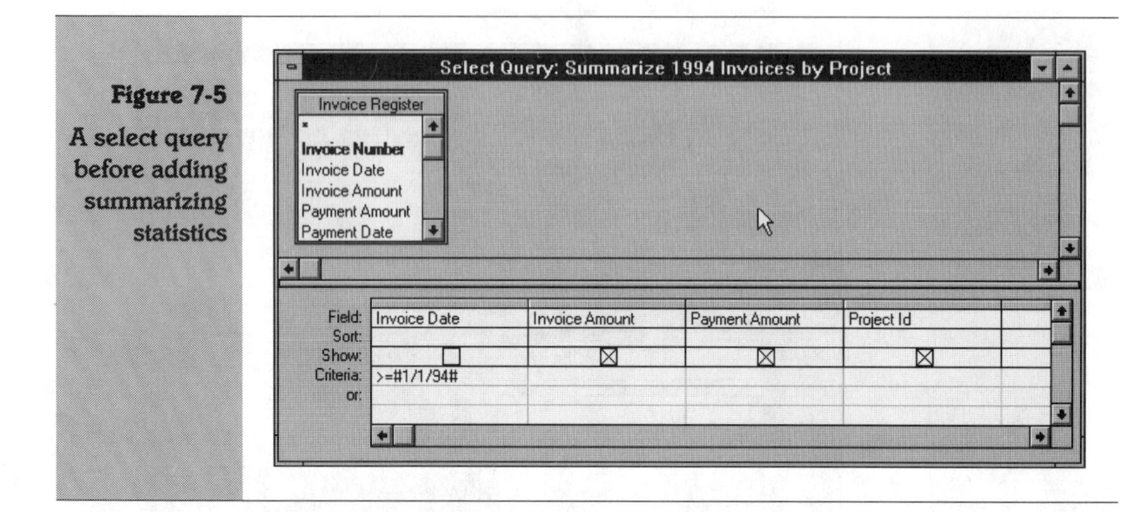


**Figure 7-5** A select query before adding summarizing statistics

## Adding Summary Statistics to a Query Design

After you add the criteria that select the records you want, add the summary statistics to the query by adding a Total row to the QBE grid. To add this row, choose Totals from the View menu or, from the toolbar, click the Totals button, which looks like this:

This command adds a Total row, as shown here:

| Field: | Invoice Date | Invoice Amount | Payment Amount | Project Id |
|---|---|---|---|---|
| Total: | Group By | Group By | Group By | Group By |
| Sort: | | | | |
| Show: | ☐ | ☒ | ☒ | ☒ |
| Criteria: | >=#1/1/94# | | | |
| or: | | | | |

The Group By entries in this row can be replaced with other choices that summarize and select fields, once the Total row is added. When the query design contains criteria like the >=#1/1/94# below Invoice Date, the Total row needs to change to tell Access to use this field's criterion but not to summarize this field. Do this by changing Group By to Where in this column. Since you do not want to summarize the data in this field, clear the Show check box. The criterion is still part of the query, but you will not see its field in the datasheet. You should also change the entries in the Total row for fields that you want to summarize. For these fields, replace Group By with one of these operators:

| **Operator** | **Effect** |
|---|---|
| Sum | Adds the values of that field |
| Avg | Averages the values of that field |
| Min | Returns the smallest of the values in that field |
| Max | Returns the largest of the values in that field |
| Count | Counts the number of records for that field |
| StDev | Calculates the standard deviation of the values in that field |
| Var | Calculates the variance of the values in that field |
| First | Returns the first of the values in that field |
| Last | Returns the last of the values in that field |
| Expression | Calculates a formula's value that is entered like a calculated field in the Field row |

For the query in Figure 7-5, you replace the Group By entries with Sum for the Invoice Amount and Payment Amount fields.

Leave Group By in the Total row for the fields you want to use to divide the data into groups that are summarized by the other fields. For the query in Figure 7-6, which has the Total row completed, the Project Id field retains Group By in the Total row. When you display this query's dynaset, the records that match the query are divided into groups according to the Project Id field values and then summarized.

Once you have made all of the changes you want to the Total row in the QBE grid, you are ready to display the query's dynaset. Switch to the Datasheet view just as you have for other queries. Figure 7-7 shows the dynaset that the query in Figure 7-6 creates. The dynaset contains the records selected by the criteria entered in columns with Where in the Total row. Access divides these records into groups according to the field values of the columns that have Group By in the Total row. For all of the records in each group, Access calculates the summary statistic for the columns in the query that have a summary statistic in its Total row. For the dynaset shown in Figure 7-7, this means that the invoice records with dates on or after 1/1/94 are divided into groups according to project numbers. For each group of recent invoices for a project, Access totals the Invoice Amount and the Payment Amount fields. Also, notice that this datasheet does not have a row at the bottom to add new data. The dynaset data cannot be changed.

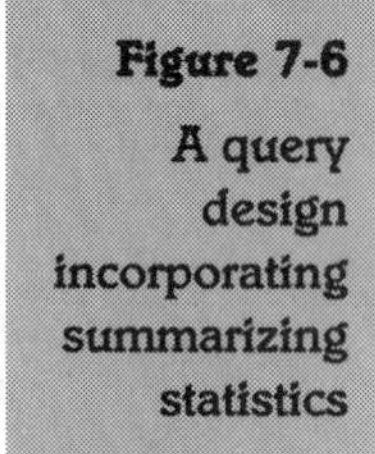

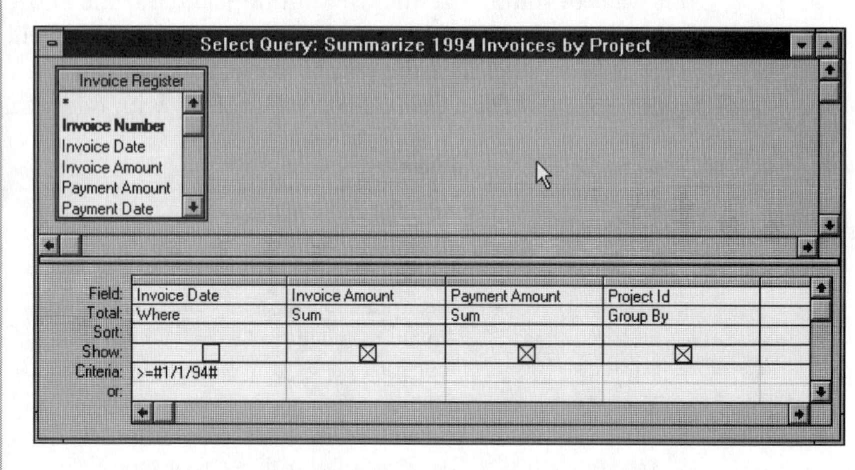


**Figure 7-6** A query design incorporating summarizing statistics

**caution:** *Do not use an asterisk (*) in the Field row of the QBE grid for a query that will use a Total row.*

**tip:** *Make sure the Total row is still visible when you save the query so that all of the settings made in the Total row are saved as part of the query design.*

## USING MORE THAN ONE FIELD FOR GROUPING RECORDS

The query shown in Figures 7-6 and 7-7 groups the records according to the values of only one field. You also can use more than one field's values to group the records. For example, suppose instead of just looking at the total invoices and paid amounts for the current year, you wanted to see the total invoices and paid amounts for each of the projects for each year. Calculate the

Select Query: Summarize 1994 Invoices by Project

| SumOfInvoice Amount | SumOfPayment Amount | Project Id |
|---|---|---|
| $2,300,000.00 | $2,000,000.00 | 1 |
| $3,900,000.00 | $1,900,000.00 | 2 |
| $1,800,000.00 | $0.00 | 3 |
| $2,500,000.00 | $2,300,000.00 | 4 |
| $198,000.00 | $0.00 | 5 |
| $1,500,000.00 | $1,500,000.00 | 6 |
| $1,800,000.00 | $1,800,000.00 | 7 |

Record: 1 of 7

**Figure 7-7** A query datasheet including summarizing statistics (dynaset for the query design in Figure 7-6)

year by creating a calculated field using the Year function, which returns the year from a date. This calculated field can be entered as **Invoice Year:Year(Invoice Date)** in the Field row of the query. Now you can remove the Invoice Date field and its criterion from the query. The new calculated field also uses Group By in the Total row of the query shown here:

| | | | | |
|---|---|---|---|---|
| Field: | Project Id | Invoice Year: Year([ | Invoice Amount | Payment Amount |
| Total: | Group By | Group By | Sum | Sum |
| Sort: | | | | |
| Show: | ☒ | ☒ | ☒ | ☒ |
| Criteria: | | | | |
| or: | | | | |

When you display this query's dynaset, Access divides the records according to the values of two fields. Access calculates the summary statistics of records for each unique combination of field values for the two fields. The result of the query you just saw is shown in Figure 7-8. In this query, all of the table's records are divided into groups since the query does not include criteria to exclude records. Each group includes the records for a project for a particular year. Several of the projects have several rows in Figure 7-8 so that each year of the projects' billing is totaled.

When you group by fields, Access divides the records according to the unique combination of field values for the fields that contain Group By in the Total row. When you group by only one field, the groups are divided solely by that field's values. When you group by two groups, the groups are divided by the unique combination of values in the two fields. If you group by more than two

**Figure 7-8** Grouping by two fields with summarizing statistics

Select Query: Summarize Invoices by Project and by Year

| Project Id | Invoice Year | SumOfInvoice Amount | SumOfPayment Amount |
|---|---|---|---|
| 1 | 1993 | $1,700,000.00 | $1,700,000.00 |
| 1 | 1994 | $2,300,000.00 | $2,000,000.00 |
| 2 | 1994 | $3,900,000.00 | $1,900,000.00 |
| 3 | 1992 | $250,000.00 | $250,000.00 |
| 3 | 1993 | $5,750,000.00 | $5,750,000.00 |
| 3 | 1994 | $1,800,000.00 | $0.00 |
| 4 | 1994 | $2,500,000.00 | $2,300,000.00 |
| 5 | 1994 | $198,000.00 | $0.00 |
| 6 | 1994 | $1,500,000.00 | $1,500,000.00 |
| 7 | 1993 | $1,400,000.00 | $1,400,000.00 |
| 7 | 1994 | $1,800,000.00 | $1,800,000.00 |
| 8 | 1992 | $2,600,000.00 | $2,600,000.00 |
| 8 | 1993 | $500,000.00 | $0.00 |
| 9 | 1991 | $3,000,000.00 | $3,000,000.00 |
| 9 | 1992 | $200,900.00 | $200,900.00 |

Record: 1 of 15

fields, the records are grouped by as many unique combinations of field entries as exist among the fields that have Group By in the Total row.

**tip:** *You can summarize calculated fields as well as the fields that come from the table or query the current query uses.*

## OTHER TYPES OF CRITERIA IN A SUMMARY SELECT QUERY

Besides the criteria you add to columns when you change Group By in the Total row to Where, you can add criteria in other locations. You also may want to add criteria in two other locations: to columns that contain Group By in the Total row and to columns that contain summary statistics in the Total row.

If you add a criterion to a field that has Group By in the Total row, only the groups of records that match the criterion are displayed. For example, if you put 2 and 7 in two criteria rows below the Project Id field in the query shown in Figure 7-5, the query's dynaset only includes the groups of records for projects 2 and 7. Therefore, you only have two lines in the query datasheet. The criteria in a Group By column selects which of the groups that the query creates are included in the dynaset.

You also can put the criteria in the columns that summarize the values. These are all of the columns that do not use Group By or Where in the Total row. In these cases, the criteria is applied to the results the dynaset would otherwise show. As an example, suppose you entered **>500000** in the Criteria row below Invoice Amount in the query design shown in Figure 7-7. When you display the dynaset, the datasheet looks like this:

Select Query: Summarize 1994 Invoices by Project

| SumOfInvoice Amount | SumOfPayment Amount | Project Id |
|---|---|---|
| $2,300,000.00 | $2,000,000.00 | 1 |
| $3,900,000.00 | $1,900,000.00 | 2 |
| $1,800,000.00 | $0.00 | 3 |
| $2,500,000.00 | $2,300,000.00 | 4 |
| $1,500,000.00 | $1,500,000.00 | 6 |
| $1,800,000.00 | $1,800,000.00 | 7 |

Record: 1 of 6

Notice how the numbers are almost the same as the ones you saw in Figure 7-7; the only difference is that the row for project 5 is missing. When you look at the dynaset in Figure 7-7, you can see that the total Invoice Amount for project 5 is less than $500,000. Since you have added >500000 in the Criteria row, the dynaset excludes the records whose summary statistics do not match this criterion.

**tip:** *If you want to use summary statistics on the output of a query that shows unique records, create a query that shows the unique records. Then use the query you have just created as the basis for the query to which you add the summary statistics.*

## Parameter Queries

The queries you created in Chapter 6 always use the same entries in the criteria. Here you will see how to create *parameter queries* that let you change the criteria added to a QBE grid every time you use a query. In a parameter query, you are prompted for the criteria. The query uses the criteria you enter just as if you entered those criteria into different parts of the query's QBE grid.

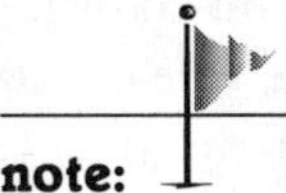

**note:** *There is actually no separate class of queries called parameter queries; you are actually adding parameters to some other type of query. However, since queries that use parameters work so differently from other queries, they are commonly referred to as parameter queries.*

To create a parameter query, first create a select query as if you do not intend it to be a parameter query. You may want to enter sample criteria where you will eventually have criteria that change every time you use the query. Using sample criteria in these locations lets you test that the parameters for the query criteria are in the correct place. For example, your QBE grid at this point may look like this:

| Field: | Completed | Operational | Est Cost |
|---|---|---|---|
| Sort: | | | |
| Show: | ☒ | ☒ | ☒ |
| Criteria: | | Between #1/1/93# And #1/1/94# | |
| or: | | | |

Next, replace the temporary criteria you added to the QBE grid with the prompts you want to see when you run the query. Enter the prompts enclosed in brackets, as in **[Enter the first date:]**. These prompts will ask for entries and replace prompts in the QBE grid with the entries you supply. For example, if you type **[Enter the first date:]** in a cell in the QBE grid, when you run the query, you will see a message box with the prompt **Enter the first date:**. Your response to this prompt replaces the **[Enter the first date:]** in the QBE grid. Each time you run the query, you can enter a different response to the prompt, and Access will substitute the different responses for the prompt in the QBE grid. The same query, after you replace some of the criteria with prompts, might look like this:

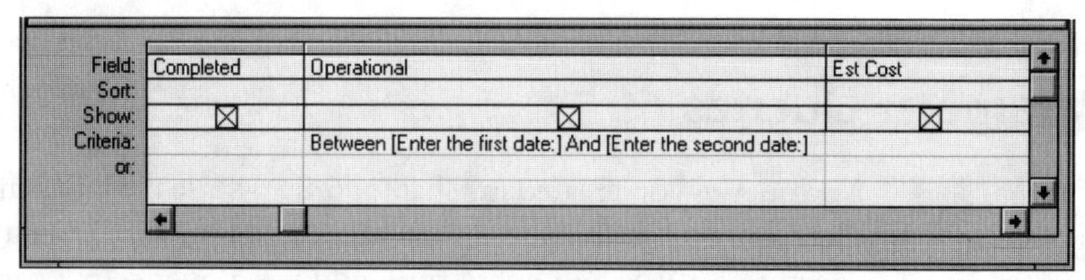


Notice how the prompts in the brackets are placed anywhere you would normally have a value. For example, the criterion entered under the Operational field is **Between [Enter the first date:] And [Enter the second date:]**.

After you have entered the prompts, you need to tell Access the type of data that is allowable for each prompt. Selecting the data types of the query's parameters lets Access confirm that your entries are acceptable when you run the query. To set the data type of the parameters in a query, choose Parameters in the Query menu. The dialog box (with some entries made) looks like this:

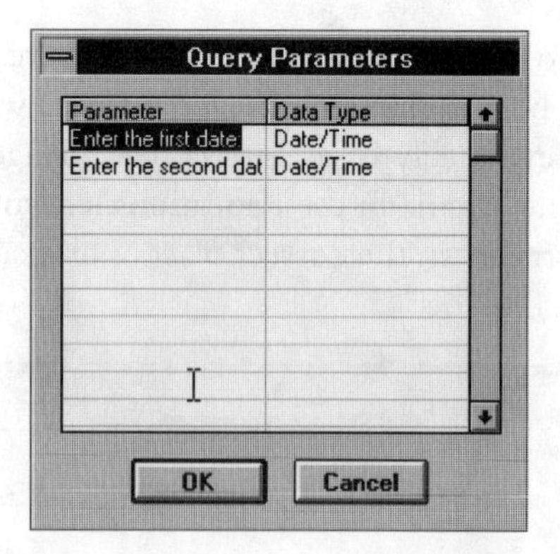


In the left half of the dialog box, type the parameter prompts without the brackets. Your entries must exactly match the prompts entered in the QBE grid, including whether letters are in uppercase or lowercase. In the right half of the dialog box, select one of the data types available from the drop-down list box. The choices are Yes/No, Byte, Integer, Long Integer, Currency, Single, Double, Date/Time, Binary, Text, Memo, OLE Object, and Value.

You can see that Number data types are selected by their field size. After filling in the parameters and data types, select OK. Make sure that the entries in the Parameters dialog box exactly match the text in the QBE grid. If you forget part of the entry—even something as small as a colon at the end—you will see the prompts appear twice, once for the prompt stored in the QBE grid and then again as the prompt stored in the Parameters dialog box. The completed dialog box for the example query contains **Enter the first date:** and **Enter the second date:** in the first column and **Date/Time** for both prompts in the second column.

Now that you have the parameter query created, you are ready to use it. When you click the Datasheet View button in the toolbar or choose Datasheet in the View menu, Access prompts for the parameters. The prompts are displayed in the order in which they are added to the Parameters dialog box. The first prompt for the sample query looks like this:

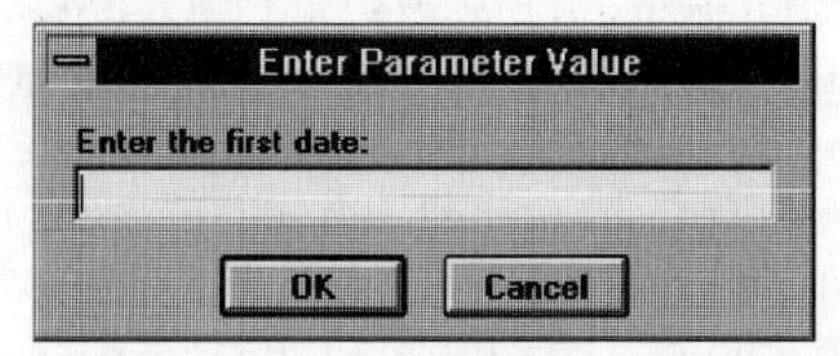


You can enter any valid date in response to this prompt. The date will be entered in the query in place of the **[Enter the first date:]** prompt. After you select OK, Access displays another prompt for the second date. When you select OK the second time, Access displays the dynaset created by the query using the other criteria in the QBE grid as well as the dates you have provided as part of the criterion under the Operational field. Every time you display the dynaset for this query, Access displays the two prompts and then displays the appropriate data.

If you enter invalid dates to either of the two prompts, Access displays a message that the value you have entered is inappropriate for the field. Access checks that the data is valid because you used the Parameters command in the Query menu. If you do not use this command, Access lets you make any entry in response to the prompts; in this case that will result in the display of an empty dynaset since none of the records will fall within the range of an invalid date.

**tip:** *You can select the prompt in the QBE grid and copy it to the Clipboard. Once the prompt is in the Clipboard, paste it into the Parameters dialog box. Copying the prompt ensures that the prompt in the parameters exactly matches the prompt in the QBE grid.*

## Crosstab Queries

Another method of summarizing your data in a query is through a *crosstab query*. Crosstab queries create tables out of your data with one set of entries in the left column, another as the column headings, and the table filled in with values. For example, suppose you want to show how many hours each of the employees worked on each project. You could create a query like the one shown in Figure 7-9 that uses the Total row in the QBE grid to group records by their combination of project number and employee number. This query may not supply the layout you want. To create a datasheet that has the project numbers across the top and the hours each employee works on the project filling in the columns, create a crosstab query.

A crosstab query is like the summary statistic select queries you saw before. The difference is that the field values of one of the fields used to group records are shown across the top of the datasheet as if they are field names. The different summary statistics are shown at the intersection of the column of the field value of one of the grouping fields and the row of the field values of the other grouping fields. A crosstab query only calculates a summary statistic on one field at a time. Figure 7-10 displays the same data as Figure 7-9 contains, presented as a crosstab query.

To create a crosstab query, first create a select query that selects the records you want to summarize. Creating this select query first lets you check that the query only includes the records you want. Once the query chooses the appropriate records, remove the fields that you don't want included in the

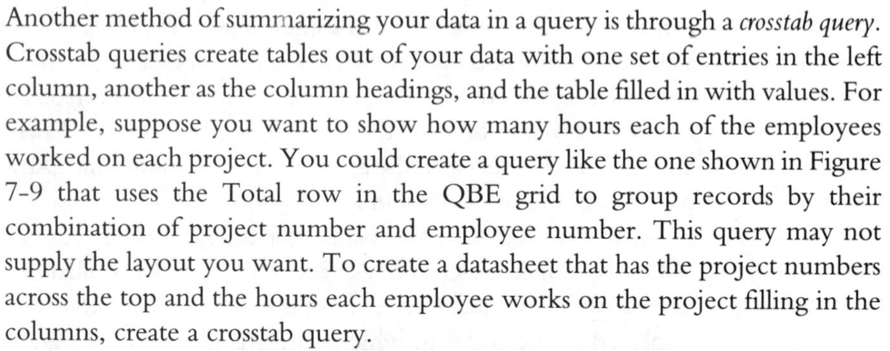

Select Query: Hours by Employee and Project

| Employee Id | Project Number | SumOfHours |
|---|---|---|
| 1 | 1 | 24 |
| 1 | 4 | 12 |
| 1 | 5 | 36 |
| 1 | 7 | 8 |
| 2 | 2 | 63 |
| 2 | 3 | 5 |
| 2 | 7 | 12 |
| 3 | 5 | 80 |
| 4 | 5 | 60 |
| 4 | 6 | 20 |
| 5 | 2 | 30 |
| 5 | 3 | 18 |
| 5 | 4 | 6 |
| 5 | 8 | 23 |
| 6 | 4 | 42 |
| 6 | 5 | 38 |
| 7 | 2 | 80 |
| 8 | 5 | 15 |

Record: 1 of 21

**Figure 7-9** Using summary statistics to group records by two fields

**Figure 7-10** A crosstab query showing the same information as shown in Figure 7-9

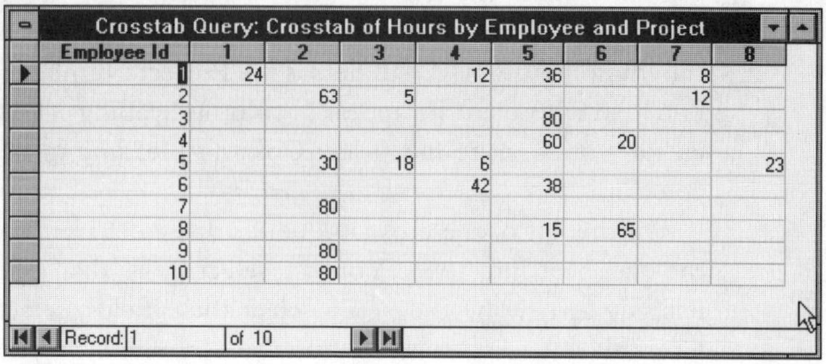

Crosstab Query: Crosstab of Hours by Employee and Project

| Employee Id | 1 | 2 | 3 | 4 | 5 | 6 | 7 | 8 |
|---|---|---|---|---|---|---|---|---|
| 1 | 24 | | | 12 | 36 | | 8 | |
| 2 | | 63 | 5 | | | | 12 | |
| 3 | | | | | 80 | | | |
| 4 | | | | | 60 | 20 | | |
| 5 | | 30 | 18 | 6 | | | | 23 |
| 6 | | | | 42 | 38 | | | |
| 7 | | 80 | | | | | | |
| 8 | | | | | 15 | 65 | | |
| 9 | | 80 | | | | | | |
| 10 | | 80 | | | | | | |

Record: 1 of 10

crosstab query. The only fields you want to remain are the fields that contain criteria, that you want to summarize, and that you want to border the top and left side of the results.

Once you remove the extra fields, you can change this select query into a crosstab query. If you are using all the records from the Employee Time Log table as the basis for this crosstab query, your query will contain the Employee ID, Project Number, and Hours fields.

Once you select the fields to appear in the crosstab query, change the select query to a crosstab query by choosing Crosstab from the Query menu or by clicking the Crosstab Query button in the toolbar. The Show row you saw in Figure 7-5 is replaced by the Crosstab row, as you can see here:

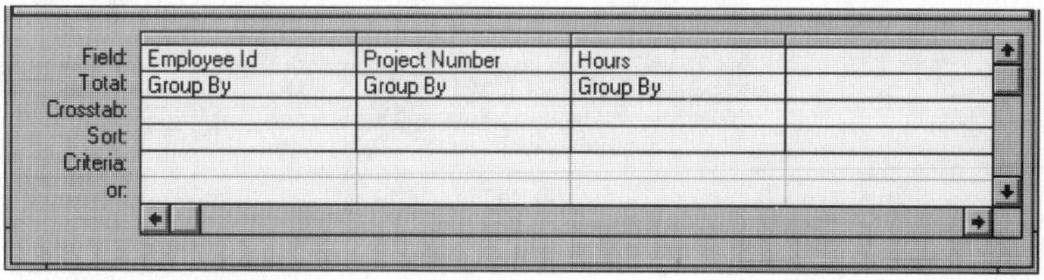

| | | | | |
|---|---|---|---|---|
| Field: | Employee Id | Project Number | Hours | |
| Total: | Group By | Group By | Group By | |
| Crosstab: | | | | |
| Sort: | | | | |
| Criteria: | | | | |
| or: | | | | |

If the QBE grid did not previously include the Total row, it is added at this time. Once the Crosstab row is added, you can make entries in this row to tell Access how you want the data to appear in the crosstab query. Three entries can be put in the Crosstab Row—Row Heading, Column Heading, and Value—or you can leave the entry blank.

If the QBE grid includes criteria to select the records used by the crosstab query but you do not want these fields used in the crosstab query, leave the Crosstab rows in these columns empty. You can later change the entry in the Crosstab row to (not shown) if you want to hide a field.

At the top of the crosstab query's datasheet are the field entries that you use to divide the crosstab entries into columns. For the crosstab query datasheet shown in Figure 7-10, this field is the Project Number field. You can have only one field whose entries appear as column headings. To tell Access which field's entries you want to use, select Column Heading in the Crosstab row for that column.

On the left of the crosstab query's datasheet are the field entries that divide the datasheet into rows. You can select more than one field to appear on the left side as row headings. To select these fields, select Row Heading in the Crosstab row. Access creates the rows by presenting the unique combinations of field value entries just as if the fields you use as row headings are in their own query with the Unique Values Only check box selected for the query properties. To create a crosstab query for the data shown in Figure 7-9, the Employee Id field has its Crosstab row changed to Row Heading.

The remaining field to change the Crosstab row for is the field that you want to summarize. For this field, change the Crosstab row to Value and then select, from the Total row, one of the choices that summarize data. These choices are Sum, Avg, Min, Max, Count, StDev, Var, First, Last, and Expression. At this point, with the crosstab query designed, your QBE grid may look something like this:

| | | | | |
|---|---|---|---|---|
| Field: | Employee Id | Project Number | Hours | |
| Total: | Group By | Group By | Group By | |
| Crosstab: | Row Heading | Column Heading | Value | |
| Sort: | | | | |
| Criteria: | | | | |
| or: | | | | |

To view the crosstab query, switch to the Datasheet view just as you do for other query types. The design just shown creates the crosstab query shown in Figure 7-10.

## Adding Fixed Column Headings for Crosstab Queries

Besides letting Access create the field headings for the fields in a crosstab query, you can enter these field headings yourself. You may want to do this when you want the field headings to appear in a different order. Even when you set the field headings yourself, you must enter the same numbers that Access would add. You cannot enter text which would explain what those values are. You will also want to use fixed column headings when you use the crosstab query as the basis for a report (Chapter 13 shows an example of this).

To set the fixed column headings that appear in a report, choose Properties from the View menu while in the query's Design view or click the Properties button. A new property is Column Headings (Fixed Column Headings in Access version 1). You can add the fixed column headings by entering them in this property. In Access version 1, you first need to select the Fixed Column Headings check box. When entering, separate the column headings by a semicolon or a comma or by pressing CTRL+ENTER, which puts the column headings on separate lines.

## Creating Crosstab Queries Using the CrossTab Query Wizard

While you can create your crosstab queries using the instructions given earlier, Access version 2 offers you the shortcut of using the CrossTab Wizard.

To use this Wizard, start by selecting Queries and then New in the Database window or by selecting the New Query button in the toolbar. Then select Query Wizards instead of New Query. In the first dialog box presented, highlight CrossTab Query in the list box and select OK. The CrossTab Query Wizard will now prompt you through the process of creating a crosstab query. Select Back and Next to move between the different dialog boxes.

- First you are prompted to select the table or query to base the crosstab query on. You cannot select more than one table or query.
- Next you are asked to select the fields to use as the row headings. You can select up to three fields as row headings.
- You are then prompted to select the field to use as a column heading.
- Next you are asked to select the field to use in filling in the crosstab table, and for any functions you want to use with that field. You cannot insert a formula or expression you create. You can also choose to show grand totals for each row in the crosstab table.
- The last dialog box lets you choose a name for the query. You can choose the Open the query to view the data option button and Finish to open the query in Datasheet view, or the Modify the query's design option button and Finish to open the query in Design view.

# Creating Action Queries

Besides using queries to present data, you can also use queries to perform actions with data. Using action queries, you can put the contents of a query's datasheet into another table, delete records, add data to another table, or change many records in a table at once. Action queries are permanent database objects, so every time you want to perform an action you have the query ready to perform the action for you.

**tip:** *Make backup copies of your database when you first start working with action queries. You can make tremendous changes to your database with action queries. If you make the wrong changes, removing the effects of the changes may take a long time.*

Action queries look different than select and crosstab queries in the database windows. The different icons used in Access version 2 are shown here:

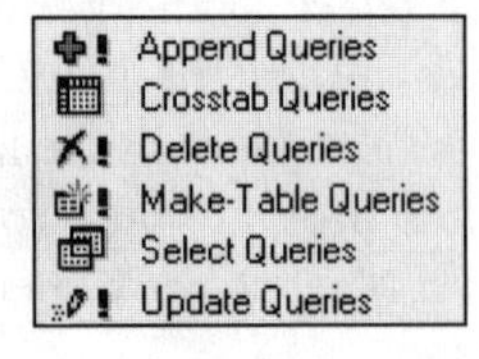

**tip:** *Access version 1 only uses two icons to distinguish between different types of queries. The same icon is used for select and crosstab queries, and an exclamation point is added to that icon for all action queries.*

## Setting Up an Action Query

The first step in using action queries is to create a select query that selects only the records on which you want the action performed. For example, if you want an action query to delete a group of records, you first create a select query that selects only the records that you want to delete. Creating a select query like this first lets you check your criteria so that you do not accidentally delete records you want to keep.

Once the query chooses the appropriate records, change the query type by choosing the type of query you want the action query to become from the

Query menu, or by selecting the button in the toolbar for the action query you want to create. After changing the query type, you may need to make further changes depending on the action the query performs. These further changes are described in the next sections, along with the different actions that these queries can perform.

When the action query design is completed, run the query by choosing Run from the Query menu or by clicking the Run button in the toolbar, which looks like this:

Before Access completes the action done by this query, Access will prompt you to confirm that you actually want this action completed. To run the query after you close the query window, select the query in the Database window and either double-click it, press ENTER, or select Open. Again, you may need to respond to a prompt warning you that running the action query will modify a table's data. You cannot undo the effects of running an action query. This is why it is so important that you create the select query *before* you convert the query into an action query. When you first run an action query, check that you get the results you expect, to be sure you have designed the query correctly.

**tip:** *You can add parameters to action queries by changing parts of the criteria, as just described for select parameter queries. Parameter action queries prompt for the data to use in the query just as parameter select queries do. The parameter action queries use the data you enter to select which data you are affecting.*

## Creating an Action Query to Create a New Table

When you create a query that contains the data that you want to save to a separate table, you can create a *make-table action query* that takes the data a query selects and puts it in a new table. You might use this type of action query when you want a table to contain a subset of information that changes every time you run the action query. For example, suppose you want to create a table from the Employee Time Log table that only includes records for the week of 6/12/94. You might want to create a separate table when you plan to export the data to another application; for example, you could export weekly payroll data to a word processing program to create a weekly expense report.

You also can use a make-table action query when you want to create a table of the records you plan to delete from a table with a delete action query. The table you create with a make-table action query will contain all of the data the select query would display in its dynaset, even if the data comes from more than one table.

To change a select query into a make-table action query, choose Make Table from the Query menu or click the Make-Table Query button in the toolbar. In the Query Properties dialog box that displays when you select this command, shown next, type the name for the new table in the Table Name text box or select an existing table name using the drop-down list box:

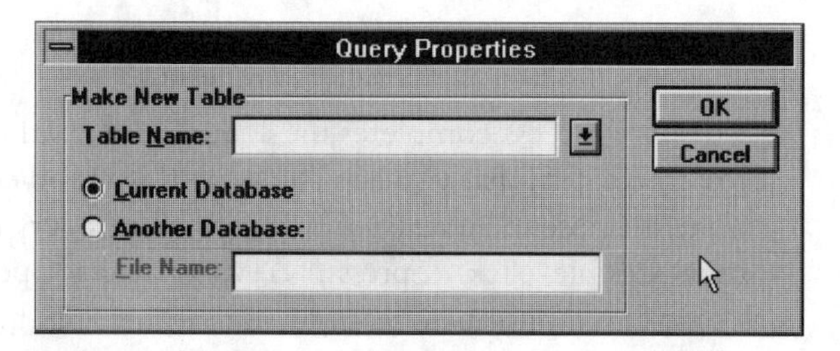

**tip:** *All blank new queries are initially select queries and must be changed to a different query type if that is what you want.*

This table is placed by default in the current database, but you can select the Another Database option button and type the filename of the other database in the File Name text box. In Access version 1, the Unique Values Only and Run With Owner's Permission check boxes are used for the same query properties as described earlier for select queries. In Access version 2, the query properties are set using the query's property sheet, as described earlier. When the table name and database name (if needed) are entered, select OK. The table is not created, however, until you run the query.

Once you have selected the new table you are creating, you are ready to run the action query. Choose Run from the Query menu or click the Run button in the toolbar. Access displays a message telling how many records it will place in the new table. Select OK to create the new table. The fields in the new table you created use the same data types and sizes as the fields in the table that originally contained the data, but the new table does not adopt any of the other table or field properties of the original.

When you run this action query a second time, Access will ask you whether it can delete the table the query created previously before continuing with the action query. Select Yes to delete the previously created table and continue the action query or No to cancel the action query and preserve the existing table.

## Creating an Action Query to Delete Records

When you want to systematically remove records from a query, you can create a query that performs this action for you. A *delete action query* quickly removes entire records that you select from one or more tables. In order to ensure that you are selecting the correct records for deletion, you will want to create the select query and then check the Datasheet view. In Access version 2, you can create a delete action query and check the Datasheet view, but Access version 1 will not show a Datasheet view for a delete action query. In Access version 1, you also need to add * (an asterisk) to the Field row of the QBE grid for the table from which you want to delete the fields. In Access version 2, all fields are deleted whether or not you add the asterisk.

To make a query a delete action query, choose Delete from the Query menu or click the Delete Query button in the toolbar. The Sort and Show rows in the QBE grid are replaced with a Delete row. This Delete row contains Where for all the columns except the one with the * (asterisk). The Where tells Access that these columns contain criteria used to select which records are deleted. The From in the Delete row for the column containing the * tells Access that this is the table from which to remove records. With this preliminary step completed, you are ready to run the action query.

Choose Run from the Query menu or click the Run button in the toolbar. Access displays a message telling you how many records it will delete. Select OK to remove the selected records.

When the query contains multiple tables, you may be able to delete records from one or both tables. If the tables have a one-to-one relationship, you can delete the matching record from both tables. Make sure you include the * (asterisk) in the Field row of the QBE grid for each table. If the tables have a one-to-many relationship, you can first use the delete action query to delete the records from the table on the many side of the relationship by including the * for that table in the Field row. After you check that the correct data is selected, run the action query to delete the records. Then replace the * for the table on the many side of the relationship with an * for the table on the one side of the relationship and run the action query again.

## Creating an Action Query to Append Data to a Table

When you have data in one table or query that you want to add to another table, you can use an *append action query* to transfer the data between tables. You can use an append action query when you have data in an attached table that you want to add to an unattached table. You also can use an append action query when you want to combine data from a separate database into a table in the current one. This may occur when someone else has entered the data at another machine.

The query you are taking data from must have certain features in common with the table you are appending the data to. First, if the appending table has a primary key, the query must contain a field with the same name and data type as well as entries that are unique. If the primary key field in the query contains duplicate information or is empty, Access will not paste the record to the table.

**caution:** *If there are text or memo fields in the source table that are longer than the equivalent fields in the destination table, you may lose data. Access will simply ignore the text that will not fit in the destination field. You will receive no warning that your entries are being truncated.*

To make a select query an append action query, choose Append from the Query menu or click the Append Query button in the toolbar. The Query Properties dialog box that appears looks just like the one that appeared when you selected the Make Table command, except that the Make New Table area is called the Append To area. Type the name of the table to append the data to in the Table Name text box or select an existing table name using the drop-down list box. Access assumes this table is in the current database, but you can select the Another Database option button and type the filename of the database containing the table in the File Name text box. In Access version 1, this dialog box includes the Unique Values Only and Run with Owner's Permission check boxes, which are used for the same query properties as described earlier for select queries. In Access version 2, of course, these are set using the query property sheet as described before, instead of in this dialog box. When the table name and database name (if needed) are entered, select OK. The data is not appended, however, until you run the query.

After you convert the query to an append action query, the Show row in the QBE grid becomes an Append To row. The Append To row selects the fields in the table to which you will append the data, while the field names for the table from which you are taking the data are shown in the Field row. You can either select the field name using the drop-down list box or type the field name. If some of the fields in the two tables have the same name, Access fills these cells with the field names for you.

All of the fields in the QBE grid must have an entry in the Append To row. If the QBE grid includes an asterisk (*) in the Field row, Access copies all of the fields from the query that have the same name as fields in the table you are appending to. If you include an asterisk (*) in the QBE grid, you don't include other fields from the same table, because Access will try to copy the fields' contents twice for each version of the field name.

When one of the fields in the table you will append to is a Counter field, do not include the Counter field in the query's data. When the records are appended, the Counter field's data is updated and renumbered in the table. You only leave this field in the query when you want the appended records to retain the same values for the Counter field in the table.

**caution:** *Do not attempt to retain Counter field values when the table you are appending the records to uses the Counter field as a primary key, or when the records you are appending contain duplicates of Counter numbers already in the Counter field in the table you are appending to. This cannot be done, since you cannot have duplicate numbers in primary keys or Counter fields.*

When the Append To row in the QBE grid is completed, you are ready to run the append action query. Choose Run from the Query menu or click the Run button in the toolbar. Access displays a message telling you how many rows it will append to the table. Select OK to add the rows. If the table has data that it cannot append to the table, the record is added to the Paste Errors table, which is created if it does not already exist.

This is the same table Access creates and adds data to every time you unsuccessfully paste data from the Clipboard to a table. After appending the data, if the table you are appending to is open, press SHIFT+F9 to display the effect of the query.

**tip:** *If the field order in the query's QBE grid exactly matches the fields in the table, copying the records from the query's datasheet and pasting them into the table is faster.*

## Creating an Action Query to Alter Data in a Table

If you have a group of records that you need to make the same change to, creating a query to select the records and then manually making the change to each record can be time-consuming. A shortcut is to create an *update action query* that selects the records and then updates them for you. All of the records selected by an update action query have selected field values altered. This type of action query lets you globally change all of the records in a group. You can also use an update query to delete the field values of specific fields.

After you create a select query that correctly selects only the records you want to update, convert the query into an update action query by choosing Update from the Query menu or by clicking the Update Query button in the toolbar. After you use this command, the Sort and Show rows in the QBE grid become the Update To row. This row is where you enter the formula of the new value you want the field to equal. These formulas are just like the criteria and calculated field formulas you have entered previously. Some of the possible entries (and the change each would perform) are listed here:

| Entry | Result |
|---|---|
| "Safety" | Changes the values of the field to the text "Safety" |
| #12/31/94# | Changes the values of the field to the date 12/31/94 |
| 7 | Changes the values of the field to 7 |
| [Actual Cost]*[1.05] | Changes the values of the field to 5 percent more than the current value of Actual Cost |

**tip:** *To double-check that the formula is correct, create a calculated field that calculates what the new values for the field will be before you change the select query into an action query. If the query's datasheet contains the correct values for the calculated field, copy the formula from the calculated field to the Update To row in the QBE grid for the original field.*

You only include entries in the Update To row for the fields whose values you want to change. With the Update To row complete, you are ready to update the field values. To update the data, you must run the query. Choose Run from the Query menu or click the Run button in the toolbar. Access displays a message telling you how many records it will update in the table. Select OK to make the changes.

**tip:** *To confirm each replacement as it is made, view the data in the table or in a query and then use the Replace command in the Edit menu to selectively make field value replacements.*

## Using Query Wizards to Create an Archive Query

Access version 2 offers a Query Wizard that will create an archive query that copies records from a table to a new table, and it can delete the records that are copied. An archive query allows you to back up records which are now outdated or to make backup copies of useful or important tables.

To use the Archive Query Wizard, start by selecting Queries and then New in the Database window or by selecting the New Query button in the toolbar. Then select Query Wizards instead of New Query. In the first dialog box presented, highlight Archive Query in the list box and select OK. The Archive Query Wizard will now prompt you through the process of creating an archive query. Select Back and Next to move between the different dialog boxes.

- First you are prompted to select the table you want to archive.
- Next you are asked to select which records you want to archive. To do this, you can use the three drop-down list boxes to select the field to test, an operator, and a test value. Records that pass this test are archived, while those that don't are not archived. To use all of the records in the table, you can also select the Archive all records in table check box.
- Next, the Archive Query Wizard displays the records that are selected to be archived. At this point, you can still select Back to return and change the criteria used to select records to be archived.
- Now you are prompted to choose whether you want the records that are archived deleted from the original table. You can select Yes to delete the records, or No to keep them.
- The last dialog box lets you choose a name for the query. Select the Archive the records option button and Finish to proceed with archiving the records, or select the Modify the query's design option button and Finish to view the query's design.

## Quick Reference

**To Add Tables to a Query** Choose Add Table from the Query menu. Select a table or query from the Add Table dialog box and then select Add. Repeat until you have added all the tables you want to the query and then select Close. You can also drag a table or query name from the database window onto the query design.

**To Remove Tables from a Query** Select the field list from the table or query you want to remove. Press DEL or choose Remove Table from the Query menu.

**To Join Tables in a Query** Drag the field from one field list to the field in the other field list you want to use to join the records in the tables. Access automatically joins tables for which you have already defined a relationship. In Access version 2, fields with the same name and field type are also automatically joined.

**To Display Unique Records in a Query** Create the select query to select the records you want and set the QBE grid to only display the fields you are interested in. Choose Properties (Query Properties in Access version 1) from the View menu or click the Properties button in the toolbar, and select Yes for the Unique Values property—in Access version 1, select the Unique Values Only check box—and then select OK.

**To Add Summary Statistics to a Query** Choose Totals from the View menu or click the Totals button in the toolbar to add the Total row to the QBE grid in the query design. For columns that contain criteria selecting which records you want to summarize, change Group By in the Total row to Where. For the columns in the QBE grid you want to summarize, change Group By to Sum, Avg, Min, Max, Count, StDev, Var, First, Last, or Expression. Display the datasheet just as you normally do. The query displays the summary statistics for the records grouped according to the unique field value combinations of the columns that contain Group By in the Total row.

## Quick Reference

**To Add Parameters to a Query** Create the query. Replace the entries you want to change each time with the text you want to appear as a prompt enclosed in brackets. Choose Parameters in the Query menu. In the Parameter column, enter the prompt, and in the Data Type column, select one of the available data types. Select OK after entering the prompts and data types for each parameter value. The parameter prompts will appear every time you display the query's datasheet.

**To Create a Crosstab Query without the Crosstab Wizard** Choose Crosstab from the Query menu or click the Crosstab Query button in the toolbar to change the select query to a crosstab query. In the Crosstab row, change the column's entry to Column Heading for the field whose values you want to appear as the column headings in the crosstab query. Change the column's entry in the Crosstab row to Row Heading for the fields whose combinations of unique values you want to divide the crosstab query into rows. Change the column's entries in the Crosstab row to Value for the field that you want summarized and change the entry in the Total row to Sum, Avg, Min, Max, Count, StDev, Var, First, Last, or Expression for the summary statistic you want calculated for the different combinations of row heading and column heading values. You can display the crosstab query by switching to the Datasheet view as you normally do.

**To Create a Make-Table Action Query** After creating a select query that correctly chooses the records you want placed in another table, change the select query to a make-table action query by choosing Make Table from the Query menu or click the Make-Table Query button in the toolbar. In the Query Properties dialog box, type the name for the new table in the Table Name text box or select an existing table name using the drop-down list box. If the table is to be added to another database, select the Another Database option button and type the filename of the other database in the File Name text box. Select OK. Run the query by choosing Run from the Query menu or by clicking the Run button in the toolbar. Select OK to confirm that Access is copying the number of rows copied to the new table.

Quick Reference

**To Create a Delete Action Query** After creating a select query that correctly chooses the records you want deleted, change the select query to a delete action query by choosing Delete from the Query menu or by clicking the Delete Query button in the toolbar. The Delete row contains Where to indicate columns containing criteria to select the records to delete and From to indicate which tables contain the records to delete. Run the query by choosing Run from the Query menu or by clicking the Run button in the toolbar. Select OK to confirm the number of rows to be deleted.

**To Create an Append Action Query** After creating a select query that correctly chooses the data you want added to another table, change the select query to an append action query by choosing Append from the Query menu or by clicking the Append Query button in the toolbar. In the Query Properties dialog box, type the name of the table to append the data to in the Table Name text box or select an existing table name using the drop-down list box. If the table is in another database, select the Another Database option button and type the filename of the other database in the File Name text box. Select OK. In the Append To row, select the field names from the table you have selected in the Query Properties dialog box where you want the query's data appended. Run the query by choosing Run from the Query menu or by clicking the Run button in the toolbar. Select OK to confirm that Access is adding the number of rows copied to the table.

**To Create an Update Action Query** After creating a select query that correctly chooses the records in which you want to change the data, change the select query to an update action query by choosing Update from the Query menu or by clicking the Update Query button in the toolbar. In the Update To row, enter formulas that calculate the value you want the current field values replaced with. Run the query by choosing Run from the Query menu or by clicking the Run button in the toolbar. Select OK to confirm the number of records to be updated by the query.

# III

# Forms and Reports

# Chapter 8

# Creating a Basic Form

a *FORM* is a definition of the data that you want to work with and an arrangement of how and where you want the information to appear on your screen. You can design a form by yourself or get help from Microsoft Access's Form Wizards. Form Wizards can provide the beginning of a customized form. By creating a form with a Form Wizard and then modifying it, as you will learn to do in later chapters, you can create a customized form like the one shown in Figure 8-1.

Forms let you present and input information in a layout that is easier to use than the tabular datasheet format. You use forms to present or input one record at a time. You can easily switch between a form and a datasheet to change between looking at one record and looking at a dynaset.

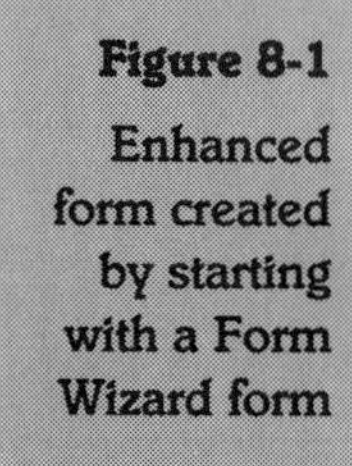

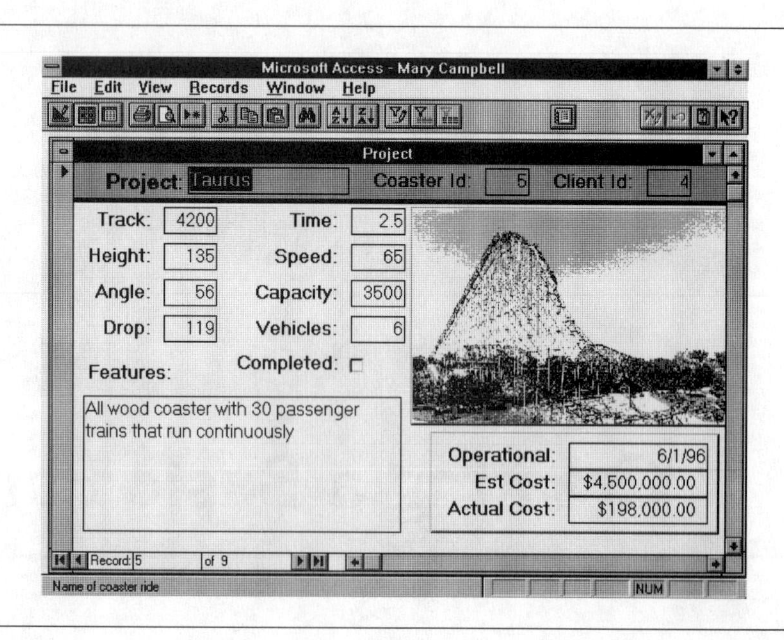


**Figure 8-1** Enhanced form created by starting with a Form Wizard form

Forms are usually used to display the information on the screen, but you can also print the form when you want a hard copy of a record's information.

**tip:** *When you want to create a customized output of a dynaset, create a report rather than printing a form. You will learn about reports in Chapter 9.*

How products are marketed provides a good analogy for how fields can be used in forms. When advertising a product to one group of consumers, marketers might stress its health benefits. When advertising the same product to another group of consumers, low cost and quick preparation time might be emphasized instead. Different advertising campaigns focus on different features of the same product. Similarly, with a database table you might have several different form designs that you use with the same set of fields; which form you use for a given task depends on the task.

You will often have multiple forms and reports so that you can enter your information differently depending on what you are doing. The forms you create with Access let you select which data from a table or query you present and how this information is presented. For example, if updating a mailing list for a client, you only need to show the customer name and address on the form. If you are updating account balances for the same client, the best form design would show the client's name and other identifying information along with the account balances. Tailoring the form to the activity makes the task of updating information easier. You don't need to show every field within a table on a form unless you are adding new records to the table and need to be able to enter data in each field.

In this chapter you'll learn the basics for creating a form. Most of the forms discussed can be created with Form Wizards, which you will learn how to use next. You will also see how to name, save, and print the forms you create. Since forms and reports share many aspects of design and creation, what you learn in this chapter will be applicable to creating reports in Chapter 9.

## Creating an AutoForm with Access Version 2

The simplest way to create a form is to let Access create it for you. The new AutoForm feature in Access version 2 creates a form using the selected table or query. The form will include all of the fields from the selected table or query. To create an AutoForm:

1. Select the table or query the form will use.

   You can either select the table or query's name from the Database window or you can switch to a window showing the table or query you want for the form.

2. Click the AutoForm button, which looks like this:

Access builds a form for the currently selected table or query. When Access is finished, the form appears in a new window like the one shown in Figure 8-2. Once you have this form, you are ready to use it.

## Using the Form

Once a form displays in a window, using the form is just like using the datasheet for the table or query. You use the navigation buttons at the bottom of the window to move between records or to move to the first or last one. You can also enter a number after Record to move to that record.

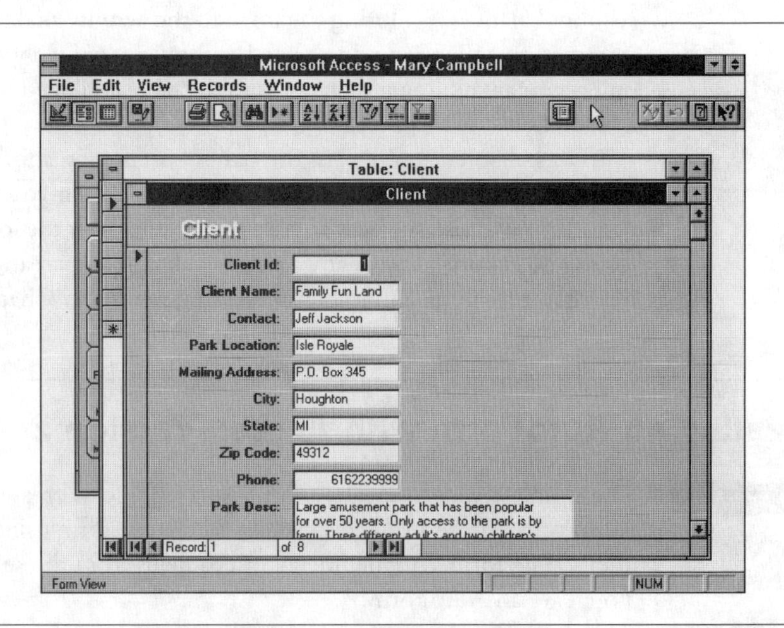


**Figure 8-2** Form created using the AutoForm button

The data that you see in a form is the data from the table or the query's dynaset. Any change you make to the data in the form is applied to the data in its original table. While you are working with the data in the form, you can quickly sort the data. When you click the Sort Ascending or Sort Descending buttons in the toolbar, Access changes the order of the records in the dynaset according to the currently selected field. For example, when the insertion point is on the Last Name field and you click the Sort Ascending button, the records are put into ascending order according to the Last Name field.

Forms pick up some of the properties of the table from which the data in the form originates. For example, when you create a form for the Employee table of the Coasters database, the entries in the Last Name, First Name, and Middle Initial fields appear in uppercase even if you type them in lowercase. These three fields have a Format property of >. The properties that a form picks up from a table or query are called *inherited properties.* Other inherited properties include Validation Rule and Default Value.

As you learned in Chapter 3, there are many variations for the data types and properties that you can use for your data. The current setting for these when your form is created determines exactly how your data looks on the form. Once created, the form continues to have the properties it picked up from the table or query when you created it. Later, you can change the properties of the table or query without changing the properties of the form. If you want a change in properties to apply to both a table or query and a form, you must change the properties of the form yourself or recreate the form after changing the table or query properties: Access does not make this change for you.

When you add a field to a table or query, the new field is not added to existing forms based on the table or query.

## Saving and Closing a Form

When you have a form you want to use again, you need to save it. Saving a form makes a custom-designed form available at a later point. To save a form:

1. Choose Save Form in the File menu.

   Access also asks if you want to save a form when you try closing the window containing the form. Selecting Yes at the prompt saves the file just as if you chose Save Form in the File menu.

2. Type a name for the form, following the same rules for naming tables.
3. Choose OK.

Forms display their names in the title bars. If you later want to save the form with a different name, save it again by choosing Save Form As in the File menu.

You can close a form just as you would close other windows in Access. You can double-click the window's control box, press CTRL+F4, or choose Close from the File menu. If the form has changes to its design, you are prompted about saving the form.

### Renaming a Form

You can rename forms just as you can any other objects in the database. If you use the default name for forms, rename them as you add more to provide descriptive names. To rename a form:

1. Close any window in which the form or its design appears.
2. Select the form from the Database window.
3. Choose Rename from the File menu or right-click the form name and select Rename.
4. Type the new name you want for the form in the Form Name text box.
5. Select OK.

## Creating a Form with Form Wizards

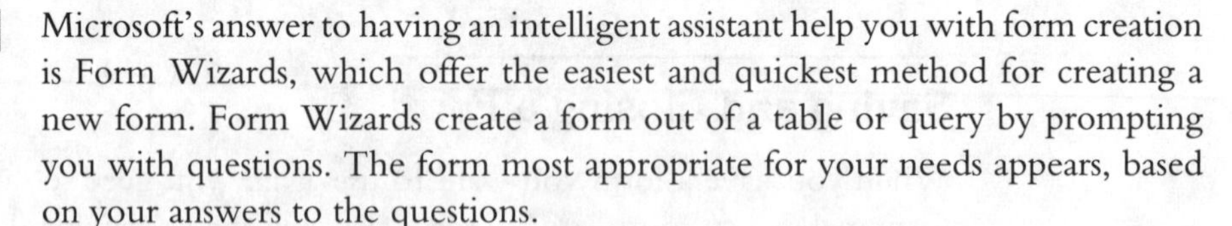

Microsoft's answer to having an intelligent assistant help you with form creation is Form Wizards, which offer the easiest and quickest method for creating a new form. Form Wizards create a form out of a table or query by prompting you with questions. The form most appropriate for your needs appears, based on your answers to the questions.

Access has four types of forms that you can create with Form Wizards. Figure 8-3 shows the four different Wizard types. If none of the Form Wizards options meet your exact needs, you can still save time by creating a form with Form Wizards and then changing the design to better suit your needs. The general

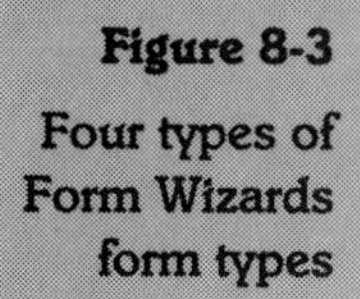

**Figure 8-3**

**Four types of Form Wizards form types**

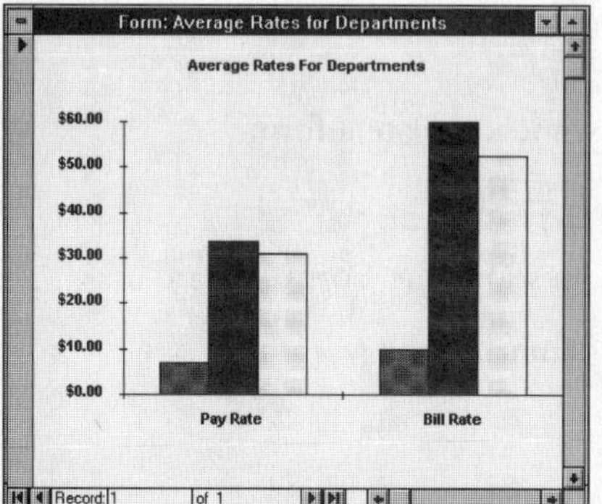


Graph form

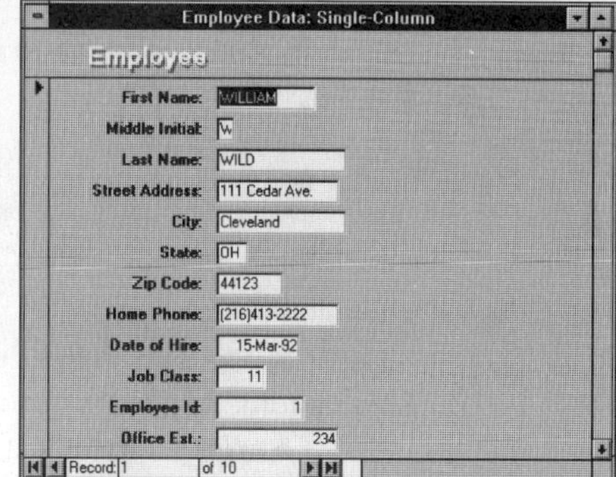


Single-Column form

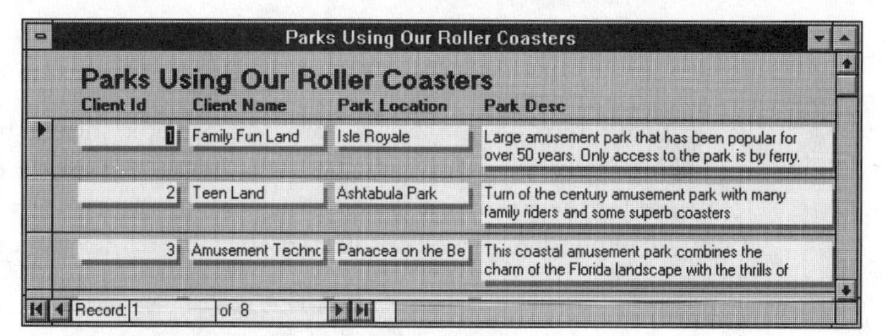


Tabular form

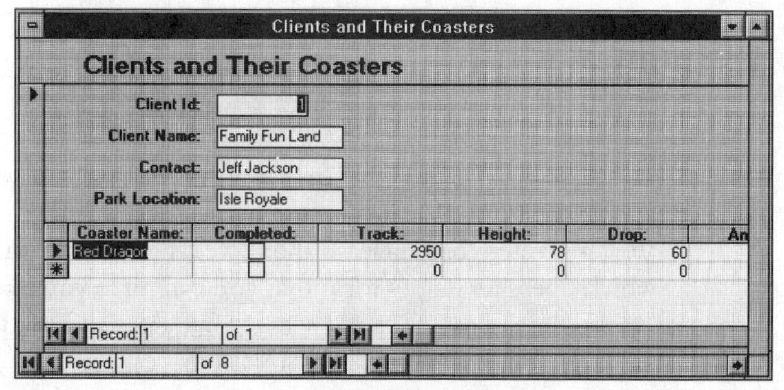


Main/Subform form

procedure you will follow for creating a form with the Form Wizards is the same for each type of form:

- Tell Access you want to create a form.
- Select the Form Wizard to use.
- Respond to the questions the Form Wizard asks.
- Give the table a name.
- Open the form.

In the sections that follow you will have an opportunity to look at how the detailing steps vary for different types of forms with the Form Wizard.

To create a form with the Form Wizard, begin by clicking the New button at the top of the Database window when displaying forms. Another way is to choose New from the File menu and then select Form. A third option to create a form is to click the New Form button on the toolbar, shown here:

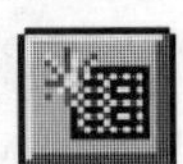

Access displays the New Form dialog box shown below. The Select a Table/Query drop-down list box tells Access the source of the data you want to use for the form you are creating. When you create a form with a table or query window displayed or selected, the table name or query is already supplied.

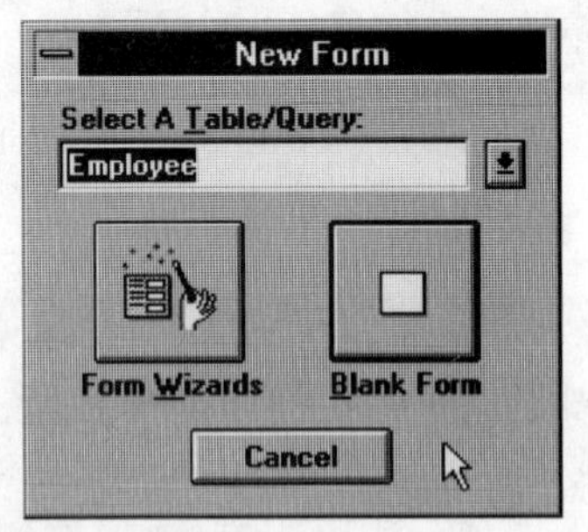


After selecting the table or query whose data you want to use in the form, choose the Form Wizards button to create the form using one of the four Form Wizards. Later you will learn about creating a form with the Blank Form button which opens an empty form that you can fill as you like.

Once you select the Form Wizards button, choose which Form Wizard form you want to create. Access offers five choices—Single-Column, Tabular, Graph, Main/Subform, and AutoForm. These five selections allow you to create four different types of forms. (The AutoForm is not actually another form type, since selecting it creates a single-column form without prompts just as if you clicked the AutoForm button.) These form types result in basic forms that you can later embellish. When you select the Form Wizard you want to use, it asks questions about the information that will appear in the form. The questions vary depending on which Form Wizard you select.

## Single-Column and Tabular Form Wizard Forms

Single-Column and Tabular Form Wizard forms are created the same way. A *single-column form* puts all of the fields you select into a single column. This form is just like the form created by clicking the AutoForm button, except that you can select the fields you wish to include and the general appearance of the form. A *tabular form* puts all of the fields you select into a row. A tabular form is similar to the table format of datasheets, but the form includes more space between each field and record. Both types of forms let you select a style for the boxes that contain the field's contents and a selected title.

From the first dialog box, you select the fields to appear in the form.

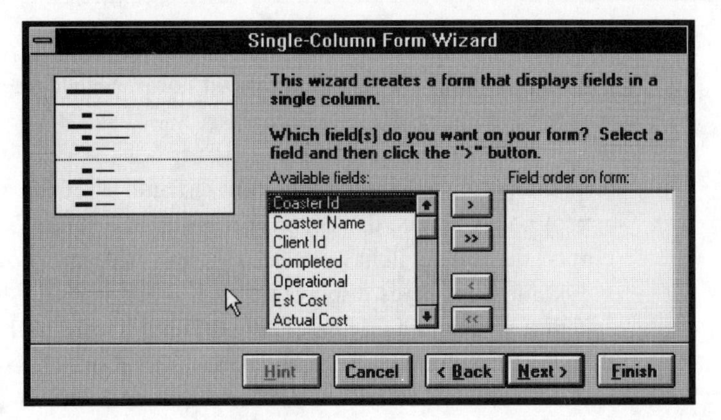


Add the fields to the form in the order you want them to appear. When you select the field in the Available fields list box and select the > button, the field is added to the form. Select the >> button to add all of the fields. You can also select a field in the Field order on form list box and the < button to remove the field from the form. The << button removes all fields from the Field order on form list box. Once the fields you want the form to use appear in the order you want, select the Next button.

Now select the look for the form. A Single-Column or Tabular Form Wizard form has five predefined looks, each shown in Figure 8-4 and named with the descriptions in the five title bars. The look decides the style of the box for each of the fields in the form; where the fields' names appear relative to the fields,

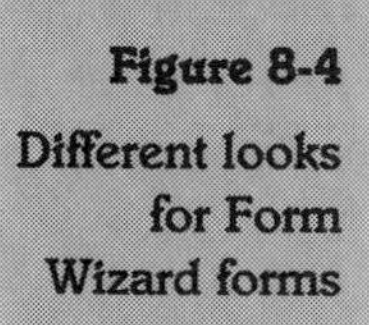

**Figure 8-4** Different looks for Form Wizard forms

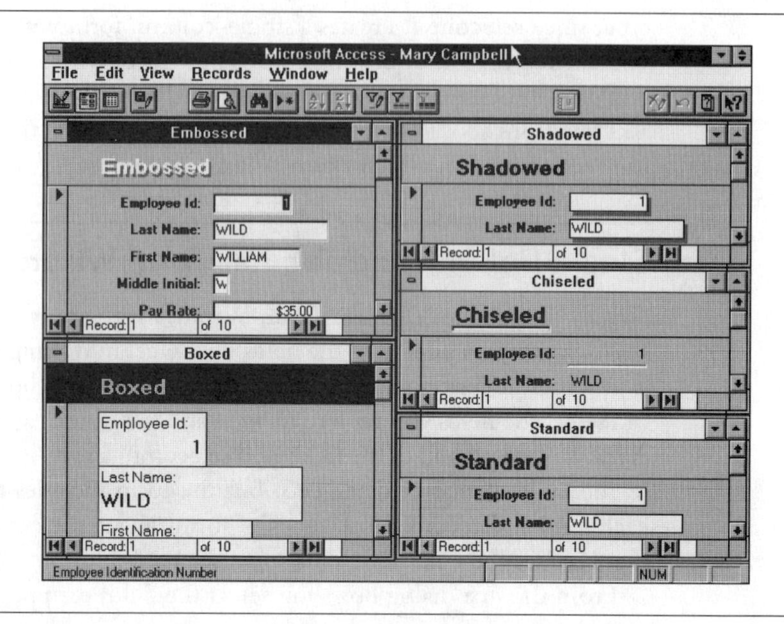


the lines added, and the background color. Select one of these styles and then select Next.

All Access needs to complete the form is the title, which appears at the top. The title is separate from the form's name. You can type any text you feel is appropriate or leave the default of the table or query's name. If this text box is empty, the form will have an empty area at the top. You can also select whether you want Cue Cards displayed as you work with the form.

Once you have a title, select the Open the form with data in it option button, then Finish (Open in Access version 1) to display the form. You are ready to use the form as described above. Figure 8-5 shows a Single-Column Form Wizard form that includes all of the fields in the Employee table of the Coasters database in a different order. Figure 8-6 shows a Tabular Form Wizard form that includes some of the fields in the Clients table of the Coasters database. You can also select the Modify the form's design option button and Finish (Design in Access version 1) to display the form's design, which you have created through the Form Wizard.

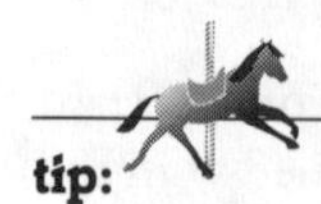

**tip:** *Use the title to add a heading to the form so that the purpose of the form is clear to the user.*

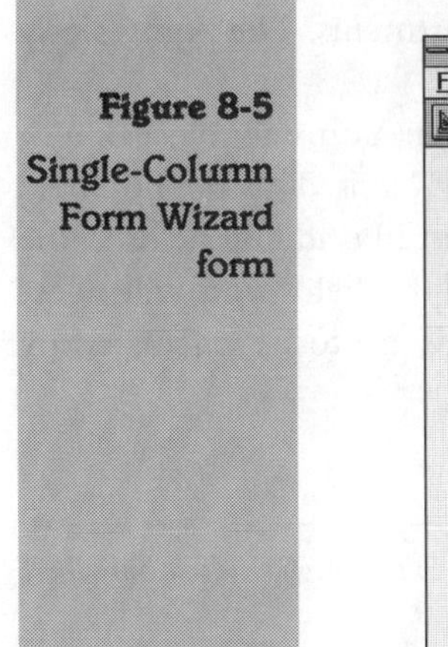

**Figure 8-5**
Single-Column Form Wizard form

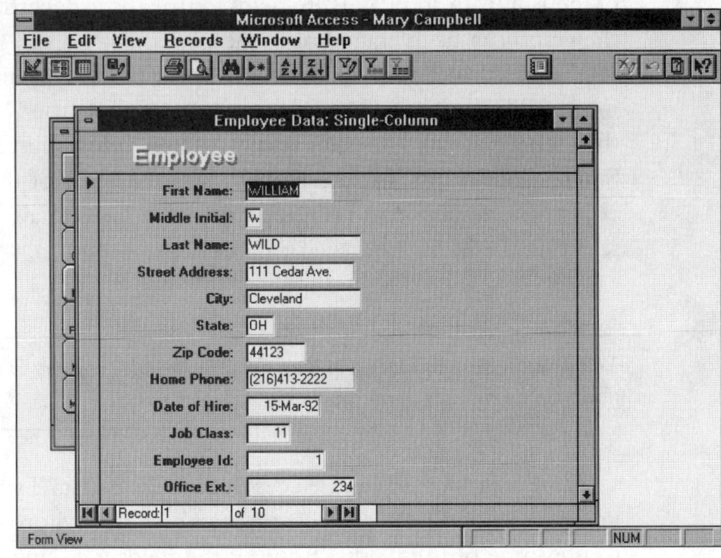


## The Graph Form Wizard Form

A *graph form* creates a graph out of the data in a table or query. This Form Wizard lets you choose from 15 graph types. Figure 8-7 shows an example of a Form Wizard graph form. In this example, the X axis is the axis along the left side of the graph since the graph is rotated. Entries on the X axis match the departments in the Department field. Each of the bars represents the average of the values

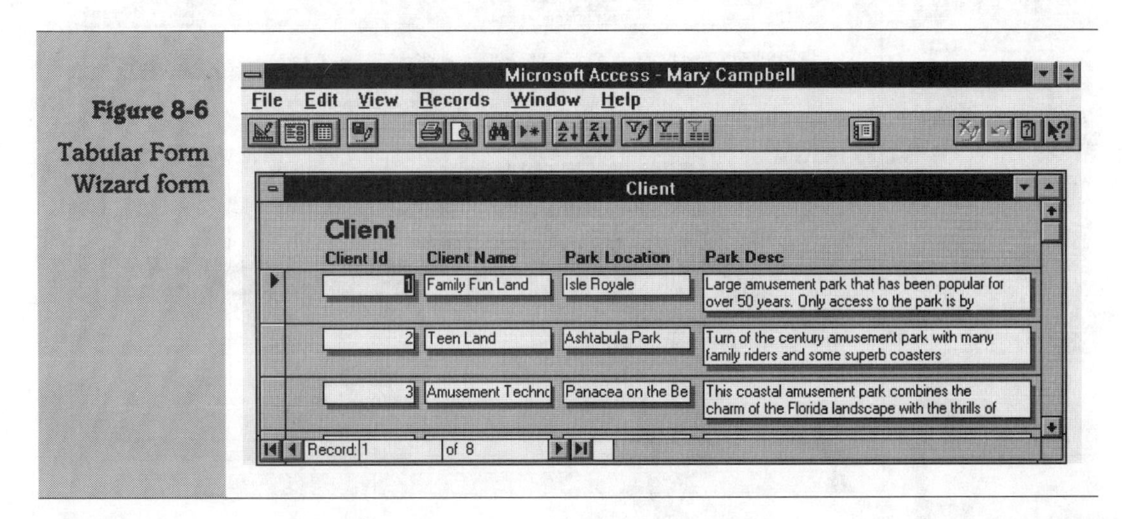


**Figure 8-6**
Tabular Form Wizard form

of the Bill Rate and Pay Rate fields for the three departments. The points along the graph can be averaged or totaled.

You need to select the fields to appear in the graph. You will select one or more fields containing the values you want along the X axis. This can be a field that contains text, values, or dates. Adding fields is just like adding fields in the Single-Column or Tabular Form Wizards. Most of the fields you will select contain numbers. You also need to select how totals are to be calculated by selecting the Sum, Average or Count option button.

**tip:** *You do not have to include all of the fields from the table or query in the graph. Include only those fields you want to see in the graph.*

When you select Next, Access looks at the Data Type property of the fields you have selected. At this point Access may need more information about how to use some of the fields. If one of the fields is a Text data type or if all fields are Number data types, the Graph Form Wizard prompts for the fields to use for labeling the points on the X axis. Usually, you will select a single field, so that the points along the X axis are labeled with the entries in that field. Select more than one field when you want the field names to label the X axis, as Pay Rate and Bill Rate label the X-axis in Figure 8-8. After selecting these fields, select Next.

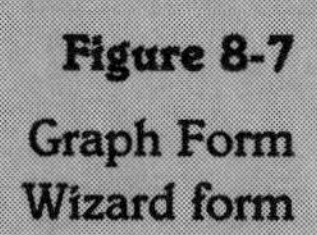

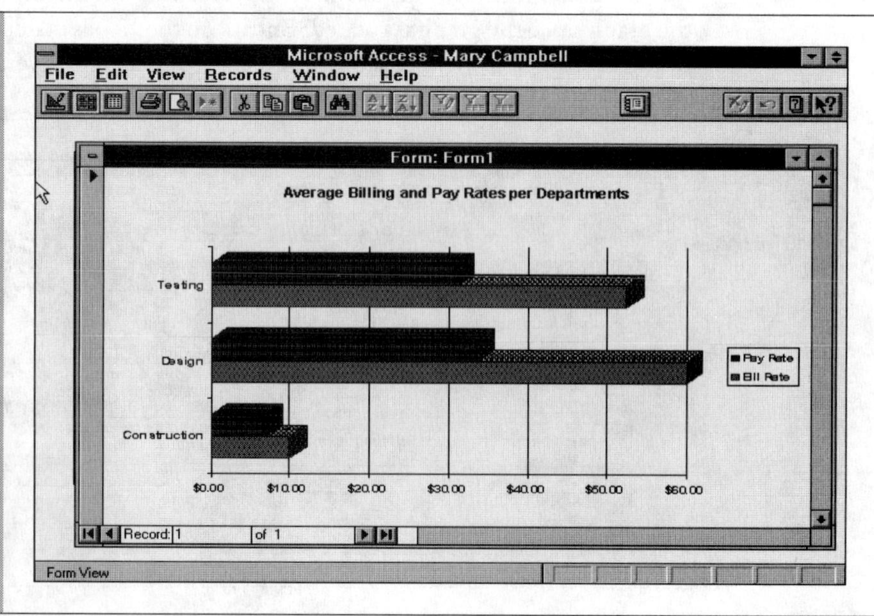


**Figure 8-7** Graph Form Wizard form

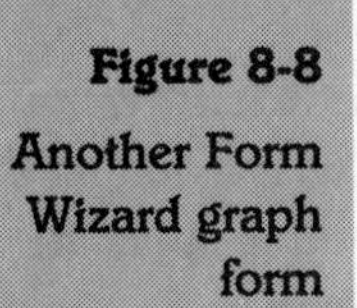

**Figure 8-8**

**Another Form Wizard graph form**

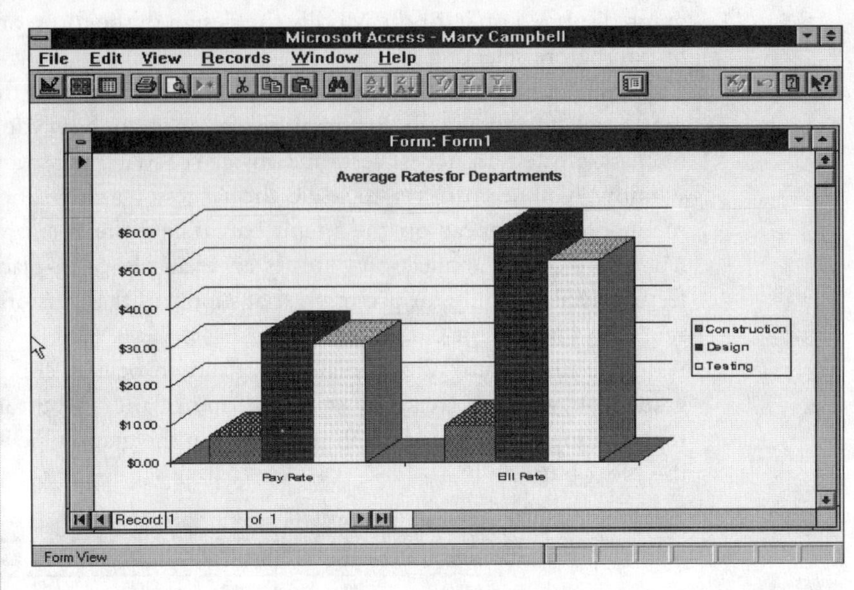


If one of the selected fields is a Date/Time data type, Access assumes you want the dates or times to identify the different points along the X axis. Access will prompt you for how to group the dates. You can choose how the dates or times in the Date/Time data type field are grouped by selecting a term in the Group field By drop-down list box. You can group dates or times by years, quarters, months, weeks, days, hours, or minutes. You can also choose to use either all the dates and times or only those within a range. The default is to use all of the dates and times but you can select the Use Data Between option button and modify the dates and times to select the range of dates and times you want to use. The range of dates and times select which records the graph uses from the table or query. When finished selecting options for the Date/Time data field, select Next.

Depending on the data types of the remaining fields, you may be prompted for the fields you want to use for the legend. Select one field to use the contents of the field as the legend entries or select multiple fields to use the field names as the legend entries.

Access now asks you how you want data totaled for the graph, and how you want the graph opened. You can select the Add (sum) the numbers, the Average the numbers or the Count the number of records in each category option button to choose how the total will be calculated. This total will be used if you select a graph style that indicates proportions. You also need to select how the graph form will be opened. You can do this by selecting the Open the form with the graph displayed on it, or the Modify the design of the form, or the graph option button before selecting Next.

Now Access starts the Microsoft Graph program, and the Chart Wizard, which will prompt you for further information about how you want your graph, or chart, created. In Access version 2, instead of switching to another application window, you seem never to leave the Access window, though several new menu options appear on the menu bar. These are menu options from the Microsoft Graph application. This is an example of in-place editing, a new feature available only for programs that support OLE version 2, as Access version 2 and Microsoft Graph do.

In the first Chart Wizard dialog box shown below, choose which type of graph you want to create by selecting one of the 15 buttons shown below, representing the different graph types. When the graph type is selected, choose the Next button.

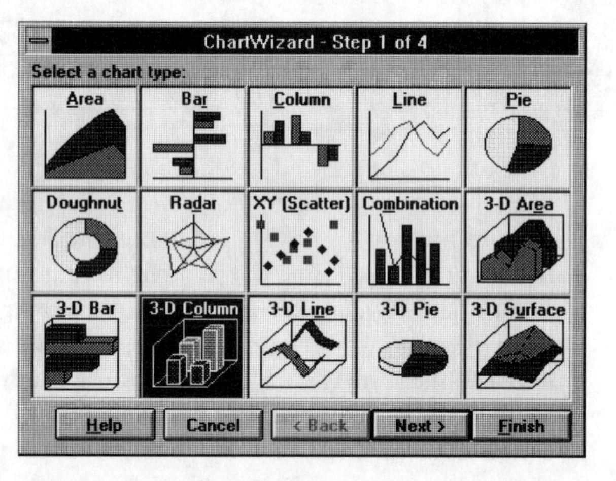


You are now prompted to select a specific format for the type of graph you selected. The available formats depend on the type of graph you selected. After choosing a format, select Next again.

You are now prompted for how the data is arranged, in rows or columns. You can choose whether the first row or column of data is used as a data series or to label the X axis or legend. You can view the effects of your selections in the sample graph, to make sure that you are presenting the data the way you want to. After making these selections, choose Next. You are now prompted for whether you want the legend, to enter a chart title, and, if appropriate, to choose titles for the different axes. When are finished with these selections, you can select Finish to create your graph form.

## The Main/Subform Form Wizard Form

A *main/subform form* combines two tables or queries. One of these is the main part of the form and the second is the subform portion of the form. Usually you have a link that connects the items from the main form to the subform.

When you create this type of Form Wizard form, the table or query you select when you create the form is the one used for the main form. After you select Main/Subform, you must select the table or query you want the form to use as the subform. Select one of the listed tables or queries, and then select Next.

Now Access needs to know which of the fields from the main table or query you want to use for the main form. Just as you selected fields for single-column and tabular forms, you select the fields you want the main form to use. After selecting the fields and Next, select the fields from the second table or query that will appear on the subform. You do not have to include the field that the two tables or queries share. After following the same steps to add the fields you want the form to use, select Next.

At this point, Access looks at the two tables or queries to see how they are related. Usually the two table or querys each have a field with the same type of data. For example, if you are creating a form that combines your Client and Project tables, use the Client Id field to select which records from the Project table appear in the subform when a record with the matching value in the Client Id field appears in the main form. If you have created a relationship between fields that appear in the main and subform, you do not have to tell Access anything. Access uses this information to select which records from the subform table or query appear for each record in the main table or query. Access version 2 will guess how the records from the two are related. If Access version 1 does not know how the data from the main and subform tables or queries are related, you will have another step at this point. This step defines how the data in the main form and subform are related. To create this link, select the field from the main form's table or query in the first column that matches the values in the field you select from the subform's table or query you select in the second column. Select Next to continue.

The next step is to select the look for the form. You can choose from the same five predefined looks available for the Single-Column or Tabular Form Wizard forms, as shown in Figure 8-4. The look decides the appearance of both the main form and the subform. Once one of the looks is selected, you can select Next.

Finally, enter the title for the form in the Form Title text box. The title is the title that appears above the main form. You can also select whether Access

Cue Cards appear as you use the form. Select the Open the form with data in it option button and Finish (Open in Access version 1) to open a Main/Subform Form Wizard form. As the Form Wizard creates the form, Access will prompt you about naming the subform. When prompted about saving the subform, select OK, type a name for the form, and select OK again. Figure 8-9 shows this main/subform type form created for the Client and Project tables. The table displays the selected information from the Client table at the top and shows the selected fields from the Project table below it. Since the two tables are related by their client identification numbers, the table only shows the projects that apply to the client shown on top. The buttons that move you from record to record for the Client table are different than the ones that move you between records for the Project table. When you use a Main/Subform Form Wizard form, you can edit the data from either the main form or the subform's table or query that appears on the form.

**tip:** *When you save a form that is a subform to another form, indicate that in the name of the subform. For example, if you name the main form Clients and Their Coasters, name the subform Subform of Clients and Their Coasters.*

## Looking at the Form's Design

Even if you use Form Wizards to create forms, usually you will change the form's design somewhat. Working with a form design lets you adjust the

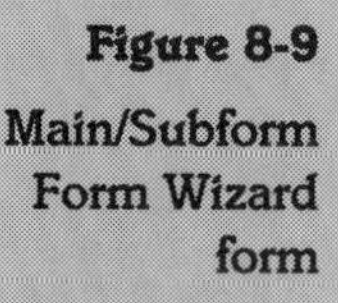

**Figure 8-9** Main/Subform Form Wizard form

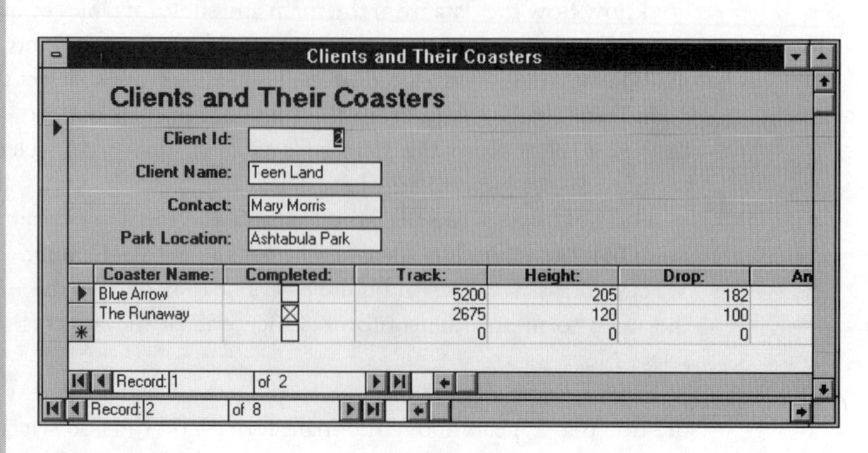

content, size, and position of everything that appears in the form. You can adjust form design and put in additional features that do not appear in a form created with Form Wizards. You can also display an empty form design and add everything you want the form to contain one piece at a time. Each small piece of a form or report is called a *control.* Controls can display a field's data, text, pictures, and calculations.

The steps for looking at a form design of an existing form differ from the steps you take to look at a new form. To look at an existing form design:

1. Select the form you want in the Database window and Design button.
2. With the form already open, click the Design View button or choose Form Design in the View menu.

Figure 8-10 shows the form design for the Employee Data form created for the Employee table of the Coasters database using Single-Column Form Wizards.

To look at the form design of a new form, you tell Access you want to create a form just as you did for a Form Wizards form:

1. Click the Form button in the Database window or choose Forms from the View menu.
2. Click the New button in the Database Window or choose New from the File menu and then select Form.

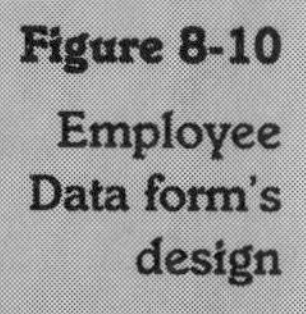

**Figure 8-10**
Employee Data form's design

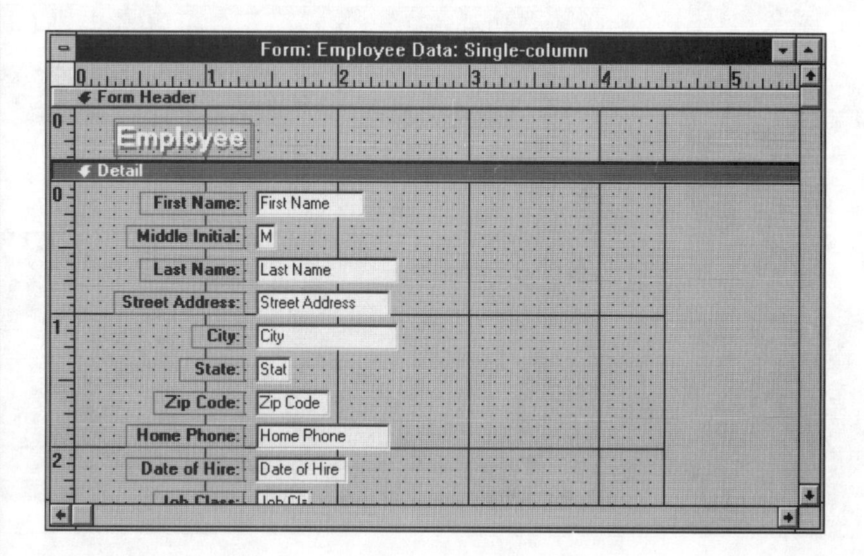

You can also create a form by clicking the New Form button on the toolbar.

3. Select the table or query you want to use from the Select a Table/Query drop-down list box.
4. Select the Blank Form button.

Selecting the Blank Form button opens the blank form in Design view that you can fill as you want. Figure 8-11 shows an empty form in Design view.

You can have several extra windows open while you design forms that make creating and modifying forms easier. One of these is the toolbox, shown in Figure 8-11, which includes the arrow at the top of it. You can display this window by choosing Toolbox from the View menu or by clicking the Toolbox button in the toolbar. Later you will learn about other windows such as the field list, which lets you list the fields you can add to the form. Chapter 10 discusses the palette and the property sheet, which allow you to change the colors and other features of the form's controls.

The rest of this chapter focuses on basic form design features. These include changing the size of the form, moving and sizing the controls you place in the form design, and adding fields to the form.

When you have the design you want, save the form using the same Save command in the File menu that you use to save a form created using a Form

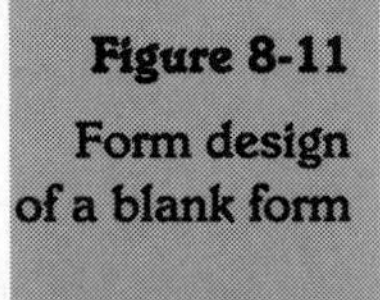

**Figure 8-11**
**Form design of a blank form**

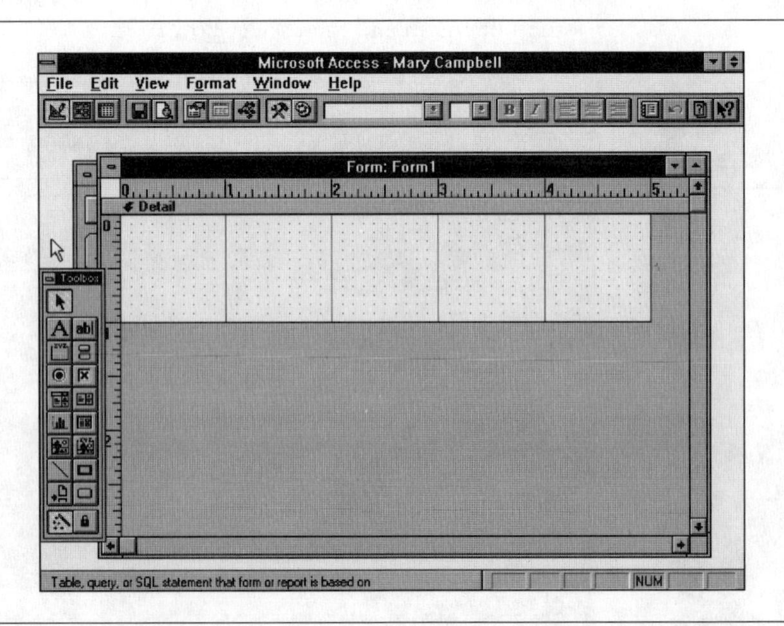

Wizard. When you want to see the form you are designing, choose Form from the View menu. You can also click the Form View button, which is the second button in the toolbar.

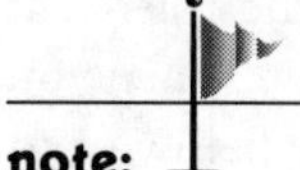

**note:** *For the sake of legibility, the text in several of the forms shown in this chapter has been enlarged. In Chapter 14, you will learn how you can make this change to your forms.*

## Selecting Form Controls

To work with any control in a form, you need to select it. Once an object is selected you are ready to move it, size it, or make any change to it. You can also select multiple controls when you want to move, size, or alter several controls at once.

Selecting a single control is as simple as clicking it. As you select controls, the selected controls are marked with handles, as shown here:

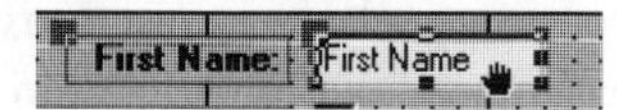


These handles show which controls you have selected. Some controls, like the one above for the First Name field, are part of a compound control. These controls have a label control and another control that belongs with the label. In this example, the First Name: label is part of a compound control with the text box for the First Name field. When you click a compound control, you are often selecting the label of the field name as well. Compound controls move together, so the text that describes a field moves with it when you move the field to another location. Other changes to a control will only affect the part of the compound control you select.

When you want to select more than one control, select the first control you want and then hold down the SHIFT key while you continue clicking the other controls you want to select. Another option for selecting a group of controls is to draw a box on the form design that selects every control included in the box. To draw this box, click an empty area of the form design near the controls you want to select and drag the mouse so that the box you are drawing contains the controls you want to select, as you can see here:

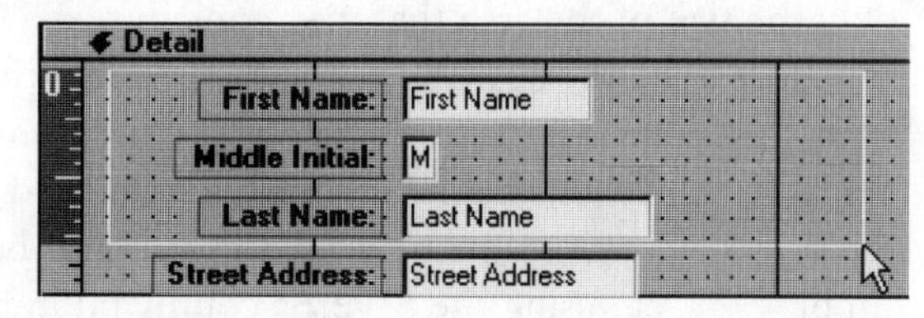

The box only appears while you are drawing it, so as soon as you release the mouse the box disappears as Access selects all of the controls that appeared in the box.

A new way to select controls in Access version 2 is to use the ruler that appears at the top and left side of the Form window in Design view. When you drag the mouse in the ruler, you select all of the controls that are below or to the right of the area of the ruler you dragged through. If you just click the mouse in the ruler, then you select all the controls that intersect a line drawn from where you clicked the mouse to the opposite side of the window. You can use these rulers to quickly select controls that are near each other.

## Moving and Sizing Controls

Most of the controls you place on a form can be moved and sized to improve the form's appearance. Before you move or size a control in a form, you must select it, as described above.

Once you have selected the controls you want to move, all you have to do is drag the controls to a new position. Move the pointer to one of the selected controls so that the pointer looks like a flat hand. When you drag this hand from one position to another, all of the selected controls are moved with it.

You can also move a part of a compound control, such as moving the text for the field name from its position relative to the field it describes. To move one part of a compound control, move the pointer to the upper-left corner of the part of the compound control you wish to move. The pointer looks like a hand holding up one finger. Drag the pointer to a new position and the part of the control is moved to that new location. If you have multiple controls selected, only the part of the compound control you are pointing to moves.

You can size selected controls just as easily. First, move the pointer to one of the control handles so that the pointer looks like a double-headed arrow. Drag the pointer to where you want the new corner of the control to be. Since the opposite corner remains in place, the selected control is resized to fit the rectangle set by the two corners. If you have multiple controls selected, resizing one of them only affects the size of the control you are pointing to. Changing the size of a control containing text does not change the size of the text but only the size of the area that may contain text.

Figure 8-12 shows a single-column form for the Employee Data table created with the Single-Column Form Wizard after moving and sizing some of the fields. In this form, the fields have been dragged to new positions and some of the boxes have been enlarged. This form also has been renamed to Modified Employee Data using the Save As command in the File menu.

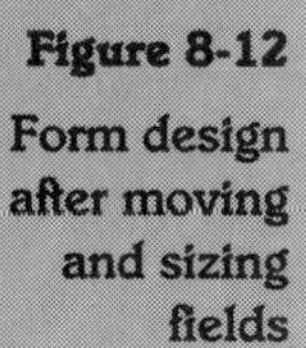

**Figure 8-12**
**Form design after moving and sizing fields**

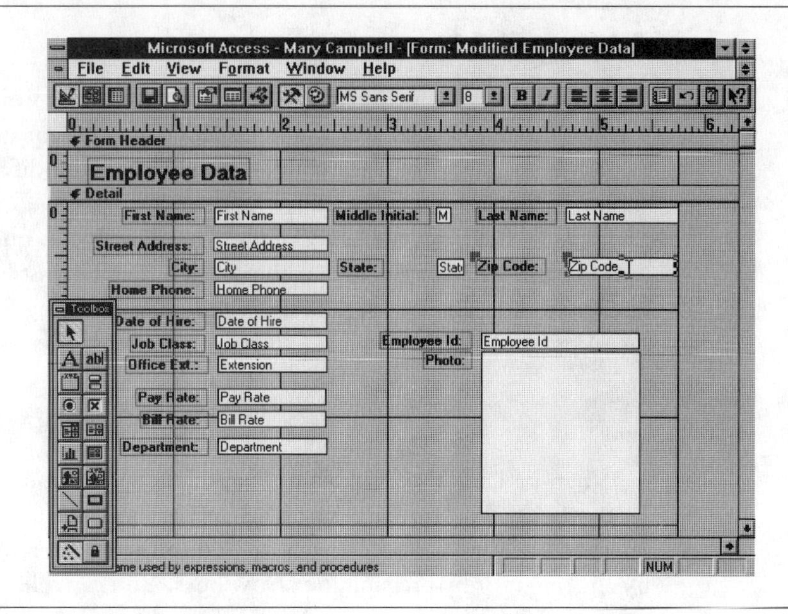

**tip:** *The style you select with Form Wizards often adds extra controls that you may not initially consider when you want to move fields and field names. For example, the Shadowed style adds a grayed box slightly to the right and below the box containing the field. The Boxed style adds an extra box around the field name and field. When you move the field name and field, you will want to include these additional controls.*

## CHANGING THE FORM'S AREA

A form has a default size that is only a starting point for the amount of space the form occupies. You can change the size of the form when you need to put more or less information on it. A form initially occupies a small part of the window, so you may want to enlarge the form as you put more information on it. You can resize a form by moving the mouse to the form's boundary. Notice that the pointer changes to a double-headed arrow. When you drag the mouse to a new location, the edge of the boundary moves with the mouse but the opposite boundary remains stationary, so the form expands. A form will also expand when you move a control into an area the form does not currently use. Access will expand the form to include the area where you move the control.

## Adding Fields to a Form

When you create a form from scratch, you add fields from the table or query it is based on. You can add any fields from the table or query. You also need to add fields as part of a form's design when you modify existing forms after adding fields to the table or query that the form uses.

To add a field, get the list of fields from the table or query that you can add to the form. This list of fields is shown in a field list just like the field lists you have used in queries. This field list is added by choosing Field List in the View menu or by clicking the Field List button in the toolbar, shown here:

When you add the field list to the Access application window, it looks like Figure 8-13. The primary key field appears in boldface. From this window, select the field or fields you want to add to the form. You can select one field by clicking it or by pressing the arrow keys. You can select more than one field from the list simultaneously by holding down CTRL while you click the additional fields. A quick method of selecting all the fields is to double-click the field list title bar.

When you have selected the fields you want to add to the form, drag one of the selected fields from the field list to where you want the fields to start. The field names are added to the left of the controls containing the fields. You can repeat the field selection and addition to the form as many times as you want so you don't have to add all the fields you want the form to use at once. When the fields are added to the form, you can size and move as you learned to do earlier.

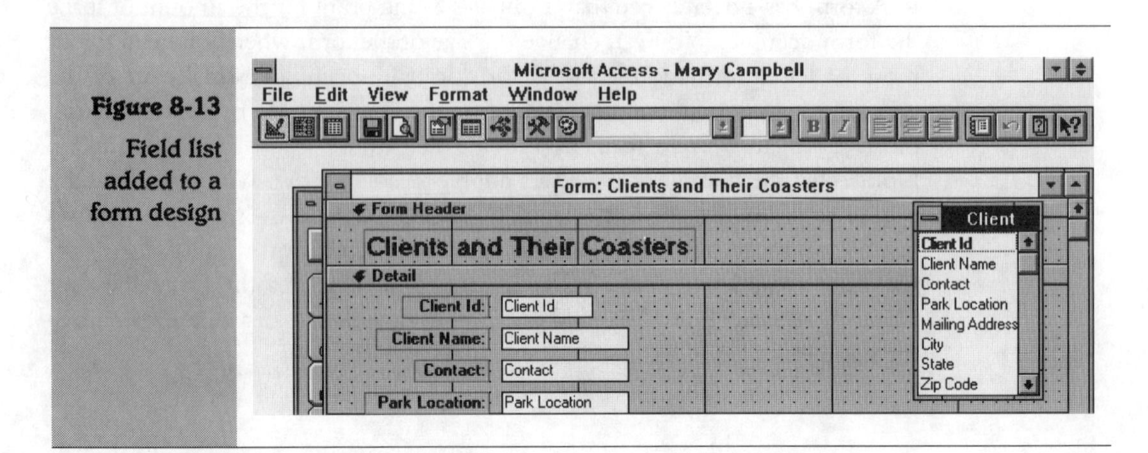


**Figure 8-13** Field list added to a form design

When finished adding fields, hide the field list. Do this by double-clicking its Control box, pressing ALT+F4 when the window is active (with the default colors, the title bar is blue when active), choosing Field List in the View menu, or clicking the Field List button in the toolbar again. When you add a field using the field list, the field appears as a text box of a default size. For some field types, you can create other types of controls that are better suited to making entries in the form. For example, Chapter 11 discusses other controls such as check boxes for Yes/No fields, option buttons for fields that have few possible entries, and list boxes to choose from a more extensive list.

## Deleting Fields from a Form

Besides adding fields that you need to include, you may have some on the form that you want to remove. For example, if you created a form by clicking the AutoForm button in the toolbar it includes all of the fields in the table or query and you may want to remove some of them. You remove a field by selecting the field and pressing DEL or by choosing Delete from the Edit menu. When you delete a compound control, you delete both the field name and the field when the part that is not a label is not selected. When you select the label for a compound control and delete that, you only delete the label without deleting the other part of the compound control.

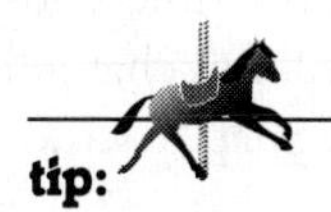

**tip:** *You can duplicate controls in a form. Select the controls to duplicate. If you want the copy in the same form, select Duplicate from the Edit menu. You can also copy the selected controls to Windows' Clipboard using the Copy command in the Edit menu. You can put the controls in another form by selecting Paste in the Edit menu.*

## Tools to Help Design a Form

The Design view for forms has several tools that make creating a form easier. One of these is the ruler that measures the distance from the top and left corner of the form. The other is a grid, which is an organized layout of dots. Use the ruler and grid to make placing or sizing the controls you add to the form easier. A third method of quickly sizing controls is by using the menu to align controls relative to one another.

If you do not find the ruler helpful, remove it so you have more room for the form design. To remove the ruler, choose Ruler from the View menu. If you want to add the ruler back, choose Ruler from the View menu again. This command is a toggle switch that turns the display of the ruler on and off.

Another command that operates as a toggle is the one that activates the grid. You may have noticed that when you move and size controls on the form, the controls hop from one location to another as you slowly drag the control. The form has a grid pattern; every time you move or size a control, Access hops to the nearest grid point. You can see this grid by choosing Grid from the View menu. When you choose the command again, the grid disappears. The horizontal and vertical lines marking each inch are part of the grid lines. You will also see dots for the grid points when they are spaced far enough apart. In Chapter 10, you will learn how you can set the distance between grid points. Displaying the grid does not affect the form; the grid only appears when you are working on a form's design.

The controls hop to the nearest grid point because the Snap to Grid command in the Format menu (Layout menu in version 1) is chosen. If you turn off Snap to Grid (removing the check mark next to Snap to Grid), the controls are then placed exactly where you drag them. This command is also a toggle, so when you choose it again, the check mark is added again and the controls you subsequently move and size hop to the nearest grid point.

You can temporarily ignore the grid when you move or size a control by holding down the CTRL key while dragging the control you are moving or sizing. The grid setting only controls the position of controls at the time you move or size them so when you turn the Snap to Grid on, you will not change the size and position of controls you sized and moved while the Snap to Grid was off.

Another grid feature that controls the size of controls is the Size to Grid command in the Layout menu in Access version 1. When you choose this command so the command has a check mark next to it, all four corners of every control hop to the nearest grid point. Usually Size to Grid does not have a check mark next to it. Both Size to Grid and Snap to Grid operate whether or not you are displaying the grid in the form design. You can continue using the default grid placement or you can change its size. In Access version 2, you can select controls, then select Size and to Grid. However, there is no set option that will size all new controls to the grid.

Besides using the grid or the ruler to position controls, you can use Align in the Format menu (Layout menu in version 1) to position controls relative to each other. For example, if you have several fields you want left-aligned, you can tell Access to left-align those controls rather than placing them individually. To align the controls, select the controls you want aligned relative to one another. Next, select Align in the Format menu (Layout menu in version 1) and choose how you want the controls aligned. Left moves all of the controls to the left edge of the control furthest to the left. Right moves all of the controls to the right edge of the control furthest to the right. Top moves all of the controls up to the top edge of the highest control. To Grid moves all of the controls to start at the closest grid point. In version 2, you can also align controls by right-clicking one of the selected controls and choosing Align and then the alignment for the controls.

## Changing the Tab Order

When you use a table or query, every time you move from one field to another you are moving to the fields in the order they appear in the table or query. In a form, you might put the fields in a different order but you will still want to move through them in the order they appear. To change the order of fields you move to as you move through the form, you change the tab order. Initially, a form's tab order is the same order in which you add the fields to the form. To change a form's tab order, select Tab Order from the Edit menu. This opens the Tab Order dialog box. In this dialog box, the fields are shown in the order that you will move between the fields in the form.

If a field uses a form header or form footer, you can also set the tab orders for those sections of a form by first selecting the Form Header or Form Footer option buttons. To rearrange the fields, point to the box to the left of the first field you want to move and drag the mouse down to cover the fields you want to move. Next, click one of these selected fields and drag the fields up and down in the list to where you want the fields placed. As you drag the mouse this time, Access draws a line indicating where the selected fields will be in the tab order. Release the mouse when the line is where you want the fields and the fields are moved from their prior location to the location of the line. Continue moving fields in the tab order until the fields are in the order you want.

You can select the Auto Order button as a shortcut. When you select this button, Access reorders the fields in the form to match the order in which they appear on the form design. The new order after selecting the Auto Order button is left to right and top to bottom.

## Changing the Text of a Field Name Label

Sometimes the field name labels that Access adds to a control in the form may be exactly what you want—but when they're not you can change the text that appears in this label. Once you have selected the field name label control, changing the text is easy; you click at the point in the label where you want to add the insertion point just as you do when editing an entry in a table or query. You can modify the field name label just as if you are making an entry. Continue to edit the label and then press ENTER or click another part of the form design to finish the changes. In Chapter 10, when you learn how to add other types of label controls to a form, you can modify the text in these controls the same way.

**tip:** *Change field name labels to put & in front of a letter. The letter after & will be underlined. For example, &First Name appears as First Name in the Form view. When you press* ALT *and the underlined letter, the insertion point will move to the field that is part of the compound control.*

## Adding Form Headers and Footers

If you look at the form designs of the forms you created with Form Wizards, you will notice that the title you have provided for your form appears in a section called Form Header. A form that has a Form Header section also has a Form Footer section that appears at the bottom of every form. You can use these two sections to include a title or any other information you want. These two sections are added by choosing Form Header/Footer in the Format menu (Layout menu in version 1). In Access version 2, you can also add these sections by selecting Form Header/Footer from the shortcut menu Access displays when you right-click the form's title bar. As you learn to add controls and change properties of forms, keep in mind that you can also add controls and change the properties of the controls in the Form Header and Form Footer sections.

Forms can also have a page header and page footer, which you will learn about in Chapter 9 when you create reports. You can add controls to these sections, as you have learned how to do in this chapter and will learn more about in subsequent chapters. A Page Header section and Page Footer section only appear when you print the form. You will not see these sections when you look at the form in a window. These two sections can be added by choosing Page Header/Footer in the Format menu (Layout menu in version 1). Figure 8-14 shows a form design that includes Page Header and Footer and Form Header and Footer sections. This command is a toggle, so selecting it again removes these sections from the form.

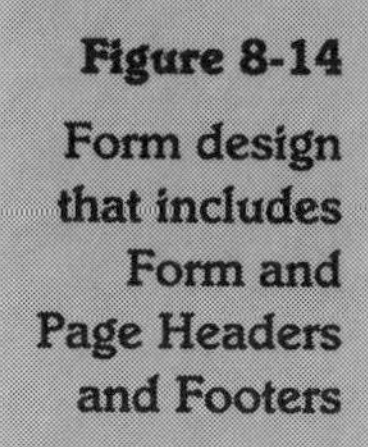

**Figure 8-14**
Form design that includes Form and Page Headers and Footers

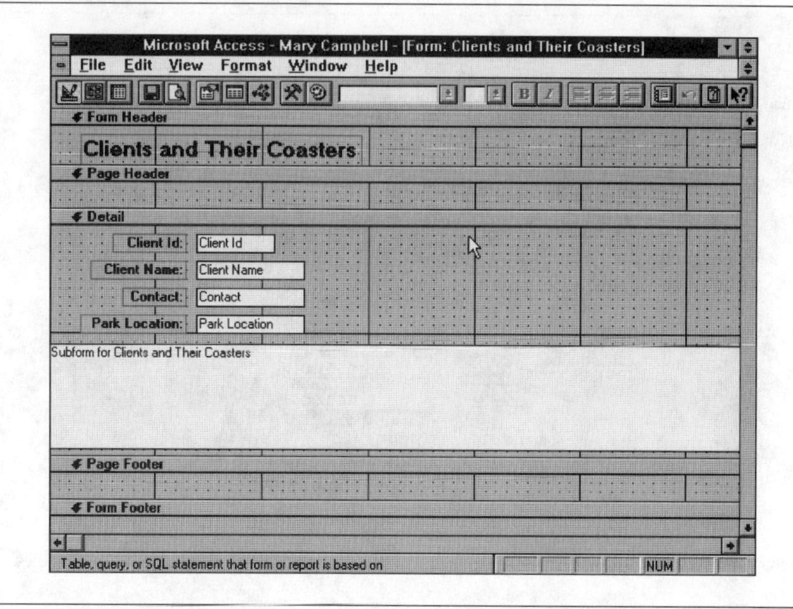


## Printing a Form

Besides using the form to input new data and display data, use the forms you create to print the information in the table or query. Printing a form is just like printing databases and queries, and, as you will learn in Chapter 9, printing reports. Printing a form has no new options over printing tables and queries.

To print data using a form:

1. Select the form from the Database window or switch to a window displaying the form or the form's design.
2. Choose Print from the File menu.

   From the Print dialog box, you have the same choices for the print range, print quality, printing to a file, number of copies, collating copies, and printer setup that you have for printing tables and queries.
3. Change any settings you want to alter.
4. Select OK to print the form.

Access prints the form for all of the records in the table or query it is based on. Figure 8-15 shows a sample printout of one of these forms for the first example. In Chapter 10, you will learn how you can add a page break at the end of the detail band so that the form skips between pages.

**Figure 8-15**
A printed form

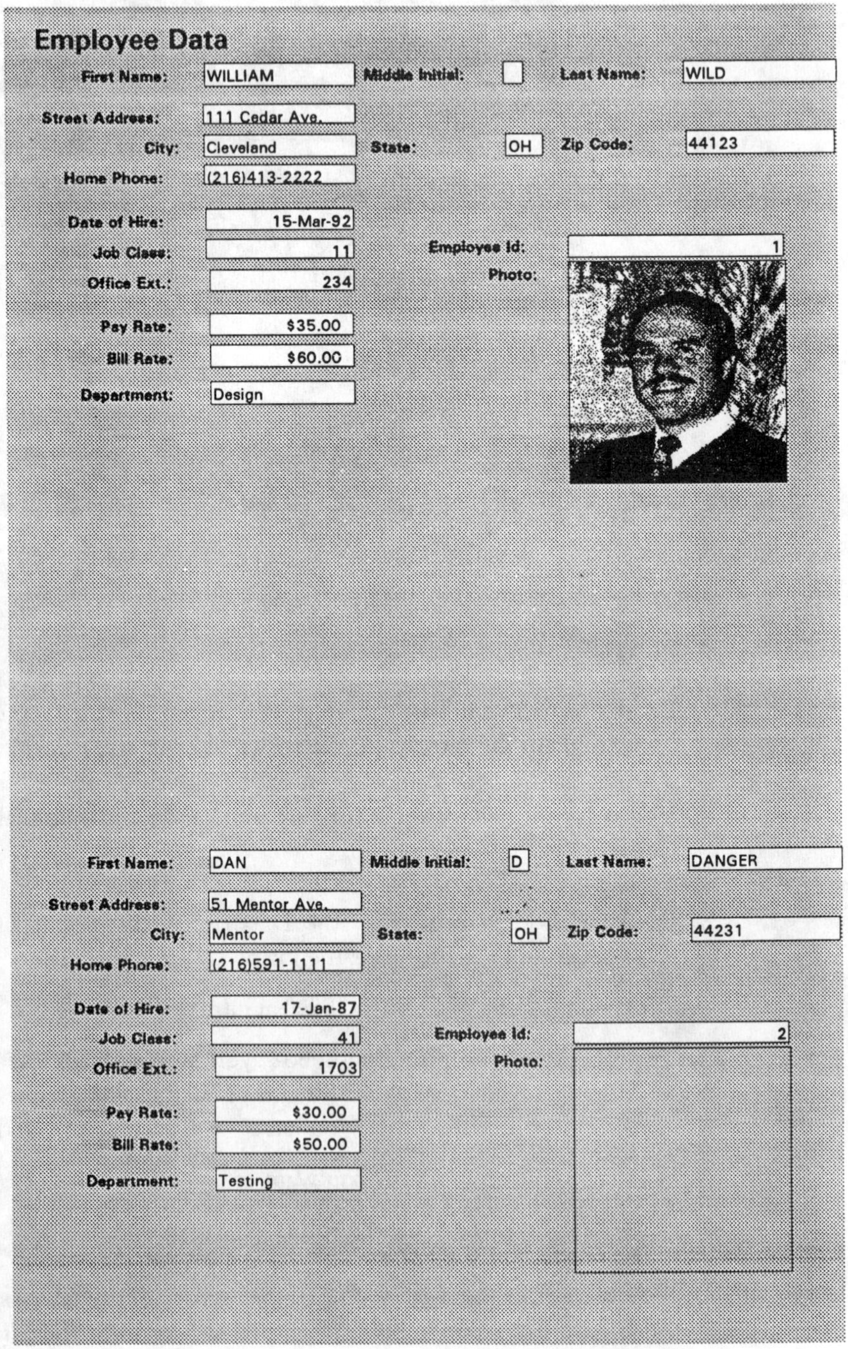

## Employee Data

First Name: WILLIAM    Middle Initial:    Last Name: WILD
Street Address: 111 Cedar Ave.
City: Cleveland    State: OH    Zip Code: 44123
Home Phone: (216)413-2222
Date of Hire: 15-Mar-92
Job Class: 11    Employee Id: 1
Office Ext.: 234    Photo:
Pay Rate: $35.00
Bill Rate: $60.00
Department: Design

First Name: DAN    Middle Initial: D    Last Name: DANGER
Street Address: 51 Mentor Ave.
City: Mentor    State: OH    Zip Code: 44231
Home Phone: (216)591-1111
Date of Hire: 17-Jan-87
Job Class: 41    Employee Id: 2
Office Ext.: 1703    Photo:
Pay Rate: $30.00
Bill Rate: $50.00
Department: Testing

## Previewing a Form

You can also preview how the printed copy will appear. Use the Print Preview command in the File menu to see a screen showing how the form will appear when it is printed before you actually print it. While previewing the printed form, you can change the setup. When you see that the format of the printout is what you want, select the Print button to print the form. Usually, if you see something you do not want in the form, you will change the form's design rather than the print settings you use to print the form.

### Quick Reference

**To Use an Existing Form** Select the form to use in the Database window while displaying forms. Double-click the form name or select Open in the Database window.

**To Create an AutoForm with Access Version 2** Select the table or query to use for the form by selecting the table or query's name in the Database window or by switching to the window showing the table or query. Click the AutoForm button on the toolbar. Access will create a form for the table or query that includes all fields.

**To Create a Form with a Form Wizard** Click the New button at the top of the Database window while displaying forms, click the New Form button on the toolbar while looking at a table or query, or choose New from the File menu and then Form. Select the table or query the form uses from the Select a Table/Query drop-down list box. Select the Form Wizards button. Next select the type of Form Wizard form you want to create. For each of the subsequent dialog boxes, select the information it requests, such as the fields the form includes, its looks, and its title. When you select the Finish button from the final dialog box, the form opens in either Design or Form view.

Quick Reference

**To Create a Form Starting with an Empty Design** Click the New button at the top of the Database window while displaying forms, click the New Form button on the toolbar while looking at a table or query, or choose New from the File menu and then Form. Select a table or query the form uses from the Select a Table/Query drop-down list box. Select the Blank Form button. In the Form window in Design view, add the controls you want to appear in the form. You can use the toolbar, toolbox, and other features that make designing forms easier. When you want to see the data displayed with Form view, you can choose Form from the View menu or click the Form View button in the toolbar.

**To Rename a Form** Select the form that you want to rename from the Database window. Choose Rename from the File menu or right-click the form. Type the new name for the form and select OK.

**To Display a Form's Design** Select the form in the Database window. Click the Design button in the top of the Database window. If you already have the form displayed, click the Design button in the toolbar or choose Form Design from the View menu.

**To Move a Control on a Form** Click the control in the form design you want to move. Point to the control so the mouse pointer looks like a hand. Drag the control to a new position. To move only half of a compound control, point to the upper-left corner of the control so that the pointer looks like a hand holding up one finger. At this point you can drag it to a new location.

## Quick Reference

**To Size a Control on a Form** Click the control in the form design you want to resize. Point to one of the handles on the control so that the pointer looks like a double-headed arrow. Drag the handle to a new location.

**To Add a Field to a Form** With the field list showing in the form design, select the fields you wish to add from the field list. Drag one of these fields to where you want the fields to appear on the form design.

**To Delete a Control on a Form** Click the control in the form design you want to remove, and then press DEL or choose Delete from the Edit menu.

**To Change the Text of a Field Name of a Control on a Form** Click the field name control in the form design. Click again where you want the insertion point added. Make the changes to the text and press ENTER or select another control to finish the editing.

**To Print a Form** Display the form or form design, or select the form name in the Database window. Choose Print from the File menu and make changes to the Print dialog box if you wish. Select OK to print the form. You can also preview your form by clicking the Preview button in the toolbar or by choosing Print Preview from the File menu.

# Chapter 9

Creating an AutoReport with Access Version 2

Creating a Report with Report Wizards

Looking at the Report's Design

Using the Report

# Creating a Basic Report

A *REPORT* is a description of how you want the data in a table or query presented. Unlike forms, reports are meant to be printed rather than displayed onscreen. You can design a report by yourself or use Microsoft Access Report Wizards for help. Even if you want to create a customized report, you might want to use the Report Wizards to create the beginning of the report. You can take the report you create with a Report Wizard and then modify it, as you will learn to do in later chapters, to create a report like the one shown in Figure 9-1.

Reports let you present information in a format that is easy to understand. Also, reports let you select the data you want to present. You can customize your reports to produce exactly the output you want. Reports, unlike forms, usually show more than one record at a time.

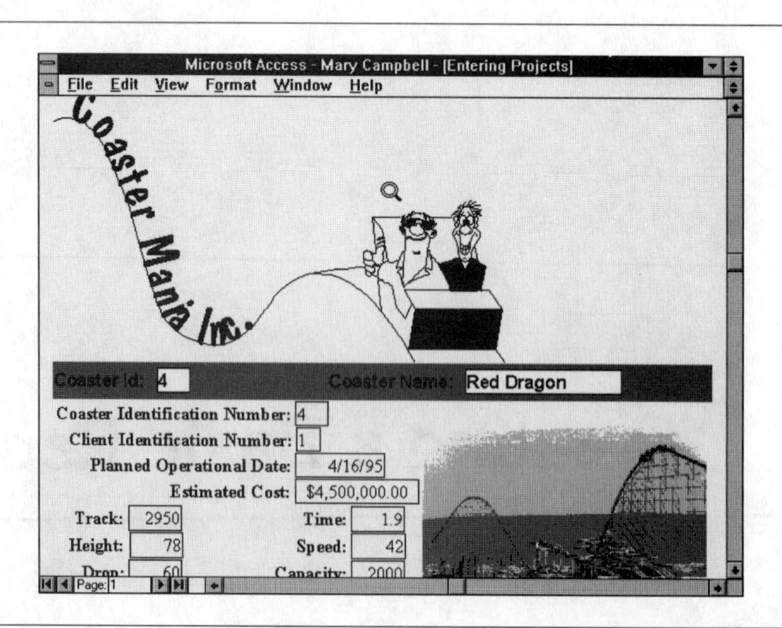


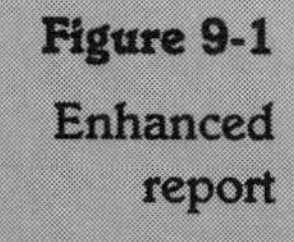

**Figure 9-1** Enhanced report

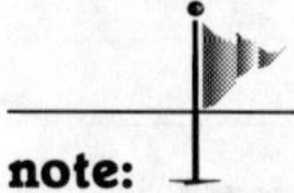

**note:** *If you want a customized presentation to display your records onscreen, create a form, not a report.*

You will create different reports in your database to match the different information requests the database supplies. The reports you create with Access let you select which data you present and how this information is presented. For example, for a mailing list of clients, you can print just the customer name and address. If you are preparing billing information, your report is likely to also include the items the clients have ordered or the services the company has rendered. A report does not need to show every field within the table or query it is based on.

This chapter covers the basics of creating and using a report. Most of the reports you will learn about and see here are created with Report Wizards. You will also learn how to name, save, and print the reports you create. Since forms and reports share many design and creation features, you will perform the same steps in designing a report that you used in Chapter 8 to design a form.

## Creating an AutoReport with Access Version 2

The simplest way to create a report in Access version 2 is to let Access create it for you. The new AutoReport feature creates a report using the selected table or query. The report will include all of the fields from the table or query. To create an AutoReport:

1. Select the table or query the report will use.

   You can either select the table or query's name from the Database window or you can open or switch to a window that shows the table or query.

2. Click the AutoReport button, shown here:

Access builds a report for the currently selected table or query. When Access is finished, the report appears in a new window like the one shown in Figure 9-2. Once you have this report, you are ready to print or save it. To learn how to work with the report, see the "Using the Report" section later in this chapter.

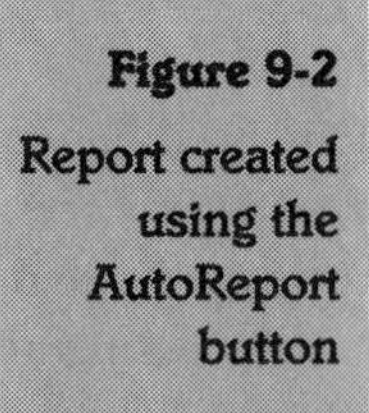

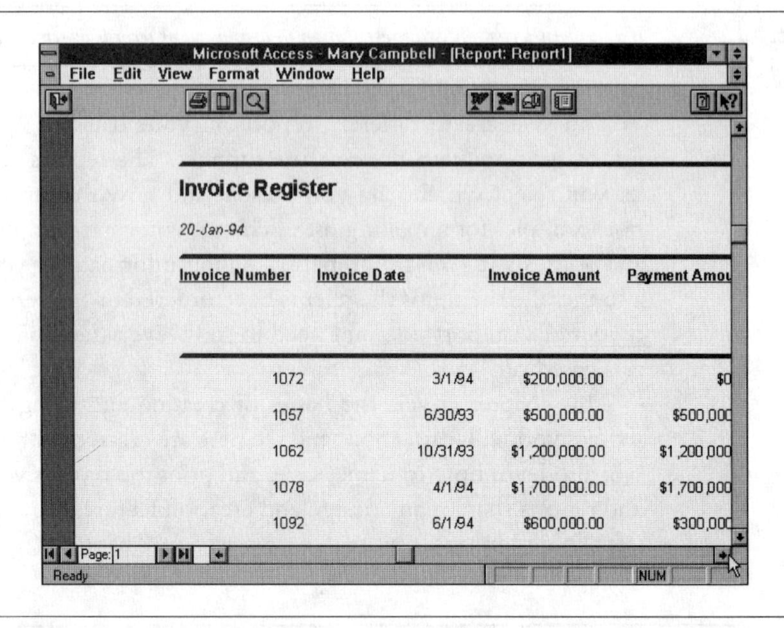


**Figure 9-2** Report created using the AutoReport button

## Creating a Report with Report Wizards

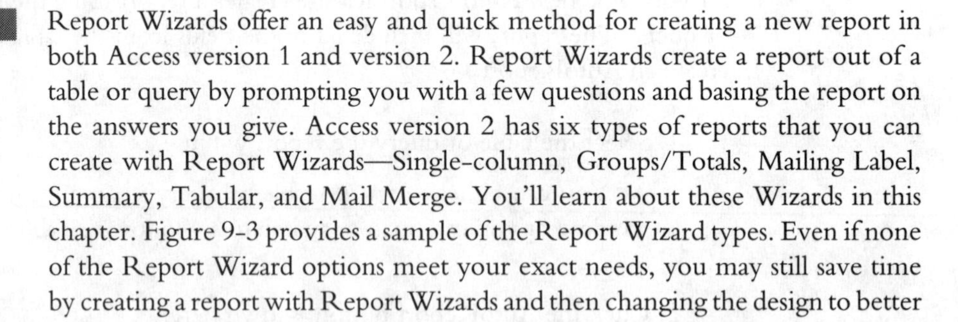

Report Wizards offer an easy and quick method for creating a new report in both Access version 1 and version 2. Report Wizards create a report out of a table or query by prompting you with a few questions and basing the report on the answers you give. Access version 2 has six types of reports that you can create with Report Wizards—Single-column, Groups/Totals, Mailing Label, Summary, Tabular, and Mail Merge. You'll learn about these Wizards in this chapter. Figure 9-3 provides a sample of the Report Wizard types. Even if none of the Report Wizard options meet your exact needs, you may still save time by creating a report with Report Wizards and then changing the design to better suit your needs.

**tip:** *Access version 1 only offers three Report Wizards—the Single-column, Groups/Totals, and Mailing Label Wizards. While these Wizards may use slightly different steps than the Access version 2 Report Wizards do, they have the same options for creating the final report. This chapter covers the Access version 2 wizards.*

**Figure 9-3**

Report types offered by Access Report Wizards

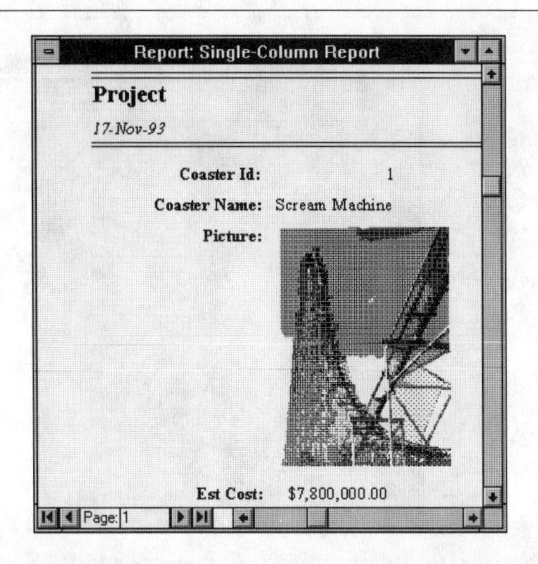


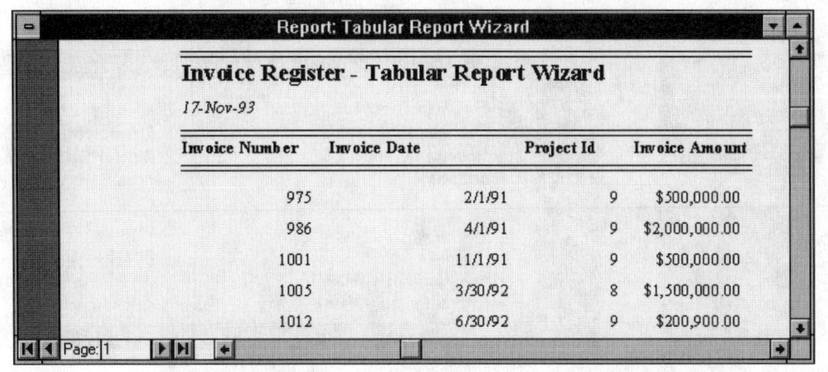


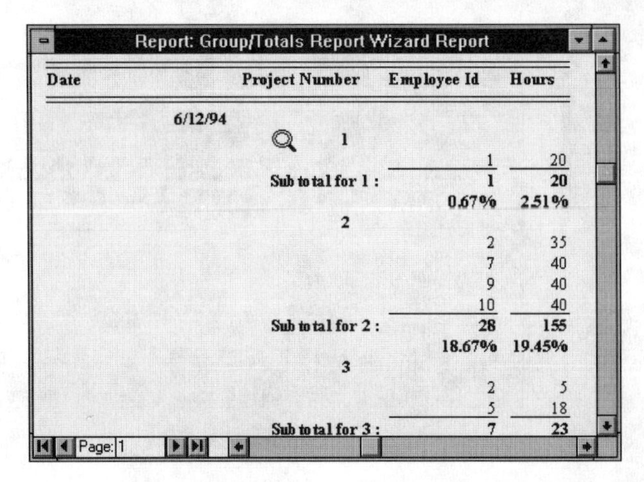

**Figure 9-3** Report types offered by Access Report Wizards (continued)

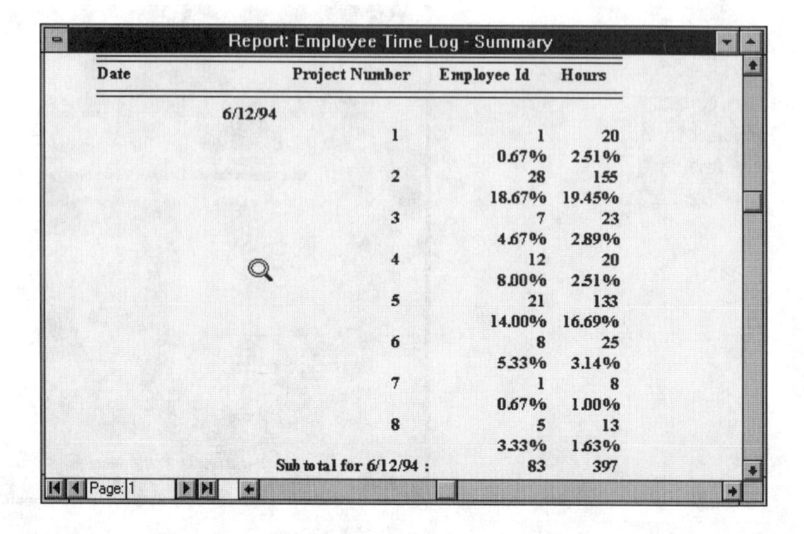


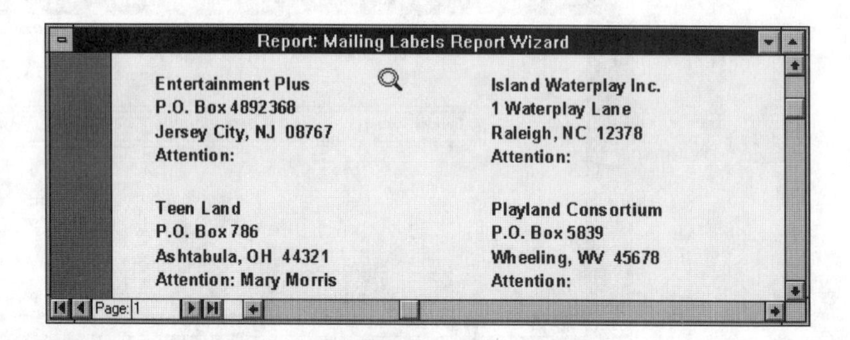


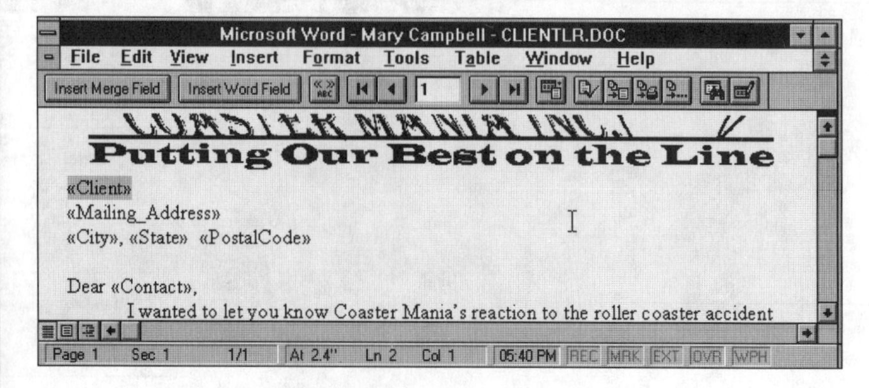


MS Word Mail Merge Report

The general procedure you will follow for creating a report with the Report Wizards is the same for each type of report:

- Tell Access you want to create a report.
- Select the Wizard to use.
- Respond to the questions the Wizard asks.
- Give the report a name.
- Open the report.

In the sections that follow, you will have an opportunity to look at how the actual steps vary for different types of reports created with the Report Wizards.

There are three ways to begin creating a report with a Report Wizard:

- Click the New button at the top of the Database window when displaying reports.
- Choose New from the File menu and then Report.
- Click the New Report button on the toolbar, shown here:

Access displays the New Report dialog box, shown in the following illustration. Your selection in the Select A Table/Query drop-down list box tells Access which data you want to use to create the report. When you create a report while looking at a datasheet, the table name or query is supplied for you.

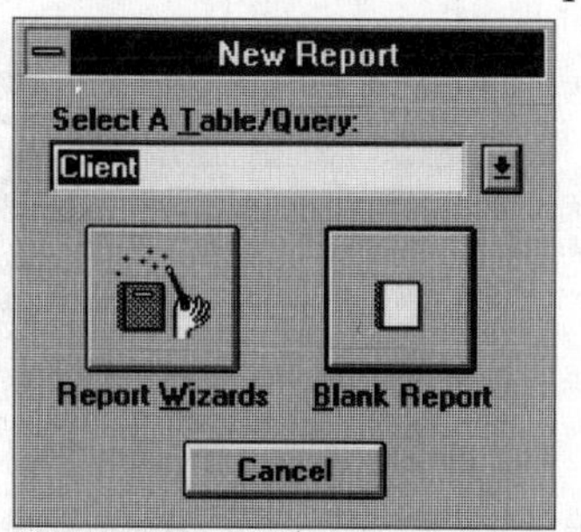


After selecting the table or query name, select the Report Wizards command button. Later you'll see how to create a report with the Blank Report button, which creates an empty report that you can fill as you want.

Once you select the Report Wizards button, choose which Report Wizard you want to use. Figure 9-3 shows some of the different report types you can create. Every one except MS Word Mail Merge has a title bar entry to describe the type of report created. Access has seven choices—Single-Column, Tabular, Groups/Totals, Summary, Mailing Label, AutoReport, and MS Word Mail Merge. The AutoReport is not actually another report type, since selecting it creates a single-column report without prompts just as if you clicked the AutoReport button.

Each of these report types gives you a different basic style of report, which you can embellish as you like. When you select which Report Wizard you want to use, the Report Wizard asks questions. Your answers to those questions determine the information that appears in the report. Each Report Wizard asks a different set of questions appropriate for the specific type of report being created.

## Single-Column and Tabular Report Wizard Reports

Single-Column and Tabular Report Wizard reports are created the same way. A *single-column report* puts all of the fields you select into a single column, with their field names to the left. A *tabular report,* available only in Access version 2, puts all of the fields you select into a row. A tabular report is similar to the table format of datasheets, but the report includes more space between each field and record. This report is just like the report created by clicking the AutoReport button except that you can select the fields you will include and the general appearance. Both types of reports let you select a style for how the field names and the contents are displayed and let you choose the title that appears at the beginning of the report.

From the first dialog box, shown here, select the fields you want to appear in the report:

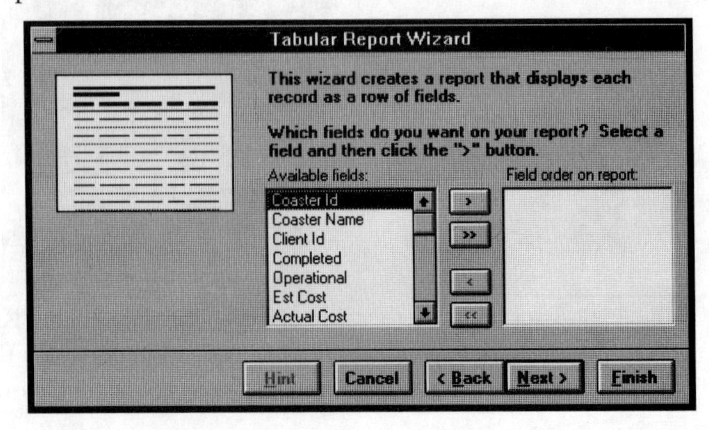

To add fields to the report, highlight the field in the Available fields list box and select the > button. The field name then appears in the Field order on report list box, wherever the highlight is. The order of the field names in the Field order on report list box determines the order of the fields in the report. Select the >> button to add all of the fields.

You can select a field in the Field order on report list box and choose the < button to remove the field from the report. The << button removes all fields from the Field order on report list box. Once all of the fields you want the report to use appear in the Field order on report list box in the order you want, select the Next button.

Now decide how the records in the report will be sorted. The records can be arranged using the values of up to ten fields. Access version 1 can sort using the values of up to three fields. From the dialog box, select the fields that you want to use to sort the records. The first field you select is the field that sorts all of the records. The second field you select sorts records that have the same value in the first field. The subsequent fields you select only control the order of the records when the records have the same values for the preceding fields. In effect, each field serves as a tie-breaker for the fields before it. You do not have to select any fields if you want the report to present the information in the order the data appears on the table or query. After selecting the fields you want to use to sort the records, select Next.

Now you can select the look for the report. The Single-Column and Tabular Report Wizards offer you three predefined looks—Presentation, Executive, and Ledger—shown in Figure 9-4. The look you choose sets the appearance of the field names and the field contents in the report. You can also set how much space you want between fields and records in Access version 2 by selecting a distance from the Line Spacing drop-down list box. Select one of the styles and choose Next.

All Access needs to complete the report is the title. The title appears at the beginning of the report and is separate from the report's name. Type any text you feel is appropriate. If you do not type a title, the Report Header section that is part of the report's design will only contain the current date. Access version 2 initially provides the name of the table or query the report is based on as the title.

In Access version 2, this last dialog box also has several check boxes you can select. For single-column reports, you can choose that each record starts on a new page or that the title appears on every page. Selecting the Show the title on each page check box puts the heading that would normally be in the Report Header section into a Page Header section that appears at the beginning of each page. For tabular reports, you can select whether you want all of the fields to

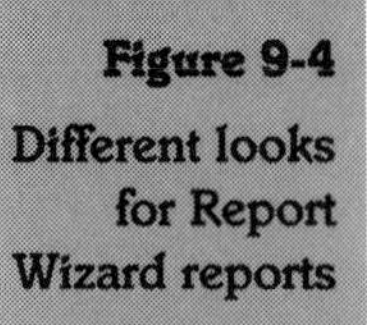

**Figure 9-4** Different looks for Report Wizard reports

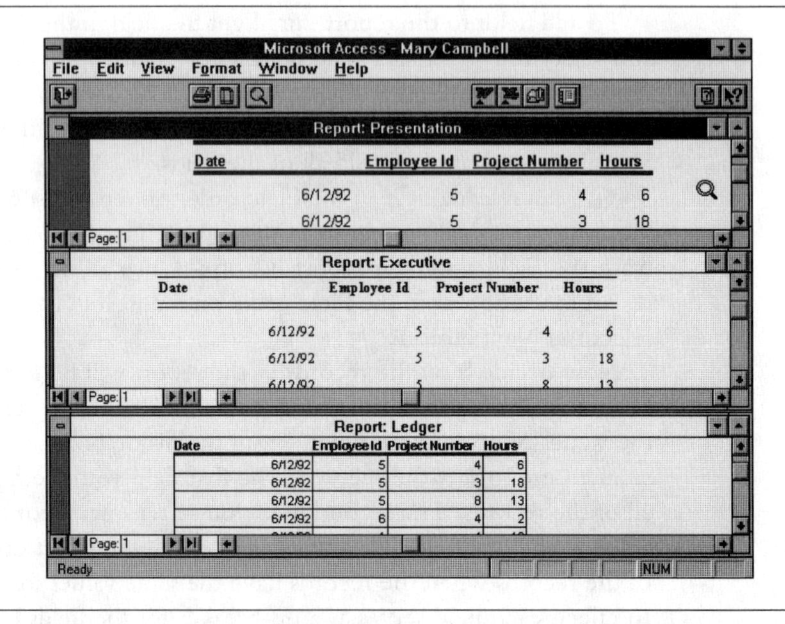


fit on one page. When this check box is selected, fields are shortened so that all fields fit on the page. For both types of reports, you can also select whether you want Cue Cards displayed as you work with the report.

Once you've entered a title, select the See report with data in it option button and then Finish to display the report in the Print Preview window. In Access version 1, select the Print Preview button to do this. At this point, you are ready to print the report, as described in the "Using the Report" section later in this chapter. Figure 9-5 shows a Single-Column Report Wizard report that includes all of the fields in the Project table in a different order than they appear in the table.

You can also select the Modify the report's design option button and Finish (in Access version 1, select Design) to display the Design view of the report that you created with the Report Wizard. If you do this, note how Access has added the date to the report. When you move to the bottom of the page in Print Preview view or print out the report, notice how the bottom of every page contains the page number. The date and page numbers are added as expressions to the report's design. You will learn more about expressions in Chapter 12.

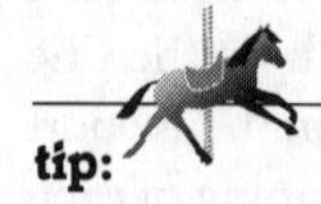

**tip:** *Use the title to add a heading to the report so that the report's user knows the purpose of the report.*

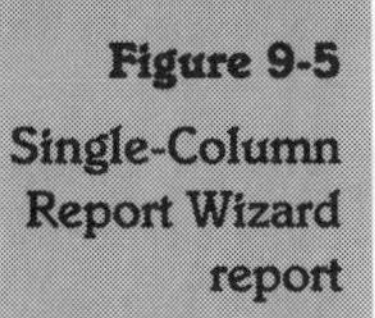

**Figure 9-5** Single-Column Report Wizard report

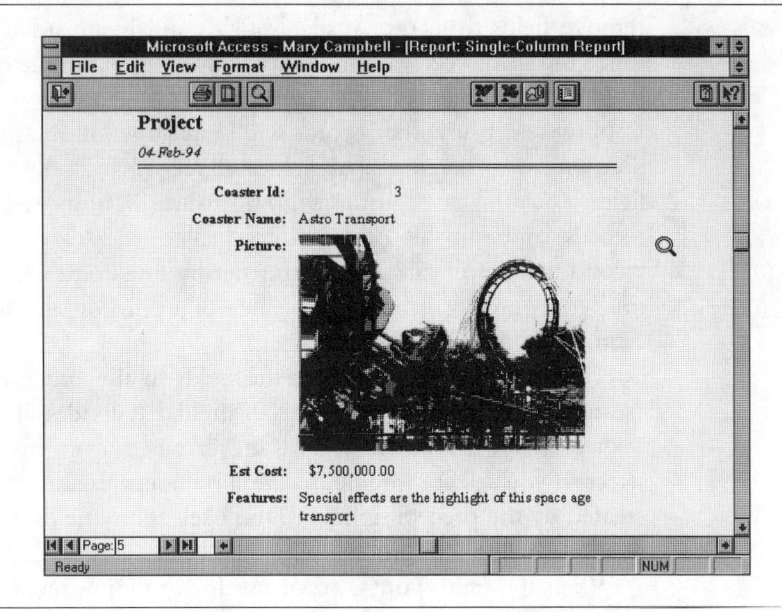


## Groups/Totals and Summary Report Wizard Reports

Groups/totals reports and summary reports are created the same way. A *groups/totals report* puts the fields you select into a row and groups the records according to the value of a field. A *summary report* is just like a groups/totals report except that the report does not include the detail information from each record. Summary reports are only available in Access version 2. You can see the difference between the groups/totals and summary report types by looking at the examples in Figure 9-3, which use the same data with the same selections made in the Report Wizards.

You can group the records using up to three different fields. Grouping fields lets you organize your data into manageable groups. As an example, suppose you want a report of all city officials for the United States and you want to be able to find the official by searching by location. You group the records for each official first by state, and then by county, and finally by city. When you want to find the official of a particular city, you can look first for the state, next for the county, and then for the city. You can select a style for how the field names and the contents are displayed, and you can choose the title that appears at the beginning of the report.

Just as with the Single-column and Tabular Report Wizards, you first select the fields to appear in the report. Use the >, >>, <, and << buttons to add and remove fields from the Available fields and Field order on report list boxes. Once the fields you want the report to use appear in the order you want in the Field order on report list box, select the Next button.

Now select how the records will be grouped in the report. The groups are divisions within a report that include all records with the same value in a specific field. You can have groups within groups. Within each primary group, the records can be further divided into smaller groups according to the value of a second field. You can take this further by dividing each secondary group into smaller groups according to the value of a third or later field. (Remember the example of the city officials report.)

From the dialog box, select the fields in the order you want the groups created. The first field you select is the field that divides all of the records. Within each primary group, the records are grouped again by the second field you select. If you select more fields, the subsequent fields further divide the groups created by the preceding fields. Don't select any fields if you do not want the records divided into groups.

When the fields you want to use for grouping records are selected, select Next. As an example, you can use groups to create the report shown in Figure 9-6. In this report, Date is selected as the first field used in sorting, and Project Number is selected as the second field used in sorting. The individual records are grouped by date and project ID.

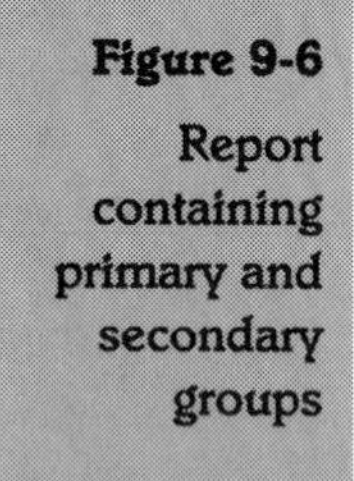

**Figure 9-6** Report containing primary and secondary groups

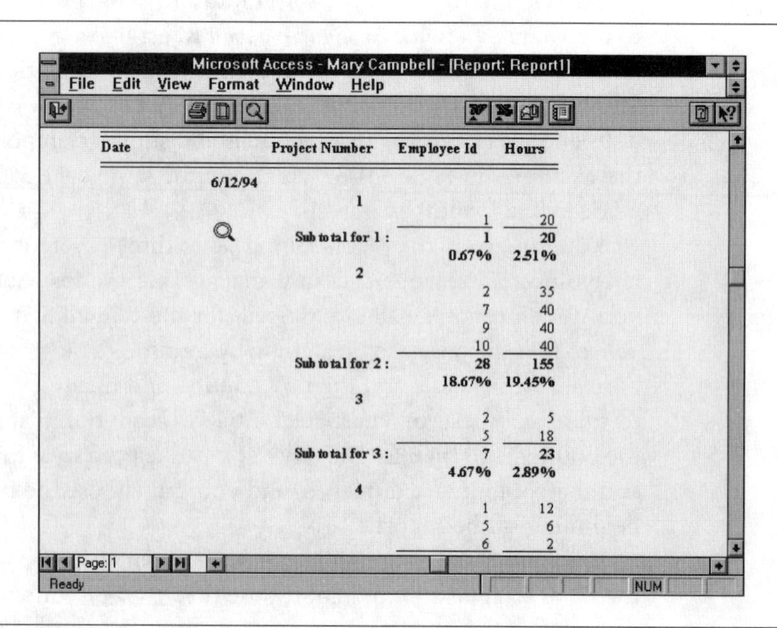

Next, decide how you want the selected fields' values divided into groups. You have different choices depending on each field's data type. With Character data fields, you can divide the data according to the entire entry in the field, the first character, the first two characters, the first three characters, the first four characters, or the first five characters. For example, when you look at a dictionary, notice that all of the entries are grouped by the first letter. When you divide addresses by a state field, you will select Normal to use the full field so that the North Dakota addresses are not intermingled with the ones from North Carolina.

Numbers can be grouped by their unique values or into groups of tens, hundreds, and so on. Dates can be grouped by years, quarters, months, and so on down to individual days. Time values can be grouped by hours or minutes.

The default selection for how to group the values in the fields used for grouping records is Normal, which means that whenever the value for the field changes, the report starts another group. To choose how the values of a field are divided into groups, select the field name in the Available fields list box and then select how you want the field values combined into groups from one of the listed choices in the Grouping Options list box (Records Will Be Grouped By in Access version 1). Repeat this for each of the listed fields, and then select Next.

You next select how the records in the report are sorted. Access organizes the records to appear in the report first by the groups the report uses and then by any fields you select to further sort the records. The fields you select to sort by only sort the records within the smallest groups of the report. For the report shown in Figure 9-6, the records are first organized by date and then by project number for the groups the report creates; then, within the smaller groups, the records are listed in order of the Employee Id field.

From the dialog box, select the fields used to sort the records. Selecting fields for sorting is just like selecting fields to appear in the report. Only the fields not used to group the records in the report are listed. You can select more than one field, and the records within each group are organized by the value of the fields in the order you select them. You do not have to use both sorting and grouping in a report, since you only select the report features you want to include. When you have selected the fields you want to further sort the records, select Next.

Once you have chosen how you want to sort the records for the report, select the look for the report. As with the Single-column or Tabular Report Wizards, you can select from three predefined looks—Presentation, Executive, and Ledger—shown in Figure 9-4. The look you choose sets the style of the box for each of the fields in the report and also determines where the lines are added. Choose one of the looks and select Next.

Now add the report's title. The title appears at the beginning of the report, and it is separate from the report's name. Type any text you feel is appropriate. If you do not add a title, the report's Report Header section, which is the part of the report design where a report's title appears, will only contain a date. Access version 2 provides a default title of the name of the table or query the report is based on, which you can use, replace, or delete.

You can also select and clear the available check boxes to set features about the report's appearance. Choose whether you want to squeeze the fields onto one page by selecting the See all fields on one page check box. When you do this, the fields in the report are truncated if Access needs more room to fit all of the fields from one record onto a page. Usually this check box is cleared, which means that when the report has many fields, some of the fields appear on separate pages. The next two check boxes are only available in Access version 2. Selecting the Calculate percentages of the total check box includes percentages for the totals within each group relative to the totals for all groups. You can also select whether you want Cue Cards displayed as you work with the report.

Once you've entered the title, select See the report with data in it option button and Finish (Print Preview in Access version 1) to display the report in the Print Preview window. Figure 9-6 shows a Groups/Totals Report Wizard report created using the Employee Time Log table. In this report, records are grouped according to the date and project number and then sorted according to the employee ID number. Each group is a separate section of the report. Also notice how the Employee Id is totaled for each group. This total is meaningless. When you learn more about report designs, you can remove it from the report. The Groups/Totals and Summary Report Wizards automatically total all numeric fields, whether the totals are meaningful or not. Like the Single-column report type, this report includes the date and page number. From the last dialog box of the Report Wizard, you can also select the Modify the report's design option button and Finish (Design in Access version 1) to display the report that you created with the Report Wizard in Design view.

## Mailing Label Report Wizard Reports

A *mailing label report* is designed to print labels; it fits the fields you select into a rectangle. The mailing label report is specifically designed to print one of various sizes of labels. This report type also makes it easy to add characters such as commas and spaces.

Once you select Mailing Label, you get a different dialog box for adding the fields than you did earlier for adding fields in the other types of Report Wizards. You'll see this dialog box:

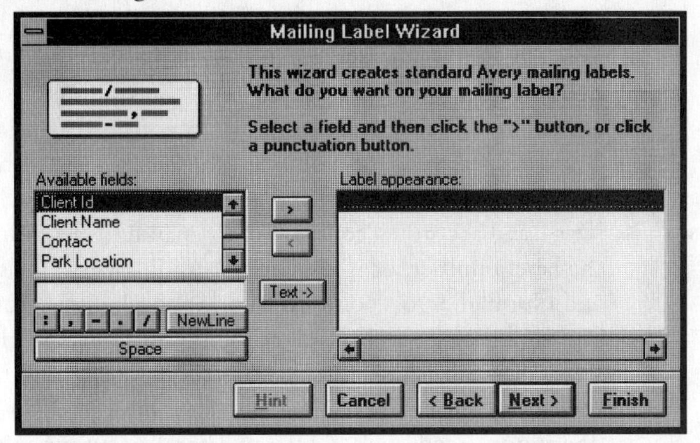


Besides selecting fields and then the > button to add them to the report, you can select which characters you want to add. The dialog box has buttons to add the characters most frequently used in a mailing label. When you click the : (colon), , (comma), - (hyphen), . (period), / (slash), or Space buttons, these characters are directly added to the current line in the report design. You can also type text into the text box below the field names and then click the Text -> button to add the text you type to the report.

Unlike the other Report Wizard reports, the fields you add do not appear on different lines. The fields appear on the same line until you select the NewLine button in version 1.

As you add fields as well as other characters to the report, you are selecting which line they appear in. Select the fields and text you want for each line. When finished with a line, select the NewLine (↵ in version 1) button to advance to the next line.

Another difference between this dialog box and the dialog box for adding fields in the other Report Wizards is that when you click the < button, Access removes the last field, character, or group of text from the current row in the Label appearance list box. You cannot insert and remove fields and characters from the middle of a row. You can shift the contents in the Label appearance list box to the left or right by clicking the arrows below this list box. When you have the fields you want in the report layout in the Label appearance list box, select Next.

Now select how the records are sorted for the report, setting the order in which records are printed onto the mailing labels. For example, you may want the printed mailing labels sorted by ZIP code. From the dialog box, select the fields to use when sorting the records from the Available fields list box. The first field you select orders all of the records. The second field you select orders the records that have the same value for the first field. The subsequent fields you select sort records when they have the same field values for the prior sorting fields. When you want the mailing labels printed in the order in which they appear in the table or query, you do not need to select any fields. When you have selected the fields you want the records sorted by, select Next.

Now select the size of the labels. The list box includes most available label sizes listed according to their Avery mailing label number. If you do not know the label number, or if you are not using Avery labels, look at the Dimensions and Number across columns to find the label size that matches your labels. By selecting the option buttons at the bottom of this dialog box in Access version 2, you can limit the list of label sizes to only those that use either English or metric measurements. You can also limit the list to either sheet-feed or continuous-feed labels. Access will handle centering the data on the label. Select one of the label sizes from the list and then select Next.

**tip:** *If Access does not provide a selection for your label size, pick the closest size and then change the design for the report before printing to match your label size and layout.*

In Access version 2, you can now choose the font for the text of the mailing label. From the next dialog box, you can select the font name, its size, its weight, its color, and whether it uses attributes such as underlining and italics. The Sample box in the dialog box shows an example of the current selected font. When the Sample box shows the font you want to use for the labels, select Next.

At this point, Access has created the label design for you. In Access version 2, you can now select the Open Cue Cards to help you print the mailing labels or modify the report design check box when you want Cue Cards available as you work with the report.

Select the See the mailing labels as they will look printed option button and Finish (Print Preview in Access version 1) to look at your mailing labels. Figure 9-7 shows a mailing label report created with the Client table. The comma, the spaces, and the text "Attention:" are added as part of the report's design. From the same dialog box, you can also select the Modify the mailing label design option button and then Finish (Design in Access version 1) to look at the design of the report that Access has created for you.

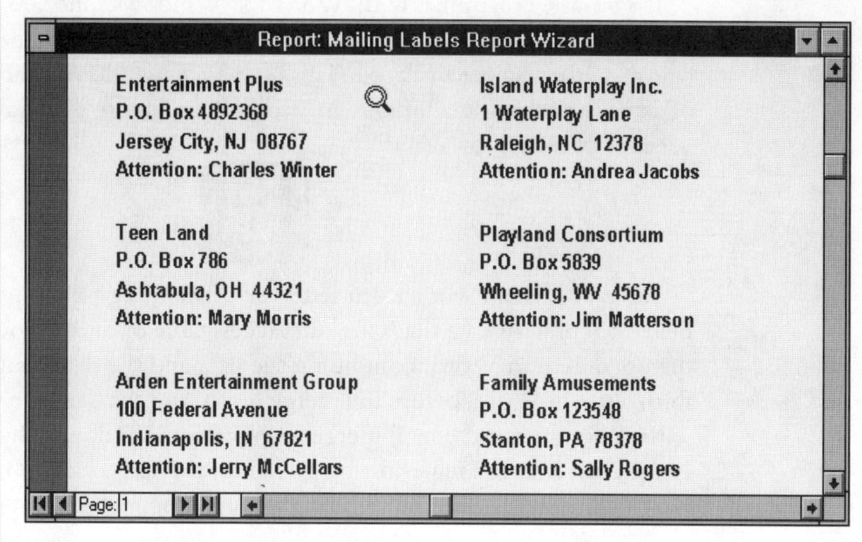


**Figure 9-7** Mailing Label Report Wizard report

## MS Word Mail Merge Report Wizard Reports in Access Version 2

A *mail merge report* sets up a Word for Windows mail merge data document to use data from a table or query. This Report Wizard sets up form letters and other types of mail merge documents in Word for Windows using the data you already have in your Access database. To use this Wizard, you must have Word for Windows installed on your system.

Once you select MS Word Mail Merge, you can select whether you want to use a Word for Windows document you have already created or one that you will create. Select one of these check boxes and OK. If you choose the Link your data to an existing Microsoft Word document option button and OK to use a Word document you already created, you then need to select the Word document and OK. If you select the Create a new document and then link the data to it option button and OK to use a new document, Word opens. Access sets up the current document to be the main document you will use in the merge process. The table or query selected for the report is set up as the data source for the letter you are creating.

When you are creating a new main mail merge document in Word, you will type the text that stays the same for all of the letters. When you want to select one of the fields from the table or query, select the Insert Merge Field button from the bottom toolbar and select the field to use in its place.

If you are unfamiliar with Word for Windows, and are using Word for Windows 6, you will want to click on the Mail Merge Helper button, shown below, in the toolbar in Word. This Helper can guide you through the process of actually running mail merge in Word. This feature is not available in earlier versions of Word for Windows.

After you create your form letter or other merge document, using merge fields to represent data fields in your Access table or query, you can then merge the document in Word, combining the data and the form. Figure 9-8 shows a form letter in Word, before the merge is run, and the database that it will merge with. You can run the mail merge in Word for Windows 6 by selecting Merge in the Mail Merge Helper dialog box and the Merge button in the next dialog box. Figure 9-9 shows the resulting merged document.

## Looking at the Report's Design

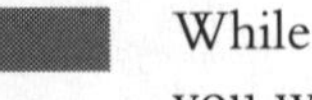

While you can continue using Report Wizards to create reports, at some point you will want to change the report's design or create your own from scratch.

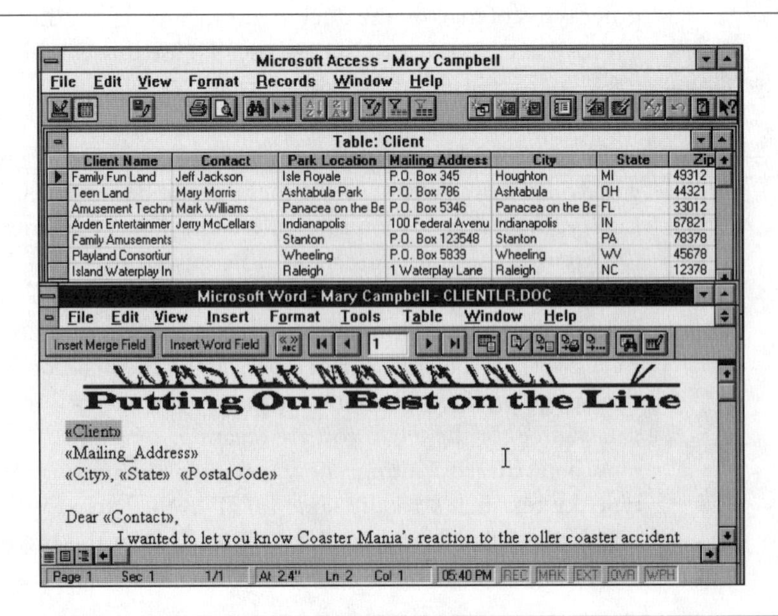


**Figure 9-8** Data and main document for form letter in Figure 9-9

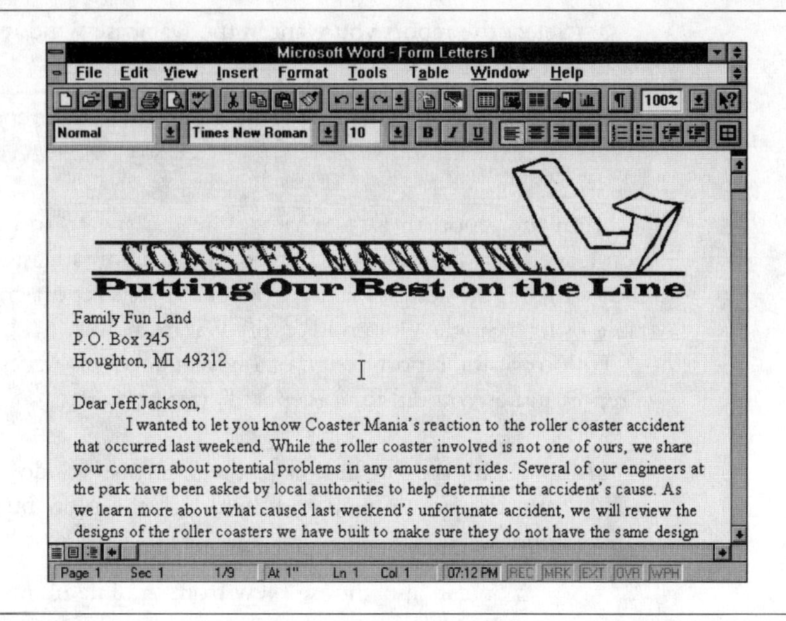


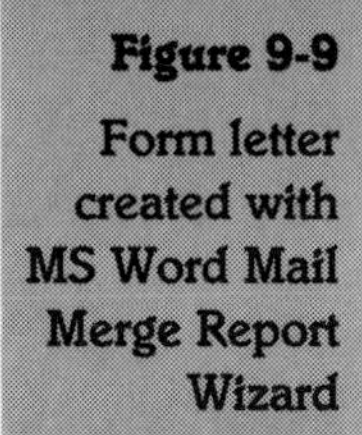

**Figure 9-9** Form letter created with MS Word Mail Merge Report Wizard

Working with the report design lets you adjust the contents, size, and position of everything that appears in the report. You can modify or add additional features that do not appear in the reports you create with the Report Wizard. You can also display an empty report design and add everything you want the report to contain, one element at a time. As with forms, each element of a report is called a *control*. Controls include a field's data, text, pictures, or calculations. Many of the features relating to forms that you learned about in Chapter 8 also apply to reports.

**tip:** *There are some printing settings that affect how your report will appear when printed; keep these settings in mind when designing your report. For example, you can print your report in columns, or change the width or height of the report, by changing print setup features. See the "Printing a Report" section, later in this chapter, to learn more about these features.*

The steps for looking at the report design of an existing report differ from those you use to look at a new report. To look at an existing report design, use one of these options:

- Select the report you want in the Database window and then select the Design button.
- In Access version 1, double right-click the report name from the Database window.

From the report in Design view, you can switch to Print Preview. When you leave Print Preview, you return to the report's Design view. Figure 9-10 shows the report design for the Coaster Projects report created for the Project table using a Single-Column Report Wizard report.

To look at the report design of a new report, tell Access you want to create a report just as you did for a Report Wizard report:

1. Click the Report button in the Database window or choose Reports from the View menu and then click the New button in the Database window.

   You can also choose New from the File menu and then Report or click the New Report button on the toolbar.

2. Select the table or query to use for the report from the Select A Table/Query drop-down list box.
3. Select the Blank Report button.

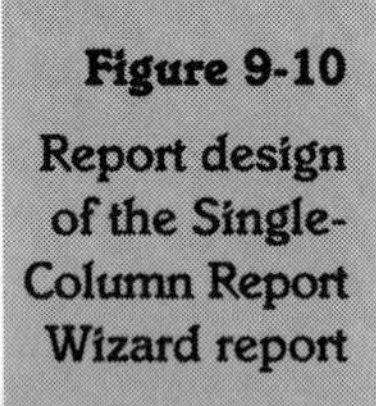

**Figure 9-10** Report design of the Single-Column Report Wizard report

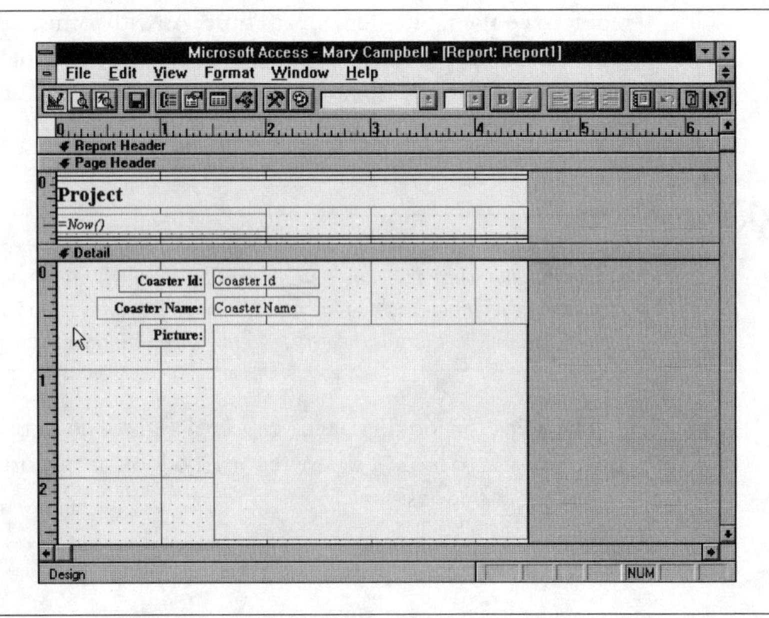

Selecting the Blank Report button opens the report design screen with an empty report that you can then fill in as you want. Figure 9-11 shows an empty report design screen.

When you look at the report design of some of the reports you create with the Report Wizard, you will notice advanced features that you will learn about in later chapters. For example, the Employees By Department report in Figure 9-6 has a Date Header and Date Footer section. In between the Date Header and Date Footer sections are Project Id Header and Project Id Footer sections. These sections start and end each group of records for the different departments in the report. You will learn about creating these sections and dividing a report's records into groups in Chapter 11. Also, when you look at the Client Mailing Label report created as an example of a Mailing Label Report Wizard report (Figure 9-7), the boxes in the report design that contain the contents of each line in the mailing label do not contain the field names, as the boxes that you see in Figure 9-10 do. Instead these boxes contain expressions. You will learn about expressions in Chapter 12.

Just like when you design forms, when you design reports you can have extra toolbars and windows open that make creating and modifying reports easier. One of these is the toolbox shown in the lower-left corner of Figure 9-11, which includes the arrow at the top of it. You can set whether the toolbox appears by choosing Toolbox in the View menu or by clicking the Toolbox button in the toolbar. You will use this toolbar in Chapter 11 to add controls

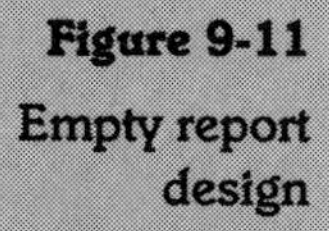

**Figure 9-11**

**Empty report design**

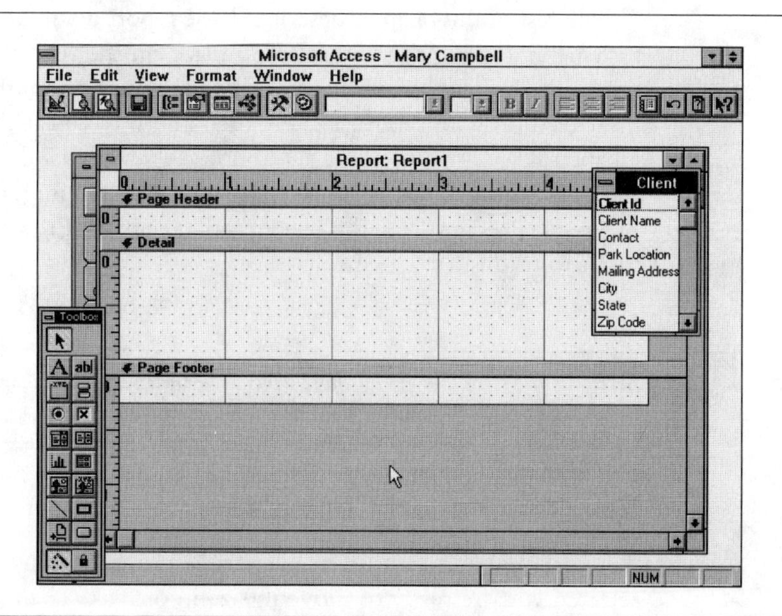

to the report. Figure 9-11 also shows the field list that you can use to quickly add fields to a report, as described later in this chapter. You can make this window appear and disappear by choosing Field List in the View menu or by clicking the Field List button in the toolbar. The following illustration shows some of the buttons in the report design toolbar that you can use to display or hide these toolboxes or windows when you are working on a report design:

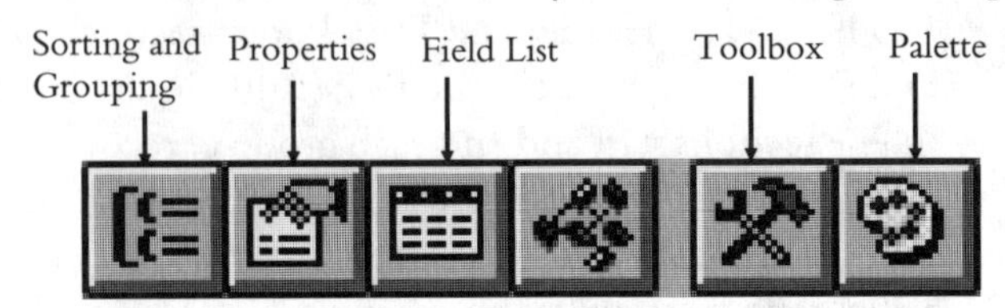


Later you will learn about other windows, such as the Palette and property sheet that you will use in Chapter 14 to change the colors and different features of the report's controls. When you display these extra windows, they remain where you put them. You can move these windows around in the Access desktop so that they are out of your way when you work on the report design. In Access version 1, displaying these windows also displays them for forms and for other database objects that use the windows. For example, if you display the property sheet for a table design, the property sheet is also open when you work on queries, forms, and reports. In Access version 2, displaying and hiding these windows in one type of object does not display or hide these windows in other types of objects.

The rest of this chapter describes basic report design features. These include moving and sizing the controls you place on the report design, changing the size of the report, and adding fields to the report in controls. You use most of these features with reports exactly the same way you used them with forms in Chapter 8.

When you want to see the report you are designing, choose Print Preview or Sample Preview from the File menu, or click the Preview or Sample Preview toolbar buttons.

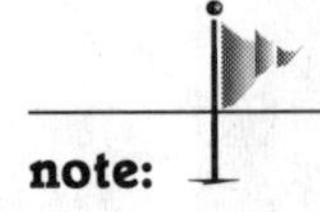

**note:** *Several of the reports shown in this chapter have their text size enlarged to make them easier to read. In Chapter 14, you will learn how you can make these changes to your reports.*

## Selecting Report Controls

To work with any control in a report, you need to select it. Once a control is selected you are ready to move it, size it, or make changes to it. You can also select multiple controls when you want to move, size, or alter several controls at once.

Selecting a single control is as simple as clicking it. As you select controls, the selected controls are marked with handles, as shown here:

These handles show which controls you have selected. Some controls, like the one for the text box for the Coaster Id field, are part of a *compound control.* These controls have a label control and another control that belongs with the label. In the example shown above, the Coaster Id: label is part of a compound control with the text box for the Coaster Id field. When you click a compound control, you are often selecting the label of the field name as well. Compound controls move as a unit, so the text that describes a field moves with the field when you move the field to another location. Other changes to a control will only affect the part of the compound control that you select.

When you want to select more than one control, select the first control you want and then hold down the SHIFT key while you continue clicking the other controls you want to select. Another option for selecting a group of controls is to draw a box on the report design that selects every control inside in the box. To draw this box, click an empty area of the report design near the controls you want to select and drag the mouse so that the box you are drawing contains the controls you want to select. The box only appears while you are drawing it; as soon as you release the mouse, the box disappears as Access selects all of the controls that appeared in the box.

Another way to select multiple controls is to drag the mouse in the ruler at the top or left of the Report window in Design view. When you do this, all of the controls under or to the right of the area you dragged through are selected. If you just click in the ruler, the controls directly under or to the right of the point you clicked are selected.

## Moving and Sizing Controls

You can move and size most of the controls you place on a report to improve the appearance of the report. Before you move or size a control in a report, you must select it as described in the previous section.

When you want to move the selected group of controls, all you have to do is drag the controls to a new position. Move the pointer to the border of one of the selected controls and it will change to look like a hand with the fingers extended. When you drag this hand from one position to another, all of the selected controls move to the new location.

You also can move a part of a compound control. For example, you can move a field without moving the field name that belongs to it. To move only part of the compound control, move the pointer to the upper-left corner of the part of the compound control that you wish to move. The pointer looks like a hand holding up one finger. Drag the pointer to a new location, and only the selected part of the compound control moves to the new location.

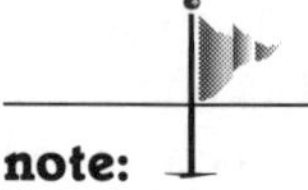

**note:** *You cannot move parts of multiple controls simultaneously; if you have multiple controls selected when you move part of a compound control, the only thing that moves is the part of the one compound control that you pointed to—the other compound controls remain the same.*

You can size selected controls just as easily. To size the selected controls, move the pointer to one of the handles around the control; the pointer changes to look like a double-headed arrow. Drag the arrow to where you want the new corner of the control to be. Since the opposite corner remains in place, the selected control is resized to fit the rectangle set by the two corners. If you have multiple controls selected, resizing one of them only affects the size of the control you are pointing to. Changing the size of a control containing text does not change the size of the text, but only the area that may contain text.

Figure 9-12 shows two copies of the same groups/totals report (which does not use any groups) for the Employee table. The report was created with the Report Wizard, and some of the fields have been moved and sized. The top window shows the preview of the report while the window on the bottom shows the report's design. In this report, fields have been dragged to new positions and some of the boxes have been enlarged or shrunk. (Also, some of the field names have been deleted and the Detail section was expanded, as described next.) Chapter 12 tells you how to create expressions so that the city, state, and ZIP code are resized to fit the contents of those fields.

### CHANGING THE REPORT'S AREA

A report design begins at a standard size, which you can change as your needs change. You can alter the size of the report when you need more or less information on the report. A report initially occupies a small part of the window, so you may want to enlarge the report as you add information to it.

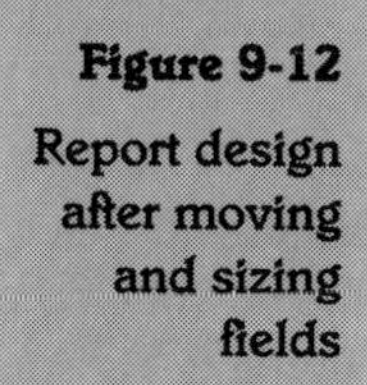

**Figure 9-12** Report design after moving and sizing fields

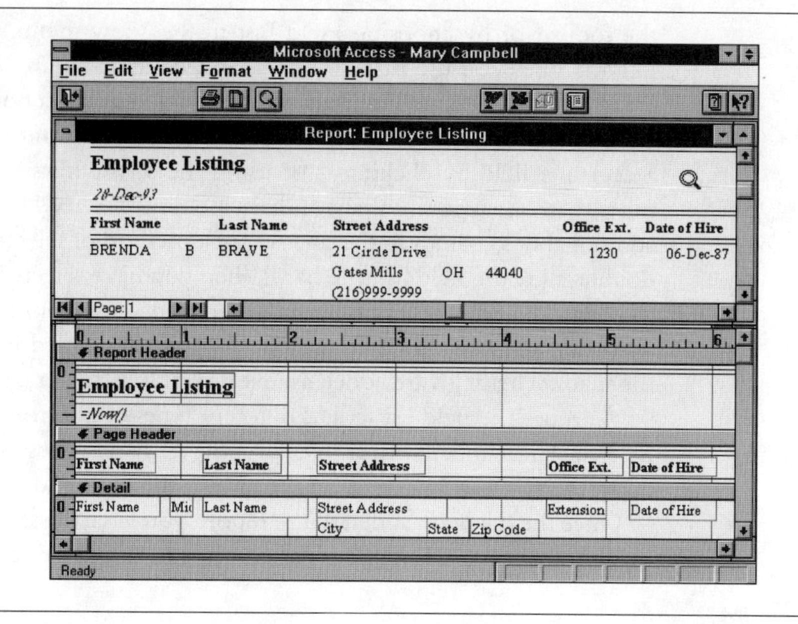


You can resize a report by moving the mouse to the report's boundary. When you do, the pointer changes to a double-headed arrow with a thick line in the middle. When you drag the mouse to a new location, the report's size widens or contracts, and the right edge of the report is placed where you release the mouse. Access will also enlarge the report's size for you when you move a control outside the report, to accommodate the control's new position.

## Adding Fields to a Report

When you create a report from scratch, you need to add the fields from the table or query it is based on. You also need to add fields when you modify a preexisting report design; for example, you might add to a report a field that you have added to the report's underlying table. You can add any fields of the selected table or query. For now, you will learn how to quickly add text boxes that are set to contain the entries of one of the table or query's fields. Chapter 11 teaches how to add fields to a report in other types of controls such as check boxes. Chapter 12 shows how to create text boxes that contain expressions, which let you add information to a report that is not directly available in one of the fields of the report's underlying table or query.

To add a field, you need the list of fields from the table or query that you can add to the report. Display the field list by clicking the Field List button in the toolbar or by choosing Field List in the View menu. This field list is just like the ones you use in query and form designs. Figure 9-11 shows the field list in a report design. The primary key field appears in boldface.

From this window, select the field or fields you want to add to the report. Select one field by clicking it or using the arrow keys to highlight it. Select more than one field simultaneously by holding down CTRL while you click the additional field names in the list. A quick method of selecting all the fields is to double-click the field list title bar. When you have selected the fields you want to add to the report, drag one of the selected fields from the field list to where you want the fields to start. The field names are added in labels to the left of the fields. The fields are added as text boxes. In Chapter 11, you will learn how you can use the field list to add different types of controls. You can repeat the field selection and addition to the report as many times as you want, and you do not have to add all the fields you want the report to use at once.

Once the fields are added to the report, you have the same sizing and moving capabilities you learned about for controls earlier in this chapter.

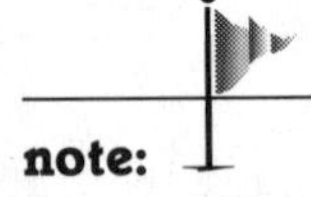

**note:** *The property sheet appears whenever you double-click a control that is not currently selected. You will want to hide the property sheet when you are not using it.*

When finished adding fields, hide the field list by either double-clicking its Control box, pressing ALT+F4 when the window is active (with the default colors, the title bar is blue), choosing Field List in the View menu, or clicking the Field List button in the toolbar again.

## Deleting Controls from a Report

You may have controls on the report that you want to remove. You can remove a control by clicking it and pressing DEL or by choosing Delete from the Edit menu. When you do this with a compound control like the ones you just learned to add, both the field name and the field are removed. You can also click the field name when you press DEL or choose Delete from the Edit menu. This deletes just the field name label without deleting the text box control for the field. Do this when you want to show a field without its field name or when you want to create a separate label that identifies the field's contents.

## Tools for Aiding Design

The report design window has several tools that make creating a report easier. One of these is the ruler, which measures the distance from the top and left corner of the ruler. The other is a grid, which is an organized layout of dots and lines. You can use the ruler and grid to simplify placing or sizing the controls you add to the report. A third method of quickly sizing controls is by using the menu to align controls relative to one another.

If you do not find the ruler helpful, remove it to give your report design more room. To remove the ruler, choose Ruler from the View menu. If you want to add the ruler back, choose Ruler from the View menu again. The Ruler command is a toggle switch that turns on and off the display of the ruler.

Another command that operates as a toggle is the Grid command. You may have noticed that when you move and size controls on the report, the control hops from one location to another as you slowly drag it. Every time you move or size a control, Access hops to the nearest grid point. Display the grid by choosing Grid from the View menu. When you choose the command again, the grid disappears. The horizontal and vertical lines marking each inch are part of the grid. The dots for the grid points will disappear when the grid points are very close together. You can continue using the default grid size or you can change it. In Chapter 11, you will learn how to set the distance between grid points. Displaying the grid does not affect the printed report, since the grid only appears when you are working on a report's design and never actually prints.

The reason the controls hop to the nearest grid point is because the Snap to Grid command in the Format menu (the Layout menu in Access version 1) is on. If you turn off this command by removing the check mark next to Snap to Grid, when you move and size controls they are placed exactly where you drag them. When you choose this command again, the check mark is added, and the controls you subsequently move and size hop to the nearest grid point. You can temporarily ignore the grid when you move or size a control by holding down the CTRL key while you drag the control you are moving or sizing. The grid setting only controls the position of controls at the time you move or size them, so when you turn the Snap to Grid on, you will not change the size and position of controls that you sized and moved while the Snap to Grid was off.

Another grid feature that controls the size of controls is the Size to Grid command in the Format menu (the Layout menu in Access version 1). When you choose this command, all four corners of every selected control hop to the nearest grid point, so the controls may enlarge or shrink, depending on the location of the closest grid points. Both Size to Grid and Snap to Grid operate whether or not you display the grid in the report design.

Besides using the grid or the ruler to position controls, you can use Align in the Format menu (the Layout menu in Access version 1) to position controls relative to each other. For example, if you have several fields you want left-aligned, you can tell Access to left-align those controls rather than placing each one individually. To align the controls, select the controls you want aligned relative to one another. Next, choose Align in the Format menu (the Layout menu in Access version 1). Choose how you want the controls aligned. Left moves all of the controls to the left edge of the control furthest to the left. Right moves all of the controls to the right edge of the control furthest to the right. Top moves all of the controls up to the top edge of the highest control. Bottom moves all of the controls down to the bottom edge of the lowest control. To Grid moves all of the controls to start at the closest grid points. In Access version 2, you can also align controls by right-clicking one of the selected controls and choosing Align and the alignment for the selected controls.

Aligning the controls does not necessarily align the contents of the fields. By default, Access left-aligns textual data and right-aligns numbers. The techniques described in Chapter 14 allow you to change how the field's contents are aligned within the control you create for a field.

## Changing the Text of a Field Name Label

The labels that Access adds when you use the field list to add text box controls to your report design may be exactly what you want on the report, but if they're not, you can change the text that appears in the label. Once you have selected the field name label control, changing the text is easy; you simply click where you want to add the insertion point in the label, just as if you are editing an entry in a table or query. Modify the field name as if you are making an entry. Continue to edit the label and then press ENTER or click another part of the report design to finish making changes. In Chapter 11, you will learn how to add other types of label controls to a report; you can modify the text in these controls the same way.

## Report Headers and Footers

If you look at most of the designs of the reports you created with Report Wizards, you will notice that the title you gave your report and the report's date both appear in a section called Report Header. A Report Header section appears at the beginning of the report design. A report that has a Report Header section also has a Report Footer section. The Report Footer section appears at the bottom of every report. When you create a groups/totals report using Report Wizards, this is the section that contains the totals of number-filled fields.

You can use these two sections to include a title or any other information you want. These two sections appear because Report Header/Footer in the Format menu (the Layout menu in Access version 1) has a check mark next to it. In Access version 2, you can also add these sections by selecting Report Header/Footer from the shortcut menu that Access displays when you right-click the report's title bar. You can choose Report Header/Footer in the Format menu (the Layout menu in Access version 1) to remove this check mark and remove the two sections from the report design.

**caution** *Remove these sections only if you do not want them at all, since removing these sections permanently destroys the contents of the report design in these sections.*

As you learn how to add controls and change properties of reports, keep in mind that you can also add controls and change properties of the controls in the Report Header and Report Footer sections.

Also, most report designs include a Page Header and Page Footer section. For reports created with the Single-Column Report Wizard, when you have selected the check box to repeat the title on every page, the title and date is placed in the Page Header section rather than in the Report Header section. The Page Footer section is where Access adds the page number for you when you create a report with the Report Wizard. When you create a Groups/Totals Report Wizard report, the Page Header section is also the section where the field names are added as column heads. You can add controls to these sections just as you've added controls earlier. Usually your reports will have these sections; they appear whenever Page Header/Footer in the Format menu (the Layout menu in Access version 1) has a check mark next to it. If you select this command to remove the check mark, the contents of these two sections are permanently removed. This command is a toggle, so selecting it again adds both sections again, but anything that was previously in those sections is no longer there.

## Using the Report

Using a report fills a report design with the table or query's data. When you generate a report, Access opens a Print Preview window showing how the report will appear when printed. You can change the part of the report that appears in the window to look at different pages, look at different sections of a page, or look at a page more closely.

AutoReports are generated after you click the AutoReport button. Reports created with a Report Wizard are generated when you select Print Preview. Access generates reports you already have in your database when you select the report name from the Database window and then double-click it or press ENTER. When you look at a report design, you can switch to the Preview view of the report by clicking the Preview button in the toolbar or by choosing Print Preview from the File menu. When you leave Print Preview, you are returned either to the Database window or to the report design.

A report design inherits some of the field and table properties from the underlying table or query at the time you create the report design. For example, when you create a report for the Employee table of the Coaster database, the entries in the Last Name, First Name, and Middle Initial fields appear in uppercase even if you typed them into the table in lowercase. This is because the three fields have a Format property of >. In Chapter 11, you will learn about other properties you can use with reports. If you later change the field and table properties in the table or query, the reports that you created from the table or query do not change. You must alter the report designs to have the new field or table properties applied to the reports.

The toolbar in the Print Preview window includes the following buttons:

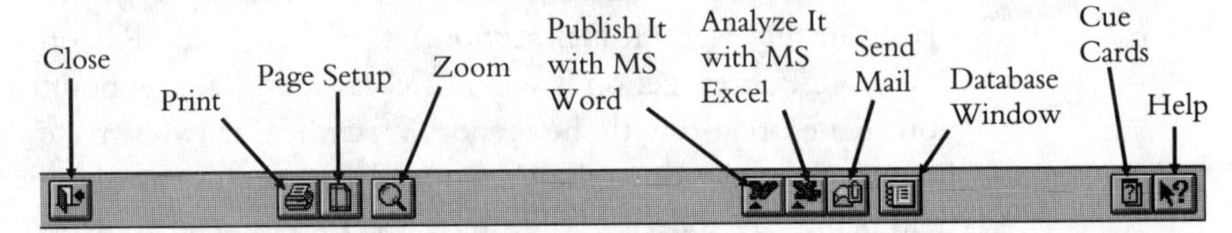


Besides selecting one of these buttons by clicking them, you can also type **C** and then press ESC to select the Close button and close the Print Preview window. Typing **S** is the same as clicking the Page Setup button, typing **Z** is the same as clicking the Zoom button, and typing **P** is the same as clicking the Print button. In Access 1, you have Print, Setup, Zoom, and Cancel buttons that perform the same functions as the toolbar buttons shown previously.

From the Print Preview window, you can change the part of the report that appears on the screen. By clicking the buttons in the bottom of the window, you can move to the first, previous, next, or last page of the report. You can click a part of the displayed page to switch between looking at the entire page and a section of the report. You can also switch between pages by pressing PGUP and PGDN. When you are looking closely at a page in the report, you can press the arrow keys to switch the part of the page that appears in the Print Preview window. Combining CTRL with the LEFT ARROW, RIGHT ARROW, HOME, or END keys moves the zoomed section of the page to the left edge, right edge, top, or bottom of the current page. You can also move to a specific page by pressing F5, typing the page number, and then pressing ENTER.

## Printing a Report

The main purpose of creating a report is to print a copy so you have a copy of the data in your database. Printing a report is just like printing other objects. You have the same options when printing a report as you have for printing tables, queries, and forms. The options you have for printing reports, as well as many of the options available for printing datasheets and forms, are described here. To print a report:

1. Check that the report appears as you want in the Print Preview window so you don't waste time printing a report destined for the garbage.

   When you are printing a report you have designed and you know it will print correctly, you do not have to open the report in the Print Preview window.

2. Select the Print button or choose Print from the File menu.

   The Print dialog box gives you the same choices about the print range, print quality, printing to a file, number of copies, collating copies, and printer setup that you have for printing tables, queries, and forms.

3. Make any necessary changes to the layout of the report by selecting Setup, making changes, and selecting OK.

   Selecting Setup opens the Print Setup dialog box. You can also open this dialog box by choosing Print Setup in the File menu. You have used some of these options when printing your datasheets or forms, but this dialog box also has other options that you will use, most often with reports. Some of these options display when you select the More button, which expands the dialog box to appear as shown in Figure 9-13.

4. Select OK.

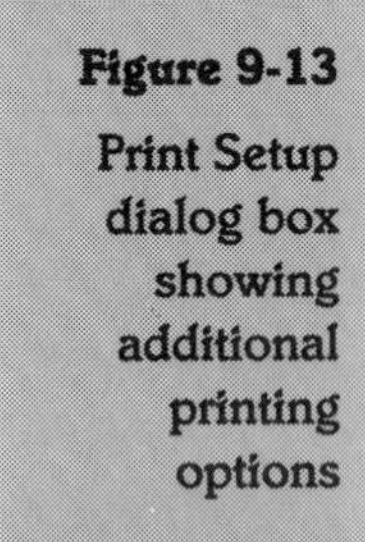

**Figure 9-13** Print Setup dialog box showing additional printing options

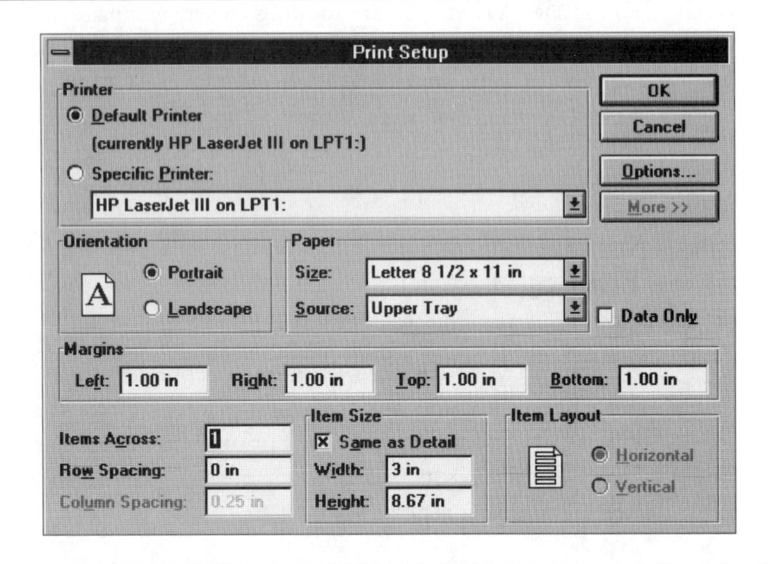


## CHANGING THE REPORT LAYOUT

Most of the top half of the Print Setup dialog box provides basic layout changes that you have probably used for other applications. Under Printer and Paper, you can select the printer you will use to print the report and the size as well as the source of the paper. The choices you have depends on the printers you have installed in Windows.

Orientation in the Print Setup dialog box sets whether the report is printed top to bottom or sideways. Portrait prints the report from top to bottom on the page. Landscape prints the report from one side to another as it goes through the printer so the top of the printed material is on the left side of the page.

Margins are set by entering measurements in the Left, Right, Top, and Bottom text boxes. For example, some of the reports in this book are printed on letterhead paper with the top margin increased to two inches.

## PRINTING MULTIPLE COLUMNS

The report shown in Figure 9-2 was created to illustrate an AutoReport; notice that the report has a lot of empty space because the report information takes little space on the page. You can arrange the data of the report into several columns. Your telephone directory is an example of a report that uses multiple columns. If phone books used a single column to list names and numbers, only weight lifters could move them. Using multiple columns makes phone books a more manageable size. Apply this same principle to your reports and display your information in several columns whenever appropriate.

To print your reports in multiple columns, display the Print Setup dialog box and select the More button. In the Items Across text box, select how many columns you want to display the report's information. For example, if you type **2** in this text box, after the data that would otherwise appear solely on the first page is printed, the data that would appear on the second page is printed to the right of the first column of information, as shown in Figure 9-14. You can use higher numbers when the columns in the report are narrow. When a report uses half of the page, you can fit only two columns on a page.

With the report shown in Figure 9-14, you may have to make other changes. You can set the amount of space that appears between the columns. Enter this distance in the Column Spacing text box in inches. When more than one record fits in a column, generally you will add space between the records. This distance between records in the same column is entered in the Row Spacing text box. When you select OK, the report uses the number of columns you select (assuming the columns can fit on the page). Figure 9-15 shows a previewed report where the report is divided into two columns with 0.5 inch between columns and rows. While you cannot see the detail of the records, you can see the groups of data that make up each record. You can limit the size of a record

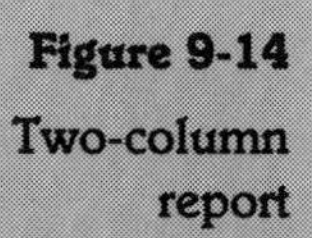
**Figure 9-14** Two-column report

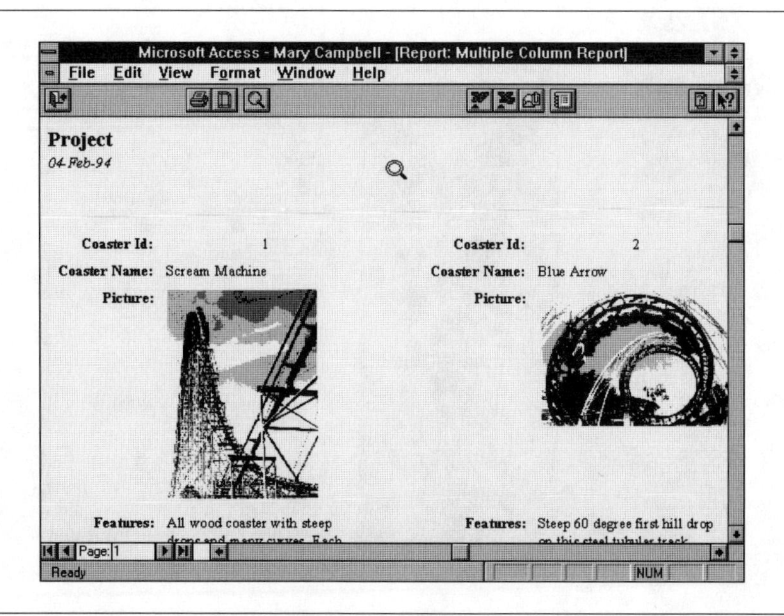

in the report by entering height and width dimensions in the Width and Height text boxes. The default is to have the Same as Detail check box selected. When this check box is selected, Access enters a number in the Width and Height text boxes based on the size of the section of the report design called the Detail section.

**tip:** *When printing multiple columns or printing a Mailing Label Report Wizard report, you can select whether the records are added to the report from top to bottom in the first column before going to the second column, or whether they are added left to right going across columns. If you select the More button in the Print Setup dialog box when the value in the Items Across text box is more than 1, you can select whether the records are added to the report from top to bottom or left to right by selecting the Horizontal or Vertical option button under Item Layout.*

## SAMPLE PREVIEW PRINTING

When you have a report for a large table or query, you may not want to use the usual Preview view to check the report's appearance because it will take Access too long to generate the report. With large reports you have the option of using the sample preview. The sample preview quickly inserts data into the report while ignoring criteria and joins. This feature is useful if you want to

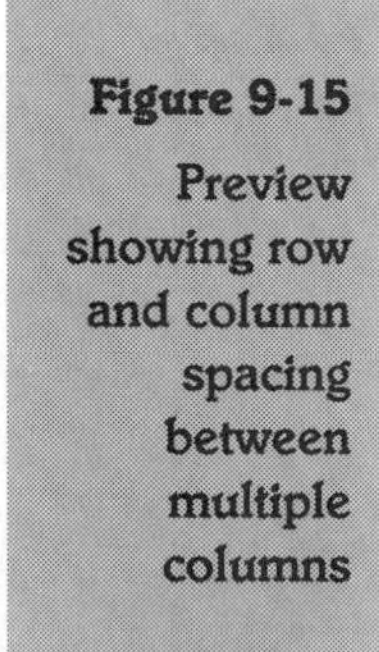

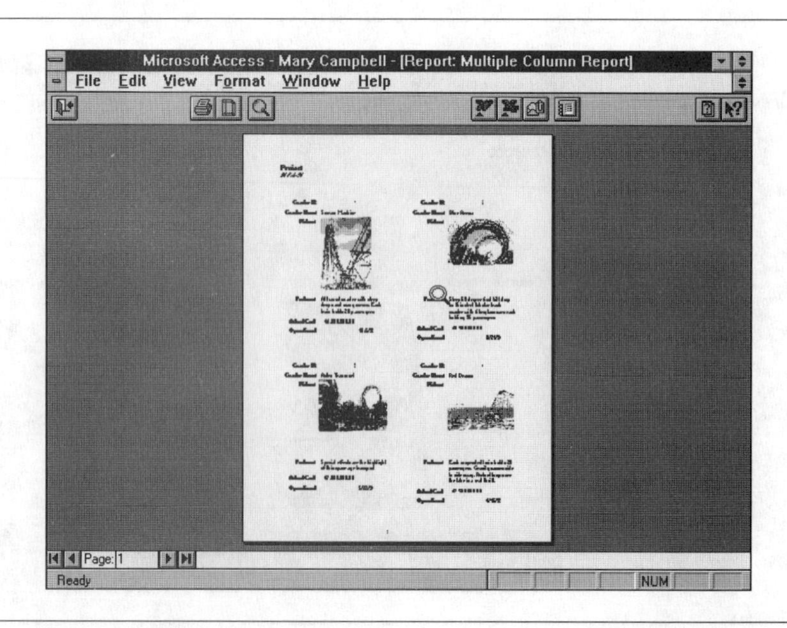


**Figure 9-15** Preview showing row and column spacing between multiple columns

check the overall look of the report rather than the specifics of the data in the report. When you print the report, Access will use the appropriate records from the table or query.

To display the report using the sample preview instead of the regular preview, choose Sample Preview in the File menu. In Access version 2, you can also display a sample preview by clicking the Sample Preview button in the toolbar. You can only do this from the report design, which you learned how to display in the "Looking at the Report's Design" section earlier in this chapter. Access displays a Print Preview window just like the regular Print Preview window. The difference is that here you may see records that the report otherwise excludes, since the sample preview ignores criteria and joins. If you print from the sample preview, the report will contain exactly the data that appears in the Print Preview window. When finished looking at the sample preview, click the Cancel button or choose Sample Preview in the File menu.

### COLLATING COPIES

You can choose how many copies you want to print of your datasheet, form, or report. To print multiple copies, type the number of copies you want in the Copies text box in the Print dialog box. When you print multiple copies, you can have Access collate the pages to produce complete copies of reports or print all of the copies of each page separately. If you do not request that the pages be collated, Access prints multiple copies of the first page, and then the second, and so on for each page. When the report is collated, which is the default setting, Access prints all of the pages in one copy of a report and then prints all of the pages for the next copy, and so on until Access has printed the number of copies you have selected. When you print large reports, Access prints multiple copies of lengthy datasheets, forms, and reports faster when it prints all of the copies of the first page, and then the second, and so on. To print your reports without collating, clear the Collate Copies check box from the Print dialog box. Select this check box to print each copy of the report, form, or datasheet separately (but more slowly).

### PRINTING TO A FILE

Access can also print reports to a file. When you print the report to a file, you can do it two ways. One way is to create a file that contains the information that Access and Windows will send to the printer. The other option is to create a file to use with other applications.

You print to a file for two reasons: to delay printing—if, for example, your computer is not currently connected to a printer—or to bring the report into another application. To print the report to a file, select the Print button or choose Print from the File menu. Select the Print to File check box. When you select OK, you are prompted for a filename. Type the name of the file and then select OK. The file will contain exactly the same information that would have been sent to the printer. You don't have to worry about clearing the Print to File check box after you have printed to a file; Access clears it for you.

The other way to print to a file creates a file containing the report data in a format for another application, such as Word for Windows or Excel. To do this, select Output To from the File menu. Select one of the formats to put the report into for the file you will create and select OK. MS-DOS Text can be used by most applications. Rich Text Format is accepted by most Windows applications and, unlike MS-DOS Text, it retains font formatting, such as the font name and font size. Then enter the name for the file and select OK.

**tip:** *In Access version 1, if you want to print to a file in order to bring the report into another application, change the printer to which you are printing to Generic/Text Only by selecting the Setup button or choosing Print Setup from the File menu, and then selecting the Specific Printer option button and Generic/Text Only from the drop-down list box. You may need to install this printer with Windows' Control Panel application if it is not already installed.*

### PRINTING ONLY THE DATA

When you print a report, the report includes all of the information included in the report design. When using a report to print the data for a preprinted form, you will not want to include information such as field names. Omit field names (and other information in a report that is not a field or expression) by selecting the Data Only check box from the Print Setup dialog box. When you print the report, the field and expression values are the only information that prints. The default is for the Data Only check box to be cleared so that all of the report's information is printed.

## Saving and Closing a Report

When you have a report you want to use again, you need to save it. Saving the report makes the custom-designed report available at a later point. To save a report:

1. Choose Save in the File menu.

    Access also asks if you want to save a report when you try closing the window containing the report. Selecting Yes at the prompt saves the file just as if you chose Save in the File menu.

2. Type a name for the report, following the same rules you would for naming tables.
3. Choose OK.

    If you later want to save the report with a different name, save it again by choosing Save As in the File menu.

You can close a report to put it away just like you close other windows in Access. You can double-click the window's Control box, press CTRL+F4, or choose Close from the File menu. If the report has changes to its design, you are prompted about saving the report.

## Renaming a Report

Just like the other objects in the database, you can rename reports. If you use the default name for reports, rename them as you add more so that you can rely on descriptive names to know which one you want even when selecting from a long list of report names. To rename a report:

1. Close any window in which the report or its design appears.
2. Select the report from the Database window.
3. Choose Rename from the File menu or right-click the report name and select Rename.
4. Type the new name you want for the report in the Report Name text box.
5. Select OK.

**tip:** *If a report has frequent blank pages, look at the report design. The report's width should be less than the page width minus the right and left margins.*

Quick Reference

**To Preview a Report** Select the report name in the Database window. Either double-click it, press ENTER, click the Preview button, or select Print Preview from the File menu to display the report in a Print Preview window.

**To Print a Report** Preview the report as described in the previous section. Choose Print from the File menu or the Print button from the toolbar. Make any changes to the Print dialog box. Select OK to print the report.

**To Create an AutoReport with Access Version 2** Select the table or query to use for the report by selecting the table or query's name in the Database window or by switching to the window showing the table or query or its design. Click the AutoReport button on the toolbar. Access will create a report for the table or query that includes all fields.

**To Create a Report With a Report Wizard** Click the New button at the top of the Database window while displaying reports, click the New Report button on the toolbar, or choose New from the File menu and then Report. Select a table or query that the report uses from the Select a Table/Query drop-down list box. Select the Report Wizards command button. Next select the type of Report Wizard report you want to create. For each of the subsequent dialog boxes, give the information you are prompted for, such as the fields the report includes, its look, and its title. When you select the Print Preview button from the final dialog box, the report is created.

**To Create a Report Starting with an Empty Design** Click the New button at the top of the Database window while displaying reports, click the New Report button on the toolbar, or choose New from the File menu and then Report. Select the table or query the report uses from the Select a Table/Query drop-down list box. Select the Blank Report button. In the Report Design window, add the controls you want to appear in the report. You can use the toolbar, the toolbox, and other features that make designing reports easier. When you want to see the data

**Quick Reference (continued)**

that is used in the report, choose Print Preview from the File menu or click the Preview button.

**To Rename a Report** Select the report to rename from the Database window. Choose Rename from the File menu or right-click the report. Type the new name for the report and select OK.

**To Display a Report's Design** Select the report in the Database window. Click the Design button in the top of the Database window.

**To Move a Control on a Report** Click the control in the report design you want to move. Point to the control so the mouse pointer looks like a hand. Drag the control to a new position. When the control is part of a compound control (such as a field and its field name), move only one part of the control by pointing to the control so that the pointer looks like a hand holding up one finger before you drag the mouse to a new location.

**To Size a Control on a Report** Click the control in the report design you want to resize. Point to one of the handles on the control so the pointer looks like a double-headed arrow. Drag the handle to a new location.

**To Add a Field to a Report** With the field list showing in the report design, select the fields you wish to add from the field list. Drag one of these fields to where you want the fields to appear on the report design.

**To Delete a Control from a Report** Click the control that you want to remove from the report design. Press DEL or choose Delete from the Edit menu.

**To Change the Text of a Field Name Label Control in a Report** Click the field name label control in the report design. Click again where you want the insertion point added. Make the changes to the text and press ENTER or select another control to finish the editing.

# Chapter 10

Adding Controls to Forms

Working with Form Properties

Selecting and Sorting Records for a Form

Saving a Form as a Report

# Customizing Forms with Controls and Other Settings

THE forms that you create with Access's Form Wizards may meet your exact needs, but usually you will want to make changes. To change a form, you add, alter, or remove controls that are part of its design. The techniques you use to modify a form by adding controls are also used to build a form starting with a blank form, without the Form Wizards.

You can customize forms further by setting properties for the entire form, for sections of the form, and for controls in the form. Properties can affect how you work with a form or how it will print.

Another way of customizing forms is by splitting a form into multiple pages. Using multiple pages in forms that have many controls lets you divide a large form into more manageable pieces.

## Adding Controls to Forms

As you used Form Wizards in Chapter 8, a control was added to the form for every field that you selected. You can add more of these text box controls if you have forgotten a field or two rather than starting over again with a new Form Wizard design. You can also add other types of controls to a form.

Access offers three types of controls: *bound controls* that refer to a field in a database table, *unbound controls* that refer to other objects such as lines or text that you have added, and *calculated controls* that perform a computation. Bound controls are like the text boxes for the fields in the forms you created with Form Wizards. Unbound controls are like the text that describes the fields you add to a form. Calculated controls are like the date and page number you add to reports created with Form Wizards.

## Types of Controls

The forms you create in Access can include various controls similar to the dialog box elements you are accustomed to seeing as you work with Windows and Windows applications. You can add the same check boxes, option buttons, list boxes, and drop-down list boxes to your forms.

Regardless of the type of control that you add, you will use the toolbox shown in the lower-left corner of Figure 10-1. You can choose from these different controls the one that best fits your data. These are the controls you can add to a form: labels, text boxes, option groups, toggle buttons, option buttons, check boxes, combo boxes, list boxes, graphs, subforms, bound and unbound object frames, lines, rectangles, page breaks, and command buttons. The following sections describe the functions that the various controls provide.

Access version 2 offers Control Wizards for creating command buttons, option groups, list boxes, and combo boxes. The Control Wizards guide you through the steps of adding these controls to your form. The Control Wizards are only available when the Control Wizards button in the toolbox is selected. When it is not selected, controls are added directly to the form, just as they are in Access version 1.

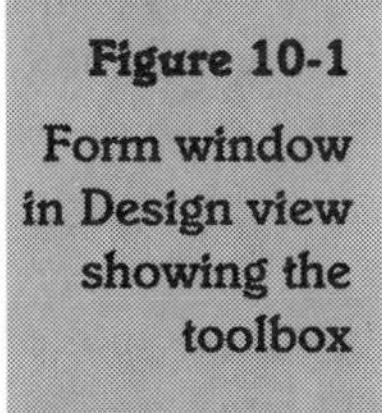

**Figure 10-1** Form window in Design view showing the toolbox

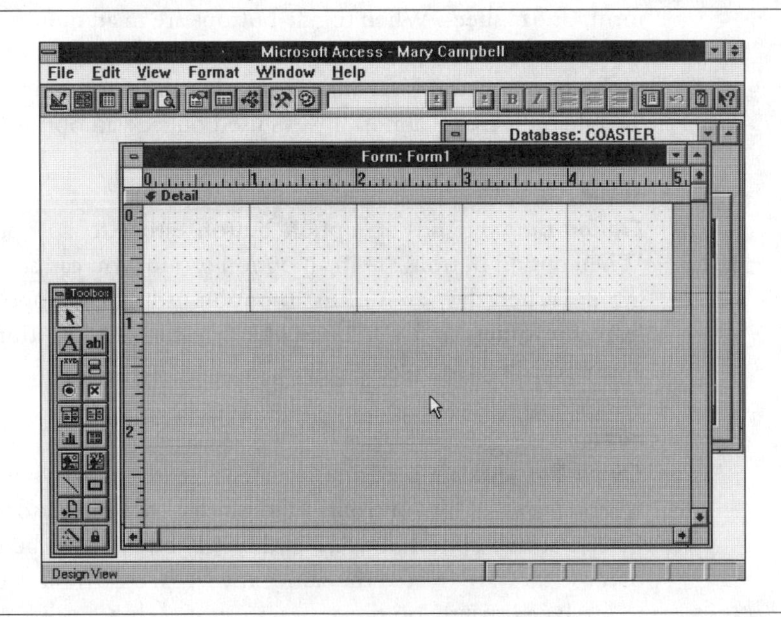

- ***Label*** Adds text that does not change from record to record. Labels often identify other controls and can appear in other sections such as the Form Header, Form Footer, Page Header, and Page Footer sections. You add labels to a form when you add most other types of controls.

- ***Text Box*** Adds a box containing the value of a field that changes from record to record. This type of text box is a bound control. Text boxes can contain other types of entries, such as the expressions you will learn about in Chapter 12. A text box that contains an expression is a calculated control.

- ***Option Group*** Adds a box that you can subsequently fill with option buttons, check boxes, or toggle buttons. When option buttons, check boxes, or toggle buttons are in an option group, you can select only one from the group.

- ***Toggle Button*** Adds a command button that looks recessed when selected and stands out when it is not. The first three buttons in the Form Design toolbar are toggle buttons that show whether you are looking at the form's design, form, or datasheet. When toggle buttons are in an option group, you can select only one from the group. When toggle buttons are not in an option group, each option button is separate from the others and functions like a check box. Toggle buttons are almost always used outside an option group.

- ***Option Button*** Adds an option button either to an option group or alone. When option buttons are in an option group, you can select only one from the group. When they are not in an option group, each option button is separate from the others and functions like a check box. Option buttons are almost always used inside option groups.

- ***Check Box*** Adds a box that is marked with an X when selected and empty when cleared. This control is used just like option buttons and toggle buttons. Check boxes, option buttons, and toggle buttons can be used interchangeably because they are treated the same way by Access. You decide which you want to use based strictly on the appearance of each. Check boxes are almost always used outside option groups.

***Combo Box*** Adds a text box with a down arrow after it. Like other drop-down list boxes, you can enter a field's value in a combo box by selecting one of the items in the drop-down list or by typing an entry in the text box.

***List Box*** Adds a box containing a list of the available choices for a field. Using a list box lets you choose the field's value by selecting one of the listed items.

***Graph*** Adds a graph that you create with the Graph Form Wizard. When you select a location for the graph, the Graph Form Wizard is started. You are prompted for information to put in the graph just as you are when you create a Graph Form Wizard form, as described in Chapter 8.

***Subform*** Adds a box that contains a subform or a form created from another table or query. You'll learn how to create subforms in Chapter 13.

***Bound and Unbound Object Frames*** Adds a box that contains an object such as a picture or an OLE object. You will learn more about adding these types of objects to your forms in Chapter 15.

***Line*** Adds a line to a form. You'll learn more about adding lines in Chapter 14.

***Rectangle*** Adds a rectangle to a form. You will learn about adding rectangles in Chapter 14.

***Page Break*** Adds a page break giving you several pages within the form design. A page break control is added on the left edge of the form design and divides forms into multiple pages. Later you will learn how to set whether the form uses the page break on the screen, when you print the form, or a combination of both. You can use page breaks in a form to divide a large area of data into smaller areas.

***Command Button*** Adds a command button that performs a macro or procedure when you select it. Macros are introduced in Chapter 16 and procedures are introduced in Chapter 19.

This chapter teaches you how to use most of these controls but not all of them. You will use the Subform tool in Chapter 13 to combine multiple tables into a form. You will learn about the controls to add lines and boxes in Chapter 14. In Chapter 15 you will learn about adding pictures and graphs to your forms. In Chapter 16 you will learn about macros, and in Chapter 19 you will learn about procedures.

## Adding a Control to a Form Design

In Chapter 8 you learned how to add a control that represents one of the fields from the table or query by dragging the field name from the field list. Dragging fields from the field list adds text boxes for the field plus adjoining labels that describe the field's contents. Besides using the field list to add controls, you can use the toolbox. You can also combine the toolbox and the field list to quickly create controls of different types that represent the different fields.

To add a control without the field list, display the toolbox by choosing Toolbox from the View menu. Next, select the button for the type of control you want to create from the toolbox. These buttons are identified in Figure 10-2. Then click the part of the form design where you want the control you are adding to begin.

With some types of controls that can be resized, you can set the size of the control when you add the control to the form design by dragging the mouse from where you want the control to start to where you want the opposite corner of the control. You may not want to set the size of label controls (including the labels that are part of other controls), because Access adjusts the control's size as you change the text that appears in the control. When you add these controls, Access puts an empty control in the location, as shown in Figure 10-3. As soon as you add a label, immediately type the text you want to appear in the label.

When adding an option group without Access version 2's Control Wizards, you are creating a group to which you will later add other check box, option button, or toggle button controls. When you add these controls to the option group, the option group will reverse its colors to indicate that the area to which you are pointing is the correct place to add the control to the option group. When you add check boxes, option buttons, or toggle buttons to an option group, don't worry about whether the box will fit the controls you are adding.

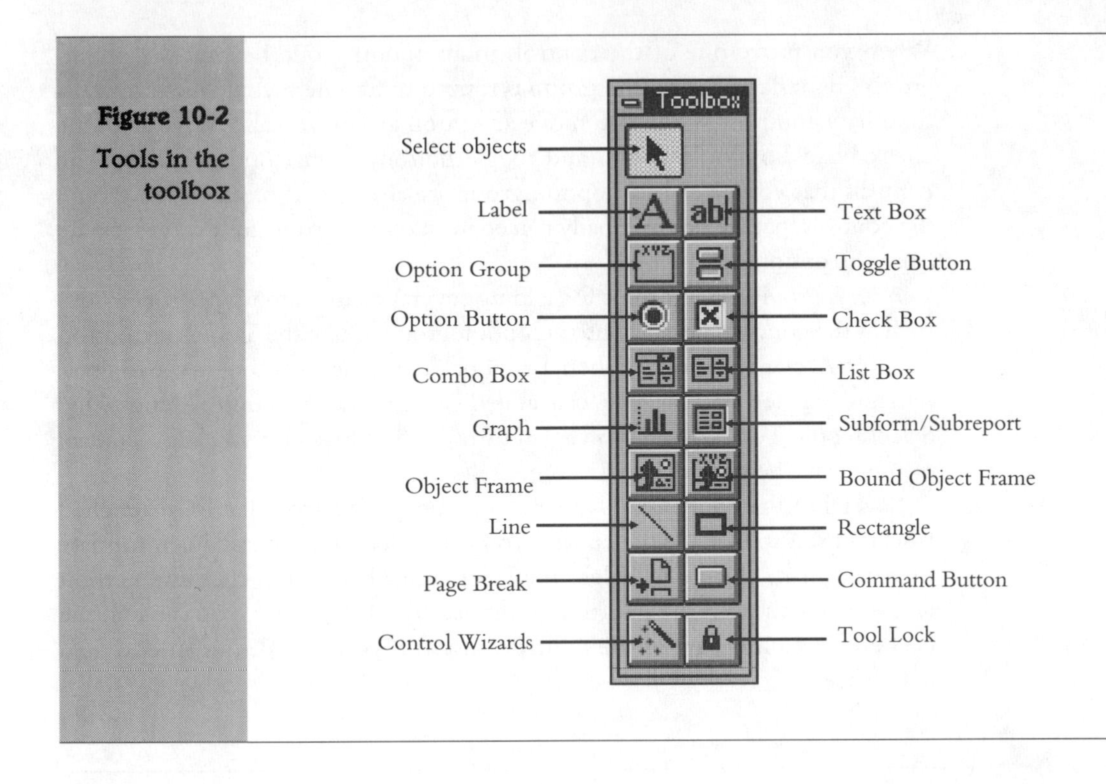


**Figure 10-2** Tools in the toolbox

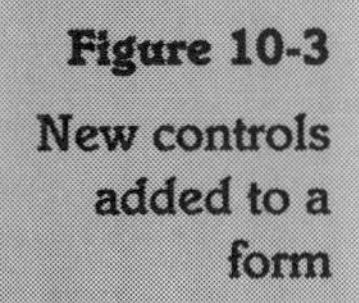

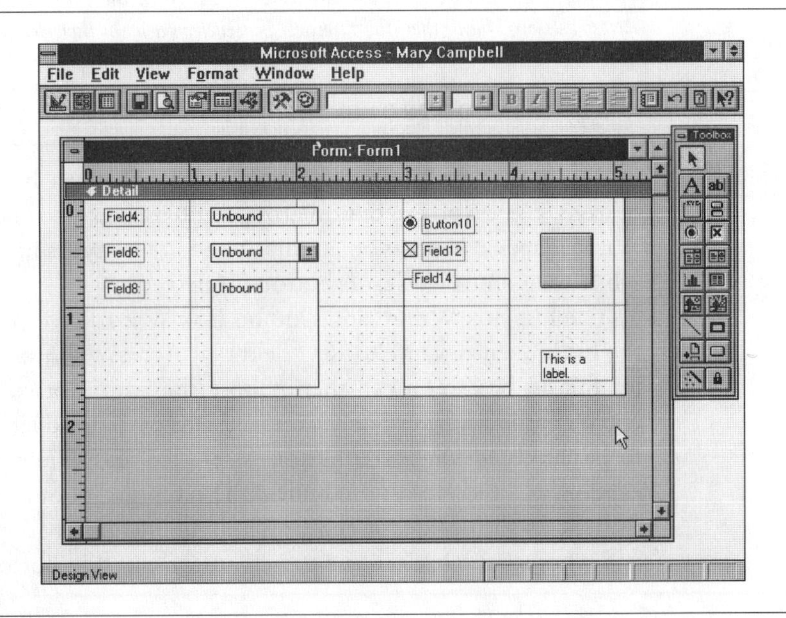


**Figure 10-3** New controls added to a form

When you move one of the controls in an option group beyond the option group's boundary, the option group is resized to fit where you have moved its subsidiary controls. When you move an option group, you also move all of the check boxes, option buttons, and toggle buttons in that option group. The controls that you place in an option group are always part of an option group; the controls that are not originally placed in an option group are always separate from the option group.

Access provides a shortcut for adding several of the same type of controls, such as the controls you put into an option group. Click the Tool Lock button (Lock in Access version 1). When Tool Lock is on, the same tool in the toolbox remains selected so that you can add the same type of control repeatedly. Selecting the Tool Lock button again turns it off so that after you add a control to the form, the pointer tool becomes selected.

Several of the controls are added as compound controls that have attached label controls to identify the control you just added. If this text is inappropriate for your form, change it. Select the label control and then click the current text where you want the insertion point placed. At this point, you can edit the content, which is part of the control, just as if you are editing an entry on a datasheet.

**tip:** *Remember to align the check boxes, option buttons, and toggle buttons that you add to a form. You can align controls you select by choosing Align in the Format menu (the Layout menu in Access version 1) and then the direction in which you want the selected objects aligned.*

## ADDING CONTROLS USING THE CONTROL WIZARDS

Access version 2 offers Control Wizards that can help you add command buttons, combo boxes, option groups, and list boxes to your form. The Control Wizards appear when you attempt to add these types of controls to your form while the Control Wizards button is selected.

The List Box Wizard and Combo Box Wizard give you the chance to enter the list box entries or choose a field that Access will use to provide the entries for the list box. You can then choose the widths of columns containing the entries in the list box. The Command Button Wizard lets you select the action to be executed when the button is selected and whether to display a button caption or a picture on the button. The Option Group Wizard lets you enter the text for the options to appear within in the option group, a default selection, and whether the options use toggle buttons, option buttons, or check boxes.

**tip:** *In Chapter 13, you will learn how to add both text and a picture to a command button.*

## Adding Different Controls with the Field List

Access has a shortcut for adding fields to a form using different types of controls. Earlier you learned how dragging a field name from the field list to the form design adds the field as a text box with the field name as an attached label. You can change the type of control you add when you drag a field name from the field list. By selecting a control from the toolbox and then selecting the field name from the field list, you add that field as the selected control type.

As an example, you can use this shortcut to create the form shown in Figure 10-4. First, make sure that both the toolbox and the field list appear. To add the toggle button, click Toggle Button in the toolbox and then drag the Completed field from the field list to the form design.

## Setting the Field That a Control Represents

Now that you have added a control to a form, tell Access which field you want the control to represent. Some controls, such as labels, do not represent fields because they do not change from record to record. For text boxes, toggle buttons, option buttons, check boxes, option groups, list boxes, combo boxes,

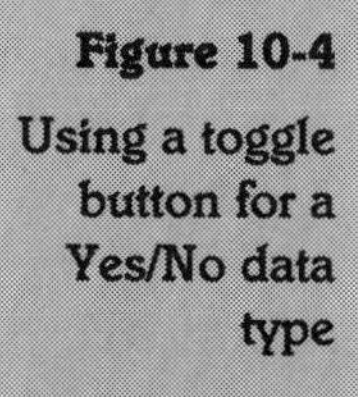

**Figure 10-4** Using a toggle button for a Yes/No data type

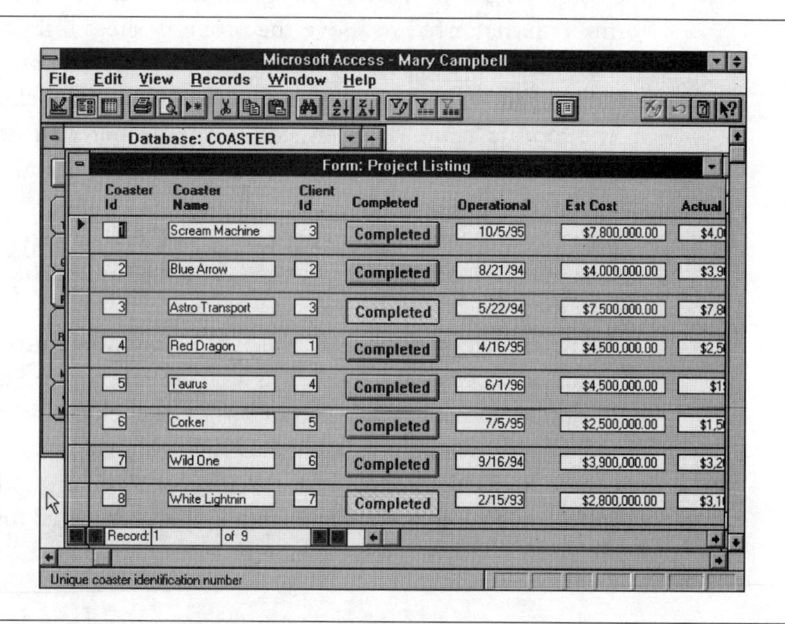

and bound object frames, you tell Access which field you want to use with the control. Which field a control represents is one of the control's *properties*. If you added the control by using a Control Wizard in Access version 2 or by dragging a field from the field list, you set the field that the control represents as part of creating the control.

To set or change the field for a text box, edit the text box's contents and change the Unbound text to one of the table or query's field names. You can also change the Control Source property, which sets what field is displayed in the control.

For all types of controls that represent a field in the table or query, you can change the control's Control Source property. First, display the property sheet by choosing Properties from the View menu or by clicking the Properties button in the toolbar. The Properties button looks like this:

When you display the property sheet in the form's Design view, the property sheet looks like the one shown in Figure 10-5. In Access version 2, you can select which set of properties you want to see from the drop-down list box at the top of this property sheet. In Access version 1, all properties are displayed at once. As you click controls or sections in the form design, the properties and the values of the properties change to match the selected control, section, or form. You may need to move the property sheet if it covers the control you want to select. The property sheet remains displayed in the form's Design view until you choose Properties from the View menu or click the Properties button in the toolbar again. The left side of the property sheet shows the property names appropriate for the selected control or section, and the right side contains the properties' values.

The Control Source property is the property that selects which field a control represents. You can either type the field name or use the down arrow to select one of the fields from the drop-down list.

How you select the field for check boxes, option buttons, and toggle buttons depends on whether these controls are part of an option group. When a check box, option button, or toggle button is not included in an option group, the controls behave as an on/off switch, which you will usually use for your Yes/No data type fields. Set the field for the control by entering the field name for the Control Source property. For example, the Completed toggle button in Figure 10-4 has its Control Source property set to Completed, so the form shows the

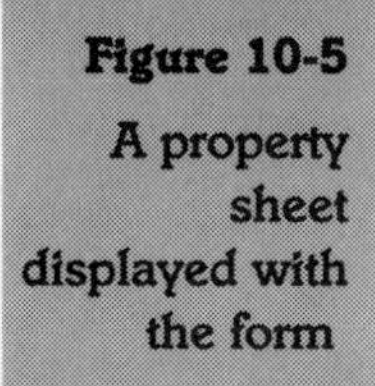

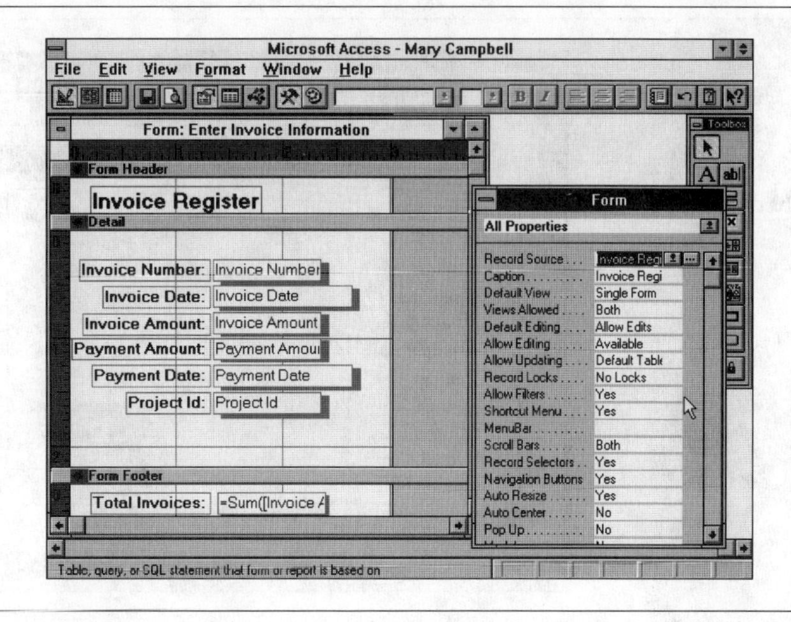


**Figure 10-5** A property sheet displayed with the form

button pressed down when the coaster is completed and raised when the coaster is still in progress.

The other way to use check boxes, option buttons, and toggle buttons is to put them in an option group to indicate which of several values a field equals. Instead of setting the field for the individual check boxes, option buttons, and toggle buttons, you set the Control Source property for the option group and then set the values of each of the check boxes, option buttons, or toggle buttons. Of course, this has already been done if you've used the Option Group Wizard in Access version 2.

Figure 10-6 shows a form that uses option groups for two fields. On the left half are option buttons in an option group. The Control Source property for the option group is Employee Id. The Control Source property for the option buttons is the numbers 1 through 10. The employee names are added as the option buttons' labels to match their identification numbers.

**tip:** *Unless your company is certain of never hiring another employee or starting another project, this form isn't a good idea. If you did hire a new employee or start a new project, you would have to redesign the form. This form was used only to demonstrate how option groups work; unfortunately, the limited information in the Coasters database doesn't offer many good examples of option groups.*

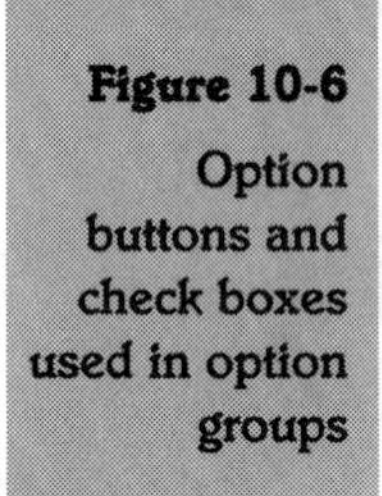

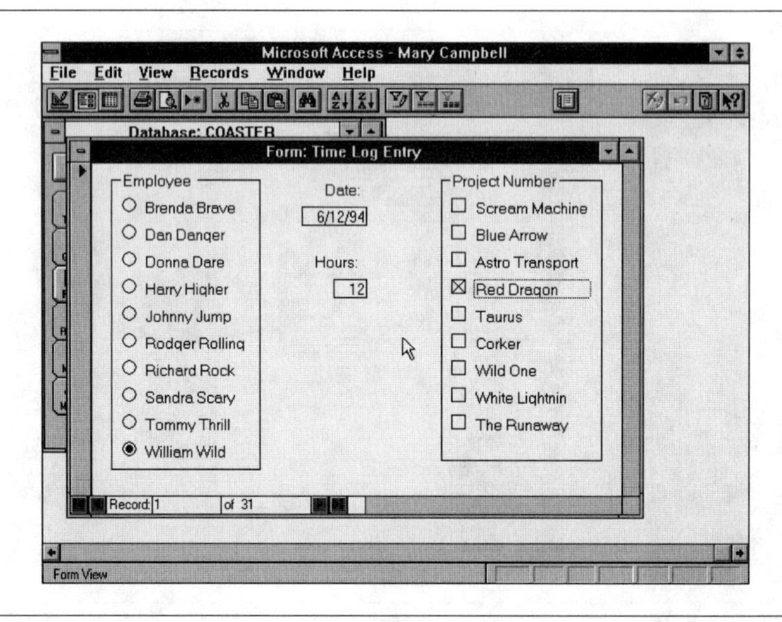


**Figure 10-6** Option buttons and check boxes used in option groups

The employee names were originally entered in the order they appear in the Employee table, but once they were all entered, the names and option buttons were rearranged in alphabetical order within the option group to make data entry easier. Access does not care that you have rearranged the option buttons in the option group; the number for the Control Source property and any text that belongs to the option button continue to belong to the option button as you move it in the option group.

On the right side of the form, the Control Source property for the option group is Project Number. The Control Source property for the check boxes is the numbers 1 through 9. The label that belongs to each of the check boxes for the different projects is replaced with the project's name to make data entry easier. With both option buttons and check boxes, you as the form designer—not Access—make the connection between the employee and project numbers and the employee and project names.

When check boxes or option buttons are added to an option group, they are numbered sequentially. This means the label of the first check box or option button is Button1, the second check box or option button has a label of Button2, and so on for all of the check boxes and option buttons in the option group. You can put both check boxes and option buttons in the same option group, when you are not using a Control Wizard, but your form will look more professional when you use only check boxes or option buttons within an option group.

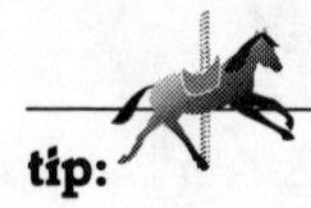

**tip:** *Remember that the goal of designing a form is to make entering and using the data as easy as possible. When designing your own forms, keep this goal in mind.*

## Using Mnemonics with Controls

In dialog boxes, you can move the focus to an element by pressing ALT and an underlined letter. Access gives you the ability to create forms that work the same way. You can add underlined letters to the labels for compound controls, which lets users press ALT and the underlined letter to move to the control attached to the label.

When you edit the label of a compound control, put an ampersand (&) in front of the character you want underlined. When you switch to Form view from Design view, the ampersand does not appear, but the following character is underlined. When you press ALT and the underlined character, the focus moves to the control marked by that label. For example, in the form shown in Figure 10-7, each of the fields has an underlined letter.

**tip:** *In the window in Figure 10-7, there are two copies of the form. The underlined letters, of course, only work for the current copy. You will have to take the usual steps to switch to the next copy of the form, such as pressing the DOWN ARROW in the last field or using the navigation buttons.*

When you underline characters in labels, try to underline the first letter in the label, the first letter of a word in the label, or a distinctive letter. If you make these true mnemonics, users will find your form easier to use, making data entry faster and more accurate. Also, try not to underline letters with *descenders,* or lines that go down below the baseline of the text, such as the *j* in Project Id. You can see in Figure 10-7 that it is hard to tell that the *j* is underlined because the descender crosses the underscore.

**Figure 10-7** Using underlined letters to select controls

Form: Invoice Listing - Underscores

| | | | |
|---|---|---|---|
| Invoice Number: | 975 | Payment Amount: | $500,000.00 |
| Invoice Date: | 2/1/91 | Payment Date: | 3/13/91 |
| Invoice Amount: | $500,000.00 | Project Id: | 9 |
| Invoice Number: | 986 | Payment Amount: | $2,000,000.00 |
| Invoice Date: | 4/1/91 | Payment Date: | 6/2/91 |
| Invoice Amount: | $2,000,000.00 | Project Id: | 9 |

Record: 1 of 28

**tip:** *Don't underline letters that are also used in the Access menu bar. When you press ALT and an underlined letter that appears both as part of a label and in the menu, you will move the focus to the compound control rather than selecting the menu.*

## Working with Form Properties

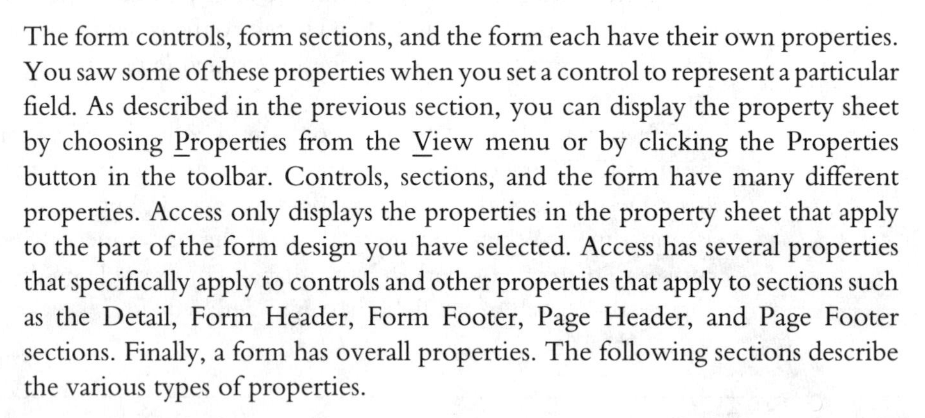

The form controls, form sections, and the form each have their own properties. You saw some of these properties when you set a control to represent a particular field. As described in the previous section, you can display the property sheet by choosing Properties from the View menu or by clicking the Properties button in the toolbar. Controls, sections, and the form have many different properties. Access only displays the properties in the property sheet that apply to the part of the form design you have selected. Access has several properties that specifically apply to controls and other properties that apply to sections such as the Detail, Form Header, Form Footer, Page Header, and Page Footer sections. Finally, a form has overall properties. The following sections describe the various types of properties.

**tip:** *Access has a shortcut to display the property sheet. You can double-click a control or section that is not currently selected to open the property sheet and display the properties for that control or section. The mouse pointer must be in the shape of an arrow or a hand, not the I-beam, in order for this to work. In Access version 2, you can also right-click a control or section and select Properties from the shortcut menu to display the property sheet.*

### Control Properties

Controls have properties that affect how the controls behave and appear in the form. These properties provide many different features. Some of the properties are designed for advanced uses; for example, macros or procedures can change the Visible property to display a control when another value, such as a quota, is met. Other properties such as Left, Top, Width, and Height set the control's position and size. You will find it easier to use the mouse to adjust the control's position and size rather than making entries. Another group, event properties such as Before Update and After Update, select the macro or procedure to perform as you work with a control on a form. You will learn more about macros in Chapter 16 and about procedures in Chapter 19.

Some of the control's properties set the control's appearance. (You will learn in Chapter 14 how to create professional-looking forms.) You usually do not need to use these properties, because the most frequently used appearance properties are available through dialog boxes and toolbar buttons. The Help Context ID property lets you select which help topic is displayed when you press F1.

**tip:** *When you want several controls to have the same property settings, you can select all of the controls and change a property setting for all of the controls at once. This is easy in Access version 2, since you can select controls by dragging your mouse in the ruler while the mouse pointer looks like a small, dark arrow. You will select all of the controls beside or below the part of the ruler you drag in.*

You will learn how to use some of the more useful properties now. These properties include changing the control's name, changing properties shared with the underlying table, expanding controls to fit long entries, adding scroll bars to a control, changing how the form prints versus how it appears in a window, and changing how the list box and combo box data appear.

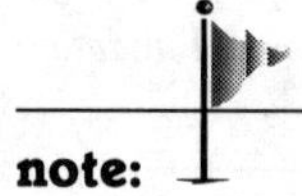

**note:** *In Access version 2, you can either display all of the properties at once, just as is done in Access version 1, or you can choose to display a subset of the properties. Rather than list the subset the following properties can be found in, it is assumed that you are displaying all properties in the property sheet.*

### CHANGING A CONTROL'S NAME

Most controls have a Name property (Control Name in Access version 1) that identifies the control on the form. Either use the default Access has provided or enter an acceptable object name. You will only be concerned about the control's name when creating an expression that uses another control, as described in Chapter 12 for expressions, or when you are developing macros and procedures that modify a control's properties.

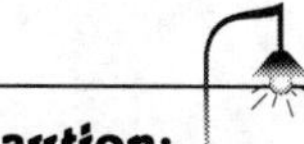

**caution:** *You cannot have two controls with the same name.*

If you are using a control for a purpose other than having a bound control represent a field, do not use a field name. Label controls have a Caption property in place of the Control Source property that other controls use. This is the property that sets the text that appears in the label control. The property can also be changed by editing the text in the label on the form design rather than on the property sheet.

## PROPERTIES ALSO USED BY TABLES

A control has several properties that you are already familiar with because you have already used these properties in the tables you have created. When you add controls with the field list or with Form Wizards, the form controls adopt the Format, Default Value, and Input Mask properties from the underlying table. The controls also pick up the field's description for the Status Line property. The control's Decimal Places property is Auto even if the underlying field's Decimal Places property is set to some specific number.

**tip:** *In Access version 1, a control cannot pick up the Input Mask property, since this property is not supported. However, controls in Access version 1 do inherit the Validation Rule and Validation Text properties from the table.*

You can change these properties for the control to override the table properties. Changing the properties does not change these same properties in the table or query. The entries you can make for the properties match the type of entries you could make for the properties in a table. You will learn more about validation rules and default values in Chapter 12.

The Status Line property sets the text that appears on the status line when the focus is on a field. Use the Status Line property to override the field's description and provide a better description for the type of entry the user should make. This text only appears when the focus is on that control. For example, in Figure 10-6, the text in the status line can switch between displaying information about selecting an employee, entering the date and hours, and selecting one of the projects.

## ALLOWING CHANGES TO A CONTROL

Two of the properties you can use for controls set whether you can move to the controls and make changes to the controls. The Locked property determines whether you can make changes to the control's value. The Enabled property determines whether you can move to the control. The defaults for most controls are No for the Locked property and Yes for the Enabled property, so you can both move to the control and change its value. The only exception is the unbound object frame, whose defaults are No for Enabled and Yes for Locked, since unbound object frames are not meant to be changed. The following illustration shows a form where these properties are changed for the four possible combinations.

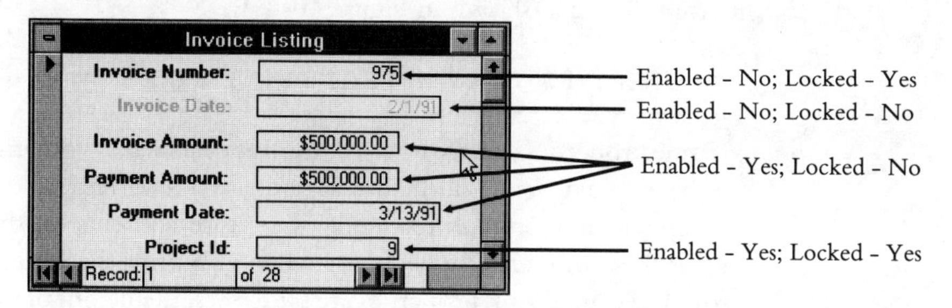


For the Invoice Number text box, Enabled is set to No and Locked is set to Yes; thus the control displays as normal although you cannot change it or move to it. The Invoice Date control has Enabled and Locked both set to No; the control appears dimmed to indicate that you cannot select it. The Invoice Amount, Payment Amount, and Payment Date fields have the default of Yes for the Enabled property and No for the Locked property, so you can change the values of these controls. Finally, the Project ID control has the Enabled and Locked properties both set to Yes, so you can move to the control but you cannot make any changes.

When you have controls that users cannot move to, make the fields look different so that the form's users will not be disappointed by seeing fields that they cannot manipulate. You may also want to comment on those fields that cannot be changed because their Locked property is set to Yes. Do this by adding text that appears in the status line to tell users that specified data cannot be changed. Another way to distinguish Locked controls is by using colors in the form to indicate controls that cannot be changed. This method is very effective and doesn't depend on users reading the status line.

**tip:** *Don't use underlined characters in the labels for controls that cannot be changed. This will help prevent users from trying to change that control.*

## ADDING SCROLL BARS TO TEXT BOXES

When you have a larger form displaying in a small window, the form has scroll bars so you can change which part of the form appears in the window. You can display similar scroll bars for text boxes. To add scroll bars to a text box, change the Scroll Bars property from None to Vertical. When you display the form, the text box contains the scroll bar when it contains the focus or the insertion point, as shown in Figure 10-8.

## PROPERTIES THAT AFFECT PRINTING

Some properties change how a control appears when you print a form. When you have a text or memo field that contains a long entry, you may not want the control large enough to display the entire contents on the screen, just as long as the entire entry will appear when you print the form. When the Can Grow and Can Shrink properties are set to Yes, the height of the control grows or shrinks to fit the field's contents when you print the form. The control extends as far down as the entry needs. Access also adjusts the height of the Detail section to match the size needed for the long entry.

When these two properties are set to No, the control's size cannot change. When you set Can Grow to Yes and Can Shrink to No, the control can expand to fit the size of the field's contents, but it cannot shrink below the size it was originally given. When you set Can Grow to No and Can Shrink to Yes, the

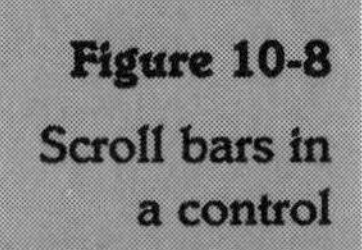

**Figure 10-8** Scroll bars in a control

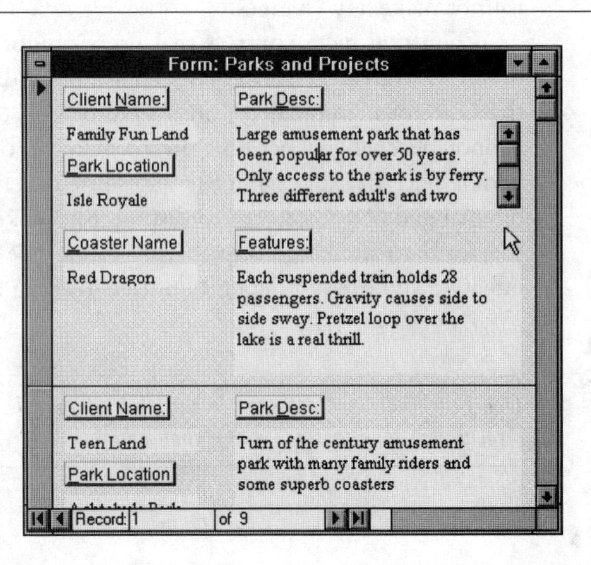

control will shrink so that there is not extra space used when the field entries are short, but longer field entries will be truncated because the control will not expand beyond its original size to match their length.

Figure 10-9 shows the Print Preview of a form that has the Can Grow and Can Shrink properties of the Features field set to Yes. In this form, the control is set to show one line. Most of the records have data in this field that is longer than the control on the form. If a record does not have an entry for the Features field or if it has a short one, the field will only occupy one line and the Detail section will shrink to use only one line. The default for Can Shrink and Can Grow is No. These two properties affect the form only when you print it. When you display the form on the screen using Form view, the control stays the same size regardless of the properties' settings and the field's contents.

Most controls give you three choices for when they appear: you can have them appear only when you display the form in a window, only when you print the form, or always. For example, you may want to use one control to represent the Employee ID field when you print the form and have another control represent it when you display it on the screen. When you print the form, you are using the form as a report; when you display the form in a window, you may want to use the form to enter data so that the controls you select will change.

As an example, you might use a combo box for the Coaster Name field to let someone make a selection using the drop-down list box, but you want to

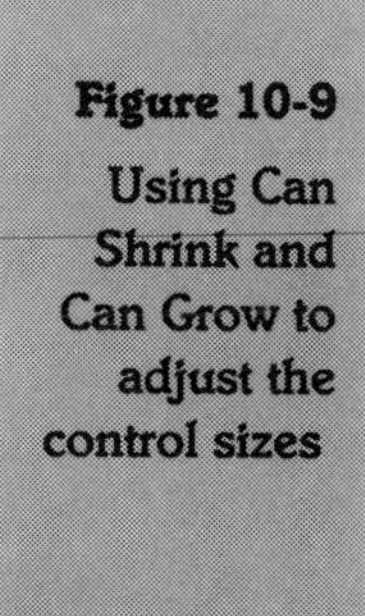

**Figure 10-9** Using Can Shrink and Can Grow to adjust the control sizes

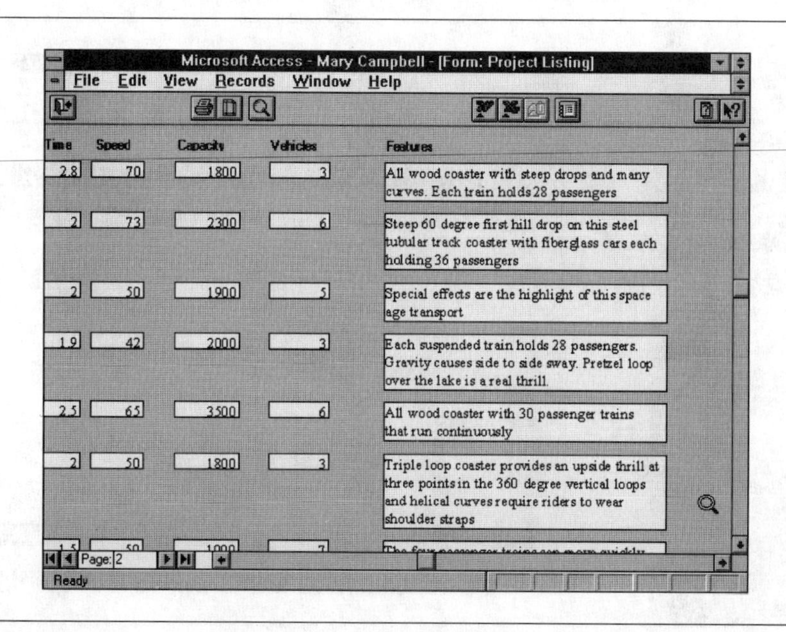

display the Coaster Name field contents as a text box when you print the form so that the extra choices do not appear in the printed copy, where they would serve no purpose. Do this by changing the control's Display When property. This property has three choices that let you determine when the control appears: Always, Print Only, and Screen Only.

To use both a combo box and a text box for the Coaster Name field, you would set the Display When property for the combo box to Screen Only and the Display When property for the text box to Print Only. The Display When default setting is Always, so by default the controls you add to a form appear both when you print and when you display the form in Form view. An example, shown in Figure 10-10, has two controls for the Coaster Id field. The control for the Coaster Id field on the left is a combo box that has its Display When property set to Screen Only. The control for the Coaster Id field on the right is a text box that has its Display When property set to Print Only.

## SETTING LIST BOX AND COMBO BOX CONTENTS

You have three ways to select what appears in the combo and list boxes: enter the values yourself, take the values from other field names, or take the values from another table or query. When you use the Control Wizards, you are prompted to select or enter the contents of combo and list boxes. If you are adding your controls without using a Control Wizard or if you want to change

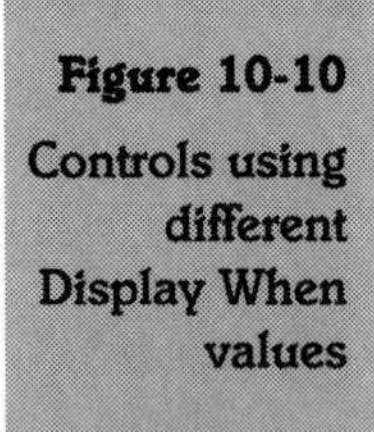

**Figure 10-10** Controls using different Display When values

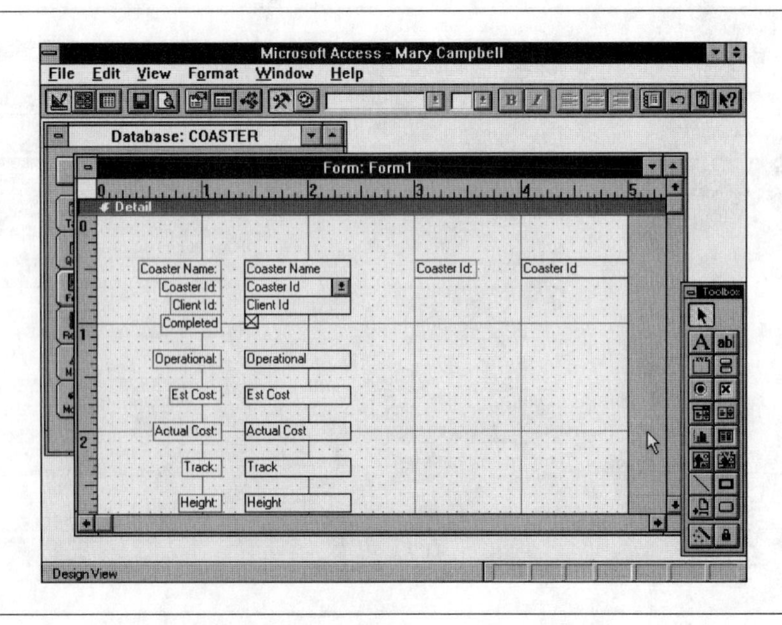

the contents, you can change the properties that set the source of the contents. To tell Access the source of the data for a list box or combo box, provide the name of the field for the Control Source property. To describe what you want in the list box for these two controls, use the Row Source Type and Row Source properties.

The Row Source Type property has three choices: Table/Query, Value List, and Field List. Table/Query lists the records from a selected table or query. Value List displays the values you enter for the Row Source property, and Field List lists the field names from a selected table or query. For either Table/Query or Field List, you must select the table or query containing the records or field names to use for the list values in the Record Source property. You can also enter the SQL statement that selects what you want to see in the Record Source property. For Value List, you can enter the values you want to appear in the list in the Record Source property.

For example, you can use a combo box or list box control to select the department of an employee. In this case, you set this control in one of two ways. You can select Table/Query for the Row Source Type and then select the name of the query that you create to contain the unique department names in the table. This method includes new departments in the list box or combo box control as they are added to the table. Figure 10-11 shows the query design for the Unique Department Names query with the Unique Values property selected.

Access has another method for you to easily extract the information you need without creating a query. You can use an SQL (Standard Query Language) statement, which functions as a query, and add it as the entry for the Row Source property. The quickest way to create this statement in Access version 1 is to create the query, choose SQL from the View menu, select the entire statement, press CTRL+INS to copy the statement to the Clipboard, and then switch to the form design and paste the SQL statement for the Row Source property for the combo box control. Access version 2 also offers the Query Builder, which appears when you click the Build button at the end of the property. This builder lets you create a query using the QBE grid and converts this query into SQL code, which becomes the property entry.

**tip:** 

*You can learn more about SQL in Appendix D.*

The second method of including the department names is to select Values List and then enter **Construction;Design;Testing** for the Row Source

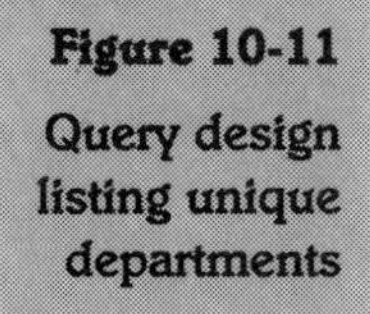

**Figure 10-11**

**Query design listing unique departments**

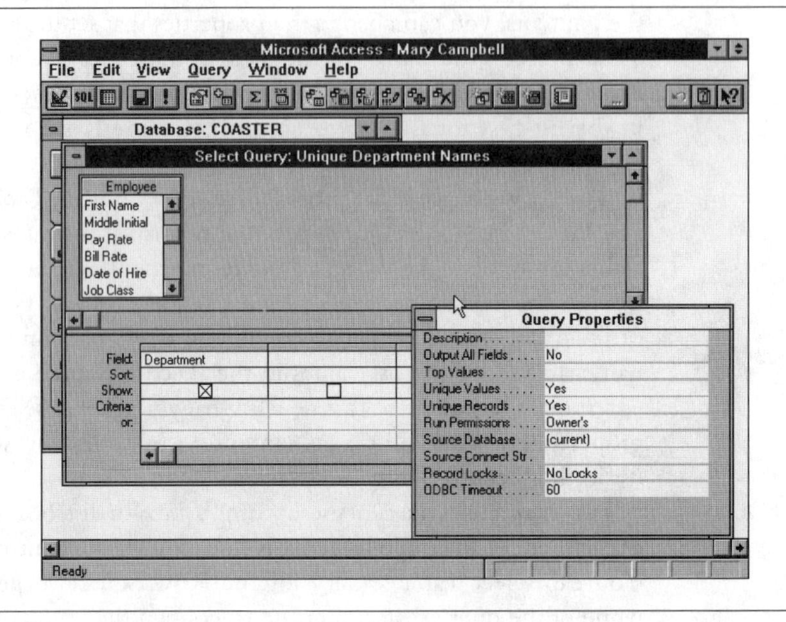


property. Note that different possible values are separated by a semicolon. You can use a value list instead of a query to provide the entries for a list box or combo box when you only have a few entries and when they do not change very often.

When you add another department, if you use the department names from a query or SQL statement, the department is included. If you use the department names from a value list, you must add the new department to the list of choices.

## USING MULTIPLE COLUMNS IN LIST BOXES AND COMBO BOXES

A special feature of combo boxes and list boxes is that they include entries in the list box describing the contents of the list, just as Employee Id, First Name, and Last Name do in the list box shown in Figure 10-12. These descriptions are *column heads*. To use a column head, change the Column Head property to Yes. When you do this, Access displays a column head using the field names from the query for a Table/Query row source type, the first field for the Field List row source type, and the first entry in the Row Source property for a Value List row source type, as shown in Figure 10-12. Column heads cannot be selected.

Another special feature of combo and list box controls is that they have more than one column of data in the control. You may use more than one column

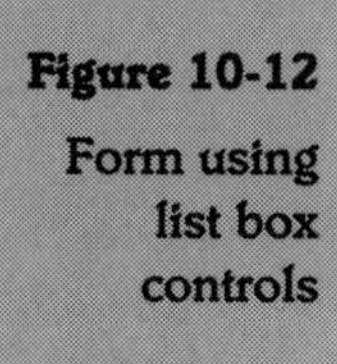

**Figure 10-12** Form using list box controls

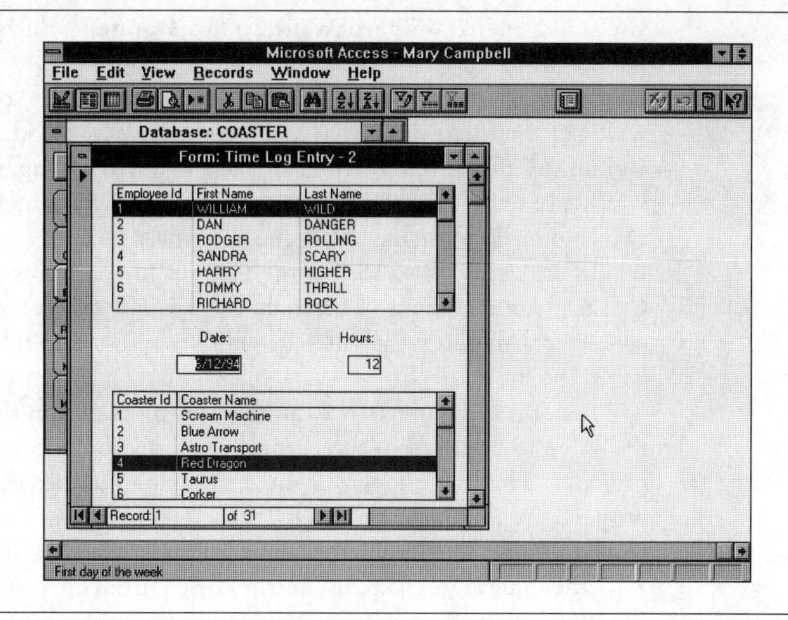


when a list box or combo box lists many items, to make it easier to select the correct item. You can use more than one column in a list box or combo box to display a series of related field entries that the form's user can select as an entire row. For example, in the modified Time Log Entry form shown in Figure 10-12, the two list boxes both use more than one column. The top list box has the Column Count property set to three while the bottom list box has the Column Count property set to two.

**tip:** *Again, you can easily create combo and list box controls that use more than one column when you use the Control Wizards to create these controls.*

The data that appear in the top list box are in a query named Employee Numbers and Names, which lists the Employee ID, First Name, and Last Name fields from the Employee table. The top list box has the Row Source Type set to Table/Query. The bottom list box also has the Row Source Type set to Table/Query, but uses the Project Numbers and Names query that lists the Coaster ID and Coaster Name fields from the Project table as the Row Source property. When using Value List as the Row Source property, set the values for more than one column by entering all of the values that appear in a row before entering the next row of values. For the top list box in Figure 10-12, you could enter **1;William;Wild;2;Dan;Danger** as the beginning of the Row Source property.

In multiple column list boxes and combo boxes, the columns have a default width of one inch, however, you can enter new widths for them using the Column Widths property. In the list box in the top of Figure 10-12, the column widths are set to .75;1;1 so that the first column is .75 inch wide and the other two columns are 1 inch wide. In the bottom list box in Figure 10-12, the column widths are set to .6;1.9 so that the Coaster Id column is .6 inch wide and the Coaster Name column is 1.9 inches wide. The last column may be wider or narrower than you set it, since its width is adjusted to fill the remaining space left in the list box control.

The form in Figure 10-12 can tell which column in the list boxes provides the value to be saved in the control's field by looking at the Bound Column property. This value ranges from zero to the number in the Column Count property. When the value is zero, the value entered in the control's field is the record number of the selected row in the list. When the value is more than zero, the value entered in the control's field is from the column number selected. For example, in Figure 10-12, the Bound Column property for both list boxes is 1, so the first list box returns the employee number for the Employee Id field in the Employee Time Log table and the second list box returns the coaster or project identification number for the Project number field in the Employee Time Log table.

## SPECIAL COMBO BOX PROPERTIES

A combo box also has additional properties that apply only to combo boxes. By default, when you click the down arrow of a combo box, the drop-down list box shows eight rows and is as wide as the combo box. You can change how many rows the list box displays by changing the List Rows property setting from the default 8 to another number. You can make the drop-down list box wider than the combo box control by entering the width you want for the List Width property. The default is Auto, which makes the list box as wide as the combo box control.

The other special property for a combo box control sets what is happening when you type in the text box. You can either be selecting one of the items listed in the list box or entering a new item. For example, when you create a table and select the data type for a field, you must select one of the available data types. Anything you type is either converted to one of the data types or rejected as an entry.

On the other hand, when you are entering a table or query name for the Row Source property, you can select one of the names listed in the drop-down list box or type the name of a table or query that does not necessarily match one of the listed ones. You can type the table or query name when you want to use a query or table that has not yet been created for a list box or combo box control.

You can put the same limit on the combo boxes controls you place into your forms. To set a combo box to accept as valid only one of the items listed in the drop-down list box, change the Limit To List property to Yes. The default of No means that you can either select an item from the list or type a new entry in the text part of the combo box control.

**tip:** *If you want the entries in the list box in a particular order and these values come from a table or query, create a query that sorts the records, as described in Chapter 6. Then use the query for the Row Source property.*

## Section Properties

Sections in a form also have properties. Since sections do not represent field values, the section properties are very different from the ones used for controls. The Detail, Form Header, and Form Footer sections all have the same properties. The Page Header and Page Footer sections have a subset of these properties because these two sections do not use the Force New Page, New Row or Col, Keep Together, Display When, Can Shrink, and Can Grow properties. You can select any one of these sections by clicking part of the section that does not include a control. Figure 10-13 shows the properties for the Detail section.

When you print forms, you may want to print the information for each record on a separate page. Rather than adding a page break control to the form's design, you can set a property to start a new page at the beginning or end of each section. To add a page break to a section, change the Force New Page property. For example, to have the contents of the Detail section printed using a separate page for each record, select Before & After for the Force New Page Property. The default for the property is None, so the form only starts another page after filling the current one. Select Before Section to have the form start on a new page every time the current section is printed. Select After Section to have the form start on a new page after printing the current section. Finally, select Before & After when you want a new page started every time you start and end the current section.

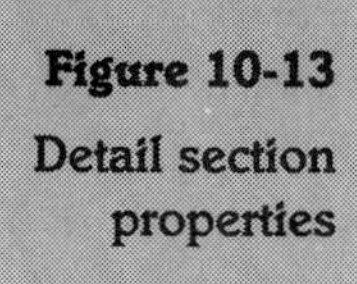

**Figure 10-13** Detail section properties

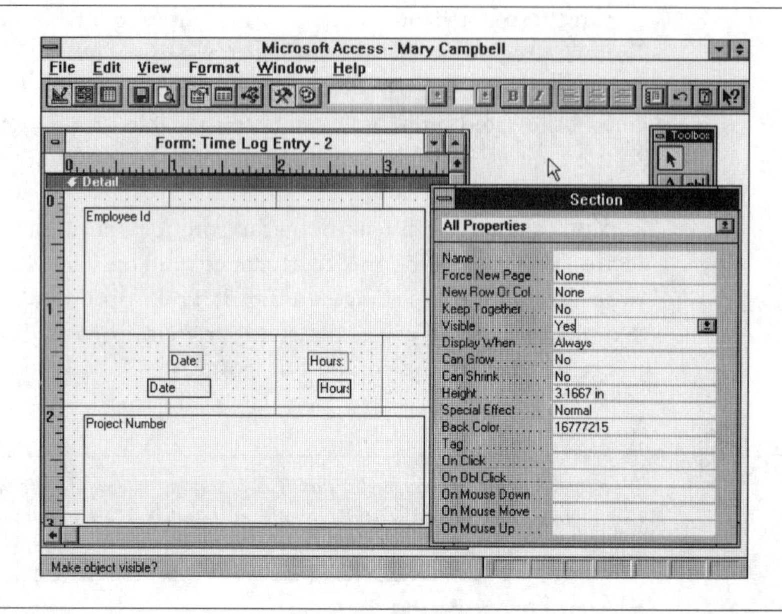


An unfortunate result of splitting a form between pages when you print can be having part of a section print on one page and the rest on the next page. You can change the form design so that when Access cannot fit the entire section on the current page, Access automatically starts the section on the next page. Usually, you will want all of the data from one record printed on the same page so that you do not have to flip between pages to look at the record's contents. To make this change to the form's design, change the section's Keep Together property from No to Yes. When you print the form, Access moves information to the next page whenever there is not enough space on the current page to print the entire section.

When you print a form, you can print the data in several columns, just as a newspaper is formatted. When you print data in a form, you can select whether each section starts at the top of the column or row or whether each section starts where the previous one left off, like the classified ads in a newspaper. Figure 10-14 shows a form that starts each Detail section at the top of the column. You would set up this form for two columns by choosing Print Setup from the File menu, selecting More, and typing **2** in the Items Across text box.

The records in Figure 10-14 are filled in from top to bottom because the Vertical option button in the Print Setup dialog box is selected. Each record starts in a new column because, for this form, the Detail section has the New Row or Col property set to After Section. The default is None so that when you have a form divided into columns, each column is filled completely before

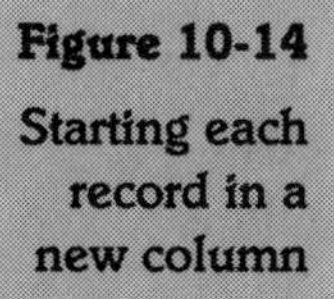

**Figure 10-14**
Starting each record in a new column

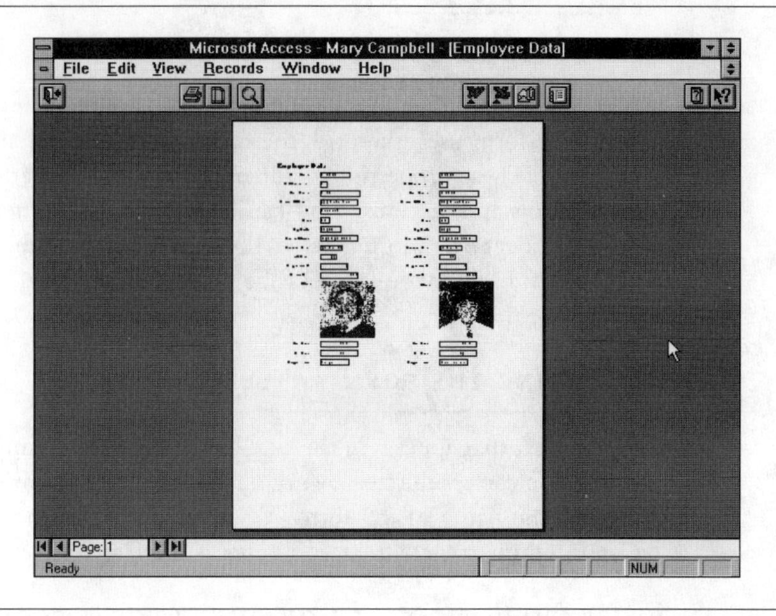


starting another column. You can also set this property to Before Section when you want a new column started after printing the current section. The other choice is Before & After, which starts in a new column before the section is printed, and after it is printed as well.

Some of the section properties are the same as properties with the same names that you used for controls. The Visible property sets whether a section appears. You can create macros that select when this section appears based on other criteria. You have the same choices as with controls for the Display When property (Always, Print Only, and Display Only), which determine whether individual sections appear when the form is displayed in a window or printed.

The Can Shrink and Can Grow properties perform the same function in a section as when applied to individual controls. The default for a section's Can Shrink property is No. For a section's Can Grow property, the default is No unless the Can Shrink property for one of the controls in the section is set to Yes.

The Height property sets the section's height just as you set the section's height, by dragging the bottom of the section up or down. You might use this property rather than the mouse when you want to be sure that two sections are the same height or sections appearing in different forms are the same height. The Special Effect and Back Color properties are described in Chapter 14, which tells you how to change the color and graphic appearance of a form.

## Form Properties

Forms also have their own properties. These properties include the table or query the form uses, the grid, the form width, its size, and the views you can switch to. These properties are different from the properties you learned about for controls and sections. You can display the properties for the form in the property sheet by choosing Select Form in the Edit menu or by clicking an area of the Form window outside of the design. Figure 10-15 shows the properties for the form.

### SETTING THE FORM'S TITLE BAR TEXT

The text that appears in the title bar of the Form window can be set in two ways. You can set the text by saving the form; the Form window title bar then displays the name of the form. You can also enter the text using the form's Caption property; any text you enter as the Caption appears in the title bar.

### SETTING THE TABLE OR QUERY FOR A FORM

Usually you will base a form on the table or query you select when you start creating it. However, if you change your mind or you select the Blank Form button from the New Form dialog box without selecting a table or query, you will need to select a table or query.

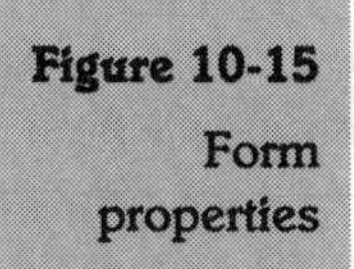

**Figure 10-15** Form properties

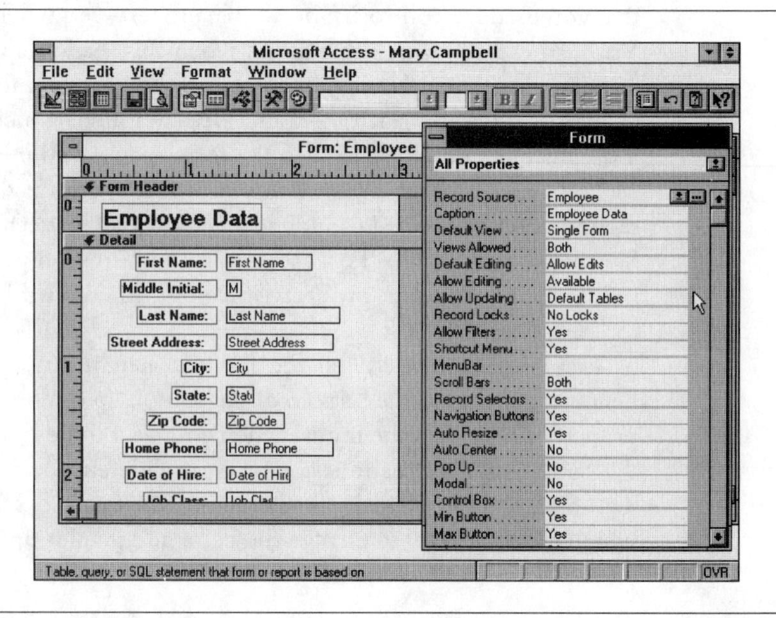

Selecting a table or query controls the fields shown in the field list. To set which table or query the form uses, change the Record Source property. You can select any of the tables and queries available in the database. You can also enter an SQL statement that selects the data for the form. In Access version 2, you can add the SQL statement by clicking the Build button at the end of the Record Source property and entering the query design to convert into an SQL statement. When you change the table or query, the fields listed in the field list change to match the new table or query, but the fields from the old table or query in the form design do not change. For example, you might change the table or query a form uses when you have copied or imported a form designed to work with one table or query that you want to use with another. You may want to use a form you have created for the names and addresses of the Employee table to list the names and addresses of the parks listed in the Client table.

## SETTING WHERE A FORM STARTS

Several of the properties let you select what you will do with the form when you use it. The Default Editing property tells Access whether you plan to use the form to enter data, to update existing information, or just to look at the data. The choices are Data Entry, Allow Edits, and Read Only; in Access version 2 there is another option, Can't Add Records. Data Entry starts the form at the end of the table or query so you can start entering data, but you cannot look at earlier records. In Access version 1, you could look at earlier records with this setting by choosing Show All Records in the Records menu. Allow Edits opens the form at the beginning of the table or query and lets you both look at the data and make changes. Read Only lets you look at the data but does not allow you to change or add records until you choose Allow Editing (Editing Allowed in Access version 1) in the Records menu. Can't Add Records lets you view and update existing records, but does not let you add new records.

You can also turn off and on whether users can make changes to the data with the Allow Editing property. When this property is set to Available, you can choose Allow Editing (Editing Allowed in Access version 1) in the Records menu to switch between having Access allow changes or not allow them. When this property is set to Unavailable, users cannot choose Allow Editing (Editing Allowed in Access version 1) in the Records menu. These two properties are often combined. For example, setting Default Editing to Read Only and Allow Editing to Unavailable makes the form read-only, since users cannot select the command that would allow them to change the table's or query's information. You may also want to set Default Editing to Data Entry and Allow Editing to

Available when you plan to use the form primarily for entering new records rather than looking at older ones.

### SETTING THE INITIAL VIEW OF A FORM

When you look at the forms you create with Form Wizards, you may notice that the Single-Column Form Wizard forms only show one record at a time while the tabular form shows as many records as can fit in the window. The reason these two Form Wizard types change between displaying one record and many is the Default View property.

The Default View property sets how many records initially appear in the form. You can switch between Single Form, Continuous Forms, and Datasheet. When the Default View property is set to Single Form, the default for the Single-Column Form Wizard forms, the form only displays one record at a time, as shown here:

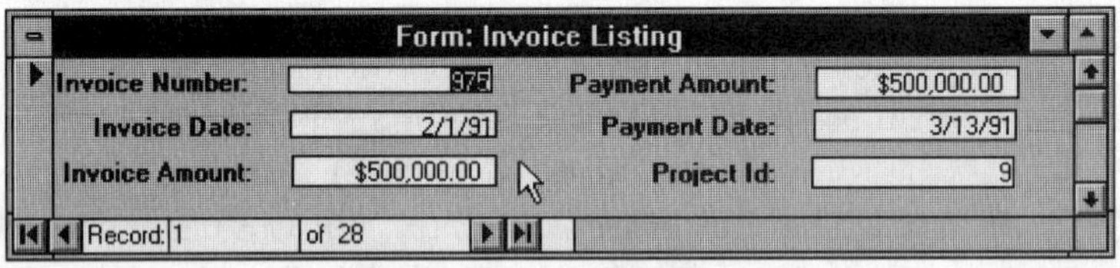

When the Default View property is set to Continuous Forms, the default for the Tabular Form Wizard forms, the form design repeats in the form window to display as many times as possible, as shown in Figure 10-16.

When the Default View property is set to Datasheet, the default for the subform in a Main/Subform Form Wizard form, the table or query's data appear in a table format, just as you can see the table or query by opening the table or query.

You can also use the Views Allowed property to limit which views the form's user can switch between. The choices are Form, Datasheet, and Both. Form lets the form's user display only the form without switching to the datasheet. You use Form when a form is designed to display only a few fields so that users don't have to go through all of the fields to find the ones they want.

Datasheet lets the form's users display the table in a datasheet without switching to the form. Both, the default, lets users switch between the datasheet and the form. Regardless of this property's setting, you can still switch to the form's design.

When the view setting for a form is Datasheet or Continuous Forms, the window has scroll bars to change which records and which parts of the form appear in the window. In a single-record form, the window contains scroll bars only when the form design is larger than the form window's area. The scroll

**Figure 10-16** Continuous Form as the Default View property

bars appear because the Scroll Bars property is set to Both. This property sets which directions in the form have scroll bars. You can also select Horizontal Only or Vertical Only when you want a scroll bar in just one direction, or choose None when you do not want scroll bars.

The Record Selectors property in a form displays or hides the record selector. The record selector is the bar containing the small triangle at the left side of the record. These appear because the form has the default of Yes for the Record Selectors property. Select No for this property when you do not want the record selectors to appear.

The following illustration shows a form that has the scroll bars and the record selector removed:

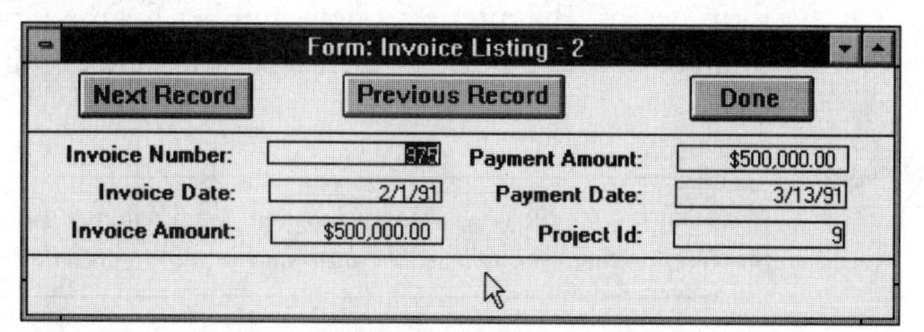


The scroll bars are not needed since the Form Header section has command buttons that let you switch between records, and all of the controls appear in the window. Removing the record selector means you do not have the border on the left side of the record that you can click to select the entire record. In

Chapter 16, you will learn how to assign macros to the Next Record, Previous Record, and Done command buttons shown in the previous illustration.

As you work on your form designs, notice that when you open a form, the window is sized to fit the form's design. The Auto Resize property handles this. When the Auto Resize property is set to Yes, every time you open the form, Access sizes the window to fit the Form Header, Detail, and Form Footer sections, if possible. If you set this property to No, the window you open when you open a form is the same size it was when you last used the form. Setting this property to Yes means that as you change the form's size, the Form window also changes. However, once you have finished designing the form, you do not need Access to readjust the window size. Also, once the form is open, Access does not readjust the window's size until after you reopen it, so changing the size of the form's design does not affect the window's size until after you close the window. When you want to update the form's window size to make it appropriate for the form's design, choose Size to Fit Form from the Window menu.

The Width property sets the form's width just as you can set the form width using the mouse, by dragging the right side of the form to the left or right. You might use this property rather than the mouse when you want the form to be a specific width. Changing the width changes the width of all sections in the form.

## CHANGING THE GRID

In Chapter 8, you learned how to use the grid for placement. You can change the size of the grid by selecting the number of grid points per inch that appear vertically and horizontally on the form design. The number of dots per inch is set with the Grid X and Grid Y properties. By entering a new number for the Grid X property, you set the number of grid points per inch that fit across the form design. By entering a new number for the Grid Y property, you set the number of grid points per inch that fit up and down the form design.

**tip:** *If you do not see the grid, choose Grid from the View menu to display it. If the grid points are too close together, you will see the inch markings but you will not see the individual grid points.*

## KEEPING THE FORM ON THE TOP

You know that you can switch easily between windows using the Window menu, the mouse, or various keyboard shortcuts. However, you can set a form to prevent users from switching to other windows inside Access. To do this, set the Modal property to Yes. When you change the Modal property, the change does not take effect until after you close the window and save the changes to the modified form. When you open the form again, the Design View and Datasheet View buttons in the toolbar are dimmed, as are the Form Design and Datasheet commands in the View menu.

When you display the Window menu, the bottom of the window includes only the current form and ignores any other windows in your Access window. Also, you cannot click other windows to activate them. You can only move to other windows by closing the form. Continue using the form, and close it when you are finished with it. To change the form's design, select the form name and the Design button from the Database window. When you do not want the current form to remain constantly in the front anymore, change the Modal property to No. This change will not take effect until you have saved the updated form.

## SETTING THE FONTS THAT THE FORM USES

The fonts that the entries in the form can use depend on the fonts you have installed for Windows. Windows has some fonts designed for printing and others intended for displaying information on the screen. You select whether you use the screen or the printer fonts for the form. The default for the Layout for Print property is No, which tells the form to use screen fonts. You can select Yes for this property when you want the form to use printing fonts. When you print the form using screen fonts, Windows substitutes a similar printer font. When you use a TrueType font such as the ones available in Windows 3.1 or through accessory packages such as Facelift or Adobe Typeface Manager, changing this property has no effect because TrueType fonts look the same on the screen as they do when printed.

## LOCKING RECORDS

If you are sharing a database with other users, you may want to make sure other users don't change the data appearing in your form. Prevent others from changing your records by selecting All Records for the Record Locks property. While you are using the form, all of the records included in the form are locked so that other users cannot change the data. The default of No Locks means other users can continue editing the data while you are using the form. If you and another user try saving changes to the same record, the one who saves second will be alerted and can choose to either save over your changes, discard their own changes, or copy the record to the Clipboard.

Another choice just for forms is Edited Record. This locks the record or group of records you are working with as soon as you make any change to the current record. Other users will not be able to make a change to the locked records until you have unlocked them. To unlock them, you must move to another record or close the form.

## MAKING FORMS RESEMBLE DIALOG BOXES

Often you will create a form to make it easier for a person who is not familiar with a database application to enter, update, or review data without really knowing much about how Access works. You can create forms that look more like dialog boxes, making them easier for users who know Windows techniques but have not previously used Access. Access version 2 offers several new properties that can help you do this. Among the properties you can set are the Auto Center, Control Box, Min Button, Max Button, and Scroll Bars.

When you set the Auto Center property for a form to Yes, Access automatically displays the form in the center of the Access window. When it is set to No, it takes the location it had when you last closed it. Automatically centering the form can make it easier for someone to use, particularly if you often move or size the form window while working with it.

To make your form look more like a dialog box, you can remove the control menu box and minimize and maximize buttons by setting the Control Box, Min Button, and Max Button properties for the form to No, the settings used for the form shown in Figure 10-17. The default setting for these properties is Yes. These buttons are hidden in Form view, but not in Datasheet or Design view.

## OTHER FORM PROPERTIES

The form has other properties that provide miscellaneous features. Some of these features are covered later in this chapter and in other chapters.

Form properties such as On Current and On Open trigger performing macros or procedures as you use the form. Chapter 16 introduces macros and Chapter 19 introduces procedures. Chapter 17 includes examples of adding macros to these properties.

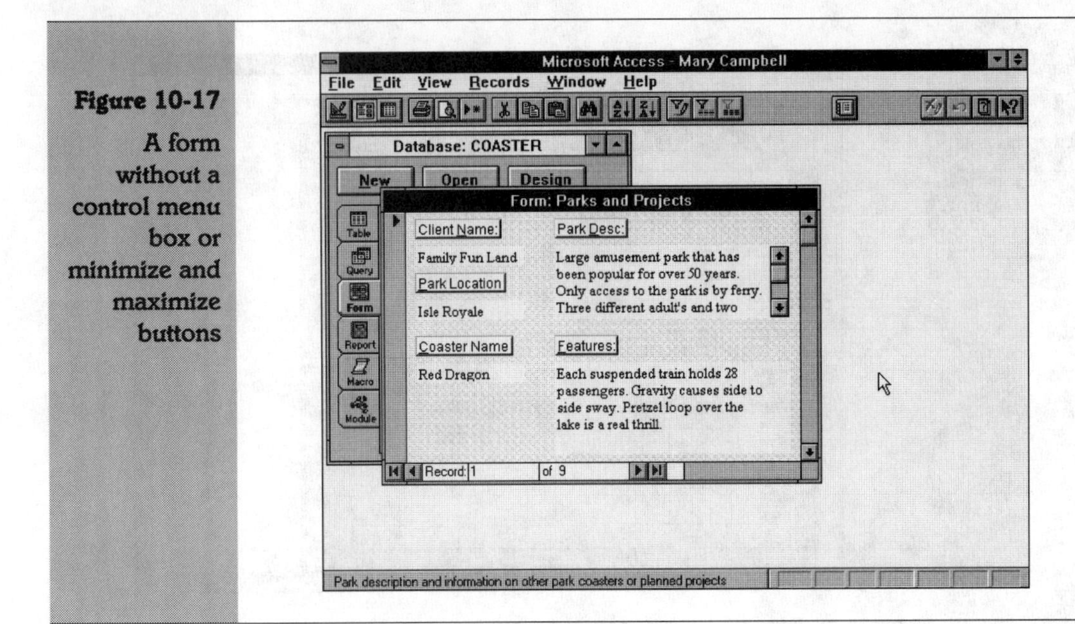


**Figure 10-17** A form without a control menu box or minimize and maximize buttons

In Chapter 13, you will learn about using multiple tables and popups in a form. Having multiple tables in a form means you can change the Allow Updating Form property to select which tables from the multiple tables you can edit. Chapter 13 describes this process fully, and you will also learn about using the Pop Up property when you create popup forms.

## Using Multiple Pages in a Form

When you have many fields that you wish to include in a form, you may find using the form easier by dividing the Detail section into pages. Each page can show a different related group of controls. For example, when adding another roller coaster project, the table has 17 fields for you to fill in. Rather than having a single crowded window that contains all of the information you need, divide the form into pages and have each page process a smaller, more manageable unit of the information.

To divide a form into pages, add page breaks to the Detail section where you want the section divided. Since the form's window size is set by the size of the first page of the Detail section plus the form's header and footer, if any exist, you will want each page to be the same size. Ensure that each page is the same

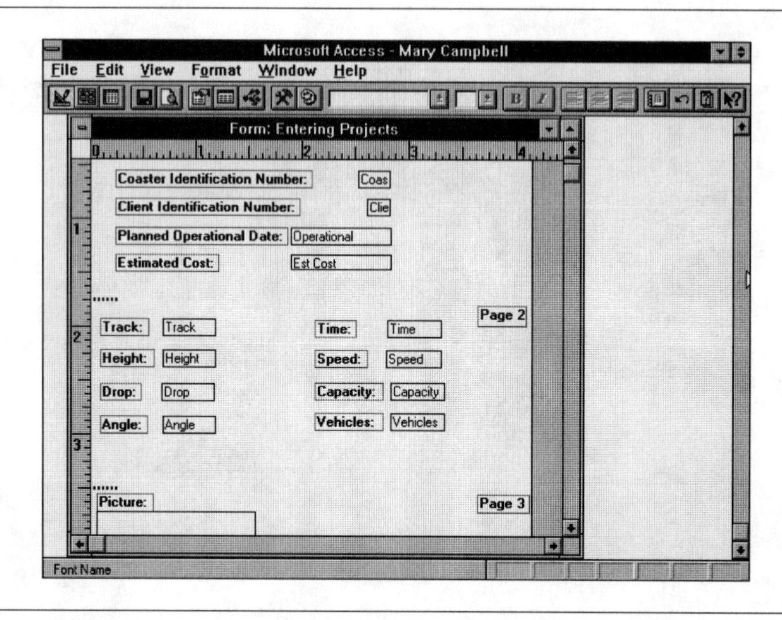


**Figure 10-18** A form using more than one page

height by adding the page breaks and entering the values for the Top property so they are an even increment. For example, for the form design in Figure 10-18, the first page break is set at 1.75 and the second page break is set at 3.5. These page break controls appear as a series of six dots next to 1.75 and 3.5 along the vertical ruler of the form design. Once you make this change, choose Size to Fit Form in the Window menu when you display the Form view.

When using multiple pages in a form, include information that serves as a reminder for the record you are using. For example, in the form shown here, the coaster name and identification number are repeated in the Form Header section:

Form: Entering Projects
Coaster Id: 1 Coaster Name: Scream Machine
Page 1
Coaster Name: Scream Machine
Coaster Identification Number: 1
Client Identification Number: 8
Planned Operational Date: 10/5/95
Estimated Cost: $7,800,000.00
This form has three pages.
Record: 1 of 9

Also, the three pages are identified so users know where they are as they use the form. The label controls containing the page numbers have their Display When property set to Screen Only, so they do not appear when you print the form.

When you use a form with multiple pages, switch between pages by using PGUP and PGDN or by clicking the scroll bar.

**tip:** *Leave a border of empty space at the beginning and end of the pages. The empty space ensures that information from one page does not accidentally appear on the next or previous page. Also, leaving the empty space before and after the page break ensures that a page break control does not divide any other controls in the middle.*

## Selecting and Sorting Records for a Form

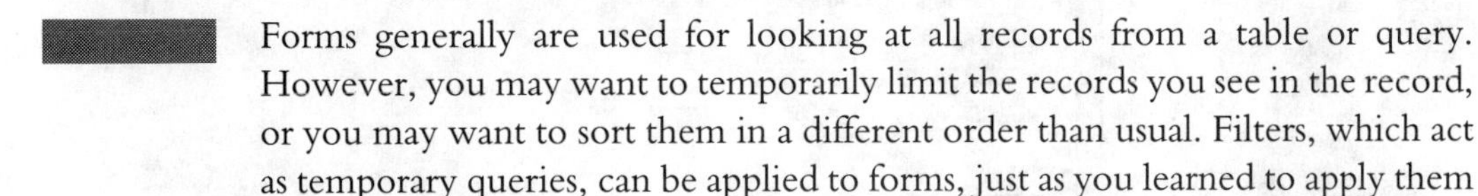

Forms generally are used for looking at all records from a table or query. However, you may want to temporarily limit the records you see in the record, or you may want to sort them in a different order than usual. Filters, which act as temporary queries, can be applied to forms, just as you learned to apply them to tables in Chapter 6.

Use filters when you want to use a subset of data once, but don't forget that if you want to repeatedly use a query to limit or sort the records you see in a form, you need to create that form using a query that selects or sorts the information the way that you want it. Filters can be saved as queries, but they cannot be saved as actual filters.

## Saving a Form as a Report

Some of the forms you create will be exactly what you want to use as reports in Access. Rather than re-creating the form as a report, you can save a form as a report. First, display the form you want to convert in Design view. Next, choose Save As Report in the File menu. Access prompts for a name for this report using the form's name as a default. Either use this name or replace it with another before you select OK to complete the command. After selecting OK, Access creates a report with the same appearance as the form.

When you look at the reports in your database, you will see the one you have just created. Once this new report is created, use it and make design modifications just as you do for the reports created from scratch. You will learn more about customizing reports in Chapter 11. As an example of saving a form as a report, Figure 10-19 shows the report design created by saving the form design shown in Figure 10-18 as a report.

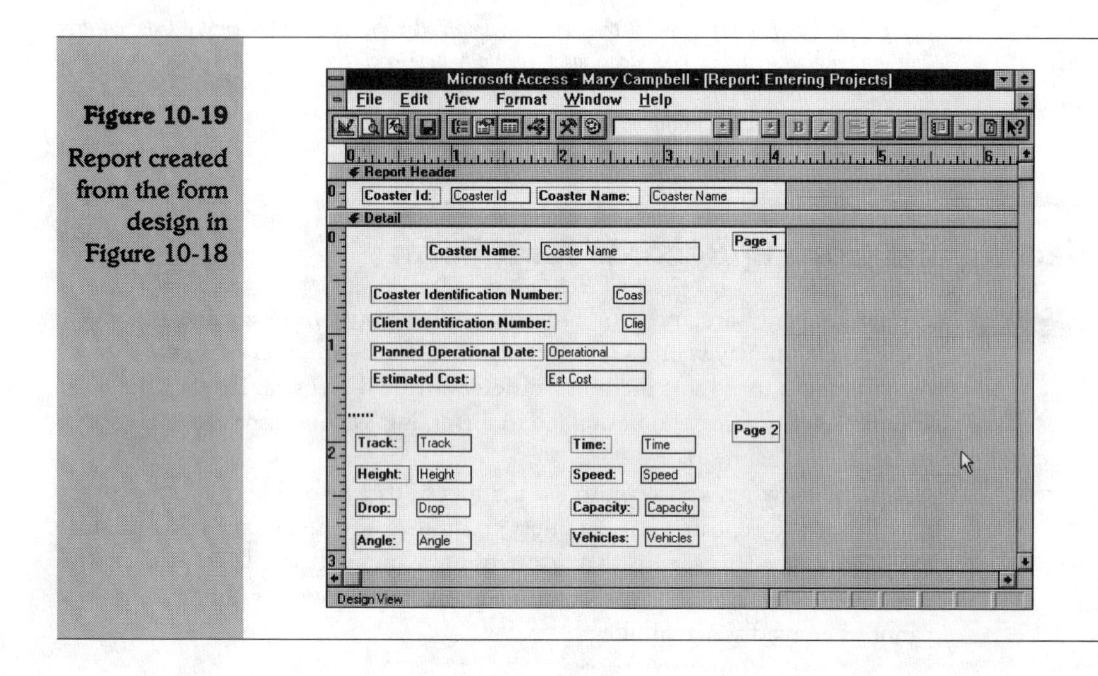


**Figure 10-19** Report created from the form design in Figure 10-18

Quick Reference

**To Add a Control to a Form** Display the toolbox by choosing Toolbox from the View menu. Click the tool for the control you want to add and then click the form design where you want the control placed.

**To Set a Property in a Form** Display the property sheet by choosing Properties from the View menu. Click the control, section, or overall form whose properties you want to change in the form design. Click the property you want to change in the property sheet. Type the new entry for the property, select one of the choices available by clicking the down arrow, or click the Build button in the property sheet to invoke a Builder to create the new entry.

**To Create Multiple Pages in a Form** Add page controls where you want each page break. You will want to add some enhancements, such as making the pages the same size and adding identifying information in the page header and footer.

**To Save a Form as a Report** Display the Form Design window for the form you want to convert. Choose Save As Report in the File menu. Modify the report name from the default of the form's name if you wish. Select OK.

# Chapter 11

Adding Controls to Reports

Working with Report Properties

Sorting and Grouping the Report's Output

# Customizing Reports with Controls, Sorting, and Grouping

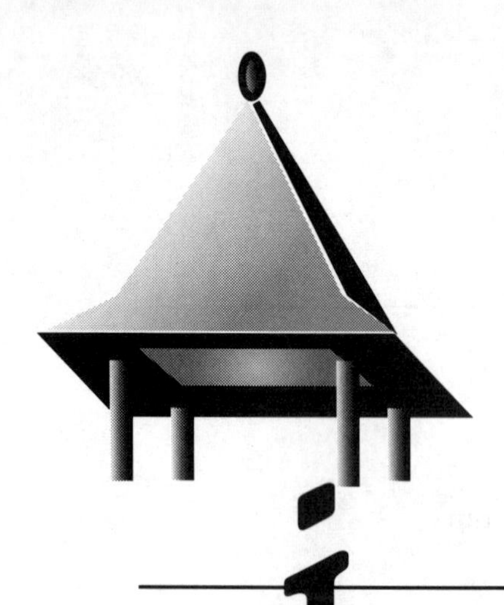

JUST as with forms, the reports you create with Report Wizards might meet your exact needs or you may have to make some changes. Instead of starting with a completely new design, you can often make adjustments to the report created with Report Wizards—by adding controls, for example. The techniques you use to modify a report by adding controls are the same techniques you use to build a report containing exactly what you want from a blank report. When you add a control, you can change its properties to alter how the control's information is presented.

You can also customize reports by sorting the records that appear in them. You can combine sorting with *grouping,* in which records that have the same values for one or more fields are placed together in a group.

## Adding Controls to Reports

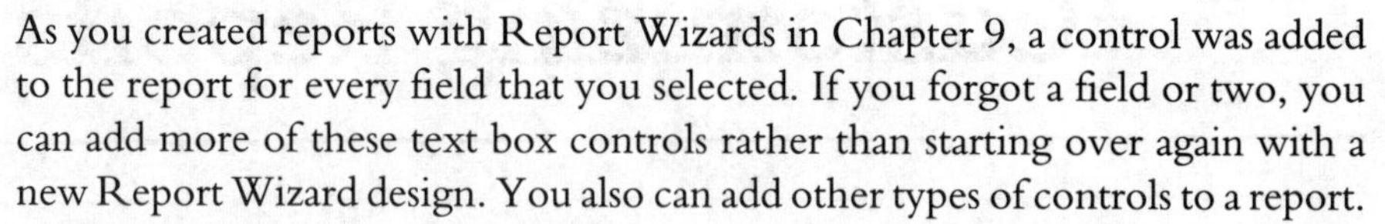

As you created reports with Report Wizards in Chapter 9, a control was added to the report for every field that you selected. If you forgot a field or two, you can add more of these text box controls rather than starting over again with a new Report Wizard design. You also can add other types of controls to a report.

Access divides controls into three groups: *bound* controls display a value from a field in a database table or query, *unbound* controls display other objects such as lines or text that you have added, and *calculated* controls perform a computation.

Regardless of the type of control that you add, you will use the toolbox shown in Figure 11-1. Some of these controls do not apply to reports. The toolbox can appear anywhere in the Access window and remains in the same location unless you move it. With reports, you usually will use label, text box, option group, option button, check box, and page break controls. Controls such as list boxes are available for use with reports but are more often used for forms.

**Figure 11-1**
**A blank report design showing the toolbox**

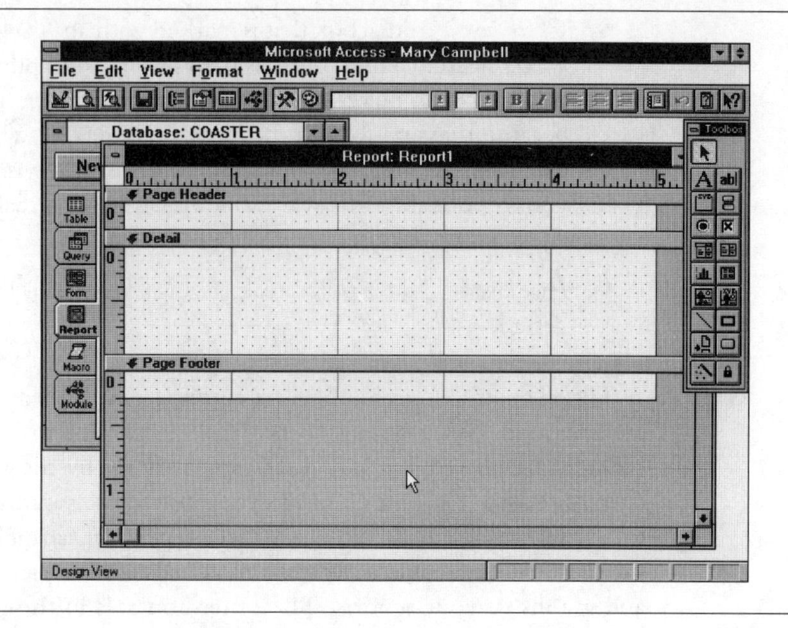


When you add controls to a report, you usually use one of six types of controls:

- *Label* Adds text that does not change from record to record. Labels are often used for sections such as the Report Header, Report Footer, Page Header, and Page Footer.
- *Text box* Adds a box that displays the value of a field and changes from record to record. Text boxes can contain other types of entries such as totals, which you will learn about later in this chapter, and expressions, which you will learn more about in Chapter 12. A text box that contains the result of a computation is a calculated control.
- *Option group* Adds a box that you can later fill with option buttons or check boxes. When option buttons or check boxes are in an option group, only one of them can be selected at a time.
- *Option button* Adds an option button either to an option group or outside any option groups. When option buttons are in an option group, only one can be selected at a time. When option buttons are not in an option group, each option button is separate from the others and functions as a check box.

- *Check box* Adds a box that is marked with an X when selected or empty when cleared. This control is used just like an option button. In a report design, check boxes and option buttons can be used interchangeably because they are treated the same. You decide which you want to use based on the appearance of these controls. It is wise, however, to design your reports the same way Windows designs its dialog boxes and reserve check boxes for use outside of option groups.
- *Page break* Adds a page break, giving you several pages within the report design.

This chapter focuses on these six controls. The label and page break controls are unbound, because they do not change from record to record. The other controls are bound, because their values are set by the values of fields in the current record. Chapter 13 shows you how to use subform/subreport controls to add subsidiary forms and reports to a report. In Chapter 14 you learn about the controls to add lines and boxes, and Chapter 15 explains how to add pictures and graphs to your reports. The other controls in the toolbox are not used in reports.

## Adding a Control to a Report Design

In Chapter 9, you learned how to add a control that represents one of the fields from the table or query by dragging the field name from the field list. Dragging fields from the field list adds text boxes for the field and adjoining labels that describe the field's contents. To add other types of controls, use the toolbox. You can combine the toolbox and the field list to quickly create controls of different types that represent the different fields.

To add a label, text box, option group, option button, check box, or page break control, first display the toolbox by choosing Toolbox from the View menu or by clicking the Toolbox button in the toolbar. Next, select the type of control you want to create from the toolbox. These buttons are identified in Figure 11-2. Then click the report design where you want the control you are adding to begin. This adds the control using the default size of the control. Access will change the size of labels and option groups as their contents change. Another option is to set the size yourself by dragging the mouse from where you want the control to start to where you want the opposite corner of the control. When you add controls, Access puts an empty control in the location you indicate, similar to the ones shown in Figure 11-3. When adding a label, you can immediately start to type the text you want to appear in the label.

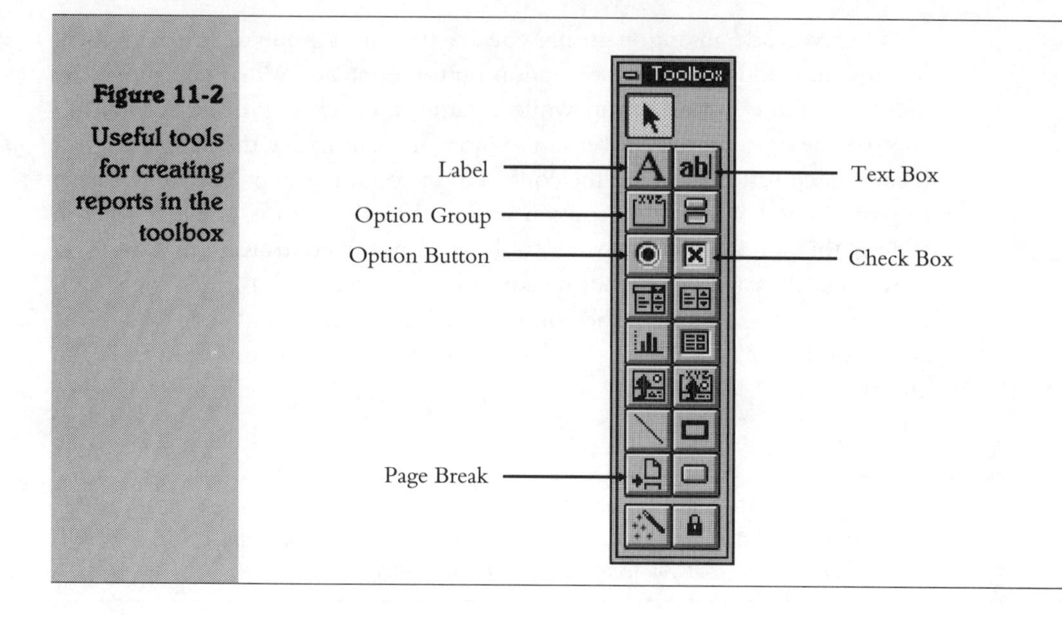


**Figure 11-2** Useful tools for creating reports in the toolbox

In Access version 2, when you add an option group to the report design while the Control Wizards button in the toolbox is selected, the Option Group Control Wizard starts. This Control Wizard, like other Access Wizards, will prompt you to enter the information and make the choices needed to create an option group and the check boxes or option buttons added to it.

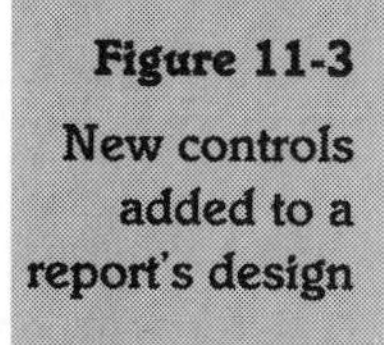

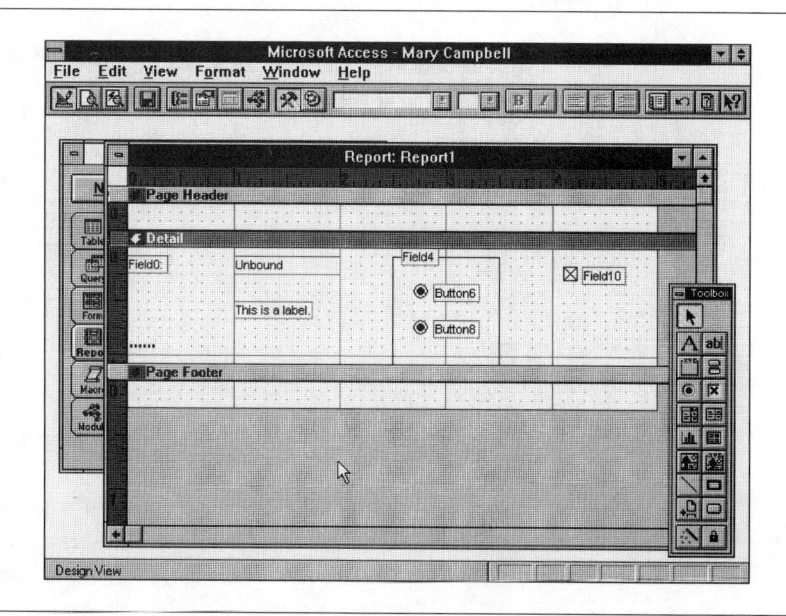


**Figure 11-3** New controls added to a report's design

When you add an option group, you are creating a group to which you will subsequently add check box or option button controls. When you move the mouse over the option group while creating a check box or option button control, the option group reverses its colors, indicating that the mouse pointer is correctly positioned to add the control to the option group. You do not have to worry about whether the option group's box will fit the controls you are adding; the option group expands to show all of the controls in it. When you move a check box or option button control outside the option group, the option group is resized to fit all of the controls, including that one. When you move an option group, you move all of the check boxes and option buttons in the group.

**tip:** *Remember to align the check boxes and option buttons that you add to a report. You can align controls that you select by choosing Align in the Format menu (the Layout menu in Access version 1) and then the direction that you want the selected objects aligned.*

When you add a page break, the page break symbol is added on the left edge of the report design. This page break control lets you divide lengthy reports into several pages. A multiple-page form letter, for example, uses page break controls to divide the Detail section into different pages. The following illustration shows part of the design of a report that breaks the Detail section into pages.

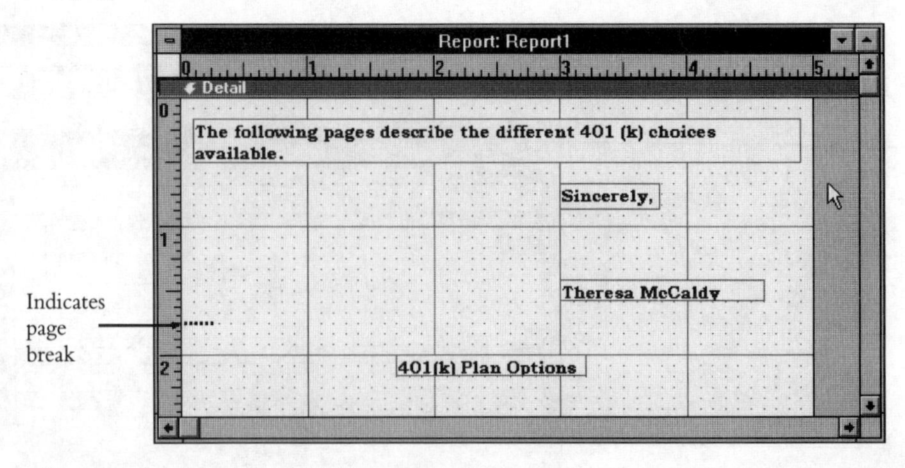


Most controls, including text boxes, option buttons, and check boxes, are compound controls. This means that when you insert the control, a related label is inserted at the same time. These labels currently have text that is inappropriate for your report. Change this text by selecting the label control and then clicking the text where you want the insertion point placed. At this point, you can edit the contents of the control.

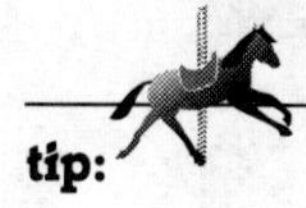

**tip:** *You can add several controls of the same type by clicking Tool Lock in the toolbox. When Tool Lock is on, the same tool in the toolbox remains selected, even after you have inserted a tool in the report's design. Selecting Tool Lock again turns it off so that after you add a control to the report, the tool in the toolbox is unselected.*

## SETTING THE FIELD THAT A CONTROL REPRESENTS

Once you have added a control to a report, tell Access which field the control will represent. Some controls, such as labels and page breaks, do not represent fields since they do not change from record to record. With controls such as text boxes, option buttons, check boxes, and option groups, you tell Access which field you want to use with the control. The field that a control represents is one of the control's properties.

To set the field for a text box, make the change by editing the text box's contents and changing Unbound to one of the table's or query's field names. You can also change the Control Source property that you use for other types of controls.

To have any type of control represent a field in the table or query, you need to change the control's Control Source property. First display the property sheet by choosing Properties from the View menu or by clicking the Properties button in the toolbar, which looks like this:

When you display the property sheet with the report itself selected, it looks like the one shown in Figure 11-4. As you click different parts of the report design, the property sheet changes to show the properties and values of the properties for the selected item. You may need to move the property sheet if it covers a control you want to select. The property sheet remains displayed in the report design until you choose Properties from the View menu or click the Properties button in the toolbar. You can also use the Control menu box in the property sheet to close this window. The property sheet for reports is just like the property sheet for forms. The left side contains the property names and the right side contains the properties' values.

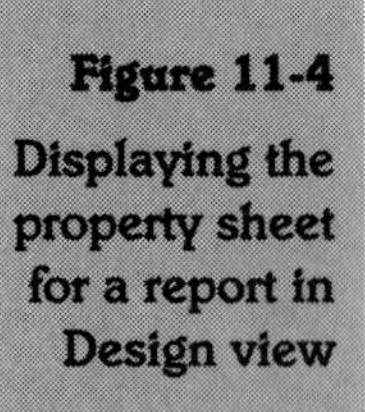

**Figure 11-4** Displaying the property sheet for a report in Design view

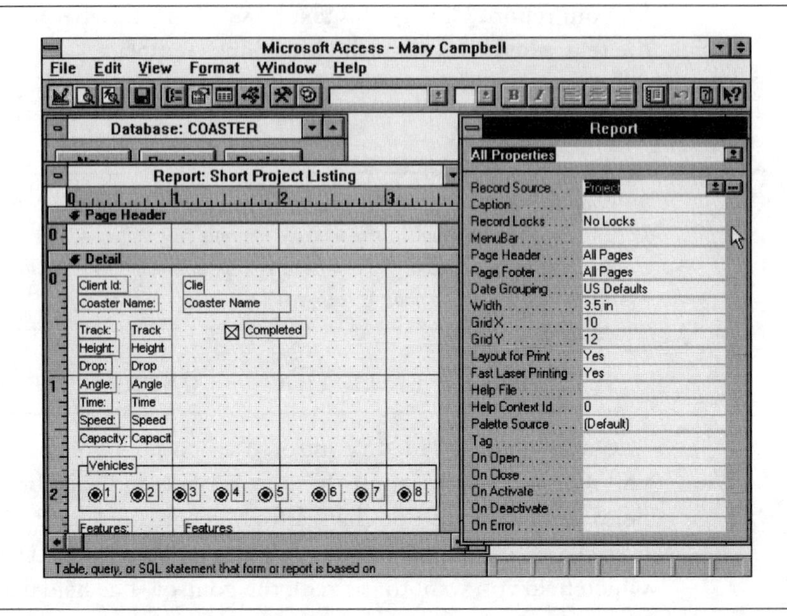


The Control Source property is the property that selects which field a control represents. You can either type the field name or use the down arrow to select one of the fields from the list.

How you select the field for a check box or option button depends on whether the control is part of an option group. When a check box or option button is not included in an option group, it is an on/off switch, usually used for Yes/No data type fields. Set the field for the check box or option button control using the Control Source property. For example, the Completed check box shown in Figure 11-5 has its Control Source property set to Completed, so the report shows the check box marked with an X when the coaster is completed and an empty box when the coaster is still in progress.

The other use of a check box or option button is for showing the value of a field; this happens when you put several check boxes or option buttons in an option group. Instead of setting the field for each check box oroption button, set the Control Source property for the option group and then set the values of each check box or option button. Figure 11-5 shows a report that does this. The option group is the box marked Vehicles. The option group's Control Source property is set to the Vehicles field. Each of the option buttons has a number for its Control Source property. For example, for the Scream Machine, the 3 option button is selected, indicating that the Scream Machine has three vehicles.

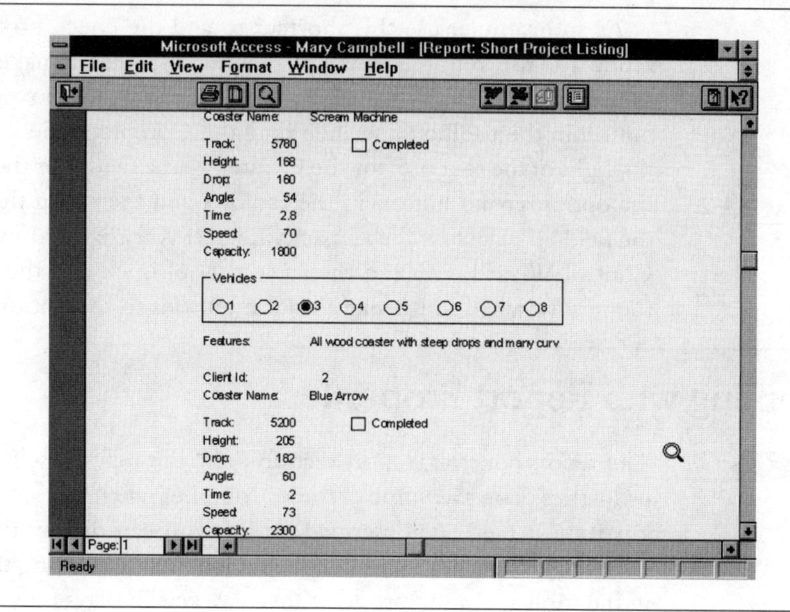


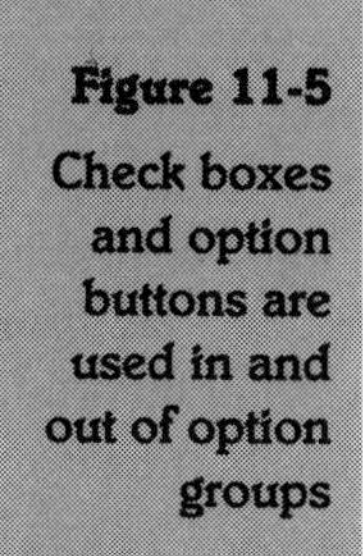
**Figure 11-5** Check boxes and option buttons are used in and out of option groups

When check boxes or option buttons are in an option group, they are numbered sequentially. This means the first check box or option button has the value of 1, the second has a value of 2, and so on for all of the check boxes and option buttons in the option group. You can put both check boxes and option buttons in the same option group, but your report will look more professional if you use only check boxes or only option buttons within an option group. Since so many people are now familiar with Windows, you may want to make sure that your report matches the basic Windows design rules. In Windows dialog boxes, check boxes almost always appear outside option groups, while option buttons almost always appear within them.

## ADDING DIFFERENT CONTROLS WITH THE FIELD LIST

Access has a shortcut for adding fields to a report using different types of controls. Earlier you learned how dragging a field name from the field list to the report design added the field as a text box with the field name as an attached label. You can choose the type of control you add when you drag a field name from the field list by selecting a control from the toolbox and then dragging the field name from the field list. This adds that field as the selected control type. This shortcut sets the Control Source property of the control to the selected field name.

As an example, use this shortcut to add the check box control and option group for the report shown in Figure 11-5. First, make sure that both the toolbox and the field list appear. To add the check box, click the check box button in the toolbox and then drag the Completed field from the field list to the right of the text box for the Coaster Name field. For the option group, click the option group button in the toolbox and then drag the Vehicle field from the field list to below the Capacity field. If you are not using the Option Group Control Wizard, you can then select Tool Lock and the option button from the toolbar and add the eight option buttons to the option group.

## Working with Report Properties

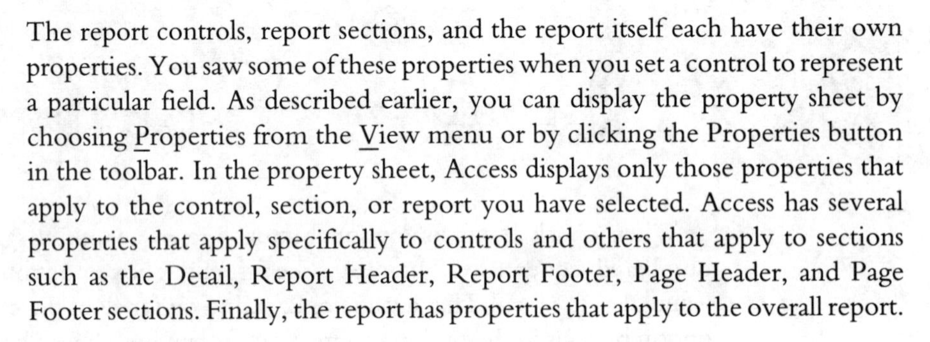

The report controls, report sections, and the report itself each have their own properties. You saw some of these properties when you set a control to represent a particular field. As described earlier, you can display the property sheet by choosing Properties from the View menu or by clicking the Properties button in the toolbar. In the property sheet, Access displays only those properties that apply to the control, section, or report you have selected. Access has several properties that apply specifically to controls and others that apply to sections such as the Detail, Report Header, Report Footer, Page Header, and Page Footer sections. Finally, the report has properties that apply to the overall report.

### Control Properties

Controls have properties that set the appearance of the information that appears in the control. The properties listed in the property sheet include all possible properties a control has. In Access version 2, you can show a subset of the properties for a control by selecting a set from the drop-down list box at the top of the property sheet, or you can select All Properties to show all possible properties for that item. Access version 1 always displays all of the available properties.

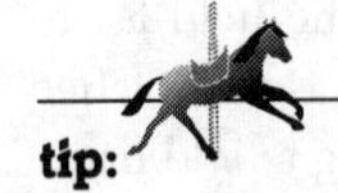

**tip:** *Sometimes you will want to select several controls at once to change a property for all of them. In Access version 2, you can drag the mouse in the vertical or horizontal ruler of the report's Design view, selecting all the controls under or to the side of where you dragged the mouse.*

Most controls have a Name (Control Name in Access version 1) property that Access uses to identify the control among the other controls in the report.

The default is the name of the field the control represents or the name of the type of control followed by a number (for example Text8), depending on how you add the control and whether the report already has the field you selected in the report. Use the default or enter an acceptable object name. You will only be concerned about control names when creating expressions that use other controls, as described in Chapter 12, or when developing macros and programs that modify a control's properties.

Label controls have a Caption property in place of the Control Source property that other controls use. The Caption property sets the text that appears in the label control. You can modify the property using the property sheet or by editing the text in the Report's Design view.

Properties such as Left, Top, Width, and Height set a control's position and size. You will find it easier to use the mouse to adjust a control's position and size rather than changing these property values. Usually, the only reason to make entries for these properties is to make several controls the same size by selecting them all and entering the values for the Height and Width properties.

Two of the properties, Format and Decimal Places, should look familiar from your earlier work designing tables. Format is initially set to whatever the field's Format property is in the underlying table. Decimal Places, which only appears when the data type uses digits after the decimal point, is initially set to Auto.

You can make another selection to change how the values appear in the report. Changing the Format and Decimal Places properties does not change the Format and Decimal Places properties of the table or query. For the Format property, select from all of the choices you have for the formats of different data types (but do select a format that is appropriate for the data displayed in the control).

Emphasize a field by only showing the field's value when the field value changes. For example, in Figure 11-6, the report shows the value of the Completed field only when the value switches between Yes and No. Hiding the duplicate field values is done by selecting the control that would contain those values, Completed in this case, and changing the Hide Duplicates property from Yes to No. When hiding duplicate values, sort the records by the field in which you are hiding the duplicates so that all of the records with the same value for that field are together.

When a text or memo field contains a long entry, you do not have to guess how much vertical space the field needs to display the entire contents. When the Can Grow and Can Shrink properties are set to Yes, the entire entry is wrapped to fit a column within the control's width. This column extends as far down as necessary to include the entire entry. Access also adjusts the height of the Detail section to match the size needed for the long entry. When these two

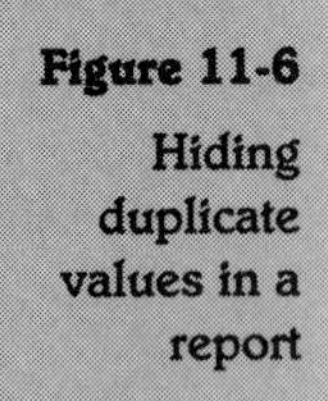
**Figure 11-6** Hiding duplicate values in a report

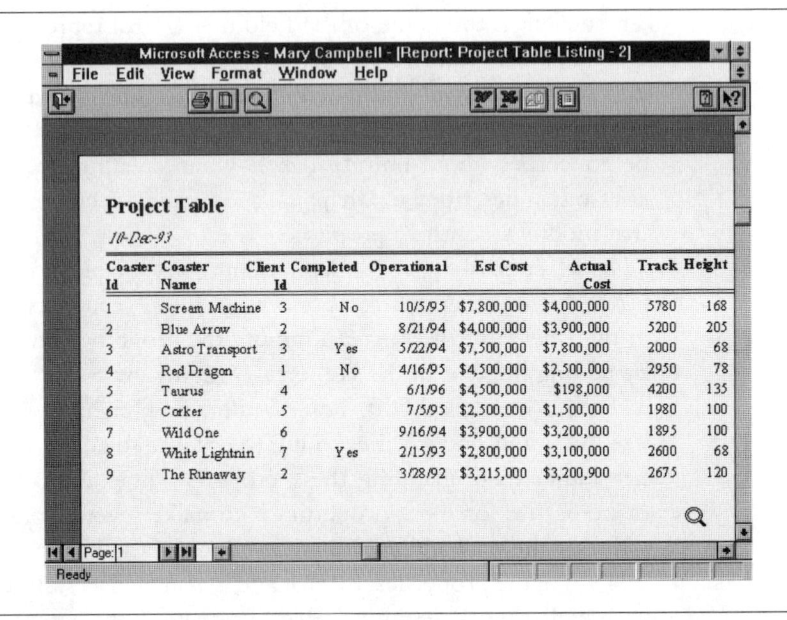


**Project Table**

*10-Dec-93*

| Coaster Id | Coaster Name | Client Id | Completed | Operational | Est Cost | Actual Cost | Track | Height |
|---|---|---|---|---|---|---|---|---|
| 1 | Scream Machine | 3 | No | 10/5/95 | $7,800,000 | $4,000,000 | 5780 | 168 |
| 2 | Blue Arrow | 2 | | 8/21/94 | $4,000,000 | $3,900,000 | 5200 | 205 |
| 3 | Astro Transport | 3 | Yes | 5/22/94 | $7,500,000 | $7,800,000 | 2000 | 68 |
| 4 | Red Dragon | 1 | No | 4/16/95 | $4,500,000 | $2,500,000 | 2950 | 78 |
| 5 | Taurus | 4 | | 6/1/96 | $4,500,000 | $198,000 | 4200 | 135 |
| 6 | Corker | 5 | | 7/5/95 | $2,500,000 | $1,500,000 | 1980 | 100 |
| 7 | Wild One | 6 | | 9/16/94 | $3,900,000 | $3,200,000 | 1895 | 100 |
| 8 | White Lightnin | 7 | Yes | 2/15/93 | $2,800,000 | $3,100,000 | 2600 | 68 |
| 9 | The Runaway | 2 | | 3/28/92 | $3,215,000 | $3,200,900 | 2675 | 120 |

properties are set to No, the field takes up exactly the space set by the control's size. Text that cannot fit in the control's allotted space simply doesn't appear.

You can also set Can Grow to Yes while setting Can Shrink to No when you want the field's size to expand to fit the entry but not to shrink below the space the control uses. Set Can Grow to No while setting Can Shrink to Yes when you want to avoid leaving empty space for short field entries but want to truncate the longer ones. Figure 11-7 shows a report that has the Features field's Can Grow and Can Shrink properties set to Yes. In this report, the control is designed to show two lines. Most of the records use more than two lines, so the Detail section expands to fit the entries. If a record does not have an entry for the Features field or if it has a short one, the field occupies only one line and the Detail section shrinks to only use one line (assuming the Detail section has its Can Shrink property set to Yes). The default for these two properties is Yes for Memo data fields and No for Text data fields.

Some of the properties are designed for advanced uses; for example, Visible is used to create a message that only appears when another value, such as a quota, is met. Many of the control's properties in the bottom half of the property sheet set the control's appearance. Chapter 14 shows how you can change the appearance of controls to create professional-looking reports. You usually do not need to use these properties, because the most frequently used appearance properties are available through dialog boxes and toolbar buttons.

**Figure 11-7** Can Shrink and Can Grow properties adjust the size of fields to match contents

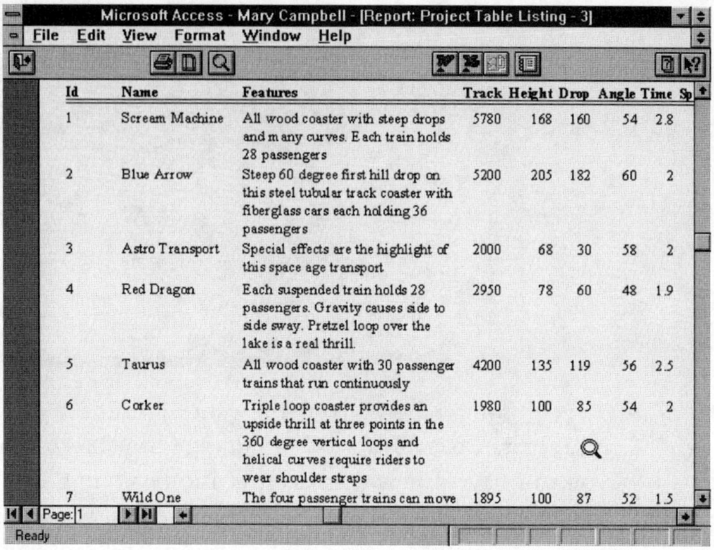

Microsoft Access - Mary Campbell - [Report: Project Table Listing - 3]

| Id | Name | Features | Track | Height | Drop | Angle | Time | Sp |
|---|---|---|---|---|---|---|---|---|
| 1 | Scream Machine | All wood coaster with steep drops and many curves. Each train holds 28 passengers | 5780 | 168 | 160 | 54 | 2.8 | |
| 2 | Blue Arrow | Steep 60 degree first hill drop on this steel tubular track coaster with fiberglass cars each holding 36 passengers | 5200 | 205 | 182 | 60 | 2 | |
| 3 | Astro Transport | Special effects are the highlight of this space age transport | 2000 | 68 | 30 | 58 | 2 | |
| 4 | Red Dragon | Each suspended train holds 28 passengers. Gravity causes side to side sway. Pretzel loop over the lake is a real thrill. | 2950 | 78 | 60 | 48 | 1.9 | |
| 5 | Taurus | All wood coaster with 30 passenger trains that run continuously | 4200 | 135 | 119 | 56 | 2.5 | |
| 6 | Corker | Triple loop coaster provides an upside thrill at three points in the 360 degree vertical loops and helical curves require riders to wear shoulder straps | 1980 | 100 | 85 | 54 | 2 | |
| 7 | Wild One | The four passenger trains can move | 1895 | 100 | 87 | 52 | 1.5 | |

The Help Context Id property determines which help topic from the help file appears when the user presses F1. The number entered for this property is between 0 and 2,147,483,647 for the number of slots for help topics available. Usually, you will only change this number when creating a custom help file using the Microsoft Windows Help Compiler, which is separate from Access. When you use a custom help file, you select the help file for the Help File report property and then enter the help topic numbers for the Help Context Id properties of the different controls. This feature is more frequently used with forms than with reports.

## Section Properties

Sections also have properties. Since sections do not focus on field values, the properties are very different from the ones used for controls. The Detail, Report Header, Report Footer, and the group headers and footers you will learn about later in this chapter all have the same properties. The Page Header and Page Footer sections have a subset of these properties because these two sections do not use the Force New Page, New Row or Col, Keep Together, Can Shrink, and Can Grow properties. You can select any one of these sections by clicking part of the section that does not include a control. The following illustration shows the properties for the Report Header Section:

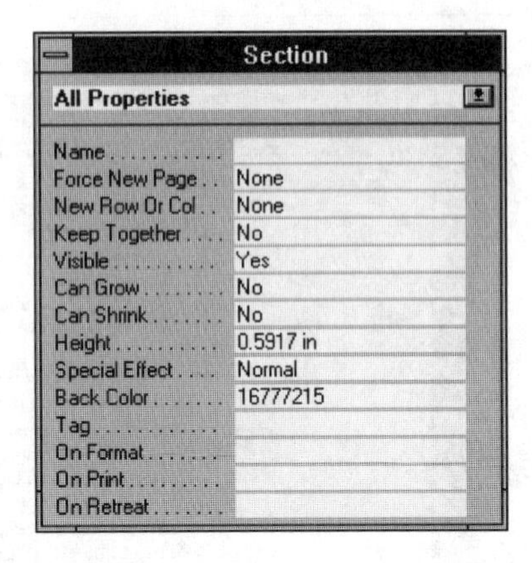


With some reports, you will want to print the information for each record on a separate page. Rather than adding a page break control to the report design, you can have a new page start at the beginning or end of each section. For example, say your Report Header, Report Footer, Page Header, and Page Footer are empty and you want the contents of the Detail section for each record printed on a separate page. To add a page break to a section, change the Force New Page property. The default for the property is None, so the report only starts another page after filling the current one. You can select Before Section so the report starts on a new page every time the current section is printed. You can select After Section so the report starts on a new page after printing the current section. Finally, you can select Before & After when you want a new page started every time you start and end the current section. To put the Detail section for each record on a separate page, you would select Before & After.

Splitting a report between pages can also result in part of a section printing on one page and the rest of the section printing on the next page. You can change the report design so that, if Access cannot fit the entire section on the current page, the section starts on the next page. You may want all of the information about a record printed on the same page so you do not have to flip between pages to look at the record's contents. To force a report to do this, change the section's Keep Together property from No to Yes. When you print the report, Access moves information to the next page whenever the current page lacks sufficient room in which to print the entire section.

Later in this chapter, you will learn how you can create groups that divide the records in a report into collections of records with the same value for a field. The report in Figure 11-8 shows an example of this. Notice from Figure 11-8 that the report uses three columns. You can use three columns by choosing Print Setup from the File menu, selecting More, and typing **3** in the Items

Across box. The records are filled into the report from top to bottom because the Vertical option button in the Print Setup dialog box is selected.

Also, each time the Client Id value changes, the report starts again in the next column even if the report leaves empty space in the current column. The report starts in the next column in this report because the group header section, which starts each group of projects for the different clients, has the Keep Row or Col property set to Before Section. The default is None so that when you have a report divided into columns, each column is filled completely before another column is begun.

You can also set this property to After Section, which has been done to the group footer section of the report in Figure 11-15, shown later in this chapter. The report then prints all records with the same Client Id value before the page break occurs. The other choice, Before & After, starts a new column before and after the section is printed. When the report fills the columns and Item Layout in the Page Setup dialog box is set to Horizontal, starting a new column causes the report shown in Figure 11-8 to put all of the records for the first client in the first row of records, all records for the second client in the second row of records, and so on.

A section also has properties that tell Access to perform a macro or user-defined function whenever certain events occur, such as when the report is formatted or printed. Reports are formatted when Access is setting up the information to appear in the report when you print or preview it. You will learn more about macros in Chapter 16.

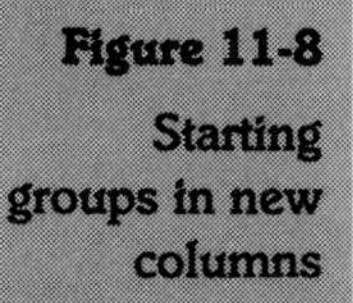

**Figure 11-8** Starting groups in new columns

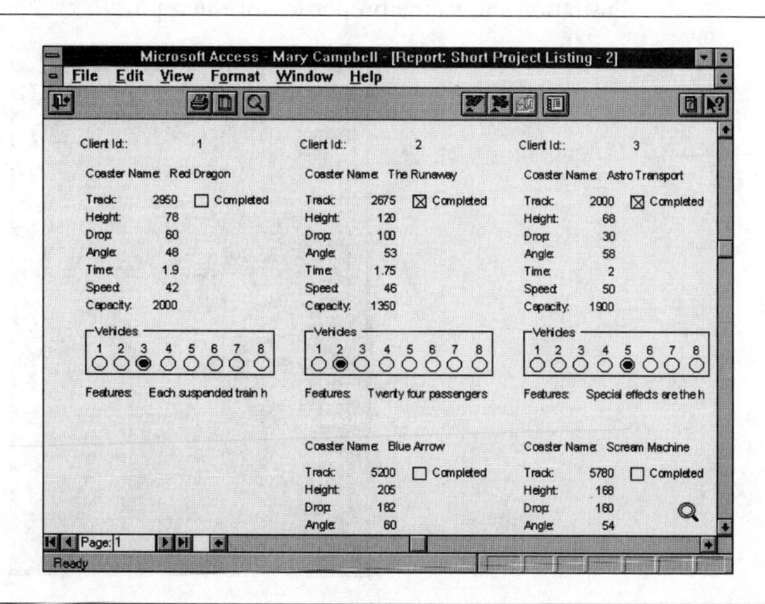

Some of the section properties are identical to the control properties with the same name. The Visible property can set whether a section appears. You can create macros that select when this section appears based on another criteria. The Can Shrink and Can Grow properties perform the same function in a section as they perform when you apply them to individual controls.

The default for a section is No for Can Shrink. For Can Grow, the default is No unless you have set the Can Grow property for a control in the section to Yes, which also sets the section's Can Grow property to Yes. The Height property sets the section's height, just as you can set the section's height by dragging the bottom of the section up or down. You might use this property rather than the mouse when you want to be sure that two sections are the same height or that sections appearing in different reports are the same height. The Special Effect, Back Color, and Font properties are described in Chapter 14, which tells how to change the appearance of a report.

## Report Properties

Reports also have their own properties. These properties include the table or query the report uses, the grid, the report width, and when page headers and footers print. These properties are different from the properties you learned about for controls and sections. Display the properties for a report in the property sheet by choosing Select Report in the Edit menu or by clicking an area in the Report window that is not part of the report design. The following illustration shows the properties for the report:

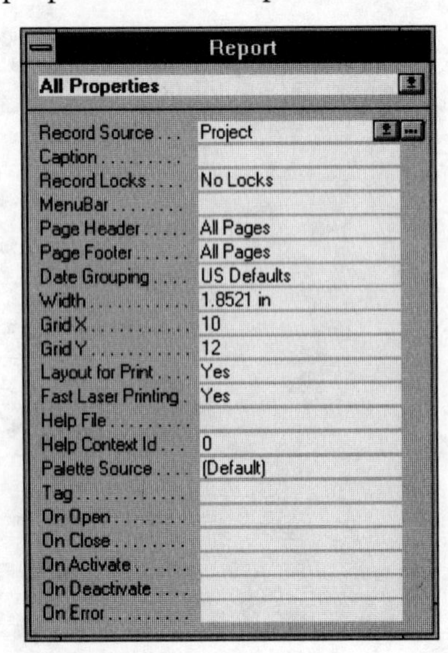

In Chapter 9, you learned how to use the grid for placement. Change the size of the grid by selecting the number of grid points per inch that appear vertically and horizontally on the report design using the Grid X and Grid Y properties. By entering a new number for the Grid X property, you set the number of grid points per inch that fit across the report design. By entering a new number for the Grid Y property, you set the number of grid points per inch that fit up and down the report design. Even when you change the numbers, the grid will not appear until you display it with Grid in the View menu.

The Width property sets the report's width, just as you can set the report width by dragging the right side of the report to the left or right. You might use this property rather than the mouse when you want the report to be a specific width. Changing the width changes the width of all sections in the report.

The fonts used to display the entries in the report depend on the fonts you have installed for Windows. Windows has some fonts that are designed for printing and others meant for displaying information on the screen. Select whether you use the screen or the printer fonts for the report with the Layout for Print property. The default for reports is Yes, so the report uses printer fonts. Select No for this property when you want the report to use screen fonts. When you print the report using screen fonts, Windows substitutes a similar printer font. When you use a TrueType font such as the ones available in Windows 3.1 or through accessory packages such as Facelift or Adobe Typeface Manager, changing this property does not affect the fonts, because TrueType fonts look the same on the screen as they do when printed.

If you share a database with other users on a network, you may want to prevent them from changing the data that appears in your report while you are generating your report. Protect your records by selecting All Records for the Record Locks property. When you generate the report, all of the records included in the report are locked so that other users cannot change their data. The default of No Locks means other users can continue using and editing the data while you generate the report.

Usually you will use the table or query you select when you start to create a report. However, if you change your mind or you have selected the Blank Report button from the New Report dialog box without selecting a table or query, you need to select a table or query to control the fields that are listed in the field list. To set which table or query the report uses, change the Record Source property. Select any of the tables and queries available in the database.

When you change the table or query, the fields listed in the field list change to match the new table or query, but the fields from the old table or query already added to the report design do not change. You may want to change the table or query used in a report when you have copied or imported a report designed to work with one table or query that you want to use with another—for example, to use a report you have created for the Employee table to print names and addresses with a roster you have in a database that keeps track of your bowling league.

The default for page headers and footers is to print on every page, but you may not want to include page headers and footers on pages that already have a report header or footer. To change whether the page header prints on every page, change the Page Header property; to change whether the page footer prints on every page, change the Page Footer property. The default for these properties is All Pages, which prints the page header or page footer on every page. When you select Not with Rpt Hdr, the page header or footer prints on every page except the one with the report header. When you select Not with Rpt Ftr, the page header or footer prints on every page except the one with the report footer. When you select Not with Rpt Hdr/Ftr, the page header or footer prints on every page except those that have a report header and report footer. As an example, you may want to change the Page Header property to Not with Rpt Hdr and the Page Footer property to Not with Rpt Ftr when you do not want to print the page header on the first page or the page footer on the last.

A report also has properties that tell Access to perform a macro or user-defined function whenever an event such as opening or closing the report occurs. You will learn more about macros in Chapter 16.

Finally, a report has Help Context Id and Help File properties to select which help topic appears when the user presses F1 and the help file containing the help topics, as described earlier for control properties. When the Help File property is empty, the report uses the same help file as the one Access uses.

## Sorting and Grouping the Report's Output

You will often want the records in a report to appear in a different order than they appear in the table or query they come from. You can sort the records in a report so that they appear in a different order and decide whether they are to be sorted in ascending or descending order. You can also *group* records, so that records with specific values in a field are separated from records with other values. Unlike filters, which are used to sort records in tables, queries, and forms, you set the sorting and grouping for records in a report from the Design view.

## Sorting Records in a Report

When you sort the records that appear in a report, you can specify up to ten fields to use as the bases of the sorting. You can choose to sort the records in ascending order, which sorts records from A to Z or 1 to 10, or in descending order, which orders records from Z to A or from 10 to 1.

To change the order of the records for the report you are designing, tell Access that you want the records sorted. The first step is to display the Sorting and Grouping box shown here:

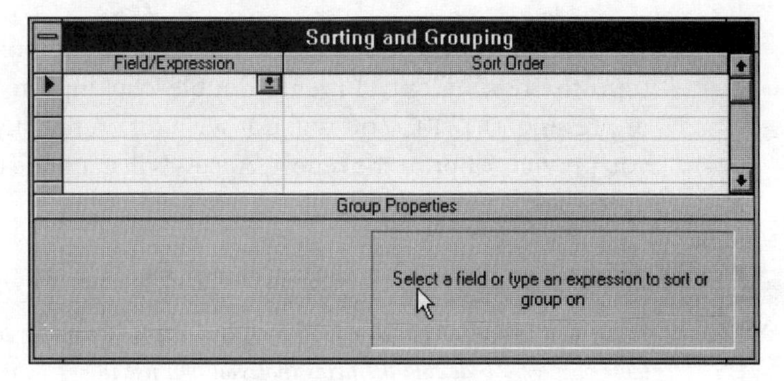


To display this box, either choose Sorting and Grouping in the View menu or click the Sorting and Grouping button shown here:

When the Sorting and Grouping box appears, you can enter the fields and expressions you will use to organize the records in the report. In the Field/Expression column, enter the fields that will organize the records by typing the field name or by clicking the down arrow and selecting the field from the drop-down list. Next, select whether the values of the field are sorted in ascending or descending order by selecting Ascending or Descending in the Sort Order column.

**tip:** *In Chapter 12 you will learn to create expressions whose values are used to sort the records in the report.*

You can use up to ten fields to sort the records by adding the fields to the Sorting and Grouping box. Access uses the fields in the order you enter them to sort the records. First Access sorts the records by the value of the first field in the Sorting and Grouping box, using the sort order you selected. When two or more records have the same entry for the first field, Access uses the second field to sort the records. When two or more records have the same values for the first and second fields, Access sorts those records using the third field, and so on.

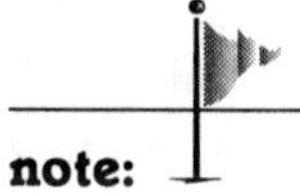

**note:** *You cannot use a Memo or OLE Object field as a field to sort the records in a report.*

After you finish selecting the fields, close the box by either selecting Close from the box's Control menu, double-clicking the box's Control menu box, or pressing ALT+F4. You will not see a difference in the report's design. When you preview or print the report, Access will generate the report using the records in the order you select.

**tip:** *If you will be sorting the records in a report, you may want to index the fields in the underlying table or query. Indexing the fields that you will use to order the records speeds up generating the report.*

## Grouping Report Records

Grouping records in a report is just like sorting records, except that the report has breaks in between each group of records. Grouped records can have header and footer sections that start and end each group of records. You were introduced to groups in records with the Groups/Totals Report Wizard in Chapter 9. Figure 11-9 shows a report that uses groups. The department name appears as the header for each group and the subtotals appear in the footer section for each group. The records are sorted by the Department field and are divided into groups when the value of the Department field changes.

You can think of using layers of grouping as organizing the report records into an outline, similar to the one shown in Figure 11-10. In this outline, the records are divided into groups according to three fields. The first set of headings divides the report's records according to their values for the first field. Within each first-level heading, the report is further divided by second-level headings according to their values for a second field. Within each second-level heading are third-level headings that further divide the records by their values for a third field. It is only after the first-, second-, and third-level headings have been used

**Figure 11-9** Records grouped by the Department field's values

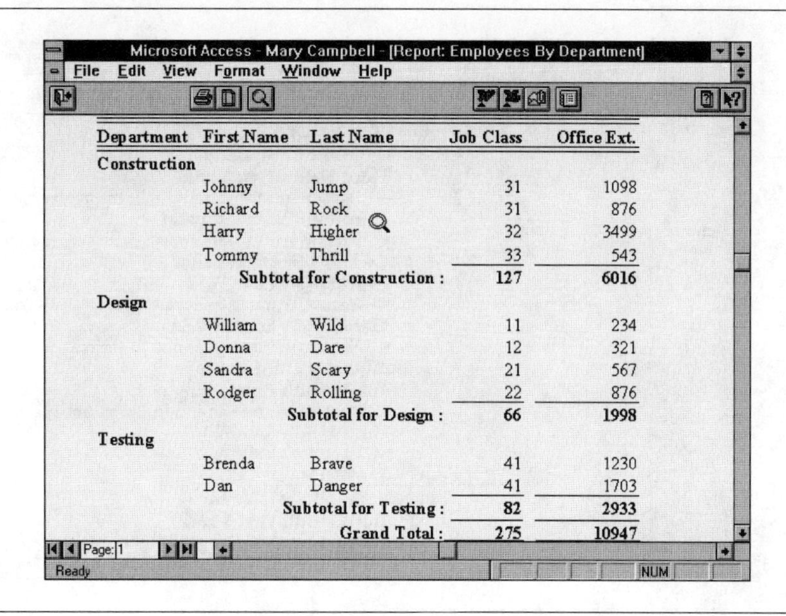


to sort the records that the report contains the records. One difference between the report outline shown in Figure 11-10 and a report in Access is that the report in Access can have a footer section at the end of a group, in addition to the group header. For example, if you have a Number data field in a report, you may want to total it at the end of every group.

Grouping and sorting records for a report are done at the same time. To group records, display the Sorting and Grouping box by clicking the Sorting and Grouping button in the toolbar or by choosing Sorting and Grouping in the View menu. Access uses the fields entered in the Sorting and Grouping box to sort the records before presenting them in the report. Next, Access adds breaks between the groups of records using the fields you choose to use for grouping in the Sorting and Grouping box.

The first step is selecting the fields used to sort the records. Just as you do for sorting, select the fields in the Field/Expression column of the Sorting and Grouping box. Each field you select to sort the records can be used to break the records into groups. To group records instead of just sorting them, change the settings of the group properties in the bottom of the Sorting and Grouping box (explained in the next section). You can include fields in the Sorting and Grouping box that are used to sort the records within the groups, simply by not changing the group properties for those fields.

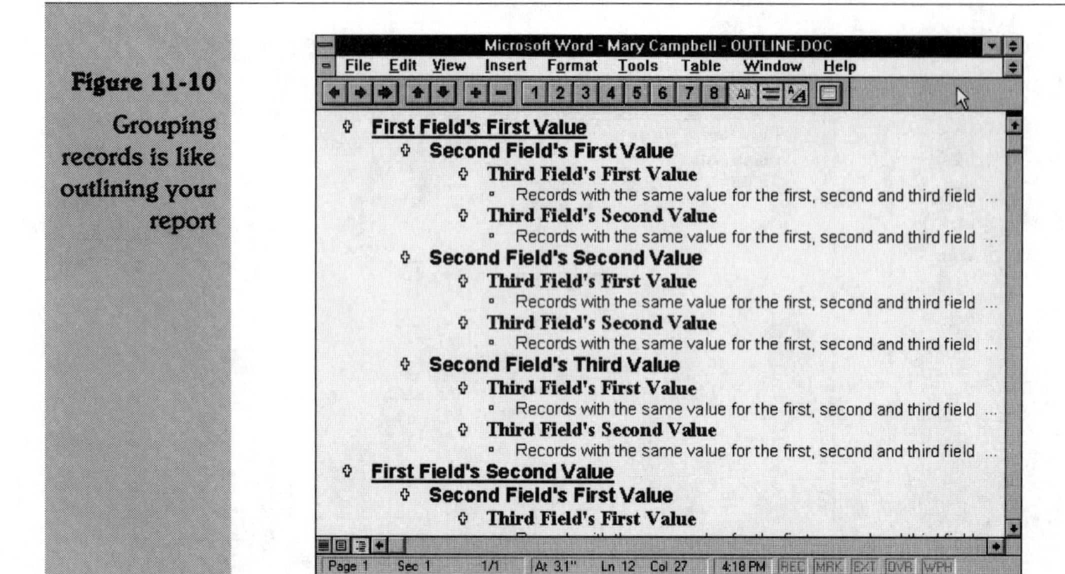


**Figure 11-10** Grouping records is like outlining your report

For example, in the report in Figure 11-11, the records are grouped by the Client Id field. The records are also sorted according to coaster name. Both Client Id and Coaster Name are included in the Sorting and Grouping box.

## Setting Group Properties

When grouping records, you set how the records are divided by changing the group properties. These group properties are listed at the bottom of the Sorting and Grouping box. Each field in the Field/Expression list can have separate group properties.

To group records by a field, set the Group Header or Group Footer property for that field to Yes. If you set Group Header to Yes, Access adds a section to the report before each group. If you set Group Footer to Yes, Access adds a section after each group. You can add both a group header and a group footer section. You can then set how the fields divide the records into groups using the Group On and Group Interval properties. After setting the group properties, close the Sorting and Grouping box by either selecting Close from the box's Control menu, double-clicking the box's Control menu box, or pressing ALT+F4.

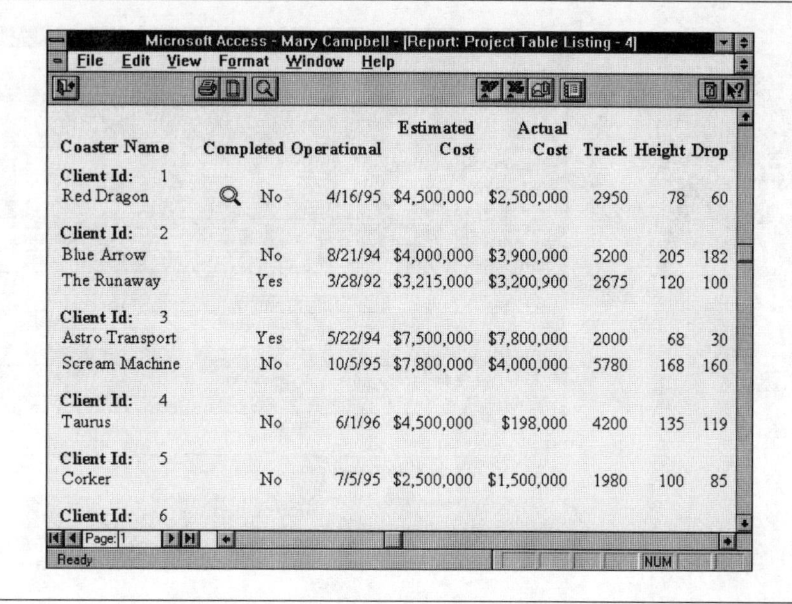


**Figure 11-11** Records grouped by Client Id and then sorted by Coaster Name

## ADDING HEADER AND FOOTER SECTIONS

The feature that makes grouping special is that you can add header and footer sections that mark the beginning and end of each group. Once these sections are part of the report design, you can add controls to them. In a header, you usually introduce the group the report will display. A footer often contains controls that summarize the records that are part of a group.

To add a group header or footer, you select the field from the Field/Expression column and then change the Group Header or Group Footer property to Yes. Once you change either of these properties, you have changed from sorting to grouping. The group header or footer appears each time the value for the selected field changes. The new sections have the name of the field followed by the word "Header" or "Footer" (whichever is appropriate). Figure 11-12 shows a report design in which the Department field has the Group Header and Group Footer group properties changed to Yes. You can see this in the report design, because the report design now includes Department Header and Department Footer sections. Department is the field that divides the records into groups. Figure 11-13 shows how the report appears in Print Preview form.

**Figure 11-12** A report design using group header and footer sections

Microsoft Access - Mary Campbell - [Report: Employee Listing - 3]
File Edit View Format Window Help
Report Header
Employee Listing
=Now()
Page Header
First Name | Last Name | Home Address | Office Ext. | Date of Hire
Department Header
Department: | Department
Detail
First Name | Mi | Last Name | Street Address | Extension | Date of Hire
City | State | Zip Code
Department Footer
End of listing for | Department | Department
Page Footer
Report Footer
Design View

When the group header and group footer sections are added to the report's design, the order in which they appear is controlled by their position in the Sorting and Grouping box. The group header sections appear before the detail section, while the group footer sections appear after the detail section. The first

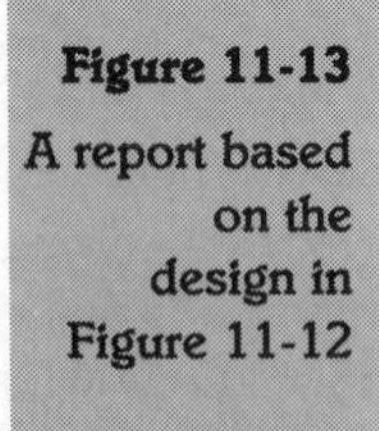

**Figure 11-13** A report based on the design in Figure 11-12

Microsoft Access - Mary Campbell - [Report: Employee Listing - 3]
File Edit View Format Window Help

| First Name | | Last Name | Home Address | | | Office Ext. | Date of Hire |
|---|---|---|---|---|---|---|---|
| **Department:** Construction | | | | | | | |
| HARRY | H | HIGHER | 321 Wood Ave. | | | 3499 | 16-May-90 |
| | | | Mayfield | OH | 44120 | | |
| JOHNNY | J | JUMP | 78 Fordham Drive | | | 1098 | 06-Nov-90 |
| | | | Austinburg | OH | 42124 | | |
| RICHARD | R | ROCK | 45 Eagle Lane | | | 876 | 03-Apr-89 |
| | | | Solon | OH | 44019 | | |
| TOMMY | T | THRILL | 213 25th St. | | | 543 | 07-Jun-88 |
| | | | Cleveland | OH | 44037 | | |
| **End of listing for** Construction | | | **Department** | | | | |
| **Department:** Design | | | | | | | |
| DONNA | D | DARE | 111 Weaver Ave. | | | 321 | 05-Mar-91 |
| | | | Columbus | OH | 43514 | | |
| RODGER | R | ROLLING | 886 Larch Street | | | 876 | 15-Apr-90 |
| | | | Cleveland | OH | 43212 | | |
| SANDRA | S | SCARY | 1232 Hillside Rd. | | | 567 | 01-Feb-92 |
| | | | Gates Mills | OH | 44040 | | |
| WILLIAM | W | WILD | 111 Cedar Ave. | | | 234 | 15-Mar-92 |
| | | | Cleveland | OH | 44123 | | |
| **End of listing for** Design | | | **Department** | | | | |

Page: 1
Ready

group header section is for the first field in the Sorting and Grouping Box with the Group Header property set to Yes, while the second group header section would be for the second field with a Group Header, and so on. However, the first group footer section is for the last field in the Sorting and Grouping box with a group footer, while the second group footer section would be for the second-to-last field with one, and so on. This works out so that the first field in the Sorting and Grouping box would have the first group header and the last group footer section in the report's design, assuming that both of these properties were set to Yes.

## SETTING HOW RECORDS ARE DIVIDED INTO GROUPS

When you created reports with Report Wizards in Chapter 9, you learned that you can divide records into groups according to field values in different ways, depending on the field's data type. For example, text fields can be divided into groups according to their unique entries or by the first few characters in the entries.

The groups you create using the Sorting and Grouping box can have the same types of divisions. Setting how the records are divided into groups is done with the Group On and Group Interval properties.

When you set the Group On property, you are selecting when you want to start a new group. The default setting for this property is Each Value, so every time the value for the field changes, the report starts a new group.

What other choices you have for this property depend on the field's data type. For Text data fields, you can create a new group each time the entry changes or according to the first several characters. To group according to the first several characters in the entry, change the Group On property to Prefix Characters and type the number of characters to compare in the Group Interval property. The default of 1 for the Group Interval property means that you will start a new group every time the first letter of the selected field changes.

For Counter, Currency, Number, and Yes/No fields, you choose between Each Value and Interval. Interval lets you group the records into sets. When you use the Groups/Totals Report Wizard to create a report that creates groups based on one of these field types, you have the choice of Normal and values such as 10s, 50s, and 100s. These numbers are the same types of numbers you can enter for the Group Interval property. For example, if you enter **25** for the Group Interval property, the first group has records with values for the field of 1 to 25, the second group has records with values for the field of 26 to 50, the third group has records with values for the field of 51 to 75, and so on for all of the values the field has.

For Date/Time fields you have these choices: Each Value, Year, Qtr, Month, Week, Day, Hour, and Minute. When you select one of the choices other than Each Value, you can use the Group Interval property to create groups of the selected date or time interval. For example, entering **30** for Group Interval when Group On is set to Minute groups the records by 30-minute intervals for the Date/Time field. As an example, the report in Figure 11-14 groups the projects by year in the Operational field. The Operational field is shortened in the Operational Header section, so only the year shows. Figure 11-15 shows the part of the report for the projects completed in 1994. In the next section, you will learn how to add the formulas that total the estimated costs and actual costs.

## Using Groups in a Report Design

Once you have added group header and group footer sections to your report, you are ready to fill these sections with controls. You add controls to the group header and group footer sections the same way you add them to the other sections.

Usually the header section introduces the group. You might add a text box control labeled with the name of the field the sorting is done by. The text box would display the value of the field for the current group, as shown in the Operational field in Figure 11-14. However, when you add a text box control

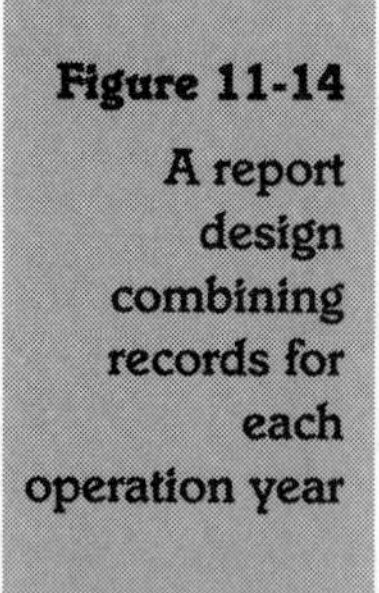

**Figure 11-14** A report design combining records for each operation year

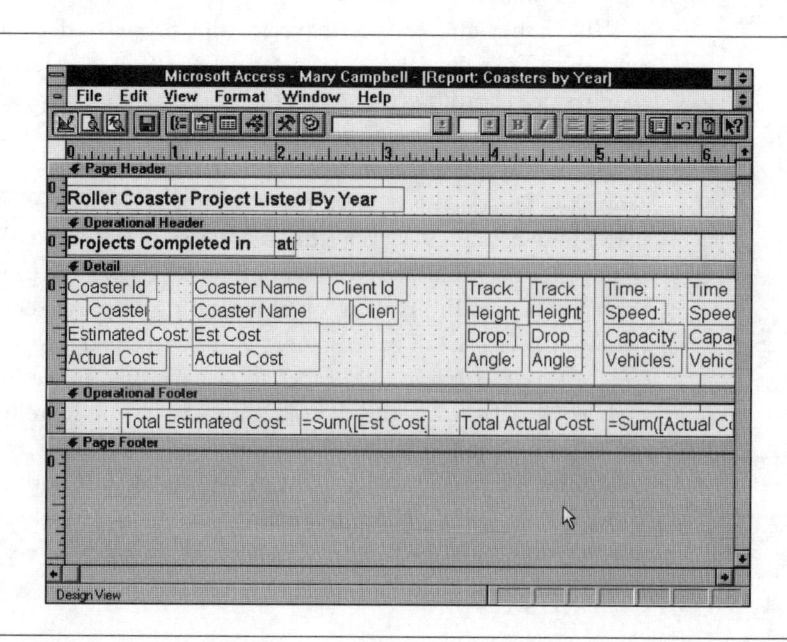

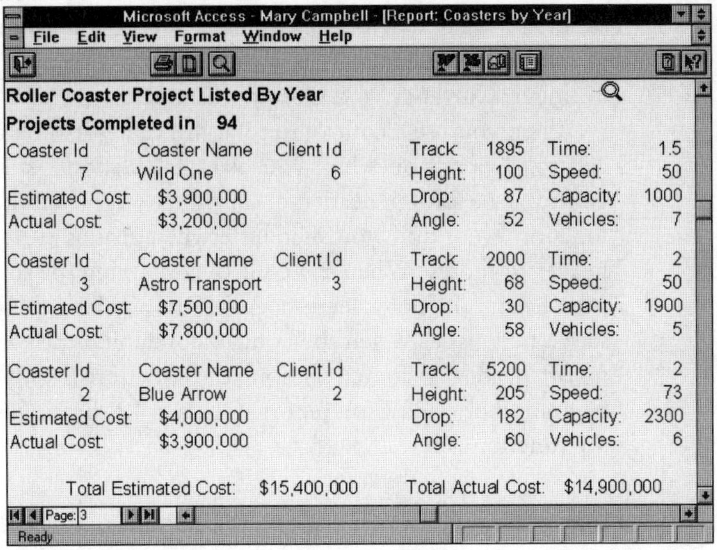

**Figure 11-15** A report based on the design in Figure 11-14

for that field in the group footer section, it displays the value of the last record of that group. The group footer section indicates that the report has listed all of the records for that group. This section often includes summary information.

To add a summary field like the Total Estimated Cost and Total Actual Cost fields in the report in Figure 11-14, you need to add a text box control. To make it a summary field, enter an expression for the Control Source property instead of the field name. *Expressions* are calculations such as totals, averages, or more complicated equations. You will learn more about expressions in Chapter 12.

When you create group footers, you will often use expressions that total a field's values for that group. A *function* is a special type of expression. You will often use functions such as Sum and Count when you include an expression in a group header or footer section. When you enter a function for the Control Source property, you first enter an equal sign and then the name of the function, an open parenthesis, followed by brackets enclosing the field name or other information needed to perform the function and a closing parenthesis. For example, to sum the estimated cost and actual cost fields for the roller coaster projects you have grouped by Client, the expressions are =Sum( [Est Cost] ) and =Sum( [Actual Cost] ). You can type these expressions in the text box or enter them in the Control Source property in the property sheet. To enter them in the Control Source property, you can either type the function or start the Expression Builder by clicking on the Build button at the end of the property.

While creating summary fields may seem new, you created reports that use summary fields when you created a report using the Groups/Totals Report Wizard in Chapter 9. This report type automatically summarizes all of the Number, Currency, and Counter data fields.

When you use a control to total the values in a report, where you place the control depends on when you want calculation restarted. When you put the control in a group header or group footer section, Access recalculates the function every time you switch between groups created by the selected group header or footer. When the control containing the summary function is in the page header or footer section, Access recalculates the function every time you start a new page. When the control containing the summary function is in the report header or footer section, the function is only calculated once, at the beginning or end of the report. Chapter 12 shows you how to change where the function is reset.

## Quick Reference

**To Add a Control to a Report** Display the toolbox by choosing Toolbox from the View menu or by clicking the Toolbox button in the toolbar. Click the tool for the control you want to add and then click the report design where you want the control placed.

**To Set a Control's Properties** Display the property sheet by choosing Properties from the View menu or by clicking the Properties button in the toolbar. Click the control whose properties you want to change in the report design. Click the property you want to change in the property sheet. Type the new entry for the property, or select one of the available choices by clicking the down arrow.

**To Sort Records in a Report** Display the Sorting and Grouping box by choosing Sorting and Grouping from the View menu or by clicking the Sorting and Grouping button in the button bar. Select the field you want to use for sorting in the Field Name/Expression column. Select Ascending or Descending in the Sort Order column. Continue adding fields and sort orders for up to ten fields in the order you want the records sorted. Close the box with ALT+F4 or by choosing Close from the Control menu.

**Quick Reference**

**To Group Records in a Report** Display the Sorting and Grouping Box by choosing Sorting and Grouping from the View menu. Select the field you want to use for grouping in the Field Name/Expression column. Select Ascending or Descending in the Sort Order column. Add group header and footer sections by changing the Group Header and Group Footer properties for the fields from No to Yes. You can also change how the values of the fields are grouped by making changes to the Group On and Group Interval properties. After closing the box, add controls to the group's header and footer sections to supply the contents of these sections. Close the box with ALT+F4 or by choosing Close from the Control menu.

# Chapter 12

Expression Builder

Expression Rules

Using Expressions in Forms and Reports

# Using Expressions in Reports and Forms

**b**ESIDES using field contents and fixed text entries, you can add *expressions* to your forms and reports. An expression is a formula where you tell Access what you want placed at a specific location in your form or report. You have already used expressions. The queries you created used expressions to select which records would match the criteria you set. Also, many of the reports you created with Report Wizards have expressions added to supply the date, page number, and totals of Number, Currency, and Counter data field types. You will often use expressions to provide information not directly supplied in a dynaset. For example, if you want to combine the city, state, and ZIP code for your employees' addresses in a report or form, create an expression that combines the three fields and adds the commas and spaces that you want.

Expressions in a form or report can perform several different functions. An expression can put a calculation's result in a form or report. Expressions can set the default value of a field. Use expressions to check the validity of an entry or total field values for groups of records. You also can use expressions to calculate totals or averages in a report. Access has several predefined functions you can use in a form or report's expression to return information such as the current date or page number.

Think of expressions in reports and forms as computations you might perform with a calculator. The calculations Access expressions perform are more extensive than simple addition and multiplication of two numbers. Access expressions include *field names* and *functions*. Field names are references to the data from a record, and functions are predefined calculations.

Rather than remembering every possible feature you can use in an expression, Access version 2 puts these features at your fingertips with the *Expression Builder*. This Expression Builder is like a set of building blocks from which you can construct the expression you want. You can add operators, field names, and functions to an expression by clicking the buttons in the Expression Builder.

# Expression Builder

The easiest way to add an expression to a form or report is by using the Expression Builder because you can select the elements you need rather than typing all of the entries yourself. When you need a field name, you avoid the possibility of misspellings by selecting the name instead of typing it. When you add a function with the Expression Builder, you will add prompts for the arguments the function uses. The Expression Builder is available in Access version 2 whenever it is appropriate to add an expression. In Access version 1, you must type the expression yourself.

## Activating the Expression Builder

You can display the Expression Builder by clicking the Build button at the end of the property where you want to add the expression. The Build button displays ellipses as shown here:

After clicking this button, or selecting Build from the shortcut menu, the Expression Builder window shown in Figure 12-1 is displayed. Sometimes when you click the Build button, you may need to select Expression Builder if you have a choice between this builder and other ones. The top part of the window shows the expression that you are building. You can transfer the expression you see here to the location where you were working (such as the Control Source property) by selecting OK. You can add to the expression by typing what you want or selecting it from another part of the window. To add something in the list boxes you can either double-click the entry you want or highlight it and select Paste. To add something on a button, you only have to click the button once.

## Using the Expression Builder to Add a Function

Although you can enter any formula you want with the Expression Builder, you will save the most time when a function can meet your computational needs. Functions come in two varieties: *built-in functions* that are part of Access and *database functions* that you can create as part of the database. Every Access user will have the same set of built-in functions, but database functions are

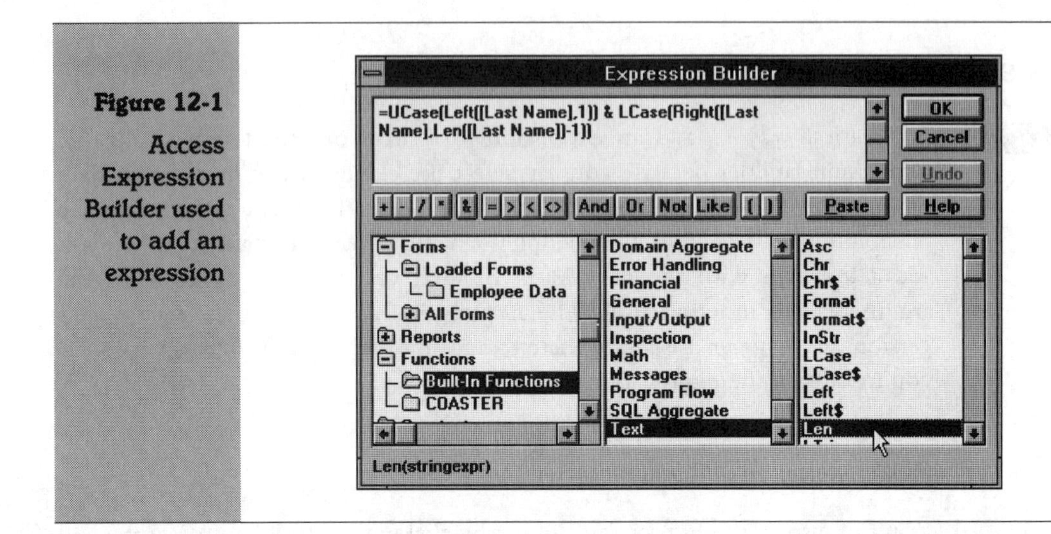


**Figure 12-1** Access Expression Builder used to add an expression

created in a module using the Access Basic language. Database functions are stored in a database you create them in.

You can put the built-in functions to work immediately for tasks such as financial computations or string manipulation. For example, if you want to select the middle section of a string, Access provides the MID function that can perform the task for you. When you double-click the Functions file folder icon in the first column of the lower half of the Expression Builder's window, you will see two more options: Built-In Functions and another entry with the name of the database. The option displaying the database name only offers functions if you have already created them. If you click Built-In Functions, the second column shows the different categories of functions that Access provides. Clicking one of the categories changes which group of functions appear in the third column. If you select Text, the MID function will appear in the third column as one of your options. You can click a function to see a description or double-click it to add it to the expression. If you double-click MID or highlight it and select Paste, the top of the Expression Builder will look like this:

The <<string>>, <<start>>, and <<length>> are placeholders for the information that the function needs. These placeholders are called *arguments*. You can click one of these and type the replacement entry, or you can make another selection such as a field name to replace one of these.

### Adding Fields with the Expression Builder

The Expression Builder can also save you some time when you need to add fields such as when you need to add a field to a property. The Expression Builder can automatically add extra information when you select a field name. For example, if you type a field name from a form for a property, you need to include the form name, the field name, and the control name. Selecting the field name from the bottom of the Expression Builder adds all three pieces of information at once. The Expression Builder handles adding the appropriate characters for the form name, field name, and control name. When you are adding a field to an expression and you want it to refer to the current record, select it from a form or report rather than from the table or query that the data comes from. Usually the top item in the first column is the query, form, or report you are working with. You can click the desired entry in the first list box to have the second and third columns change to show items from the table, query, form, report, or the available functions. For example, while creating a form or report you can click <Record Source> in the second column, and then double-click the field you want from the third column to add the field to the expression. You can also select a control from the second column for a field or for any control you want to change, then select the property from the third column.

**note:** *You can also select the field name from column two and select <Value> from column 3 in order to change what the field shows.*

## Expression Rules

Expressions have several rules. These rules let Access know what types of data and information you are using. Expressions in forms and reports usually start with an equal sign followed by a description of what you want the expression to equal. When you build an expression with the Expression Builder, the Expression Builder will add the equal sign if it is appropriate. The types of entries that follow the equal sign include field and control names, operators such as < and +, and function names.

## Using Controls and Field Names in Expressions

Expressions often include control or field names to work with controls in a form or report. For example, you might have expressions in a report that total actual and estimated costs of roller coasters. These expressions include field names and other controls you add to a form or report.

In an expression, Access needs to know where an object, field, or control name starts and ends. Since you can have up to 64 characters in a name, you enclose the name in special characters to let Access know when you have finished entering a name. Field and control names are enclosed in brackets as in [Last Name]. Form and report names also use brackets as in [Clients and Their Coasters]. You will want to include a form name as part of an expression when you are using subforms in Chapter 13.

To separate a field name from a report name, use an exclamation point (!) as in [Employee Data]![Last Name]. If you are providing the form name for an expression, you may need to tell Access that the name is for a form as in Forms![Employee Data]![Last Name]. If you need to include a property name after the control name, separate the control name and property name with a period as in [Last Name].Format. Property names in expressions do not include spaces, so the Control Source property appears as ControlSource.Expressions use properties to change a control in a form or report. For example, you can create an expression for a form or report to make a control disappear or appear depending on the value of another control.

## Data Types in Expressions

Like fields, expressions have data types. Some of these data types are just like field data types. These include Integer, Long, Short, Double, and Currency. Access has three other types: *String, Variant,* and *User-defined.* String contains characters just like the characters you store in Text and Memo data type fields. Variant stores any type of data. For example, a Variant variable can store the text "Name," the number 5, and the date 6/12/94 at different points. User-defined types are used in macros and modules.

Usually you do not need to worry about data types since most of the expressions you create are the Variant type; Access adjusts the data type to the results returned by the expression. For example, if you want to combine the text "Phone Number" with a phone number stored as a number, using a Variant data type in Access means you do not have to convert the text and number to the same data type.

Expressions also contain *literals,* which indicate text, numbers, or dates to be used exactly as you enter them. Text literals must be enclosed in quotes as in "This is text". Dates must be enclosed with number signs as in #06/03/93# but you can enter the date in any of the acceptable date formats between the number signs. Numbers do not need any special characters. Access assumes the remaining characters in an expression are function names and other expression operators.

## Expression Operators

Expressions can have *operators*. The operators are like the buttons on a calculator that tell the calculator the function you want to perform with the numbers you have entered or will enter. Access has six categories of operators: arithmetic, comparison, concatenation, logical, pattern matching, and miscellaneous. Some of these are added using the buttons in the middle of the Expression Builder window, while others are added by selecting Operators in the first list box in the bottom half of the Expression Builder window.

Unlike other database programs where additional spaces cause formulas using the same types of operators to be incorrect, you can include spaces before and after the expression operators. Access will even add them for you after you enter the expression so the expression is easier to understand.

Several of the operators return true or false results. This means Access looks at the expression and decides whether it's true or false. True expressions have the numeric value of –1 and false expressions have the numeric value of 0. As an example, Access looks at an expression such as =3>5 and decides it is false. When an expression that is evaluated contains field names, Access substitutes the field's value in the current record into the expression.

### ARITHMETIC OPERATORS

The easiest expressions to understand are the ones that use the basic arithmetic operators. These operators include many of the mathematical functions you find on even the smallest calculators such as addition (+), subtraction (–), multiplication (*), division (/ and \), exponentiation (^), and modulo (mod). These are the same operators that you learned about in Chapter 6 for queries.

Figure 12-2 shows an example of the results of an arithmetic operator used for calculating the differences in the form. In this form, the formula for the entry after Amount Still Due is =[Total Invoices]– [Total Payments].

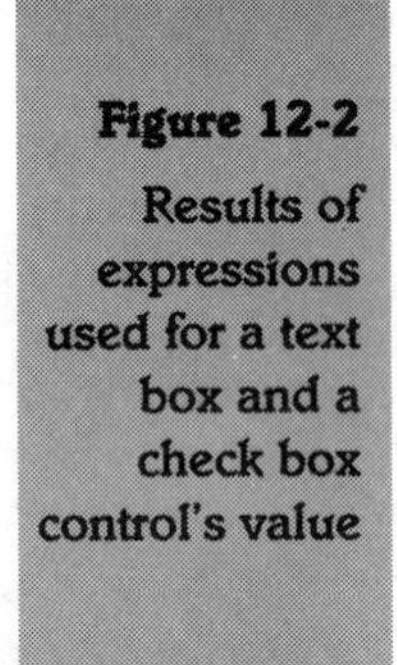

**Figure 12-2** Results of expressions used for a text box and a check box control's value

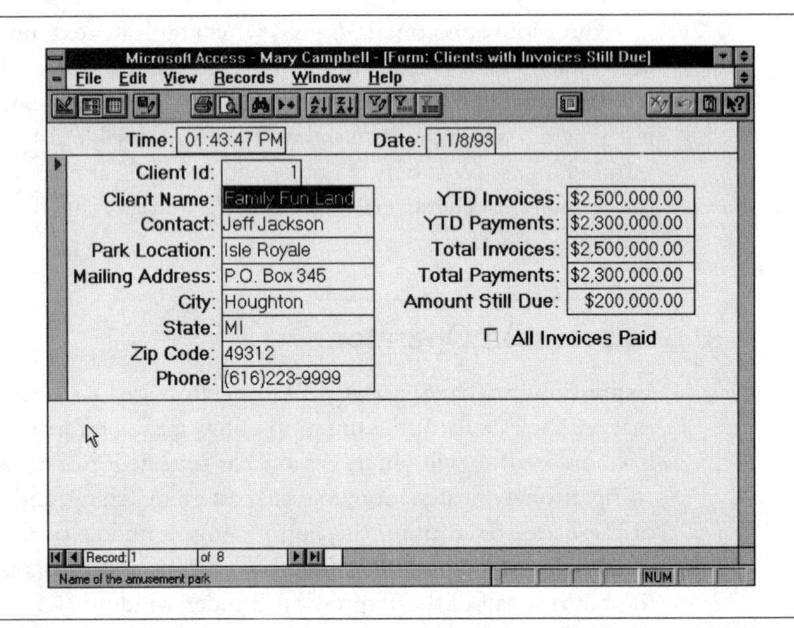



## COMPARISON OPERATORS

Comparison operators are also easy to use. The comparison operators include < (less than), <= (less than or equal to), > (greater than), >= (greater than or equal to), = (equal), and <> (does not equal). You use these operators when you want to use one of two values. For example, if you want to show whether all invoices are paid, you use the expression =[Total Payments] = [Total Invoices]. This expression is true when total payments equal total invoices and false otherwise. This expression is the expression used by the check box in Figure 12-2.

**tip:** *The Between . . . And operator is considered a comparison operator in Access version 2. Since it is considered a miscellaneous operator in Access version 1, however, it is covered under "Miscellaneous Operators" later in this chapter.*

In Figure 12-2, for the first record where the Amount Still Due control has the value of 200,000, the All Invoices Paid check box is cleared. For a record where all of the invoices are paid, this check box is selected. When the expression containing the comparison operator is true, the check box, toggle button, or option button is selected. When the expression containing the comparison operator is false, the check box, toggle button, or option button is false. If you used this comparison operator expression in a text box, the text box will display –1 or 0 to indicate true or false.

The other purpose of comparison operators is to use the value of true or false for subsequent calculations. For example, if you want to add a late fee to overdue invoices, you create an expression that compares the current date to the invoice date. If the invoice date is 60 days ago, you add a late fee. You can add a late fee by multiplying the –1 or 0 the comparison operator returns by the amount of the late fee. The late fee is a negative number so when you multiply it by –1, the late fee becomes a positive number. This expression looks like this:

```
=([Invoice Date]+60<Date ( ))*-.01*[Invoice Amount]
```

This expression tests if the invoice date plus 60 days occurred before today's date. When the invoice is still current, the rest of the expression equals zero since the 0 from the comparison operator part of the expression is multiplied by the other values. When the invoice is overdue, the comparison part of the expression equals –1, which is multiplied by –1 percent of the invoice amount. The parentheses tells Access to perform the comparison before multiplying the values. Later in this chapter in "Using Functions to Return More than One Value" you will learn about the IIF function that you can use to return one of two results depending on a logical expression such as the comparison shown above. For the expression above, calculating the same result using the IIF function has the expression =IIF([Invoice Date]+60<Date(), [Invoice Amount]*.01,0). The advantage of using the IIF function instead is that you do not need to know the numeric results of true or false.

Sometimes you will run into situations using comparison operators where the data type of what you are comparing matters. Access decides how it will compare the data by looking at the data types of the data you are comparing. When the data types are both Number and Currency types, Access determines which number is larger or smaller than the other. When you compare text, Access compares the text left to right, one character at a time. When you use comparison operators, you will want to use them with data that it makes sense to compare.

## THE CONCATENATION OPERATOR

Access has only one concatenation operator, the ampersand (&). In the Expression Builder, you add this operator using a button above the list boxes. The ampersand joins two entries as if they are one. For example, when you add an address to a report, you do not want a big gap between the city and the state. Instead of leaving the space between the city and the state, put the state right next to the city by using an expression that uses the concatenation operator.

You have already seen this operator in use when you use the Mailing Label Report Wizard report type. When you add fields and text to a line in a mailing label, the Mailing Label Report Wizard builds expressions that combine the text and fields you select. For example, in Chapter 9, the example of the Mailing Label Report Wizard using the Client table creates the line containing the city, state, and ZIP code with the expression of =[City] & ", " & [State] & " " & [Zip Code]. To use the concatenation operator, put the ampersand between the two entries you want to combine. Usually, you do not have to worry about the type of data you are combining; you can combine Text data types with Number data types without converting the data as you do with other products.

Figure 12-3 shows a report design that uses this operator to produce the report shown in Figure 12-4. The expressions combine text with some of the values in the Project table so the report presents them as complete sentences. Rather than having gaps between the text and the field values, the text boxes contain expressions that combine them into a stream of characters with no extra spaces. These are some of the formulas used in the report:

```
="The track is " & [Track] & " feet long."
="The height is " & Height & " feet high."
="The greatest drop is " & [Drop] & " feet."
="The greatest angle of descent is " & [Angle] & " degrees."
="Ride time is " & [Time] & " minutes."
="Greatest speed is " & [Speed] & " miles per hour."
```

## LOGICAL OPERATORS

Another type of comparison you will want to make is comparing two true and false values you have from other calculations. For example, you can have comparisons that check both whether an invoice is overdue and, if so, whether the amount is over 100,000. With this example, you may want a true response

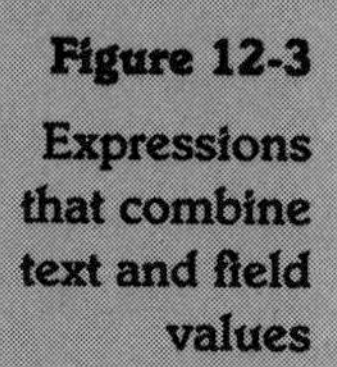

**Figure 12-3** Expressions that combine text and field values

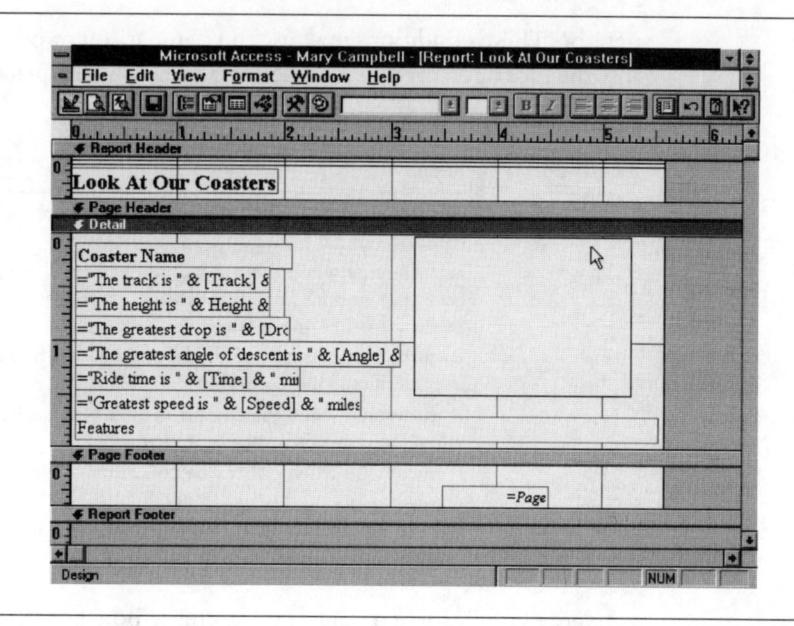


when both conditions are true or a false response when either or both of the conditions are false.

To make this type of evaluation, you use logical operators. Most of the logical operators compare two true or false conditions placed on either side of the

**Figure 12-4** The report created from the design shown in Figure 12-3

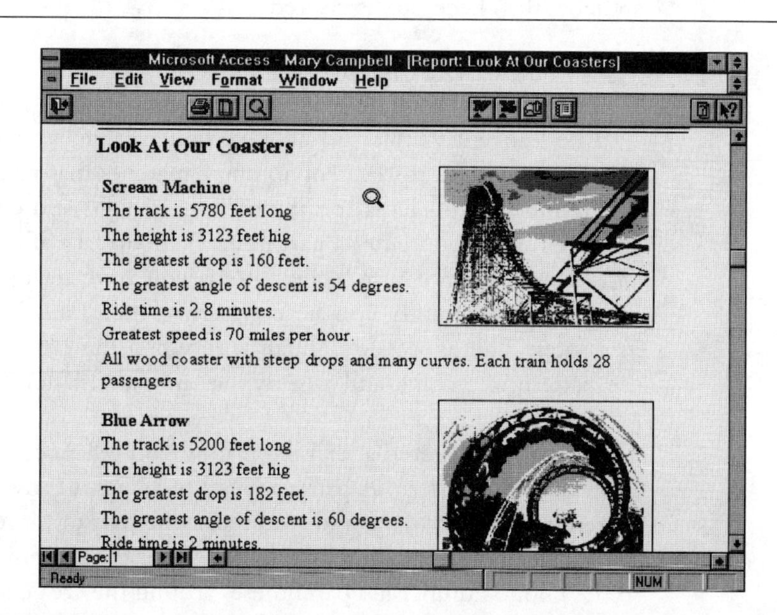

operator. These conditions may use the comparison or other types of operators. Only the Not operator uses a single condition, which is placed after the operator. Here are the logical operators and their results:

| Operator | Result |
|---|---|
| And | Returns true only when the conditions before and after the And are true and returns a false on all other occasions |
| Eqv | Returns true when the conditions before and after the Eqv are either both true or both false, and returns a false when either condition is true while the other one is false |
| Imp | Returns a true or false value depending on whether the first condition implies the second condition |
| Not | Returns true when the condition after Not is false and returns false when the condition after Not is true |
| Or | Returns true when either one condition or both conditions are true |
| Xor | Returns true when either of the conditions before and after Xor is true and returns false when the conditions before and after Xor are both true or both false |

As an example, when you want a check box in a form or report for the Invoice Register table to be selected when both the invoice is over 60 days old and the invoice amount is over $100,000, you can enter the expression =([Invoice Date]+60<Date( )) And [Invoice Amount]>100000.

Only when the results from both comparisons are true will the entire expression be true and the check box selected. When either or both conditions are false, the check box is cleared.

## PATTERN MATCHING OPERATOR

When an entry must match a certain pattern, you use the Like pattern matching operator to test that an entry matches that pattern. For example, a part number may have a specific pattern of digits and characters. A form can easily tell when you enter a part number incorrectly if the pattern of numbers and letters does not match the pattern you have set up. To use this pattern operator, use the entry you are comparing, then Like followed by the pattern in quotes. The expression equals true when the entry before Like matches the pattern after Like and false when the pattern does not match the entry preceding Like.

The pattern entered after Like is how you tell Access which characters are allowed in the pattern. A pattern uses ? to represent any single character, # to represent any digit (0–9), and * to represent zero or more characters. You can also include characters directly as in (###) for the beginning of a phone number so the phone number has parentheses around the area code. Another option is to include a group or range of characters by including the characters or range of characters in brackets ([ ]). An example of several characters is [abc] and an example of a range of characters is [A-Z].

**note:** *Access distinguishes between uppercase and lowercase characters in the brackets so [abc] is not the same as [ABC].*

One requirement of a range is that the characters be in ascending order so you can use [A-Z] but not [Z-A]. You can also use the brackets to exclude characters by putting an exclamation point after the opening bracket as in [!A-Z] to not match an uppercase letter. You do not want to use [ ] with only a space in between the brackets since Access only ignores that combination. You can include a space when other characters are in the brackets as in [abc ].

An example of this operator is used in Figure 12-5. In this form, the phone number is entered with the area code in parentheses and a hyphen after the exchange (three digits after the area code). The expression [Home Phone] Like "(###)###-####" tests whether the home phone number is entered correctly. The form uses this expression by using Like "(###)###-####" as the control's Validation Rule property. The Validation Rule property does not need [Home Phone] since it is implicitly provided.

## MISCELLANEOUS OPERATORS

Finally, Access has some miscellaneous operators that provide many different features. These features test if one entry is in a range, whether an entry is a member of a set of entries, or whether an entry is empty. These operators make working with an expression easier since they often combine the features of comparison operators and logical operators.

When you need to test whether an entry falls inside or outside of a range, you can combine the logical and comparison operators or you can use the Between . . . And operator. In Access version 2, the same operator is called the Between operator and is considered a comparison operator. This operator tests whether the value before Between is within the range set by the entries before and after the And. When the tested entry is in the range, this operator returns a true value. When the tested entry is outside of the range, this operator returns a false value. You can always flip the result of this operator by putting the Not logical operator before the entry so a true value becomes false and vice versa.

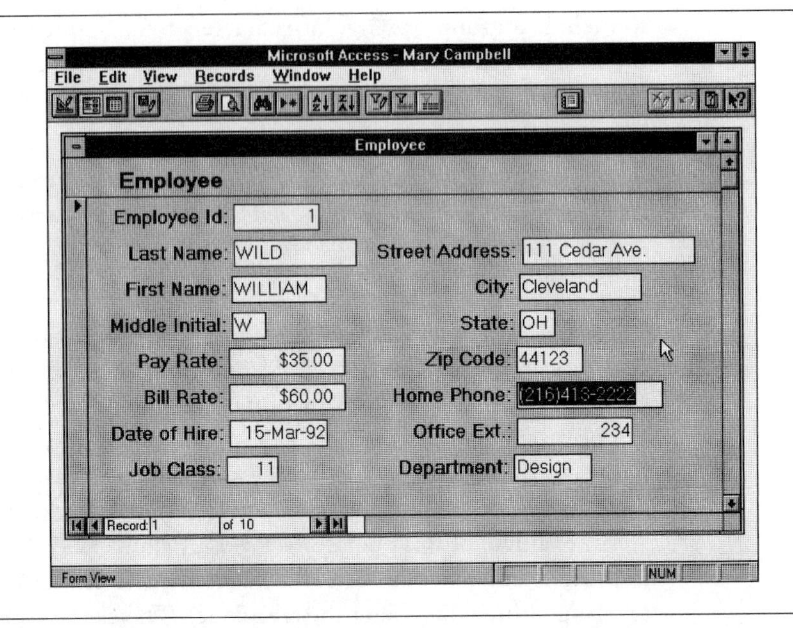


**Figure 12-5** A form using the Like operator to check for a pattern

As an example, you can have an expression =[Height] Between 2000 And 3000 in place of the expression =[Height] > 2000 And [Height] < 3000.

If you need to test whether an entry is part of a group, use the In operator. For example, if you have a Health field in your Employee table to indicate which of four health insurance plans each employee participates in, this field might contain the letters A, B, C, and D. One method of testing that an entry is made correctly is to create an expression such as = [Health] = "A" Or [Health] = "B" Or [Health] = "C" Or [Health] = "D" that checks whether Health is one of these four letters. A better alternative is to use the In operator in an expression like this: = [Health] In ("A", "B", "C", "D"). This expression equals true when Health equals one of the four letters and false when it equals something else.

Access has one last miscellaneous operator. The Is operator combines with Null to test if an entry is empty. For example, if you are entering amounts paid on invoices for the Client table, you do not want to add payments until you add invoices. Use an expression for total payments that tests whether Total Invoices has an entry. The expression = [Total Invoices] Is Null returns a true value when Total Invoices does not contain an entry and a false value when Total Invoices has an entry. This operator is often combined with the IIf function (which you'll learn about later in this chapter) to return another value depending on whether the expression you are testing contains an entry. Access also has the IsNull function, which can test if an entry is empty. While you get the same results, the expression is constructed differently. For example, the expression = [Total Invoices] Is Null can be entered = **IsNull [Total Invoices]**.

### OPERATOR PRECEDENCE

When you have several operators in an expression, Access makes decisions for the order it uses to evaluate them. The decisions are based on operator precedence. The operator precedence for expressions is the same as operator precedence for queries as you learned about in Chapter 6. In the "Comparison Operators" section earlier in this chapter, you saw comparison and arithmetic operators combined in the second example of comparison operators. In that example, the expression included parentheses to tell Access to make the comparison before multiplying the numbers. If you did not include the parentheses, Access would multiply the numbers and then use the resulting values for the comparison. Access does this because in Access's precedence order, multiplication is evaluated before comparison operators. By including parentheses, the comparison is performed first.

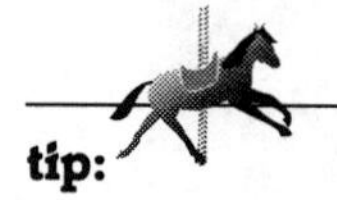

**tip:** *Where you place the expression determines where the field values the expression uses are reset. For example, when you put the expression in the Detail section, the expressions are updated for every record. When you put an expression in a header for a group in a report, the expression is recalculated when you start a new group. You can change when an expression is reset by changing the expression's Running Sum property as described later in the chapter.*

## Functions

Functions are included in expressions to provide ready-made formulas and return information that is not readily available. Functions are used for queries, forms, reports, macros, and modules. Some of the functions are not often used with forms and reports. This section focuses on some of the functions most frequently used in forms and reports.

Functions have the format of the function name followed by its *arguments* surrounded in parentheses. The function's argument(s) is the information you must supply for the function. The arguments a function uses depends on the function since each function may need different information. Function arguments are often field names, or literals such as a number, date, or a string.

**tip:** *If you have used spreadsheet applications such as Excel, Lotus 1-2-3, or Quattro Pro, you may already know about many of the functions available through Access. Functions such as Left, Right, and Npv perform the same function in both Access and these spreadsheet products although the format for entering them differs.*

## USING FUNCTIONS TO RETURN PART OF A STRING

Access has several functions that return part of a text entry. If you want to create mailing labels to your employees that use the first letters of their first and middle names, you can use a function to return only one character out of the first name. You can also use other functions to return the last few characters or a section of characters from the middle of a string or text field. The Left function returns a selected number of characters starting from the left side of the text and the Right function returns a selected number of characters starting from the right side of the text. The Mid function returns a selected number of characters starting from a position in the text that you select.

An example of using one of these functions is if you want to combine the first letter of the first and middle name with the last name for mailing labels. For this purpose, the expression that creates the name looks like this:

```
Left([First Name],1) & "."& [Middle Initial] & ". " & [Last Name]
```

The Left function returns the first character from the First Name field because the function has a 1 as the second argument. The ampersands join the field names and the strings containing the periods and spaces. When you use this expression in a form or report for the Employee table, the results for the first two records are W. W. WILD and D. D. DANGER.

Two other functions you may want to use with text and strings are the LCase and UCase functions, which convert text to lowercase and uppercase, respectively. For example, the Format property for the Last Name, First Name, and Middle Initial fields in the Employee table is >, which displays the entries entirely in uppercase. If you want to display these names, such as in a report in proper case where the first letter is uppercase and the rest is lowercase, use the LCase, UCase, and Len functions to do so. The Len function returns the number of characters in a string. This is the expression you will use for the Last Name field:

```
=UCase(Left([Last Name],1)) & LCase(Right([Last Name],
Len([Last Name])-1))
```

This expression uses the Left function to return the first character of the field and convert it to uppercase. This uppercase letter is combined with the lowercase letters created by the second half of the expression. In the second half, the LCase function converts the letters into lowercase. But before that happens, the Right function returns the remaining number of characters. To decide how many characters the Right function uses, the second argument is the Len function to return the number of characters in the field less one for the letter the UCase function turns into uppercase. This example is only for the Last Name field but it can be repeated for any field you want presented in proper case as it has been for the Last Name and First Name fields in the report in Figure 12-6. The only problem this function has is with a name like McMillan that has two uppercase letters.

A special feature of this example is how you can put one function inside another. The functions are evaluated from the one furthest inside the expression outward. Putting one function inside another is called *nesting*. When you nest functions, each function must be entirely inside the other. This means that the Right function is entirely contained within the LCase function.

## USING FUNCTIONS TO RETURN PART OF A DATE

Access has many functions that work with dates. You have already seen the Date function in Chapter 9 since this is the function that Report Wizards adds

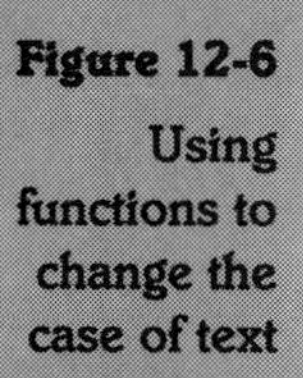

**Figure 12-6** Using functions to change the case of text

to several report types in the Report Header section to add the current date. Access has other date functions that work with dates. The Day function returns the day part of a date, the Month function returns the month part of a date, and the Year function returns the year part of the date. These three functions require a date entered in the parentheses.

In Chapter 11, you saw an example of a report that grouped records by date. By changing the group interval, Access grouped the records by looking at the date and ignoring the day and month portion. However, when you put the date in Operational in the Operational Header section, the only reason that the report omitted the day and month was because the text box was shortened so only the year appeared.

You can use the Year function so the text box can be as large as you want without the day and month appearing. The Year function requires that the date be entered in the parentheses. Figure 12-7 shows the same report after modifying the design. In this report, the text box after Projects Completed In contains the expression =Year([Operational]). When the report is generated, the text box shows only the year.

The date and time in the upper-right corner of the report in Figure 12-7 is created by the Now function in a text box in the Page Header section. When you generate the report using the Now function, you always know the date and time it was created. The Now function does not use any arguments so the parentheses are optional.

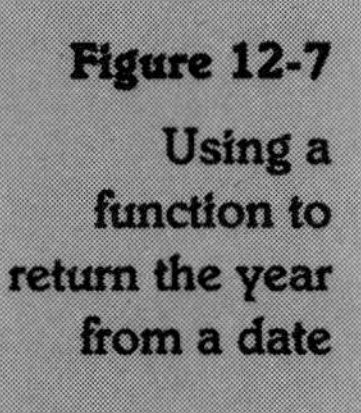

**Figure 12-7** Using a function to return the year from a date

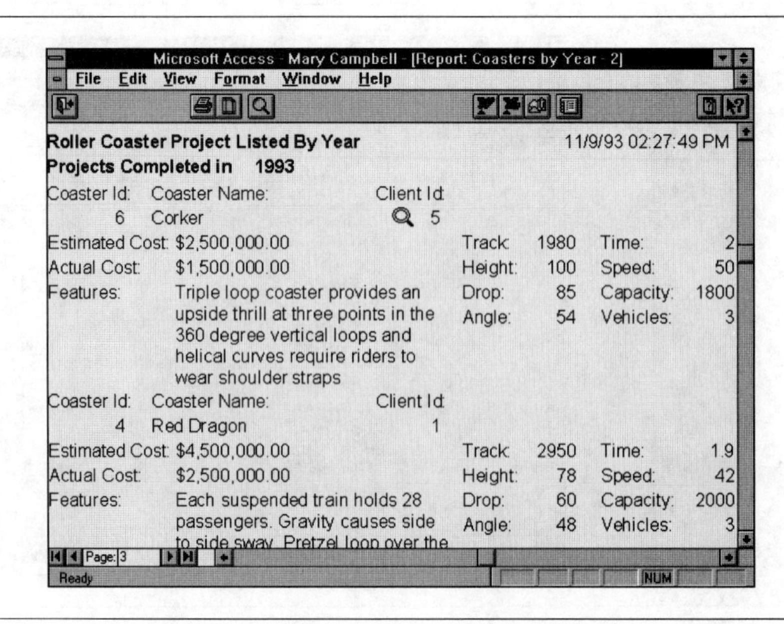

## USING FUNCTIONS TO RETURN MORE THAN ONE VALUE

The values for most controls are simply plugged in from fields and then calculated. You can use functions that change the value the expression returns depending on another expression's value. You can also use expressions to create calculated fields in queries. One of these functions is the IIf function. This function returns one value when another expression is true and another value when the same expression is false. The other function is the Choose function, which returns one of several values depending on the result of the first argument.

The IIf function is used for switching between two expressions at once depending on another expression's value. The format of this function is IIf(expression, truepart, falsepart). This formula evaluates the expression and decides whether it is true or false. The value this function equals when the expression is true is truepart. The value this function equals when the expression is false is falsepart. As an example, suppose you are creating a form that includes a text box indicating whether the invoice is overdue. When the invoice date is more than 30 days past, you want the text box to display "Invoice is overdue." When the invoice date is less than 30 days ago, you want the text box to display a null value (the equivalent of containing nothing). This is the expression you would use:

```
= IIf([Invoice Date]+30<Date(), "Invoice is overdue", Null)
```

You can see the text box this expression creates in Figure 12-8, which shows the form for two records of which the first invoice is overdue and the second one is current. If you need more than two choices, nest the IIf functions. For example, if you only want to display different messages for overdue invoices depending on the invoice amount, you might have an expression like this:

```
= IIf([Invoice Date]+30<Date(), IIf([Invoice Amount]>50000,
"Send copy of invoice to collections","Invoice is overdue"), Null)
```

Access evaluates the outer IIf function to test whether the Invoice Date is more than 30 days past. When the invoice is overdue, then Access evaluates the truepart argument of this expression. For this example, the truepart argument is another expression that Access must evaluate. Access then evaluates the second IIf function to compare the amount of the invoice with 50,000. When the invoice is more than 50,000, the entire expression equals the truepart argument of the inner IIf function, Send copy of invoice to collections. When the invoice is less than or equal to 50,000, the entire expression equals the

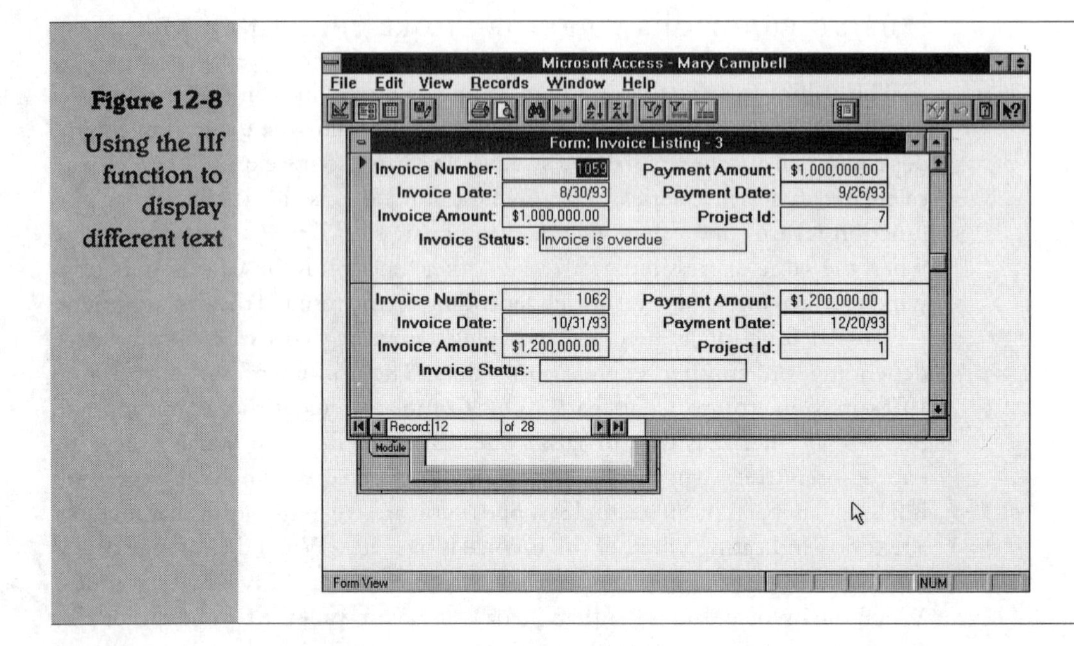


**Figure 12-8** Using the IIf function to display different text

falsepart argument of the inner IIf function, "Invoice is overdue". When the invoice is not overdue, the outer IIf function evaluates to Null.

## USING FUNCTIONS FOR STATISTICS

Access has several functions that provide statistical information about the values in a record or the values in several records. You have already seen the Sum function used for totaling the records in a group of records on a report. Besides the Sum function, Access has functions that calculate the average, count the entries, find the smallest or largest entries, and calculate how much the values vary from the mean. These statistical functions use the same format of a function name followed by parentheses enclosing the expression on which they perform their statistical evaluation.

You can use these functions to calculate statistics among the values in a record. If you have a table that contains salespeople's sales for three products, you can average the sales for the projects for each salesperson with a formula such as this: =Avg([Product 1], [Product 2], [Product 3]).

You are more likely to include the statistical functions in different locations than the Detail section. For example, by including one of these functions in the Form Footer, Report Footer, or Group Footer sections, you can summarize the records for an entire form, report, or group. The following shows a form that uses the Sum function in the Form Footer section to total the value of the Invoice Amount field:

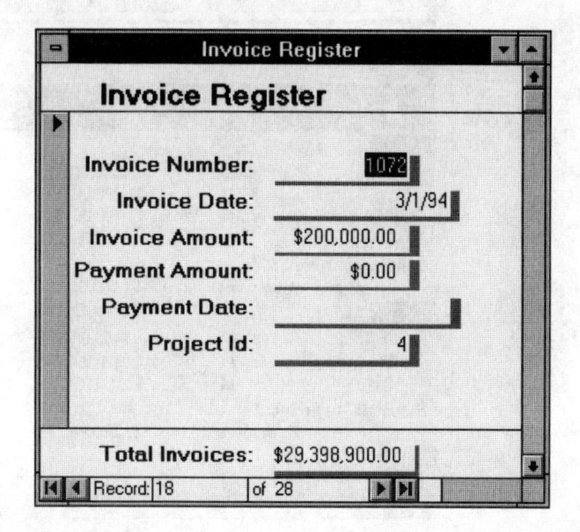


The expression for the Total Invoices text box is =Sum([Invoice Amount]). The results are calculated for all of the records in the selected dynaset. This total is updated as you change the Invoice Amount field's values. Figure 12-9 shows a report that uses several statistical functions to summarize each group or records for a particular project. The design for this report is shown in Figure 12-10. The four expressions in the Project Id Footer section are shown here:

```
="Subtotals for Project " & [Project Id] & " : "
=Count(*) & " Invoices"
=Sum([Invoice Amount])
=Sum([Payment Amount])
```

The Count function counts the number of records in the group. Since it counts any type of data, Access does not care which field you place in the parentheses. Since you want to count all records for the group—even ones that do not have an entry for the Payment Date field—use * as the function's argument as in =Count(*).

## Resetting an Expression

When Access calculates the value of an expression that is displayed in a text box control in a report, it must decide when the expression is reset. Resetting a

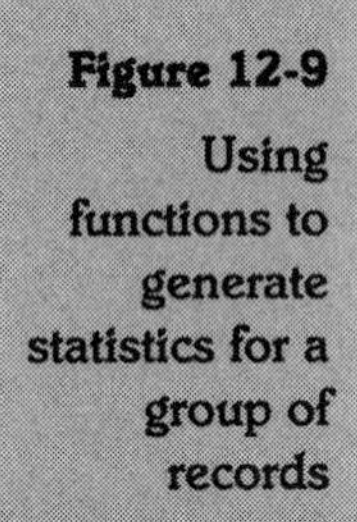

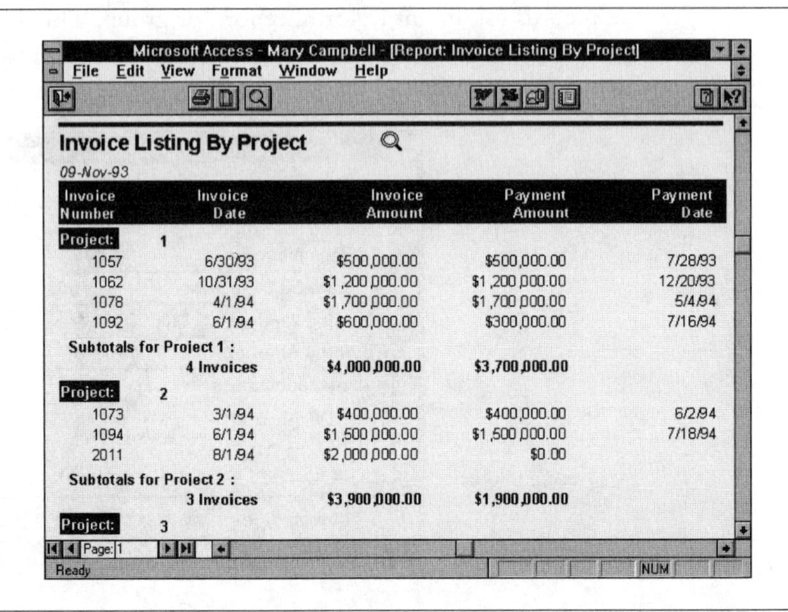


**Figure 12-9** Using functions to generate statistics for a group of records

control displaying an expression sets the expression's value to zero so the next time it is calculated, it does not include the value from the previous calculation. The location of an expression determines when Access recalculates the values. When an expression appears in a control that included in the Detail section of a form or report, the expression is usually calculated for each record. When you

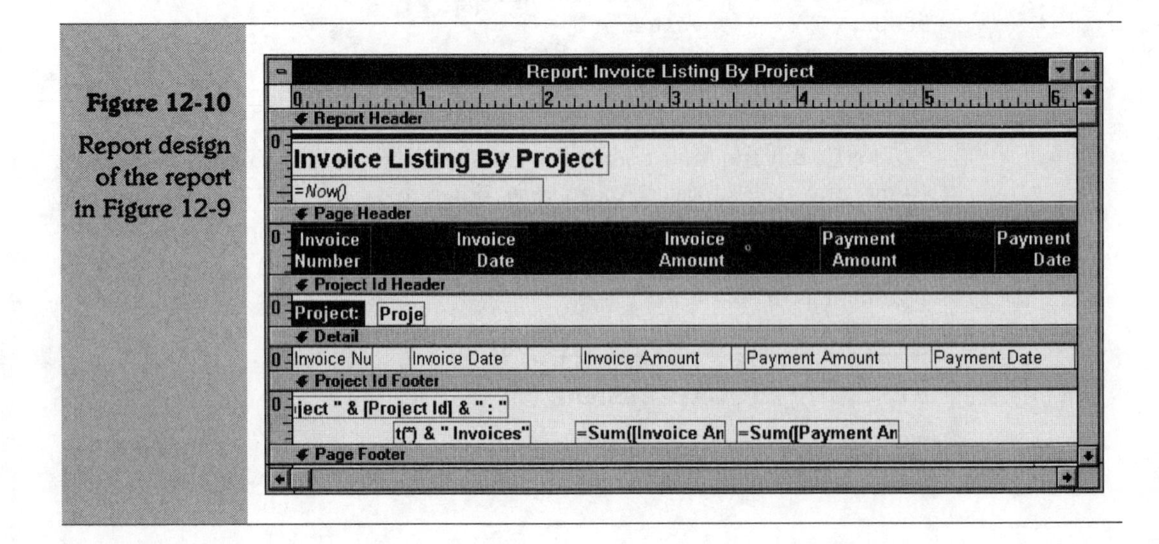


**Figure 12-10** Report design of the report in Figure 12-9

switch to another record, Access clears the expression's value and recalculates it for the next record. For Page Header and Page Footer sections, these expressions in controls are reset every time you start a new page. For Form Header, Form Footer, Report Header, and Report Footer sections, these expression-displaying controls are reset and recalculated when you start using the form or report. Of course, the expressions are also updated when the values the expressions use change.

In reports, you can override when an expression displayed in a control is reset. To change where an expression is reset, change the control's Running Sum property. The default is No so the expression is reset according to the control's location. Controls in the Detail section are reset every record; controls in a group's Header or Footer section are reset every time the group changes; controls in the Page Header and Page Footer sections are reset every page; and controls in the Report Header and Report Footer sections are reset every report.

The other choices are Over All and Over Groups. Over All tells Access to restart the expression's calculation only at the beginning of the report. Over Groups tells Access to restart the calculation when the group level above the one with the control containing the expression changes groups. This means that if you have a report that groups time log records first by project and then by date, a control in the Date Footer section that totals the hours and has the Running Sum property set to Over Groups, resets when you change project groups but not when you change date groups. The expression keeps a running total within each project even as you change date groups.

## Using Expressions in Forms and Reports

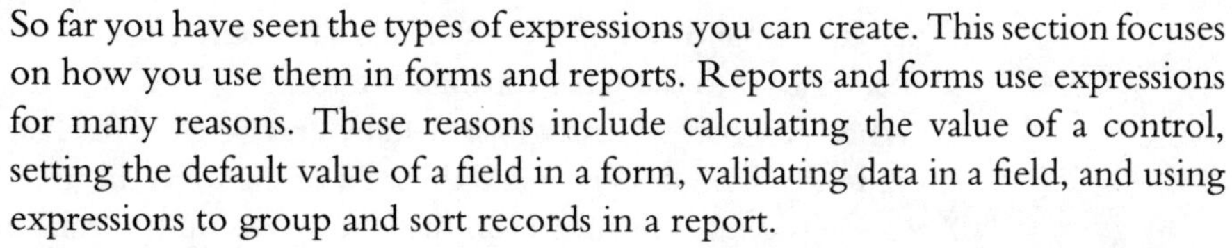

So far you have seen the types of expressions you can create. This section focuses on how you use them in forms and reports. Reports and forms use expressions for many reasons. These reasons include calculating the value of a control, setting the default value of a field in a form, validating data in a field, and using expressions to group and sort records in a report.

You have already seen several expressions added to reports you have created. For example, the reports you create with Report Wizards often include expressions for dates and page numbers. Also, the Groups/Totals Report Wizard report type totals the values of data types containing numbers.

Where you enter an expression into a form or report design is based on what you want the expression to do. Expressions can be entered as the value of the

Control Source property and as the Default Value property of a control. When you use an expression to check the validity of an entry in a form, you will enter the expression in the Validation Rule property.

**tip:** *An easy way to add an expression to a form or report is to modify one of the existing controls. When you do so, change the Control Name property from the field name the control previously represented to another name. If you do not change the name, the expression won't be properly calculated.*

## Setting the Default Value of a Field

The Default Value property for a field in a table sets the default value for that field when you add records onto a datasheet. This Default Value property is adopted in forms that you create by the controls you add through the Form Wizards or by dragging the field name from the field list in the form design. You can override the table's default value by entering a different expression for the Default Value property in the field's control on the form. For example, when entering invoices you have billed, you may want the current date as a default for the invoice date. To do this, the Default Value property for the Invoice Date control is =Date (). As you add new invoices, the current date is placed in this field.

## Using Expressions for Validation Rules in a Form

In Chapter 3, you learned about adding validation rules to a table. You can also use validation rules for a form. A form's validation rules are separate from the validation rules of a table. The table's validation rules apply when you enter data to the table through the datasheet. The form's validation rules apply when you enter data to the table through the form.

When you add a control for a field by dragging the field name from the field list onto the form design or add the field to the form through Form Wizards in Access version 1, the control in the form picks up the validation rule the field has in the table. You can subsequently modify the validation rule to add one, delete one, or modify it. When you enter a validation rule as a control's Validation Rule property, you do not need the equal sign to tell Access you are entering an expression since Access assumes the entry for the Validation Rule property is an expression.

You can add an expression for a validation rule when you want to make sure that an entry is made into a field. The form in the following illustration has the controls for the First Name, Last Name, and Date of Hire fields using the validation rule of Is Not Null:

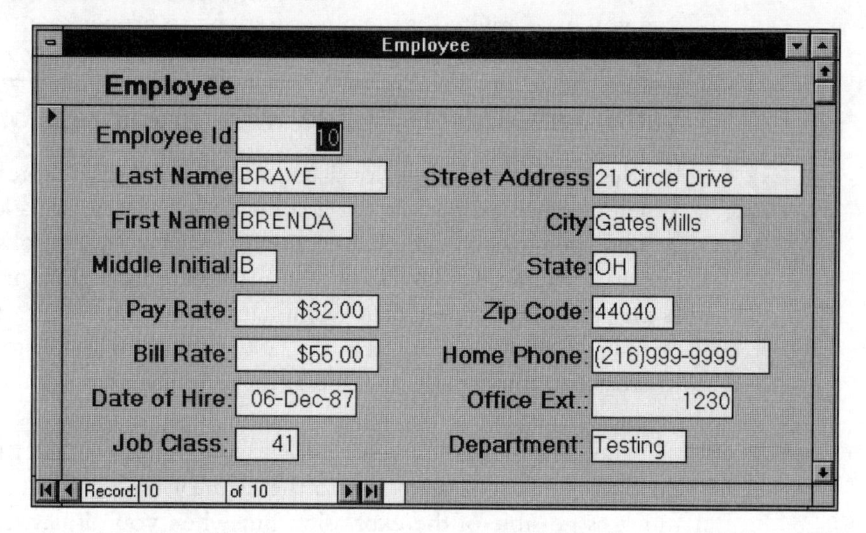


This rule prevents the form's user from leaving these four fields empty when any changes to the field is made. Access also has an IsNull function you can use for the purpose of testing whether you have made an entry or not. For these controls, you can also enter this validation rule using the IsNull function as in Not IsNull([First Name]) for the First Name field. While these only test for an entry when the existing entry has changed, you can use macros as described in Chapter 17 to test whether an entry is made when you leave a field or when you leave a record.

Another example of using expressions for the Validation Rule property is the validation rule used for the home phone number. The Home Phone control uses the validation rule of Like "(###)###-####" so the area code is surrounded by parentheses and the number has a character between the first three digits and the last four digits of the phone number. You do not need the field's control name, Home Phone, before the Like operator since the field name is implied by the expression's location. Using this validation rule is an alternative to using the (###)###-#### input mask.

If you want a field to have more than one validation rule, you can join the expressions you want to evaluate the field with AND or OR. The OR operator makes the validation rule true for a field when the expression on either side of the operator is true. The AND operator makes the validation rule true only when the expression on both sides of this operator are true.

In Chapter 16, you will learn about using macros for data validation. Most of the time you will enter an expression for the Validation Rule property. You will find macros helpful when you want to perform data validation that is more complex than the expressions can handle. You can also use macros to convert data you have entered as in converting text to proper case.

## Setting a Control's Value with an Expression

Besides using field values for a control, you can use expressions in controls. When you use expressions for a control's value, you are adding a control for one of three purposes. First, use an expression for a control's value to provide information that is not otherwise available from the table or query's data such as the page numbers and date. Second, use expressions for calculated values that operate on the values stored in the table. The third reason to use expressions is to create summary calculations that involve more than one record in the table or query.

When you use an expression for a control's value, enter the expression for the Control Source property. In the form or report design, Access displays as much as possible of the expression but when you display the form or report, the control displays the current value of the expression.

A control that contains an expression rather than a field value cannot be edited. With the controls in Figure 12-11, the time and date cannot be changed so the Status Line property is set to tell the user this. Also, when one expression depends on the value of another record, the expression is immediately updated as the value it depends on changes.

**tip:** *When you design a form with a control that cannot be changed, let the user know they cannot edit it. You may want to shade controls that cannot be changed or remove the box around a text box showing the control's value.*

### SETTING A CONTROL'S VALUE FROM ANOTHER SOURCE

When you create reports with Report Wizards, the report contains controls that print the page number and report date. Controls like the one for the date use a function to create the value that appears in the report. You can create expressions that use function results as the control's value.

Another special value you can have in a form or report is the Page property. When included in an expression, this property is replaced by the current page

**Figure 12-11** Including controls in a form that you cannot modify

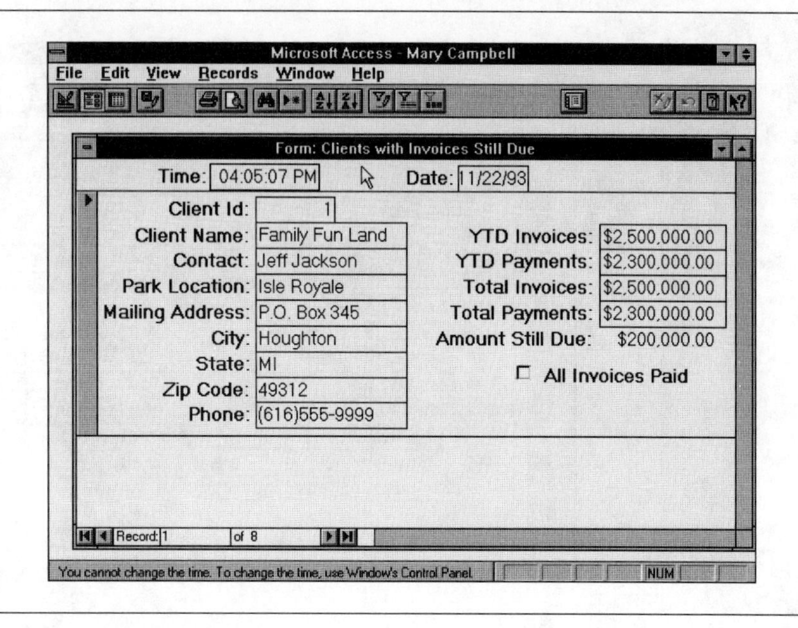


number. Page is not a function so you do not want to include any parentheses. You can combine Page with other parts of an expression so you can include the word Page or whatever text you want to place next to the page number. Access version 2 has another property, *Pages*, that returns the total number of pages within the report.

**tip:** *Although this feature is called the Page property, it is not a property that appears on a property sheet. Instead, it is entered as part of an expression, like a function or operator.*

Figure 12-11 shows a couple of fields that are created using values that do not appear in the underlying table. In this form, the date and time at the top are added with the expressions =Date() and =Time(). You can also see these expressions in the form design shown in Figure 12-12.

## CALCULATED CONTROLS

In Chapter 2, when you designed your database, the chapter mentioned how you do not want to include fields in a table that contains values that can be calculated. For example, if you offer a two-percent reduction in account

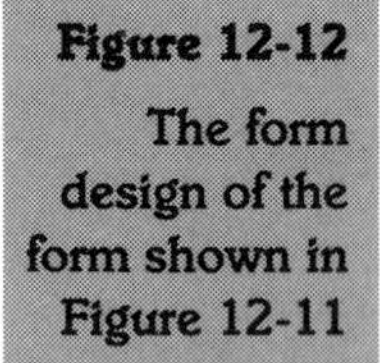

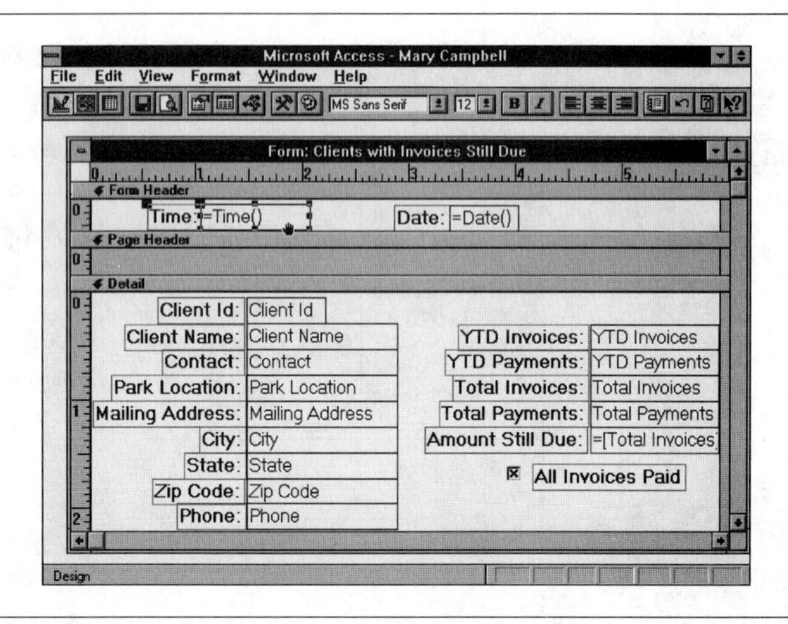


**Figure 12-12** The form design of the form shown in Figure 12-11

receivables when they are paid promptly, you do not want to include a field in your accounts receivable table that calculates the potential discount of every account receivable. Simply calculate these values whenever you need them so you do not have to consume disk space to store values that are readily available. You can create calculated controls that work with the data from a single record or with the data from multiple records, which is described later in this chapter.

A calculated control in a form or report often uses the field names of the table. For example for the form shown in Figure 12-11, the control after Amount Still Due is the result of subtracting Total Payments from Total Invoices. This calculated control uses the expression of =[Total Invoices]–[Total Payments]. This control has the Enabled property set to No so you cannot move to this control. Chapter 14 tells how to change the colors of controls and sections in a form so the user will realize that calculated fields are different from the other ones.

When you have a control that relies upon another control that does not directly contain one of the fields from the table or query, you have two choices for how to refer to that calculated control. For example, suppose you have a form like the one shown in Figure 12-13. The control below Difference contains the expression =[Bill Rate]–[Pay Rate]. The control below Percentage Markup contains the amount of the difference divided by the Pay Rate. You can enter this expression in one of two ways. You can use the expression =([Bill Rate]–[Pay Rate])/[Bill Rate]. Another option is to use the name of the control below Difference. This control has the default name of Field followed by the next unused number. You can give it a better name by entering a new name for the control as the control's Control Name property. You can use up to 64 characters just as you have with other objects that you've named in Access.

If you have named the control that subtracts the two rates as Difference, enter the other expression as **=[Difference]/[Bill Rate]**. Using the control names instead of repeating the formula makes the calculations easier to understand and giving descriptive names to the controls makes it easier to use the control names.

## USING EXPRESSIONS FOR CONTROLS IN OTHER SECTIONS

So far, many of the examples have focused on adding expressions to the Detail section of forms and reports. Expressions are often used in other form and report sections. You can also include expressions in the Form Header, Form Footer, Report Header, and Report Footer sections when you want an expression to appear at the top or end of a form or report. For example, the form in Figure 12-11 includes controls to display the time and date in the Form Footer section. Page Header, Page Footer, and Group Headers and Footers are other sections that you can add controls to. For example, you can include controls in the Page Header or a Group Header section to summarize the reports on the page or group.

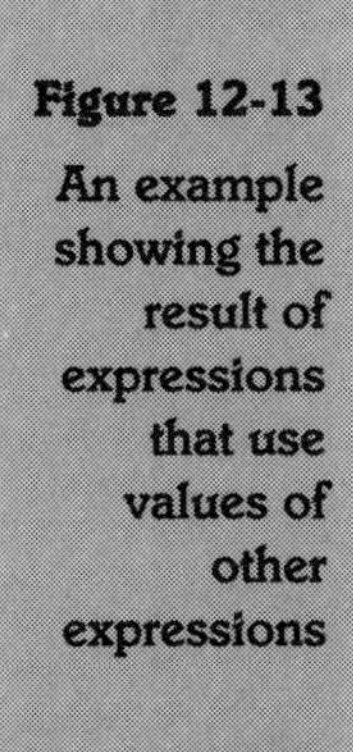

**Figure 12-13** An example showing the result of expressions that use values of other expressions

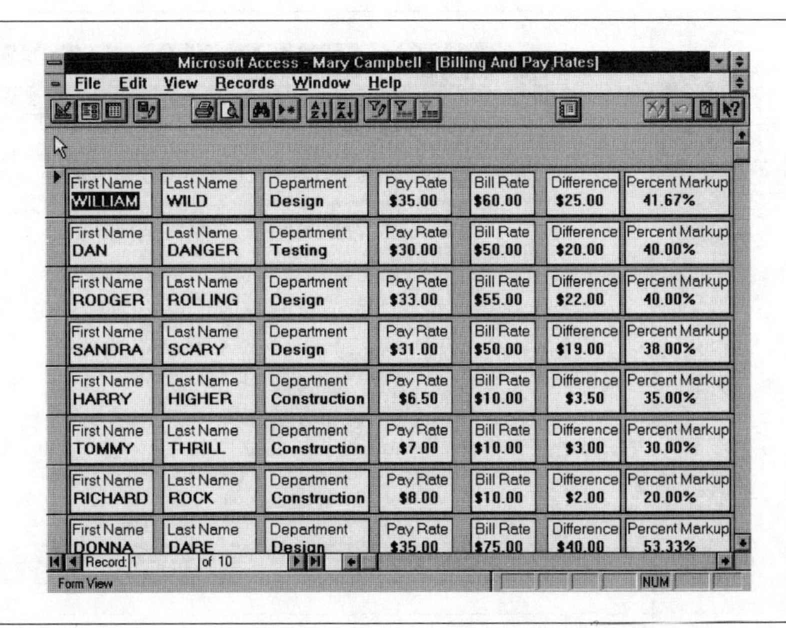

## Using Expressions to Sort and Group Records in a Report

In Chapter 11, you learned how you can sort records using the values of fields but you can also create expressions whose values for the records determine the order of the records in the report. To use an expression to sort the records in a report, enter the expression in place of the field name in the Sorting and Grouping box. Just like when sorting records by field contents, you can select whether the sorting is performed in ascending or descending order, and whether to divide the records into groups based on the expression's values. Think of using an expression for organizing records in a database as having a temporary field in the table or query that contains the values of the expression. Other than the fact that you enter the expression in place of a field name, sorting and grouping records in a report using an expression is just like using a field name to sort and group records.

As an example of using an expression to sort and group records in a report, the report in Figure 12-14 uses the expression = [Invoice Date] – [Payment Date] to sort the records. The entries in the first column are the result of the expression =[Payment Date]–[Invoice Date] & " days" with its Hide Duplicates property set to Yes.

**Figure 12-14** Using an expression to sort records in a report

Microsoft Access - Mary Campbell - [Report: Unpaid Invoices Grouped by Amounts

File Edit View Format Window Help

**Clients and Unpaid Invoices**

| Age | Client Number and Name | Project Number and Name | Invoice Amount |
|---|---|---|---|
| days | 4 Arden Entertainment Group | 5 Taurus | $198,000 |
| | 3 Amusement Technologies | 3 Astro Transport | $1,800,000 |
| | 1 Family Fun Land | 4 Red Dragon | $200,000 |
| | 2 Teen Land | 2 Blue Arrow | $2,000,000 |
| | 7 Island Waterplay Inc. | 8 White Lightnin | $500,000 |
| 13 days | 1 Family Fun Land | 4 Red Dragon | $400,000 |
| 16 days | 7 Island Waterplay Inc. | 8 White Lightnin | $1,500,000 |
| 20 days | 1 Family Fun Land | 4 Red Dragon | $300,000 |
| 27 days | 6 Playland Consortium | 7 Wild One | $1,000,000 |
| 28 days | 3 Amusement Technologies | 1 Scream Machine | $500,000 |
| | 2 Teen Land | 9 The Runaway | $200,900 |
| 29 days | 6 Playland Consortium | 7 Wild One | $1,800,000 |
| 33 days | 3 Amusement Technologies | 1 Scream Machine | $1,700,000 |
| 36 days | 1 Family Fun Land | 4 Red Dragon | $1,600,000 |

Page: 1

Ready NUM

## Quick Reference

**To Enter an Expression** Start the Expression Builder in Access version 2 by clicking the Build button in the toolbar or property sheet. Then you can create the expression. To add an operator, you can click the buttons for operators in the middle of the window. You can also type what you want added to an expression or double-click what you want to add from the list boxes at bottom of the Expression Builder or highlight one of those options from the list boxes, and select Paste.

To enter an expression without the Expression Builder, type an equal sign (=) followed by the control names, field names, operators, and functions you want the expression to evaluate.

**To Use an Expression as a Control's Default Value** Enter the expression in the control's Default Value property.

**To Use an Expression to Validate an Entry in a Form's Control** Enter the expression in the control's Validation Rule property.

**To Enter an Expression as a Control's Value** Enter the expression in the control's text box or as the control's Control Source property. The control cannot be altered in a form.

**To Use an Expression to Sort Records in a Report** Display the Sorting and Grouping box by choosing Sorting and Grouping from the View menu. Type the expression you want to use for sorting in the Field Name/Expression column. Select Ascending or Descending in the Sort Order column. Repeat adding fields or expressions and sort orders for up to ten fields in the order you want the records sorted.

# Chapter 13

Combining Tables with Subforms and Subreports

Queries to Combine Data from Different Tables

# Using Multiple Tables and Queries in Reports and Forms

WHILE the reports and forms you have created thus far have focused on one dynaset or table at a time, you also can use data from multiple dynasets and tables in a report or form. In Chapter 8, you learned how to do this using the Form Wizards to create a main/subform form type. You can create other types of multiple dynaset and table reports and forms. One option for doing this is to insert a form or report inside another report or form. A second option is to create a query that provides the data from all of the data you want to combine.

## Combining Tables with Subforms and Subreports

You can actually combine forms and reports when combining multiple dynasets and tables in a form or report. You can put one form inside another, a report inside another report, or a form inside a report. You can also make one form a pop-up form to another one. You do this by adding a subform/subreport control to your form or report design. This control shares many of the same properties as other controls in forms and reports that you have learned about in earlier chapters. When you make these combinations, the principal form or report is the *main form* or *main report*. The form or report contained within the main form or report is called a *subform* or *subreport*.

### Adding a Subform to a Form

The main/subform form types you designed with the Form Wizards create a main form that contains a subform inside of it. You can also create these types of forms without using the Form Wizards.

The first step in creating a main/subform form is creating the two forms you will later combine. Decide in advance which will be the main form and which the subform, and then create the two separately. When you finish designing your main/subform form, you will have two separate forms listed in the

Database window. Ideally, you would complete one of the two forms before starting the other, but realistically, you probably will switch between designing the two forms. You can continue making enhancements to either form's design after you add a subform/subreport control.

Usually you leave an area in the main form in which you will later place the subform. For best results, make the subform as small as practical. Figure 13-1 shows three form designs. The form designs on the bottom and top right will be added as subforms to the form designs on the top left. The Invoice Generation form uses the Project table as its record source. The Form 1 for Invoice Generation form uses the Client table as its record source, matching the records in the Project table by the Client Id field in both tables. The Form 2 for Invoice Generation form uses a query that combines the Employee Time Log table with the employee names from the Employee table. The records in the query match the records in the Project table by the Project Number field in the query and the Coaster Id field in the Project table.

**tip:** *When creating a subform that you intend to use as a datasheet, don't worry about the size of the form or the placement of the controls in the form. However, make sure the tab order of the controls matches the order in which you want the fields listed as part of the subform.*

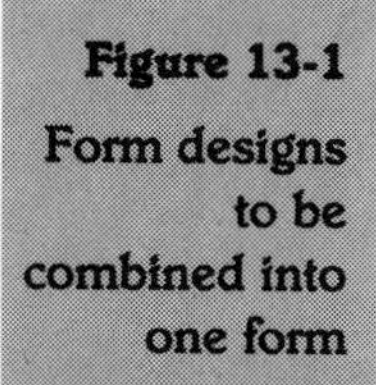

**Figure 13-1** Form designs to be combined into one form

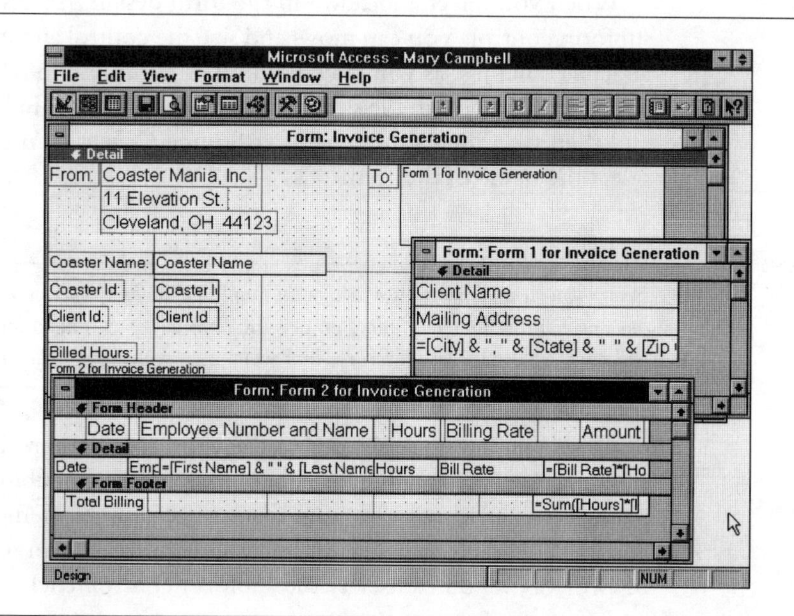

Once you have both forms designed, you can add one form to the other. Select the main form and switch to the Database window. Since you will drag the form from the Database window to the form design, make sure the windows are not maximized. Next, display the forms in the Database window and highlight the subform. Drag the form name from the Database window to the Design view of the main form.

When you drag the form name, the mouse pointer changes to a form icon. When the icon is where you want the subform, release the mouse. If the Default View property of the form you are pointing at is set to Continuous Forms, Access warns you that it is changing this property to Single Form. Select OK to continue adding the form as a subform. Access adds a subform control to the form's design that is the subform's size. An attached label control is also added, displaying the subform's name. At this point, switch to the main form's design and make changes to the main form. You can also change the subform control by moving and sizing it. Figure 13-2 shows a form design after adding two subform controls.

You also have another method available for adding a subform to the current form you are designing. When you display the toolbox, select the Subform/Subreport button, which looks like this:

When you select a location in the form design, Access adds an unbounded subform control. You can move and size the control and change the text in the attached label just as you have with other controls. To tell Access which form you want to appear in the subform control's location, display the property sheet and then type the form name after Source Object or use the down arrow to select the name of the form.

**tip:** *Before you create forms to use as a main form and subform, look over your existing forms. You can save yourself time by finding an existing form to use as a main form or subform or one that will serve as the basis for the form, which you can subsequently modify to meet your current needs.*

Once you add the subform to the main form, the main form continues to use the same subform design. When you change the subform's design with the main form open, tell the main form to refresh its memory of the subform's design. You can tell Access to update the current form for a subform's design in two ways. You can select the subform control, click the form name in the

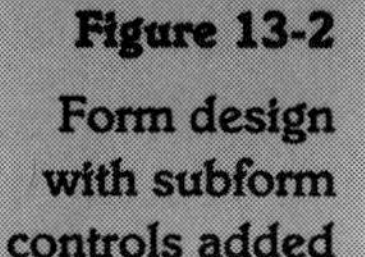

**Figure 13-2**
**Form design with subform controls added**

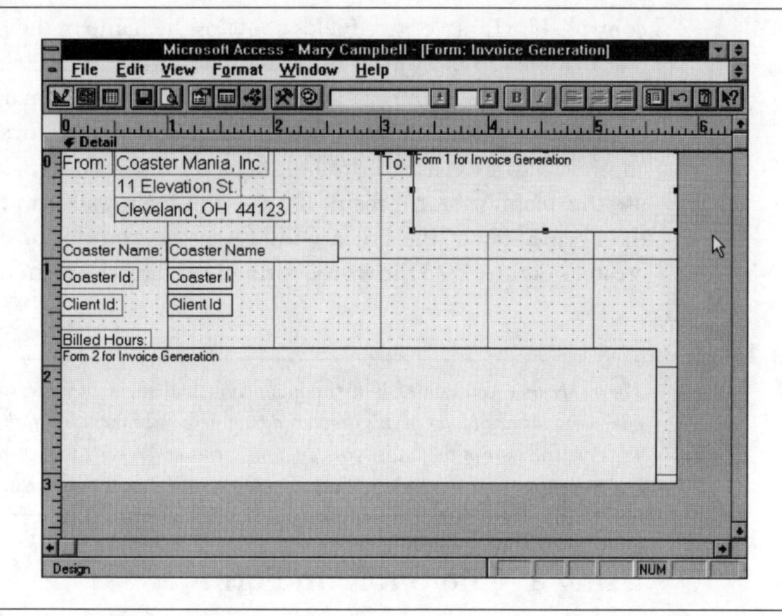


subform control, and then press ENTER or click another part of the form design. You can also display the list of form names with the Source Object property in the property sheet and select the same form again. If you double-click a subform control when it is not selected, you will open a Form window in Design view for that subform's design.

The link between the main form and the subform selects the records from the subform's dynaset that appears as you change records in the main form. This link means that when you switch clients in a main form when the subform displays the projects, the projects change to show only the projects for the currently displayed client.

Depending on how you added the subform to the form, either Access will create the link between the main form and the subform or you will have to create this link. When you add a subform to a form by dragging the form's name from the Database window to the main form's design, Access first checks to see if you have already established a relationship between the two tables or the underlying tables in a query. If you have not, and the tables for the two forms have fields using the same name and data type, Access creates the link that way.

When you select a subform for the Source Object property of the subform, if the underlying tables of both forms use a field with the same name and data type, Access creates the link that way. In other cases, you must define the link. The link between the main form and the subform is created with the Link Master Fields and Link Child Fields properties of the subform/subreport control. The Link Master Fields contains the name of the field in the main form that matches a field in the subform. The Link Child Fields contains the name of the field in the subform that matches a field in the main form.

Once you have created both forms, added one form as the subform to another, and established the link between the two dynasets, you are ready to use this main/subform form. Display the main/subform form by switching to the Form view of the Form window just as you do for other forms you have created. Figure 13-3 shows the form created by the form design in Figure 13-2.

**tip:** *The fields that you use to link the main form and the subform (as well as main reports and subreports described later in this chapter) do not need to be included in the design. Since the linking fields are still part of the underlying data the forms and reports use, Access can link the two tables or dynasets without the linking fields appearing in the form or report design.*

## Using a Main/Subform Form

While you are using the main form and subform, you can switch between the main and the subform parts of the form. To switch the insertion point to the subform, click any area of the subform. To switch the insertion point to the main form, click one of the controls in the main form. If you click the main form's background, you will not reposition the insertion point. You can switch

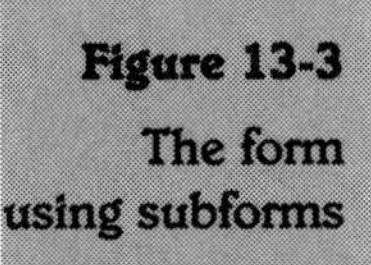

**Figure 13-3** The form using subforms

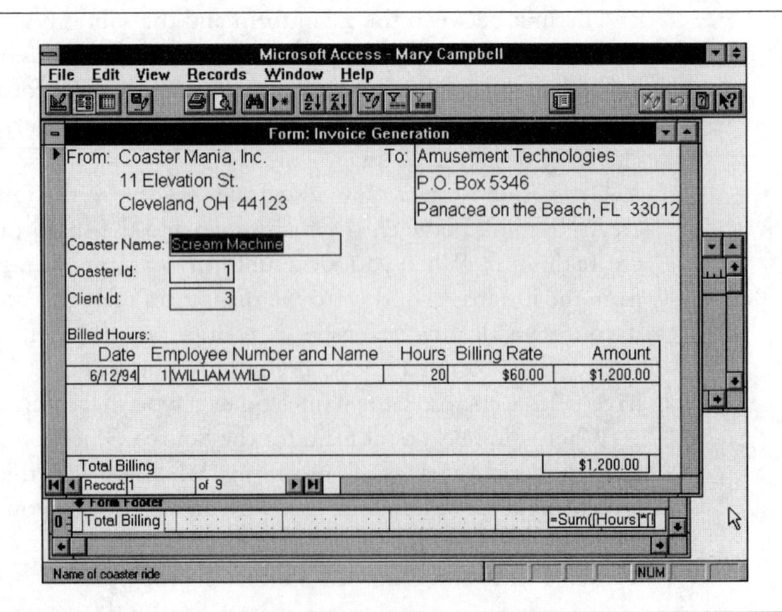

between the two parts of the form to add, edit, and delete records in either part. You can also press TAB until you move to the section of the form you want, since the tab order of the main form selects when the insertion point will move to the subform. The subform's own tab order sets how pressing TAB moves you from one field to another within the subform. If the subform shows query data rather than table data, you may need to reapply the query so you are only seeing the applicable records. You can apply the query while the insertion point is on the subform by pressing SHIFT+F9. Any filter you use only applies to the main form and does not affect the subform.

You can switch subforms that can appear as either a form or datasheet by choosing Subform Datasheet in the View menu. When this command has a check mark by it, the subform data appears as a Datasheet view. When this command does not have a check mark by it, the subform's data uses the Form view. This command is only available when the insertion point is in the subform. This command can be disabled by changing the properties of the subform.

## PROPERTIES IN A MAIN/SUBFORM FORM

When you are using a main/subform form, the main form and subform have their own properties. You are familiar with most of these properties because you have used them in other forms. Some of these properties are particularly useful for a main/subform form. You can use them to effect the kinds of changes that are made to the records and how the data appears in the subform. These changes are made by displaying the subform's form design and modifying the properties for the overall form.

In a subform, you select whether the data appears as a datasheet or uses the form design. Change whether the subform can use one or both of these views by changing the Views Allowed property. The default is Both, but you will want to change it to Datasheet or Form if you only want the subform to appear using either Datasheet view or Form view regardless of the view used by the main form. When you have selected Datasheet or Form, the Subform Datasheet command in the View menu is not available. When Views Allowed is set to Both, you can also select the default view by changing the Default View to Single Form, Continuous Forms, or Datasheet.

For example, the main/subform forms you create with the Form Wizards have the Views Allowed set to Both while the Default View is set to Datasheet. In Figure 13-3, the subform controls for both subforms have Views Allowed set to Form, so you cannot switch between displaying the subform in a Form view and a Datasheet view. Also, Default View is set to Continuous Forms for the subform that appears below Billed Hours, so the Detail section is repeated for each record that appears in the subform. The column headings and the total at the bottom of the subform are part of the Form Header and Form Footer sections in the subform's design, as you can see here:

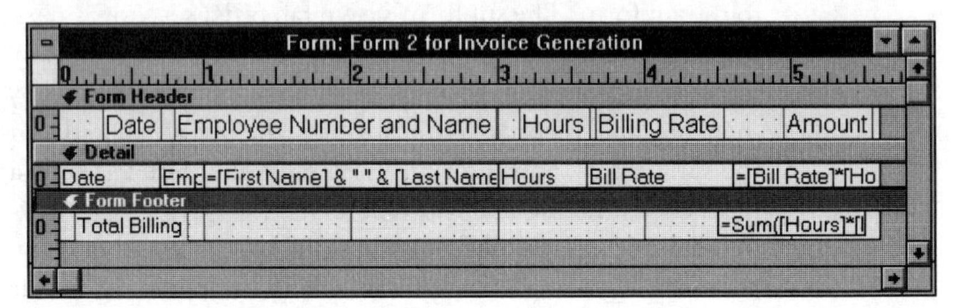


You might also want to change whether edits are allowed. You can prevent editing in specific parts of the form. For instance, you cannot edit the subform form shown in Figure 13-3 because the Default Editing property of the subform's form design is set to Read Only. Also, for this subform's form design, Allow Editing is set to Unavailable and Allow Updating is set to No Tables, so you cannot use menu commands to change the contents of the subform. If these changes were not made to the subform form design, this section of the form would appear differently to show that you can add records, as shown here:

Billed Hours:

| Date | Employee Number and Name | | Hours | Billing Rate | Amount |
|---|---|---|---|---|---|
| 6/12/94 | 1 | WILLIAM WILD | 20 | $60.00 | $1,200.00 |
| | 0 | | 0 | $10.00 | $0.00 |

Total Billing $1,200.00

## Pop-up Forms

There is a special type of main/subform form in which the subform is a pop-up form. A pop-up form does not appear as part of the main form. For example, in Figure 13-4, New Roller Coasters is the main form. If you click the New Client command button, the New Client pop-up form appears, as shown in Figure 13-5. Pop-up forms can be used to display a message or prompt for more information. In the examples in Figures 13-4 and 13-5, the pop-up form lets you add a new client to your Client table at the same time you add a new roller coaster to your Project table. Pop-up forms use macros, which you will learn about in Chapter 16.

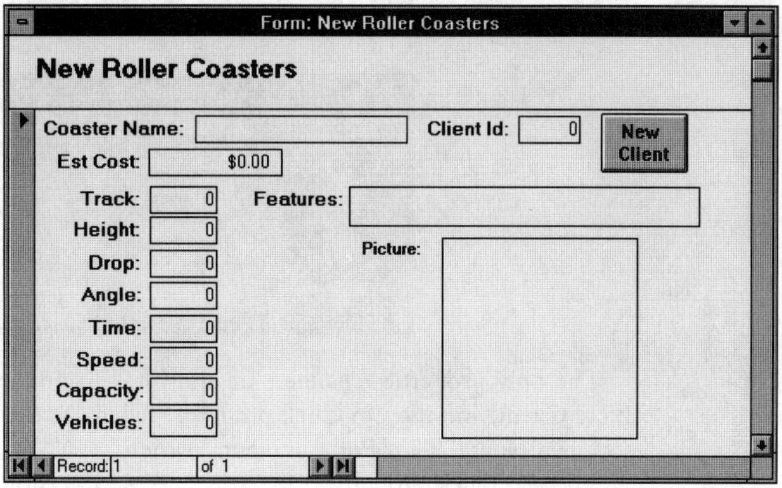

**Figure 13-4** A form that invokes a pop-up form

Form: New Roller Coasters
New Roller Coasters
Coaster Name:
Client Id: 0
New Client
Est Cost: $0.00
Track: 0
Height: 0
Drop: 0
Angle: 0
Time: 0
Speed: 0
Capacity: 0
Vehicles: 0
Features:
Picture:
Record: 1 of 1

The examples of pop-up forms shown in Figures 13-4 and 13-5 are very easy to create. The New Roller Coasters form contains the fields shown and has a command button added. This form does not show the Coaster Id field because Access will assign the next unused number for this counter field and you do not need to know the number it is assigned. The command button is added just as

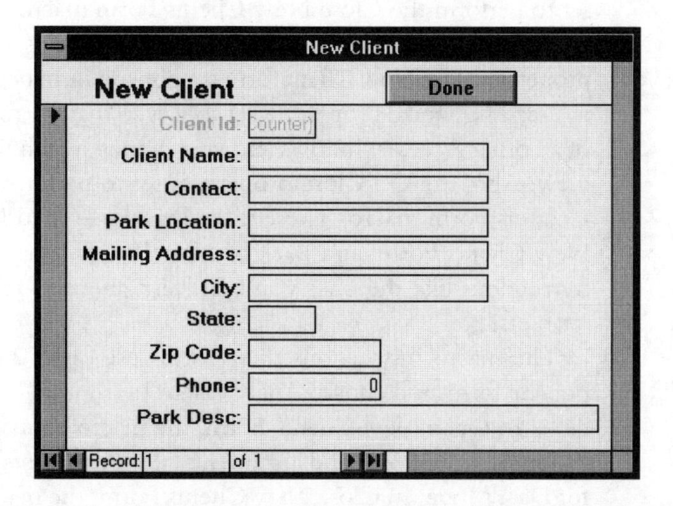


**Figure 13-5** Pop-up form

you would add a toggle button, which you learned about in Chapter 10. This button and some of its properties are shown here:

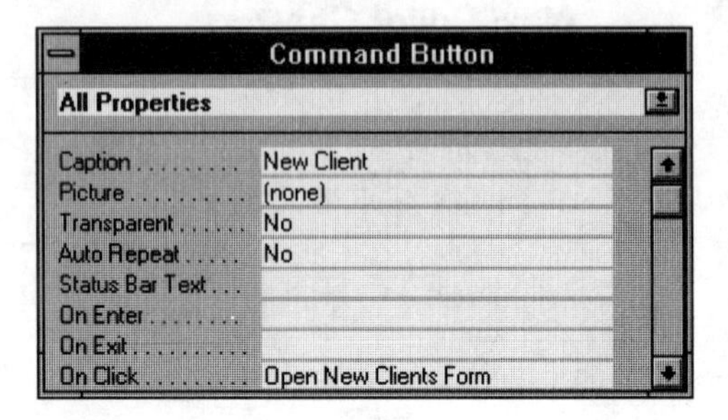


The only properties changed are the Caption property, which changes to New Client, and the On Click property (called On Push in Access version 1) to Open New Clients Form, a macro name.

The On Click property (On Push in Access version 1) tells Access which macro to perform when you click the button. The macros are a set of instructions that are recorded as a separate object in the database. You can click the Build button then select Macro Builder and OK to display a macro window to help enter the macro to perform.

The New Client form is created using the fields shown in Figure 13-5. The Client Id has the Enabled and Locked properties set to No so that the form's user cannot make changes to it. Also, this form has a Done command button, which is added just like the New Client one in the New Roller Coasters form. This command button has its On Click (On Push in Access version 1) property set to perform the Close New Clients Form macro.

The only other special feature about this form is a few changes of the form's properties. The New Client form is a pop-up form because the Pop Up property is Yes. The Modal property is set to Yes so that the form always remains on top of all other Access windows and you cannot switch to the Design or Datasheet view. Also, the On Close property is set to perform the Back to New Roller Coasters Form macro. These three macros—Open New Clients Form, Close New Clients Form, and Back to New Roller Coasters Form—contain macro instructions like the ones you will learn about in Chapter 16 and subsequent chapters.

The macro instructions these forms use open the pop-up form, close the pop-up form, and copy the new Client Id from the Clients table to the Projects table. In Open New Clients Form, the macro contains the instruction with an action of OpenForm and arguments of New Clients for Form Name and Add for Data Mode. In Close New Clients Form, the macro contains an instruction with an action of DoMenuItem and arguments of Form for the Menu Bar, File for the Menu Name, and Close for the Command. In Back to New Roller Coasters Form, the macro contains an instruction with an action of SetValue and arguments of Forms![New Roller Coasters]![Client Id] for Item and Forms![New Clients]![Client Id] for Expression. This last macro sets the new Client Id number for the record you have just added with the New Client form to the record you are entering in the New Roller Coasters form. In a macro, the actions tell Access what you want the macro to do and the arguments give Access the information it needs to complete the action.

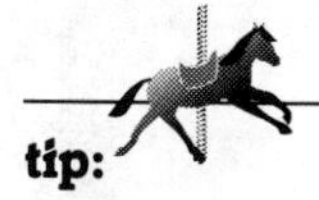

**tip:** *Change the Display When property of the command buttons you use to display the pop-ups to Screen Only, since you do not want these buttons to appear when you print the form.*

## Adding a Subreport to a Report

Just as you can create a form that contains another form, you can create a report that contains another report. You can use the combined reports to create unique-looking reports you could not otherwise create.

Just as with main/subform forms, the first step for creating a main/subreport report is creating the two reports you will later combine. You may already have reports you want to use for this purpose. These two reports are separate reports that are listed separately in the Database window. Expect to make changes to both reports as you work on them; what makes a report look good by itself may not be attractive when you combine it with another. Usually you leave an area in the main report in which you will place the subreport. Figure 13-6 shows the report that will become the main report. Figure 13-7 shows the report that will become the subreport.

Once you have designed both reports, you are ready to add one report to another. Select the report that will be the main report and then switch to the Database window. Since you will drag the report from the Database window to the Design view of the report, you do not want the windows maximized. Next, display the reports in the Database window and highlight the report you want to use as the subreport. Drag the report name from the Database window to the Design view of the main report.

When you drag the report name, the pointer changes to a report icon. When the icon is where you want the subreport, release the mouse. Access adds a subform/subreport control that is the size of the subreport to the report's design. The report's size is the total of the height of the Report Header, Report Footer, Detail, and any group header and footer sections. The subform/subreport's

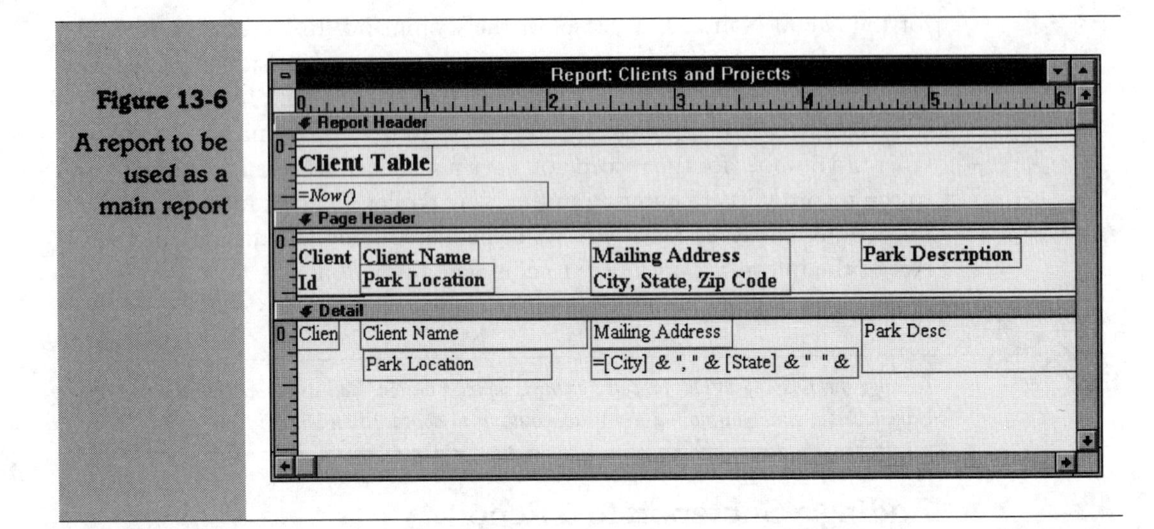


**Figure 13-6** A report to be used as a main report

Can Grow property has a default of Yes so that the subreport's size adjusts according to the number of records printed by the subreport. This control also has text above the control that is the same as the subreport's name. At this point, switch to the main report's design if you need to make any changes to the main report. You can change the subreport control by moving and sizing it. Figure 13-8 shows a report design after adding a subform/subreport control and changing the text above it.

There is also another method available for adding a subreport to the current report you are designing. From the toolbox, select the subform/subreport

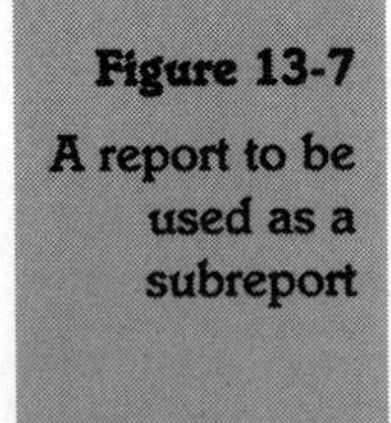

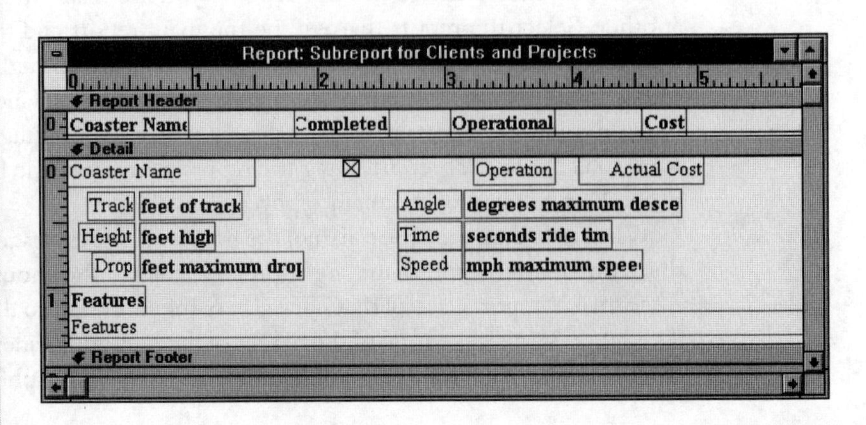


**Figure 13-7** A report to be used as a subreport

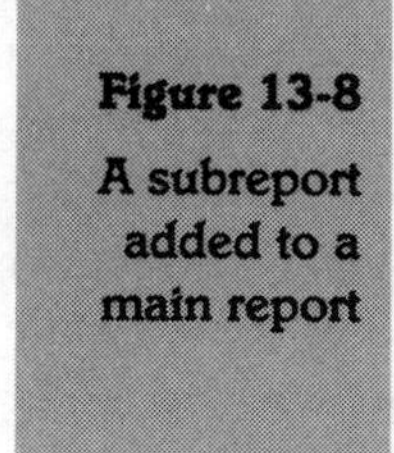

**Figure 13-8** A subreport added to a main report

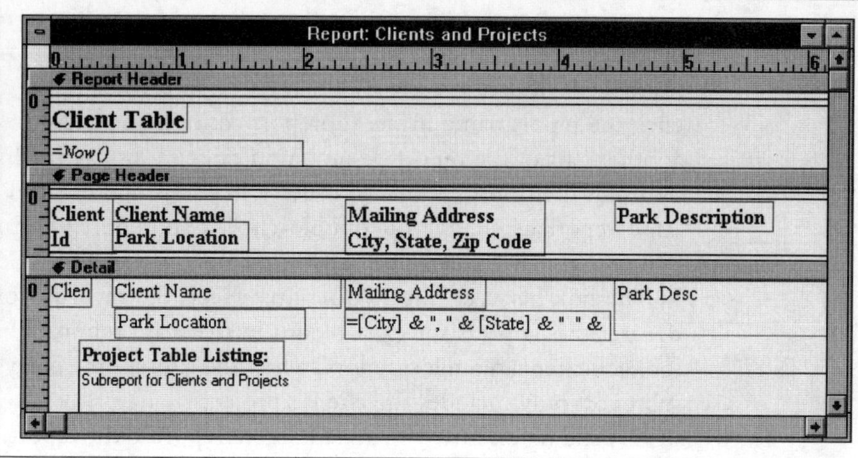


control and then select the location where you want the subform/subreport control placed. When you select a location, Access adds an unbounded subform/subreport control. As with other controls, you can move and size the control and change the text that appears above it. To tell Access which report you want to appear in the subreport control's location, display the property sheet and type the report name after Source Object or use the down arrow to select the name of the report.

Notice that the list for Source Object now includes both reports and forms, with each preceded by Form or Report and a period. Also, when you edit the control's Source Object property by editing the text that appears in the subform/subreport control, the name of the form or report has the same Form or Report and a period to distinguish whether the control's contents are a form or report.

**tip:** *When you create a subreport, you may want to make some changes to where you place controls in the report design. Remove the date from the Report Header section of the subreport and the page number from the Page Footer section, since this information should be part of the main report. Also, any information in the Page Header or Page Footer sections that you want to appear in the subreport should be moved to another section. Page Header and Page Footer sections appear in a subreport at the beginning and ending of the subreport section rather than at the top and bottom of the page.*

Once you add the subreport to the main report, the main report continues to use the same subreport design. When you change the subreport's design and the main report is open, you need to tell the main report to refresh its memory of the subreport's design. Tell Access to update the current report for a subreport's design in one of two ways. You can select the subreport control, click the report name in the subreport control, and then press ENTER or click another part of the report design. You can also display the list of report names by using the Source Object property in the property sheet and selecting the same report again. If you double-click a subreport control when it is not selected, you will open a window containing that report's design.

The link between the two reports selects the records from the subreport's dynaset that appears for each record in the main report. This link means that for each client in a main report, when the subreport displays the projects, the subreport only includes the client's projects.

Depending on how you added the subreport to the report, either Access will create the link between the main report and the subreport or you will have to create this link. When you add a subreport to a report by dragging the report's name from the Database window to the main report's design, Access first checks to see if you have already established a relationship between the two tables or the underlying tables in a query. If you have not, and the tables for the two reports have fields using the same name and data type, Access creates the link that way. Also, when you select a subreport for the Source Object property of the subreport, if the underlying tables of both reports use fields with the same name and data type, Access creates the link. In other cases, you must define the link.

The link between the main report and the subreport is created with the Link Master Fields and Link Child Fields properties for the report. The Link Master Fields contains the name of the field in the main report that matches a field in the subreport. The Link Child Fields contains the name of the field in the subreport that matches a field in the main report. Once you have created both reports, added one report as a subreport to another, and established the link between the two dynasets, you are ready to use this main/subreport report just as you would use any other report. Figure 13-9 shows the part of the report for the third client with the information from both of the client's projects created by the subreport.

**tip:** *If you want the subreport to display only summary data, change the subreport Detail section's Visible property to No. The report will continue to create the Detail section and perform any calculations required, but the Detail section will not be included in the report.*

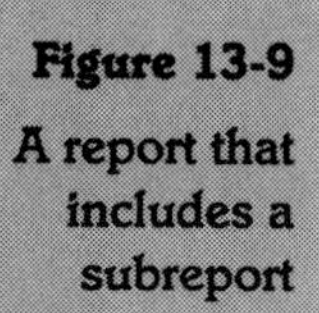

**Figure 13-9**
**A report that includes a subreport**

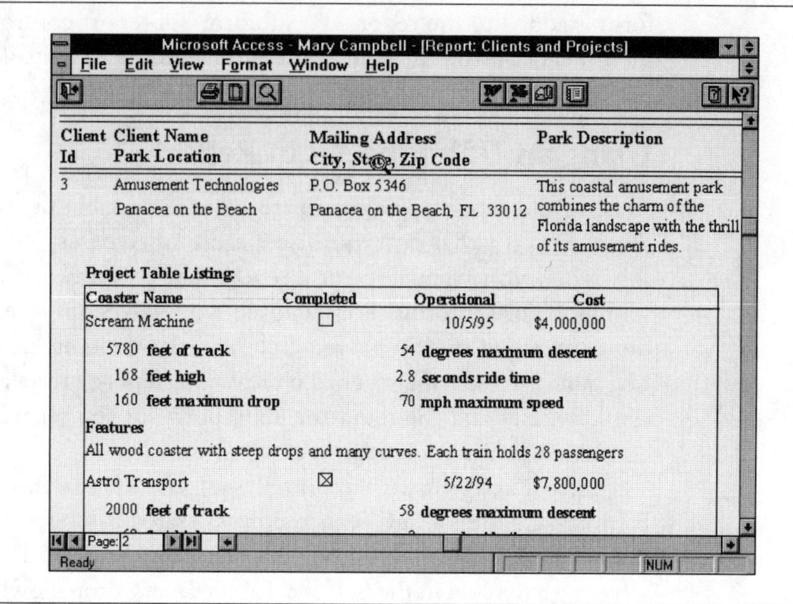


## Adding a Subform to a Report

Another possible combination for using multiple dynasets in a report is adding a subform to a report. This is just like adding one form to another or adding a report as a subreport to another report. When you use a subform in a report, you are not using the form to enter and edit data; you use a subform in a report strictly to affect how the data in the other table or dynaset appears. You can end up with a report/form combination like this by saving a main/subform form with the main form as a report using Save As Report in the File menu. The new report continues to use the same subform even though the main form is now the main report.

Most of the steps are identical to creating main/subform forms or main/subreport reports. First, create the main report and the subform. Next, add the form to the report by either dragging the form from the Database window or by adding a subform/subreport control and changing the control's Source Object property to the name of the form. This time the form name is preceded by the word Form and a period.

Next, check the link between the Link Master Fields and Link Child Fields properties. These two properties link the data in the main report and the subform so that the subform contains related information to the record shown in the report. Figure 13-10 shows the designs of a form and a report. When the form is added to the report as a subform/subreport control below the Department field control, the resulting report looks like Figure 13-11.

## Using an Unbound Main Report

Most of the reports you create are based on a table or dynaset. You can also create a report that does not use a table or dynaset. You might want to do this when you want to print a report that contains other reports or forms as subreports or subforms. For example, you may want a report that prints both the contents of the Employee table and the contents of the Employee Time Log table for a specific week. To create this report, create a report that does not use a dynaset and then add the subreports for the separate reports you want combined into a single report.

Figure 13-12 shows a report design created for this purpose. The Main Report - Coasters and Clients report is created by choosing New from the File menu and then choosing Report and selecting the Blank Report button without selecting a dynaset in the Select a Table/Query drop-down list box. Next, after the controls that appear in the Report Header and Report Footer sections are added, add the subform/subreport controls. The first one is for the Look At Our Coasters report. This is added the same way you added other subreports, as described earlier in this chapter. The second one is for the Coaster Mania

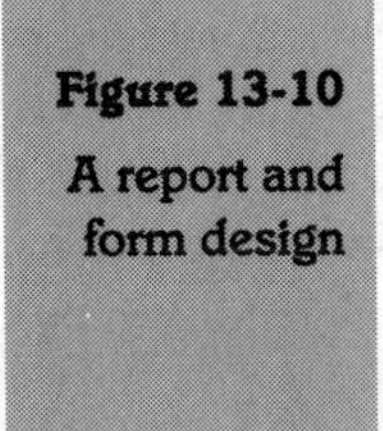

**Figure 13-10**
**A report and form design**

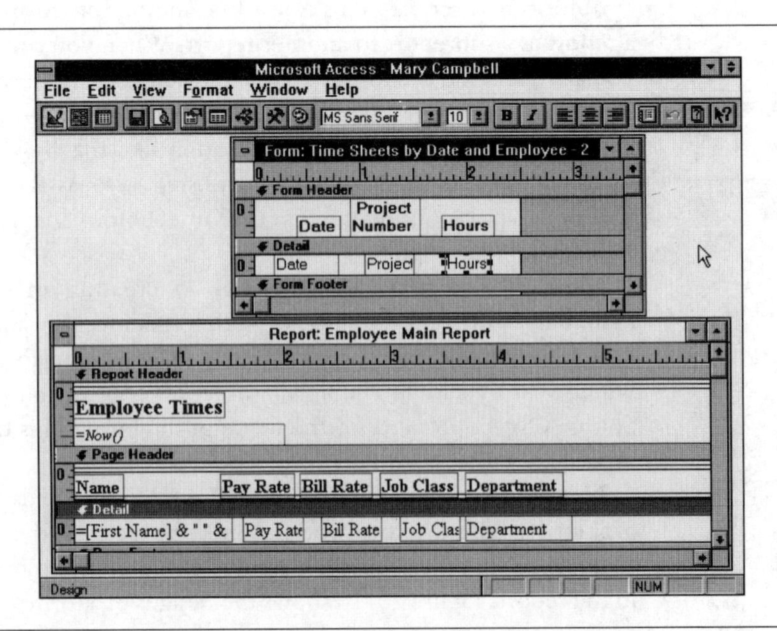

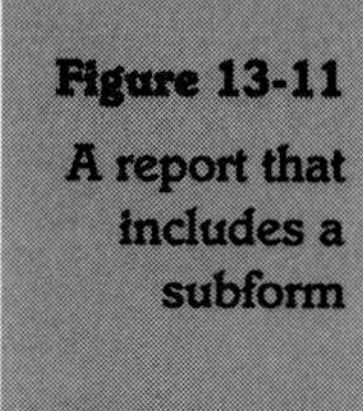

**Figure 13-11** A report that includes a subform

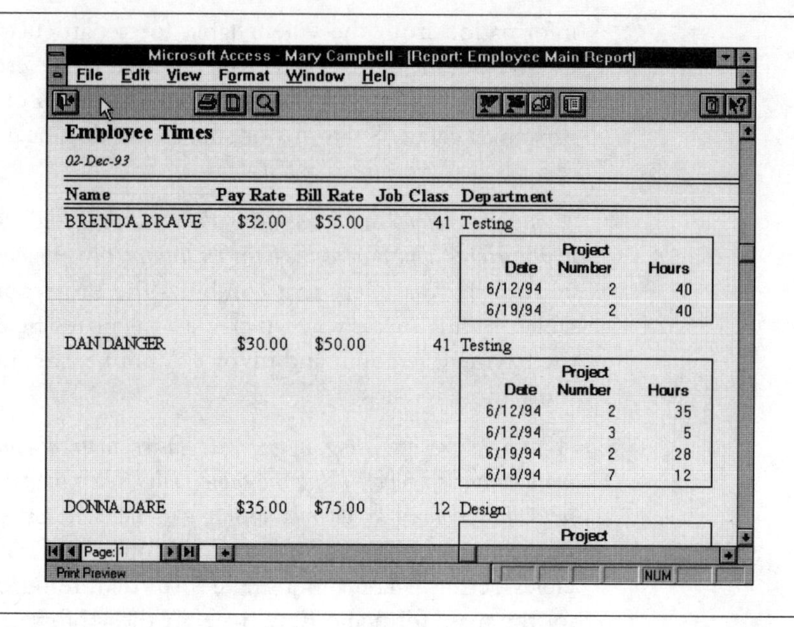


Client List - Plain form. This is added just as you add other subforms, also described earlier in this chapter. Reports can have both subforms and subreports.

**tip:** *You can have nested subforms and subreports. A subform can contain other subforms and a subreport can contain other subforms and subreports. Use this feature to create composites of several tables.*

## Queries to Combine Data from Different Tables

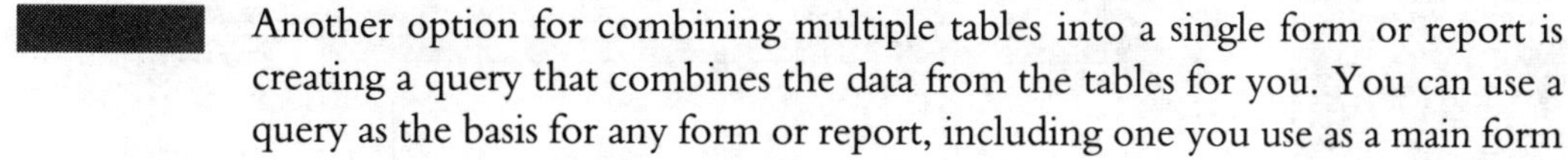

Another option for combining multiple tables into a single form or report is creating a query that combines the data from the tables for you. You can use a query as the basis for any form or report, including one you use as a main form or report or as a subform or subreport.

Using a query over a subform has several advantages over subforms and subreports in some circumstances. Sometimes using a query is better than using a subform or subreport and other times the reverse is true. Using a query for a form or report has these advantages:

- *A query can be more selective about the data from the selected tables that appears in the reports or forms.* For example, if you want a form or report to include information from the Client table for a particular client and all their invoices for the current year from the Invoice Register table, use a query. In a subform or subreport, you would display all of the invoices for that particular client. Subforms or subreports do not use filters to limit the records that appear.

- *A query can have calculated fields that you use either as the basis for selecting which records appear or as the basis for linking two or more tables.* For example, you can have a query that combines the Project and Invoice Register tables. In this query, you can create a calculated field to determine when the Payment Amount and Invoice Amounts are different and then only show those records.
- *A form or report using a query is faster than a main/subform form or a main/subreport report using the same tables when the table for the main form or report has a many-to-one relationship with the table for the subform or subreport.* For example, a query that joins the Employee Time Log and Employee tables performs faster in a single form than using Employee Time Log for the main form and Employee for the subform.
- *A form using a query creates a single datasheet versus the two separate datasheets that you have in a main/subform form.* If your intended form uses the

**Figure 13-12** Report design for a report without an underlying table or dynaset

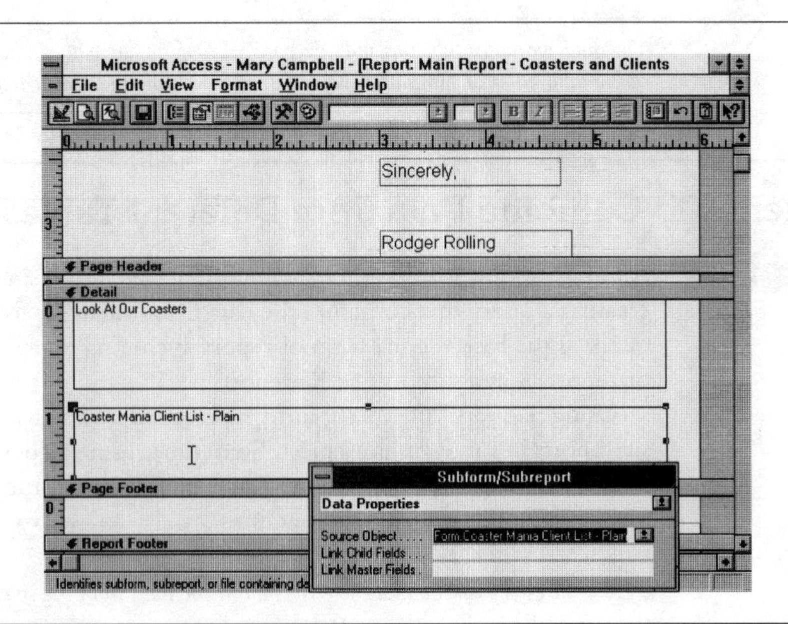

Datasheet view rather than the Form view, you will see all of the fields from both tables using a query.

- *A form or report using a query lets you put fields from any of the tables anywhere in the design.* When you have a main/subform form or a main/subreport report, the fields from the main form or main report are not placed where the subform or subreport control is located and the fields from the table of the subform or subreport only appear within the subform/subreport control's boundaries. Using a query lets you intermingle the fields from both tables.
- *Creating a form or report can be quicker when you already have a query that combines the two or more tables you would otherwise combine with forms and reports.*

Figure 13-13 shows a report using a query that combines the data from the Employee and Invoice Register tables. The fields from the two tables are placed among each other. Also, the records are grouped according to project number and only the records from the Invoice Register table with a Date field of 6/12/94 are included.

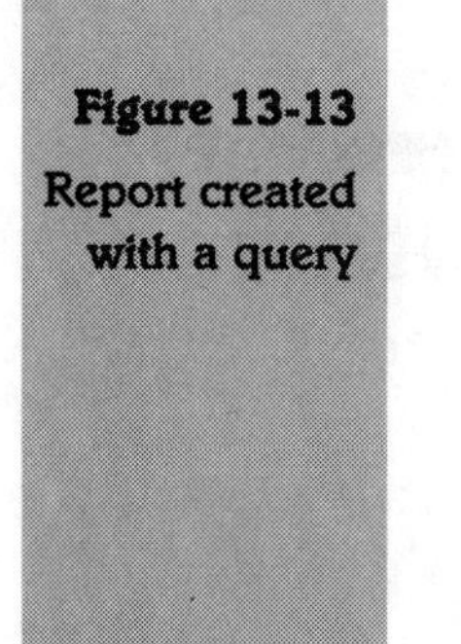

**Figure 13-13**
**Report created with a query**

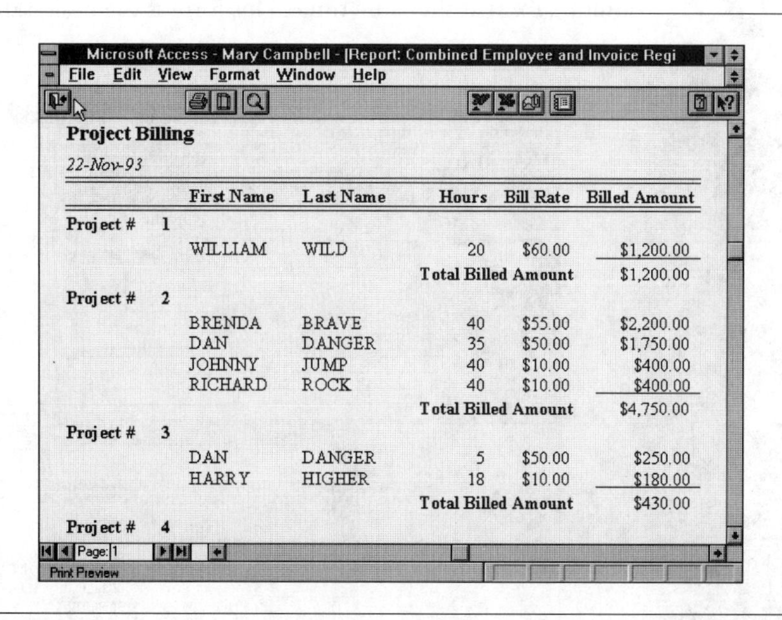


**Project Billing**

*22-Nov-93*

| | First Name | Last Name | Hours | Bill Rate | Billed Amount |
|---|---|---|---|---|---|
| Project # 1 | | | | | |
| | WILLIAM | WILD | 20 | $60.00 | $1,200.00 |
| | | | Total Billed Amount | | $1,200.00 |
| Project # 2 | | | | | |
| | BRENDA | BRAVE | 40 | $55.00 | $2,200.00 |
| | DAN | DANGER | 35 | $50.00 | $1,750.00 |
| | JOHNNY | JUMP | 40 | $10.00 | $400.00 |
| | RICHARD | ROCK | 40 | $10.00 | $400.00 |
| | | | Total Billed Amount | | $4,750.00 |
| Project # 3 | | | | | |
| | DAN | DANGER | 5 | $50.00 | $250.00 |
| | HARRY | HIGHER | 18 | $10.00 | $180.00 |
| | | | Total Billed Amount | | $430.00 |
| Project # 4 | | | | | |

## Using a Crosstab Query as a Subform

One particular time you may want to use a query as a subform is when you want the results from a crosstab query combined with another table. In Chapter 7, you learned how to create crosstab queries that calculate totals of groups of records. You can create a crosstab query that totals the values for groups in a table and then use that query in a subform or subreport when you want the totals in another form or report.

Figure 13-14 shows both Design and Datasheet views of the same crosstab query. This query groups the records in the Invoice Register by project number and then totals the project's invoices for each year. You can see how the project numbers label each of the rows in the resulting dynaset. The column headings of the crosstab query are created by extracting the year from the invoice dates. This query has the Column Headings query property set to 1991, 1992, 1993, 1994. (In Access version 1, choose Query Properties from the View menu and enter the column headings after Fixed Column Headings.) The fixed column headings are necessary when you plan to use the query in a report. If you do not have fixed column headings, the headings will constantly change and the form or report design will not adjust for the altered headings.

The form that this example uses (you can do the same thing with a report) is shown in two copies in Figure 13-15 so you can see the design and the resulting form at the same time. This form is the design that will be used as the

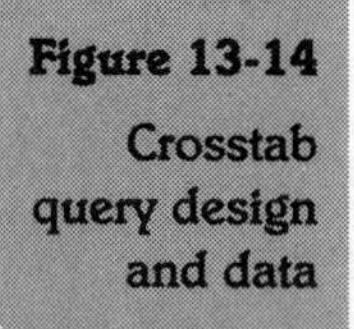
**Figure 13-14** Crosstab query design and data

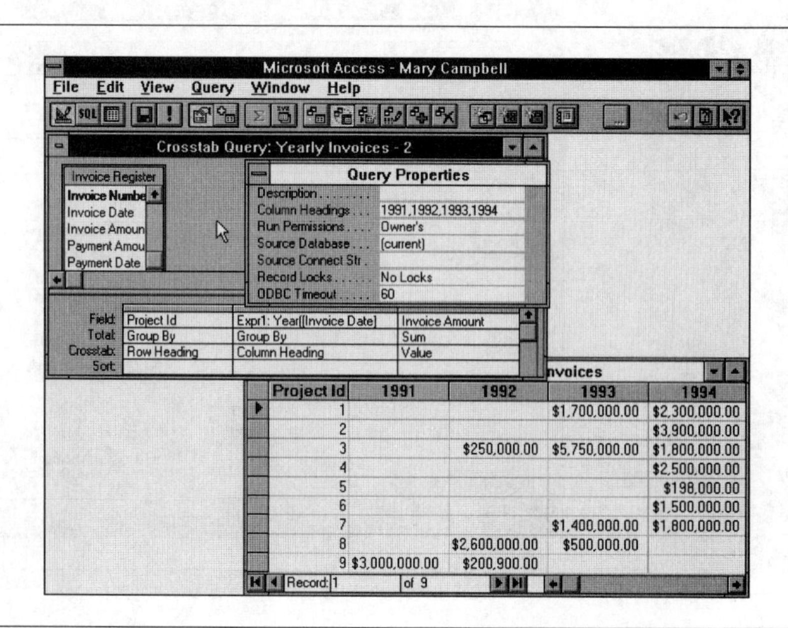

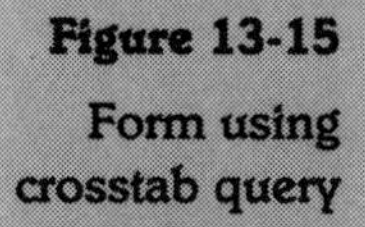

**Figure 13-15** Form using crosstab query

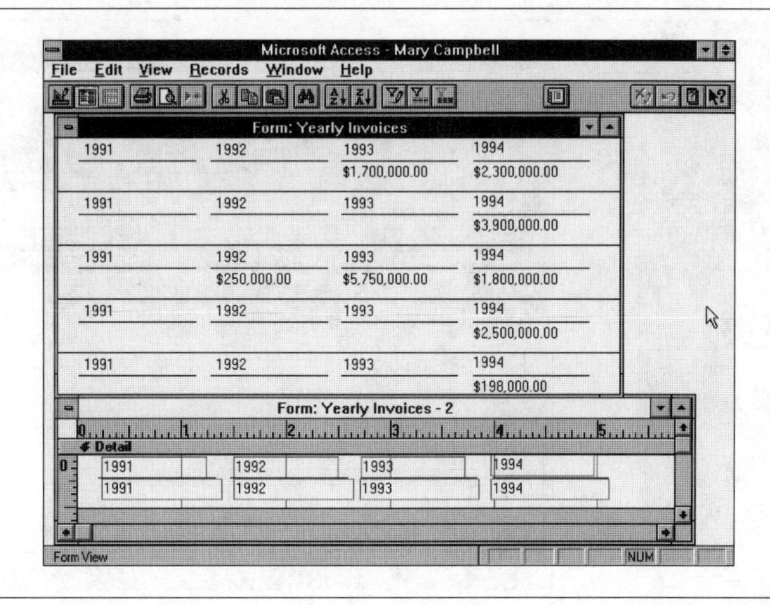


subform. The form is created by using the Tabular Form Wizard and making a few changes to the design.

The report design is shown in Figure 13-16. In this design, the subform/subreport control has the Source Object property set to Yearly Invoices, the Link Master Fields property is set to Coaster Id, and the Link Child Fields property is set to Project Id. Other than the subform/subreport control, the rest of the report is created with the Groups/Totals Report Wizard report and then moved closer together. Also, the control for the Completed field is replaced with an option button. When this report's design is complete, the finished report looks like Figure 13-17.

In this case, you can present the same information using groups in a subreport. Figure 13-18 shows a report that uses the subreport shown below. In this report, the report groups the records together according to the year; the expression for grouping the records is =Year([Invoice Date]). The =Year([Invoice Date]) Footer section contains label and text box controls that display the total in a set format, such as "Total Invoices for 1993: 9350000".

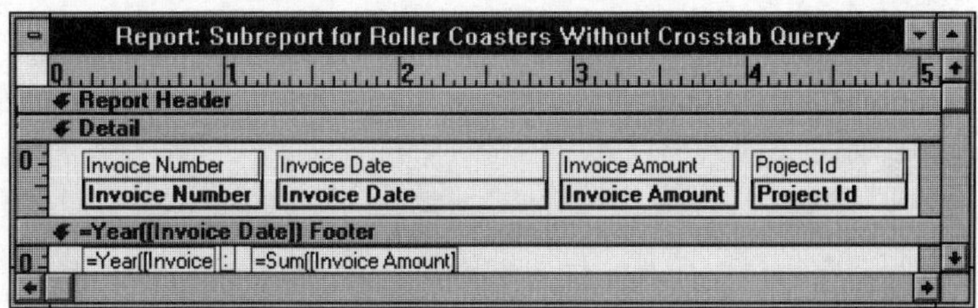

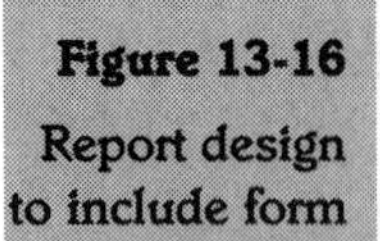

**Figure 13-16**

Report design to include form

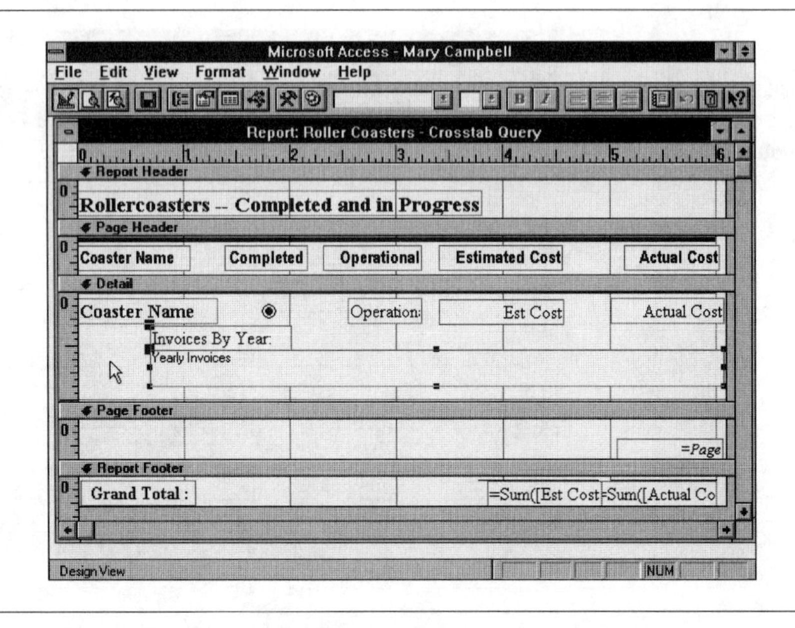


**Figure 13-17**

Report using a subform of a crosstab query

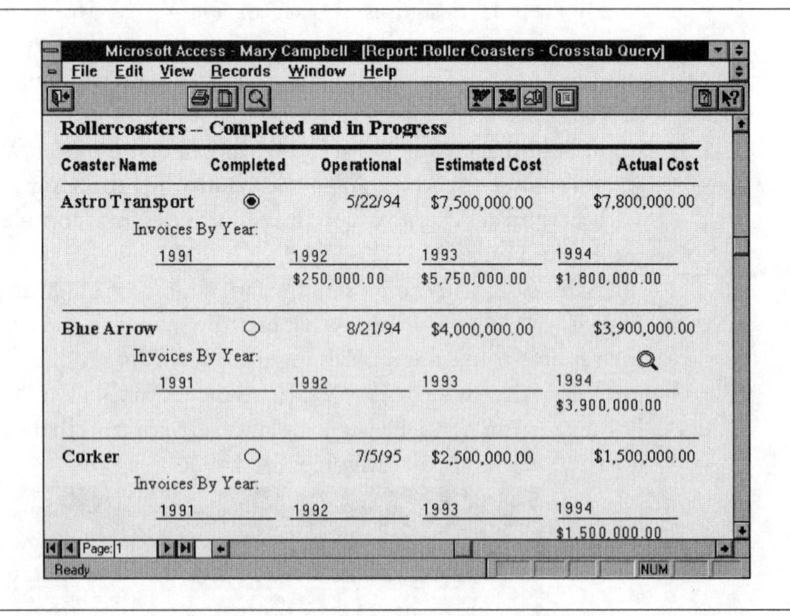

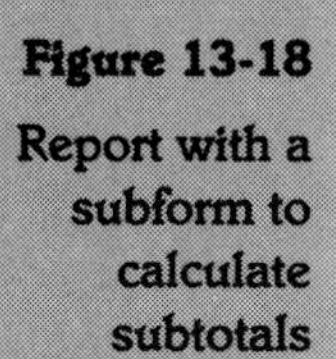

**Figure 13-18** Report with a subform to calculate subtotals

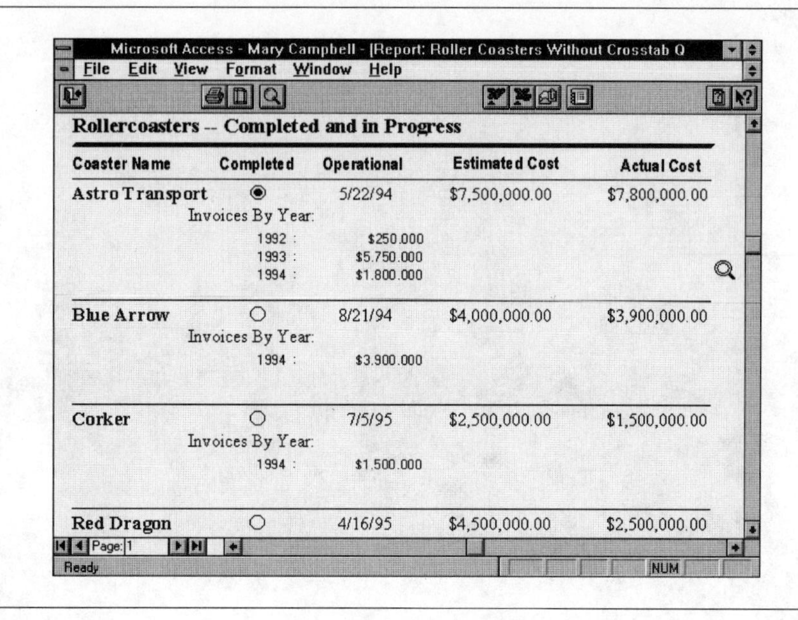


The other special feature of the subreport is that the Detail section's Visible property is set to No. Hiding the Detail section means that the report only produces the =Year([Invoice Date]) Footer section for each year. When you combine this report with the report in Figure 13-18, the yearly totals are calculated for the invoices of each of the projects separately. Figure 13-18 shows the beginning of the resulting report. You can see that the year's total invoices are listed vertically instead of horizontally, but the results are the same.

**Quick Reference**

**To Add a Subform or Subreport to a Form or Report** Drag the form or report name from the Database window to where you want the subform or subreport to start in the main form or report. You can also select the subform/subreport tool from the toolbox. Point to where you want the subform or subreport to start and then change the Source Object property for the control to the name of the form or report.

# Chapter 14

# Using Color and Effects in Reports and Forms

THE form and report features you have learned about so far let you choose the information you want to present. This chapter shows how to adjust the appearance of the information. You can add boxes and lines to add emphasis and to separate different parts of a form or report. You can also enhance forms and reports by changing alignment and fonts and adding three-dimensional effects, colors, and borders. While all of these features can be applied to both forms and reports, some features are used more often with forms and others are used more often with reports.

The features described in this chapter—adding lines and boxes, using different font styles and sizes, and adding color or shading—improve your form's or report's appearance without changing its contents. Think of these features as similar to those that distinguish a Mercedes-Benz from a pared-down budget-oriented car. Both cars will get you where you are going, but the Mercedes-Benz has features that make the drive more enjoyable. The enhancements that you add to your forms and reports make using them easier and more pleasant.

Figure 14-1 shows a very simple form. This same form can be enhanced to look like Figure 14-2 using the features described in this chapter.

Besides changing the appearance of your forms and reports through style enhancements, you can set the appearance of your forms and reports by changing the defaults. You change the defaults for a single form or report by changing the default properties of the controls you plan to add. You can also change the appearance of new forms and reports by using a *template,* which is a model that sets up how the form or report appears.

## Adding Lines and Rectangles to Forms and Reports

The forms and reports you create using Access Wizards use lines to separate sections and indicate totals. The lines and rectangles you add to forms and reports can emphasize portions of the form or report or separate one part from another.

**Figure 14-1**
**A plain report showing contents of the Client table**

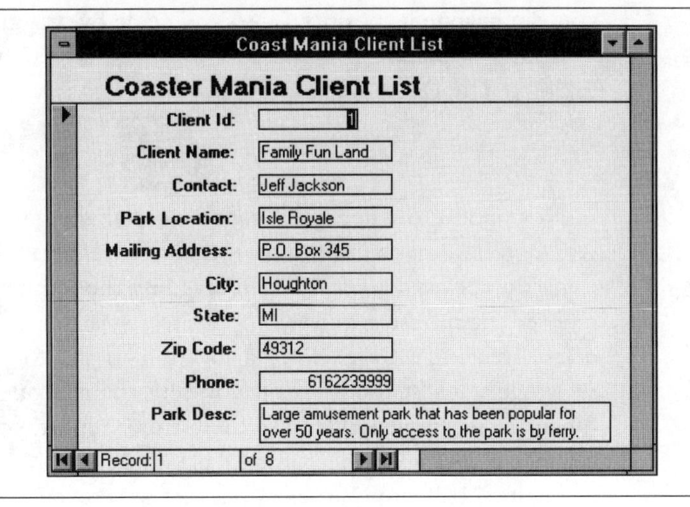


You add lines by selecting the Line tool in the toolbox, which looks like this:

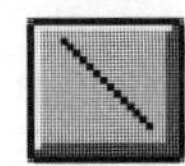

Next, point to where you want the line to start and drag the pointer. The Line tool draws a straight line from where you start dragging the pointer to where you release the mouse. You also can add a default line by clicking a location in the form or report design. This default line is a horizontal line starting at the location you select and continuing for one inch. Once the line is added,

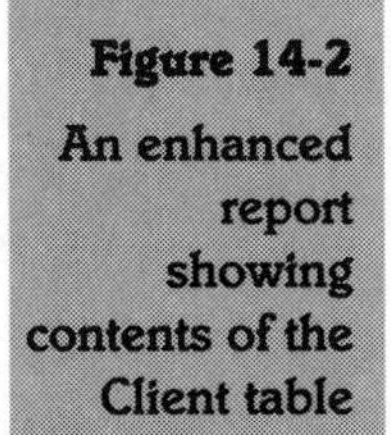

**Figure 14-2**
**An enhanced report showing contents of the Client table**

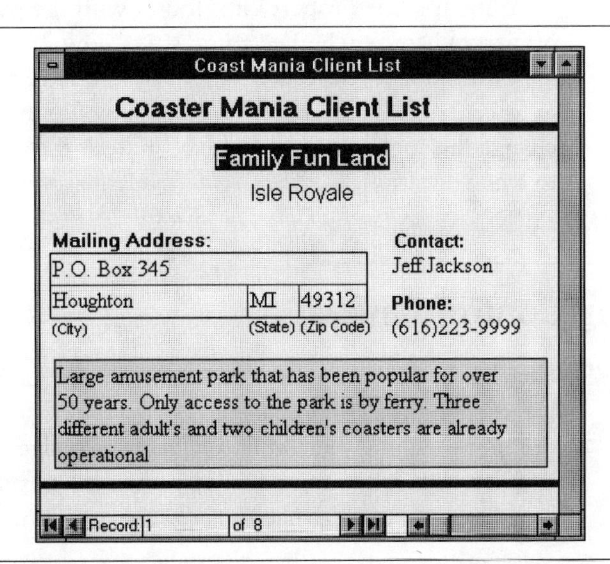

you can change its position, size, and angle by dragging the control's handles.

Adding a rectangle is just as easy. First, select the Rectangle tool in the toolbox. The Rectangle tool looks like this:

Next, point to where you want the rectangle to start and drag the pointer to where you want the opposite corner. The Rectangle tool draws a rectangle using the spot where you began dragging the pointer and the spot where you released the mouse as the two opposite corners of the box. You also can add a default rectangle by clicking a location in the form or report design. This rectangle starts at the location you select and is one-half inch tall and wide. Once the rectangle is added to the form or report, you can change its position and size by dragging the control's handles.

Figure 14-3 shows an example that uses several lines and boxes. The lines are made thicker than the default; you will learn how to change line thickness later in this chapter. In this report, the boxes group different pieces of data. The lines are added to the Report Header section to emphasize the report's title (not shown in the report design in Figure 14-3) and in the Detail section to separate the park information from the coaster information. When you add boxes like the ones in Figure 14-3, they are initially placed on top of any other controls. For example, the box in the upper-left corner of Figure 14-3 is covering other controls that lie beneath it. The next section shows how to move a control from the top layer to the bottom layer. Later in the chapter, you will learn how to change the thickness and color of the lines and rectangles.

A line has one property not found with the other controls. The Line Slant property changes whether a line slants down or up. Select \ to have the line slant from upper left to lower right or / to have the line slant from upper right to lower left. Use this property to quickly flip the direction of a line's slant. To change the angle of a line, drag a handle at the end of the line with the mouse to a new location.

## Changing Control Layers

Each of the controls you add to a form or report is placed on top of whatever was there before. This is like creating a collage out of the controls in the form or report design. When children create a collage, they glue one item on top of another without concern for what they are covering. With a form or report, you may need to see what you are covering. You can take one control and put

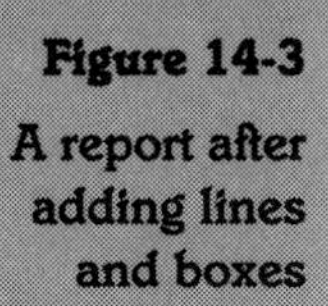

**Figure 14-3**
**A report after adding lines and boxes**

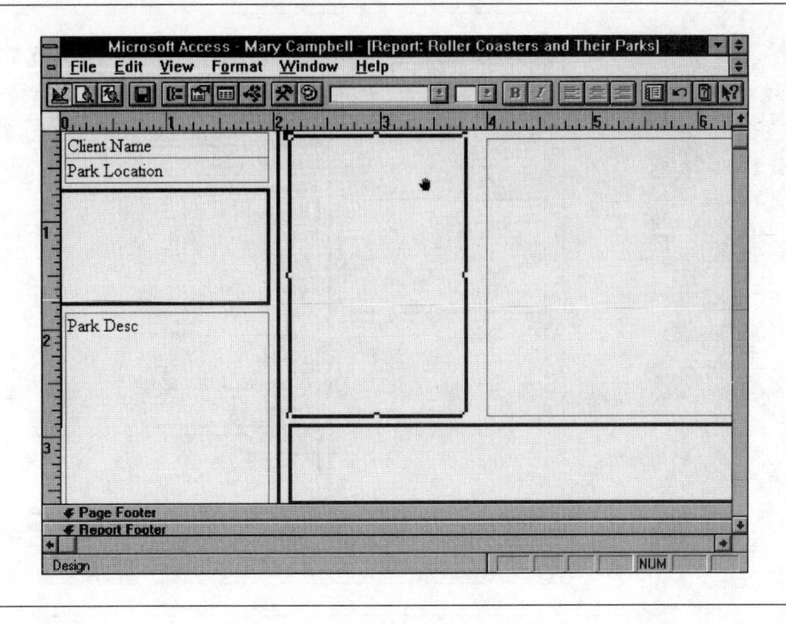


it behind another—for example, move a rectangle behind other controls that it was covering. You can also move the other controls on top—for example, move controls hidden by a rectangle on top of the rectangle.

To move a control from the front to below the other controls, choose Send to Back from the Format menu (the Layout menu in Access version 1). For example, the rectangle chosen in Figure 14-3 covers the controls for the mailing address, phone, and contact fields. When you choose Send to Back from the Format menu (the Layout menu in Access version 1), the report design changes to show the mailing address, phone, and contact fields, as shown in Figure 14-4. When you use the report design shown in Figure 14-4 after putting the rectangles behind the other controls, the report looks like Figure 14-5. Now the rectangles are behind the controls that they previously covered. Conversely, you can take a control from behind other controls and put it on top by choosing Bring to Front from the Format menu (the Layout menu in Access version 1).

## Adding Style to Your Forms and Reports

The style enhancements you can make to controls include alignment, color, three-dimensionality, fonts, and borders. These properties are listed in the bottom half of the property sheet and in the property sheet by themselves when you select Layout Properties at the top of Access version 2's property sheet.

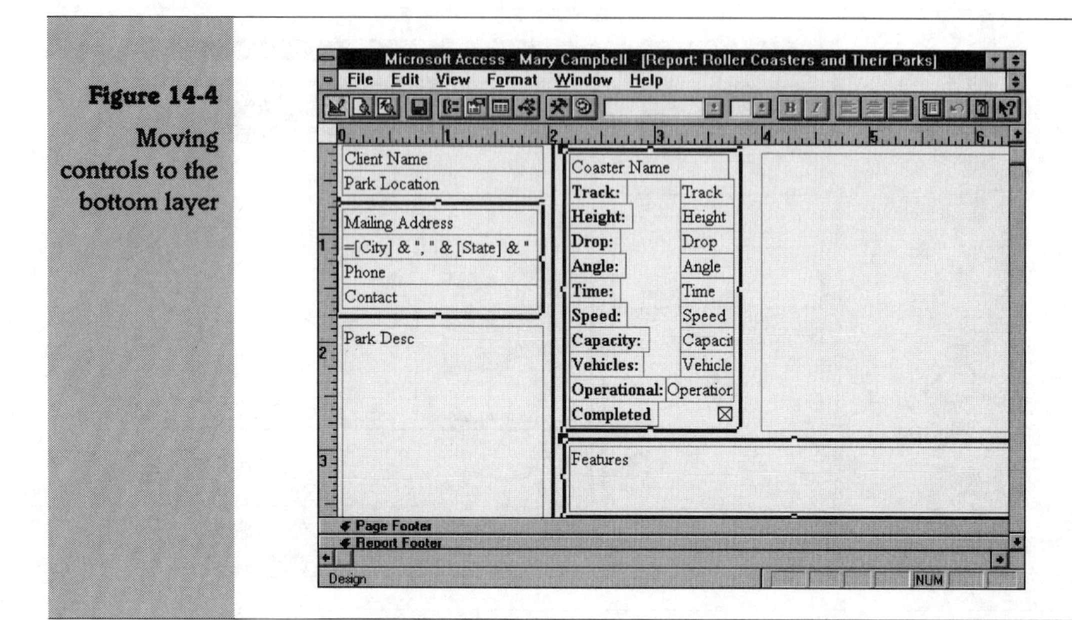


**Figure 14-4** Moving controls to the bottom layer

Access also has buttons in the toolbar to make these style enhancements even easier to use. Style changes such as color and borders can be made with the Palette. You add styles to a form or report by changing the properties of the control either through the property sheet or through the toolbar. When you

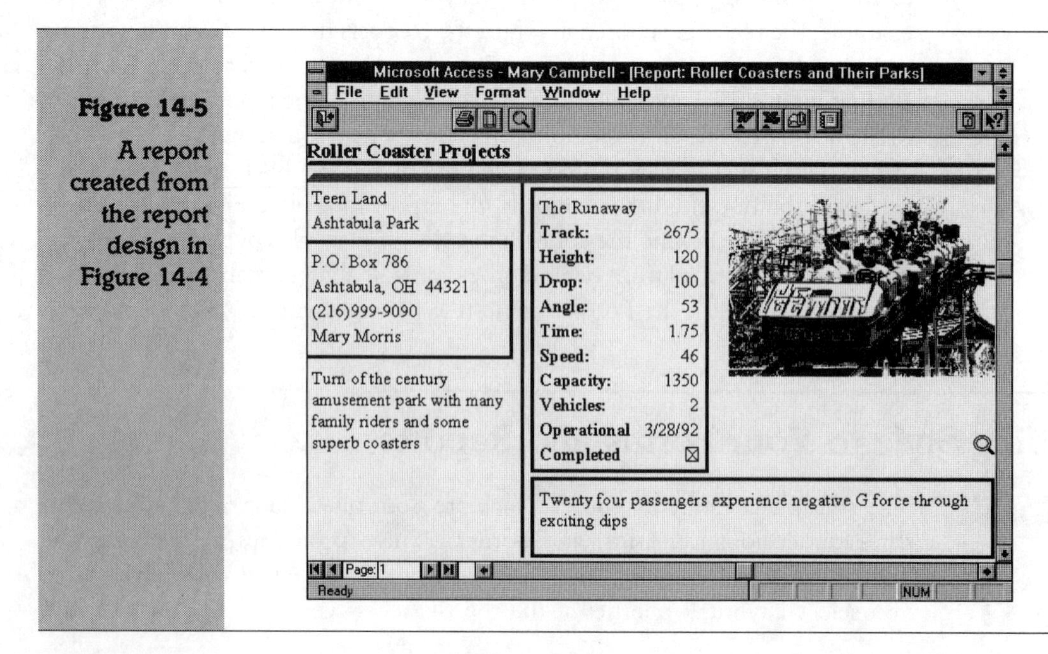


**Figure 14-5** A report created from the report design in Figure 14-4

select a control that uses the style enhancements described in this section, the middle and right sections of the toolbar change to look like this:

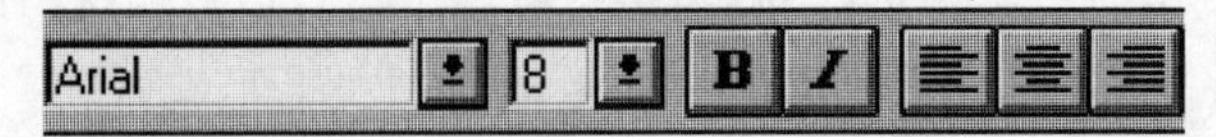


These new toolbar boxes and buttons let you easily change the font, font size, weight, italics, and alignment of the selected control. (Access version 1 has two more buttons that underline text and return alignment to the general setting.) Also, when you change the style of a control, the control in the form or report design appears with the alignment, font, color, three-dimensional effect, and borders that you have added or changed.

**tip:** *You can change the appearance of several controls at once using the toolbar and the Palette. When you select multiple controls in a form or report design and then select buttons in the toolbar or Palette, the changes affect all selected controls. If you look at the property sheet while multiple controls are selected, many of the properties are empty because they do not have the same setting for all of the selected controls.*

## Setting Alignment

You can change the alignment of any control that uses text. Alignment determines whether the characters that appear in the control start at the left side of the control, end at the right side of the control, or are centered in the control's position. The default of general alignment is to right-align data fields that contain numbers and dates and to left-align all other controls. Change the alignment of a control by clicking one of these three buttons:

The first button left-aligns the text in the control, the second button centers the text in the control, and the third button right-aligns the text in the control. Access version 1 has a fourth button that returns the control to general alignment. You can also change the alignment by changing the Text Alignment property in the property sheet and then selecting General, Left, Center, or Right.

Figure 14-6 shows a report that uses different alignments. The controls for the Employee Id and Hours fields use general alignment. The label and field for Project Number use center alignment. The control for the Date field uses left alignment, and the controls for the Employee Id and Hours labels use right alignment.

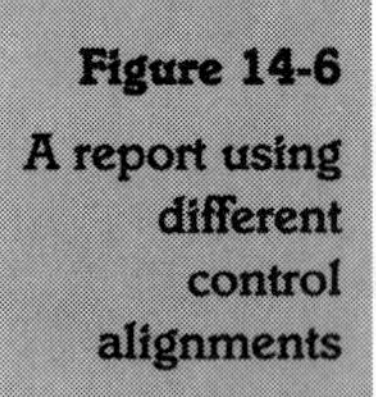

**Figure 14-6** A report using different control alignments

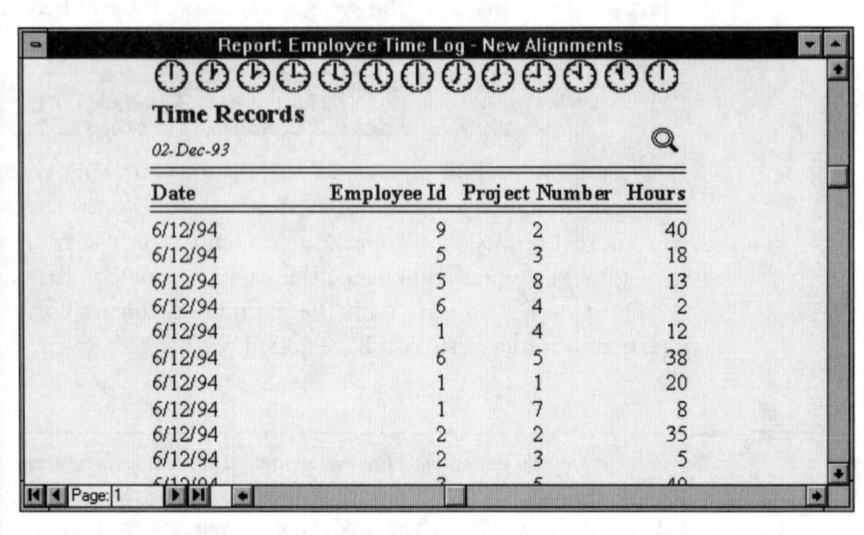

**tip:** *Set the headers to use the same alignment as the entries below them. Your forms and reports look more professional when the column headings align with the data. Usually, you will change the alignment of labels that are used for column headings of date and numeric fields to right alignment so that the text aligns with the dates and numbers.*

## Setting the Font for Controls

Using the same font for all of the text in a form or report is dull. Using several kinds of type enlivens your form or report and lets you emphasize important information. For our purposes, a *font* is a collection of features that describe how the text appears. The name of a font tells you the font's general appearance, but a font also has size and weight. (*Weight* is simply the boldness of the type—a very thin, lightweight type is useful for copy that you don't want to stand out; a heavy, very bold type draws the reader's attention to text you really want to emphasize.) The fonts you use can have other features such as italics and underlining. Each control has its font properties set separately, so changing the font of one control does not affect the others.

A font's name sets the style of the characters in a form or report. The default is Helv (Helvetica) in Windows 3.0 and Arial or MS SanSerif in Windows 3.1, depending on whether the Layout for Print property of the form or report is Yes or No. To change the font style, select one of the font names from the Font

Name drop-down list box in the property sheet or from the Font Name box in the toolbar, which looks like this:

The list of names includes all of the fonts available to Windows. These fonts include the fonts installed as part of Windows, the fonts available through your printer, and any fonts you have added to Windows. If you do not see a font style that you think should be available, check the Windows Control Panel program to see if the font is correctly installed.

Figure 14-7 shows a few of the fonts you can use. Some of these are available through Windows 3.1, so if you are using Access version 1 using Windows 3.0, your fonts will have different names. Also, several fonts in Figure 14-7 are provided through CorelDraw, which includes additional TrueType fonts as well as extensive clip art. Several companies make additional fonts that—once installed—are available to Access as well as to other Windows applications.

When selecting a font for a control, keep two ideas in mind. First, don't use more than two or three fonts in a form or report since too much variety focuses attention on the different fonts rather than on the information you are trying to present. Second, select the font that fits the purpose of the form or report. For example, the calligraphy font in Figure 14-7, while pretty, is inappropriate for most business situations.

Which font names are listed depends on the Layout for Print property of the form or report. The default for this property is No for forms and Yes for reports. When this property is set to Yes, the font names list includes all of the screen fonts and any installed scalable fonts. When this property is set to No, the font names list includes all of the printer fonts and any installed scalable fonts.

When you use a screen font to print or a printer font to display the information on the screen, Windows makes the closest substitution possible. Since the substitution is not exact, you'll see differences between how the form or report appears on the screen and how it looks on paper.

**tip:** *If you have TrueType fonts, use them. These fonts look the same when displayed on the screen and when printed. Also, Access does not have to make substitutions depending on whether you are looking at the form or report on the screen or printing it. When you use TrueType fonts and preview the output, the preview matches much more closely what you get when you print the form or report.*

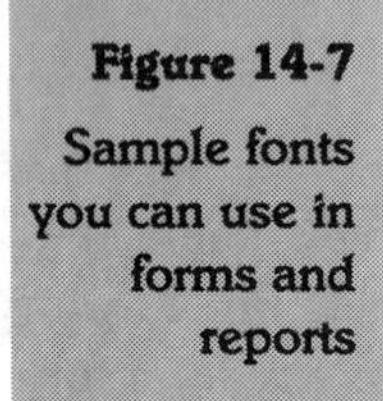

**Figure 14-7** Sample fonts you can use in forms and reports

You can also select the size of the font for a control. The font size is set by the Font Size property in the property sheet or from the Font Size box in the toolbar, which looks like this:

The list of sizes includes many of the font sizes available for the selected font name. Not all font names have every size possible. One of the advantages with scalable fonts such as TrueType fonts is that you can use any size. Use the Windows Control Panel program to check whether the selected font is scalable. When setting the size of a scalable font, you can type the size of the font you want, so you can have other font sizes than the ones listed.

The remaining features seem more like those you would expect from a word processor than a database product. The Font Weight property sets how heavy or light the characters appear. Select between Thin, Extra Light, Light, Normal, Medium, Semi-bold, Bold, Extra Bold, and Heavy in the Font Weight drop-down list box. A shortcut to quickly change the Font Weight property of a control to Bold is to click the Bold button in the toolbar, which looks like this:

You can also italicize the text in a control by changing the Font Italic property from No to Yes. A shortcut for changing this property is clicking the Italic button in the toolbar, which looks like this:

You also can underline the text in a control. Note that you underline the *text* in the control rather than underlining the control. (If you want a line under

the control itself, add it using the Line tool.) To underline text in a control, change the Font Underline property from No to Yes or click the Underline button in the Access version 1 toolbar, which looks like this:

Use these font properties to draw attention to the important parts of a form or report. The following illustration shows a form that is enhanced with various font properties:

Invoice Register
Coaster Mania
Invoice Register
Invoice Number: 975
Invoice Date: 2/1/91
Invoice Amount: $500,000.00
Payment Amount: $500,000.00
Payment Date: 3/13/91
Project Id: 9
Total Invoices: $29,398,900.00
Record: 1 of 28

In this form, the controls for the fields use the Times New Roman font while the controls for the field names use Arial. The font size for the fields and their labels is 14 points while the font size for the two label controls in the Form Header section is 16 points. Also, the Invoice Register label is underlined and the control for the Invoice Number field is italicized.

Access remembers the printer that is currently selected when you create a form or report. Access does this because the form or report may use fonts that are specific to the selected printer. For example, if you switch from printing a report that uses the CG Times font available on a Hewlett-Packard LaserJet Series III to printing the report on a Hewlett-Packard LaserJet Series II, Access must substitute another font for the CG Times font selection.

## Setting Dimensions, Colors, and Borders

Forms and reports can look bland without something to liven them up, but there are many ways to make a form or report look more interesting. You can make a control appear three-dimensional. You can use colors to brighten the forms (and also to separate sections of a form or report). You can use different colors for different forms so users know immediately that they are using the correct form. Since most printers do not print colors, you will primarily use colors for forms. Borders for controls can be set to different widths; you don't have to use the default hairline border, which you have seen up to this point in the book.

While you can make entries for a control's colors and borders when you change a control's properties, Access has a better way. Select Palette from the View menu or select the Palette button to display this Palette:

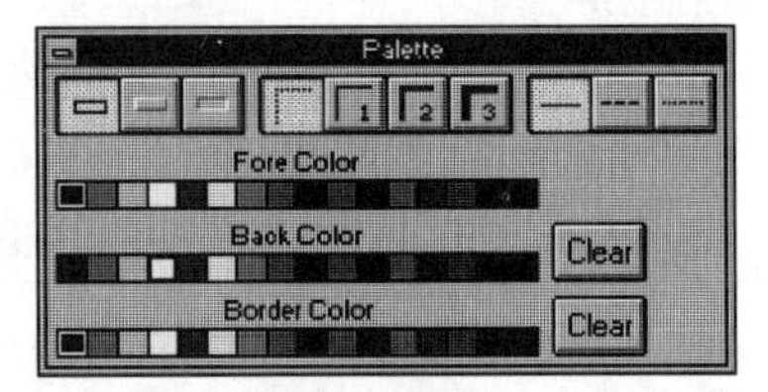


This Palette sets the color, the border, and the three-dimensional appearance of a control. In Access version 1, the Palette looks different but provides the same features.

## ADDING DIMENSIONS TO CONTROLS

You can give controls a three-dimensional appearance in one of three styles. These three types—Normal, Raised, and Sunken—are exaggerated here:

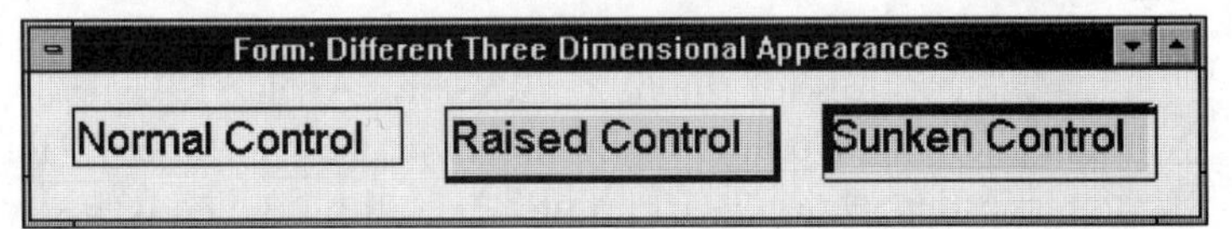


Select one of these by clicking one of the first three buttons in the Palette shown previously. In Access version 1, you set the style by selecting the Normal, Raised, or Sunken option button. You can also select one of these types for the control's Special Effect property. In Access version 1, the Normal choice is called Color. Normal is the default for most controls. Raised has a white border on the top and left sides and a dark gray border on the bottom and right sides, while Sunken has a dark gray border on the top and left sides with a white border on the bottom and left sides. When you select Raised or Sunken for a control's appearance, the control uses the same colors as buttons in the toolbar and command buttons. These colors are set by the Control Panel program. Also, when a control's appearance is Raised or Sunken, changing the border (described later in the chapter) has no effect. When you create your own macros, you can design them to change the three-dimensional appearance for controls as you work with the control's data.

**tip:** *Command button, toggle button, and raised and sunken border colors are set through the Control Panel. The Button Face, Button Highlight, and Button Shadow screen elements set the front, top, and bottom appearance of these controls. When you change the button colors with the Control Panel, you also change several other colors in Access, as well as changing the button colors used by all Windows applications.*

## SETTING COLORS OF CONTROLS

Using the Palette, you can set the color of text, the border around controls, and the background color of a control. Once you select the control, the Palette indicates the selected colors of the control. A control can have different colors for the text, fill, and border.

Not all of the options are available for all controls. For controls that have a raised or sunken appearance, you can only change the text color by changing the Fore Color (Text, in Access version 1). Other color changes have no effect. Several controls use the Back Color to select the colors that fill the control. In Access version 1, the back color is set by selecting a color after Fill. Option groups, rectangles, and labels also use the Clear button or check box at the end of the back color. When you select Clear, the control is transparent, so the control shows whatever controls are behind it. When this check box is cleared, which is the default, the control is filled with the selected color even if the color is white.

You can see the color settings after Fore Color, Back Color, and Border Color in the property sheet. These properties contain a number representing the selected color. Since you probably don't want to memorize the color code for each color, it's easiest to select colors using the Palette. The Back Style property matches the Clear button or check box after the back color in the Palette.

**tip:** *Do not use the Fore Color, Back Color, and Border Color properties in the property sheet to change color. These properties use a number that represents the red, green, and blue that create the color. You can't necessarily understand the color a number indicates. Selecting the color using the Palette lets you see the color you are selecting. You can set a color with the Palette when you want to know the number for a specific color. You will need to know the number for a color when you set the color of a control in a form or report through a macro or procedure. For example, you can change the color of a control depending on a field's value.*

The following illustration shows a form that has the colors of several controls (which appear as shades of gray) and sections altered:

Entering Projects

Coaster Id: 1 Coaster Name: Scream Machine

Page 1

Coaster Name: Scream Machine

Coaster Identification Number: 1

Client Identification Number: 3

Planned Operational Date: 10/5/95

Estimated Cost: $7,800,000

This form has three pages.

Record: 1 of 9

In this form, the color of the Form Header section is changed to cyan and the Form Footer section is changed to black; the text in the Form Footer section is changed to white. When you print a form or report with colors, how the colors look when printed depends on how your printer converts colors into shades of gray.

**tip:** *When adding color to a form or report, choose a light color. The people who read the forms and reports will find it easier to read characters against a light background rather than a dark one.*

## CHANGING THE BORDER OF A CONTROL

All controls have borders that you can adjust. Some controls, such as the labels for check boxes, option buttons, and text boxes, have as a default not to display any border. Other controls, such as option groups, list boxes, and combo boxes, have as a default to display a thin black border. You can set the thickness and color of the border and whether it displays.

To select whether a border appears around a control, clear or select the Clear button to the right of Border Color in the Palette. You can also change the Border Style property in the property sheet. When Clear is selected or the Border Style property is Clear, the control does not display the control's border in the form or report. In the form or report's design, you will still see the thin border, although it is dimmed to indicate that it will not appear. When Clear is not selected or the Border Style is Normal, the control's border appears in the form or report. Also, any color or border width setting appears on the form's or report's design.

Select the border's width with the buttons at the top of the Palette or with the Border Width property. In Access version 1, the border width buttons are at the bottom of the Palette. You can visually select the border's width by clicking one of the buttons. If you use the Border Width property in the property sheet, select between Hairline and 1 pt through 6 pt. The buttons in Access version 2's Palette make a border width hairline, 1 point, 2 points, or 3 points. The buttons in Access version 1 match the seven choices available for the Border Width property.

The border's color is set by the color button for Border Color in the Palette or through the Border Color property in the property sheet. Selecting a border's color is just like selecting the foreground and background color for a control.

Figure 14-8 shows a report that uses different border styles. The Employee Id and Last Name boxes use thicker borders than the remaining fields. The labels that identify the fields have borders that appear onscreen and when printed, since Clear is not selected in the Palette for the border. The graphic on the left side of the employee data is added as an unbound object frame; you will learn about those in the next chapter.

## Setting the Default Properties of Form and Report Controls

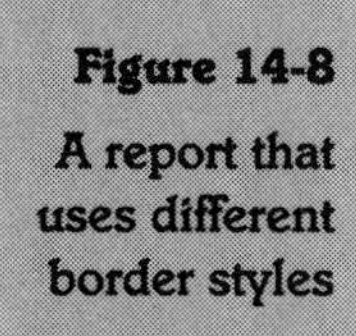

You can set the properties as you add controls to a form or report or before you add them. Set the default for controls by changing the properties of the tools in the toolbox. The default properties apply to all of the controls of that

**Figure 14-8** A report that uses different border styles

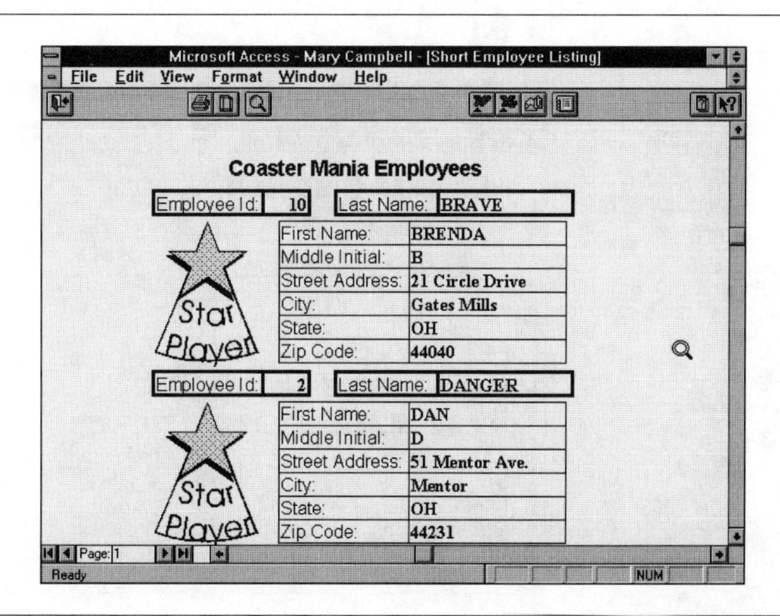

type that you add to the current form or report. When you want to use a set of default control properties for multiple forms or reports, you can create templates that store default settings. Use these templates, as described later in the chapter, whenever you create forms and reports.

## Setting Property Defaults

Setting property defaults for a form or report is just like setting property settings for a control added to a form or report. Simply click the tool in the toolbox while the property sheet appears. The property sheet changes to show only the properties you can set as the default for controls of the selected type. Figure 14-9 shows the property sheet displaying the default properties for a text box in a report. You can see that the title bar changes to Default and the name of the type of control. Most of the properties you see listed are a subset of the properties you can set for the individual controls. You have learned about these properties in prior chapters; later you will learn about the properties that are specifically default properties. At this point, change the properties in the property sheet just as you change the properties for specific parts of forms and reports. Any control of that type that you subsequently add to the form or report uses the new settings you have made to the control.

Figure 14-10 shows a report created by changing the default properties. Changing text font and size is easier if you change the default properties because

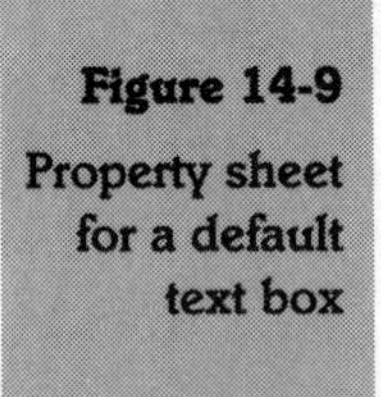

**Figure 14-9** Property sheet for a default text box

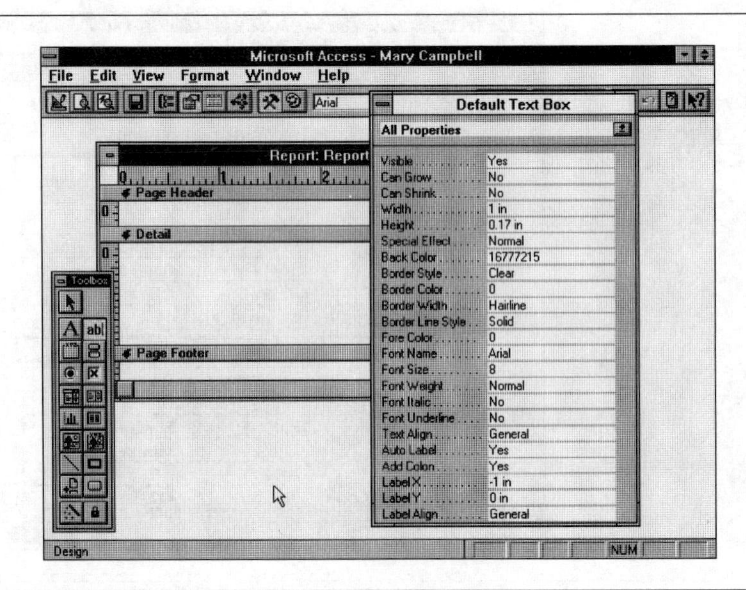

you make the change to the tool in the toolbox, which applies the change to all controls of that type that you subsequently add. When you create forms and reports using Form Wizards and Report Wizards, each Wizard sets the default properties of the controls it adds such as labels, text boxes, and check boxes. By changing the default properties, all of the controls added with the Form Wizards and Report Wizards have the same appearance.

**tip:** *You can change some properties of labels and text boxes for forms and reports you create with the Wizard. In Chapter 18, you will learn how you can use the Add-in Manager to customize Access Wizards. Changing the Wizards provides another way to change the properties of labels and text boxes besides changing the default control properties or using a template.*

## Control Properties Specific to Default Control Settings

When you set default settings for different types of controls, you will notice as many as five new properties that you have not seen before: Auto Label, Add Colon, Label X, Label Y, and Label Align. These properties can only be set as part of the default settings.

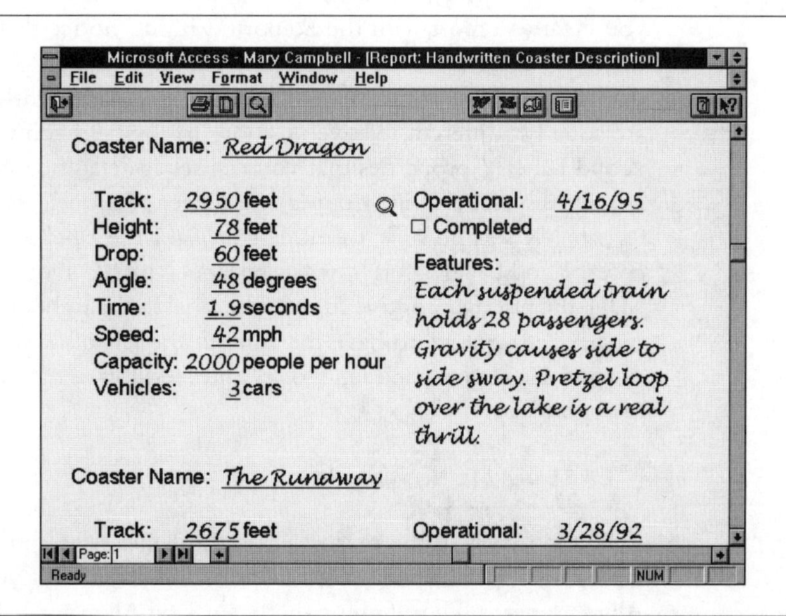


**Figure 14-10** A report created by changing the default properties

### AUTO LABEL

When you have added compound controls up to this point, the controls have included an attached label control. This label includes its own text and colon. These labels appear with the control because the Auto Label default control property is set to Yes. This default property is set to Yes for text boxes, option groups, option buttons, check boxes, combo boxes, list boxes, and subforms, but it is set to No for toggle buttons and command buttons. Change this property when you want toggle buttons and command buttons to add the label controls as part of the control or if you don't want to add the label controls as part of the other control types.

### ADD COLON

When label controls are added as part of a compound control, they have a colon after them if the Add Colon property is Yes (the default for text boxes, option buttons, check boxes, combo boxes, list boxes, and subforms). Changing this property to No omits the colon from the label in the compound control.

### LABEL X AND LABEL Y

When you create a form with the Form Wizards, notice that the Boxed look for the form (described in Chapter 8) puts field names above the fields. When you create a report with the Report Wizards, notice that the labels added for the fields using the Ledger look puts the labels closer to the text box controls than the other report looks and that the labels are right-aligned. These labels are added at different relative positions to the field controls because the Label X and Label Y properties that you can set as default control properties set the relative distance from the upper-left corner of the selected control.

Label X sets how far to the left or right the label is placed relative to the control, and Label Y sets how far the label is placed above or below the control. Make the number positive to have the label to the right of or below the control, or make it negative to have the label to the left of or above the control. The distance is measured in inches or centimeters just as the other parts of the form or report are.

### LABEL ALIGN

The position of the text is set by the Label Align property. You have the same choices of General, Left, Center, and Right that you have for the Text Align property. The difference between Text Align and Label Align is that Label

Align sets the alignment of the label control added next to a control and Text Align sets the alignment of the characters that appear in the control.

The following illustration shows a form created by changing these default settings:

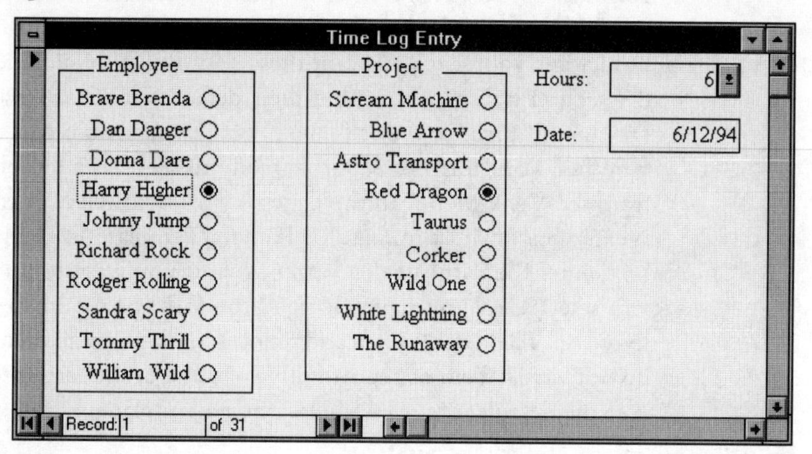


In this form, the Label X and Label Y properties are changed so that the labels are added to the left of the option buttons rather than to the right. Also, the Label Align property is changed to Right, so the employee names and project names are right-aligned.

# Templates

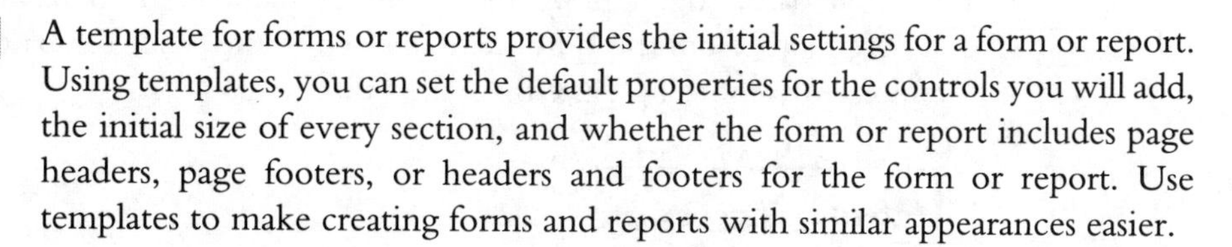

A template for forms or reports provides the initial settings for a form or report. Using templates, you can set the default properties for the controls you will add, the initial size of every section, and whether the form or report includes page headers, page footers, or headers and footers for the form or report. Use templates to make creating forms and reports with similar appearances easier.

## Creating a Template

When you want several of your forms or reports to have a similar appearance, you can create a template. The template determines the default settings for form, report, section, and control properties, section sizes, and whether the form or report includes headers or footers. A template is really nothing more than using an existing form or report as the basis for a new form or report.

To create a template, create a form or report in which the settings for the different types of controls are set as you want them to be. (You may already have a form or report that contains all of the settings that you want to use as defaults. If so, use this for the template; you do not need to create another one just for this purpose.) Display the form or report header and footer and the page header and footer if you want these sections to be included as the default. Set the section sizes to determine their default size if you want. When you have created this form or report, save it just as you would other forms or reports.

When your form or report is ready to serve as a template, choose Options from the View menu. In the Category list box, select Form & Report Design. Next, after Form Template or Report Template in the bottom of the dialog box, enter the name of the form or report you want to use as a template. Once you select OK, you have changed the form or report design that is used as a template. The default form and report templates are named Normal. When you do not have a form or report with the name of the template, the form or report uses the default settings without using a template.

**tip:** *You can also create a form or report template by renaming a form or report design to Normal. Normal is the initial form or report name Access expects to use as a template.*

When you want to use the same style for forms and reports in more than one database, you will want to use the same template in the other databases. You can transfer a form or report template by copying the form or report to the Clipboard. Highlight the form or report name in the Database window and choose Copy from the Edit menu. Switch to the other database and paste the template by choosing Paste from the Edit menu.

## Using a Template

To use the template, create a form or report without using the Wizards. The form or report you create uses the same default settings for all of the controls you add through the toolbox. Also, the form or report has the headers and footers that the template has as well as the same section sizes.

The new form or report you create does not have any of the controls added to the form or report you are using as a template. That is why you can use an existing form or report as a template without the individual controls from the template form or report affecting the current form or report. The new form or report does not have any of the property settings of the individual controls in the template form or report. As an example, if you have set all of the controls in a form to use the Courier font by changing the Font Name property of the individual controls of text boxes, using the form as a template does not set the Font Name property of all text boxes to Courier in the new form unless you also have set the Font Name property for the default text box.

**tip:** *If you want to use the same template for both forms and reports, create the template for the form and then save the form as a report by choosing Save As Report in the File menu when looking at the form's design. Both the form and report templates will have the same settings.*

Figure 14-11 shows a report created using the report in Figure 14-10 as a template. In Figure 14-11, the text boxes automatically use the same handwriting font used in Figure 14-10. The labels also use the same Arial font in both reports. These settings are not altered in the report in Figure 14-11 because the text boxes and labels have these properties set by the report in Figure 14-10.

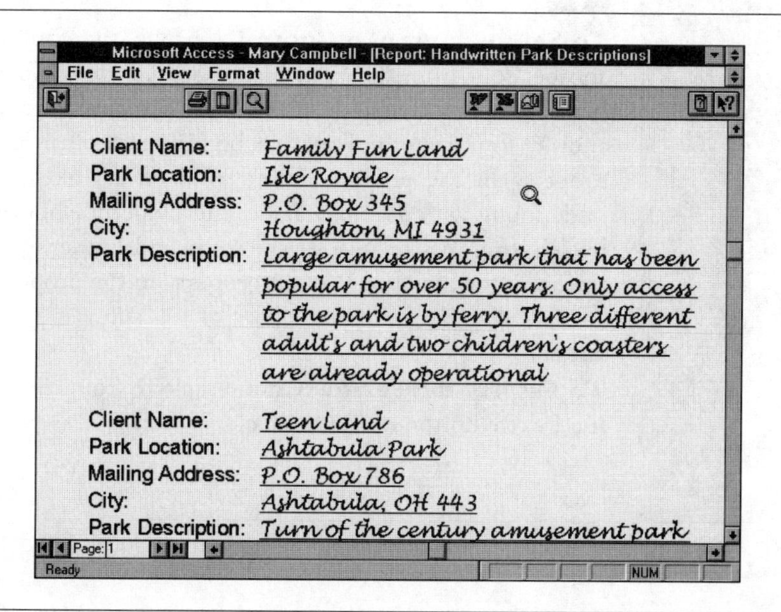


**Figure 14-11** A report created using the report in Figure 14-10 as a template

Quick Reference

**To Add a Line or Rectangle to a Form or Report** Select the line or rectangle tool from the Tool box. Point to where you want the line or rectangle to start and then drag the mouse to where you want the line or rectangle to end.

**To Change the Layer of a Control** To put a control on the bottom layer of the form or report, select Send to Back from the Format menu (the Layout menu in Access version 1). To put a control on the top layer of the form or report, select Bring to Front from the Format menu (the Layout menu in Access version 1).

**To Set the Alignment of a Control** Click the Left-Align Text, Right-Align Text, Center-Align Text, or General alignment buttons in the toolbar (the General button is only in Access version 1) or change the Text Alignment property in the property sheet to Left, Right, Center, or General.

**To Set the Font of a Control** Change the font name by selecting another font from the Font Name box in the toolbar or from the Font Name property in the property sheet. Change the font size by selecting another font from the Font Size box in the toolbar or from the Font Size property in the property sheet. Add effects like boldface, italics, and underlining with the Bold, Italic, and Underline buttons in the toolbar or by selecting Yes or No for the Italic and Underline properties and the thickness for the Font Weight property in the property sheet.

**To Display the Palette** Choose Palette from the View menu or click the Palette button in the toolbar.

Quick Reference

**To Set the Color, Border, and Three-Dimensional Appearance of a Control** Select the three-dimensional appearance you want for the control by selecting between the Normal Appearance, Raised Appearance, and Sunken Appearance buttons in the Palette or by setting the Special Effect property to Normal, Raised, or Sunken. Then select the color you want for the text, fill, and border from the Palette. You can also select the first Clear in the Palette or Clear for the Back Style property in the property sheet to select whether the control is transparent and will display the ones behind it. To select the width of the border, select one of the border width buttons in the Palette or select a width for the Border Width property in the property sheet. You can also select the second Clear in the Palette or Clear for the Border Style property in the property sheet to select whether the border appears when you print the report or form.

**To Set the Default Properties of a Control** Display the property sheet and then click the tool in the toolbox. The properties listed in the property sheet are the properties you can set for the defaults for all controls of that type that you subsequently add to the form or report.

**To Create a Form or Report Template** Choose Options from the View menu. Select Form & Report Design from the Category list box. After Form Template or Report Template, enter the name of the form or report that you want to use as a template for all forms or reports you subsequently create without using the Form Wizards or Report Wizards. The form or report adopts the control properties, default size, and settings for whether headers and footers appear for the page as well as for the form and report.

# Chapter 15

Embedding Versus Linking

Adding OLE Objects to Form and Report Designs

Adding OLE Objects as Data in Your Database

Working with OLE Objects

Adding Graphs to Forms and Reports

# Adding OLE Objects to Forms and Reports

ACCESS is one of the many Windows applications that support OLE (Object Linking and Embedding). OLE lets you add pictures, charts, and other data created in other applications to your tables, forms, and reports. OLE adds the functionality of other packages to the one you are presently using.

You can either link or embed objects into Access. Windows 3.1 allows both linking and embedding, but Windows 3.0 only allows linking. To use OLE objects in Access, first decide whether you want to link or embed the data from the other applications into Access. After deciding, you add these objects to your database.

You use the linked and embedded objects you add to a database either in tables or in forms and reports. The embedded and linked data can be part of the table's data, such as pictures of employees or projects. The embedded and linked data added to forms and reports can be graphics such as a company logo. You can continue to edit these objects. A graph like the one you created in Chapter 8 for the Graph Form Wizard form is a special type of OLE object that you will learn more about in this chapter.

In this chapter, you will learn the different ways you can add OLE objects to your tables, forms, and reports. You will also learn about the different properties that change how you work with these objects. Finally, you will learn more about the Microsoft Graph application that accompanies Access. This is the same application the Access Graph Form Wizard uses.

## Embedding Versus Linking

When you want to take data from another application and put it into your Access tables, forms, and reports, you first must choose whether to embed or link the data. (You choose between linking and embedding only if using Windows 3.1—if using Windows 3.0, the choice is made for you, because Windows 3.0 only supports linking.) You decide based on where you want the data stored and whether you plan to use the data in applications besides Access or in other Access databases.

Figure 15-1 shows a diagram of how embedding and linking differ. Embedded data is stored in the database file along with other objects such as tables, forms, and reports. This data is still in the format used by the application you created the data with. When you use the creating application, called the *server application*, to edit the embedded data, the server application gets the data to work with from the Access database. The embedded data is not available for sharing with other applications or databases.

When you link data, the data is stored in the server application's format and it is maintained in a file separate from your Access database. The tables, forms, and reports that use that data store links to that file rather than storing the actual data. When you use the server application to edit the linked data, the application gets the data from the separate file—not from the Access database. Also, other applications can use the file. For example, a Paintbrush file containing a company logo can still be linked to Excel worksheets and Word documents.

If you plan to use the data solely in one Access database, embed the data. This keeps the data in the database that uses it even while the data is being edited by the server application used to create it. If you plan to use the data in other applications or databases, link the object. Linking keeps the data in the format of the server application and in its own file, which allows other applications and databases to use it for their own links.

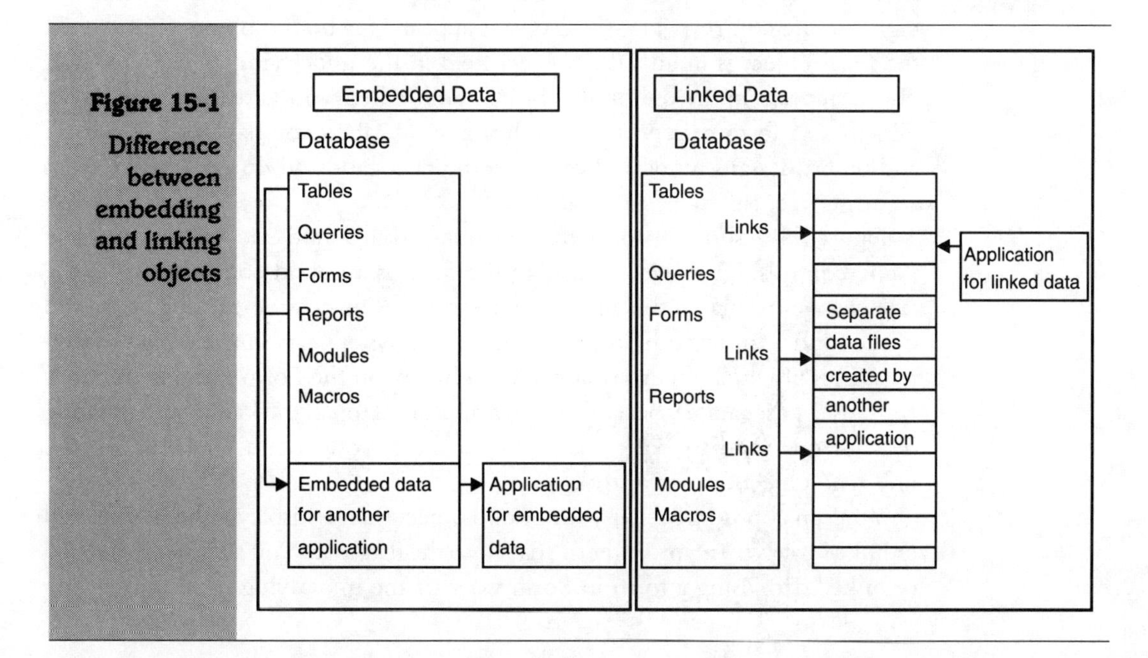


**Figure 15-1** Difference between embedding and linking objects

An application must have the ability to link or embed objects before you can link and embed objects from that application into Access. Some applications can only make data available for linking and embedding in another application, while some applications can only link and embed data from other applications; some applications can do both, and some can do neither. An application that accepts data to embed or link is a *client application.* An application that provides data to be embedded or linked is a *server application.*

Access is only a client application. The Access package also provides one or two applications that can only be server applications. Microsoft Graph creates graphs like the ones you made with the Graph Form Wizard in Chapter 8. Paintbrush, which Access version 1 provides, replaces an older version provided with Windows, giving you graphic drawing and editing capabilities.

**tip:** *If you have the Microsoft Office package, you have more server applications available. Some of the applications in the Microsoft Office set can serve as client and server applications. Microsoft Office includes Microsoft Word, Microsoft Excel, Microsoft PowerPoint, and Microsoft Mail.*

## Adding OLE Objects to Form and Report Designs

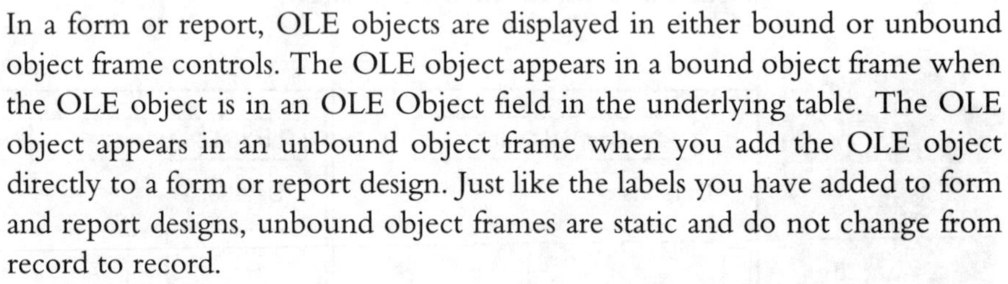

In a form or report, OLE objects are displayed in either bound or unbound object frame controls. The OLE object appears in a bound object frame when the OLE object is in an OLE Object field in the underlying table. The OLE object appears in an unbound object frame when you add the OLE object directly to a form or report design. Just like the labels you have added to form and report designs, unbound object frames are static and do not change from record to record.

Figure 15-2 shows a form that includes both bound and unbound object frame controls. The person's face in the form is a bound control because the face changes to match the employee described. The coaster tracking at the top of the form is an unbound control since it always appears in the same position regardless of which record is displayed. The text in the Form Header section is composed of separate label controls that appear on top of the Paintbrush drawing because the Send to Back command in the Layout menu was used on the unbound object frame control.

You can choose whether your bound object frames display either embedded or linked data when you enter the data into the database. You add the embedded or linked data using a form in Form view or the underlying table or query in

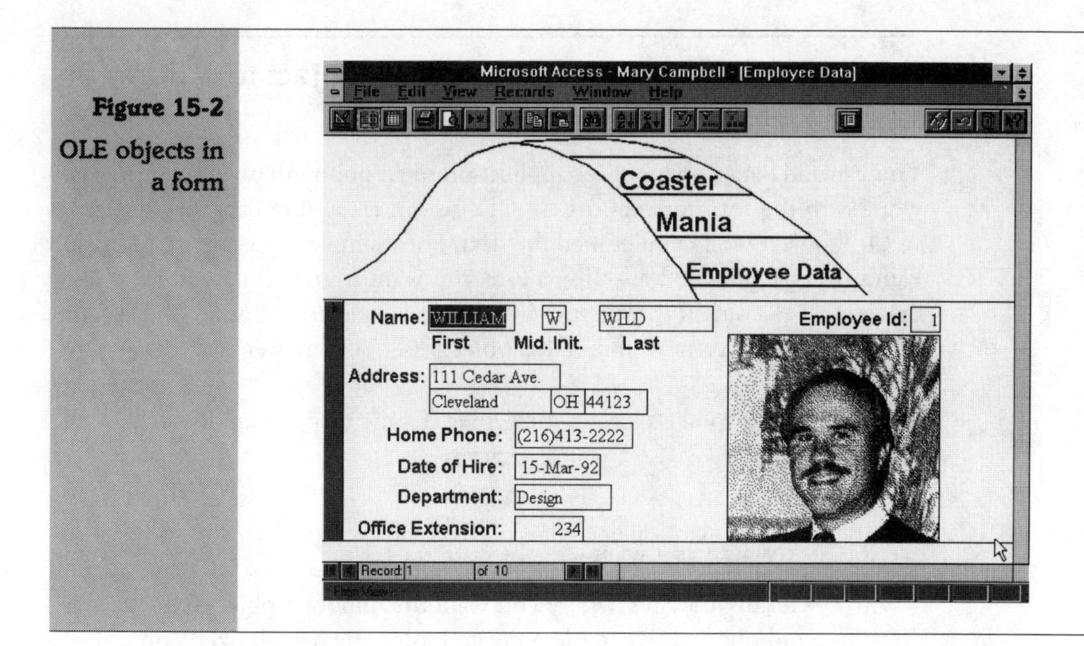


**Figure 15-2** OLE objects in a form

Datasheet view. You set whether the contents of an unbound object frame are embedded or linked when you add the control to the form or report in Design view.

You can tell whether the unbound object frames display embedded or linked data by looking at the control's properties. In Access version 2, the read-only OLE Type property contains Linked or Embedded to describe whether the data is embedded or linked. Controls containing linked OLE objects have an Update Options (Update Method in Access version 1) property that does not appear when the object frame contains an embedded object. Also, linked objects may look different than embedded objects that use the same application. This difference in appearance varies by application. When you initially add an unbound object frame to a form or report design, the control may appear empty. When you look at the form or report design after displaying the form in Form view or previewing or printing the report, an unbound object frame displays its contents. Bound controls always look empty in the form or report design because they are filled by the data from the underlying table, just as text boxes are. In Access version 2, you can select whether a bound or unbound control for OLE objects will contain linked data, embedded data, or either by changing the OLE Type Allowed property.

## Adding New Data as an Embedded Object to a Form or Report Design

You can add data from another application to an unbound object frame as you work with the form or report design. You can create the data that appears as an OLE object while you embed the data. For example, you can use Microsoft Paintbrush to quickly draw the picture you want to use while you are adding the control to contain that picture in Access. To add an unbound object frame control to contain a new embedded object, follow these steps:

1. From the toolbox, select the Object Frame tool, which looks like this:

2. Click where you want the object to start.

   If you just click where you want the unbound object frame to start, the unbound object frame is created using the default size. You can also drag the mouse from where you want the object to start to where you want the lower-right corner of the object frame to set the size of the object frame. After you insert the unbound object frame, Access displays the Insert Object dialog box. Another way to insert an unbound object frame and open the Insert Object dialog box is by choosing Insert Object in the Edit menu. When you use this command, the object frame starts at the upper-left corner of the current section in the form or report design and uses the default object frame size. After the object is added, you can drag the frame to its proper location and resize it.

3. Select the application to use in creating the data you want to embed from the Object Type list box.

4. Create the data you want to appear as the embedded object in the application you selected.

5. Choose Exit or Return from the File menu of the application you are using to create the data to embed. When prompted about updating or saving the changes, select Yes.

You can see the OLE object in the unbound object frame control in your report or form's Design view. Figure 15-2 shows the results of following these steps to add a Paintbrush picture (the curves and lines at the top) to the Form Header section of a form.

## Adding Existing Data as an Embedded Object to a Form or Report Design

If you already have the data you want to embed saved in a file created with a server application, embedding that data is easy. You can add an entire file as an embedded object.

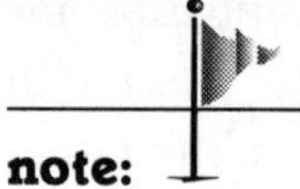

**note:** *Existing files must have been created by an application that can serve as an OLE server if you want to embed them in your Access database.*

To add an unbound object frame control to a form or report design and display an existing file as an embedded OLE object, follow these steps:

1. Select the Object Frame tool from the toolbox.
2. Click where you want the unbound object frame control to start.

   When you click the form or report design to create an unbound object frame control, the control uses the default object frame size. Another option is to drag the mouse from where you want the object frame control to start to where you want the lower-right corner of the object frame control to be. Access displays the Insert Object dialog box.

**tip:** *Instead of following steps 1 and 2, you can choose Insert Object command in the Edit menu to add the object frame control in the upper-left corner of the currently selected section using the default object frame size.*

3. Select the Create from File option button (the File command button in Access version 1).
4. Select the type of file you want to display from the List Files of Type drop-down list box. This list includes all of the file types for applications that support linking and embedding.

**tip:** *The Microsoft ClipArt Gallery is an application that comes with Microsoft Office. It can review all of your clip art images. You can easily locate the image you want to use, even if you don't remember the correct file name. You can use this application to visually select the clip art you are adding.*

5. Select the name of the file that you want to use and then OK.

You will see the embedded OLE object in your form or report design. Figure 15-3 shows an example of a report design that has an embedded CorelDRAW! graphic. This drawing uses CorelDRAW!'s extensive graphics editing capabilities and clip art. In this case, after the Create from File button was selected in step 3, the file COASTER.CDR was selected. You would want to link rather than embed a logo like this if you planned to use it in several locations or if you planned to change it later.

**tip:** *When creating a small graphic for an OLE object, keep it simple. A complex drawing becomes a blur when it is scaled down. For example, the gentlemen in the Coaster Mania logo shown in Figure 15-3 originally had more detailed faces and clothing, but the details were removed because the facial expressions were obscured by the other details.*

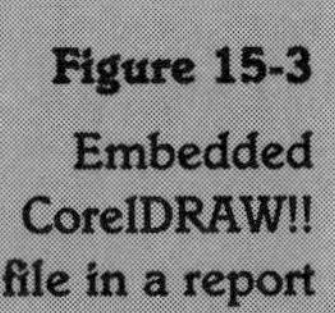

**Figure 15-3** Embedded CorelDRAW!! file in a report

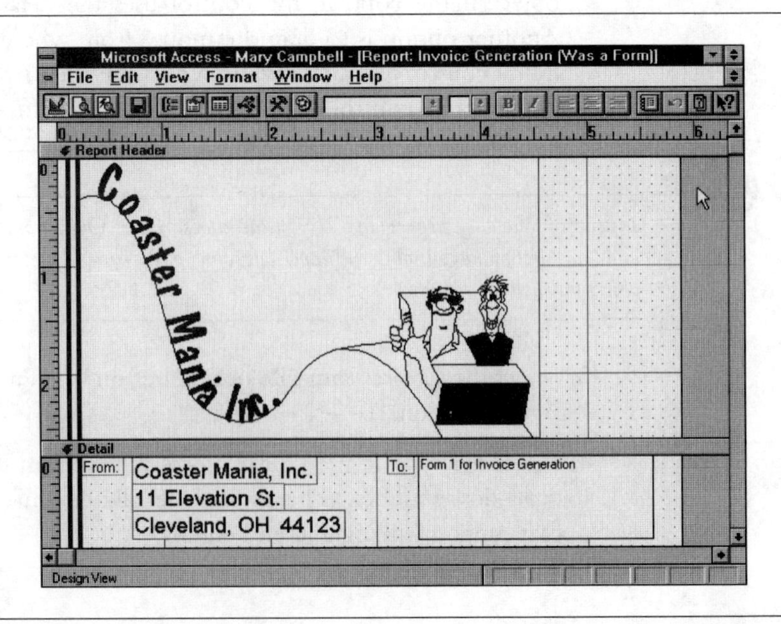

## Adding a Section of Existing Data as an Embedded Object

When you want to embed only a section of data from a file rather than an entire file in an unbound object frame control, you use different steps than you do when embedding a new object or an entire file. You will use the Clipboard to select how much of the data you want to embed. To add an unbound control for a section of data from a file to a form or report design, follow these steps:

1. Switch to the application displaying the data you want to embed in an unbound object frame on a form or report.
2. Select the data you want to embed.
3. Choose Copy from the server application's Edit menu to copy the selected data to the Clipboard.
4. Switch to Access and the form or report design where you want to embed the data in an unbound form or report control.
5. Choose Paste from the Edit menu.

If the data can be embedded, Access creates an unbound object frame control containing the selected section of data as an embedded object. If the type of data cannot be embedded, Access tries adding the Clipboard's contents as a label or as a picture that you cannot edit. Whichever type of control is created, it appears in the upper-left corner of the currently selected section.

Figure 15-4 shows a form that has a section of an Excel worksheet embedded in an unbound object frame. The cells A1:C11 were selected in Excel and then copied to the Clipboard. The application was switched to Access, and then the data was pasted into the form's design.

**tip:** *When you embed part of an Excel worksheet, the entire worksheet is embedded even though only part of it appears on the form or report design. When you attempt to edit the section of data, the entire file appears—not just the data you copied using the Clipboard, though this is the only data that appears in the form or report.*

These steps also work for copying data from other applications that do not support OLE. You can use these steps as another way to put the logo shown in Figure 15-3 into the report design. If you create the logo with CorelDRAW! 2.0,

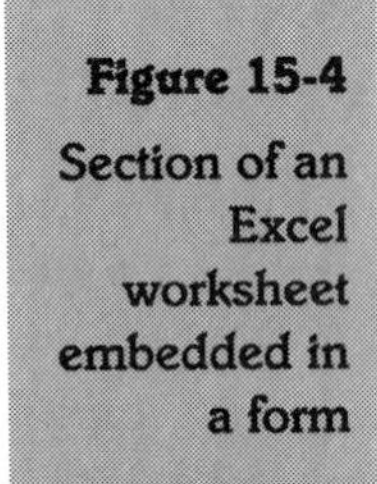

**Figure 15-4** Section of an Excel worksheet embedded in a form

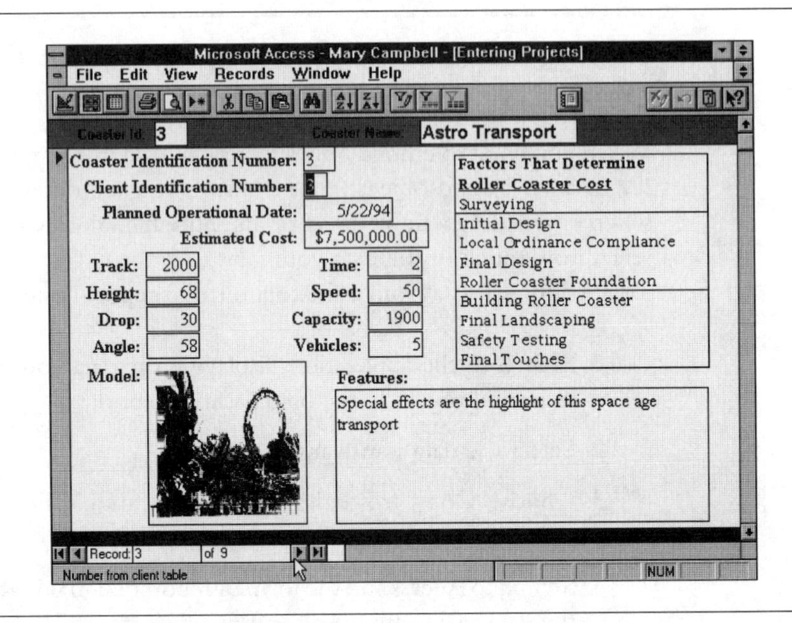


which does not support OLE but does support the Clipboard, you can transfer the drawing by copying it to the Clipboard and then pasting it into the report. Later versions of CorelDRAW! can be directly embedded and linked. The difference is that the pasted image from the Clipboard cannot be edited with CorelDRAW!, as the embedded .CDR file can.

## Linking Unbound Objects to a Report or Form Design

Linking data to an unbound control in a form or report design is a lot like embedding a section of data from a file, because you use the Clipboard to create the link. To link data to an unbound control from a file created with another application, follow these steps:

1. Switch to the application that displays the data you want to link.

   Before you create the link, you must save the data in a file. If it is not saved in a file, you cannot link this data, you can only embed it.

2. Select the data you want to link.
3. Choose Copy from the application's Edit menu to copy the selection to the Clipboard.

4. Switch to Access and the form or report design where you want the linked unbound object frame.

5. Choose Paste Special from the Edit menu in Access version 2 or Paste Link from the Edit menu in Access version 1.

   In Access version 2, you need to select the Paste Link option button. In Access version 1, this is not necessary. In Access version 1, this command is only available when the data in the Clipboard is from an application that you can link to Access.

6. Select OK.

The data may look different than it would if you embedded it. For example, in Figure 15-5, the Excel data includes the row and column borders, which would be omitted if the data was embedded. The difference between how the data looks when it is linked or embedded depends on the application providing the data. The form in Figure 15-5 is just like the one in Figure 15-4 except that the worksheet was linked instead of embedded. The other difference between the two forms is that some controls were rearranged to fit the larger OLE object in Figure 15-5. The worksheet in Figure 15-5 is still separate, so you can continue to use the worksheet in Excel, and other applications or databases can have links to this worksheet.

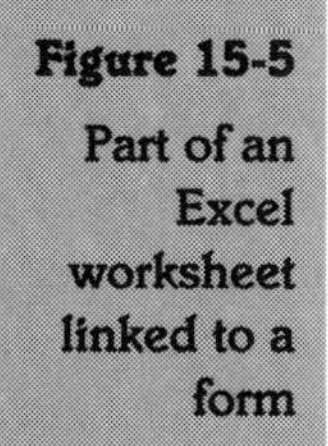

**Figure 15-5**

**Part of an Excel worksheet linked to a form**

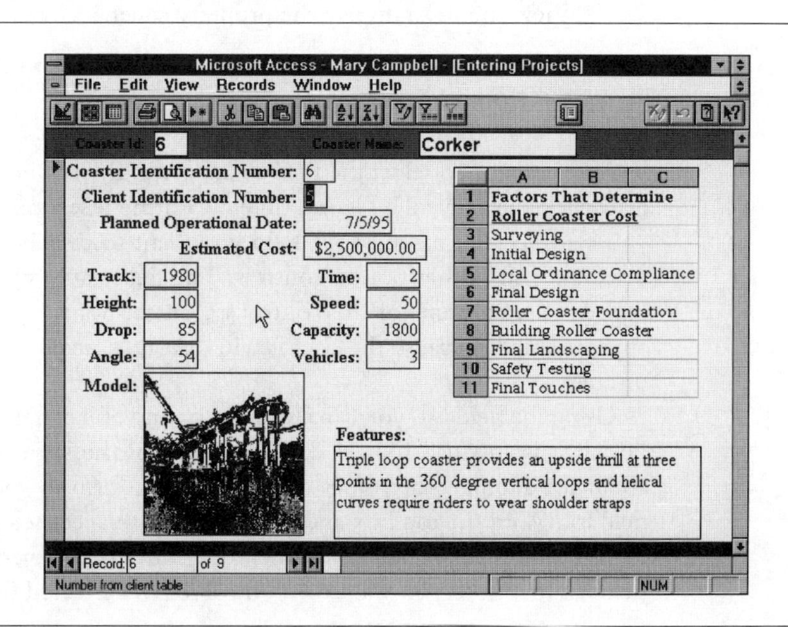

## Adding a Bound Object Frame Control to a Form or Report

When you add a bound object frame control to a form or report design, you do not decide whether the data that will appear in the control is linked or embedded. A bound object frame control will display OLE object data that is already entered in the underlying table or query. Thus you determine whether you are linking or embedding the OLE object when you enter the OLE object in the table or query, or in a form. To add a bound object frame control to a form or report design, follow these steps:

1. From the toolbox, select the Bound Object Frame tool, which looks like this:

2. Click where you want the object frame to start.

   Clicking creates an object framing using the default object size. You can also drag the mouse from where you want the object frame to start to where you want the lower-right corner of the object frame to be.

3. Click the Properties button in the toolbar or choose Properties in the View menu to display the property sheet.

4. Select the name of the field you want to appear in the object frame for the Control Source property.

Another way to select the field to appear in the bound object frame control is to click the control a second time. With the insertion point in the control, you can type the name of the field you want to display, just as you can with text boxes and other bound controls. The field name you type in the control replaces the contents of the control's Control Source property. This control appears empty because the data it will display is saved in the underlying table or query.

Using the field list, you can also add a bound object frame control for a table's field if it is an OLE Object data type. This is the same shortcut you learned about for adding other types of controls to a form or report design with the field list. With the toolbox and the field list displayed, select the Bound Object Frame tool in the toolbox and then drag the OLE Object data field from the field list to where you want the control for the selected field added.

## Adding a Linked or Embedded OLE Object with the Clipboard

Another option for adding a control to contain an OLE object is to use the Clipboard and select whether you want the object linked, embedded, or simply pasted in as a label or picture that cannot be edited. To select how Clipboard data is copied to an unbound object frame control, follow these steps:

1. Switch to the application that displays the data you want to link, embed, or copy.
2. Select the data you want to link, embed, or copy.
3. Choose Copy from the application's Edit menu to copy the selection to the Clipboard.
4. Switch to Access and the form or report design where you want to link, embed, or copy the data into an unbound object frame.
5. Choose Paste Special from the Edit menu to display this dialog box:

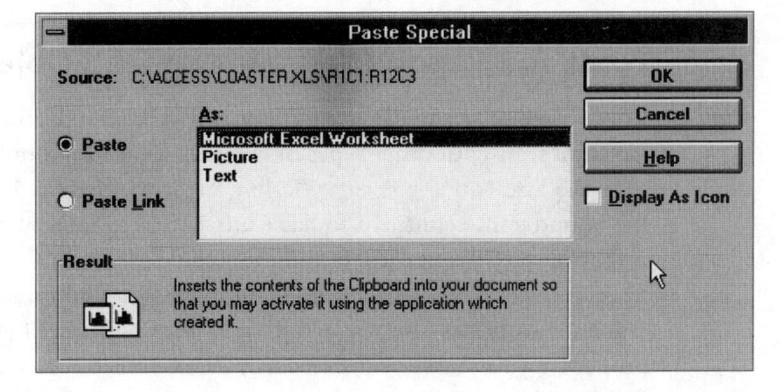

**tip:** *If you are using Access version 2, you used this command before in the "Linking Unbound Objects to a Report or Form Design" section.*

Under As (Data Type in Access version 1), select the format you want to use when pasting the data in the Clipboard in your form or report. You can also select the Paste or Paste Link buttons to select when you want to copy the data to the field. Paste pastes either the embedded data or the image of the Clipboard's contents. Paste Link links the data in the selected format. Paste Link is only available when the selected data type supports linked OLE objects.

6. Select OK in Access version 2, or Paste or Paste Link in Access version 1.

   In Access version 2, the Paste and Paste Link buttons are option buttons; you still have to select OK after selecting one of these buttons and the data type. In Access version 1, they are command buttons that you select after selecting the data format to use.

The OLE object is added in the upper-left corner of the currently selected section.

You may want to select Text as the data type when you want to link to the text in another application without linking to how that application presents the data. For example, you may want to use text from a Word for Windows document and omit the formatting. In that case, you would paste the link using the Text data type instead of Microsoft Word 6.0 Document or Picture, so that the text would appear in the form or report but the character formatting would not appear.

## Form and Report Properties for OLE Objects

Bound and unbound object frame controls have additional properties that you have not seen with other types of controls. Bound and unbound frame controls have the Size Mode property (Scaling in Access version 1). In Access version 2, the bound frame control also has Auto Activate, Display Type, Verb, and OLE Type Allowed properties. Unbound controls have an OLE Class property and, in Access version 2, an OLE Type property. Unbound controls containing embedded objects also have the same Row Source Type and Row Source properties you saw for list and combo box controls, as well as the Link Master Fields and Link Child Fields properties. Unbound controls containing linked objects also have Source Object, Item, and Update Options properties.

When the area you have selected for a bound or unbound object frame control is smaller or larger than the size of the image, you can select how the image is reduced to fit in the area or how the extra area is used. How the object fits in the control is set by the Size Mode property (Scaling in Access version 1). When this property is set to Clip, Access fits as much of the image as possible in the area provided. When this property is set to Stretch, the height and width are altered to fit the area provided even if the height-to-width proportion of the original object must be altered. When this property is set to Zoom, the height and width are altered to fit the area provided while retaining the original height-to-width proportion. Figure 15-6 shows the three different scaling choices operating on the same original object. You can always make the object frame's size the size of the OLE object by choosing Size and then to Fit from the Format menu (Size to Fit in the Layout menu in Access version 1). This command expands or contracts the control's size to match that of the OLE object.

**tip:** *You can use the Palette to add a border around a bound or unbound object frame control. Choose Palette from the View menu or click the Palette button in the toolbar to display the Palette.*

The Display Type property in Access version 2 will also change how the OLE object appears, since you can either display the OLE object as an icon or as its contents. For example, if the OLE object is an Excel worksheet, when the Display Type property is Icon, the Excel worksheet appears as the icon for Excel. When the Display Type property is Contents, the form or report shows the Excel worksheet data.

You can also use the Auto Activate property to change how you edit the OLE object. The default of Double-Click for this property allows you to edit OLE objects by double-clicking them. When Auto Activate is set to Manual, you must use the menu or a shortcut menu to edit the OLE object. The Verb property can contain a number that describes how the server application is used when you activate an OLE object.

**Figure 15-6** Different scaling options with the same OLE object

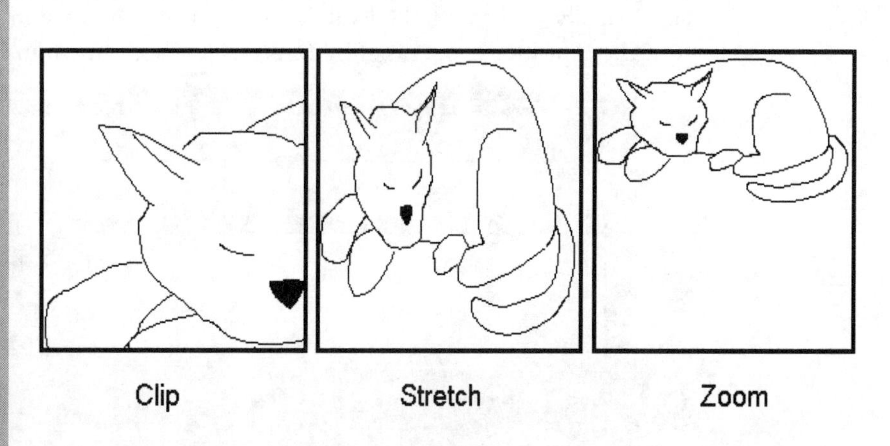

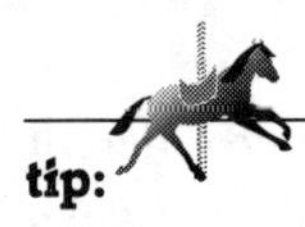

**tip:** *Use the OLE Type Allowed property in a bound object frame control for a form to limit whether OLE Object data fields contain embedded or linked data. The default of Either for this property lets you add either type of OLE object to the field.*

Unbound object frames have properties that select the source of the data appearing in the object frame. The OLE Class property selects the application used to edit the OLE object data. The object frame's current setting matches the choice you made from the As (Object Type in Access version 1) list box in the Paste Special dialog box. This property is read-only, so you cannot change the setting. When the OLE object is linked rather than embedded into the control, the control has the Source Object and Item properties.

The Source Object property selects the file the link is made to and the Item property selects the part of the file that appears in the object frame. When you are linking an entire file to the object frame, the Item property is empty. When you are only linking a section of a file, the Item property describes the section of the file displayed, using the format the server application uses to describe a section of data. For example, for the link to the Excel worksheet shown in Figure 15-5, the Item property is R1C1:R11C3 to indicate that you want to link a range that starts in the first row and column and extends to the eleventh row in the third column.

The remaining property that is specific to object frames containing linked OLE objects is Update Options (Update Method in Access version 1), which selects when the object in the control is updated. Your choices are Automatic and Manual. Automatic updates the object displayed in the control as the object changes in the application that created it. Manual updates the object only when you choose to. This property is initially set to Automatic, although bound OLE objects are updated manually regardless of the Update Options property setting. To manually update a linked OLE Object in Access version 2, choose Links from the Edit menu, opening the Links dialog box shown in here:

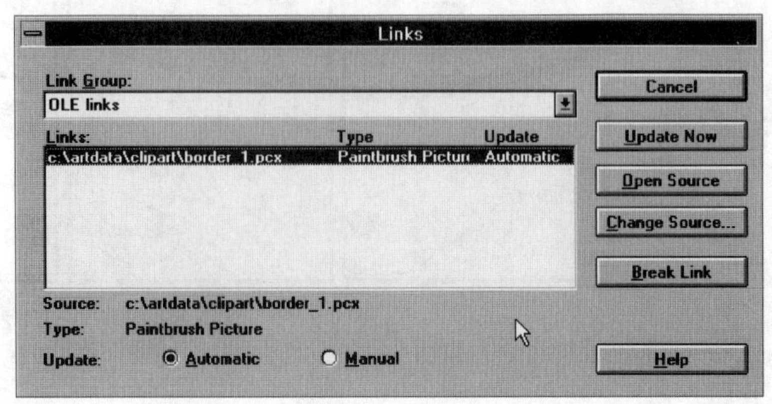

Select the link or links you want to update in the Links list box. Then select Update Now. Notice that this dialog box also lets you set what file the link is to, and when the file is updated. You can break the link or change which file the link is to. You can also edit the linked file using this dialog box.

In Access version 1, you choose *OLE Class* Object from the Edit menu and Update Now. *OLE Class* is replaced by the name of the application that the object is created with.

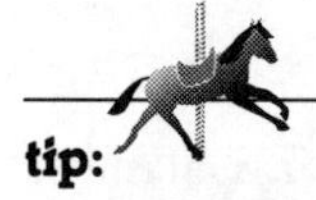

**tip:** *In Access version 1, the Update Method options match the check boxes in the Paste Link dialog box. Selecting Automatic is the same as selecting the Auto Update check box in the Paste Link dialog box, while choosing Manual has the same effect as clearing the Auto Update check box in the Paste Link dialog box.*

## Adding OLE Objects as Data in Your Database

Adding bound OLE objects in Form or Datasheet view is slightly different from adding unbound OLE objects in a form or report's Design view. When you add OLE objects to a table in the Datasheet or Form view, these OLE objects are part of the table's data. The difference between adding OLE objects in a datasheet or in Form view is how the OLE object appears. In a datasheet, the field displays the source of the OLE object. This is the same information that would appear for the OLE Class property if the same object were added to a form or report design. In Form view, the contents of the OLE object appear.

In either view, you can edit, add, or remove the OLE object. The only exceptions are unbound OLE objects, which you can modify in the form's Design view instead of the Form view, and pictures that are not OLE objects, which you can remove but not edit.

### Adding New Data as an Embedded Object

You can add data created by another application as you work in Datasheet or Form view. You can also create the data that appears as an OLE object while you embed the data. For example, use Microsoft Paintbrush to quickly draw a picture you want to use. To add an embedded object for a field that has the OLE Object data type, follow these steps:

1. Choose Insert Object in the Edit menu to display the Insert Object dialog box.
2. Select the application for the type of data you want to add from the Object Type list box.
3. Create the data you want to appear as the embedded object.
4. Choose Exit or Return from the File menu. When prompted about updating or saving the changes, select Yes.

You can see the OLE object on your screen in Form view; in Datasheet view, the field shows the name of the application you selected in step 2.

## Adding Existing Data as an Embedded Object

If the data you want to embed is already saved in files created with a server application, embedding that data is easy. You can add an entire file as an embedded object. For you to add existing objects, they must have been created by an application that supports OLE. To add an OLE object to an OLE Object data field in the Form or Datasheet view, follow these steps:

1. Move the insertion point to the OLE Object data type field for the record you want to add the data as the OLE data.
2. Choose Insert Object in the Edit menu to display the Insert Object dialog box.
3. Select the Create from File option button (the File command button in Access version 1).
4. Select the name of the file that you want to use and then OK.

In Form view, you will see the OLE object on your screen. In Datasheet view, you will see the name of the application used to create the OLE object.

Figure 15-7 shows the Preview of a report after several roller coaster pictures have been added to the Project table.

## Adding a Section of Existing Data as an Embedded Object

When you want to embed as an OLE object only a section of data in a file rather than the entire file, use the Clipboard to paste the data to the OLE Object data

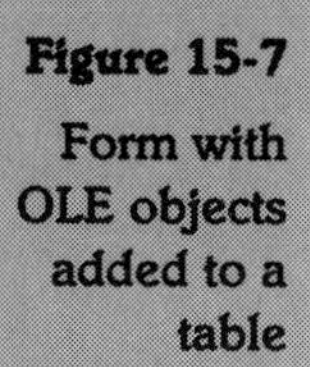

**Figure 15-7** Form with OLE objects added to a table

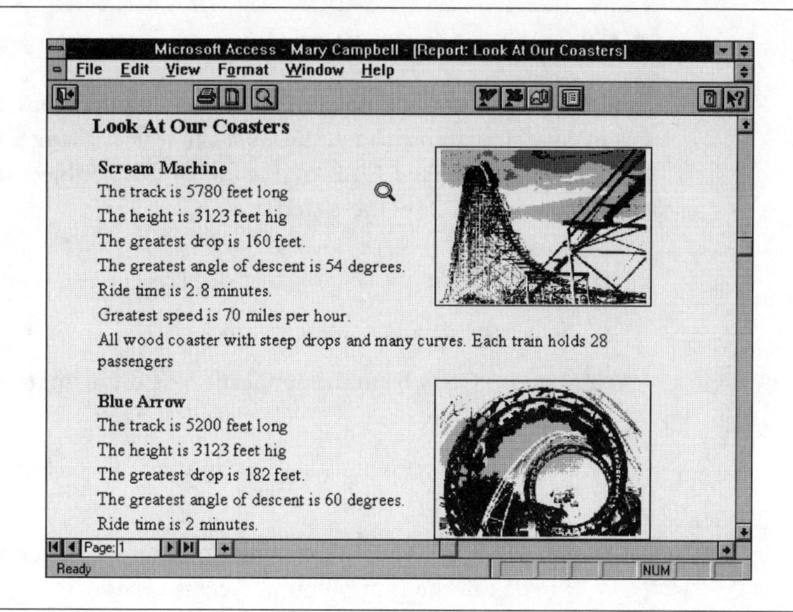


field. To add an embedded OLE object that contains a section of another file, follow these steps:

1. Switch to the application that displays the data you want to embed in a table.
2. Select the data you want to embed.
3. Choose Copy from the application's Edit menu to copy the selection to the Clipboard.
4. Switch to Access and move to the field where you want to embed the selected data in the table.
5. Choose Paste from the Edit menu.

If the data can be embedded, Access adds the embedded data as the OLE object for the field. The data appears in the Form view and the object's application appears in the Datasheet view. If the type of data cannot be embedded, the Paste command is not available.

## Adding Linked OLE Objects to a Field

Entering a linked OLE object for a field's value keeps the reference to the original file so that the data in the table can reflect changes made to that original file. To create a linked OLE object for an OLE Object data field in Form or Datasheet view, follow these steps:

1. Switch to the application that displays the data you want to link.
2. Select the data you want to link.
3. Choose Copy from the application's Edit menu to copy the selection to the Clipboard.
4. Switch to Access and the field in the table or form where you want to enter the OLE object.
5. Choose Paste Special from the Edit menu in Access version 2, and Paste Link from the Edit menu in Access version 1.

   In Access version 2, you now need to select the Paste Link option button. This is not necessary in Access version 1. In Access version 1, the Paste Link command is not available if the data in the Clipboard cannot be linked.
6. Select OK.

The linked data may appear different than it does when embedded. For example, embedded Excel worksheet data does not include the row and column borders that appear when the same data is linked.

Figure 15-8 shows a form that includes different Paintbrush files. You add each Paintbrush file to the form's table by adding records and linking the Paintbrush picture to the form's bound object frame control. You can update these linked files to display the most current version of the Paintbrush files.

## Adding a Linked or Embedded OLE Object with the Clipboard

A final method of entering an OLE object in an OLE Object data field is to use the Clipboard and select whether the data is to be linked or embedded as you copy it. You can select between embedding the data or linking the data as text

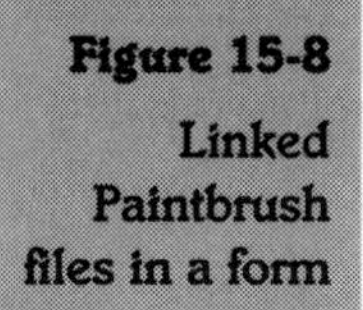

**Figure 15-8** Linked Paintbrush files in a form

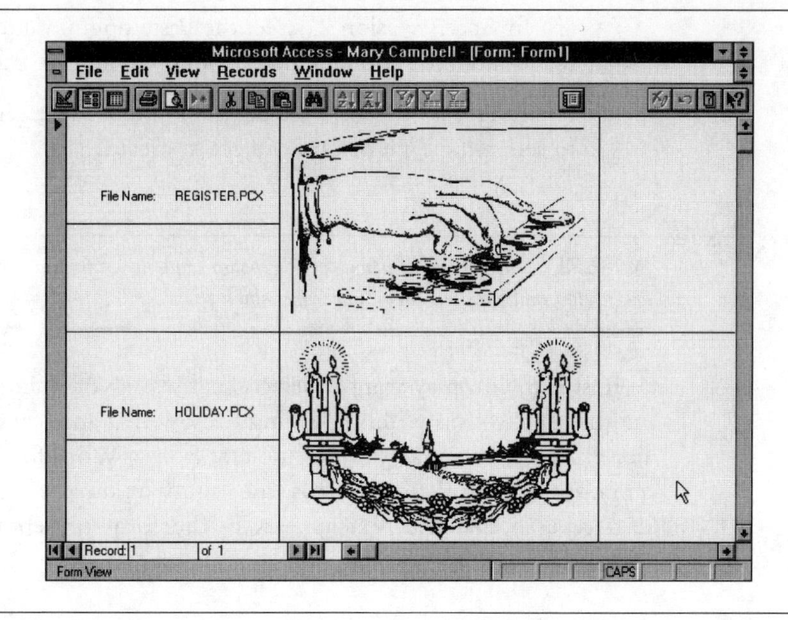


or in a picture or bitmap format. To select how Clipboard data is copied to an OLE Object data field in Form or Datasheet view, follow these steps:

1. Switch to the application that displays the data you want to link or embed.
2. Select the data you want to link or embed.
3. Choose Copy from the application's Edit menu to copy the selection to the Clipboard.
4. Switch to Access and the field where you want to add the OLE object.
5. Choose Paste Special from the Edit menu.

   Under As (Data Type in Access version 1), Access lists the available formats you can use to paste the data from the Clipboard to the field.
6. Select the data type you want to paste from the As (Data Type in Access version 1) list box.
7. Select the type of OLE object you want to create in one of the following ways:

a. In Access version 2, select the Paste option button to embed or copy the data or the Paste Link option button to link the data. Then select OK.

b. In Access version 1, select the Paste or Paste Link command button to select the type of OLE object to create.

**tip:** *Paste Link is only available when the Clipboard contents are from a document created by a server application that supports providing OLE objects.*

In step 6, you may want to select Text when you want to link to the text in another application without linking to how that application presents the data. For example, you may want to use text from a Word for Windows document and omit the formatting. In that case, you would paste the link using the Text data type so that the text appears in the form or report but the character formatting does not appear.

**tip:** *In the Paintbrush application, change a picture from color to black and white by copying the color picture to the Clipboard, changing the image attributes to black and white, and then copying the Clipboard's contents back into Paintbrush.*

## Working with OLE Objects

As you work with OLE Objects in tables, forms, and reports, you will use many features that are common to all settings. You will be able to convert an OLE object into a picture, edit OLE objects, and change the file of a linked OLE object.

### Making an OLE Object Unchangeable

If you have finished editing an OLE object either in a form or report design or in a table, you can freeze the object so that nobody can edit it. Access can switch between records in Form or Datasheet view faster when the OLE objects in the records being shown can no longer be edited. You can convert your OLE object into a picture of the data it presents so that it is no longer an OLE object. Converting an OLE object into a picture is a one-time event; you cannot convert the picture back into an OLE object, even if you choose Undo from the Edit menu immediately. To make the OLE object uneditable, choose *OLE Class* Object from the Edit menu or from the shortcut menu in version 2 and then choose Change to Picture. *OLE Class* is the name of the application the object is created with.

After you select this command, you cannot edit the picture of the data that displays in that location. When you convert an OLE object in an object frame in a form or report design to a picture, you may notice that the object frame no longer has the OLE Class, Source Object, and Item properties. These properties are no longer in use because the object frame no longer contains an OLE object.

You can insert a picture as if it is an OLE object in two other situations. One is when you paste the contents of the Clipboard using Paste Special from the Edit menu and you select Picture for the data type. The other is when you paste the Clipboard's contents into an OLE Object data type field or an object frame in a form or report design and the Clipboard's contents cannot be embedded. For example, when you paste a CorelDRAW! 2.0 drawing into an object frame in Access, Access pastes an uneditable picture. Another example is if you copy the screen's image to the Clipboard using the PRINT SCREEN key. You can do this to copy a picture of the structure of your tables to a field. The report in Figure 15-9 is created by copying pictures of the tables' Design views. Once the picture is in the Clipboard, you can switch to the report's Design view and choose Paste in the Edit menu.

## Editing OLE Objects from Access

When you want to change the data that is part of the OLE object, you can edit the data directly from the Design, Form, or Datasheet view.

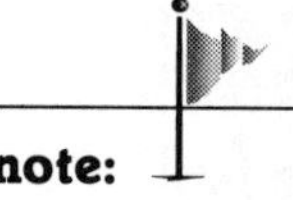

**note:** *OLE objects in unbound object frames can only be edited from Design view. OLE objects stored in a table can only be edited in Form or Datasheet view.*

You can change the OLE object by double-clicking it or by selecting the OLE object and choosing *OLE Class* Object from the Edit menu or from the shortcut menu in version 2, and then choosing Edit. Access opens the application for the object and puts the data in that application. When the OLE object is linked, you will notice the object's filename in the title bar. When the OLE object is embedded, as in Figure 15-10, the title bar for the application or the document indicates that the data belongs to an Access object. For the Paintbrush

**Figure 15-9** Uneditable pictures of Access windows added to a report

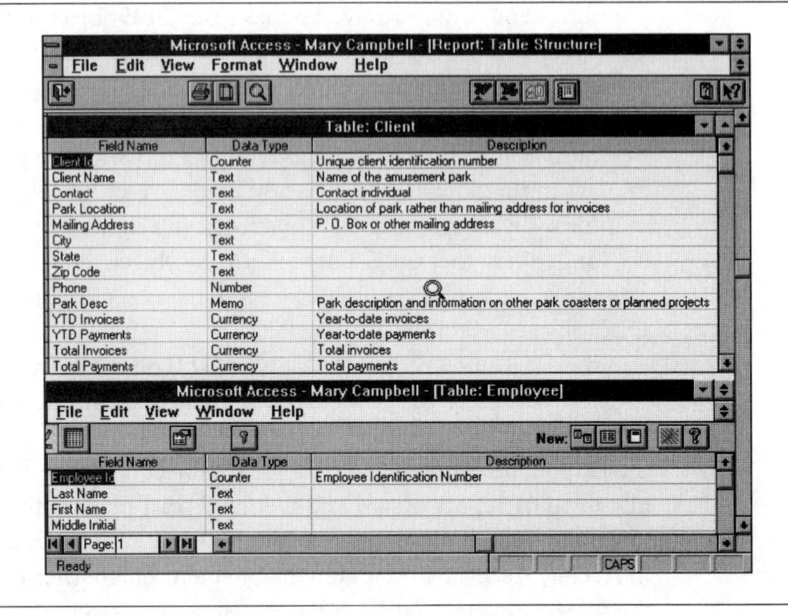


drawing in Figure 15-10, the drawing is embedded in the Employee table. In Access version 2, you can set a form to only accept embedded or linked data for an OLE Object data field by changing the OLE Type Allowed property for the bound object frame control to either Embedded or Linked, rather than the default of Either.

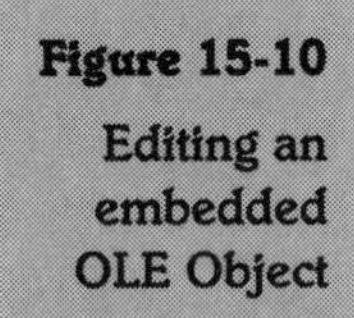

**Figure 15-10** Editing an embedded OLE Object

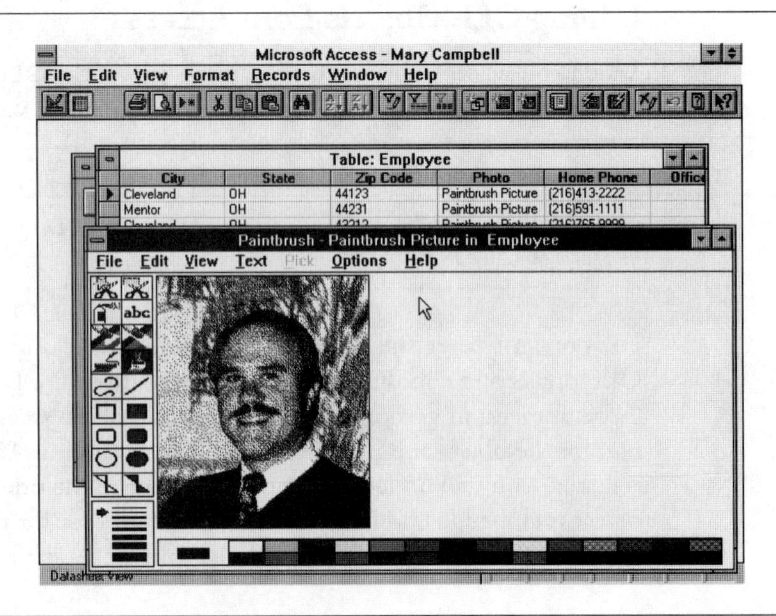

When you finish editing a linked object, choose Save from the server application's File menu. You can then exit that application or leave it open and switch back to Access, just as you would normally. When you finish editing an embedded object, choose the Exit or Update command from the server application's File menu (the exact command depends on the application) to leave the application and return to Access. Select Yes when given the confirmation message box asking whether you want to update the object in Access.

**tip:** *Sometimes you will not see a title bar for the server application while you are editing the OLE object. Some applications, such as Microsoft Graph, support in-place editing. When an application uses in-place editing, instead of opening a new application window, the server application's menu bar replaces the Access menu bar or a new toolbar appears, letting you edit the OLE object. When you use in-place editing, all of the features normally available in the server application are still available. When you are finished editing the OLE object, click outside of the area the object uses. If you want to use a separate application window to edit the selected OLE object instead of doing in-place editing, choose* OLE Class *Object from the Edit menu or from the shortcut menu, and then choose Open.*

## MODIFYING THE OLE LINK FOR LINKED OLE OBJECTS

You can change the file for linked OLE objects in a form or report design or in a table's OLE Object data field. In Access version 2, choose Links from the Edit menu, select the link in the Links list box and then select Change Source, and select a new file. In Access version 1, choose *OLE Class* Object from the Edit menu and Change Link. From the Change Link dialog box, you can select another file.

You may need to change the source of the OLE object's data when you rename the file the link uses. You can also change the source of the link of an OLE object added to a form or report design by changing the Source Object property. If you want to change the section of the object displayed in an unbound object frame control in a form or report, change the Item property for the control. If you want to change the section of the object displayed as a field's value, you must re-create the link.

Access version 2 offers you further ways to modify the link itself for an unbound linked OLE object in an Access form or report design. When you open the Links dialog box by choosing Links from the Edit menu, not only can you change the source of the OLE object's data, but you can also change how the OLE object is updated, convert the OLE object into a picture, edit the source, or update the OLE Object. To change how the link is updated, select the Automatic or Manual option button. To update the link automatically, select Update Now. To convert the link into a picture, select Break Link. To edit the linked file, select Open Source.

## Adding Graphs to Forms and Reports

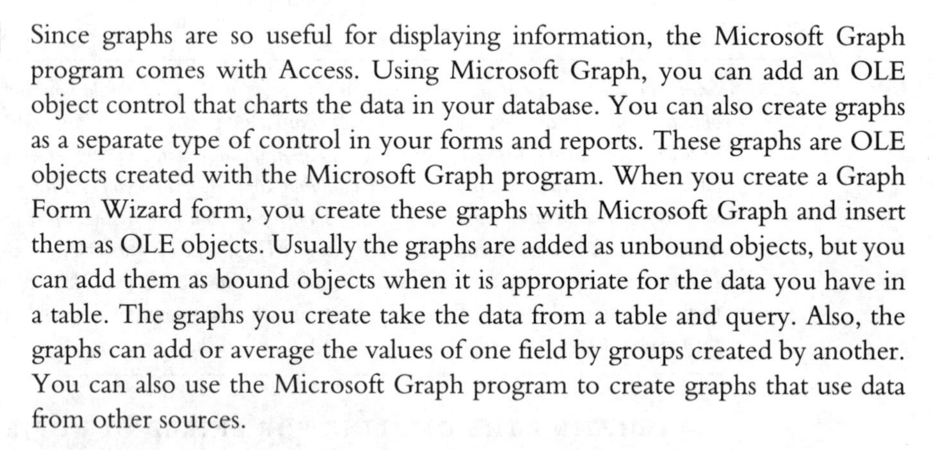

Since graphs are so useful for displaying information, the Microsoft Graph program comes with Access. Using Microsoft Graph, you can add an OLE object control that charts the data in your database. You can also create graphs as a separate type of control in your forms and reports. These graphs are OLE objects created with the Microsoft Graph program. When you create a Graph Form Wizard form, you create these graphs with Microsoft Graph and insert them as OLE objects. Usually the graphs are added as unbound objects, but you can add them as bound objects when it is appropriate for the data you have in a table. The graphs you create take the data from a table and query. Also, the graphs can add or average the values of one field by groups created by another. You can also use the Microsoft Graph program to create graphs that use data from other sources.

### Adding a Graph Control to a Form or Report

A graph is added to form and report designs by adding a control for the graph, just as you added controls for other parts of a form or report. After you add a graph control to a form or report design, Access starts the Graph Wizard, which prompts you for the graph type and the data that will appear in the graph. These are the same prompts you see when you create a Graph Form Wizard form. Figure 15-11 shows a report design that includes a graph control. This control is added to the Report Header section, so it appears at the beginning of the report. Figure 15-12 shows the beginning of the report that this report design creates. Every time you print or preview the report, Access recalculates the values the graph displays.

To add a graph control to a form or report design, select the Graph tool from the toolbox, which looks like this:

Next, select where you want the graph to start. As with other controls, you can drag the mouse from one corner to another of the area you want the graph

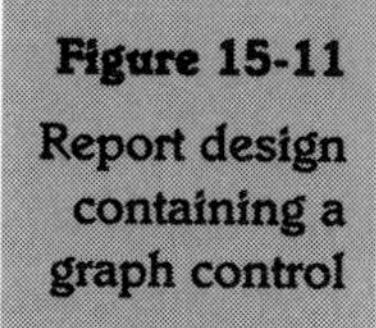

**Figure 15-11** Report design containing a graph control

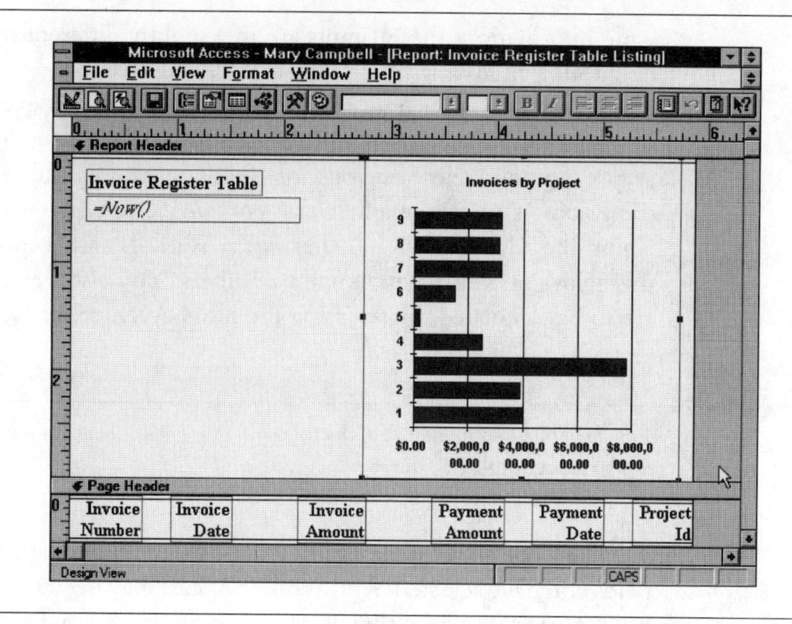


to fill. Clicking one location adds a graph of the default size, which you can later move and size.

At this point Access starts the Graph Wizard, which prompts you for the information to include in the graph. While Access versions 1 and 2 request the

**Figure 15-12** Report that incorporates a graph control into its design

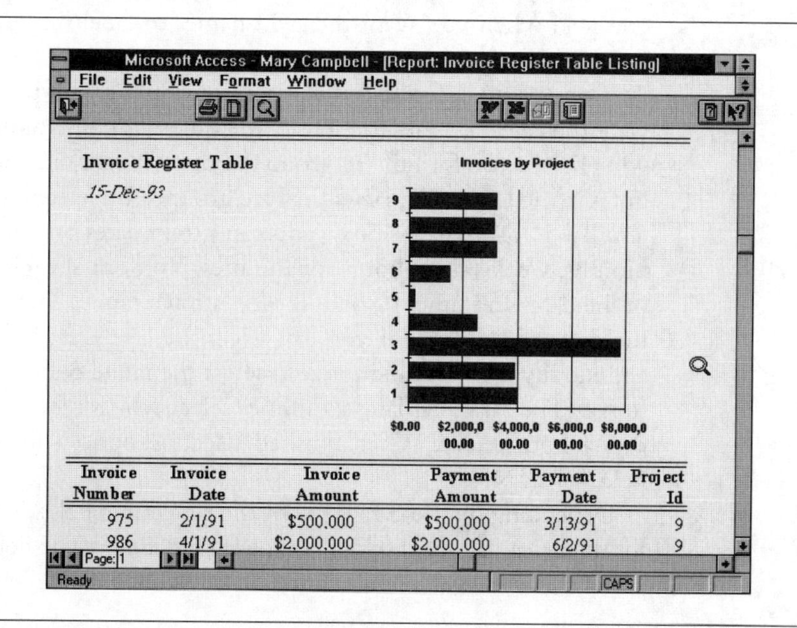

same information, the prompts are in a slightly different order. The following description follows the prompts in Access version 2.

Select the table or query used for the data in the graph by choosing a table or query. Then select Next. Now you need to select the fields to appear in the graph. You will select one or more fields containing the values you want along the X axis. This can be a field that contains text, values, or dates. Adding fields is just like adding fields in other Form Wizards and Report Wizards. Most of the fields you select will contain numbers. You also need to select how totals are to be calculated, by selecting the Sum, Average, or Count option button.

**tip:** *You do not have to include all of the fields from the table or query in the graph. Include only those fields you want to see in the graph.*

When you select Next again, Access looks at the Data Type property of the fields you have selected. At this point Access may need more information about how to use some of the fields. If one of the fields is a Text data type or if all of the fields are Number data types, the Graph Wizard prompts for the fields to use for labeling the points on the X axis. Usually you will select a single field, so that the points along the X axis are labeled with the entries in that field. For example, in Figure 15-11, the contents of the Project Id field label the X axis. This axis appears vertical because the graph's axes are rotated. Select more than one field when you want the field names to label the X axis. After selecting these fields, select Next.

If one of the selected fields is a Date/Time data type, Access assumes you want the dates or times to identify the different points along the X axis. Access will prompt you for how to group the dates. You can choose how the dates or times in the Date/Time data field are grouped by selecting a term in the Group *field* By drop-down list box. You can group dates or times by years, quarters, months, weeks, days, hours, or minutes. You can also choose to use either all of the dates and times or only those within a range. The default is to use all of the dates and times, but you can select the Use Data Between option button and modify the dates and times to select the range of dates and times you want to use. The range of dates and times select which records the graph uses from the table or query. When finished selecting options for the Date/Time data field, select Next.

Depending on the data types of the remaining fields, you may be prompted for the fields you want to use for the legend. Select one field to use the contents of the field as the legend entries or select multiple fields to use the field names as the legend entries.

Access displays a confirmation message box asking if you want to link the graph with one of the fields in the form or report. Select Yes when you want only the records selected by the current record in the form or report to be included in the graph.

For example, if you want separate graphs for each of the projects, select Yes, since you will use the records only for specific projects that change as the project numbers change. Select No on other occasions. If you select No, Access proceeds to open Microsoft Graph and start the Chart Wizard (as described below), just as Access will do after you choose how to link the graph to fields in the form or report.

If you select Yes in the confirmation message box, Access needs to know how to link the fields in the graph with the fields in the form or report; the dialog box shown in Figure 15-13 appears. If the graph uses the same table or query as the form or report, you usually are connecting the same named fields. If the graph uses a different table or query as the form or report, you are often connecting the same fields you would use to link the two tables or queries if you used them in a main/subform form or main/subreport report. Under the Form fields and Graph fields list boxes, select the fields you want to link and then select the <=> button. The link you have just created appears in the Link(s) list box below. You can create one link or many links. In a report that uses groups, you may want many links for each of the different groups the report uses. After the links are created, select Next.

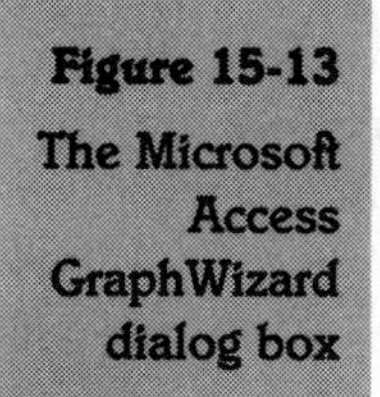

**Figure 15-13** The Microsoft Access GraphWizard dialog box

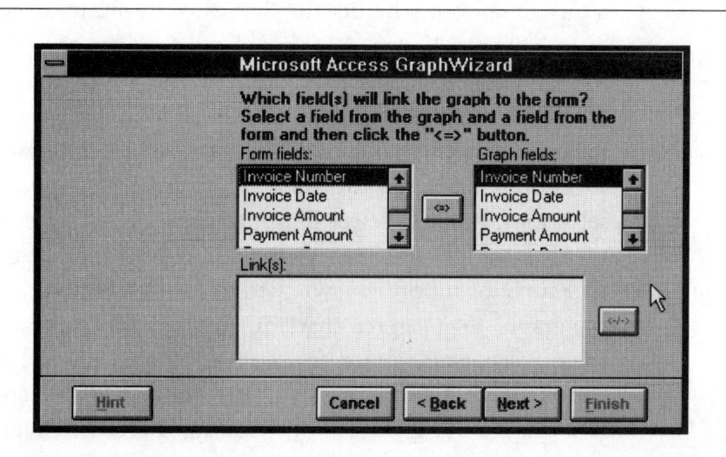

Now Access starts the Microsoft Graph program and the Chart Wizard, which will prompt you for further information about how you want your graph or chart created. Notice that, while you never seem to leave the Access window, several new menu options appear on the menu bar. These are menu options from the Microsoft Graph application. Choose which type of graph you want to create by selecting one of the 15 buttons shown next, which represent the different graph types. These are the same types you saw with the Graph Form Wizard. After selecting the graph type, choose the Next button.

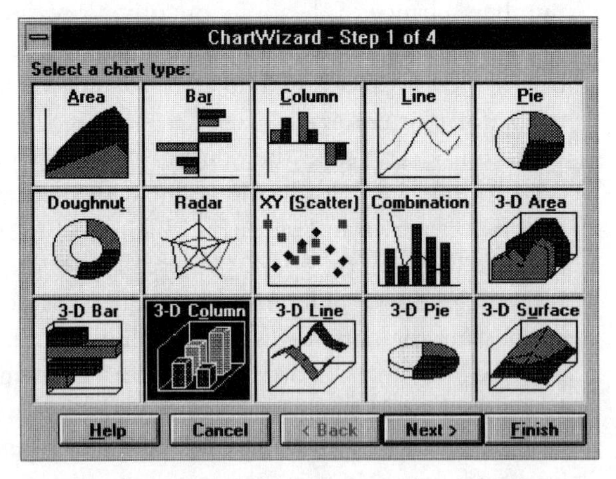


You are now prompted to select a specific format for the type of graph you selected. The available formats depend on the type of graph you selected. After choosing a format, select Next again.

You are now prompted for how the data is arranged, in rows or in columns. You can choose whether the first row or column of data is used as a data series or to label the X axis or legend. You can view the effects of your selections in the sample graph, to make sure that you are presenting the data the way you want to. After making these selections, choose Next. You are now prompted to decide whether you want the legend, to enter a chart title, and, if appropriate, to choose titles for the different axes. When you are finished with these selections, you can select Finish to create your graph control.

After the graph is added, the graph control appears on the form or report. The form or report has switched to Form or Preview view so that you can see the graph. You can tell that you are in Form or Preview view because of how the other controls in the form or report appear and because the Access toolbar has changed. The Microsoft Graph commands still appear in the menu bar, as you can see in Figure 15-14, because Microsoft Graph is still open.

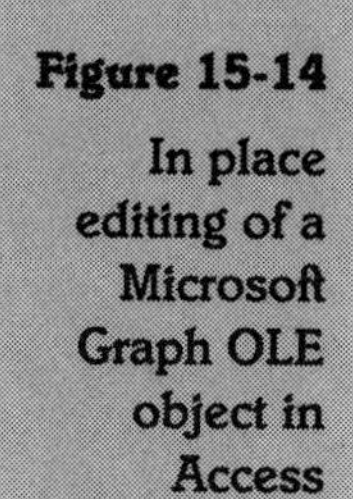

**Figure 15-14** In place editing of a Microsoft Graph OLE object in Access

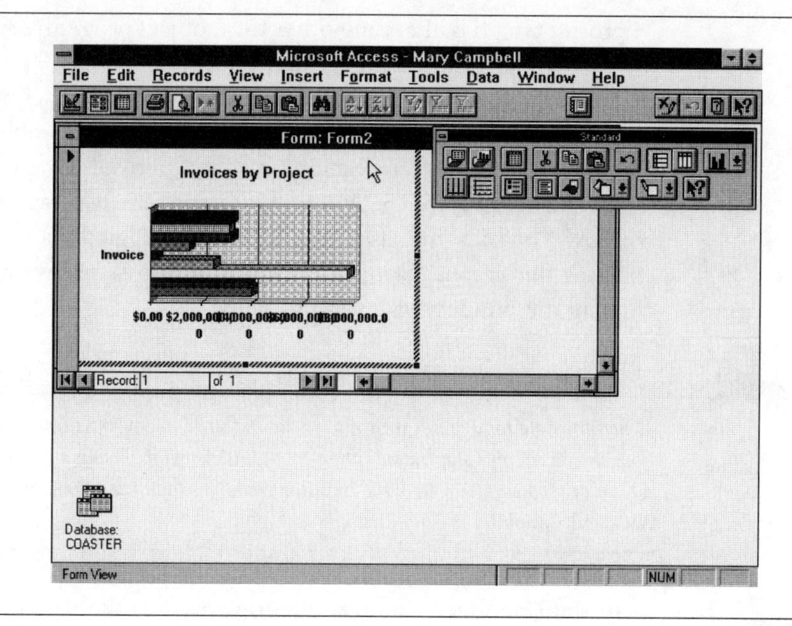


To close Microsoft Graph and return to working in Access only, click somewhere on the form or report outside of the graph. When you look at the properties for this control, notice that OLE Class is Microsoft Graph, Row Source Type is Table/Query, and Link Master Fields and Link Child Fields are set to create any link. The Row Source property contains an SQL statement. This statement selects the data from the selected table/query that appears in the graph. You will learn more about SQL statements in Appendix D. The Graph Wizard creates the SQL statement for you using the selections you have made. The graph control may appear shaded if you change this graph by opening Microsoft Graph in a separate application window.

## Adding a Graph Using Other Data

When the data you want to appear in a graph is not part of a table or query, you create a graph differently. You can create a graph for a form or report that does not use data from a table or query. A graph that does not use data from a table or query is added to forms and reports by adding an unbound object frame control that you fill with the Microsoft Graph OLE object. Adding this unbound control adds an embedded Microsoft Graph object. All of the data that is part of the graph must be entered in the Microsoft Graph program. Using

Microsoft Graph is like using other OLE object programs, since you are creating the object you want to appear in the form or report.

To add a graph control to a form or report design, choose Insert Object in the Edit menu just as if you are adding another OLE object. From the list of object types, select Microsoft Graph. The Microsoft Graph application window looks like Figure 15-15. Microsoft Graph has two windows: the Datasheet window contains the data displayed by the graph and the Chart window contains the graph. Switch between the two windows by pressing F6 or by clicking the window you wish to be in.

**tip:** *When the data for a graph is in Access, do not use Insert Object in the Edit menu to add a graph from the Microsoft Graph application to a form or report. Using a graph control to add a graph to a form or report lets Access handle putting the data from the form's or report's table or query into Microsoft Graph.*

In the Datasheet window, the top row lists the data to appear along the X axis, and the data in the left column makes up the entries that appear in the legend. The rest of the datasheet window contains the data that is graphically displayed in the graph. You can type entries in each of the cells of the datasheet. You also can paste data from other applications that you have copied to the

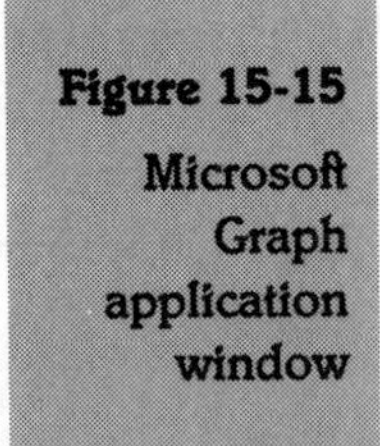

**Figure 15-15** Microsoft Graph application window

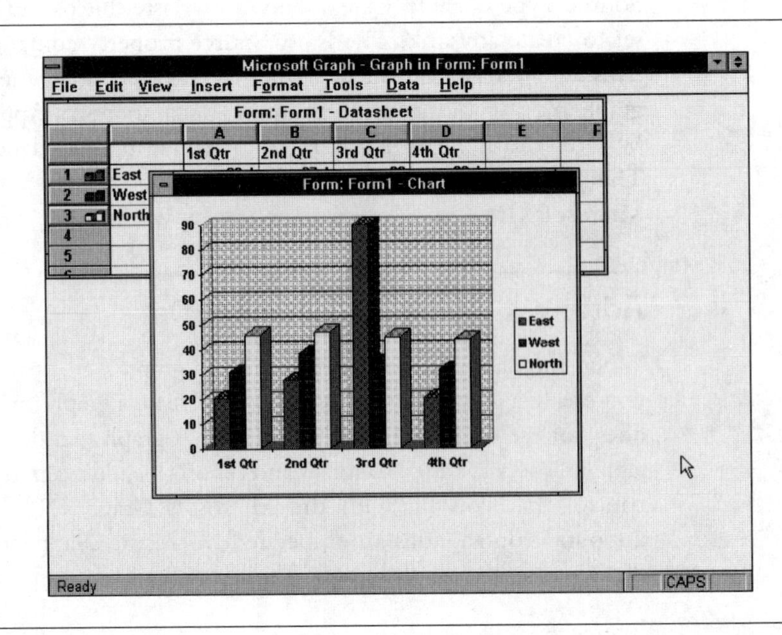

Clipboard. Since you are copying the values of the Clipboard entries, if the values change in the applications you created them in, the values in the graph are not updated. As you change the entries in the Datasheet window, Microsoft Graph updates the chart in the Chart window. When finished adding the data, choose Exit and Return to Microsoft Access in the File menu and then choose Yes from the confirmation message box to update the changes in Access. The graph looks just like the graphs you have added to forms and reports using the graph control.

**tip:** *If you want to use values from another application's file that you want updated in Access as the data changes, attach the data from the file into a table in Access, as described in Chapter 5. This works for all of the formats that support attaching tables, including Excel, dBASE, Btrieve, and SQL databases.*

## Making Changes to the Graph

You can make several changes to the graphs you create for your forms and reports. The best way to change which data appears in the graph is to create a new graph control as a replacement for the old one. Creating a new graph control means you do not have to decipher the SQL statement that selects the table's or query's data to use in the graph. If the graph contains data that is not stored in a table or query, you can start Microsoft Graph by double-clicking the control and then change the data that needs to be updated.

Make other changes to the graph's appearance using the Microsoft Graph program. Some of the changes you can make include selecting colors, adding labels to identify data points, and adding grid lines. To make these changes, first double-click the graph in the form or report design. To change the size of the graph the control represents, drag the boundary of the graph window to the size you want for the report.

Once in Microsoft Graph, you can use the menus to change the graph's appearance. Select Data Labels in the Insert menu (Chart in Access version 1) and then select the option button for how you want the data labels to appear. Figure 15-16 shows a graph in a report that displays data labels; the legend has been removed.

Change the graph's type by selecting another type after choosing Chart Type from the Format menu in Access version 2, or by selecting a chart type from the Gallery menu in Access version 1. Once you click part of the graph to select it, you can use the Format drop-down menu to change how the selected graph object appears. In Access version 2, for example, when you select a series, choose

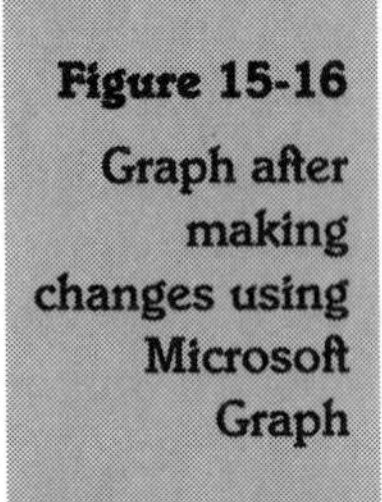

**Figure 15-16** Graph after making changes using Microsoft Graph

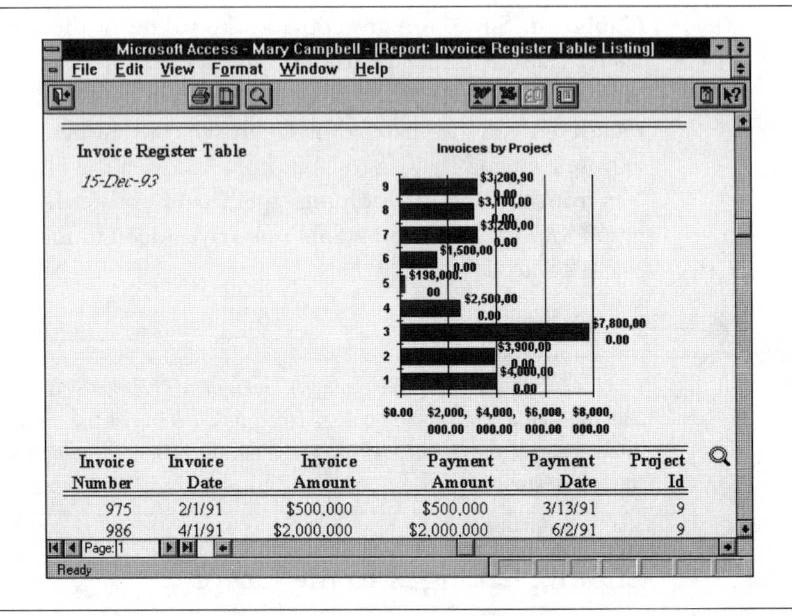


Selected Data Series from the Format menu to change the color and pattern of the series. In Access version 1, you would select the series and then select Patterns from the Format menu. A *series* is a set of values that use the same color or pattern.

You can also set the font of a selected graph object with Font in the Format menu. As you work with the Microsoft Graph program, try out the different features. You can always return to Access without saving the changes you have made to the graph by selecting No from the confirmation message box when you leave Microsoft Graph. Update the graph in Access as you work on it in Microsoft Graph by choosing Update from the File menu. When finished with your changes, choose Exit and Return to Microsoft Access in the File menu, and then choose Yes from the confirmation message box to update the changes in Access.

The graph title will probably be the only change you make by modifying the SQL statement. If you look at the graph's current title and then look at the SQL statement, you can see which part of the SQL statement you need to change. When you look at the Row Source property, you can see the entire SQL statement by pressing SHIFT+F2 to display the statement in a Zoom dialog box.

Quick Reference

**To Add an Unbound Control for a New Embedded OLE Object to a Form or Report Design** Select the Object Frame tool from the toolbox. Click where you want the object to start. Select the application for the type of data you want to add from the Object Type list box. Create the data you want to appear as the embedded object. Choose Exit or Return from the File menu. When prompted about updating or saving the changes, select Yes.

**To Add Existing Data as an OLE Object to an Unbound Control in a Form or Report Design** Select the Object Frame control from the toolbox. Click where you want the object to start. Select the Create from File button (the File button in Access version 1). Select the name of the file that you want to use and OK.

**To Add the Clipboard's Contents as an Embedded OLE Object to a Form or Report Design** Move to the section of the form or report design where you want to embed an unbound form or report control. Choose Paste from the Edit menu.

**To Add a Linked OLE Object to a Form or Report Design** Copy the data you want to appear in the linked OLE object to the Clipboard. Switch to Access and move to the section of the form or report design where you want the linked unbound form or report control. In Access version 2, select Paste Special from the Edit menu and then select the Paste Link option button and OK. In Access version 1, choose Paste Link from the Edit menu and select OK.

**To Add a Bound Control for a New Embedded OLE Object to a Form or Report Design** Select the Bound Object Frame tool from the toolbox. Click where you want the object to start. Change the Control Source property of this control to the name of the field you want to appear in the object frame.

**To Add a New Embedded OLE Object to a Field** Choose Insert Object in the Edit menu. Select the application for the type of data you

Quick Reference

want to add from the Object Type list box. Create the data you want to appear as the embedded object. Choose Exit or Return from the File menu. When prompted about updating or saving the changes, select Yes.

**To Add Existing Data as an Embedded OLE Object in a Field** Choose Insert Object in the Edit menu. Select the Create from File button. Select the name of the file that you want to use and OK.

**To Add the Clipboard's Contents as an Embedded OLE Object to a Field** Move to the OLE Object data field and choose Paste from the Edit menu.

**To Add a Linked OLE Object to a Field** Copy the data you want to appear as the linked OLE object to the Clipboard. Switch to Access and move to the field where you want the linked OLE object. In Access version 2, select Paste Special from the Edit menu and then select the Paste Link option button and OK. In Access version 1, choose Paste Link from the Edit menu and select OK.

**To Make an OLE Object Uneditable** Choose *OLE Class* Object from the Edit menu and Change to Picture.

**To Edit an OLE Object** Double-click the OLE object in the Datasheet or Form view. OLE objects that are part of a form's or report's design must be edited from the Design view.

**To Add a Graph Control to a Form or Report** Click the Graph tool in the Tool Bar and then click where you want the graph to start. For each of the subsequent dialog boxes, select the information you are prompted for, such as the fields the report includes, its style, and its title. When you select Finish from the final dialog box, the graph is created. You can also add a graph by adding an unbound object frame control and selecting Microsoft Graph as the application. When you create the graph using this method, you must enter the data the graph charts.

# IV

# Macros and Programming

# Chapter 16

# Macro Basics

ACCESS makes it easy to create macros to automate any task. You can either select from a list of actions or drag the appropriate object to the Macro window to record the action that you want to perform. Once created, you execute the macro to perform the action. Each time you use the macro, you are guaranteed the same results. Since Access macros are so easy to create, they do not require the attention to detail required in earlier macro products.

Macros are especially suited to creating your own custom menus and controlling the use of forms and reports. These topics are covered in Chapters 17 and 18. This chapter addresses a few quick basics that will work with macros regardless of where you decide to use them. Master these building blocks and you will be ready to look at more sophisticated examples of their use.

## Why Use Macros?

Increased productivity is the most important reason to use macros. You can record the steps for a task that you perform often. When you need the task performed, you can simply run the macro, often by pressing only a few keys.

Macros also provide capabilities that are not otherwise possible. For example, you can use macros to validate data entered on forms before the record is saved. You can also update a second form based on the values entered and saved in the first form. You can attach macros to command buttons that you add to forms to make it easy to select a task. You can also create a custom menu bar and pop-up forms for the collection of information, and customize your workspace in other ways with macros.

Access macros are easier to record than macros in other packages. Most other macro features require a significant amount of typing on your part and have required entries where a slight mistake results in a syntax error and a failed macro. This is not the case with Access since everything is menu selectable.

## Creating and Using Macros

Access macros consist of a series of actions that can be selected from a list to make up each macro instruction. You can add comments to your macro to explain the need for each step. Actions can have *arguments,* which define the objects that will be used with each action.

You enter macros in the Macro window that is displayed when you click the Macro button in the Database window and then click the New button. Macro windows have different sections to organize the entry of actions, comments, and arguments as shown in Figure 16-1.

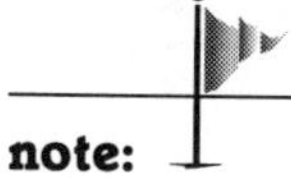

**note:** *When you create macros for a network environment, you should complete the macro and any of the objects it refers to before making it available to network users. Also, when you modify macros that users may be working with, you will want to insure that you have exclusive use of the database while you make the modifications.*

The entries in the Action column tell Access what you want to do. The entries in the Comment column document your selection of different actions. Arguments in the bottom half of the Macro window further specify how an action works. Arguments do not display until you have selected an action. The list of arguments that displays within the window depends on which action has

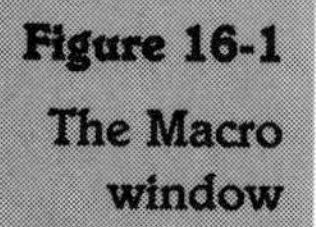

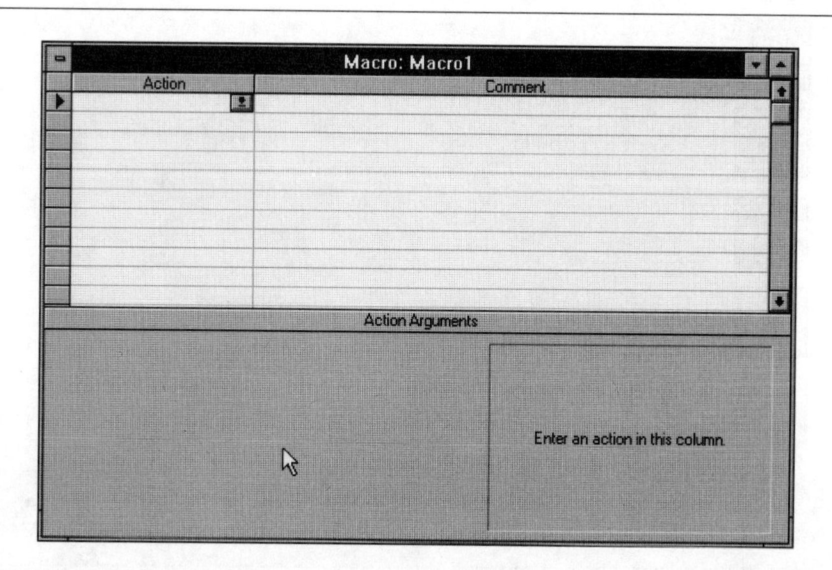


**Figure 16-1** The Macro window

the focus, the insertion point that indicates the macro action you are working with. The toolbar is different since the toolbar now contains the buttons for macro tasks shown in Table 16-1.

## Creating the Macro

You must record the actions that you want a macro to perform before you can use it. Macros are always created in a special Macro window. At a minimum,

| Button | Tool Name |
|---|---|
| 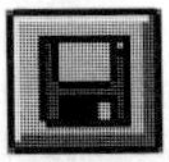 | Save |
|  | Macro Names |
| 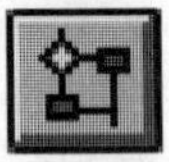 | Conditions |
|  | Run |
|  | Step Into |
|  | Database Window |
|  | Build |
|  | Undo |
|  | Cue Cards |
|  | Help |

**Table 16-1**
**Macro Window Toolbar Buttons**

this window has two columns at the top for actions and comments and a bottom section for the arguments associated with each action. Optionally, you can display two additional columns in the top part of the window as you learn to show macro names and conditions that affect whether or not actions are executed. The display of these columns and the entries that you place in them are discussed later in this chapter. With all the help that Access provides, the process is really quite easy once you have created a few macros.

You enter actions in the top part of the window by typing them or using the drop-down list box to select the action you want. To supply values for arguments use F6 to move to the bottom of the window and complete each argument entry. Use F6 when ready to move back to the top part of the window.

To create a macro you must open the Macro window as your first step. From the Database window, follow these steps:

1. Click the Macro button in the Database window.

   If you have already created macros, a list of their names appears in the Database window.

2. Click the New button shown in Figure 16-2.

   A Macro window that looks like Figure 16-1 will appear. Record macro actions in the order in which you want them to execute.

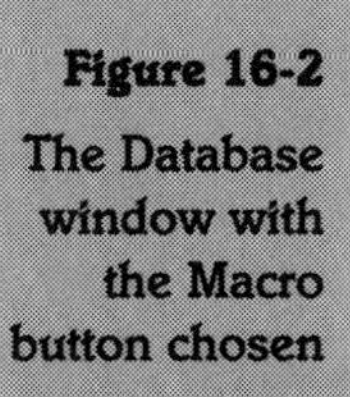

**Figure 16-2**
**The Database window with the Macro button chosen**

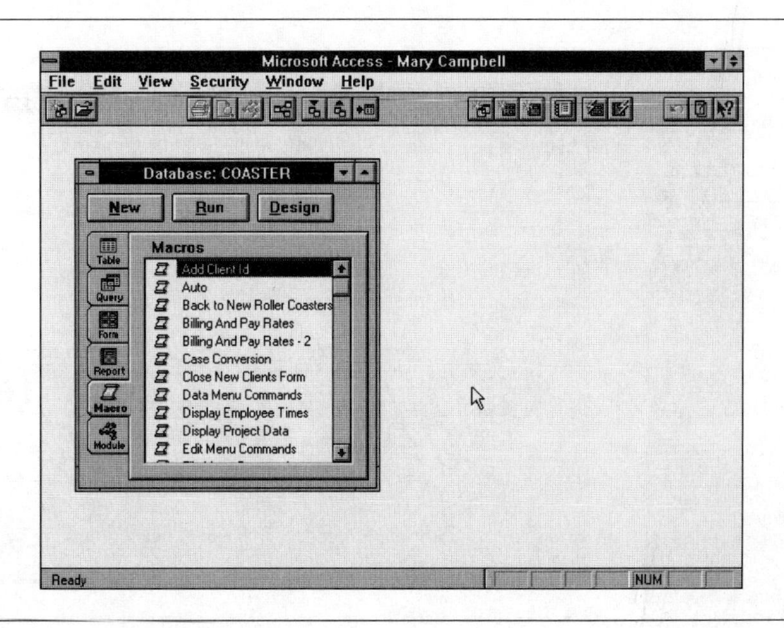

3. Click the arrow to display the action list shown here:

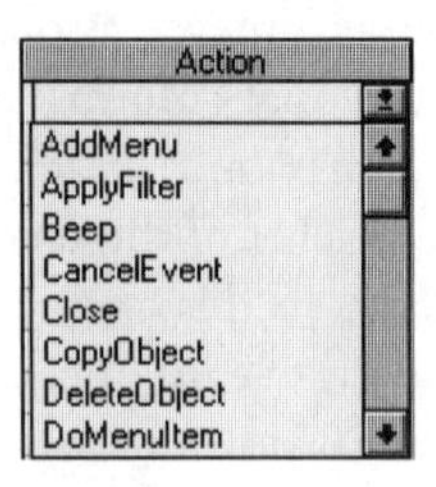


4. Select the action you want or type the name of the action.

   If you display the Database window, you can also select actions by dragging an object from the Database window to an action row. You will first need to click the button for the type of object you want to drag. Dragging a table, form, report, or query adds an open action and supplies an argument for the specific object selected. When you drag a macro, a run action is added.

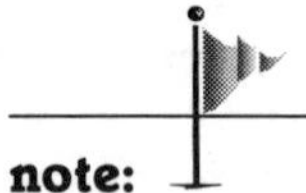

**note:** *If the Database window is not easily accessible, press* F11 *or click the Database Window button in the Access version 2 toolbar. You can use the function key or toolbar button in place of the Window menu to display it quickly.*

**Figure 16-3** A comment entered for the Hourglass action

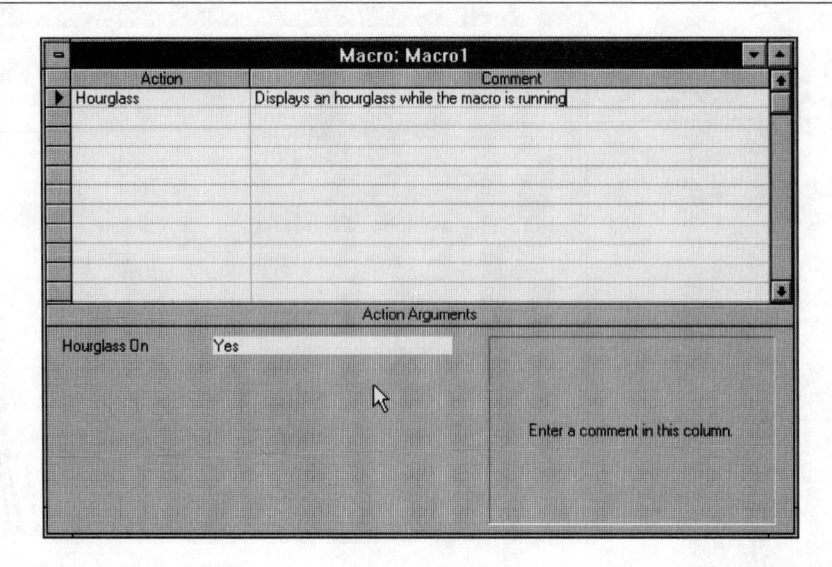

The Hourglass action selected in the example will display an hourglass while the action runs.

5. Type a comment in the Comments column as shown in Figure 16-3, where the comment reflects the Hourglass action.

   Comments are optional but you should include them. Comments let you know how a macro works months after you create it. When a complex macro does not have comments, the macro will be difficult to modify if you need to make revisions in the future.

6. Press F6 to move to the arguments or click the argument that you want to change.

7. Complete the argument entries.

**tip:** *In Access version 2 if you make a mistake while entering an action or an argument, you can use the Undo button in the Macro toolbar.*

Figure 16-4 shows the argument entries for the Print action. Access initially sets the Print Range argument to All, which means the Page From and Page To arguments are empty. After Print Range is changed

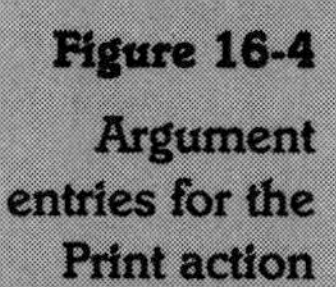

**Figure 16-4**
**Argument entries for the Print action**

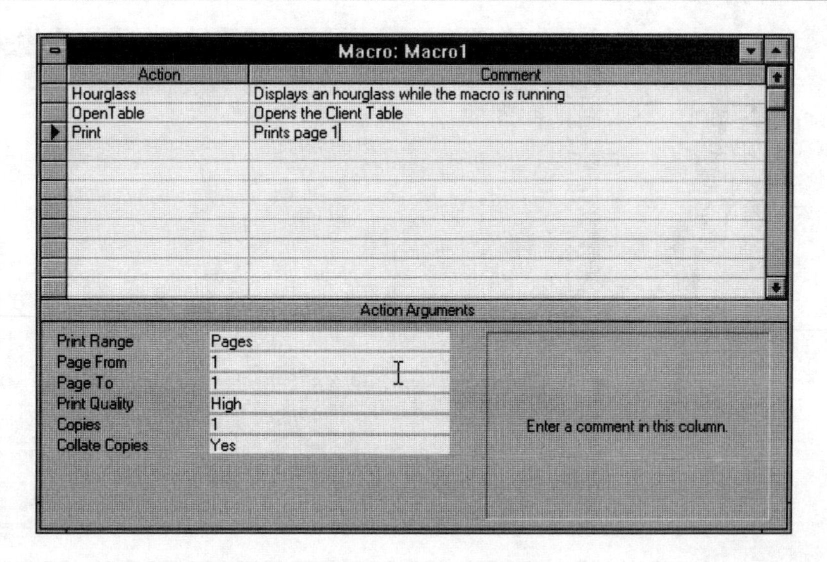

to Pages, complete these arguments by typing **1** after each of them. The other actions, Hourglass and OpenTable, have their arguments set separately.

8. Press F6 to move to the top and use the DOWN ARROW or TAB to move to the next row and select another action.

   Figure 16-5 shows the macro with another action. This one requires that you specify an object type and name.

With the macro entries complete, save the macro, close the Macro window, and try executing the macro.

## Saving the Macro

Like other Access objects, macros are stored with the database but you will need to save each macro with a unique name. Use the Save command in the File menu to save the macro. If you have Access version 2, you can also click the Save button in the toolbar. You will need to supply a name for the macro if you have not saved it before. Restrict your entry to no more than 64 characters. Leading spaces and control characters are not acceptable in macro names.

Close the Macro window after saving by choosing Close from the File menu. The name that you assign to the macro displays in the Database window. Notice

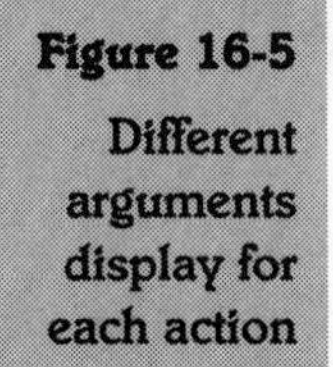

**Figure 16-5** Different arguments display for each action

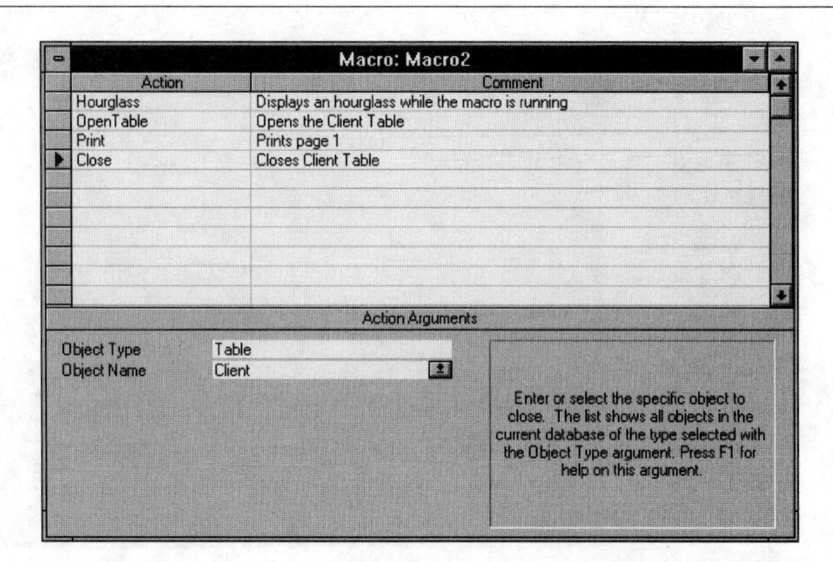

that two new buttons are now available: Run and Design. Use the Run button to execute the macro from this window and the Design button when you want to modify your entries. You also can double-click a macro's name to run the macro or double-click the macro's name using the right mouse button in Access version 1 button to open the Macro window and make changes to the macro's design.

## Executing the Macro

You can run a macro from the Macro window or from other locations. To run a macro from the Macro window, simply click the Run button in the toolbar (the Run button has what looks like an exclamation point on it, as shown in Table 16-1). To run a macro from the Database window click the Macro button, select the macro, and click the Run button. From other locations, choose Run Macro from the File menu, select the macro to run, and select OK.

## Actions and Arguments

An action is nothing more than an instruction that tells Access to perform a task for you. The task might be opening a table, saving a report design, displaying an hourglass, or closing a table. So you don't have to worry about the syntax of action entries, they are all prerecorded for you in a list that you can select from. Many actions are specified as two words with no space between them where initial capital letters are used for each word, such as OpenTable.

### CATEGORIES OF ACTIONS

Access categorizes actions into five different groups depending on how they are used. These groups are *Data in forms and reports, Execution, Import/export, Object manipulation,* and *Miscellaneous.*

Actions in the Data in forms and reports category either restrict data or move from record to record. The ApplyFilter action restricts data. The FindNext, FindRecord, GoToControl, GoToPage, and GoToRecord actions all move you from one record to another.

Actions in the Execution category either perform or stop a task. You can use the DoMenuItem to execute a menu command. Macro procedures can be executed with either OpenQuery, RunCode, RunMacro, or RunSQL. You can even run another DOS or Windows application with the RunApp action. To stop execution, you can use CancelEvent, Quit, StopMacro, or StopAllMacros.

The Import/export action category transfers data between Access and other applications. The actions are TransferDatabase, TransferText, and Transfer-Spreadsheet.

Object manipulation actions are the largest category. You can use SetValue to set the value of a field, property, or control. To update objects use the RepaintObject, Requery, and ShowAllRecords actions. To select an object use the SelectObject action. Objects can be copied or renamed with CopyObject and Rename. You can open or close an object with OpenForm, OpenQuery, OpenReport, OpenTable, DoMenuItem, and Close. You can use the Print action to print an object once you open it. To work with windows use the Minimize, Maximize, MoveSize, and Restore actions.

The Miscellaneous actions are those that do not fit into the other categories. Echo, Hourglass, MsgBox, and SetWarnings all display information. SendKeys generates keystrokes and Beep sounds a beep noise. The AddMenu action creates a custom menu bar.

## SETS OF ARGUMENTS

Each action has its own set of arguments. These arguments define the data that should be used for the action or how it is to take place. Think of arguments as the specifications for the action. For example, if you wanted to have a tailor make a suit, the making of the suit is the desired action and the measurements of the individual it needs to fit are the arguments. When you use the OpenTable action, the arguments are the table to be opened, the view that you want the table to display in (datasheet or design), and the Data Mode with the default being Edit.

**tip:** *Arguments that require expression are easier to enter with Access version 2 since you can click the Build button in the toolbar and utilize the Expression Builder for your entries.*

Just as you can pick actions from drop-down list boxes, many arguments have drop-down list boxes providing a choice of options. You can click the arrow or press ALT+DOWN ARROW to see the list of possibilities if an arrow displays at the right side of the argument entry area. Table 16-2 shows the arguments for each of the actions supported by Access.

| Action | Arguments | Use |
|---|---|---|
| AddMenu | Menu Name<br>Menu Macro Name<br>Status Bar Text | Adds a drop-down menu |
| ApplyFilter | Filter Name<br>Where Condition | Restricts or sorts an underlying table or query |
| Beep | No arguments | Sounds a beep |
| CancelEvent | No arguments | Cancels the event that caused Access to run the macro |
| Close | Object Type<br>Object Name | Closes the active window or the specified window |
| CopyObject | Destination Database<br>New Name<br>Source Object Type<br>Source Object Name | Copies a database object |
| Delete Object | Object Type<br>Object Name | Deletes a database object |
| DoMenuItem | Menu Bar<br>Menu Name<br>Command<br>Subcommand | Executes an Access menu command |
| Echo | Echo On<br>Status Bar Text | Determines whether or not the screen is updated |
| FindNext | No arguments | Finds the next matching record |
| FindRecord | Find What<br>Where<br>Match Case<br>Direction<br>Search As Formatted<br>Search In<br>Find First | Finds the record specified by the arguments |
| GoToControl | Control Name | Moves the focus to the field or control specified |
| GoToPage | Page Number<br>Right<br>Down | Moves the focus to the specified page |
| GoToRecord | Object Type<br>Object Name<br>Record<br>Offset | Moves to the specified record in the table, form, or query |
| Hourglass | Hourglass On | Changes the mouse pointer to an hourglass to indicate the macro is running |
| Maximize | No arguments | Maximizes the active window to fill the Access window |
| Minimize | No arguments | Minimizes the window to an icon |

**Table 16-2**
**Macro Actions and Arguments**

| Action | Arguments | Use |
|---|---|---|
| MoveSize | Right<br>Down<br>Width<br>Height | Moves or resizes the window |
| MsgBox | Message<br>Beep<br>Type<br>Title | Displays one of several styles of message boxes |
| OpenForm | Form Name<br>View<br>Filter Name<br>Where Condition<br>Data Mode<br>Window Mode | Opens a form in the specified view |
| OpenModule | Module Name<br>Procedure Name | Opens a module |
| OpenQuery | Query Name<br>View<br>Data Mode | Opens a crosstab or select query |
| OpenReport | Report Name<br>View<br>Filter Name<br>Where Condition | Opens the specified report |
| OpenTable | Table Name<br>View<br>Data Mode | Opens a table |
| OutputTo | Object Type<br>Object Name<br>Object Format<br>File<br>Auto Start | Specifies the object and the output file |
| Print | Print Range<br>Page From<br>Page To<br>Print Quality<br>Copies<br>Collate Copies | Prints the active object |
| Quit | Options | Exits Access |
| Rename | New Name<br>Object Type<br>Old Name | Names the selected object |
| RepaintObject | Object Type<br>Object Name | Updates the screen |
| Requery | Control Name | Updates the data in a control |
| Restore | No arguments | Restores a window to previous size |

**Table 16-2**
**Macro Actions and Arguments (continued)**

| Action | Arguments | Use |
|---|---|---|
| RunApp | Command Line | Runs another application |
| RunCode | Function Name | Executes an AccessBasic function |
| RunMacro | Macro Name<br>Repeat Count<br>Repeat Expression | Executes a macro |
| RunSQL | SQL Statement | Runs an SQL query |
| SelectObject | Object Type<br>Object Name<br>In Database Window | Selects a database object |
| SendKeys | Keystrokes<br>Wait | Sends keystrokes to an application |
| SendObject | Object Type<br>Object Name<br>Output Format<br>To<br>Cc<br>Bcc<br>Subject<br>Message Text<br>Edit Message | Specifies the object to be sent and its destination |
| SetValue | Item<br>Expression | Sets the value of a control, field, or property |
| SetWarnings | Warnings On | Turns the system messages on or off |
| ShowAllRecords | No arguments | Removes all filters |
| ShowToolbar | Toolbar Name<br>Show | Shows or hides a custom or built-in toolbar |
| StopAllMacros | No arguments | Stops all macros |
| StopMacro | No arguments | Stops the current macro |
| TransferDatabase | Transfer Type<br>Database Type<br>Database Name<br>Object Type<br>Source<br>Destination<br>Structure Only | Imports or exports data |
| TransferSpreadsheet | Transfer Type<br>Spreadsheet Type<br>Table Name<br>File Name<br>Has Field Names<br>Range | Exports or imports data |
| TransferText | Transfer Type<br>Specification Name<br>Table Name<br>File Name<br>Has Field Names | Exports or imports data |

**Table 16-2**
**Macro Actions and Arguments (continued)**

### Speeding the Process with Shortcuts

If you choose Tile from the Window menu, you can see the Macro window and Database window on the desktop at the same time. With the database objects in view you can drag them to the Macro window to supply both actions and arguments. Create an OpenTable, OpenQuery, OpenForm, and OpenReport action by dragging the object listed in the name of the action to a blank action row. Dragging a table from the Database window creates the OpenTable action quicker than you can select it from the drop-down list box. If the row is not blank, Access inserts a row for the new action. If you drag another Macro object, Access adds a RunMacro action.

When you drag objects to macro actions, Access fills in several of the arguments for you. You can supply arguments for some actions by dragging objects to the arguments. For example, when the action is Close, you can drag the table, query, or form you want closed to supply the Object Type and Object Name arguments. The commands and arguments that support this dragging action are shown in Table 16-3.

## Modifying a Macro

You can modify macros once they are created by adding and deleting rows and changing the values of arguments. You can also change the order of the macro's

| Action | Argument | Drag |
|---|---|---|
| AddMenu | Menu Macro Name | Macro |
| Close | Object Type<br>Object Name | Any Object |
| GoToRecord | Object Type<br>Object Name | Form, Table, Query |
| OpenForm | Form Name | Form |
| OpenQuery | Query Name | Query |
| OpenTable | Table Name | Table |
| RepaintObject | Object Type<br>Object Name | Form, Table, Query |
| RunMacro | Macro Name | Macro |
| SelectObject | Object Type<br>Object Name | Any Object |

**Table 16-3**
**Arguments Supplied by Dragging Objects**

actions to change the sequence with which they execute. To choose a replacement selection for any entry, all you have to do is make another selection.

To move an entry in a macro to a different position, click the row selector to the left of the action you want to relocate, click the row selector again and drag it to the new location.

Copy and paste techniques that you have used elsewhere in Access will work in macros. Everything attached to an action—including arguments, comments, macros, and conditional expressions—remain attached to the copy or relocated action after the copy or cut and paste operation.

The strategy you use for entering new actions depends on where in the macro the new action should be added. If it goes at the end of the macro all you need to do is move to the blank row at the end of the macro and add the new action. If you need to insert an action in the middle of the macro, click the action below where you want the new action and choose Insert Row from the Edit menu. A blank row is inserted above the selected action, and you can add a new action and complete the argument entries.

To delete an action, click the action and press the DEL key. The action, its optional comment, and any arguments are removed. Macros and conditional statements attached to the action are also deleted.

# Adding Sophistication

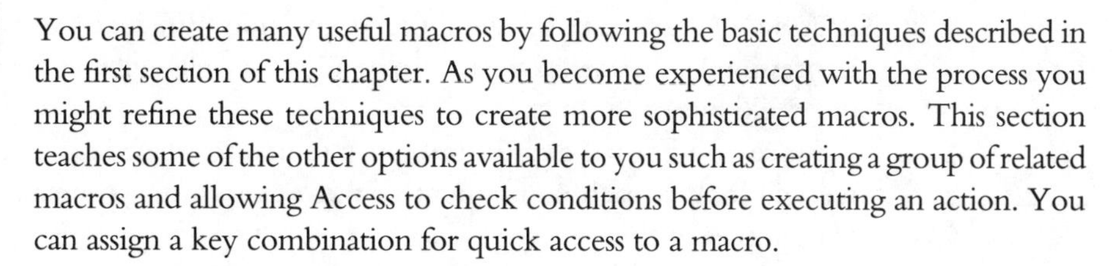
You can create many useful macros by following the basic techniques described in the first section of this chapter. As you become experienced with the process you might refine these techniques to create more sophisticated macros. This section teaches some of the other options available to you such as creating a group of related macros and allowing Access to check conditions before executing an action. You can assign a key combination for quick access to a macro.

## Using Conditions

A *condition* allows you to alter how a macro works depending upon the condition of your data. A condition is an expression Access evaluates to be either true or false. The macro will behave differently when a condition is true than it will when the condition is false.

Conditions are entered in the Conditions column of the Macro window. This column is displayed as shown in Figure 16-6 when you click the Conditions button in the toolbar or choose conditions from the view menu.

**Figure 16-6** The Conditions column displayed

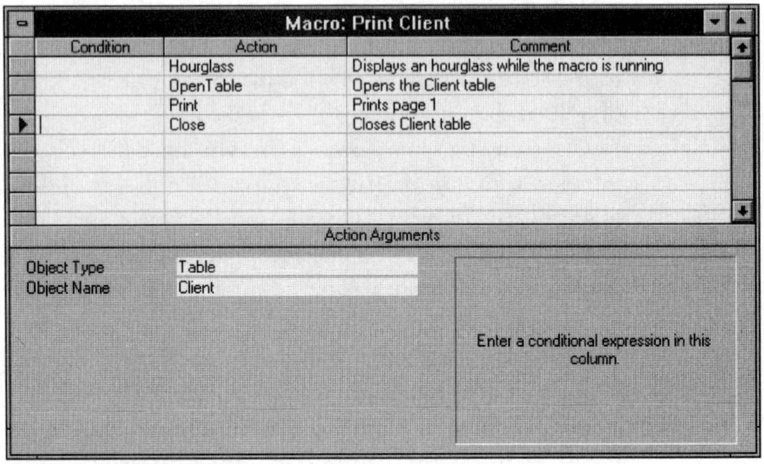

Conditions are recorded as expressions that can be evaluated as true or false. You must follow Access rules for recording expressions, constructing them carefully from allowable components, and following syntax rules when referencing database fields or controls. You have already used expressions for entering query criteria, constructing validation rules, and recording calculated controls. If you have Access version 2, you may have already seen how easy expression entry can be with the Expression Builder. You can access this Expression Builder from the macro window as well—all you need to do is select the Build button from the toolbar.

Since conditional expressions are essential to recording macro conditions, we will look at each component of these expressions in detail before looking at examples of their entry.

## COMPONENTS OF AN EXPRESSION

Like other expressions, conditions can contain operators, identifiers, functions, literals, and constants. A quick look at each component will show you how many options there are for each component of a valid expression. If you have Access version 2, the details will provide interesting background but you will be able to get the Expression Builder to handle much of the needed work.

*Operators* tell Access which operations must be performed on the elements of an expression. They can specify a comparison operation that can be evaluated as true or false and can require other operators before the expression is fully evaluated. Allowable operators in a conditional expression include the comparison operators =, <>, <, >, <=, and >=. Other types of operators such as arithmetic operators ( + – * / ^ \ and Mod), the concatenation operator (&), logical operators (And, Eqv, Imp, Not, Or, Xor) and other operators (Between, In, Is, Like) can also be used as part of these expressions.

*Identifiers* are used to reference forms, reports, fields, controls, or properties. Each identifier can have several elements with the ! and . symbols used as separators between the components. The ! is used after the name of a system object that tells what kind of object you are referring to. You will use Forms, Reports, and Screen as system object entries. The Screen object lets you refer to whatever is on the screen without identifying it by name.

Following the Forms or Reports system objects, you will enter the name of the report or form followed by the name of the field, control, or property. If you want to refer to a field, control, or property that is currently on the screen you can omit the two qualifying entries for the system object and object. The *qualifiers* are the Forms or Reports and the field or control name that appears at the beginning of the identifier. You must use brackets around these names if they contain a space and another ! between the name of the form or report and the field or control. An example is Reports![Coasters by Year]![Coaster Name]. If a property is specified the . is used as a separator.

Following the Screen system object you enter one of the three properties supported: ActiveControl, ActiveReport, or ActiveForm. Here are some examples:

*Forms![Employee Data]![First Name]* to refer to the First Name control on the Employee Data form

*Reports![Coaster Projects]![Completed]* to refer to the Completed control on the Coaster Projects report

*Screen.ActiveReport* to refer to the active report on the screen. The . is used because ActiveReport is a property

Field names that are used as part of the expression to be evaluated must be qualified. If you are checking an entry in the Pay Rate field on a form called NewEmp, an example of your condition entry might be Forms![NewEmp]![Pay Rate] <= 7.

*Functions* can be used within an expression to return a value. Access has many functions to perform mathematical or financial calculations. Avg, Count, and Date are three examples. You can also create your own function definitions through Access Basic.

*Literals* can be character strings, dates, or numbers. Numbers are entered without any special symbols to enclose them. Character strings used as part of the expression must be enclosed in quotes as in Forms![NewEmp]![Last Name]= "Smith". Number signs are used around dates as in Forms![Employee Data]![Hire Date] < #1-Jan-90#.

*Constants* represent values that do not change. True, False, Yes, No, and Null are examples of constants that can be used in expressions.

You will not use all possible components in every expression that you record. The variety of options is meant to provide flexibility. The following represent some conditions that might be entered in the Conditions column:

[Contact Name] = "John Smith"
Forms![Employee Data]![Last Name] = "Jones"
IsNull([Last Name])
[Last Name] In ("Smith", "Jones", "Walker")
LEN([Last Name]) > 1
[Park Location] = "Isle Royale" Or [City] = "Houghton"

The conditions in the previous list without system objects or form or report names all refer to the current form or report.

### PROCESSING CONDITIONS

If Access does not encounter a condition for an action, it executes the action. When a condition is present, Access first evaluates the condition. If the condition evaluates as true, the action is performed.

Access also performs any actions that follow as long as an ellipsis (. . .) is included in the Conditions column for the actions. You can enter the ellipsis by typing three periods. If the condition evaluates as false, the actions with ellipses are skipped. Figure 16-7 shows a condition entry that causes three additional actions to be performed if the condition is true. The condition IsNull([Client]![Park Location]) is true only when the Park Location control is empty. If the condition is false, only two actions are performed.

## Creating a Macro Group

A *macro group* is a macro that contains more than one macro. It is really no different than any other macro except the Macro window has multiple macro names displayed when you show the Macro Name column. Think of a macro group as a library of macros. You can execute any macro within the library. It

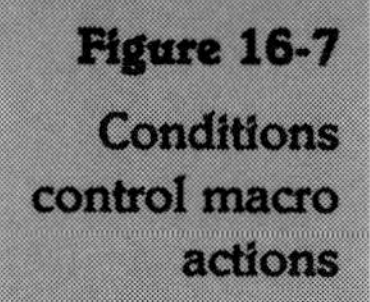

**Figure 16-7**

**Conditions control macro actions**

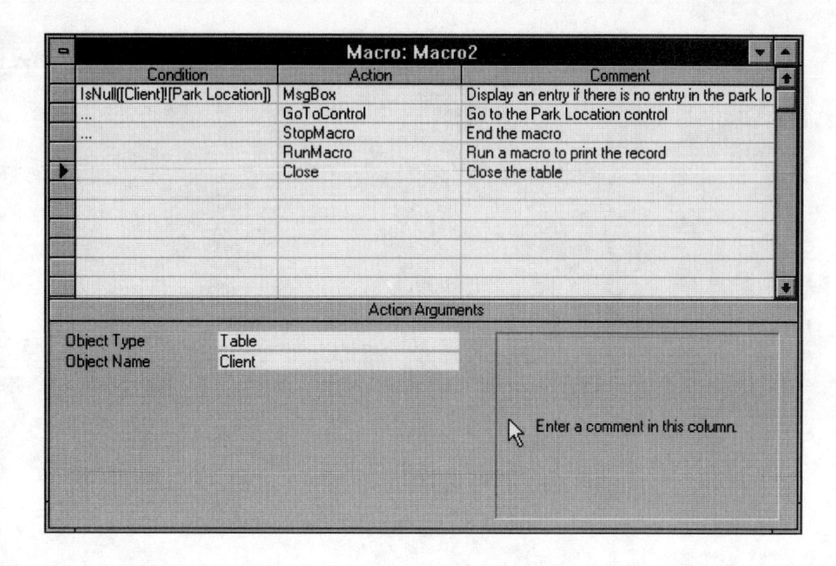


is a great solution when you have macros attached to several command buttons on a form to place all of these macros in the same group.

Creating macros within a group is no different than creating a single macro in a window except you must display the Macro Name column in the Macro window and name each macro. To display the Macro Name column, click the Macro Names button or choose Macro Names from the View menu. Figure 16-8 shows a macro group with three macro names, Print Client, Print Employee, and Print Project. Each named macro starts in the row containing the macro name and continues until the row before the next macro name. There are many modifications that you can make to these macros to add sophistication to the macros. One possibility is to add an Echo action after each Hourglass action. You can set the Echo On argument to No and provide specific status bar text such as Print Client Table.

You save the Macro window in the same way you save a single macro except the name that you assign actually refers to the group. You can execute any macro in the group by typing the macro group name, a period (.), and the macro name that you want to execute. For example, execute the Print client macro in the Print macros group by typing **Print macros.Print client** as the macro name when you want to run the macro.

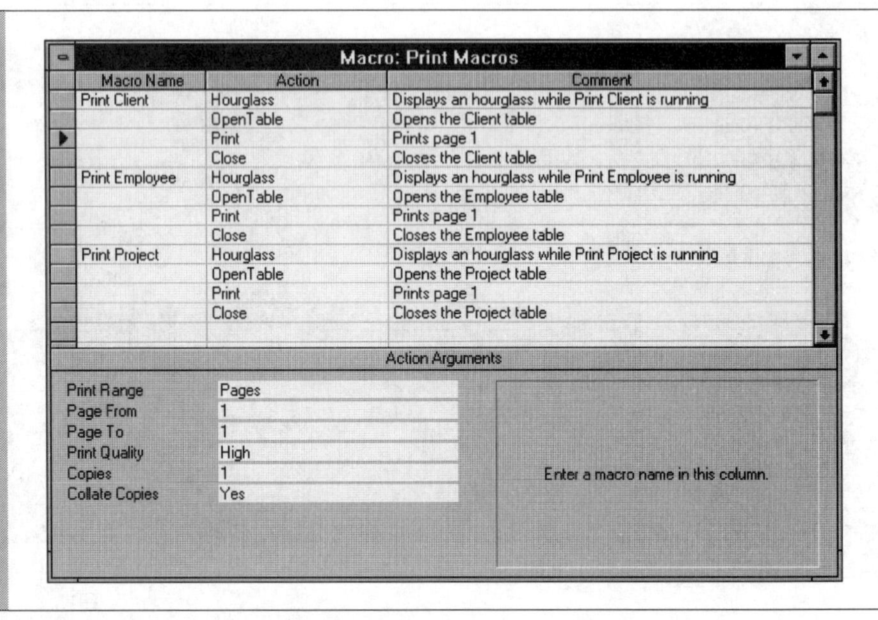


**Figure 16-8** Macro group with three macros

## Assigning a Macro to a Key

To be able to execute a macro quickly, assign it a key combination. This lets you execute the macro just by pressing the keys.

You can create one macro group that contains all of the macros that you want to assign to keys. The name of this macro group must be AutoKeys. The key combinations must be entered in the Macro Name column using the same representation as the SendKeys action. For the SendKeys representation, a single letter is represented by the letter itself, such as h. If you want to specify that the key be pressed in combination with SHIFT, CTRL, or ALT, use the symbols +, ^, or %, respectively, to represent these keys. For example, CTRL+H is represented by ^h. To use other keys such as F2 enclose the special representation in braces such as {F2}. The macro must be saved as AutoKeys. After you save the macro, when you press the key combination, these key combinations will execute the assigned macros.

## Calling One Macro from Another Macro

You can branch from one macro to another. Branching means performing another macro before the current macro has finished. To do this you include the RunMacro action in the macro that you want to branch to a second macro. You must supply the Macro Name argument. You can also use Repeat Count to specify how many times the called macro will execute, and Repeat Expression if you want an expression evaluated with each execution until the expression evaluates as No. Branching from one macro to another is often used in conjunction with conditional expressions. The condition can decide whether the RunMacro action is performed. If a RunMacro action is performed, after Access performs the actions in the other macro, Access returns to performing the macro actions in the original macro.

## Solving Problems

At times a macro will not behave as expected. In some instances you get a different result than you expect, and in others the macro actually fails during execution.

When a macro actually fails an error message displays in a dialog box that only provides the Halt option. The action causing the error is listed. After choosing Halt you can correct the action from the Macro window and try the macro again.

Walking through a macro one step at a time can help identify the cause of a problem. After opening the macro choose the Step Into button to execute one action at a time. A Macro Single Step dialog box appears as shown here:

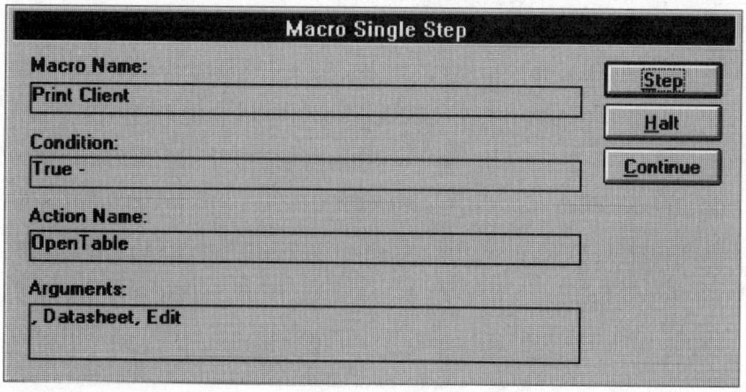

Macro Single Step
Macro Name: Print Client
Condition: True -
Action Name: OpenTable
Arguments: , Datasheet, Edit
Step
Halt
Continue

Choose Step to execute the next action, Halt to suspend execution, and Continue to execute without the single step operation.

In the next chapter, you see application examples using macros in forms and reports. You will see many of the components discussed in this chapter used in longer application examples there.

**Quick Reference**

**To Create a Macro** Click the Macro button in the Database window. Click New. Select the desired actions from the drop-down list box in the Action column. Use F6 to move to the arguments after selecting each action and completing it. Use F6 to move up and select the next action in the top part of the window.

**To Run a Macro** Choose Run from the File menu or from the Database window when it displays macros, select the macro then select Run.

**To Delete an Action** Select the action then press the DEL key.

**To Insert an Action** Move the focus immediately below where you want to add the action. Choose Insert Row from the Edit menu.

# Chapter 17

When Macros Are Performed in Forms and Reports

Adding Command Buttons to a Form

Using Macros to Hide and Display Data

Using a Macro to Synchronize Form Data

Using Macros for Data Conversion

Using Macros for Data Validation

Using a Macro to Add Data for You

# Using Macros for Forms and Reports

**M**ACROS can be used with forms and reports to save time and add flexibility to your applications. The macros you add to a form or report are performed as you use the form or report. Macros that you add to a form are performed regardless of whether you use the form in a form or in a Datasheet view. You use the events that occur when you use a form or report to determine when a macro is executed.

In this chapter, you first learn about the events to which you can attach macros. Next, you will get some insight into the different purposes for macros in your forms and reports by looking at a few examples. You will see how to use macros to validate data, enter data, change the report layout, or synchronize multiple forms.

## When Macros Are Performed in Forms and Reports

While you use forms and reports, Access constantly checks what you are doing to see when Access should perform any macros you have added. Each check that Access does to see whether it should perform a macro is called an *event*. Events occur frequently, so you have many opportunities to tell Access when you want to perform a macro.

Think of events as shopping in a mall. A mall has many stores but you do not have to go into every one of them. Also, you may go into some stores and not buy anything, while in other stores you will make purchases. Similarly, in forms and reports, although there are many events, you select only those events to which you want to attach a macro. Some events occur when you move to a control and others when you change a control. You only need to supply macros for the events in which you want a macro performed. The rest of the events will pass by without any indication that Access is checking for macros.

How often events occur depends on the focus' location. (Remember that the focus is another name for the insertion point or the indication of where you are in a form.) If you placed your finger on the screen for your current location, your finger would represent the focus.

**tip:** *Sometimes you will see event names as a single word, as in OnOpen. The property sheet where you enter macro names to occur at events displays these event names as two words. In the text in this book, you will usually see the macro names spelled as two words.*

## Report Events

The order of events in reports is simple because a report has fewer events than forms do. A report has these events:

- The On Open event occurs when you open the report but before Access determines the data that appears in the different sections.
- The second event, the On Format event, occurs for each section of the report. The On Format event occurs just before Access takes the data that it knows will appear in the section and lays it out as it will appear in the final printed report.
- The third event, the On Print event, is performed for each of the sections just before the section is printed.
- If an error occurs while creating a report in Access version 2, the On Error report event occurs.
- An Access version 2 report also has the On Activate event, which occurs when you switch to the window showing the preview of the report.
- The On Deactivate event occurs when you switch away from this window in Access version 2.
- Each section in Access version 2 also has the On Retreat event, occurring when Access returns to a previous report section that occurs in a report using groups or subform or subreport controls.
- The final event, the On Close event, occurs when you are closing the report.

The report has properties that let you select macros to perform when the On Open, On Close, On Error, On Activate, and On Deactivate events occur. Each section of the report has properties that let you select macros to perform when the On Format, On Print, and On Retreat events occur. Each section can have different macros.

To better understand when these events occur, imagine printing the report previewed in Figure 17-1 (the card file and telephone are added from Presentation Task Force graphics). When you select Clients and Projects in the Database window, the On Open event occurs. In the background, Access determines which data appears in the different sections. As Access decides on the data that appears in each section, the On Format event occurs. After the On Format event, Access decides the layout of the report. If you preview or print the report or save the report to a file, the On Print event occurs as each section is prepared for printing. When you leave the Preview window of the report or Access has finished printing the report when you are not displaying the preview, the On Close event occurs. The other four events—On Retreat, On Error, On Activate, and On Deactivate—only occur when you return to a prior section, when an error occurs, or when you switch to or from the report window.

## Form Events

The order of events is more complex in forms simply because a form has more events to which you can attach macros. Both the form and the individual controls can have events. Unlike reports, form sections do not have events. To get an idea of the possible events, first look at the events that affect the overall

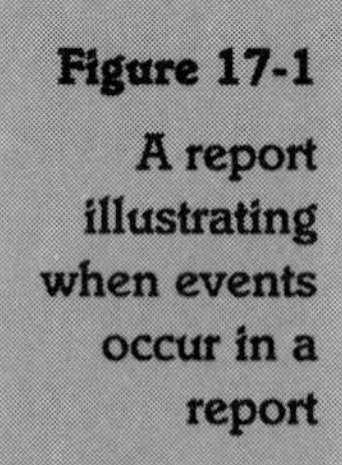

**Figure 17-1** A report illustrating when events occur in a report

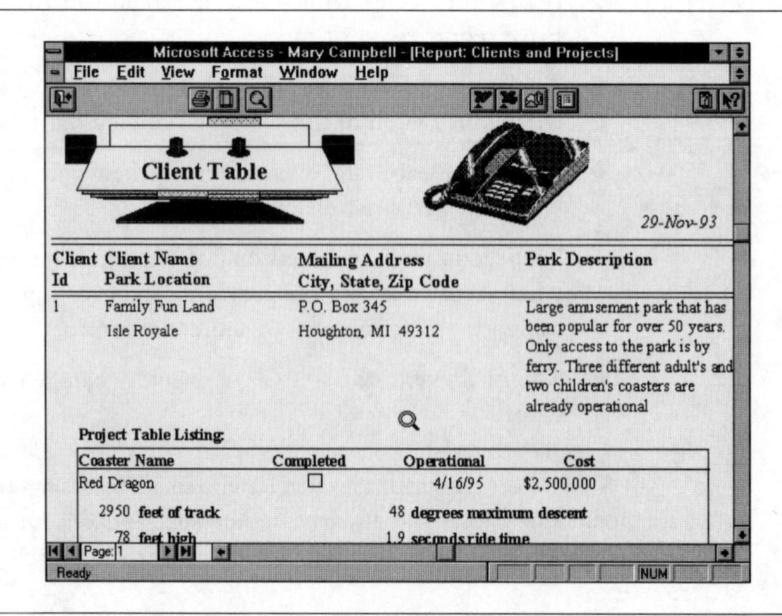

form rather than the individual controls. Table 17-1 includes the events that can happen in a form for either the form or individual controls. The events marked with asterisks indicate the new ones for Access version 2.

| Event | When It Occurs |
|---|---|
| On Current | When the focus moves to another record |
| Before Insert | Before you add the data for a new record (called On Insert in Access version 1) |
| After Insert * | After the new record is added |
| On Delete | Before removing a record from the table |
| Before Del Confirm * | Before you see the prompt about deleting a record |
| After Del Confirm * | After you respond to the prompt about deleting a record |
| Before Update | Before the record or field is updated |
| After Update | After the record or field is updated |
| On Open | When the form window is opened in Form view |
| On Load * | After the On Open event |
| On Resize * | When you resize the form |
| On Unload * | After the On Close event |
| On Close | When you leave the Form view of the form |
| On Activate * | When you switch to the form window |
| On Deactivate * | When you switch to another window from the form window |
| On Get Focus * | When the form or control gets the focus |
| On Lost Focus * | When the form or control loses the focus |
| On Click | When you click a control or form (called On Push for command buttons in Access version 1) |
| On Dbl Click | When you double-click a control or form |
| On Mouse Down * | When you hold down the mouse button |
| On Mouse Move * | When you move the mouse |
| On Mouse Up * | When you release the mouse button |
| On Key Down * | When you hold down a key while using the form or control |
| On Key Press * | When you press a key on the keyboard while using the form or control |
| On Key Up * | When you release a key while using the form or control |
| On Error * | When an error occurs that prevents from presenting a record in the form |
| On Timer * | When a time interval set by the Timer Interval property has elapsed |
| On Updated * | When the control for linked or embedded data is updated by an outside source |
| On Change * | As a control's value changes |
| On Enter | When the focus moves to a control |
| On Exit | When the focus leaves a control |

**Table 17-1**
**Events in a Form**

**tip:** 

*You can quickly see which events a form or control has in Access version 2 by displaying the property sheet. Then, change the property category at the top of the property sheet to Event Properties.*

When you open a form, the first event is On Open. In Access version 2, the next event is On Load. Next, since you have made a record the current record, the On Current event occurs. At this point the focus is in the controls of the forms so that the events of the form's controls are occurring. When you are finished with the current record, the Before Update event occurs. Access knows this event occurred because you have done something to leave the current record. This might be switching to another record, closing the window, or clicking the current record's record selector to finish any changes you have made. After the Before Update event occurs, Access updates any changed data for the current record. Next, the After Update event occurs.

At this point, you have updated the record for one of three reasons. If you are leaving the current record because you are closing the form, Access performs the On Close event and, in Access version 2, the On Unload event. If you are leaving the current record because you are switching to another record, the On Current event will occur as soon as you've switched to the next record. (Each time you move to another record, the On Current event occurs again.) The third possible reason you have updated the current record is that you have selected Save Record in the File menu. Following the After Update event, no events occur until you leave the current record or make further changes.

As an example of the events that occur in a form, suppose you are using the form in Figure 17-2. (William Wild's photo was copied from Andrew Fuller's photo in the NWIND database that accompanies Access.) When you select Employee Data - 3 in the Database window, the On Open event occurs and then the On Load event occurs in Access version 2. After the window is open, the On Current event occurs as Access displays the current record in the form. After you make changes to the record, you may finish this record and then switch to the next one. As you move to the next record, the Before Update event occurs. Next, Access updates the data saved for that record. After the updated record's data is saved, the After Update event occurs. Finally, since you have made a different record current, the On Current event occurs.

A form has other events that occur as you use it. When you delete a record, the On Delete, Before Delete Confirm, and After Delete Confirm events occur. Often the On Current event occurs just before the On Delete event, since you are selecting the record you will delete. After you delete the record, the next record is displayed and the On Current event occurs. When you insert a record,

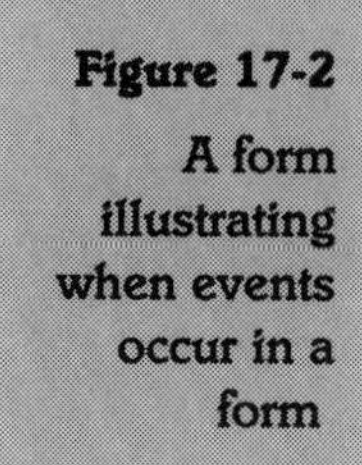

**Figure 17-2** A form illustrating when events occur in a form

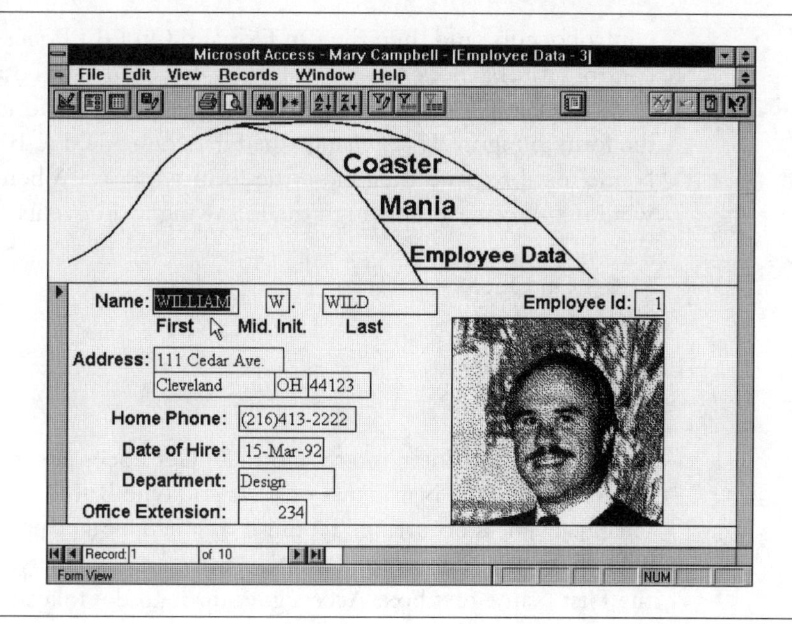


just as you type the first character for any field in the record, the Before Insert event occurs (On Insert in Access version 1). This event occurs after the On Enter event for the control you are entering the data into (the On Enter event is described later in this section). When you switch between windows in Access version 2, the On Activate and On Deactivate events occur. On Resize occurs when you resize a form by choosing Size to Fit Form in the Window menu from Form view or when Access resizes a form window because the Auto Resize property is set to Yes.

While you are editing the data of a record in a form, the events that are occurring are the ones created by the controls in the form. Each control has its own separate events. All controls except for a page break control and a line control have events. (In Access version 1, controls for labels, option groups, unbound objects, and rectangles do not have events either.) You can see the events different controls have by looking at the property sheet after selecting the control.

In most cases, when you first move to a control, the On Enter and then the On Get Focus events occur. If you move to a control by clicking it or double-clicking it, the On Click or On Dbl Click events occur after the On Get Focus event. When you switch to another control, which event occurs next depends on whether you have changed the data in the control. If the data has changed, the Before Update event occurs, the data in that control is updated, the After Update event control occurs, and then the On Exit and On Lost Focus events occur. If the control's data has not changed, only the On Exit and On Lost Focus events occur.

As an example of the events that occur as you use a form, suppose you open the form in Figure 17-2, change the First Name field to Bill, switch to the Last Name text box, and then close the form window. When you open the form window, Access runs through the following form events:

- On Open
- On Load
- On Current

Next, the On Enter and then the On Get Focus events occur as the focus is moved to the First Name text box. As you type **Bill** for the new value, the On Change event is occurring. To finish this field, you can press TAB or ENTER or click Wild to switch to the Last Name text box. When you change the data in the First Name text box, Access goes through the following events:

- The Before Update event for the First Name text box (Access then updates the data in the First Name text box.)
- The After Update event for the First Name text box
- The On Exit event for the First Name text box
- The On Lost Focus event for the First Name text box
- The On Enter event for the Last Name text box
- The On Get Focus event for the Last Name text box

At this point, if you close the form window to keep your change and close the form, Access runs the following events:

- The On Exit event for the Last Name text box
- The On Lost Focus event for the Last Name text box
- The Before Update event for the form (Access then updates the record's data.)
- The After Update form event
- The On Close event
- The On Unload event

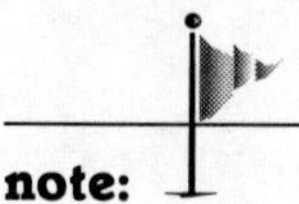

**note:** *The On Enter, On Get Focus, On Exit, and On Lost Focus events occur for a control each time it contains the focus even if you do not change the data. This means that if you use TAB or ENTER to move from one control to another, these events occur for each control you move through.*

## Adding Macros to Events

To add a macro to any one of the macro events, you need to add the macro name to the form or report design. Specifically, you will follow these steps:

1. Display the form or report design.
2. Select the form or report, section, or control in which the event you want to assign the macro to belongs.
3. If you do not currently see the property sheet, switch to it by choosing Properties from the View menu or by clicking the Properties button in the toolbar.
4. Select from the property sheet the event property when you want the macro performed.
5. Type the name of the macro or select the macro from the drop-down list.

   Remember that if the macro is part of a macro group, you must enter the macro group name, a period, and the macro name.

When you use that form or report, the macro is performed when the selected event occurs. Now that you know how to add macros to forms and report events, find out more about macros by looking at several examples.

Besides typing or selecting the macro names for events using a property sheet, you have two shortcut options with Access version 2. One of these is using a Macro Builder. The other is using a Control Wizard when you add command buttons to forms.

When you move to an event property in the property sheet, you will notice the Build button, which you have seen at other times for starting the Expression Builder. When you click this button, you can select the builder you want to use. Select Macro Builder from the list and OK to open the Macro Builder. Next, you are prompted for the name of the macro you are creating. After you type in the name and select OK, you are in a Macro window. You can create the macro to perform for the event. When you close the window, the macro name appears on the property sheet. If you click on the Build button again, you will open the Macro window for the macro the event uses. You can modify macros you have already assigned to an event by clicking the Build button. In Chapter 19, you will learn how you can create functions with Access Basic. You can add these functions to form controls to have the function test the control entry or make any changes you want. Assigning a function for a form or report event is just like assigning a macro, except that you select the Code Builder from the list after you click the Build button.

When you add a command button and the Control Wizard is selected, you see questions about what you want the button to look like and do when selected. The choices you make become the entry for the On Click property. If you subsequently look at the property sheet for the command button you add, you will see [Event Procedure] for the On Click property. This is the procedure that Access performs when you click the command button. Depending on what the procedure does, the procedure may perform the same feature as a macro.

## Adding Command Buttons to a Form

Command buttons are designed to use macros and procedures; the only action these controls take in a form is the macro or procedures that you have assigned to the different events for the command button. Command buttons offer a quick method of automating the use of forms and reports, because by selecting command buttons you can select predefined choices that perform an action for you. An example of a form that does this is one that lets you select the report you want to print and then prints that report. A form like this might look like Figure 17-3. A form like this can either use macros or procedures. You will learn about procedures in Chapter 19, so the only ones you will be using here will be the ones Access creates for you when you use the Control Wizards to create a command button.

The form in Figure 17-3 uses macros within a macro group that perform at the On Click event. You can see these macros in Figure 17-4. To create this form, follow these steps:

- Create a new form containing everything except for the command buttons.
- Turn off the Control Wizards, since the command buttons will run a macro instead of a procedure in a module.
- Select Tool Lock and Command Button in the toolbox.

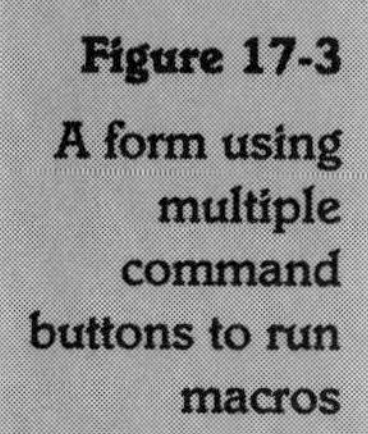

**Figure 17-3** A form using multiple command buttons to run macros

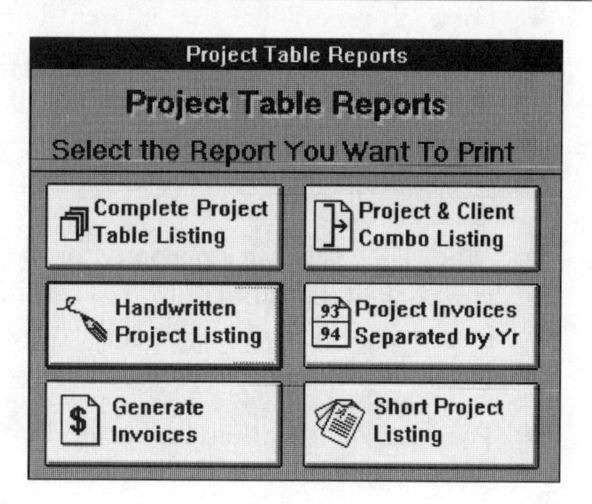


- Add the command buttons to the form. Don't worry about making them the same size, because you can use the Size command in the Format menu (the Layout menu in Access version 1) to resize the buttons.
- For each button, add the text to appear in the button as the Caption property or the picture to be the Picture property. For the form in Figure 17-3, the buttons show both text and graphics using the Paintbrush Windows accessory. The icons came from Windows and Word for Windows 6.
- Click the Build button for the On Click property after selecting one of the command buttons. Select Macro Builder and OK. Type the name for the macro group and select OK. Add the Macro Name column to the Macro window by selecting Macro Names in the View menu.

**Figure 17-4** Macros used to print reports

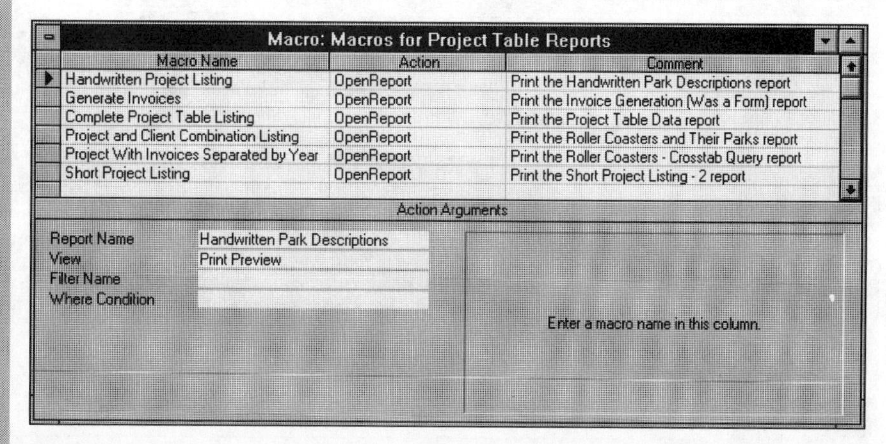

- For each report that the different buttons are to print, drag the report from the Database window to the Macro window. Type the name for the macro within the macro group in the Macro Name column.
- Close the Macro window and select Yes when prompted about saving the changed macro.
- Modify the On Click property for the command button you used when you clicked the Build button so that the macro group name includes the macro name as well. You can use the drop-down list, and you will notice that all of the macro names you entered for the macro group are available.
- For each of the other command buttons in the form, change the On Click property to the macro group name and the name of the macro within the group.
- Change any properties for the form. For the form in Figure 17-3, the Scroll Bars property is set to Neither, the Border Style property is set to Dialog, and the Navigation Buttons, Record Selectors, Max Button, Min Button, and Control Box properties are set to No. The form design looks like Figure 17-5. The labels pointing to the command buttons identify the contents of the On Click property for each button.

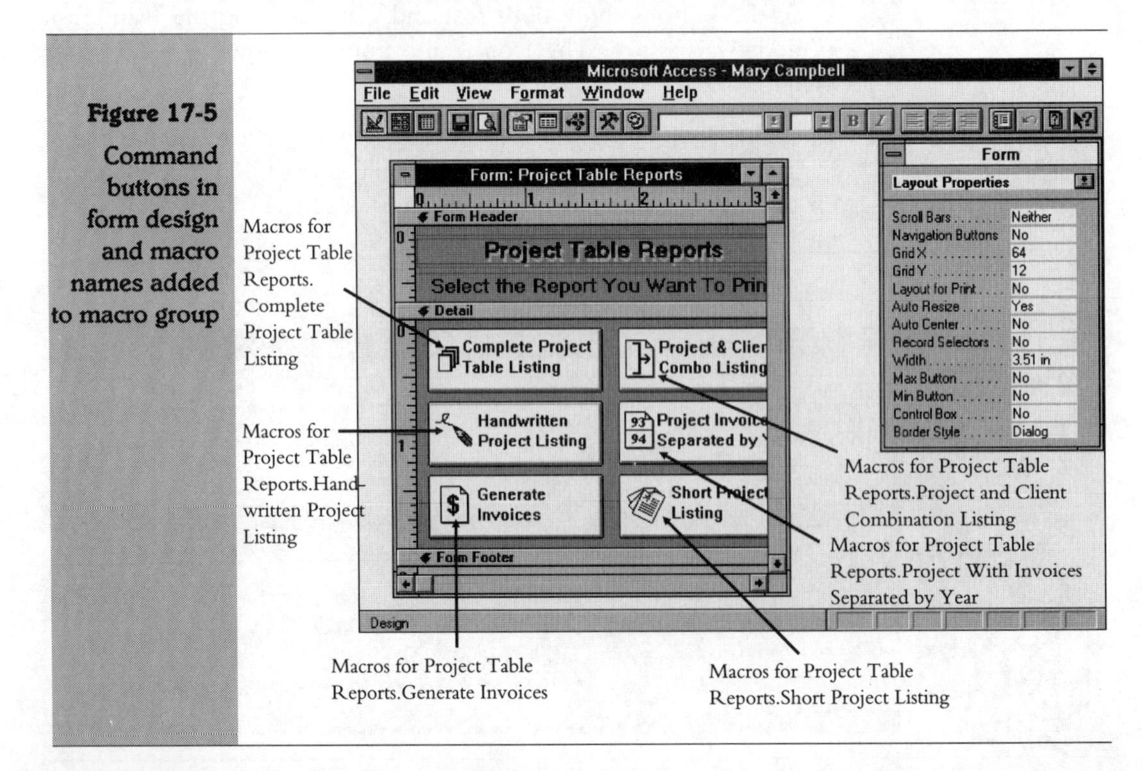


**Figure 17-5** Command buttons in form design and macro names added to macro group

When you save, close, and then open this form again, it looks like Figure 17-3. Later, when you know that all the reports print correctly without any changes, you can change the View arguments for each of the actions in the Macros for Project Table Reports macro group from Print Preview to Print.

The steps above apply to Access version 2. The only difference if you are using Access version 1 is that you will need to create the macro group name with its macros before adding the command buttons, because you do not have the Build button available to create the macros as you create the command buttons. Also, these macros are added to the On Push property instead of to the On Click property.

**tip:** *You can combine text and graphics into a single button by creating the text and graphics to put on the button with the Windows Paintbrush accessory. Create a .BMP file with the text and graphics for the button and select the .BMP file for the button's Picture property.*

## Using Macros to Hide and Display Data

One purpose for macros is selectively deciding whether other data is displayed. All controls except for page breaks have a Visible property. When this property is Yes, the control appears; when this property is No, the control does not appear. To see how you can use macros to change this property, suppose you have a form like the one shown here:

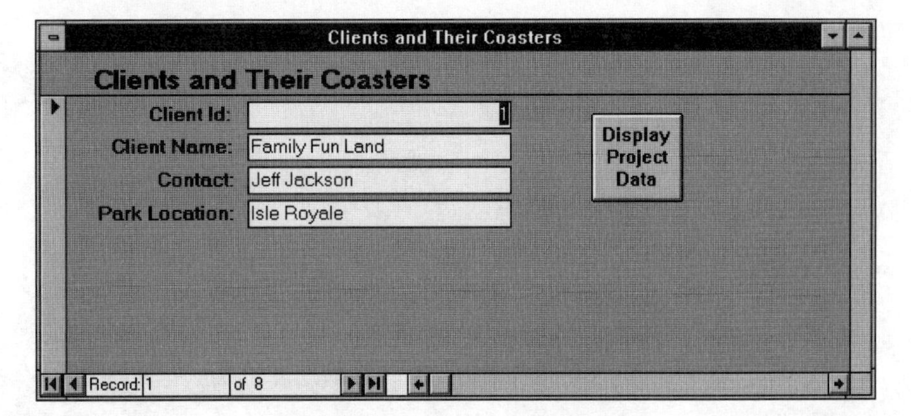


In this form, you only want to display the Project table's data for a client in a subform when the Display Project Data button is selected. You also want to be able to hide the subform. You can use command buttons that change the subform's Visible property when selected. This example uses two command buttons — one displays the subform and the other hides it. Since the command buttons are in the same location, the different command buttons look like they are the same one with its text changing as the button is selected.

For the preceding form, you need to add the command button that will display the subform. This command button is added with the Command Button tool in the toolbox. The Control Wizards are turned off, since you will add a macro to perform when the command button is selected. The Control Name for the command button is Display Button, the Caption property is Display Project Data, and the On Click property (On Push in Access version 1) is Macros for Clients and Their Coasters - 2.Display Project Data. In this example, the On Click property has the macro name rather than On Dbl Click, so you only need to click the command button once rather than double-clicking it to perform the macro.

At this point, the form design only has one command button. To add the second one, select the button and copy it to the Clipboard by choosing Copy in the Edit menu. Choose Paste from the Edit menu to make a second copy of the command button. Use the Clipboard to duplicate the command button so that the second command button is the same size and has most of the same properties as the first. Once you have the second command button, change the Control Name to Hide Button, the Caption property to Hide Project Data, and the On Click property to Macros for Clients and Their Coasters - 2.Hide Project Data.

You'll see the two command buttons slightly apart from one another. Leave them this way for now — you will find it easier to make any other necessary changes, since you can select one without selecting the other. The only other

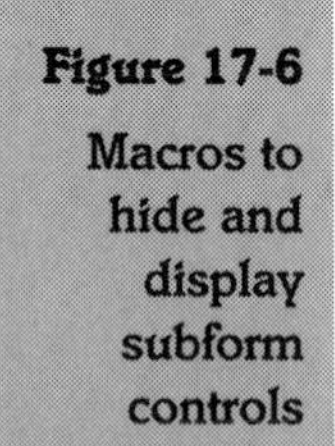

**Figure 17-6**

**Macros to hide and display subform controls**

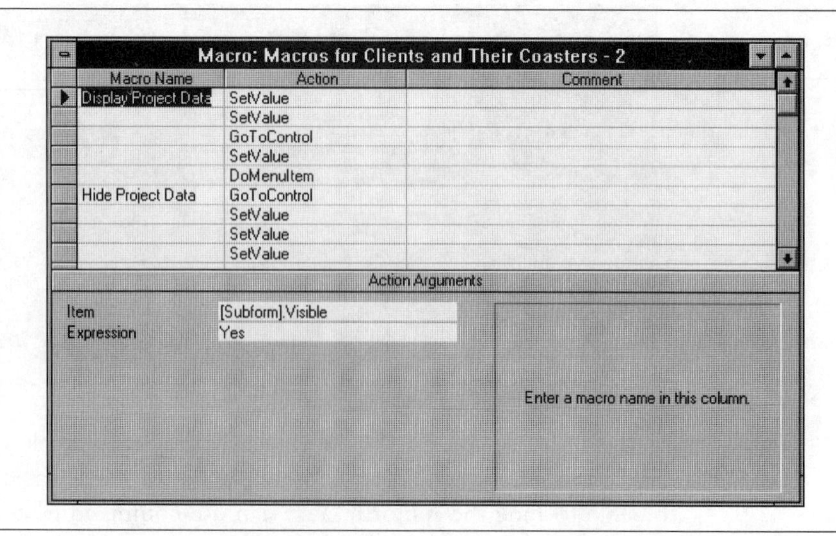

change you should make to the form's design is to set the Visible property for the subform control to No so that the default property setting is not to display the subform. This subform control has the Control Name property of Subform.

For the macro this form uses, the macro group looks like the one in Figure 17-6. You need one macro to display the subform and another to hide it. The actions for these two macros have only one or two arguments. These are the macro names, actions, and arguments:

| Macro Names | Actions | Arguments | |
|---|---|---|---|
| Display | SetValue | [Subform].Visible | Yes |
| Project Data | SetValue | [Hide Button].Visible | Yes |
| | GoToControl | Subform | |
| | SetValue | [Display Button].Visible | No |
| | DoMenuItem | Form | Window |
| | | Size to Fit Form | |
| Hide | GoToControl | Client Name | |
| Project Data | SetValue | [Subform].Visible | No |
| | SetValue | [Display Button].Visible | Yes |
| | SetValue | [Hide Button].Visible | No |

In each macro, the macro hides or displays the Display Button command button, the Hide Button command button, and the subform controls. Also, the GoToControl action moves the focus to either the subform control or the Client Name control. The focus must be moved because you cannot hide a control that has the focus. Save the macro; you cannot run the macro until you save it.

Now try the macros. Switch to the form and display the form view. The form looks like the preceding illustration. Select the command button labeled Display Project Data. The subform appears; the Display Project Data button disappears and is replaced by the button labeled Hide Project Data, as shown here:

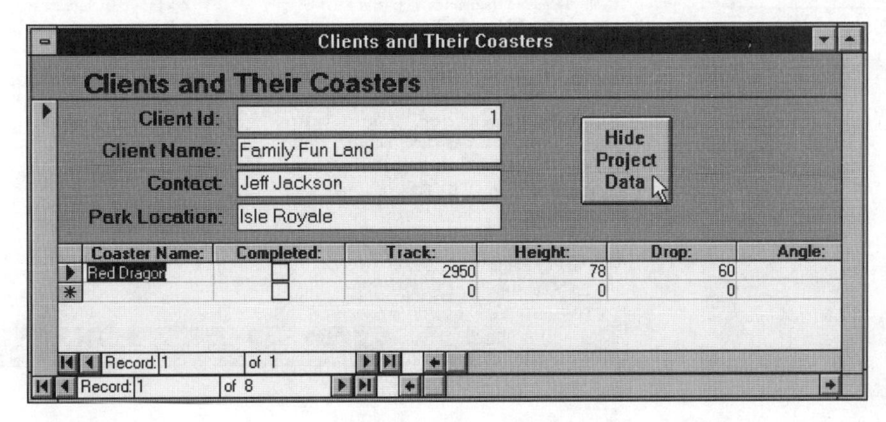

When you select this button, the subform disappears and the command button disappears, being replaced by the Display Button command button. When the two command buttons and their macros perform correctly, you will want to switch to the form design and set the Top and Left properties of both of the command buttons to the same value so that they are in exactly the same location.

When you create macros like this for your own forms, remember that you can add conditions that let the macro decide whether or not a control is hidden or displayed. The preceding example used command buttons to determine whether the subform appeared, but you can create conditions that determine this instead. Also, this example uses forms, but report controls also have Visible properties for which you can use macros to hide and display controls. For example, you can use macros for the On Format property of a control that hides or displays controls depending on another field's value. Figure 17-7 shows a report that uses this feature. The record on the left shows a description of the park that does not appear for the record on the right. The record on the right also does not show the YTD Payments. This report's On Format event runs the macro with the same name as the report. This macro decides whether to change the Visible property for several controls based on whether the contents of the fields are empty.

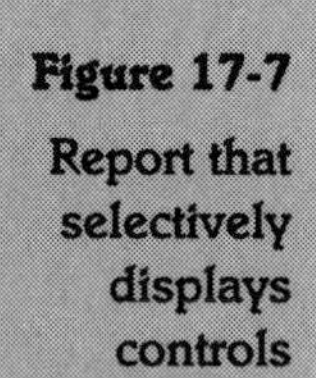

**Figure 17-7** Report that selectively displays controls

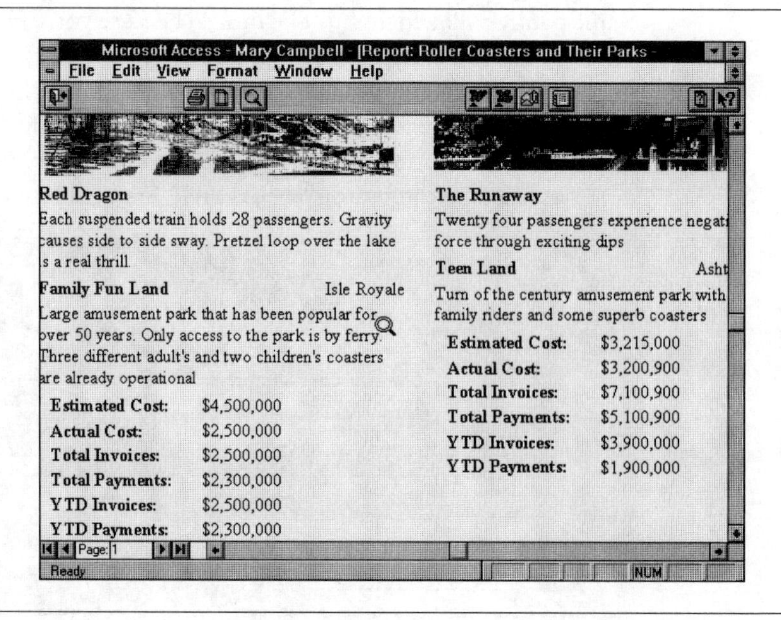

**tip:** *Use a macro group to contain all of the macros used by the same form or report. Putting the macros in a central location lets you quickly find all of the macros a single form or report uses. Give the macro group the same name as the form or report so that you can easily remember which macro group contains the macros a form or report uses.*

## Using a Macro to Synchronize Form Data

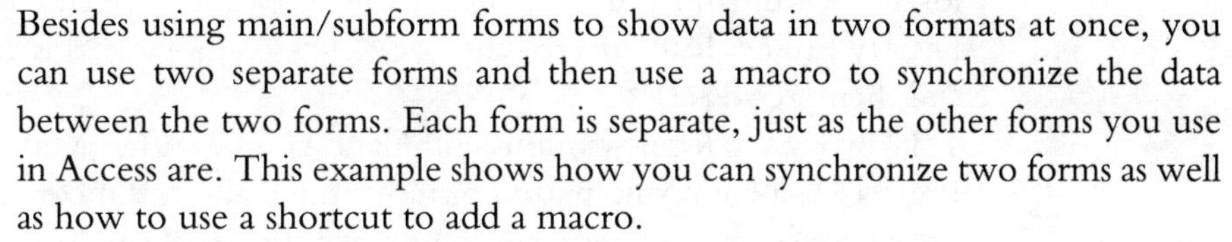

Besides using main/subform forms to show data in two formats at once, you can use two separate forms and then use a macro to synchronize the data between the two forms. Each form is separate, just as the other forms you use in Access are. This example shows how you can synchronize two forms as well as how to use a shortcut to add a macro.

To use a macro to synchronize two forms, suppose you have a form like the Clients and Their Coasters form used earlier, except that the subform control is removed, the command buttons are removed, and the form is resized. In this form, you want the Project Listing form to display the projects for just a particular client when the Display Project Data command button is selected.

When you want to create a macro like this, create the macro first and then you can try a shortcut for adding a macro and a command button to a form. The macro in this example is named Display Project Data. This macro only has one action, OpenTable, with Project Listing as its Form Name argument.

The only other argument of this macro is the Where Condition. This argument selects which records appear in the second form. This macro uses [Client Id]=Forms![Clients and Their Coasters - 3]![Client Id] as the Where Condition argument. The first [Client Id] matches one of the controls in the Project Listing form, the one the OpenTable action opens. The rest of the argument sets the value from the original form that you want to match. Since this condition matches the value of the [Client Id] control in the other form, you must supply the full identification.

### Using a Shortcut to Create the Command Button

When the macro is completed, you can create the command button using a shortcut. Display the form design and then switch to the Database window and list the macros. With both the Database and the form design windows in view, drag the macro name from the Database window to where you want the command button to start. Access adds a command button of the default size to the form and gives this button the Caption property of the macro name. This shortcut does not work when you want to add a macro in a macro group, because the command button you create will include only the macro group's name without the individual macro in the group.

Figure 17-8 shows the Database window and part of the form design after the command button has been added. You can choose Size from the Format menu and then To Fit (the Size to Fit command in Access version 1's Layout menu) to quickly adjust the command button's size to fit the text of the Caption property. The On Click property (the On Push property in Access version 1) for this command button is Display Project Data. Access will perform the Display Project Data macro when you click or move to this command button and then press ENTER.

Now try the form with this command button. When you click the Display Project Data command button or move the focus to this command button and press ENTER, Access performs the Display Project Data macro. After opening the Project Listing form and setting the form to only display the records for the same client as the one displayed in the Clients and Their Coasters - 3 form, the two forms look like Figure 17-9.

**tip:** *Use the dragging method to add command buttons to a form when the macro is stored separately rather than as part of a group.*

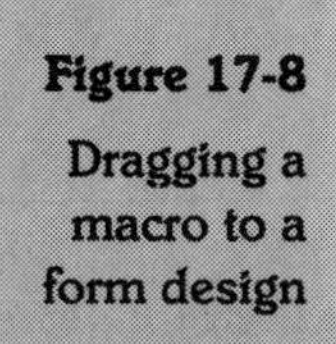

**Figure 17-8** **Dragging a macro to a form design**

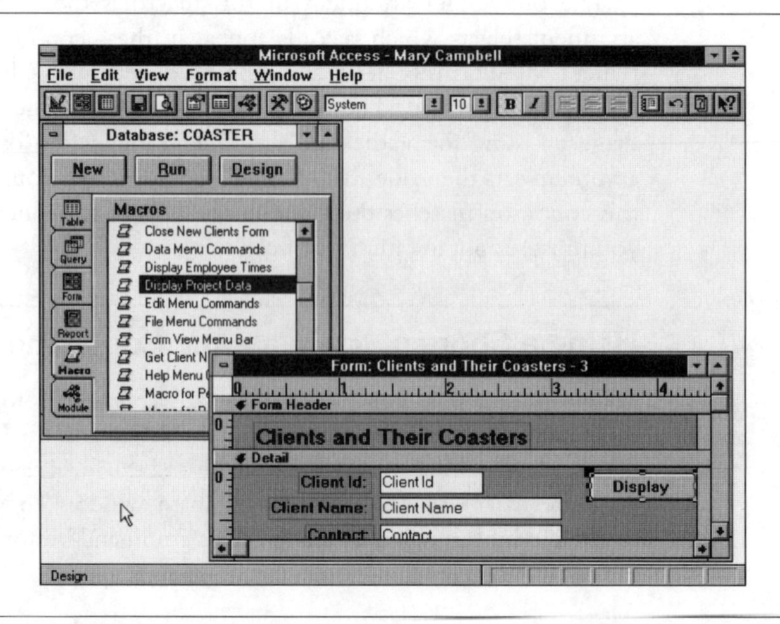

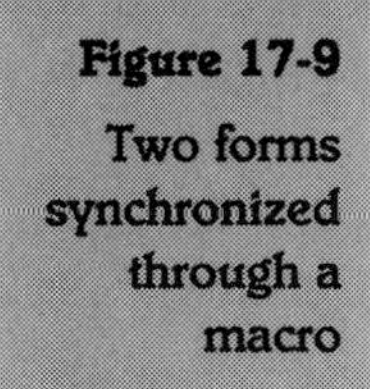
**Figure 17-9** Two forms synchronized through a macro

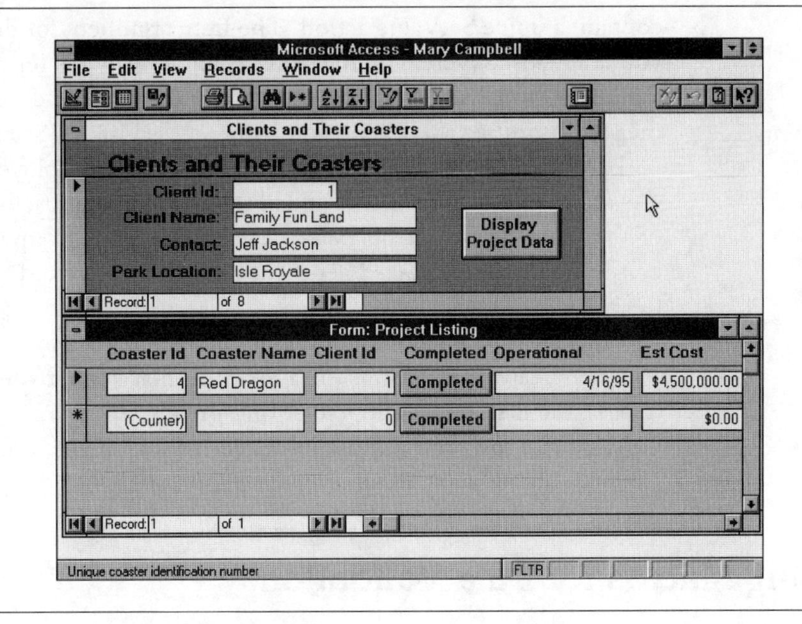


## Using Macros for Data Conversion

You can use macros to convert an entry in a control to another entry. For example, you may want to convert the names in your Employee table into uppercase. Another example is a part number for an inventory table to which you want to add characters such as hyphens in specific locations.

The macros you create for this purpose are performed at the On Exit or On Update events for a specific control. Whether you should add the macro to the On Exit or On Update event depends on if you want the data conversion performed based on whether the data in the control has changed. If you want the data conversion performed on a control's entry regardless of whether you change the field's entry, add the macro to the On Exit event. If you only want the conversion performed when you have changed the data, add the macro to the Before Update event. To see an example of using macros to convert the format of data, create a macro that converts user entry to uppercase for a form using the Employee table.

Suppose you want to convert a state entry into uppercase so that data is stored in the table as uppercase regardless of whether uppercase or lowercase letters are used to enter the data. To do this conversion, add a macro to either the On Exit property or the Before Update property, depending on whether you want to convert existing data and new data or only to convert new data. This macro contains a single SetValue action. The Item argument for this action is the field you want to convert. For the state example, it is [State]. For the Expression argument, you want this data converted into uppercase using a function. For the state example, the Expression argument is UCase([State]).

This example works for both the Client and the Employee tables. When you use a form that has this macro added to the On Exit or Before Update property of the State field control, before the data is actually updated, your entry is converted into uppercase. Then Access uses this converted entry when updating the record's values.

You can use all sorts of functions to convert data in a form. For example, you can create a procedure for a function that converts text into proper case (that is, the first letter is uppercase and the rest is lowercase). Once you have a function like this, you can use it in place of the UCase example just described.

## Using Macros for Data Validation

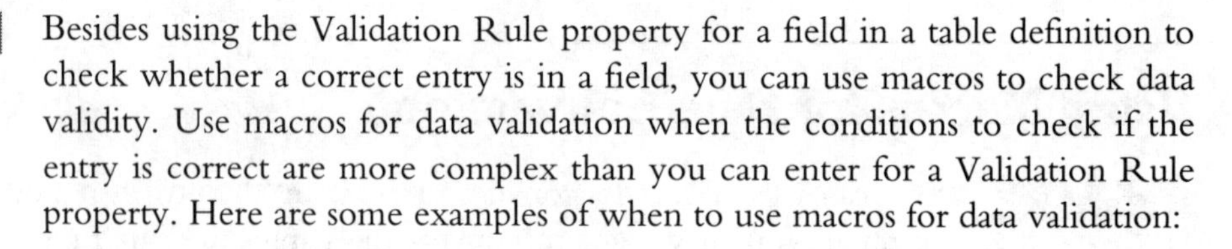

Besides using the Validation Rule property for a field in a table definition to check whether a correct entry is in a field, you can use macros to check data validity. Use macros for data validation when the conditions to check if the entry is correct are more complex than you can enter for a Validation Rule property. Here are some examples of when to use macros for data validation:

- The correct entry on the field depends on the entry of another field. For example, the billing and pay rate of your employees depends on which department they are in.
- You want to make sure the user leaves an entry in the field. For example, in a form for the Employee Time Log table, you want to be sure every field in every record has an entry.
- You want to display different messages that vary according to the incorrect entry made in a field.
- You want to let the user make decisions about whether the entered data is accepted, even if it goes against a Validation Rule.
- The condition for testing whether an entry is valid has several parts.
- You want to share the validation checking between several forms.
- A form has multiple validation checks that you want performed simultaneously.

For each of these cases, add the macro to check a control's entry for the control's On Exit or Before Update property. Use On Exit when you want the entry validated even if the entry has not changed. Use Before Update when you only want to check whether the entry is valid when the user has changed the entry.

As an example, suppose you have the following form:

Billing And Pay Rates

| First Name | Last Name | Department | Pay Rate | Bill Rate | Difference | Percent Markup |
|---|---|---|---|---|---|---|
| WILLIAM | WILD | Design | $35.00 | $60.00 | $25.00 | 41.67% |
| DAN | DANGER | Testing | $30.00 | $50.00 | $20.00 | 40.00% |
| RODGER | ROLLING | Design | $33.00 | $55.00 | $22.00 | 40.00% |

Record: 1 of 10

The Validation Rule of the form's underlying table checks whether the entry in the Pay Rate field is between 4.25 and 35 and whether the entry in the Bill Rate field is 10 percent more than the amount in the Pay Rate field. For this form, you may want to add some additional checks. Each department has a different range of what is valid for the pay and billing rates. You can add these validation checks and display different messages depending on the department. This example has separate macros for the Bill Rate and Pay Rate controls.

Figure 17-10 shows the macros this example uses. The conditions test whether the value of the Department control is Construction, Design, or Testing, and whether the value of the Bill Rate or Pay Rate falls within a certain range. The values in the Bill Rate or Pay Rate controls only meet one of the conditions when its value does not match the range for the particular department. When a condition is met, Access displays the message set by the MsgBox action and then cancels the updating. For each of the MsgBox actions, the Message describes the appropriate range and the title bar indicates that the wrong value has been entered. The CancelEvent action halts the updating process so that the form's user can make a new entry.

To make creating the two macros easier, copy the entries to the Clipboard and then paste them back, changing only the department names, ranges of valid values, and whether you are testing the Bill Rate or the Pay Rate. The ellipsis is necessary to continue the condition above them. If you omit the ellipsis, every time you make an entry in the Bill Rate or Pay Rate controls, they would not be updated because the CancelEvent action cancels the updating even when the entry is within the range appropriate for the department. The form has the Before Update properties changed to Billing And Pay Rates.Check Bill Rate

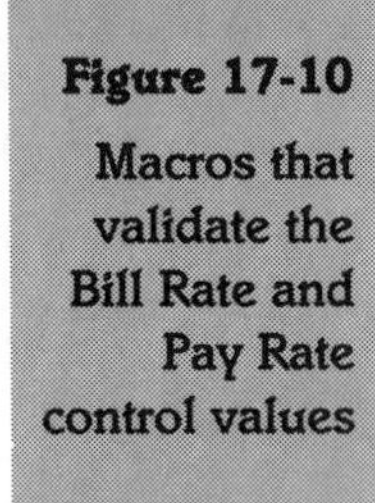

**Figure 17-10** Macros that validate the Bill Rate and Pay Rate control values

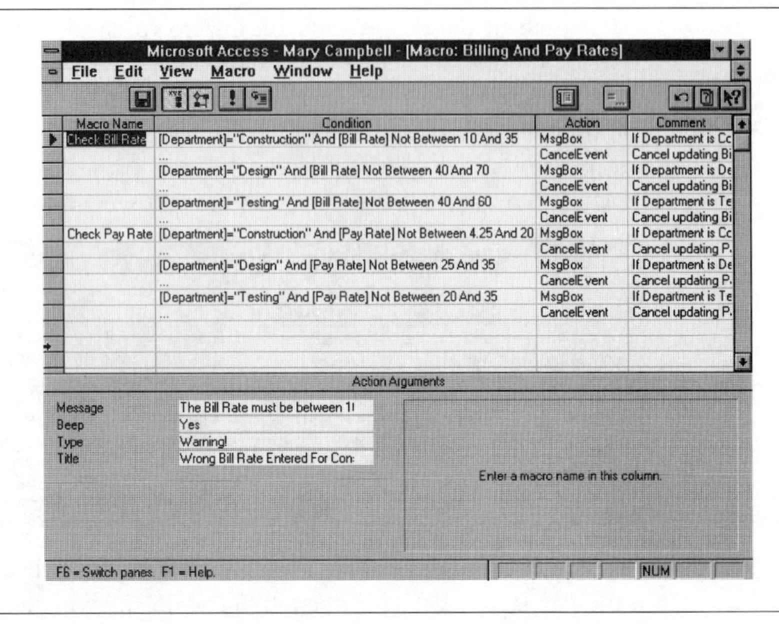


for the Bill Rate control and Billing And Pay Rates.Check Pay Rate for the Pay Rate control.

When you use the form with the macros, every entry is checked by the form's Validation Rule and then by the macro that you have entered for the Before Update property. As an example, if you type **Design** for the Department field and **5** for the Pay Rate field, Access displays this message:

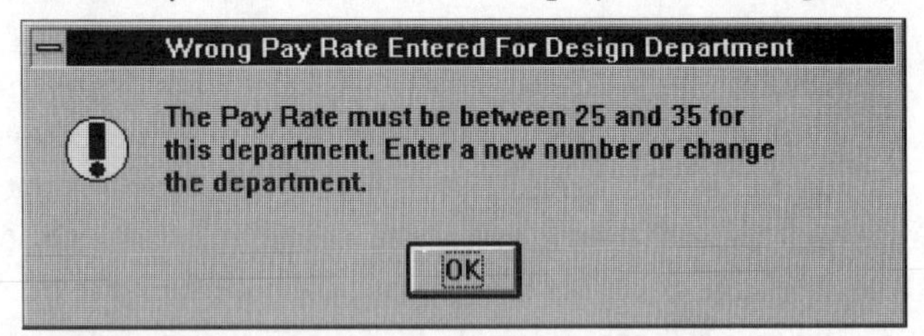


Since 5 is not in the range of valid entries for the Design department, the condition of [Department]="Design" And [Pay Rate] Not Between 25 And 35 is met. The MsgBox action displays the message box that you see above. The ! icon appears because the Type argument for the MsgBox action is set to Warning!.

The message box shown above also shows the text that is entered for the Title and Message arguments. When the form's user selects OK, the message box disappears and the updating of the control is canceled by the CancelEvent action. At this point, the form is ready for you to make another entry for this control. If you typed **3** for the Pay Rate control, you would see the Validation Text property's entry in a message box, because a control's Validation Rule is checked before any On Exit and Before Update macros are performed.

When you create macros like this for your own forms, the only difference is the condition entered in the Condition column of the macro and the text the MsgBox action displays when the condition is met. You may also want to enter the macro names for the On Exit property of controls when you want the validation performed on the controls for those fields that you do not change.

## Using a Macro to Add Data for You

You can create macros that present another form to make additional selections while you are working on a form. For example, you can create a form for adding new roller coaster projects that lets you select the name of the client and have the macro supply the client identification number. Using a macro for this means you do not have to remember all of your clients' identification numbers.

The form in Figure 17-11 lets you enter new roller coaster projects. The Coaster Id and Client Id controls have their Enabled properties set to No so that you cannot move to these controls. The Client Name control is an unbound text box control; it will contain whatever you enter in it or whatever macro commands you want to enter data into it. This unbound text box also has the

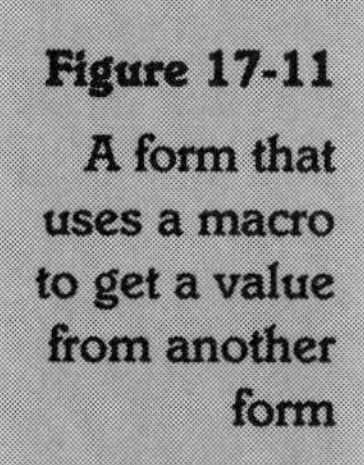

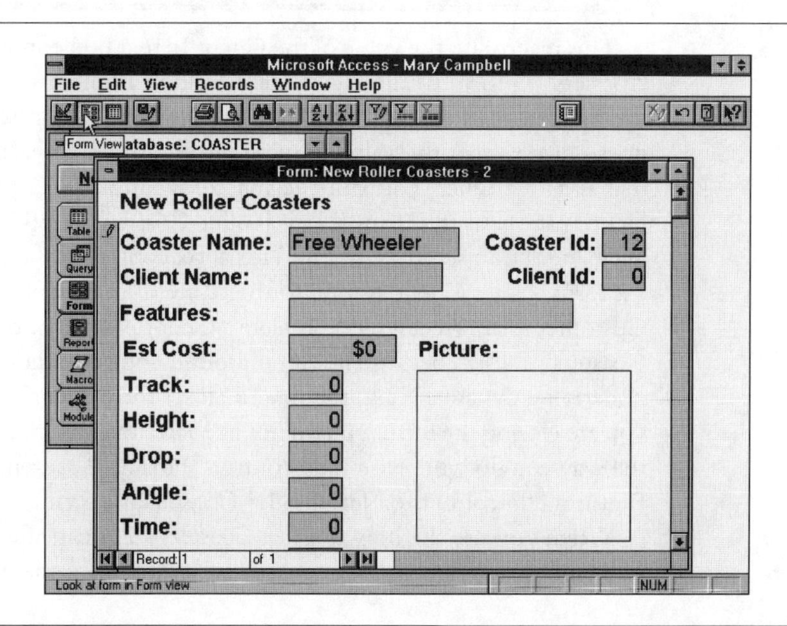


**Figure 17-11** A form that uses a macro to get a value from another form

Get Client Number macro assigned to its On Enter event. Every time you move to this control, Access performs the Get Client Number macro.

The Select a Customer form, shown in Figure 17-12, lists just the client names and park locations for all of the records in the Client table. The Client Name controls can be selected, although the entries cannot be edited, because the Locked property for this control is Yes. This form only has one macro, Add Client Id. This macro is attached to the On Dbl Click property of the Client Name text box control. Access performs this macro whenever you double-click any of the customer names.

The Add Client Id macro is added to the Client Name control in the Select a Customer form to perform when the On Dbl Click event occurs. This is the macro that performs the most work. The Add Client Id macro looks like this:

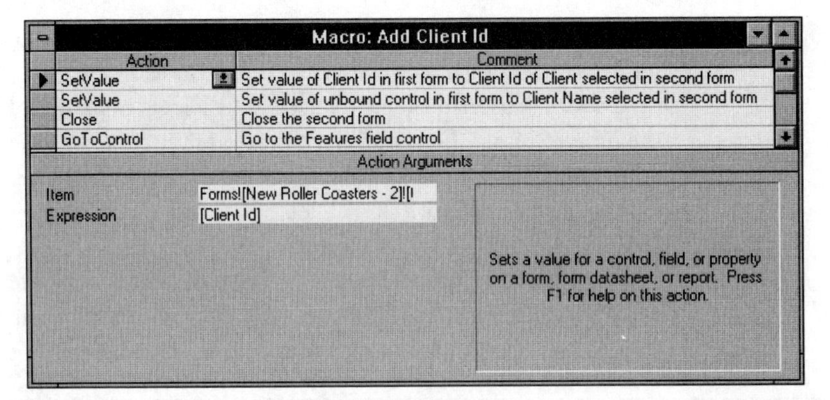


This macro sets the value of the Client Id text box control in the New Roller Coasters - 2 form to the client identification number of the client selected in the Select a Customer form. The first SetValue action sets this value. Access does not care that the value you are setting is in a different form than the one that is active when you run the macro as long as you provide the complete identification, as in Forms![New Roller Coasters - 2]![Client Id]. The second SetValue action sets the unbound text box control in the New Roller Coasters - 2 form, called Client Name, to the name of the client chosen in the Select a Customer form. Access lets you have a Client Name control in the New Roller Coasters - 2 form because it is an unbound control rather than an entry for the underlying dynaset. Next, the macro closes the Select a Customer form. Since you are closing the form, you do not need to move the focus to another location the way you do when you hide controls. Finally, Access moves the focus to the Features control in the New Roller Coasters - 2 form.

When you use the New Roller Coasters - 2 form, after you enter the name of the roller coaster, the focus moves to the Client Name unbound text control.

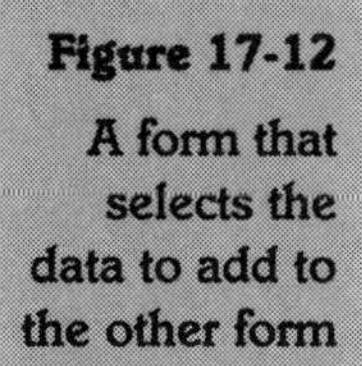

**Figure 17-12** A form that selects the data to add to the other form

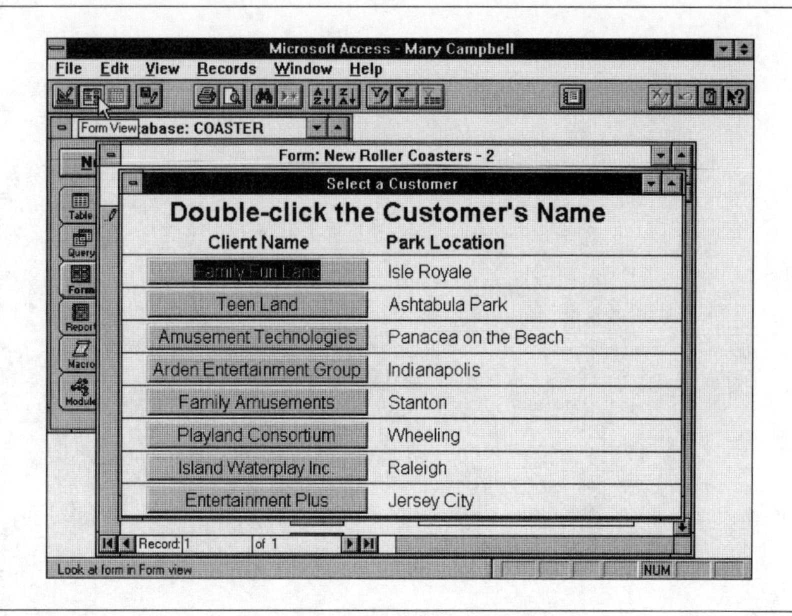


This triggers the On Enter event, so the Get Client Number macro performs and opens the Select a Customer form. When you double-click a client in the Select a Customer form opened by the macro, Access performs the Add Client Id macro. The only effect you will see from the macro is that the Select a Customer form is closed, the client name you have just selected is in the Client Name text box control, the client's identification number is in the Client Id text box control, and the focus is in the Features text box control.

## Quick Reference

**To Add a Macro to a Form or Record Event** Display the form or report design. Select the control that has the event to which you want to attach the macro. Display the property sheet and enter the macro name for the property name of the event when you want the macro to occur. In Access version 2, you can create the macro for an event by clicking the Build button, selecting Macro Builder and OK.

**To Add a Macro as a Command Button** Display the form design and then switch to the Database window. Drag the macro name from the Database window to where you want the command button to start.

# Chapter 18

Creating a Macro that Performs When You Open a Database

Adding Macros to Create Popup Forms

Macros to Define New Menus

Creating Macros that Perform with Key Combinations

Access Add-ins

# Creating Custom Applications with Macros and Using Add-Ins

CHAPTER 17 showed how adding macros can make using forms and reports easier. You can use macros for other purposes—for example, to design applications. When you use macros to design applications, you want the macros to guide the user through each step, from selecting the data through presentation of the final output.

In this chapter, you will learn about creating macros that run every time you open a database, macros that create popup forms, macros that set the menus and commands available through the menu bar, and macros that run with special key combinations. You will also learn about the add-ins that Access version 2 provides as well as the Wizards you can customize using Access' Add-in Manager.

## Creating a Macro that Performs When You Open a Database

When you open a database in Access, Access opens the Database window for that database, displaying the tables stored there. Using a macro, you can change how a database is presented. This type of macro, called AutoExec, is executed whenever you open a database. Every time you open a database, Access checks if any of the macros in the database's list of macro names is named AutoExec. If Access finds a macro named AutoExec, Access runs the macro.

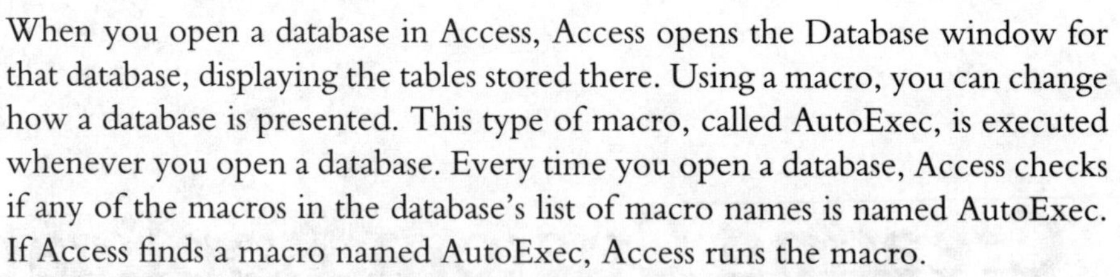

AutoExec macros can provide two functions. First, an AutoExec macro can set up a different interface, or a way to select the data you want to use other than through the Database window Access provides. Second, an AutoExec macro can provide daily reminders of tasks you need to perform.

As an example of an AutoExec macro, you can create a macro that minimizes the Database window and displays a form from which users can choose the tasks they want to perform. An example of this type of form is shown in Figure 18-1. As one of the forms in the last chapter showed, you can combine graphics, such as the ones from Presentation Task Force, with text using the Paintbrush Windows accessory. You can produce this form by using the Project Table

Reports form created in Chapter 17 and changing the command buttons and the text the form uses.

**tip:** *To open a database and not run the AutoExec macro, hold down the* SHIFT *key while you open the database.*

Each of the command buttons in the form has an On Click property (On Push in Access version 1) of Macros for Autoexec.*Command button name.* For example, when you click the Current and Prospective Customers button or highlight it and press ENTER, Access performs the Macros for Autoexec.Current and Prospective Customers macro. This form displays because the database has an AutoExec macro. This macro has only two actions. The first is Minimize, which minimizes the Database window (see the icon in the lower-left corner of Figure 18-1). The second action is OpenTable with Initial Form as the table argument. The form shows **Welcome to Coaster Mania** in its title bar instead of the form name because the form's Caption property is set to Welcome to Coaster Mania. By changing other form properties, you can hide the Control box, minimize and maximize buttons, scroll bars, record selectors, and navigation buttons. This simple macro executes every time you open the Coasters database.

From the form in Figure 18-1, you can select command buttons. These command buttons display other forms, which let you select exactly the data you

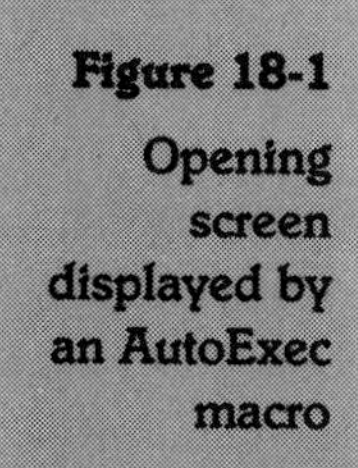

**Figure 18-1** Opening screen displayed by an AutoExec macro

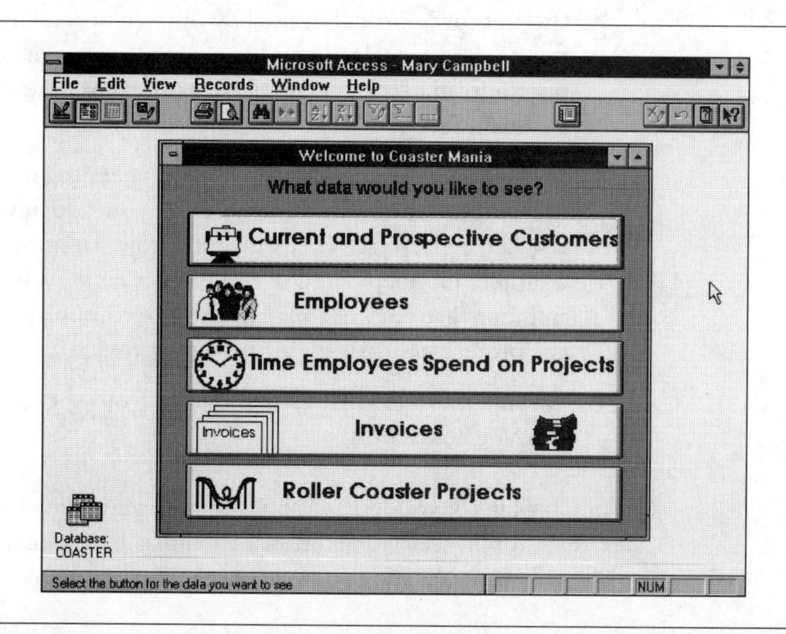

want to see and the format in which you want the data presented. Using these command buttons means you can use keystrokes and mouse selections to choose the object you want to display. You can continue to use macros throughout the application—how you use them is limited only by your imagination. Having all of these command buttons in various forms also means that someone who doesn't know how to use Access can easily use the data in the database.

**tip:** *With a macro such as AutoExec, you may want to have a keystroke combination that also executes the macro so that every time users need to return to the initial form, they can press the key combination to have AutoExec execute again. This key combination is just like pressing F11 every time you want to go to the Database window. You will learn how to assign keys to macros later in this chapter.*

## Adding Macros to Create Popup Forms

You can add popup forms with macros. These forms remain at the top of your Access window just as if you were using a command's dialog box. Popup forms can serve a variety of purposes, including these:

- Prompt for confirmation that you want to override the Validation Rules.
- Prompt for information used by other actions. The information you get can be used for selecting which records appear in a form or report. The popup form can also prompt for entries for other fields not included in the main form.
- Display another form for data entry depending on the value of a field in the current form. For example, as you add invoices to the invoice register, a macro can check that the project number you entered matches a project number stored in the Project table. When you enter a project number that does not match, the macro displays a popup form to add the project information for the new project.
- Display messages that look different from the message box created by the MsgBox action.

In Chapter 13, you learned about using a popup form in place of a subform. Below, you will see two additional examples by looking at popup forms used to override the validation rules set by another macro and popup forms used to prompt for additional information when an entry does not match a field's value in another table.

## A Popup Form to Override Validation Rules

In Chapter 17, you learned how to use macros for validation rules, which prevent entries that do not match criteria. Sometimes you want users to be able to override a rule. Since you still want the validation rule present, you want users to be aware that their entry does not fit the validation rule and give them the choice of continuing with the entry or canceling the entry. Using macros for validation does not replace validation rules but rather provides an alternative for testing the appropriateness of the entries.

As an example, in the Billing and Pay Rates form shown next, the Pay Rate and Bill Rate field controls have validation rules just like the ones added in Chapter 17.

Billing And Pay Rates

| First Name | Last Name | Department | Pay Rate | Bill Rate | Difference | Percent Markup |
|---|---|---|---|---|---|---|
| WILLIAM | WILD | Design | $35.00 | $60.00 | $25.00 | 41.67% |
| DAN | DANGER | Testing | $30.00 | $50.00 | $20.00 | 40.00% |

Record: 1 of 10

The difference here is that, when users make an entry in the Pay Rate or Bill Rate fields, the fields' Before Update macros validate the entry instead of the field's validation rule doing it. The macros for the Before Update event of these two fields are shown in the top of Figure 18-2. The OpenForm actions in both the Check Bill Rate and the Check Pay Rate macros use the Dialog window mode for the form they open. These actions make the opened form behave as if the Pop Up and Modal properties are set to Yes regardless of the setting the form has saved as part of its design.

The Override form opened by entering an inappropriate pay or bill rate is shown here:

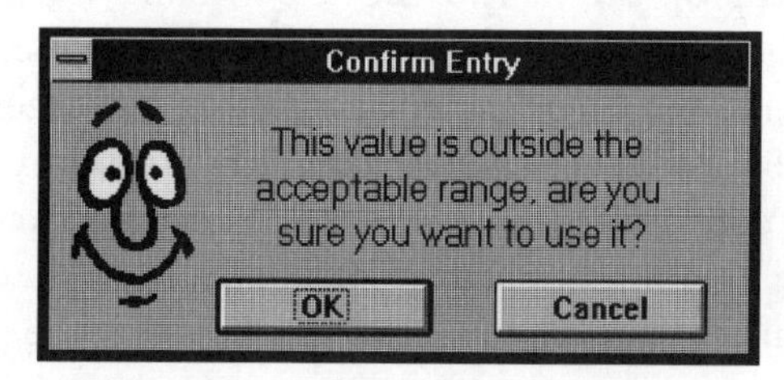

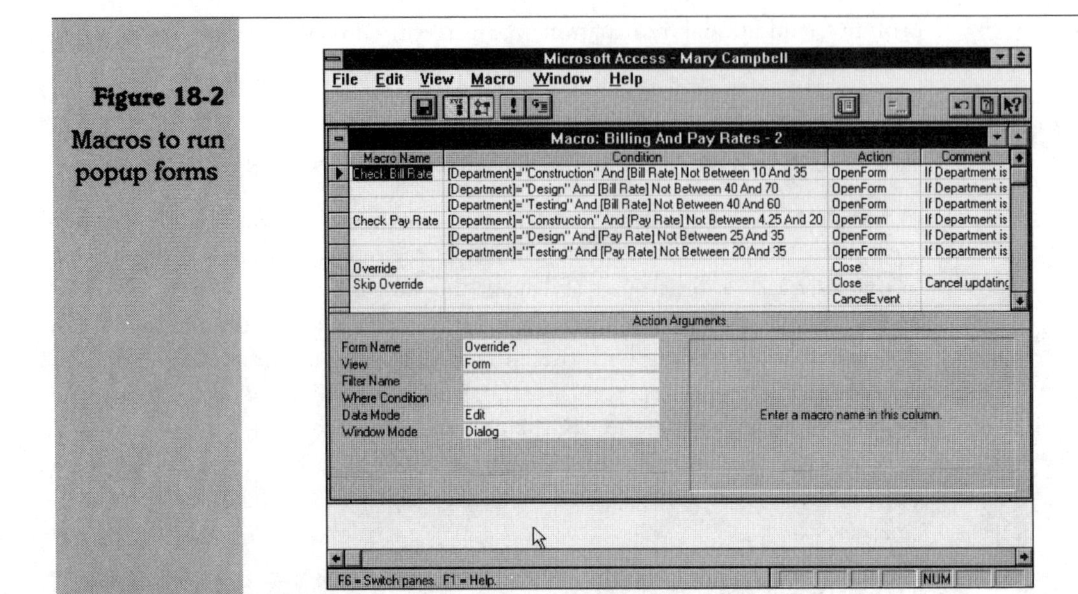


**Figure 18-2** Macros to run popup forms

This form has two command buttons. The OK button runs the Billing and Pay Rates - 2.Override macro, which closes the form and continues with the updating process in the Billing and Pay Rates form. The Cancel button runs the Billing and Pay Rates - 2.Skip Override macro. This macro closes the form and cancels the updating occurring in the Billing and Pay Rates form. Initially the OK button has the focus because of the Override form's tab order. If you want the Cancel command button to have the focus when the form is opened, edit the form design and use the Tab Order command in the Edit menu to change the tab order of these command buttons.

## A Popup Form Activated by Data Entry

When you make an entry in a field that is linked to the values of a field in another table, you want to know that the other table has a record for the appropriate value of the field that links the tables. For example, before you enter a new project, you want to know that you have the client's information entered into the Client table. Also, before you enter an invoice for a project, you must have a record in the Project table that provides information about that project. You can create a macro that checks whether the data you enter for a field in a form matches the data in a table. When the data does not match, have the macro display a popup form to supply the information added to the table.

The following shows a form used to enter invoices:

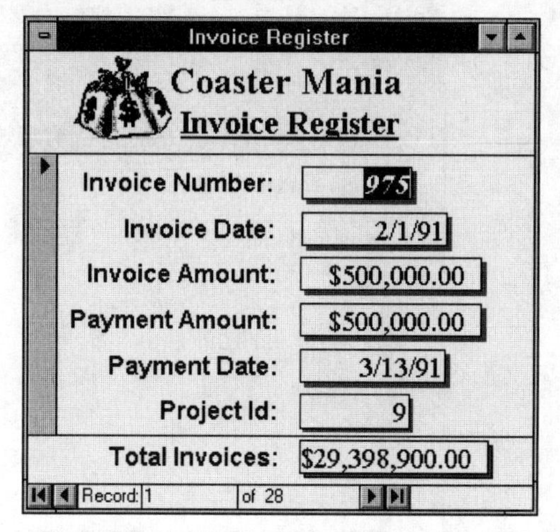


The Project Id control has a macro performed on the After Update event that checks if the entry in this control matches one of the projects in the Project table. The macro has this entry in the Condition column of its design:

```
IsNull(DLookup("[Coaster Id]","Project","Form.[Project
Id]=[Coaster Id]"))
```

The DLookup function returns a field's value (Coaster Id) from a record in the selected table (Project) that matches the condition set by the criteria (Project Id in the current form matches the Coaster Id field in the Project table). This function returns a null or empty value when the DLookup function does not find a matching record. The IsNull function returns a TRUE value when the DLookup function cannot find a matching record and a FALSE value when the DLookup function finds a matching record.

When this macro's condition is met because DLookup cannot find a matching value, the action to the condition's right, OpenForm, displays a form like the one in Figure 18-3. This form has the Window Mode set to Dialog, so you cannot continue making other changes in Access until you close the popup form. This example assumes that you will add projects when you enter a project number not already in use. Another possibility is to have the macro evaluate the entry and reject it. If you were creating a macro that would reject an entry that was not available in the other table, you would use the macro for the Before Update property instead of for the After Update property. Chapter 17 includes an example of using macros to reject an incorrect entry.

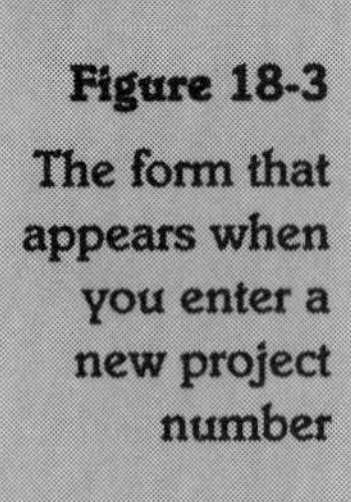

**Figure 18-3** The form that appears when you enter a new project number

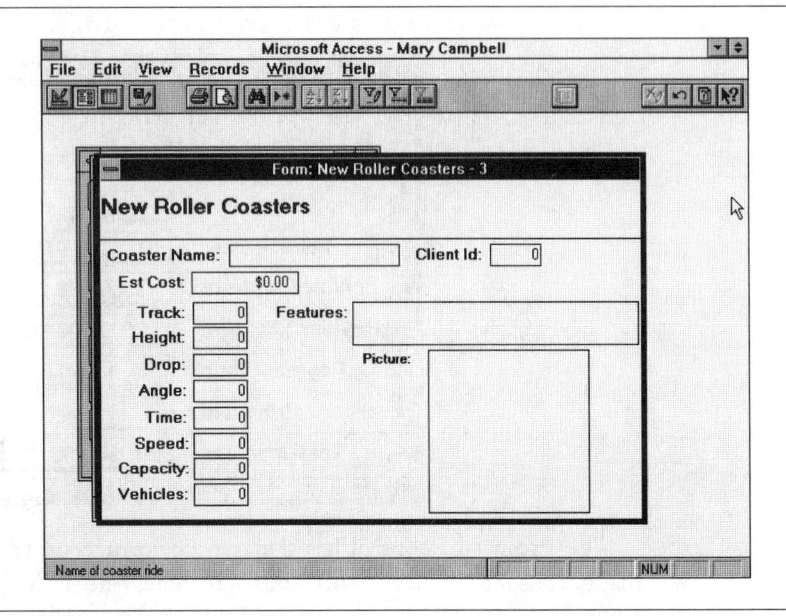


## Macros to Define New Menus

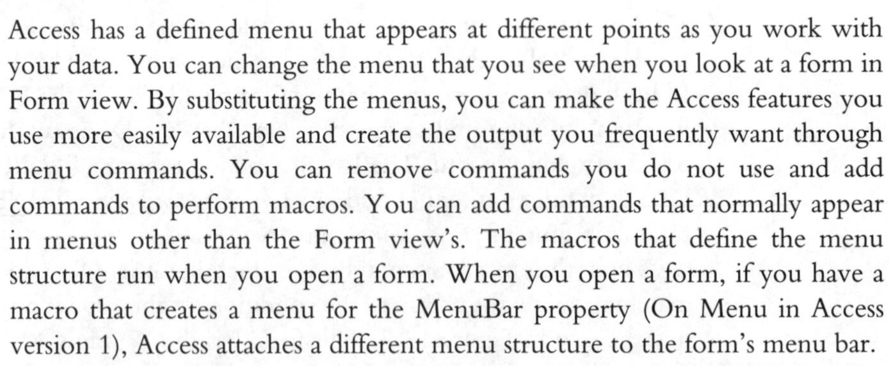

Access has a defined menu that appears at different points as you work with your data. You can change the menu that you see when you look at a form in Form view. By substituting the menus, you can make the Access features you use more easily available and create the output you frequently want through menu commands. You can remove commands you do not use and add commands to perform macros. You can add commands that normally appear in menus other than the Form view's. The macros that define the menu structure run when you open a form. When you open a form, if you have a macro that creates a menu for the MenuBar property (On Menu in Access version 1), Access attaches a different menu structure to the form's menu bar.

When you replace a menu, the menu replacement completely removes the previous menu. For example, when you replace a menu by supplying a macro's name for the form's MenuBar property, all of the commands that you previously used for the menu are absent. You see only those commands that you selected through the macros that define the menu.

The MenuBar macro is special because this macro can only contain AddMenu actions. This is the only time a macro ever uses the AddMenu action. You will use the AddMenu action only to create custom menus. The example you are shown adds a Data pull-down menu with five commands in addition to the other menus. The drop-down menu looks like this:

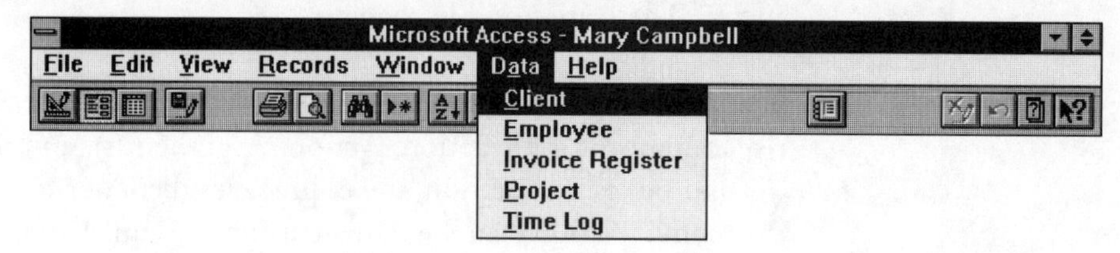


The menu is created differently depending on whether you are using Access version 1 or version 2. In Access version 2, you use the Menu Builder. The Menu Builder handles building the macros for you.

## The Menu Builder Add-In

The Menu Builder add-in lets you create and define the menus you want and creates the macros that display these menus. You cannot use the Menu Builder to alter Access' built-in menus. To start the Menu Builder, follow these steps:

1. Select Add-ins from the File menu and then Menu Builder.

   You are prompted for a menu bar to edit. The list box shows all of the macros in the database, not just the ones containing menus.

2. Select the macro name and Edit to work with one of your existing menus, or select New if you are creating a new menu.

   The first time you create a menu, you will not select a macro at this point since you will provide a new macro name when you save the menu. When you are editing an existing menu, you want to select the macro that defines the menu bar you are editing.

3. If you chose New, select the menu you want to start off with and select OK. The list box includes the standard menus that Access already has.

   Once you select one of your existing menus, or the starting menu of a new one you are creating, you will see the Menu Builder dialog box, which looks like the one shown in Figure 18-4. The bottom half of the dialog box lists the currently defined menu system. As you make changes to the menu, the new, modified, and removed menu items are reflected in the list in the bottom. You can move through the list box or use the Next button to change the item highlighted in the menu system. Your next step depends on the change you want to make to the menu. These are possible changes:

- Modifying an item - Move to the item in the list and change the contents of the Caption, Action, Argument(s), and Status Bar Text text boxes. In Caption, the & precedes the letter to underline in the menu. Action can be DoMenuItem, RunMacro, or RunCode, determining whether the menu item performs a menu command, a macro, or a module. Argument(s) provides the information needed to perform the menu command, macro, or module. You can click the Builder button when you want to use a dialog box to select the Menu Bar, Menu Name, Command, and Subcommand arguments that the DoMenuItem macro action requires, rather than entering this information separated by semicolons. When Action is Run-Macro or RunCode, enter the macro or procedure name in the Argument(s) text box. Status Bar Text sets the text that appears when the item is highlighted.
- Delete an item - Move to the item in the list and select Delete.
- Change the position of the menu item within the menu - Select the item to move in the list and click the up or down arrow. Moving a

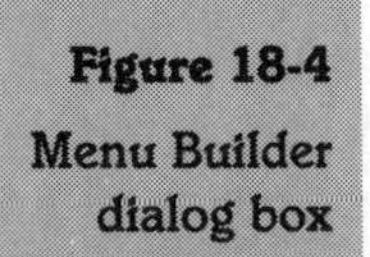

**Figure 18-4** Menu Builder dialog box

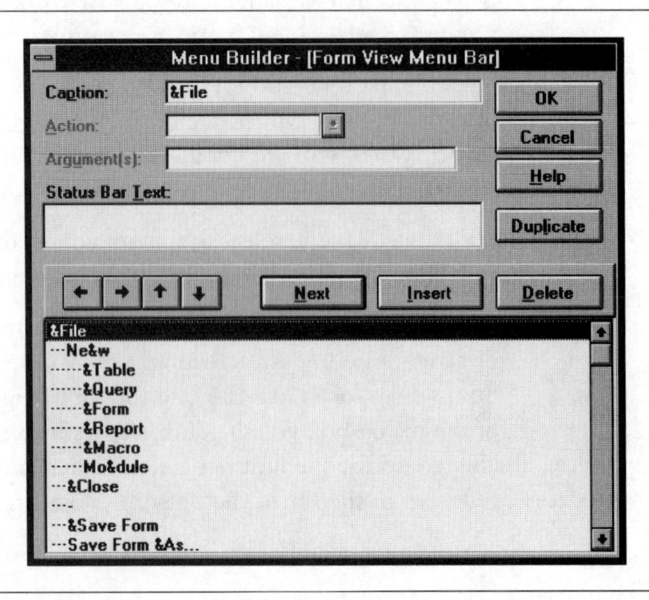

menu item does not move the items that are below it. This means that putting Edit before File does not also move the items that previously appeared in the Edit menu to before the File menu. If you want to move the items below a menu item as well, you must move them separately.

- Change the menu level of an item - Move to the item whose level you want to change and click the left or right arrow. Changing the level of a menu item changes what you must select to choose that menu item. For example, if you click the left arrow until a menu item is all the way on the left side of the list box, the menu item appears in the menu bar. When the item appears one indentation to the right, the menu item appears in the pull-down menu described by the menu item that appears above the current menu item without any indentation.

- Create a menu item similar to one you already have - Move to the similar menu item in the list and select Duplicate. Then change the contents of the Caption, Action, Argument(s), and Status Bar Text text boxes to match what you want the copy of the menu item to perform. You may also want to change the copied menu item's position and level.

- Add a menu item - Move to the menu item in the current list below where you want the new item added. Select Insert. In Caption, type the name for the new menu item using an & to the left of the letter you want underlined. Set Action to DoMenuItem, RunMacro, or RunCode to select whether the menu item performs a menu command or performs the contents of a macro or module. Click the Builder button after Argument(s) to provide the information needed to perform the menu command, or type the name of the macro or procedure to perform in the Argument(s) text box. In the Status Bar Text text box, type in the text to show in the status bar when the item is highlighted.

4. Select OK when the menu is completed.

If you selected New when prompted for the macro name, you are now prompted for the name of the macro to contain the menu bar. You can type the name of the macro for the menu bar and select OK. If you supplied a macro name when you started the Menu Builder, the macro is saved. You will notice that the macro groups that describe the commands in the pull-down menus have similar names to the macro that describes the menu bar. The Menu Builder will rename any macro groups a menu uses to match its own naming scheme.

To see how the Menu Builder sets up the menus for you, you will want to look at how you set up macros for a menu, as described in the next section.

## Setting Up the Macros for a Menu

Creating macros for a menu is done in several steps. When you use the Menu Builder, the Menu Builder creates the macros for you. However, if you are using Access version 1 or if you are not using the Menu Builder, you will have to create these macros yourself. First, create the macro that defines the menu bar to replace the existing one. Figure 18-5 shows a macro for this purpose. In this macro, the AddMenu actions add the titles of the selections you want to appear across the menu bar. For each of these actions, the Menu Name argument includes the text to appear in the menu bar.

**tip:** *The easiest way to create your own menu system in Access version 1 is by copying the menu system included with the NWind database. These macros can be added to your own database with the Import command in the File menu. Once you copy these macros into your own database, you can change only the parts of the menu system you want to change.*

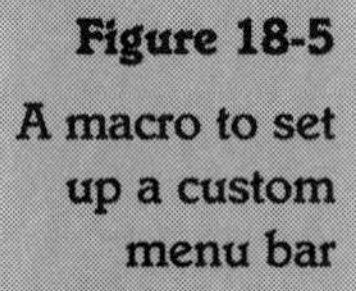

**Figure 18-5** A macro to set up a custom menu bar

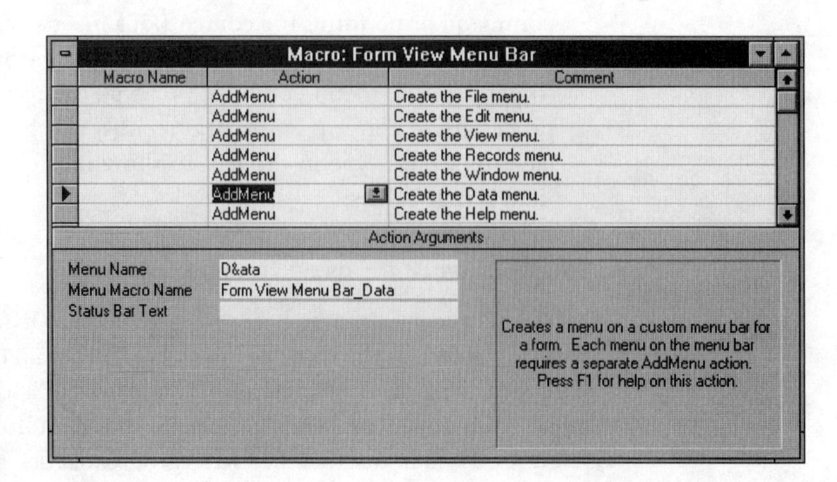

For example, the default Form view menu bar uses &File, &Edit, &View, &Records, &Window, and &Help as the arguments for the different AddMenu actions. The ampersand (&) is placed before the letter to be underlined, so for the menu bar item shown in Figure 18-5, the first item appears as Data. The Menu Macro Name argument of each of the AddMenu actions is the name of the macro group that defines the commands that appear in the drop-down menu. For example, the macro in Figure 18-5 tells Access that the Form View Menu Bar_Data macro group contains the information Access needs to determine which commands appear in the Data drop-down menu. This example uses the macro name styles set by the Menu Builder, but if you are not using the Menu Builder, you can use any acceptable macro group name.

Finally, you can supply the Status Line argument that sets the text to appear in the status line when you select the drop-down menu. If you do not supply this text, the text that appears in the status line of the commands is the text you enter for the macro's comment, which defines the command.

Each drop-down menu named in the macro for the menu bar has its own macro group. These macro group names match the Menu Macro Name arguments supplied for the different drop-down menu names. For example, the Form View Menu Bar macro in Figure 18-5 names macro groups for each of the items in the menu bar. For the Data drop-down menu, the database has a group macro named Form View Menu Bar_Data. The macro group contains macros for each of the commands that appear in a drop-down menu. The macro name is also the name of the command. Figure 18-6 shows the macro group for the Form View Menu Bar_Data macro group.

For the Form View Menu Bar_Data macro group, the commands that appear in the Data drop-down menu are Client, Employee, Invoice Register, Project,

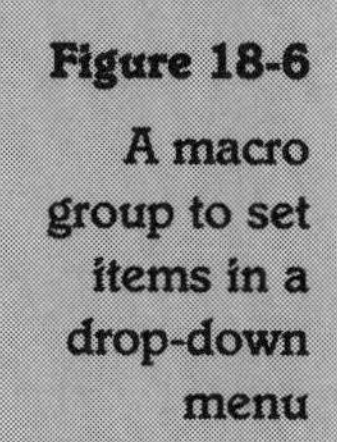

**Figure 18-6**

**A macro group to set items in a drop-down menu**

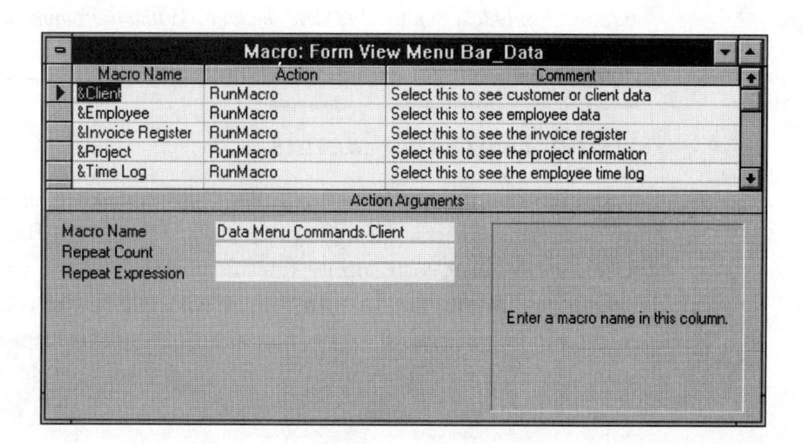

and Time Log. Like the items in the menu bar, the ampersand (&) indicates which letter is underlined. Next to the macro name is the action or actions Access performs when you choose the command in the menu bar. The actions you select for a command are the actions you want Access to perform when you select the command from the drop-down menu. When you are working with a menu using the Menu Builder, you are limited to the DoMenuItem, RunMacro, and RunCode actions. If you want to use other actions, set the action to RunMacro and the name of the macro to the macro containing the actions to perform. For example, if you choose Project in the Data drop-down menu, Access performs the RunMacro macro action to perform the Macros for Form View Menu Bar.Project macro. This macro opens the Project Table Reports form.

**tip:** *To create lines in a menu like the lines on either side of the printing commands in the File menu, create a macro name of - (a hyphen). This macro has no action.*

To have a menu perform one of the existing commands when you use the same name or a different one, use the DoMenuItem action. This action uses the menu bar name, the menu name, the command name, and any subcommand selection as arguments. For example, to have a command open another database, the Menu Bar argument is Database for the Database window, the Menu Name argument is File for the File menu, the Command is Open Database, and the Subcommand is empty.

**tip:** *Be sure to include a command to close the form. Without a command for this purpose, you can only close the form using the form window's Control menu box.*

## Using Your New Menus

When you complete the macros that will create the menus, try out your menu by displaying a form's design and changing the MenuBar property of the form. The macro name you supply for this property is the name of the macro that defines the menu bar. In turn, this macro selects the other macro groups that select the commands to appear in the drop-down menus. The macros in the macro groups are run as the different commands are selected. For example, you can change the MenuBar property of a form to Form View Menu Bar. When you display the form, the menu bar includes a Data drop-down menu, which you saw earlier.

The macro that creates the menu must be added to every form that you want to use the new menu. For example, you may want the Data menu to be included in your other forms so that you can quickly switch between the data you are viewing. To do this, enter **Form View Menu Bar** for the MenuBar property of every form you want to use the modified menu. Forms that do not have Form View Menu Bar as the MenuBar property use the standard Form view menu when you open them.

## Creating Macros that Perform with Key Combinations

You already have developed a group of commands that you can perform by pressing one or two keys. For example, you can press F11 in place of selecting the Database window from the bottom of the Window menu. You can create other key combinations that perform any macro action you assign them.

To create macros that perform when you press a key combination, name the macro group AutoKeys. This macro group contains macros named by the key combinations that perform them, like this one:

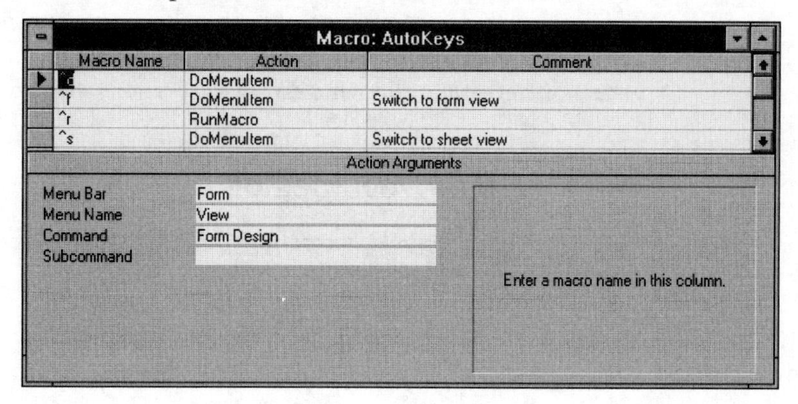


The key combinations are the same key combinations the SendKeys action uses. For numbers and letters, the keys are represented as entered. The SHIFT key is presented as + and the CTRL key is presented as ^. Most of the remaining key combinations are the name of the key in braces, as in {F11} or {INSERT}. For the macros entered in the preceding illustration, the key combinations are CTRL+D, CTRL+F, CTRL+R, and CTRL+S.

Each of these macros is followed by the macro action Access performs when you press the different key combinations. For the CTRL+D, CTRL+F, and

CTRL+S macros, the macro actions switch between the Design, Form, and Datasheet views. For the CTRL+R macro, Access performs the Project Table Reports macro. When a key combination in the AutoKeys macro conflicts with a key combination Access has assigned, the macro in the AutoKeys macro is performed instead.

Every time you open a database, Access checks whether the database has an AutoKeys macro. When Access finds an AutoKeys macro, the key combinations set in effect by the macro are in force while the database is open. When Access does not find an AutoKeys macro, only the default key combinations are in effect. When you edit an existing AutoKeys macro, the keystroke changes take effect when you save the modified macro.

## Access Add-ins

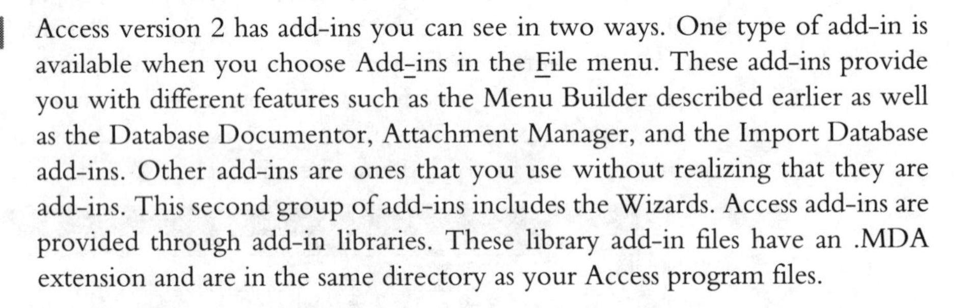

Access version 2 has add-ins you can see in two ways. One type of add-in is available when you choose Add-ins in the File menu. These add-ins provide you with different features such as the Menu Builder described earlier as well as the Database Documentor, Attachment Manager, and the Import Database add-ins. Other add-ins are ones that you use without realizing that they are add-ins. This second group of add-ins includes the Wizards. Access add-ins are provided through add-in libraries. These library add-in files have an .MDA extension and are in the same directory as your Access program files.

### The Database Documentor

Access version 2 has a Database Documentor that creates reports about tables, queries, forms, reports, macros, or reports in a database. The Database Documentor reports the same information that you can generate for individual objects with Print Definition in the File menu. The Database Documentor has the advantage that you can report on multiple objects at one time. To use the Database Documentor, follow these steps:

1. Choose Add-ins from the File menu and then Database Documentor.
2. Select the types of objects you want to print information about from the Object Type drop-down list box.

3. Double-click the names of the tables or other objects to print information. You can also highlight the name from the Print Definition of Objects list box and choose Select.
4. Select Options and choose the information to print about the object.
5. Select OK twice to generate the report.
6. Click the Print button in the toolbar and choose OK to print the report.
7. Press CTRL+F4 or click the Close button in the toolbar to close the report window.

Figure 18-7 shows the report the Database Documentor creates for the Macros for Form View Menu Bar macro group when you select Options and clear the Properties and Permissions by User and Group check boxes.

## The Attachment Manager Add-in

The Attachment Manager add-in handles updating the tables you select. As mentioned in Chapter 5, attached tables are tables that are actually in another database. Attaching tables lets you borrow the data from another database and use it as if it is in the database you are currently using. To use the Attachment Manager, choose Add-ins from the File menu and then Attachment Manager. You can select the attached tables in the database that you want to update. When you select the attached tables that you want to update, select OK and the add-in handles the updating of the attached tables.

## The Import Database Add-in

When you want to import an entire Access database into the current one, you want to use the Import Database add-in rather than using the Import command in the File menu for each object in the other database. Chapter 21 will also describe how you can use this add-in to transfer ownership of a database when you are assigning ownership to databases and database objects. After you select Add-ins from the File menu and Import Database, select the database containing the objects you want to import. As soon as you select OK, this add-in imports every object from the database you select. Unless this add-in encounters a problem, you will not see any message until the database is imported. If one of the objects cannot be imported, you will see a message and have the opportunity to select whether you want to abandon importing the database, retry importing

**Figure 18-7** Report on macros created with the Database Documentor

Wednesday, December 01, 1993 | **Macro: Macros for Form View Menu Bar** | Page: 1

**Actions**

| Name | Condition | Action | Argument | Value |
|---|---|---|---|---|
| **Client** | | | | |
| | | OpenForm | Form Name: | |
| | | | View: | Form |
| | | | Filter Name: | |
| | | | Where Condition: | |
| | | | Data Mode: | Edit |
| | | | Window Mode: | Normal |
| | *Select this to see customer or client data* | | | |
| **Employee** | | | | |
| | | OpenForm | Form Name: | |
| | | | View: | Form |
| | | | Filter Name: | |
| | | | Where Condition: | |
| | | | Data Mode: | Edit |
| | | | Window Mode: | Normal |
| | *Select this to see employee data* | | | |
| **Invoice Register** | | | | |
| | | OpenForm | Form Name: | |
| | | | View: | Form |
| | | | Filter Name: | |
| | | | Where Condition: | |
| | | | Data Mode: | Edit |
| | | | Window Mode: | Normal |
| | *Select this to see the invoice register* | | | |
| **Project** | | | | |
| | | OpenForm | Form Name: | Project Table Reports |
| | | | View: | Form |
| | | | Filter Name: | |
| | | | Where Condition: | |
| | | | Data Mode: | Edit |
| | | | Window Mode: | Normal |
| | *Select this to see the project information* | | | |
| **Time Log** | | | | |
| | | OpenForm | Form Name: | |
| | | | View: | Form |
| | | | Filter Name: | |
| | | | Where Condition: | |
| | | | Data Mode: | Edit |
| | | | Window Mode: | Normal |
| | *Select this to see the employee time log* | | | |

the object, or ignore the object causing the problem and continue importing the database. When the database already has an object with the same name as one you are importing, the imported version will have a 1 added to the object name to distinguish the two versions.

## Customizing Wizards and Other Add-Ins

In addition to simply using Wizards and the other add-ins you do not access by choosing Add-ins in the File menu, you can also customize these add-ins, install them, and remove them. To make these types of changes, choose Add-ins in the File menu and then choose Add-in Manager. From the subsequent dialog box, you can select an add-in and then select Customize to change the add-in, as described below, or select Uninstall to remove the add-in so that its features are not available (Access will then require less memory). You can also select Add New and the add-in library file for the add-in. When you are finished working with the add-ins, select Close to leave the Add-in Manager dialog box. The options for customizing the add-in libraries Access provides are described below.

### CUSTOMIZING THE TABLE WIZARD

You can customize the tables and fields in the tables you create with the Table Wizard. Change this Wizard by selecting MS Access Table from the Available Libraries list box and selecting Customize. Then, select from Customize Table Names, Customize Field Names, Customize Field Types, and Install Table Wizard Samples Database.

When you select Customize Table Names, you can change the names of existing tables, their description, and category. You can change the order of a table in the list by changing its sort order number. Within each table, you can select the fields in the sample table by entering field names for the fields in the table. Changing the sort order of the fields within the list of field names changes the order they are listed in the Table Wizard. Closing this window saves your changes and returns you to the Add-in Manager dialog box.

When you select Customize Field Names, you can rename fields provided by the sample tables, the field's description within the table Wizard, and field template. A field name can only be used once even though several sample tables use the same field. For example, several sample tables have a field for phone numbers and they all use the same field name, description, and template. Closing this window saves your changes and returns you to the Add-in Manager dialog box.

When you select Customize Field Types, you can alter the settings represented by the templates. From the next dialog box, you can select most of the properties you set for a field in a table. The settings you make here set the field property settings for all sample fields that use the field template that matches the entry in the Field Template Name text box. Closing this window saves your changes and returns you to the Add-in Manager dialog box.

When you select Install Table Wizard Samples Database, you can select the table wizard file containing the sample tables you want to add to your database. Select a file and OK and Access will add its tables to the tables in your sample database.

## CUSTOMIZING FORM AND REPORT WIZARDS

The Form and Report Wizards can be altered. For example, you can change the default font size when you want the text in new forms to be larger. By making customizing changes with the Add-in Manager, you can change how forms or reports created with a Wizard appear. To make these changes, select Form and Report Wizards from the Available Libraries list box and select Customize. The next dialog box selects whether you are changing the Form Wizard, the Report Wizard, AutoForm, AutoReport or Mailing Label size. AutoForm and AutoReport are Wizards that have different options, so they are listed separately. Once you select the Wizard, you will see a dialog box containing the features you can change.

When you have selected Customize Form Wizard Styles or Customize Report Wizard Styles, a dialog box like the one in Figure 18-8 appears. You can select options for each of the different looks available for forms or reports. From the Which Style drop-down list box, select one of the looks for forms (Standard, Chiseled, Shadowed, Boxed, and Embossed) or reports (Executive, Presentation, and Ledger). Once you select the look, the other selections you make in the dialog box change how that look appears in a form or report. These are some of the changes you can make for each look:

- The color of the Form or Report Header and Footer as well as the Page Header and Page Footer sections
- The color of the Detail section
- The foreground and background colors of label and text box controls
- The style, size, and attributes of the font of the label and text box controls

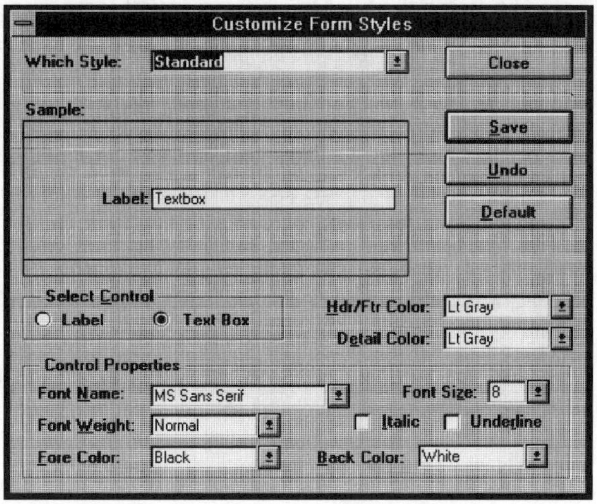

**Figure 18-8** Options for customizing a Form Wizard

You will see an example of the selections you have made in the sample section of the dialog box. When you have the changes you want, select Save. You can return to Access' defaults by selecting Default. When you are finished, select Close.

When you select Customize AutoForm, you can only select the default look and a single-column or tabular format. When you select Customize AutoReport, you can select the default look orientation, a single-column or tabular format, whether Access adjusts the formatting to fit all the fields onto one page, and the default spacing.

The Form Wizard and AutoForm choices affect each other, and the Report Wizard and AutoReport choices do as well. The default look selected for the AutoForm or AutoReport selects the initial look selected when you are responding to the questions in a Form Wizard or Report Wizard. The default spacing set for an AutoReport sets the initial line spacing for reports created with the Report Wizard. The check box for fitting all fields on a page for the AutoReport selects whether this same check box is initially selected in the last dialog box for a Report Wizard. The colors and fonts set by customizing the Form and Report Wizards sets the colors and fonts of forms and reports created with AutoForm or AutoReport. For example, you can change the Boxed look for forms to have a default label and text box font size of 14 points and AutoForm to use the Boxed look. Forms created with AutoForm will then have a font size of 14 points. When you are selecting a form's look that you are creating with the Form Wizard, the Boxed option button is initially selected.

These changes only alter the initial form or report you create using a Wizard. Once you have the form or report, you can make any change you want regardless of the settings for the Wizard.

When you customize the mailing label size, you are defining additional label sizes. By selecting New, you can add a new label design. You will type a name for the label in the Label Name text box. You can also select how many fit across the page, whether they are fed a sheet at a time or continuously, and whether their dimensions are measured in inches or centimeters. In the label diagram below, enter the measurements that define the spacing and size of the labels. Once you return to the User Label Sizes dialog box, you can continue creating, deleting, or editing the label sizes you have defined. Select Close when you are finished.

### CREATING NEW INPUT MASKS

You can create, delete, and change the available input masks you add as a property to a field or form control. When you select Control and Property Wizards from the Add-in Manager dialog box, Customize, and Customize and Input Mask, you are in a form that lets you work with the available input masks. You can modify one of the existing records to change one of the available input masks. You can also create new ones. When you enter a new input mask, add the code for the input mask, a description, a sample, a prompt to use as a placeholder, and a country code, and select the field type that uses the input mask. When you close this window, the changes you have made are included and you can see them the next time you use the Input Mask Wizard.

### CREATING NEW COMMAND BUTTONS

Besides changing the input masks when you customize the control and property wizards, you can also change the bitmapped images you have for command buttons created with the control wizard. After selecting Control and Property Wizards from the Add-in Manager dialog box, Customize, and Customize Command Button, you can change the pictures for command buttons created with the control wizard. From the Customize Picture List dialog box, you can delete existing button pictures, rename their text, and add new ones from BMP files. When you are finished, select Close.

Quick Reference

**To Make a Macro Run When a Database is Opened** Simply name the macro that you want to run whenever the database is opened AutoExec.

**To Make a Form a Popup Form** In the macro that opens the form, for the OpenForm action that displays the form, set the Window Mode property to Dialog or change the form's Pop Up and Modal properties to Yes.

**To Add a Different Menu To a Form View** Create a macro containing AddMenu actions for each item that you want to appear in the menu bar. Create macro groups for each of the menu bar items that contain macros with the name of the menu command and the actions to perform when the command is chosen. Add the macro name containing the AddMenu actions to the form's MenuBar property (On Menu in Access version 1).

**To Create a Menu with the Menu Builder** Start the Menu Builder by choosing Add-ins from the File menu and Menu Builder. Select the macro that defines the menu bar and Edit, or select New to create a new one and then select the existing menu you want to start with as the starting point for the menu you are creating. Add, modify, and delete the menu items to create the menu you want. Select OK. If you are creating a new menu, you must supply the name of the macro for the menu bar and OK.

**To Assign Macros to Specific Key Combinations** Name the macro group containing the macros for the key combinations AutoKeys. For each key combination, give the macro the same name as the key combination that, when pressed, runs the macro.

**To Customize a Wizard** Choose Add-ins in the File menu and Add-in Manager. Select the Wizard to customize and select from the options available.

# Chapter 19

Modules

Saving the Module

Printing a Module

Putting Modules in Forms and Reports

Using the Procedures

Programming with Access Basic

Finding Mistakes in Your Procedures

# Introduction to Access Basic

MOST database applications provide the user with a programming language for applications development, and Access is no exception. Access calls its programming language Access Basic. As a programming language, it has many of the same features as Microsoft's Visual Basic. If you have used other database programming languages, you will find Access Basic easy to use because it shares many programming capabilities with them.

Most of the features requiring code in other programming languages are handled automatically by the objects that an Access Basic program uses. For example, a dBASE program would have many lines that display the data, get the data, and validate the data. In Access Basic, this is all handled by the form, so a program using the form has much less work to do. You use Access Basic when you want customized functions or if you want to automate using several objects. Use Access Basic when you want to develop further actions after an event on a form or report occurs. You will also want to use Access Basic when you are creating applications within Access to work with the database objects you have created.

This chapter gets you started using Access Basic to create programs. Access Basic is a full-fledged programming language. Like most programming languages, entire books can be written on how to use it. This chapter's intent is to give you enough basic information that you can try it on your own.

The programs in Access Basic are called *procedures*. These procedures are stored in a database object called a *module*. You can put all of the procedures you use in a database into a single module, or you can split the procedures among several modules. This chapter starts with the basics of creating a module and then shows how to add procedures to it. In each procedure, the instructions telling Access the steps to perform are called *statements*. Once you have procedures, you will want to save them, print them, and use them. After learning these basics, you will learn a few of the advanced programming capabilities you can add to your procedures. Finally, you will learn about some of the tools Access provides to help you make your procedures error-free.

# Modules

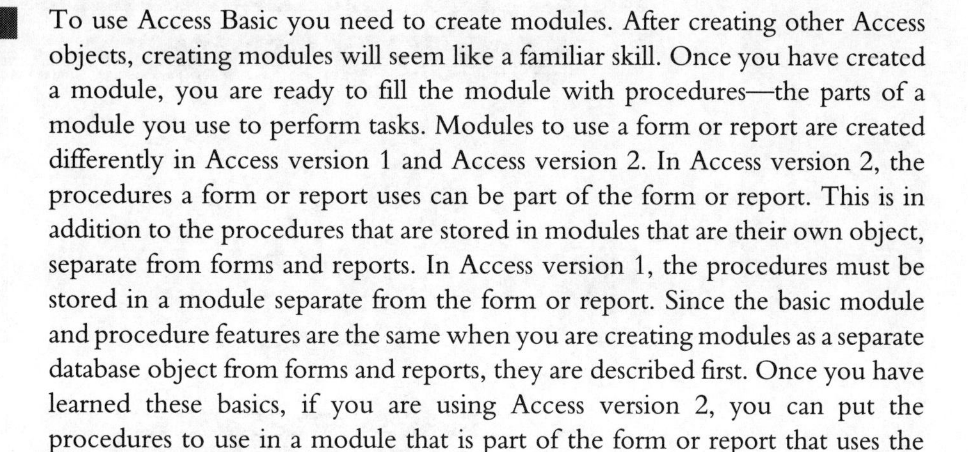

To use Access Basic you need to create modules. After creating other Access objects, creating modules will seem like a familiar skill. Once you have created a module, you are ready to fill the module with procedures—the parts of a module you use to perform tasks. Modules to use a form or report are created differently in Access version 1 and Access version 2. In Access version 2, the procedures a form or report uses can be part of the form or report. This is in addition to the procedures that are stored in modules that are their own object, separate from forms and reports. In Access version 1, the procedures must be stored in a module separate from the form or report. Since the basic module and procedure features are the same when you are creating modules as a separate database object from forms and reports, they are described first. Once you have learned these basics, if you are using Access version 2, you can put the procedures to use in a module that is part of the form or report that uses the procedures.

**note:** *Access performs procedures rather than modules. Modules are Access' approach for storing procedures.*

## Creating a Module

To create a module, begin by clicking the Module button in the Database window and the New button, or select New from the File menu and then choose Module. Access opens a window to contain this module, which looks like the one shown in Figure 19-1.

At the beginning of a module is the *declarations section*, which initially contains Option Compare Database when you open a new module. This section may subsequently contain other declarations if needed.

## Creating a Procedure

Creating a procedure is easy, since Access constantly looks at what you enter in a Module window. To tell Access you want to start a new procedure, simply begin typing an entry in the Module window. This entry is either **Sub** or **Function** followed by the name of the procedure, parentheses, and any

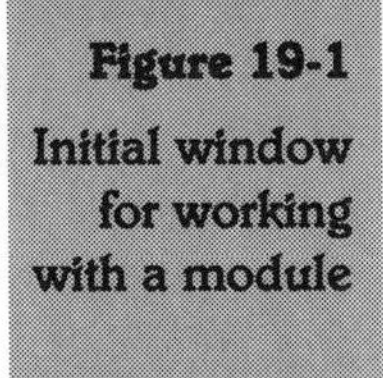

**Figure 19-1**
**Initial window for working with a module**

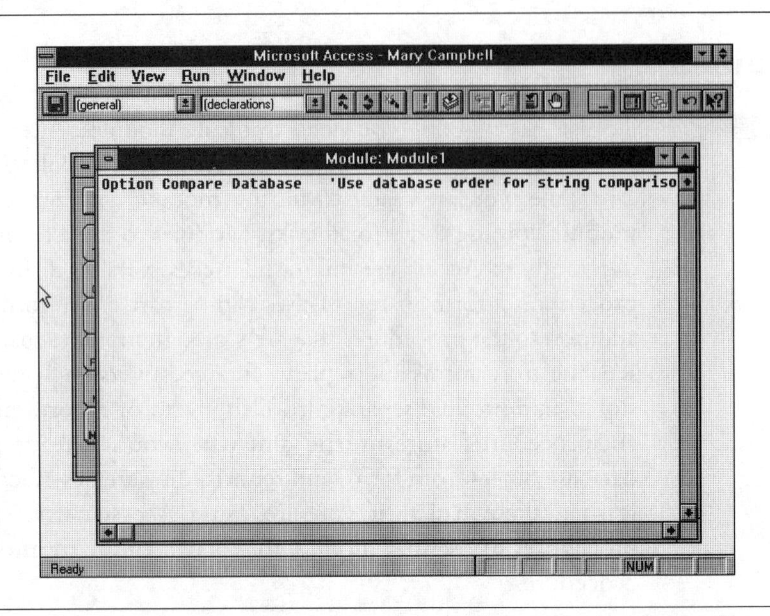


arguments the procedure uses. Sub or Function tells Access the type of procedure you want to create.

A *function procedure*, like the functions Access provides, takes zero or more arguments and returns a value that you can subsequently use in an expression. A *sub procedure* takes zero or more arguments but does not return a value. Either type of procedure can perform tasks. When creating a new procedure, you have to decide whether the procedure is a function procedure or a sub procedure. The difference between these two procedures is whether you want the procedure to return a value when completed.

For example, when you use an Access function, the function returns a value. When you create a procedure that is to be included in an expression, you want the procedure to be a function procedure. In other cases, when Access performs a procedure, the procedure does not return a value. An example of this is a procedure that changes a control's Visible property without returning information other parts of Access can use. This type of a procedure is a sub procedure.

A procedure name can be up to 40 characters long, including letters, numbers, or underscores, and must start with a letter. Procedure names cannot contain spaces. You cannot have more than one procedure in a database with the same name. You cannot name a procedure the same name as global variables or constants (defined later), or as *reserved names*. Reserved names include statements used by Access Basic, function names, operators, and methods (defined later in this chapter).

These rules for naming are explicitly for Access Basic, and differ from the database object rules you use for naming objects and controls.

When a procedure is a function procedure, you can add one of several characters as the last character of the name to indicate the data type of the result. These suffix characters are % for Integer, & for Long, ! for Single, # for Double, @ for Currency, and $ for String. If a function procedure name does not use one of these characters, the function procedure returns a Variant data type. Unless you need a specific data type result, use a Variant data type.

### USING ARGUMENTS

Parentheses surround the arguments the procedure uses. These arguments are like the arguments the Access functions use. When you use the procedure, it expects a specific number of arguments, and the information provided by the arguments often must be in a specific order. Argument names are like the names of arguments for Access functions. You want them to describe the data the argument represents. You only need as many arguments as you plan to pass to the procedure. Each of the arguments is separated with commas.

As an example, suppose you want a function procedure that takes a word and converts it to proper case. By using a function procedure for this purpose, you use the custom function procedure every time you want the results without typing the longer formula that the custom function procedure represents. In this example, you tell Access you want to create a function procedure by typing **Function Proper (OldText)**. Function tells Access to create a Function procedure, that Proper is the name of the function procedure, and that OldText represents the single argument that you pass to this function procedure every time you use it.

When you press ENTER, Access recognizes that you want to create a function procedure and adds an End Function line for you two lines below the function, as you can see in Figure 19-2. If you were creating a sub procedure, Access would add End Sub at the bottom of the procedure. The Function or Sub lines start the beginning of the procedure and the End lines end the procedure. The lines in between contain the instructions for Access to perform every time you run this procedure. Also, notice that the procedure name appears in the toolbar.

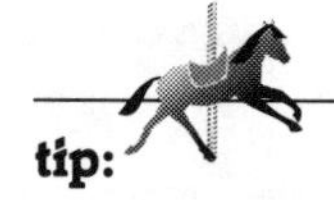

**tip:** *You can also start a new procedure by choosing New Procedure from the Edit menu or by clicking the New Procedure button in the toolbar. When you use this command, you can select whether the procedure is a sub or a function procedure and the procedure's name. This adds the top and bottom lines of the procedure without any arguments in the parentheses. You can always fill in the parentheses later as you decide the arguments the procedure will use.*

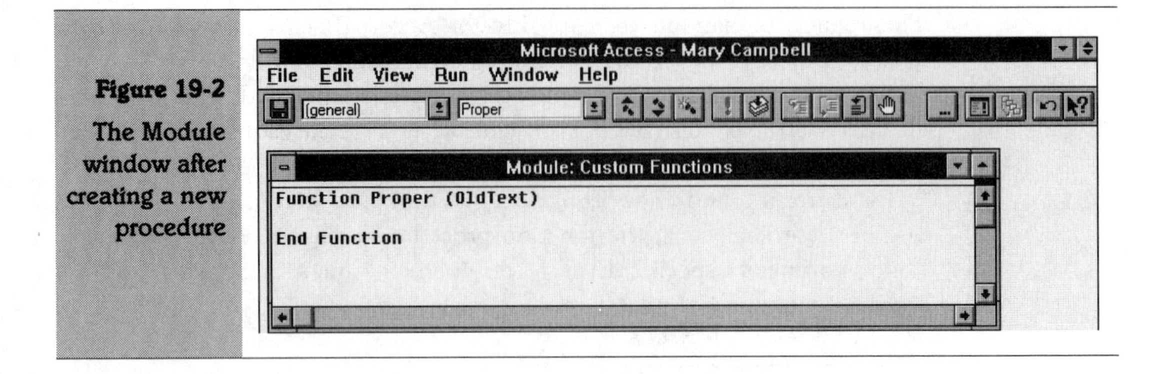


**Figure 19-2** The Module window after creating a new procedure

## CHANGING THE PROCEDURE DISPLAYED

You only see one procedure at a time in the window (later you will learn how to see two). Each procedure is like text written on separate pages of a loose-leaf notebook. You have several ways to choose the procedure that appears in the window. You can press CTRL+UP ARROW and CTRL+DOWN ARROW, which is the same as choosing Previous Procedure and Next Procedure in the View menu. You also can click one of these two buttons in the toolbar:

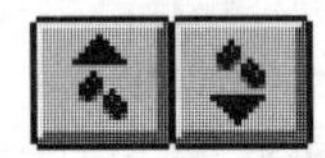

The Previous Procedure button on the left displays the previous procedure, and the Next Procedure button on the right displays the next procedure. You also can choose which procedure to display by selecting the name of the procedure or the declarations section from the second of these two drop-down boxes:

Access version 1 only has one drop-down list box, which is labeled Procedure. An additional method of selecting which procedure you are viewing is to choose Procedures from the View menu or press F2. Access displays a dialog box like the one shown next. You can select the different modules as well as which procedure you want to see.

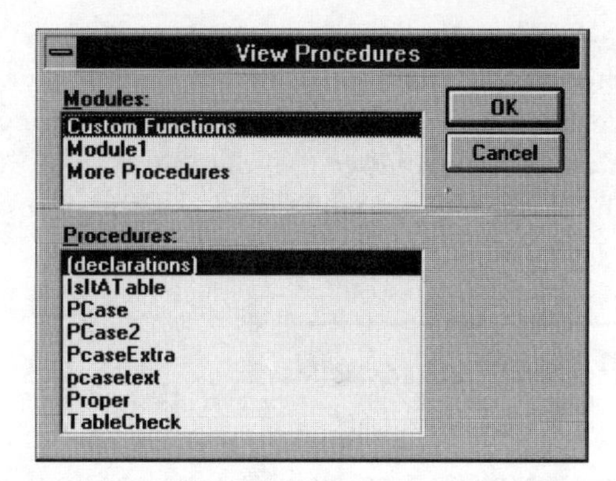

**note:** *Access alphabetizes the procedures in a module, so the order of the procedures changes from the order you enter them into the module.*

## SPLITTING A MODULE WINDOW

When you want to look at two procedures or a declarations section and a procedure from the same module, you can split the window. Splitting the window is like splitting a window of a query design, where you divide the query Design window between the field lists and the QBE grid. To split a Module window into two, drag the white bar below the title bar (the mouse will change to a double-headed arrow) to where you want the window split.

You also can choose Split Window from the View menu to divide the Module window in half. Once the window is split, switch between the two halves by clicking them or by pressing F6. Each window can show a separate procedure or declarations section from the same module. The following shows a Module window split in half to show two separate procedures:

Module: Custom Functions

```
Function TableCheck ()
'This function is solely for starting the IsItATable sub procedure
IsItATable
End Function
```

```
Function Proper (OldText)
    Proper = UCase(Left(OldText, 1)) & LCase(Right(OldText, Len(OldText)
End Function
```

While a window is split, you can change the position of the split by dragging the white bar up or down. You can return a window to showing a single declarations section or procedure by dragging the bar to the top of the window. You also can remove the split in the window by choosing Split Window from the View menu again to remove the check mark next to the Split Window command.

## Editing a Procedure

When you have the beginning and end of a procedure, you are ready to add the statements that tell Access what to do when you use the procedure. Editing in a Module window is like editing with the Windows Notepad accessory. The only difference is that Access reviews the statements you enter. When you enter a statement it cannot understand, Access displays a message indicating that the current line has a problem. This review process finds mistakes as you enter statements, catching typing errors and some incorrect entries.

Each of the lines contains a statement. Some of these statements are expressions. For example, the following Proper function procedure contains a single statement:

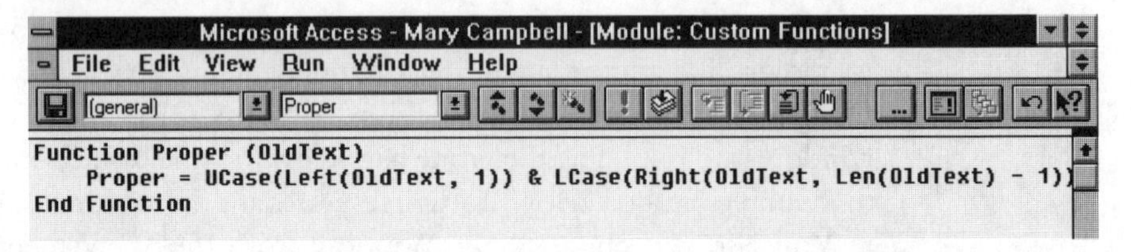


Every time this procedure is run, it needs the text to convert. Within the Proper function procedure, this text is called OldText. What the text to convert is called in the procedure or other Access feature that uses this function is not relevant to the Proper function. The expression that this statement computes is the same expression you used in Chapter 12 to convert a form or report control's entry to proper case. Access knows what value this function procedure returns, because the procedure contains an expression that equates the function procedure's name with a value. In this case, this function procedure returns the text it is sent, changing the first letter to uppercase and the rest of the letters to lowercase. Since sub procedures do not have this expression, it is this statement that separates a function procedure from a sub procedure.

This function procedure only works with single words. Later you will see a PCase function procedure that handles making each word proper case. The

PCase function procedure uses the Proper function procedure to switch individual words to uppercase.

With expressions in a procedure, you must tell Access where you want the result of the expression stored. In the module in the preceding illustration, the expression's result becomes the function procedure's return value. At other times, you will put the expression's result in a variable. Variable names follow Access Basic naming conventions (up to 40 letters, numbers, and underscores).

**tip:** *When you are entering expressions into a module in Access version 2, click the Build button in the toolbar or select Build from the shortcut menu. This opens the Expression Builder that you learned about in Chapter 12 for building an expression like the one shown earlier in this section.*

## Saving the Module

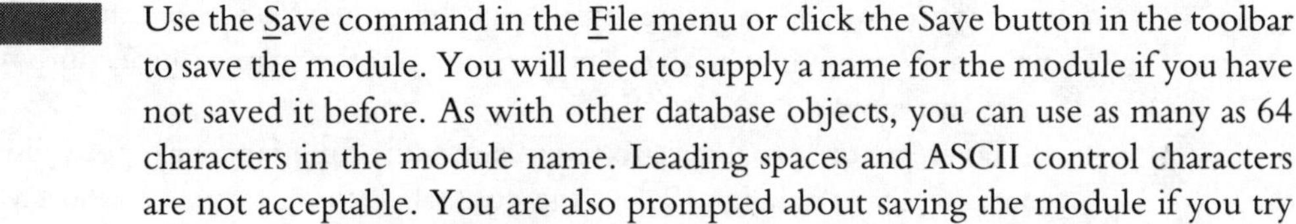

Use the Save command in the File menu or click the Save button in the toolbar to save the module. You will need to supply a name for the module if you have not saved it before. As with other database objects, you can use as many as 64 characters in the module name. Leading spaces and ASCII control characters are not acceptable. You are also prompted about saving the module if you try closing the window when the module has unsaved changes. Close the Module window by either choosing Close from the File menu, pressing CTRL+F4, or double-clicking the window's Control menu box. The module's name displays in the Database window. Now you have the Design button available. Later, when you want to edit the module, you can select the module and then select the Design button or, in Access version 1, double right-click the module's name.

## Printing a Module

To work on the procedures you create more easily, print them out. Printing a module prints the contents of the declarations section and all the procedures in the module. You can preview the appearance of the printout by choosing Print Preview from the File menu. Use Print Setup in the File menu to change how the output is printed. Choose Print from the File menu when ready to print and select OK.

**tip:** *Create a report of the contents of a module with the Database Documentor or by printing the module's definition. Start the Database Documentor by choosing Add-ins from the File menu and Database Documentor. Print the module definition by choosing Print Definition from the File menu. With the options for either choice, you can print out the contents of the module as well as printing out the properties and permissions assigned to the module.*

## Putting Modules in Forms and Reports

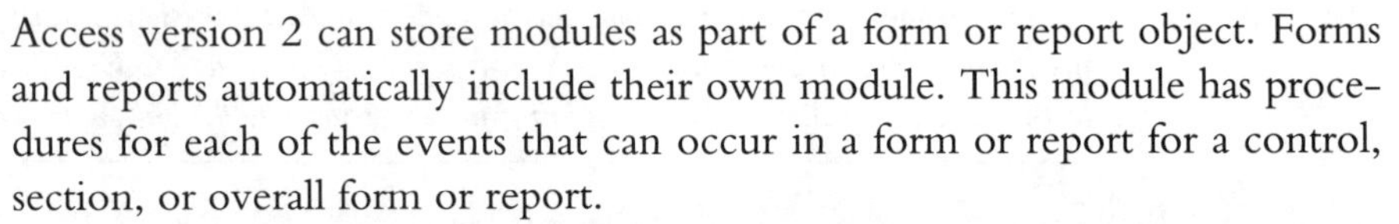

Access version 2 can store modules as part of a form or report object. Forms and reports automatically include their own module. This module has procedures for each of the events that can occur in a form or report for a control, section, or overall form or report.

Put procedures that you want to share between forms or reports in a separate module from the forms and reports. Any form or report procedure that wants to use the procedure in the module can do so. You cannot, however, use one procedure in a form or report in another one. You also cannot change a procedure name that an event performs to another named procedure within a form or report.

To create the procedure to use in a module for a form or report, display the form or report's design. Select the control, section, form, or report with the event that you want to assign the procedure to. Then do one of the following:

- Select [Event Procedure] from the property's drop-down list in the property sheet and click the Build button.
- Click the Build button, select Code Builder, and OK.

Either option opens a Module window like the one shown in Figure 19-3. This Module window has an entry of Form or Report, a period, and then the name of the form or report, as in Form.Billing And Pay Rates. Access assumes you want a sub procedure. This procedure is already named with the control, section, or form or report and then the event for the module. Spaces are replaced with underscores. For example, when you are creating a procedure for the On Change event for the First Name control, the procedure is named First_Name_Change. Do not change the procedure name. Access expects the procedure names to match the controls and event names. You can reassign a procedure to a different event by changing the procedure name to the one the form or report expects for a specific event. For example, if you change the First_Name_BeforeUpdate procedure name to First_Name_AfterUpdate, the

Before Update property for the First Name control remains [Event Procedure], but it only contains the First_Name_BeforeUpdate procedure as it existed the last time you saved the form's module. The After Update property also contains [Event Procedure] and this procedure contains the contents of the First_Name_AfterUpdate procedure as they were when you renamed the First_Name_BeforeUpdate procedure. At this point, you can enter the procedure. You will also need to enter any arguments this procedure uses.

Just as with modules you create outside of a form or report, you can switch between procedures in the form or report. You can switch to any available procedure within the form or report's module using the Object list and Procedure list in the toolbar. In the Object list in the toolbar, you select the control, section, or overall form or report. In the Procedure list in the toolbar, you can select the event for the selected control, section, or overall form or report that you want to see the procedure. However, when you switch to the next or previous procedure, the only procedures you will see are the ones you have created.

Just like procedures stored in their own module, you can split the Module window in two. You can close the form or report's Module window just like you would close other windows for other database objects. Closing the Module window for modules belonging to a form or report does not close the window for the form or report. You won't see the prompt for saving the module when you close the Module window, because the module is saved as part of the form

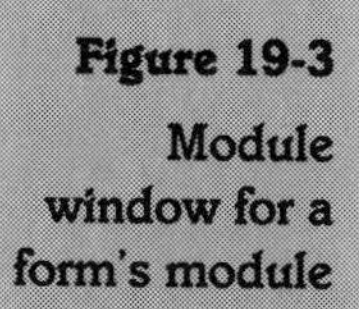

**Figure 19-3**
**Module window for a form's module**

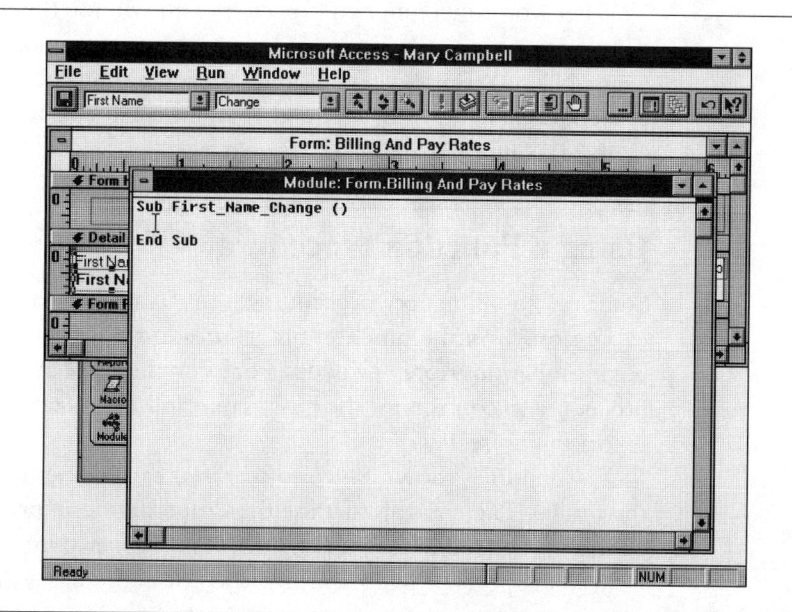

or report design. You do not see the module for the form or report in the Database window when the Database window displays modules, because the module is within the form or report.

When you print the module using Print or Print Preview from the File menu, Access prints the contents of all of the modules in the form or report. You can reopen the Module window for a form or report with the Code command in the View menu.

**tip:** *Use the Clipboard to transfer Access Basic statements between procedures as well as to transfer a procedure you have in a form or report to a module and to transfer a procedure in a module to one in a form or report. You will want to omit the Function or Sub statements as well as the End Function and End Sub statements when you copy statements between procedures.*

## Using the Procedures

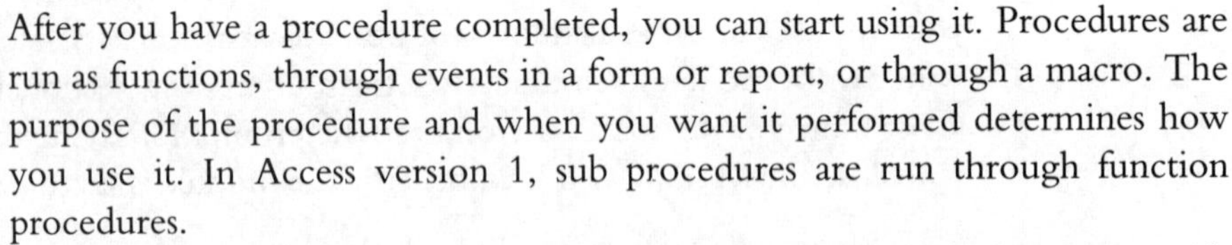

After you have a procedure completed, you can start using it. Procedures are run as functions, through events in a form or report, or through a macro. The purpose of the procedure and when you want it performed determines how you use it. In Access version 1, sub procedures are run through function procedures.

When you run a function procedure you will use the procedure name with the arguments in parentheses and separated by commas, as in CompareName ([First Name], [Employee]). When you run a sub procedure, you will use the procedure name followed by the arguments separated by commas, as in CompareName [First Name], [Employee].

### Using a Function Procedure

Some of the function procedures you create can be used as part of any expression. You use function procedures in the same locations in which you use the functions Access provides. For example, you can add the Proper function procedure to controls for the First Name and Last Name fields, as shown in the report in Figure 19-4.

This report is shown twice so that you can see both the report design and the results. The controls that use the Proper function procedure are calculated controls. The control for the first name has =Proper([First Name]) as the Control Source property; the control for the last name has =Proper([Last Name])

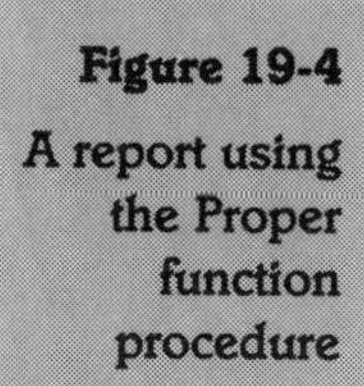

**Figure 19-4**
**A report using the Proper function procedure**

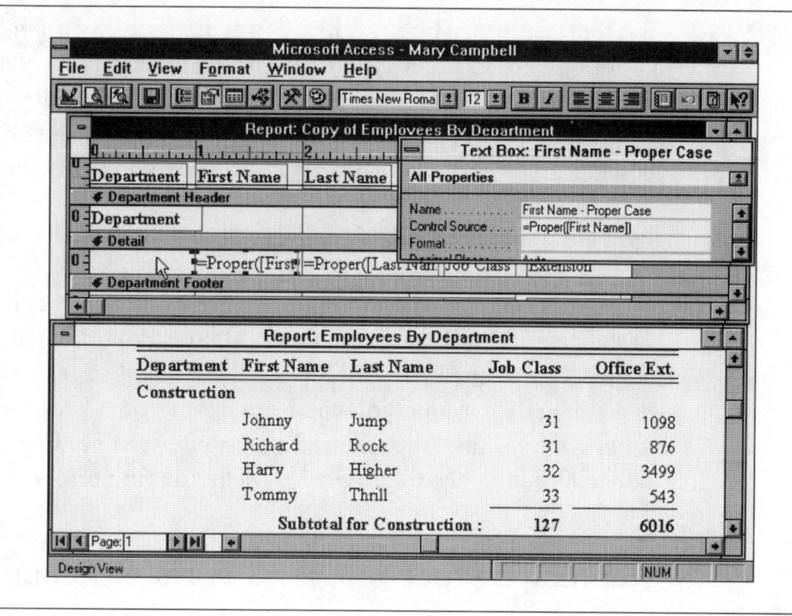


as the Control Source property. Since Access does not have a function of its own named Proper, Access checks for a function procedure in any one of the database's module objects for one named Proper. The module containing this function is in a separate module from the module that is part of the report's design. Access uses this function procedure to convert all of the first and last names to proper case. The Name properties for these controls are changed so that they are not the same as the field names.

## Running a Procedure in a Macro

A macro can use procedures in two ways. One way is running a procedure with the RunCode macro action. The other way is using a procedure as part of a condition that selects whether a macro action is performed.

To create a macro action that runs a procedure, select the RunCode action in the Action column and the name of the procedure for the Function Name argument. If the procedure uses any arguments, you must supply them in parentheses as well. For example, you might enter **Proper ([Last Name])** for the Function Name argument. The value the function procedure returns when Access performs the RunCode macro action is ignored.

If you use a function procedure as part of a macro action's condition, Access evaluates the condition to decide whether to perform a macro action. Include the function procedure just like you would use any other Access function in a condition. For example, you might have a function procedure that calculates the percentage difference between your employee billing rates and pay rates. To use this function procedure in a macro's condition to find records where the markup percentage is more than 25 percent, the condition may look like this:

```
PercentMarkUp([Bill Rate],[Pay Rate])>25%
```

In this case, Access uses the result of the function procedure, since the result of the condition that uses the function procedure determines whether a macro action is performed.

Later in the chapter, you will learn how to run a procedure from the Module window by using the Immediate window. The Immediate window is a debugging tool Access provides to help you find errors in a procedure.

### Running a Procedure for a Form or Report Event

A procedure can be run when an event in a form or report occurs. In Chapter 17, you saw several examples that attached macros to events, but you can also attach procedures. The approach is different for versions 1 and 2.

In Access version 2, when an event property is set to [Event Procedure], the procedure created for that event and stored as part of the form or report's module is automatically run. In Access version 1, you can run a procedure when a form or report event occurs by using a macro that runs the procedure, as described in the previous section.

Another option that you can use in both versions 1 and 2 is to run a procedure as an event for the event property. For example, if you have a function procedure called TableCheck, you can run this procedure when an event occurs by entering **=TableCheck()** for the property. Any arguments that the function uses must be included. Access will ignore any value this function returns.

## Programming with Access Basic

Programming in Access Basic has many possibilities. You select what a procedure does through the information you place in a procedure. When creating your own procedures, you will want to plan and comment the statements you add to your procedures. Most procedures use variables; you will learn about their types and the different information they can represent shortly. Access Basic has many statements providing repetitive and selective processing that you will incorporate into your own procedures. Access Basic also has methods that you use to work with data stored in the different Access Basic objects. Remember, this chapter is just an introduction to programming with Access Basic, so as you try to create your own procedures you will be learning about Access Basic features that are beyond the basics presented here.

## Planning and Adding Comments to Your Procedures

When creating procedures that are longer than a single line, you will need to plan the statements you will be entering. Rather than focusing on exact tasks, you will make planning procedures easier if you first think of the tasks you want to perform and later convert the tasks into exact statements.

Figure 19-5 shows the PCase procedure that has the tasks the procedure will perform. The text describes these steps as if you are describing these tasks to another person. These tasks also act as placeholders. The task descriptions temporarily fill lines that you know need to contain a statement—although you are not yet sure what that statement will be. Later, when you know what that statement is, you can add it. Using the placeholder comment marks where the statement belongs and is a reminder to prevent you from forgetting a crucial step.

All of the lines of description in Figure 19-5 start with a single quote. The single quote tells Access that the text following is a *comment.* Comments in a procedure are like comments in a macro. They describe the purpose of each of the statements. When you look back later at a procedure, you can quickly determine what each of the statements accomplishes. While Access Basic does not require them, comments are a good idea to add so that your procedures will not be abandoned when you forget what the lines represent. You can use

**Figure 19-5** Comments in a procedure to lay out the tasks to perform

Module: Custom Functions

```
Function PCase (OldText)
'for 1 to the length of OldText
'   get that numbered character out of OldText & put in CurrentChar
'   Is CurrentChar a space?
'       If so, you have a word
'           Take existing word and make it proper case
'           Add word to NewPhrase
'       If not, add character to CurrentWord
End Function
```

the descriptions of the tasks the procedure completes as the comments after you add the statements to perform the task. Figure 19-6 shows the PCase procedure shown in Figure 19-5 after the statements to complete the function procedure have been added.

## Variables and Data Types in Access Basic

*Variables* let you store the data as a procedure performs each of the statements. Variables are temporary storage facilities available to a procedure. Think of variables as sticky notes containing different information. The procedure can create these variable sticky notes and change the data placed on each one. Usually, when Access is done with a procedure, it takes all of these sticky notes that it has created and throws them out.

Variable names follow Access Basic naming conventions. This means that you can include up to 40 letters, numbers, and underscores. The variable name must start with a letter. Variable names cannot have the same name as a procedure, a global variable, a global constant, an Access Basic statement, a function, an operator, or a method.

When a procedure contains something that looks like a variable name and is in a location where a variable name is allowed, Access creates a variable with that name. To help you keep track of all of the variables in a procedure, use a *Dim statement.* Dim is followed by the variable names and possibly their type. The following is an example of a Dim statement:

```
Dim My_Number As Integer, My_Date as Variant, OldText as String
```

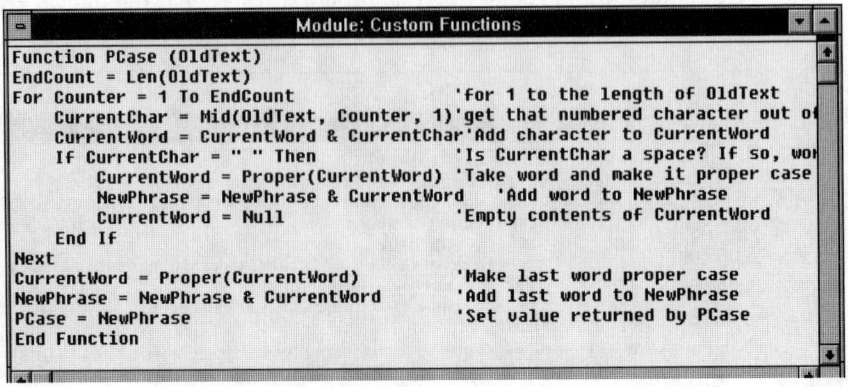

Module: Custom Functions

```
Function PCase (OldText)
EndCount = Len(OldText)
For Counter = 1 To EndCount                  'for 1 to the length of OldText
    CurrentChar = Mid(OldText, Counter, 1)'get that numbered character out o
    CurrentWord = CurrentWord & CurrentChar'Add character to CurrentWord
    If CurrentChar = " " Then                'Is CurrentChar a space? If so, wo
        CurrentWord = Proper(CurrentWord) 'Take word and make it proper case
        NewPhrase = NewPhrase & CurrentWord    'Add word to NewPhrase
        CurrentWord = Null                   'Empty contents of CurrentWord
    End If
Next
CurrentWord = Proper(CurrentWord)            'Make last word proper case
NewPhrase = NewPhrase & CurrentWord          'Add last word to NewPhrase
PCase = NewPhrase                            'Set value returned by PCase
End Function
```

**Figure 19-6** The PCase procedure after adding statements

Most of the variables you use are Variant data types. Variant data types have the wonderful ability to accept most types of data. (However, keep in mind that Access can perform procedures more efficiently when it knows the data types of the variables.) Most of the examples in this chapter use the Variant data type because this data type provides the most flexibility. The other available types are Integer, Long, Short, Double, Currency, String (for text), and User-defined (created by defining how the data is formatted). You can define the data types when you want to be sure that only a particular type of data is accepted.

## LOCAL, MODULE, AND GLOBAL VARIABLES

When you use variables in modules, some are shared by all procedures in any module (global), some are shared with any procedure within the module (module), and some are only available to a single procedure (local). The words "local" and "global," when applied to variables, simply indicate how long a variable lasts and which procedures can use the values the variables contain.

When you use the different variables in Access Basic, you initially will not have to worry about whether you are creating local, module, or global variables. The only time the variable scope makes a difference is when you try using a module variable and a local variable with the same name or a global variable with either a module or global variable. In either case, the procedure will not work.

***Local Variables*** Most variables in procedures are local variables. When you are done with the procedure, the variable disappears. If the procedure calls another one, the procedure that is called has access to all of its own variables as well as to all of the ones in the procedure that called it. Local variables, the variables you use within a procedure, are either defined with a Dim statement or not defined at all.

***Module Variables*** If you want to have a variable that all procedures in a module can share, you want a module variable. To create these variables, declare them in the declarations section of the module using the Dim statement.

***Global Variables*** Global variables are available in any procedure of any module in the database. To create global variables, declare them in the declarations section of the procedure, but use Global in place of Dim. With module and global variables, the current values of these variables remain as long as the database is open.

*Global constants* are text that represent specific values. Access has defined some of them such as True, False, and Null. You can create your own—for example, if working with circles in several procedures in a module, you might define a global constant of pi, which always equals 3.141592. Using the global constant means you use pi in a statement every time you want to use the value of 3.141592.

## OBJECT VARIABLES

Besides having variables to represent specific types of data, you can have variables representing objects. For example, instead of having a variable that equals the current value of a client name, you can have a variable that represents the Client Name control in a form or report. Object variables have eight types that select the type of object an object variable represents. These types are Databasa, Form, Report, Control, Table, QueryDef for the query definition, Dynaset for a table or query containing data you can edit, and Snapshot for a table or query containing data you cannot edit. To use an object variable in a procedure, you must define it. For example, you can have a Dim statement in a procedure that looks like this:

```
Dim My_DB as Database, My_Table as Table, My_Client as Control
```

With these variables defined, you subsequently can use My_DB for the database, My_Table for the table the procedure uses, and My_Client for the Client Name control in a form or report. Access also has two other objects that you can use in place of an object variable when you want to refer to these objects. These are like predefined object variables. *Screen* represents the current form, report, and control. *Debug* represents sending output to the Immediate window, which you will learn about later in the chapter.

To assign the object these object variables represent, you use the Set statement. The Set statement is like an expression prefix since you use Set, the object variable to assign, an equal sign, and the description of the object it represents. Often you are supplying an object identifier just like the ones you used for forms and reports. Here are some examples:

```
Set My_DB = DBEngine.Workspaces(0).Databases(0)
Set My_DB = CurrentDB()
Set My_Table = Forms![Employee Data - 3]
Set My_Table = Forms(Name_Table)
```

```
Set My_Client = Report![Handwritten Park Description]![Client Name]
Set My_Client = My_Table![Client Name]
```

The first two statements assign the current database to the My_DB object variable. The first option uses collections, so it cannot be used in Access version 1. The difference between the two assignments for My_Table is that in the first example, My_Table represents the Employee Data - 3 form. In the second example, My_Table represents the form with the same name as the entry placed in the Name_Table variable. The contents of Name_Table are either set by a previous statement or they are sent to the procedure as an argument when you use it, so the form that My_Table represents changes every time you use it. With the two examples that set the value of My_Client, the first one selects My_Client to represent the Client Name control of a specific report, while the second example selects My_Client to represent the Client Name control of the form represented by the My_Table object variable.

Object variables that are sent as an argument to another procedure must be identified in the procedure as such. For example, in the NextControl procedure, which accepts a control as an argument that NextControl identifies as This-Control, the first line of the procedure is Sub NextControl (ThisControl As Control). The word "As" indicates that you are providing the data type of this control, and "Control" identifies the variable as an object variable for a control.

This example purposefully uses a sub procedure, because you cannot use object variables as arguments for function procedures. You can send an object to a function procedure, and the function procedure uses the value of that object. For example, you can use the object variable My_Client, which represents the Client Name control of a form to a function procedure, and the function procedure uses the current value of that control.

## COLLECTION OBJECT VARIABLES

Access Basic also uses collection objects that collect objects of a specified type. Rather than describing the data that is in an object variable, Access defines the collections for you. Access has the following collections:

| Collection Name | Collection Contents |
|---|---|
| Containers | Containers |
| Databases | Open databases |
| Documents | Document objects |
| Fields | Fields within the table, query, record set, index, or relation |
| Forms | Open forms in the open database |
| Groups | Group accounts in the current workgroup |

| Collection Name | Collection Contents |
|---|---|
| Indexes | Indexes for the tables |
| Parameters | Parameters for queries |
| Properties | Properties of an object |
| QueryDefs | Queries saved in a database |
| Recordsets | Recordset objects |
| Relationships | Relations defined in the database |
| Reports | Open reports in the open database |
| TableDefs | Tables saved in a database |
| Users | User accounts that define the workgroup |
| Workspaces | Workspace objects |

For example, if you want to list all of the open reports in the current database, you would use the Reports collection. Figure 19-7 shows a procedure that displays a message box listing open reports or a message that none are open.

## Nesting Procedures

Besides running a single procedure, you can have one procedure that runs others. This process is called *nesting procedures*. For example, to run a sub procedure in Access version 1, you must use a function procedure that calls the sub procedure. This sub procedure is nested in the function procedure. At other times, you will have a group of statements that you want to run repetitively. Put the same statements into a single procedure and then run the procedure every time you want to run the statements that the procedure contains. Putting frequently used statements in a procedure that other procedures can use makes

**Figure 19-7** Procedure using a collection

Module: Custom Functions

```
Sub OpenReports ()
'This procedure displays a box listing open reports or that none are open
OverallMessage = "The following reports are open: "
If Reports.Count = 0 Then
    MsgBox "No reports are open", 0, "Open Reports"
    End
End If
For Counter = 0 To Reports.Count - 1
    OverallMessage = OverallMessage & Reports(Counter).Name & ", "
Next    'Adds next open report to the list
OverallMessage = Left(OverallMessage, Len(OverallMessage) - 2)
'Above statement removes the last comma and space
MsgBox OverallMessage, 0, "Open Reports"
End Sub
```

creating procedures faster, because you have chunks of statements that you already know run correctly.

When one procedure calls another, the procedure that has just been called begins processing. Only when the called procedure is finished does Access continue with the procedure that called the other one.

As an example, suppose you want a function procedure to convert text into proper case, but unlike the Proper function procedure you saw earlier, you want each word of the phrase in proper case. A procedure that performs this for you can divide each word in a phrase and then use the Proper function procedure to make each word proper case. This procedure might look like Figure 19-8.

This PCase function procedure uses the Proper function procedure twice. The first time Proper is used is during the loop. This loop goes through each character of the text it is given. Then, the procedure tests whether the last character of the current word is a space. If it is a space, the procedure sends this current word to the Proper function procedure to let the Proper function procedure convert the word into proper case. Then, after adding the word, the function procedure returns to the phrase and the loop continues until the procedure finds the next word. When the PCase procedure gets to the end of the text, the procedure uses the Proper function procedure one last time to make sure that the last word is proper case. Using the Proper function procedure in place of a lengthy formula makes the procedure easier to understand.

**Figure 19-8** Using For ... Next and a nested If ... Then ... Else statement in a procedure

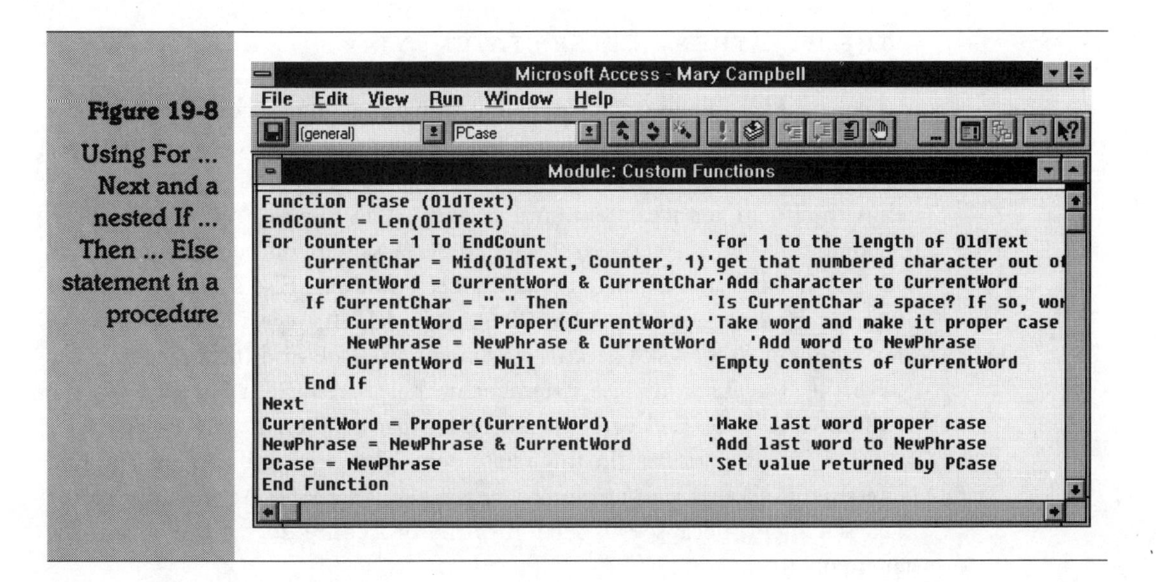

## Adding Repetitive Processing

Access has five statements you can use in a procedure to have Access repeat a section of code. These five statements have similar control structures in most other programming languages. Access has the For ... Next statement, the If ... Then ... Else statement, the Select Case statement, the Do ... Loop statement, and the While ... Wend statement. Each of these selectively performs a group of statements a specific number of times or the number of times set by a condition you create.

### THE FOR ... NEXT STATEMENT

To use the For ... Next statement, you have a counter variable that varies from one value to another. For the procedure shown in Figure 19-8, the counter is named Counter and its value ranges from 1 to the length of the text that this function accepts. After the For statement are the statements you want repeatedly performed each time Access goes through the loop. At the end of these statements is the Next statement, which tells Access that the loop is finished and to repeat the loop again if necessary.

For the For ... Next statement in the procedure in Figure 19-8, Access repeatedly performs the statements between the expression that sets the value of CurrentChar (which uses the value of Counter to select which character to return) and the End If statement.

### THE IF ... THEN ... ELSE STATEMENT

To use the If ... Then ... Else statement, you place a logical condition between If and Then. Every time this statement is performed, Access checks whether the condition is true. When the condition is true, Access performs the statements below the If ... Then statement until it arrives at an Else or End If statement. If the condition is false, Access checks whether the statements between If ... Then and End If have an Else statement. If Access finds an Else statement, Access performs the statements between Else and End If. If Access does not find an Else statement, Access skips to the statements after the End If statement.

For the If ... Then ... Else statement in the procedure in Figure 19-8, the condition is whether the current character is a space. When the current character is a space, Access performs the three statements between the If ... Then and End If statements. When the current character is not a space, Access skips to the Next statement, because this section of the procedure does not have an Else statement.

## THE SELECT CASE STATEMENT

The Select Case statement is a variation of the If ... Then ... Else statement. After Select Case, you place the expression to be evaluated. Under this statement, you place Case and a potential value of the expression. Below Case and until the next Case or End Select, you place the statements Access performs when the value of the expression equals the value given after Case. Case, followed by additional statements, can be created for every potential value you want to check. If you include a Case Else statement at the end of the cases, Access performs the statements between the Case Else and End Select statements when the expression does not equal the values of the Case statements above. The End Select statement indicates the end of the cases that the Select Case statement checks for.

The Select Case statement is usually used in place of If ... Then ... Else when you have more than one situation to test. Figure 19-9 shows the same procedure function as Figure 19-8, using Select Case in place of the If ... Then statement. For this procedure, Select Case checks the value of the entry in CurrentChar. When the character is a space, the three statements below Case " " are performed. For all other cases, Access performs any statements between Case Else and End Select.

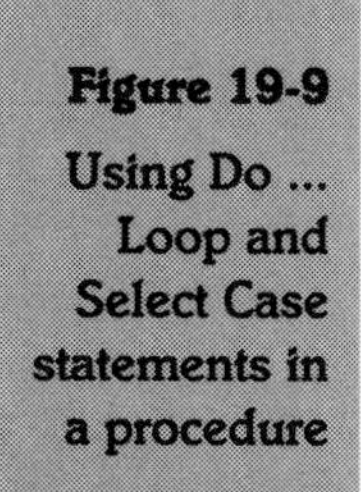

**Figure 19-9** Using Do ... Loop and Select Case statements in a procedure

```
Microsoft Access - Mary Campbell - [Module: Custom Functions]
File  Edit  View  Run  Window  Help
(general)  PCase2

Function PCase2 (OldText)
EndCount = Len(OldText)                   'Set EndCount to length of OldText
Counter = 1
Do While Counter < EndCount + 1           'Repeat for the length of OldText
    CurrentChar = Mid(OldText, Counter, 1)'get that numbered character out of
    CurrentWord = CurrentWord & CurrentChar'Add character to CurrentWord
    Select Case CurrentChar               'Is CurrentChar a space? If so, word
        Case " "
            CurrentWord = Proper(CurrentWord) 'Take word and make it proper ca
            NewPhrase = NewPhrase & CurrentWord   'Add word to NewPhrase
            CurrentWord = Null                'Empty contents of CurrentWord
        Case Else
            'This is where the statements to perform in other cases appears
    End Select
    Counter = Counter + 1                 'Increment Counter by 1
Loop
CurrentWord = Proper(CurrentWord)         'Make last word proper case
NewPhrase = NewPhrase & CurrentWord       'Add last word to NewPhrase
PCase2 = NewPhrase                        'Set value returned by PCase2
End Function

Ready                                     NUM
```

### THE DO ... LOOP AND THE WHILE ... WEND STATEMENTS

To use the Do ... Loop or While ... Wend statements, you have a condition that is tested. When Access performs the procedure, Access checks whether the condition is true, and if the condition is true, the statements between the beginning and end of these statements are performed. If the condition is false, Access skips to the statements after the Loop or Wend statement.

Figure 19-9 shows the Proper procedure function using Do ... Loop in place of the For ... Next statement. For this procedure, the variable Counter must be set and initialized. After Do While is the condition that checks whether Access has processed all of the characters in OldText. After the Do While statement are the statements you want performed each time the condition is true. At the end of these statements is the Loop statement, which tells Access that the loop is finished and to test the condition again to repeat the loop if necessary. For the procedure in Figure 19-9, the statements Access repeatedly performs during each repetition of the loop are the statements between the expression that sets the value of CurrentChar, which uses the value of Counter to select which character to return, and the expression that increments the value of the Counter variable by 1.

### NESTING REPETITIVE STATEMENTS

The procedures in Figures 19-8 and 19-9 contain two sets of repetitive processing statements. Notice how each set of repetitive processing statements is entirely placed inside the other. This is called nesting. Think of nesting as placing a set of variously sized mixing bowls inside each other. When you use multiple sets of repetitive processing statements in a procedure, they must either be sequential or nested. Sequential sets of repetitive processing statements are performed one after the other.

**caution:** *Procedures cannot start a second set of repetitive processing statements with the first one ending before the second one ends. If you try doing this in one of your procedures, you will get an error message when you use the procedure that says you are missing part of a set of a repetitive processing statement.*

## Adding Methods to Your Modules

*Methods* are the means to work with the data contained in an object. Methods are like actions or statements except that they only operate, and are combined with, specific objects. As such, you separate the method from the object variable that represents the object the method operates on with a period. An example is CreateTheSnapshot.MoveNext. MoveNext is the method that moves to the next record in the object variable represented by CreateTheSnapshot since CreateTheSnapshot is supplied as the object. Methods are like procedures in that they are provided information and possibly return some result. A method also may look like a function, because methods often have arguments that are supplied after the method's name. Each of the different object variable types can have methods.

Methods have two types of behavior. They can perform a task like a statement. These methods are entered as a statement, so you might have CreateTheSnapshot.MoveNext entered on its own line in a procedure.

The other way methods behave is like a function. The method in this case returns a result that you want to put somewhere. The method's result can be another object or a value. An example is the statement CreateTheSnapshot=My_DB.ListTables( ). In this example, Access performs the ListTables method on the database selected by the My_DB object variable. The ListTables method creates a snapshot of the tables and queries you have in a database. A *snapshot* is a dynaset that captures the information at one point in time without updating the dynaset as the underlying data changes. This example of a method that acts as a function or function procedure stores the result of the method, a dynaset, into an object variable called CreateTheSnapshot.

**tip:** *To help remember whether to use an exclamation point or period to separate parts of an identifier, look at the part of the entry that appears after the exclamation point or period. If Access has determined that name, as with object properties, use a period. If you have created that name (or someone else using Microsoft Access has created it), use an exclamation point.*

As an example of adding methods to a module, suppose you want to be able to select a command button and then enter a name and have Access tell you whether it is the name of a table or query in the current database. Figure 19-10 shows the form this example describes and the prompt that will appear to request the table name. This form is created by following these steps:

- Add the command button without using the Control Wizard.
- Next, set the On Click property to [Event Procedure].

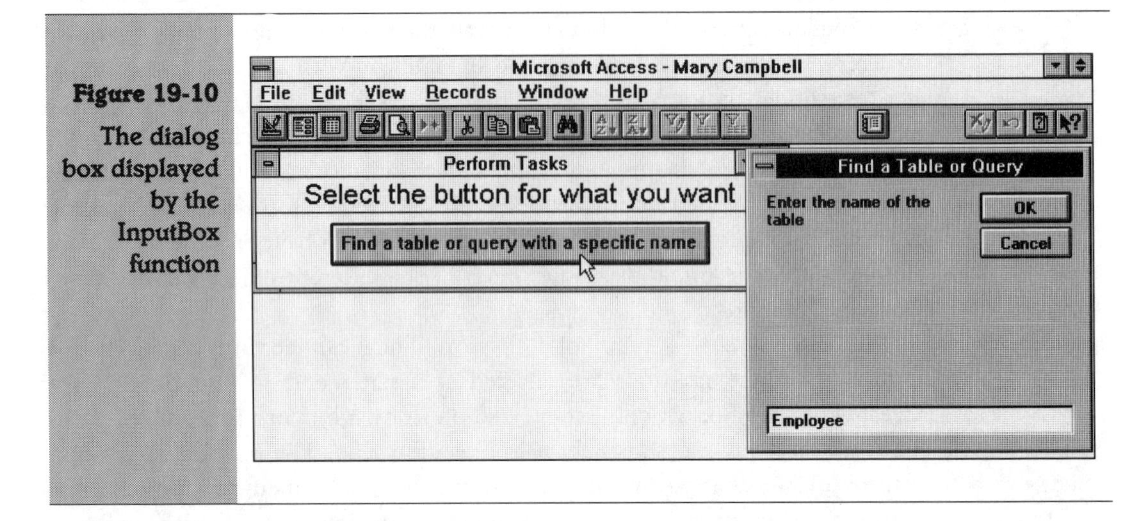


**Figure 19-10** The dialog box displayed by the InputBox function

- Click the Build button or select Build from the shortcut menu to edit the procedure for this event.
- Enter the Access Basic statements for the sub procedure, like the ones shown in Figure 19-11.
- Close the Module window and switch from the form's Design view to its Datasheet view.

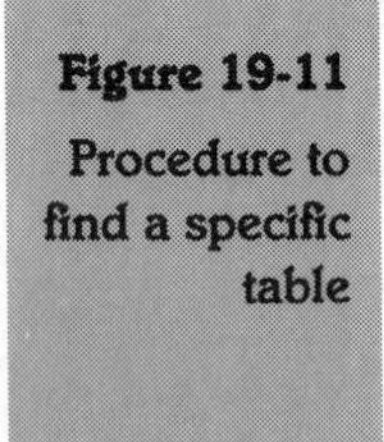

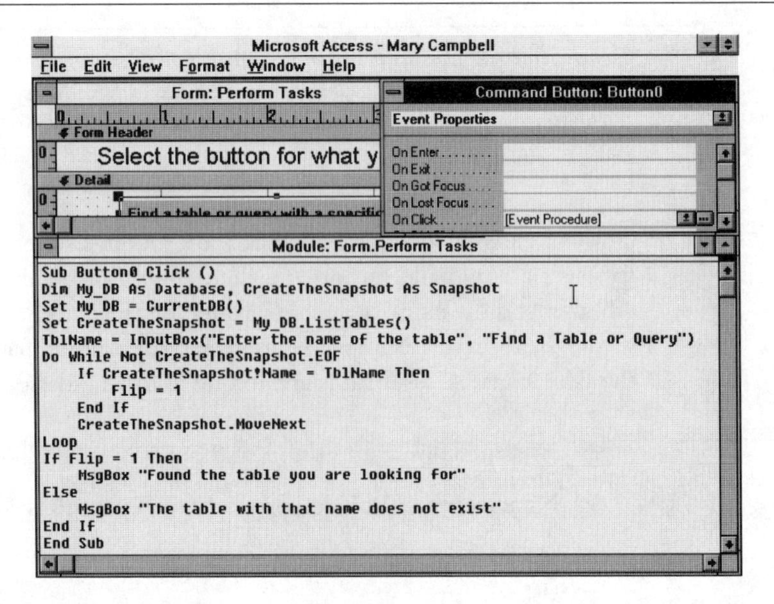


```
Sub Button0_Click ()
Dim My_DB As Database, CreateTheSnapshot As Snapshot
Set My_DB = CurrentDB()
Set CreateTheSnapshot = My_DB.ListTables()
TblName = InputBox("Enter the name of the table", "Find a Table or Query")
Do While Not CreateTheSnapshot.EOF
    If CreateTheSnapshot!Name = TblName Then
        Flip = 1
    End If
    CreateTheSnapshot.MoveNext
Loop
If Flip = 1 Then
    MsgBox "Found the table you are looking for"
Else
    MsgBox "The table with that name does not exist"
End If
End Sub
```

**Figure 19-11** Procedure to find a specific table

When you click the button you have created or press ENTER, Access performs the Button0_Click procedure, assuming the name of the command button is Button0.

In Access version 1, the steps are different. Instead of having [Event Procedure] as the value of the On Push property, the same command button in version 1 has the entry: **=TableCheck( )**. This function procedure contains the following statements.

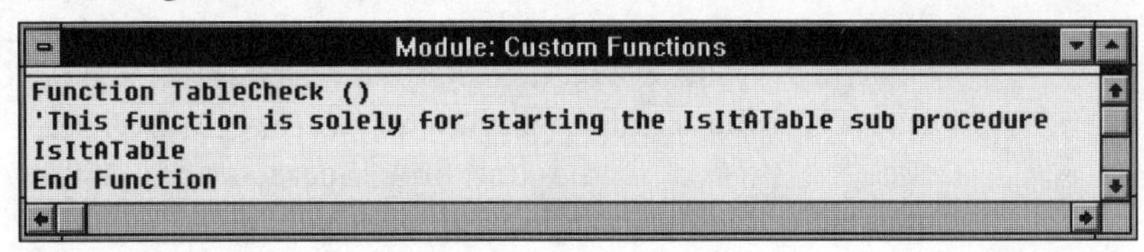


The IsItATable procedure is a sub procedure, so it is entered as a statement. It contains the same statements as the Button0_Click procedure shown in Figure 19-11. It does not use any arguments. The IsItATable or Button0_Click procedure is the real workhorse of this application.

First, the Dim statement declares all of the object variables this procedure will use. Next, the Set statement sets My_DB to represent the current database. Since you need to include the database when you work with most of the other objects in a procedure, the Dim and Set statements for the My_DB object variable often appear together. Next, the Set CreateTheSnapshot = My_DB.ListTables() statement creates a snapshot dynaset. This dynaset is created by the ListTables method. This method creates a snapshot dynaset that includes information about every table and query in the database. For this example, you are interested in the Name field of the data, since the Name field is a Text data type that contains the names of the different tables and queries in the database. The resulting dynaset is represented in this procedure by the CreateTheSnapshot snapshot object variable.

Now, the procedure prompts for the name of the table or query that you are looking for. InputBox is a function that returns the text entered in response to its prompts. When this function is performed, Access displays a dialog box like the one shown in Figure 19-10. The result is stored in the TblName variable.

The Do While statement goes through each record in the dynaset represented by the CreateTheSnapshot object variable. The statements between Do and Loop find whether the contents of the TblName variable match one of the table or query names stored in Name in the CreateTheSnapshot object. Within the Do ... Loop statements is the CreateTheSnapshot.MoveNext method. Snapshots as well as queries and tables have records that you can move between. When you open or create one of these objects, you are at the top record. The MoveNext method moves to the next record. For each record in the snapshot, the If ... End If statements check whether the value of the Name field of the data represented by the CreateTheSnapshot object variable matches what you entered in the dialog box like the one shown in Figure 19-10. When the procedure finds an entry in the Name field that matches the entry in the TblName variable, the Flip = 1 statement assigns a value to the Flip variable. This variable is *reinitialized*, or started over, every time you run the procedure.

After the procedure checks every record in the CreateTheSnapshot object variable, the second set of If ... End If statements checks the value of Flip. If Flip equals 1, the procedure has found the table name in the CreateTheSnapshot object variable during its review of every record. When Flip equals anything else, the procedure did not find the record. In either case, the MsgBox statements display an appropriate message.

Once the message is displayed and the user selects OK, Access ends the sub procedure. In Access version 1, Access would perform any remaining statements in the TableCheck function procedure if there were any.

This example shows just the basics of how to use methods. You can continue to try the different methods for each of the object variable types.

**tip:** *Up to this point, you have seen many properties with spaces in their names. When you use property names in Access Basic, make sure that you do not include a space. For example, the Display When property appears as DisplayWhen.*

## Finding Mistakes in Your Procedures

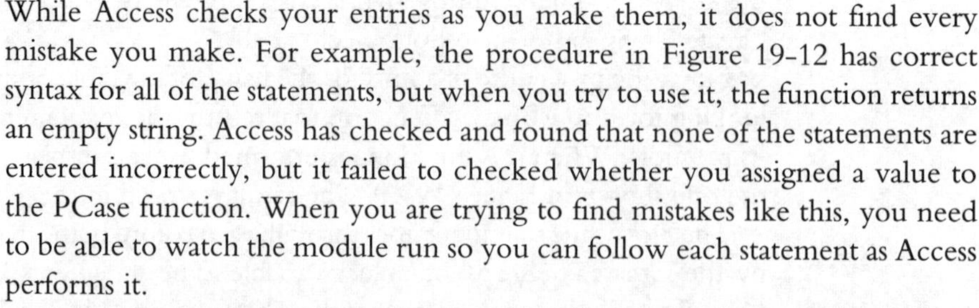

While Access checks your entries as you make them, it does not find every mistake you make. For example, the procedure in Figure 19-12 has correct syntax for all of the statements, but when you try to use it, the function returns an empty string. Access has checked and found that none of the statements are entered incorrectly, but it failed to checked whether you assigned a value to the PCase function. When you are trying to find mistakes like this, you need to be able to watch the module run so you can follow each statement as Access performs it.

Access has several features that assist you in finding errors in a module. These features include compiling the procedures, running them a step at a time, and displaying a window you can use as a scratch pad to test how a procedure is functioning.

**Figure 19-12** Procedure with a missing statement so nothing is returned

Module: Custom Functions

```
Function PCase (OldText)
EndCount = Len(OldText)
For Counter = 1 To EndCount                    'for 1 to the length of OldText
    CurrentChar = Mid(OldText, Counter, 1)'get that numbered character out of
    CurrentWord = CurrentWord & CurrentChar'Add character to CurrentWord
    If CurrentChar = " " Then                  'Is CurrentChar a space? If so, wor
        CurrentWord = Proper(CurrentWord) 'Take word and make it proper case
        NewPhrase = NewPhrase & CurrentWord   'Add word to NewPhrase
        CurrentWord = Null                     'Empty contents of CurrentWord
    End If
Next
CurrentWord = Proper(CurrentWord)              'Make last word proper case
NewPhrase = NewPhrase & CurrentWord            'Add last word to NewPhrase
End Function
```

## Compiling Procedures in a Module

When you use a procedure, Access *compiles* it, which is a process that converts the statements you have entered into the instructions it internally uses to perform the procedure. You can make a procedure run faster the first time by compiling it. Also, as you work on a module, you can compile it to find any errors you have overlooked.

To compile the procedures in all modules, select Compile All from the Run menu or click the Compile Loaded Modules button, shown here:

Access starts with the current procedure and checks each of the procedures in the module for several types of errors. If Access cannot find any errors, the compilation is finished. You will not see any message, but when you look at the Run menu again, you will see that Compile All is dimmed since the module is already compiled.

If an error is found, Access displays the procedure, highlights the statement it thinks caused the problem, and displays a message saying what it thinks the problem is. Figure 19-13 shows an example of an error message; the statement that ends the For ... Next loop is mistakenly entered as End instead of Next. You can see from this example that sometimes Access does not highlight the line with the problem.

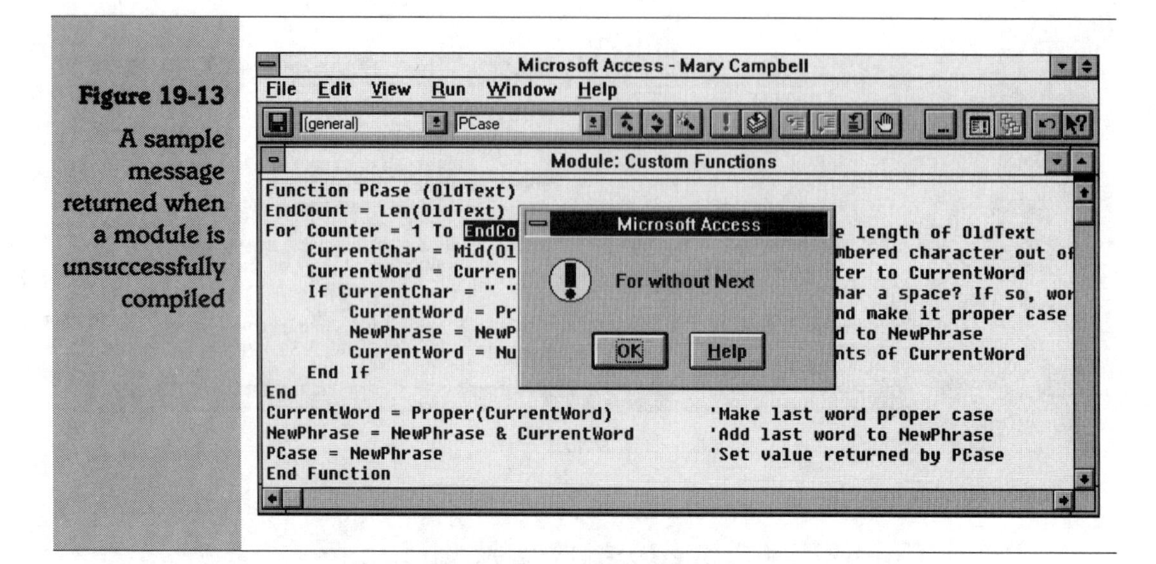


**Figure 19-13** A sample message returned when a module is unsuccessfully compiled

## Running a Procedure One Step at a Time

You often can find procedures that contain an error faster when you run the procedure a step at a time. Running a procedure one step at a time lets you watch the statements Access performs.

To set a procedure a step at a time, you need to add a *breakpoint*. A breakpoint is a statement that, when reached, tells Access to stop performing the procedure. You can choose to run the procedure one step at a time, restart, or continue running it. To add a breakpoint, add the Stop statement to a procedure. You also can move to a statement that you want to use as a breakpoint and choose Toggle Breakpoint from the Run menu, choose Toggle Breakpoint from the shortcut menu, press F9, or, from the toolbar, click the Breakpoint button, which looks like this:

When you set a breakpoint this way, the selected statement appears bold. The difference between adding a breakpoint to a specific statement and adding the Stop statement to a procedure is the permanence of the breakpoint. When you add a Stop statement to a procedure, the breakpoint remains there until you remove it. When you add a toggle breakpoint that boldfaces a specific statement, the breakpoint only remains while the Module window is open. When the Module window is closed, the breakpoint is removed. Most of the time you will use temporary breakpoints and reserve Stop for when you are working with a lengthy procedure. When the procedure with the breakpoint is in a Module window for a form or report, you will want to leave the Module window open and switch to the form or report's window. When you are in the Form's Form view or the report's Print Preview view, the breakpoint is still in effect for the procedures in the form's module, assuming that you have not closed the Module window.

Once a procedure is set to run, the procedure runs at regular speed until Access gets to the Stop statement or the statement you have set as a breakpoint. At this point, the Module window is placed on top, as shown in Figure 19-14. You can see how the temporary breakpoint is boldfaced. You also can see the box around one of the statements. This box indicates the next statement Access performs. To run the next statement, choose Step Into from the Run menu, press F8, or click the Step Into button, shown here:

In Access version 1, the command is Single Step in the Run menu and the toolbar button is called Single Step and shows a single footstep. Each time you choose Step Into from the Run menu, press F8, or click the Step Into button, Access performs the next statement. You can run the procedure at regular speed

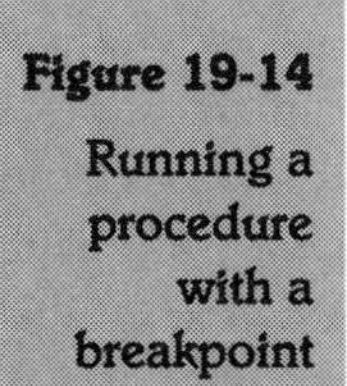

**Figure 19-14** Running a procedure with a breakpoint

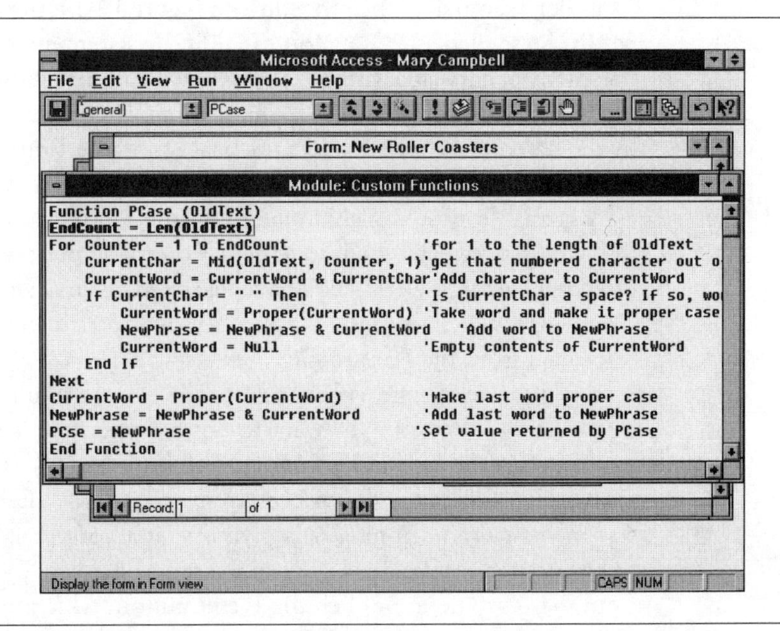

by choosing Continue in the Run menu, pressing F5, or clicking the Run button, which looks like this:

When a procedure calls another procedure, like the PCase function procedure calls the Proper function procedure in Figure 19-14, Access runs the called procedure one statement at a time as well. If you already know that the called procedure works correctly, you may want to run just the first procedure at a slower speed. For example, when the PCase procedure calls the Proper procedure, you may not want to watch the Proper procedure operate one statement at a time, since you know that Proper runs correctly. You can operate a procedure you are about to call at regular speed and continue with single-step viewing after the procedure is completed. To run a procedure at regular speed, when the box is around the statement that calls the other procedure, choose Step Over from the Run menu, press SHIFT+F8, or click the Step Over button, shown here:

In Access version 1, the command is Procedure Step in the Run menu and the toolbar button is called Procedure Step and shows two footsteps.

If you suddenly realize you have made a mistake in the procedure, you can fix it. For example, in the procedure in Figure 19-14, the next-to-last statement has PCase spelled as PCse. You can edit the statement and fix the error. If the statement occurs after the box, Access will use the updated statement. If the statement you change is before the statement with the box, the change made by the statement does not affect the procedure's performance, but it is retained, and the next time you use the procedure, the procedure will include the change.

A special feature available when you run a procedure one step at a time is that you can change which statement Access will perform next. This feature is often used when the error you have just fixed occurs before the next statement. To change which statement is next, move to that line and select Set Next Statement from the Run menu.

You also can change a procedure when you are running it one step at a time by restarting it. You might want to do this when you have just fixed an error that prevents the procedure from performing correctly. To restart a procedure, change the next statement to perform to be the one after the Function or Sub statement at the beginning. Also, you want all of the values in the procedure to be restarted as if you had not run the procedure yet. To do this, choose Reset from the Run menu or click the Reset button, which looks like this:

In Access version 1, the command is Reinitialize Step in the Run menu and the toolbar button is called Reinitialize but looks the same.

After you select the next statement to perform and reinitialize the values, you are ready to start executing the procedure. You can start the procedure at this point by clicking one of the toolbar buttons, or by using the statements in the Run menu.

## Using the Immediate Window

Watching Access perform a procedure one step at a time helps you spot a potential error; another especially helpful feature is being able to find the values of different variables as you run the procedure. For example, when you run the procedure in Figure 19-14, you may want to know the current values of CurrentChar and CurrentWord. Access provides you with this ability through the Immediate window. This window is put on top of the Module window just like a property sheet that always appears on top of the table, query, form, or report you are designing. You also can use the Immediate window to run procedures. You will find this especially useful with function procedures, since you want to try the procedure using different values.

To display this window, choose Immediate Window from the View menu or click the Immediate Window button in the Access version 2 toolbar, shown here:

Access adds a window like the one shown in Figure 19-15. Select this command or click the toolbar button again when you want to remove the window. This window is empty, but so is any scratch pad when you start to use it. The Immediate window is used either to run procedures or to test them. Most of your entries to test a value or run a function procedure in the window start with a ?. The question mark tells Access that you want Access to give you the value of the expression you enter. The ? is a shortcut for the Print Access Basic command. To run a sub procedure from the Immediate window, type the name of the sub procedure and any arguments the sub procedure uses. After you type the entry you want, test a line in the Immediate window by pressing ENTER. This tells Access to process whatever is on the line. Your entry and the result remain in the window until replaced by another entry. You can always repeat one of the entries you have made in the Immediate window by moving to the line with the arrow keys and then pressing ENTER.

To run a procedure through the Immediate window, type **?** followed by the procedure name and any arguments.

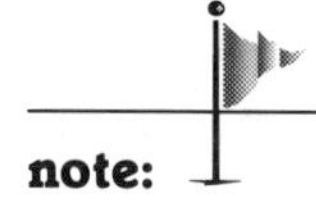

**note:** *Function procedures have their arguments enclosed in parentheses, but sub functions do not.*

To run the PCase function with the text "my new CAR", type **? PCase("my new CAR")** and press ENTER. Access performs the procedure and returns the result on the next line, as shown here:

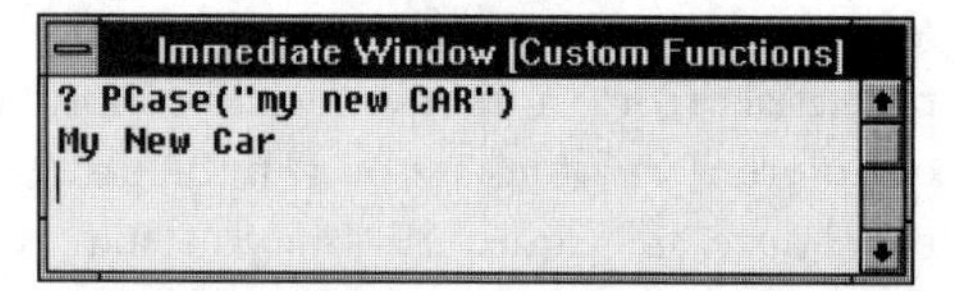


When Access returns My New Car, you know the procedure is running correctly. If you do not get that as a result, the procedure has an error; you may want to add a breakpoint to the procedure to run it a step at a time.

When testing a procedure, you can test the values of the variable in the procedure through the Immediate window. Figure 19-16 shows the Immediate

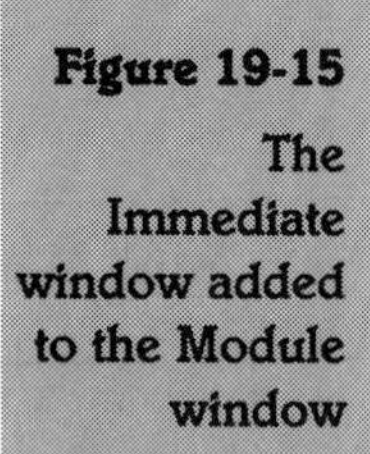

**Figure 19-15** The Immediate window added to the Module window

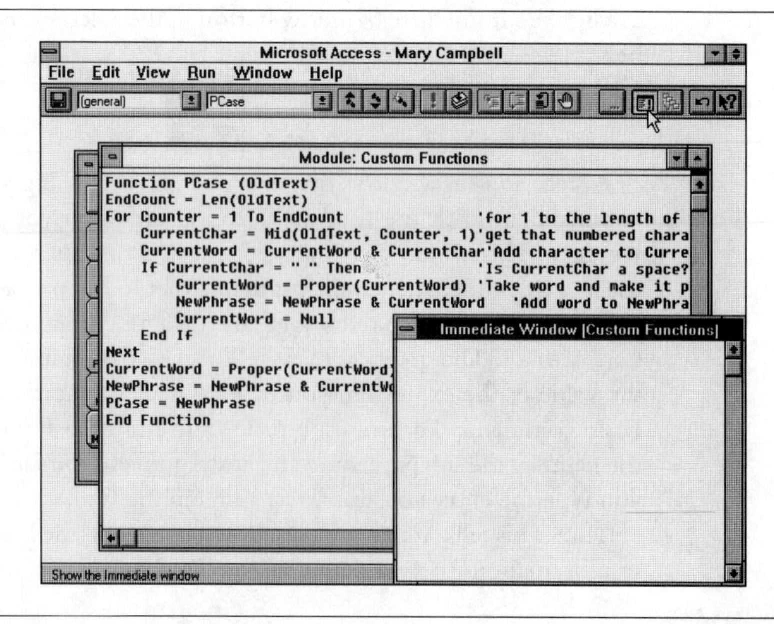

window while the PCase procedure is running one step at a time. In Figure 19-16, the Immediate window contains several prompts. These prompts are entered on several lines, since Access does not care on which line in the Immediate window you make an entry. Access decides which line to process by the line that is active when you press ENTER. For the Immediate window in Figure 19-16, this feature of the Immediate window means you can constantly move to the line containing ? CurrentChar and press ENTER to repeatedly return the most up-to-date value of CurrentChar.

You also can enter one request for information while another is processing. For example, in Figure 19-16, the request for the PCase result is not complete, yet other requests are prompting for variable values used to determine the PCase result.

One way you can use the Immediate window to find an error is to have the procedure display entries in the window. To do this, put **Debug.Print** in the procedure followed by what you want entered in the Immediate window. For example, if you want the value of TblName displayed every time you run a procedure, include the statement **Debug.Print TblName** in the procedure.

**tip:** *When using the Immediate window to find errors in a procedure, separate each entry you make by two or three lines. Leaving the extra lines means the entries remain on the window, so you can return to them and repeat them.*

**Figure 19-16** The Immediate window with several requests processed

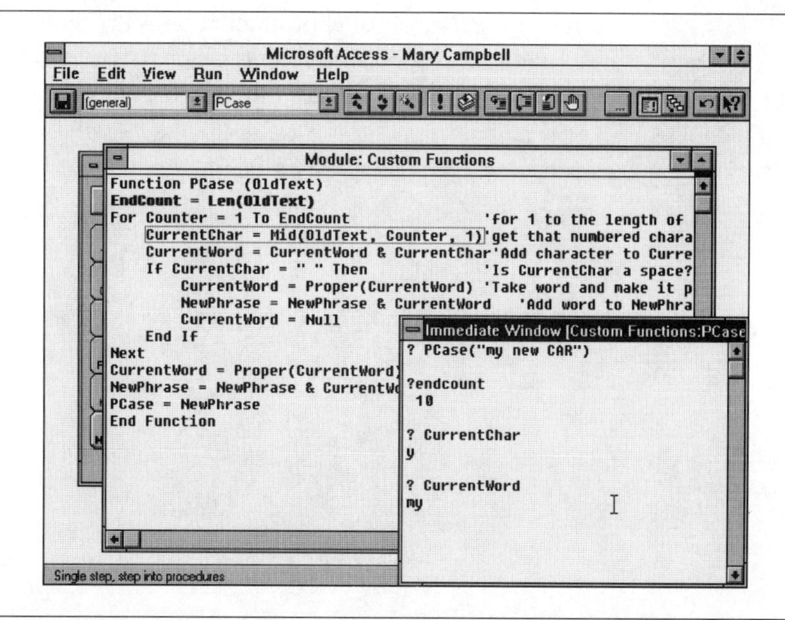

Quick Reference

**To Create a Module** Click the New button at the top of the Database window while displaying modules, or choose New from the File menu and then Module.

**To Create a Procedure** Type **Sub** or **Function** on an empty line followed by the name of the procedure and any arguments the procedure uses enclosed in parentheses. You can also choose New Procedure from the Edit menu or click the New Procedure button in the toolbar, type the name of the function, and select OK.

**To Add a Procedure to a Form or Report in Access Version 2** Display the form or report's design. Select the control, section, form, or report with the event that you want to assign the procedure to. Then select [Event Procedure] from the property's drop-down list in the property sheet and click the Build button. You can also click the Build button, select Code Builder, and OK.

**To Change the Procedure Displayed** Display the previous procedure by pressing CTRL+UP ARROW, clicking the Previous Procedure button in the toolbar, or choosing Previous Procedure in the View menu. Display the next procedure by pressing CTRL+DOWN ARROW, clicking the Next Procedure button in the toolbar, or choosing Next Procedure

Quick Reference

in the View menu. An additional method of selecting which procedure you are viewing is to choose Procedures from the View menu or press F2, and then select the procedure you want to see. You can also select the procedure name from the Procedure list in the toolbar. If you are selecting the procedure to display for a form or report's module, you can also select the control, section, or overall form or report of the object for the procedure to find, using the Object list in the toolbar.

**To Print a Module** Choose Print from the File menu and select OK. You have all the same printing options you have for printing other database objects. All of the procedures and the declarations section are printed. You can also print the procedures, properties, and permissions for a module using Print Definition in the File menu or print the information for more than one module by using Add-ins in the File menu and selecting Database Documentor.

**To Add a Breakpoint to a Module** Move to the statement that you want to be a breakpoint. Choose Toggle Breakpoint from the Run menu, press F9, or click the Breakpoint button in the toolbar.

**To Display the Immediate Window** Choose Immediate Window from the View menu or click the Immediate Window button in the toolbar.

# V

# Network and Administrative Topics

# Chapter 20

The Dangers of Lost Data

Opening a Database

Altering Database Objects

Changing Options for a Multiuser Environment

# Special Considerations for Network Use

FOR the most part, you use the same techniques to work with a database whether you are working on a stand-alone PC or in a shared environment. However, in a shared environment or network, you can share data with other users on a file server or attach the same external table to your database that other users have attached to their databases. Therefore, Access offers important features that you will want to use to ensure data integrity in a shared environment.

In a multiuser environment you have special considerations that do not apply when you are the only user who accesses and updates a database on your own PC. In a multiuser environment, it is possible that two users will want to read or update the same record at a given point in time. If you do not take the proper precautions, both users could update a record simultaneously and one user's changes could overlay the other's. Review this chapter carefully if you are not the sole user of your database to see how this situation can be prevented—and to see how many users can obtain the benefits of shared data access while avoiding the pitfalls.

You will learn how to open a database in a multiuser environment and how to choose a record-locking strategy that meets your needs. You will also learn how to change the design of database objects. This chapter shows you the features that Access provides to ensure your success in this environment.

## The Dangers of Lost Data

With the specialization that exists in many organizations today, there may not be one user responsible for updating the values in every field of a database table. If you look at the Client table in the Coasters database, you find fields that might be updated by different departments. The Contact fields may be updated by someone in Marketing while the YTD Payments and Total Payments fields might be updated by someone in Accounting. If both users happen to request the records and Accounting's changes are applied first, they will be overwritten when Marketing's change is applied. Follow through this sequence of steps with a hypothetical three-field table to see how important changes can be lost.

Both User 1 (Marketing) and User 2 (Accounting) retrieve a record with the following field entries:

| Company | Contact | YTD Payments | Total Payments |
|---|---|---|---|
| Teen Land | Mary Morris | 2300000 | 2300000 |

User 1 changes the contact name and saves the record this way:

| Company | Contact | YTD Payments | Total Payments |
|---|---|---|---|
| Teen Land | Sally Green | 2300000 | 2300000 |

User 2 changes the record, overwriting User 1's changes. The record now looks like this:

| Company | Contact | YTD Payments | Total Payments |
|---|---|---|---|
| Teen Land | Mary Morris | 2500000 | 2500000 |

When Teen Land's record is later retrieved, User 1 will be confused as to why the updated contact name that was entered no longer appears. This type of problem can be prevented by following the recommendations in this chapter.

## Opening a Database

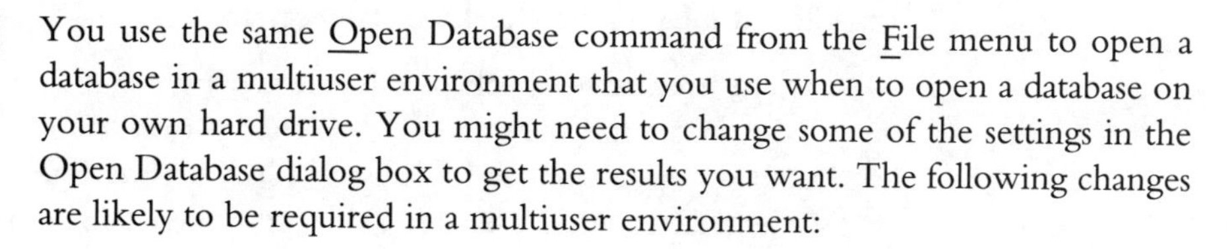

You use the same Open Database command from the File menu to open a database in a multiuser environment that you use when to open a database on your own hard drive. You might need to change some of the settings in the Open Database dialog box to get the results you want. The following changes are likely to be required in a multiuser environment:

- Setting the Drives list box to the network drive
- Clearing the Exclusive check box to allow other users to share the database
- Restricting your access to the data and database objects by selecting the Read Only check box, which prevents modifications

You will not be able to access the database file you need with an incorrect drive setting. The other options affect database performance and control whether or not users can access and update data.

To open a database that can be shared with other users, follow these steps:

1. Establish the network connection that lets you access database.
2. Choose Open Database from the File menu to display the Open Database dialog box shown here:

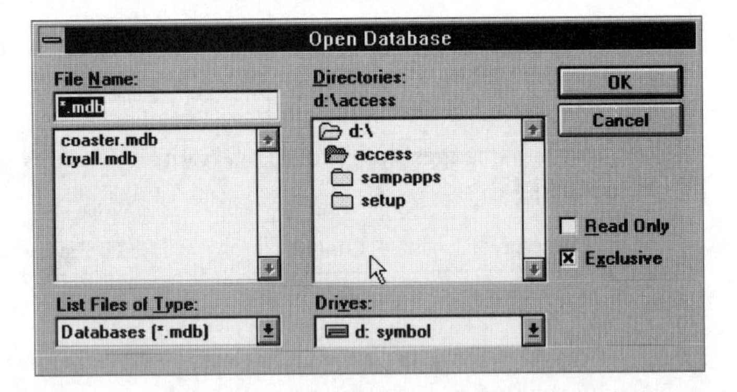


3. Select the network drive from the Drives drop-down list box.
4. Select the filename of the database that you want to open.
5. To ensure that you do not accidentally modify the database, select the Read Only check box.
6. Clear the Exclusive check box if necessary.

   The Exclusive check box is selected by default, unless you select Options from the View menu, then change the Default Open Mode for Databases option under Multiuser/ODBC. If the Exclusive check box is selected, no other users are able to use the database. If someone else already has the database opened for exclusive use, you cannot open it until they have closed it.

   If you need to modify the design of the database or database objects you should leave the Exclusive check box selected to ensure that no one else is using the database while you change the design. If you clear the check box, any open objects will not be updated until they are reopened.
7. Select OK.

The database will be opened if it is not already open for exclusive use by another user. Any user who attempts to open it for exclusive use after you open it will see an error message because the database is already open for shared use.

**tip:** *You may want to consider attaching tables on the network server to a database on your local workstation. If your local database contains all of the other database objects you need, such as reports and forms, performance will be much better. You learned the techniques for attaching tables in Chapter 5.*

Although your choice of the options for Read-Only and Exclusive use will be dictated by what you want to do with the data, you should be aware that these options affect database performance. On a continuum from best to worst performance, you can see how these settings affect response time in the chart that follows:

| | | | | | | |
|---|---|---|---|---|---|---|
| **BEST** | Exclusive: | Yes | Yes | No | No | **WORST** |
| **PERFORMANCE** | Read-Only: | No | Yes | Yes | No | **PERFORMANCE** |

## Altering Database Objects

Once a database is open you can make changes to any of the objects that it contains. Microsoft Access has some restrictions to prevent problems from occurring, including the following rules:

- Access will not allow a user to make design changes to a table while another person is using it.
- Access presents a message if you make a design change to an object that another user has changed since you last opened the object.
- Access only allows you to look at a table design as read-only if another user has its table open or is viewing a report, form, or query based on the table.
- Access presents the most recently saved version of an object if someone opens an object that has been changed.

## Altering a Table

If you are going to alter a table design, you may want the Exclusive check box checked when you open the database. This allows you to make changes to the database tables and associated objects without a conflict with other users. Stick to your task and complete it as soon as possible; remember that you are preventing others from using the database during this time. Some companies have rules that restrict exclusive use to weekends and after hours to ensure that work production is not impeded by removing a database from use during normal business hours.

Even if you open a database in nonexclusive mode, once you display the Design view for a table no other users will be able to use the table data. Minimize the time that you are in Design view to limit the restrictions you are placing on other users.

When you change the design of a table, other database objects may be affected. You will need to update each object to ensure consistency in the database.

## Altering Non-Table Objects

When you plan to alter database objects other than the tables, it is best to obtain the database for exclusive use. Although you can modify forms, reports, queries, modules, and macros without doing so, you can encounter some problems.

If you change a macro that someone is using, they may get unexpected and unacceptable results from its use.

Users working with a form, report, or query that you change must close the object and reopen it. Otherwise they will be using the old rather than the new version.

Dependency between database objects is always a consideration, but neglecting to consider this issue in a network environment can compound the problem because of the number of users affected. If you plan to modify a number of dependent objects, such as forms, reports or queries, it is important that you modify all of the objects before users work with them. If you add fields to a form or a report, the underlying query should have the fields added first. Figure 20-1 shows how the query should have fields added before the same fields are added to a report, since the report will get its information from the query results. If you modify the report first and a user works with it before you have the query modified, the field may display as **Name?**.

**Figure 20-1**

**New fields are added to a query before a report**

Last Name field must be added here first

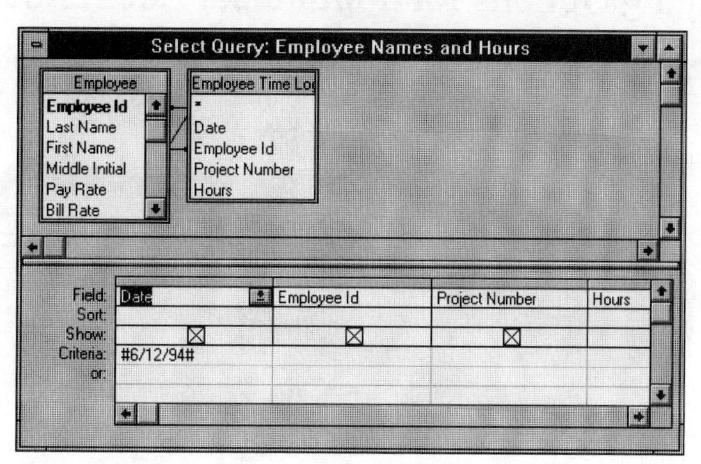


Last Name added to the report after adding it to the query

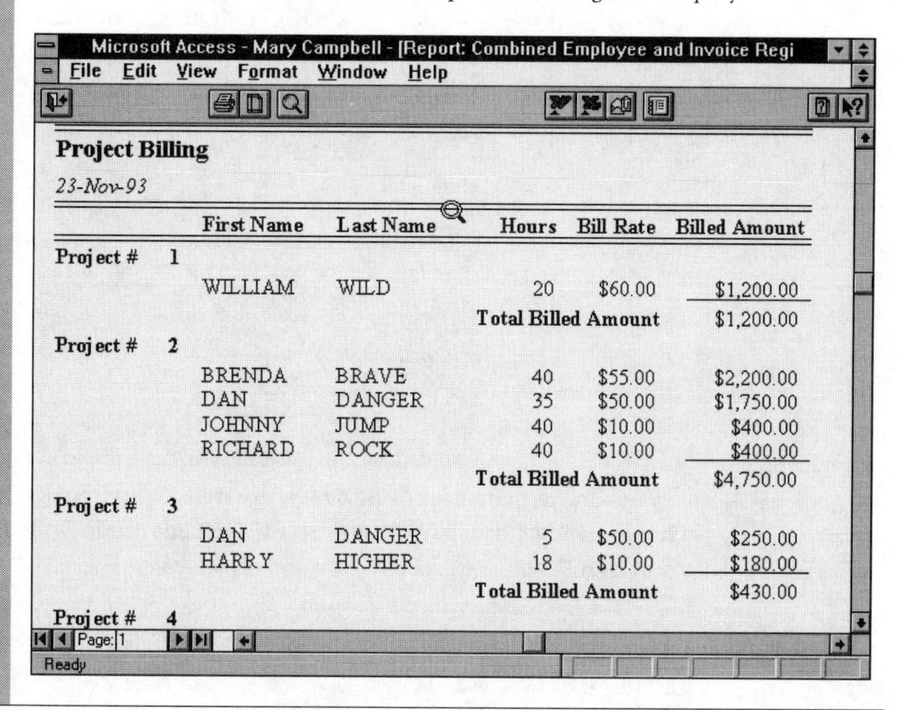

## Changing Options for a Multiuser Environment

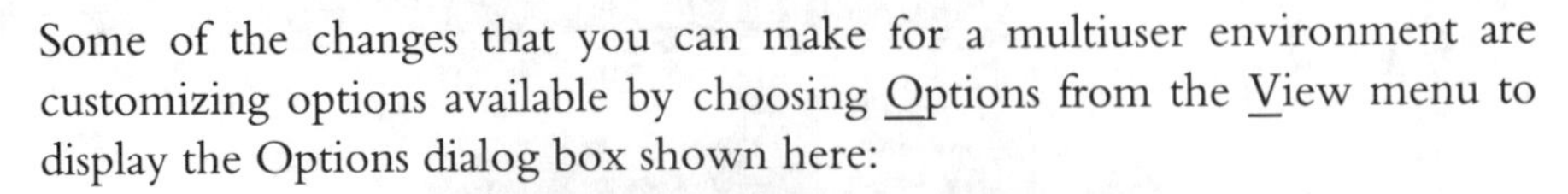

Some of the changes that you can make for a multiuser environment are customizing options available by choosing Options from the View menu to display the Options dialog box shown here:

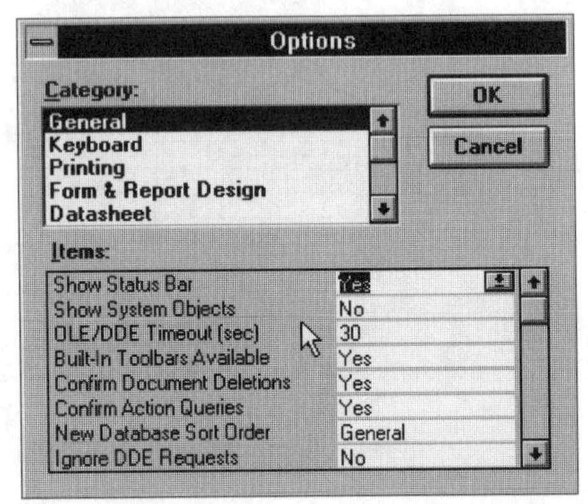


When you select Multiuser/ODBC (Multiuser, in Access version 1) in the Category list box, the options presented will match those given here:

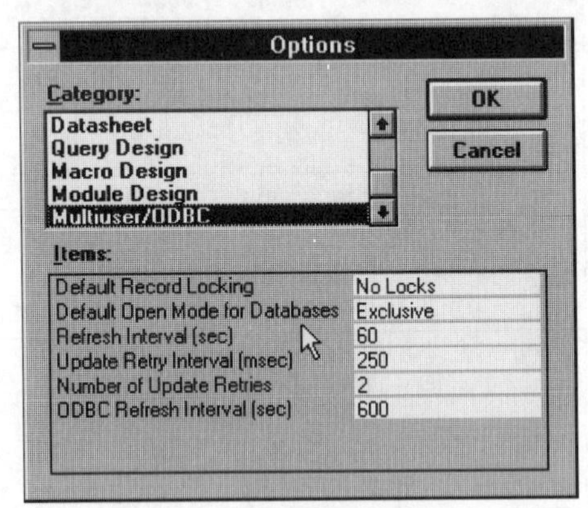


You can use these options to set the default for the Exclusive check box when opening a database or to establish a default mode for locking records and a refresh interval.

**tip:** *The changes that you make for your system do not affect other users. The network administrator must ensure that certain settings are established for all users as an organizational standard.*

## Setting Record Locking

*Record locking* determines whether other users can change a record while you are editing it. You can even use this feature to lock all records in the same table or dynaset. If a record is locked, other users attempting to update the record get a message telling them that you are updating the record or table.

You can choose a default setting for record locking that applies to all tables and queries. You can also set the record-locking feature on forms to override the default setting. The options available to you for record locking are the default setting of No Locks, Edited Record, and All Records. Each option is discussed separately in the following sections.

### THE NO LOCKS SETTING

The No Locks setting allows anyone to edit a record at any time. The No Locks setting means that as you are editing a record, it is not locked from use by other users. If another user changes this record before you save it you will see a message indicating that this has occurred. You can discard your changes, overwrite the other user's changes, or take a closer look at their changes. To look more closely, you need to copy the record to the Clipboard and look at the changes.

Another danger of the No Locks setting is that another user can overwrite your changes with their own and you will not know that your changes have been lost (remember the example with User 1 and User 2 earlier in this chapter). If another user locks a record that you are editing, you will need to wait until the other user is finished with the record before you can save your changes.

### THE EDITED RECORD SETTING

The Edited Record setting locks the record being edited until you are finished. Other users wanting to edit the same record will be prevented from doing so until you are finished.

This option prevents one user from overlaying changes made by another user. It can cause delays when many users want to edit the same records, but from most users' perspective it is a necessary precaution to prevent data loss.

### THE ALL RECORDS SETTING

The most restrictive option is to lock all the records on the form or datasheet. Other users will not be able to edit or lock any records from the table while you have the table open. Records in attached SQL Server tables cannot be viewed when the All Records option is selected. You might want to consider this option if you need to work for a short time getting totals of all the records and want to ensure that the figures do not change until you have all the totals that you need.

## Setting a Default Open Mode

The default setting when you display the dialog box for opening a database has the Exclusive check box selected. If you want the default setting to allow shared access, you can change it with the Options command in the View menu. To make the change to Shared, choose the Multiuser/ODBC category and then select Shared for Default Open Mode for Databases. The Open Database dialog box will show the Exclusive check box cleared.

## Refreshing the Data Displayed

Access automatically updates records displayed in a form or datasheet every 60 seconds if other users have updated the records. You can change this interval by choosing Options from the View menu, selecting the Multiuser/ODBC category, and then entering a refresh interval other than the 60-second default. Any interval from 1 to 32,766 seconds is possible. If you are using a table stored on a SQL server, the refresh interval is set by the number after ODBC Refresh Interval. The default setting is 600 seconds.

You can refresh the data at any time. Choose Refresh from the Records menu while the table's window is active to refresh immediately. To see added records, deleted records removed, and reordered records in a query, you will need to perform another query.

## Retrying Updates

There are two ways you can influence how Access continues to try to update a record when it cannot update it the first time it tries. You can tell Access how many times to retry the update process if someone else has a lock on the record the first time Access tries the update. The default is two retries, but you can choose any number from 0 to 10.

You can also specify an update interval in milliseconds. The default is 250 milliseconds, but you can specify any number from 0 to 1,000 milliseconds.

To make the change, choose Options from the View menu, select the Multiuser/ODBC category, and then specify an Update Retry Interval and a Number of Update Retries.

## Quick Reference

**To Open a Database in Shared Mode** Choose Open Database from the File menu. Select the network drive and filename. Clear the Exclusive check box, then select OK. You can select the Read Only check box if you want to be able to read the data without changing any of it.

**To Change Multiuser Settings** Choose Options from the View menu. Select Multiuser/ODBC from the Category list box and then change the appropriate settings before selecting OK.

**To Refresh Records Immediately** Choose Refresh from the Records menu.

# Chapter 21

Access Security

Additional Database Operations

Customizing Access

# Network Administrator's

# Guide to Access

tHE tasks in this chapter will interest the individual responsible for data in a shared computing environment. This individual may have the title of network administrator, or data management may be just one of a myriad of responsibilities. People using Access in a stand-alone fashion solely on their machine will also be interested in this information since they will want to protect the investment they have made in their data.

In a network environment, it is not possible to allow each individual user to make his or her own decisions regarding the overall system and the security of the data that it contains. These tasks must be the responsibility of the network administrator. In most organizations, the network administrator is also regarded as somewhat of a technical guru with the capability to advise users on settings for the best performance. Many organizations have allowed this individual to establish the custom settings for all software used on the system to ensure the highest level of system throughput for all users.

In this chapter you will learn all about the security settings for Access. You implement them to control who can use the system and what tasks they can perform. Backup considerations will be discussed, as will recovery and compaction procedures. If you have been in the role of network administrator for some time, you will want to focus on the procedures for each task, as you are already well versed in the need for them. If you are less experienced as a network administrator, read the entire chapter to find the reasons for the various measures.

This chapter also describes several file operations you will perform on your databases with Access. Finally, you will learn about customizing options that change how Access operates. While these features are important if you are working with Access on a network, they are also important when you are working with Access on a single computer.

## Access Security

The security that Access provides is designed to supplement the security options in your network software and hardware. It also is useful for users running Access in a stand-alone environment who want to add a measure of security to prevent unauthorized users from logging onto Access or using or changing their databases. You have already been using Access's security system, but since the default is to let you use any Access feature, you will not notice Access's security system working behind the scenes.

Access provides security options through workgroups, user accounts, and permissions. *Workgroups* are one or more databases that are part of the security you add to it. To use a workgroup, you log on and supply the password. The logon procedure ensures that you are an authorized user and tells Access your user account. Each user account has permissions that tell Access what the user can do to the database. Figure 21-1 shows a diagram of how this works.

Both users and groups have permissions assigned that describe the tasks you can perform with various database objects. Users can have separate permissions from each other and from the permissions in the groups to which they belong. Groups allow you to set the permissions for groups of users all at once, rather than setting every user's permission separately. Each user must belong to at least one group.

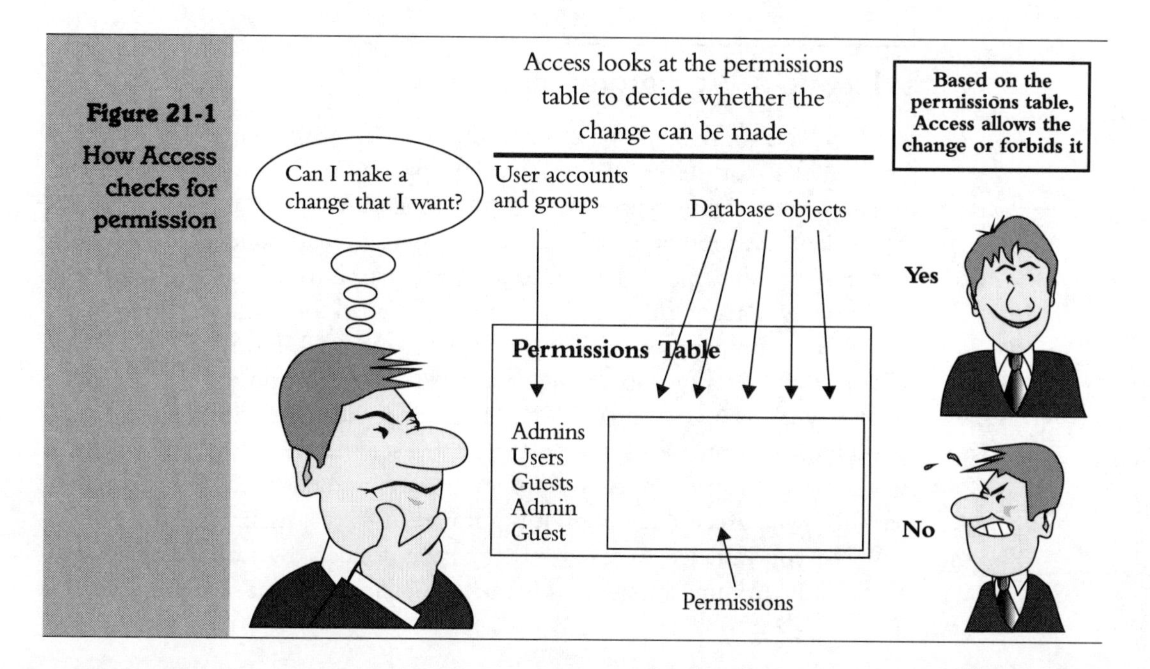


**Figure 21-1** How Access checks for permission

To use Access' security to limit how available a database is to any user, you will follow these steps:

- Select the workgroup to use
- Create or select the administrator account for the workgroup
- Create or select the owner account for the application
- Require a logon procedure to use Access
- Set the owner account for a database and its objects
- Create groups and users for the application
- Change the permissions for application objects
- Create the passwords for the user accounts
- Encrypt the database
- Make the database available to other users

Before you perform these steps to make a database secure, when you start Access, you are starting off using a user account named Admin. Initially, this user account does not have a password and has no limits on the changes you can make, so you are not seeing the effects of Access' security system.

## Selecting a Workgroup

You can have more than one workgroup in Access. Each workgroup contains the databases that the users in the workgroup will want to work with. As an example, you might set up a workgroup for all of the users in the accounting department and another workgroup for the users in the production department. It is also possible that the members of the workgroup may span different departments if many different disciplines are needed for a project. If you work in a smaller company or are using Access for personal information, you may only need one workgroup for the databases you are working with.

Each workgroup uses a SYSTEM.MDA file to store its security information. If you look at your Access directory, you will see the SYSTEM.MDA file that Access has used so far. Workgroups are created and changed with a program that ships with Access, although it is not part of Access itself.

When you installed Access, you may have noticed the icon for MS Access Workgroup Administrator. This is the application you use when creating or changing workgroups. When you double-click this icon to start the application, you will see a dialog box like this one:

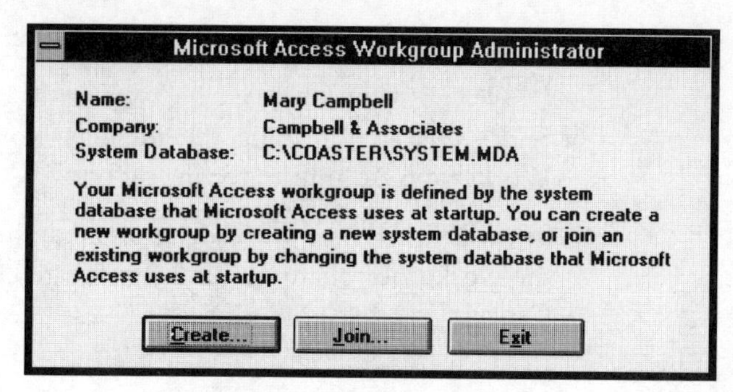


The system database is for the workgroup you use when you start Access. By changing the system database with the Workgroup Administrator, you change the workgroup you use when you start Access.

## CREATING A WORKGROUP

When you create a new workgroup, you are creating the SYSTEM.MDA file that Access uses to store the security information about the workgroup. You can create this new workgroup with the MS Access Workgroup Administrator (Microsoft Access Change Workgroup, in Access version 1) by following these steps:

1. Select the Create button.

   In Access version 1, you will select New instead.

2. From the next dialog box, make the entries for Name, Organization, and Workgroup ID.

   In Access version 1, the fields to complete are Name, Company, and Personal ID Number. Access uses these entries to identify the owner of a workgroup database.

3. Select OK.

   You are prompted for the path of the new system database. In Access version 1, you will make your entry in the Path Text box.

4. Change the path to change the location of the SYSTEM.MDA file you are creating.

   Figure 21-2 shows the two dialog boxes after the entries are made.

5. Select OK from the Workgroup System Database dialog box and then select it again from the Confirm Workgroup Information dialog box.

   The Workgroup Administrator will create the system database for you.

6. Select OK after reading the message; you are returned to the initial Workgroup Administrator dialog box.

7. Select Exit to leave the Workgroup Administrator and set Access to use the workgroup that you have just created. In version 1, you will select Cancel.

**tip:** *Account names, workgroup IDs, and personal IDs follow the same rules. You can use up to 20 characters, but you cannot include spaces, certain punctuation symbols (“ \ / [ ] : | < > + = ; , ? * ‘), or control characters that have an ASCII value of 0 to 31.*

## CHANGING TO ANOTHER WORKGROUP

If you are a member of more than one workgroup, you will want to change workgroups before working in the databases of another group. When you want to switch from one workgroup to another, you must exit Access and use the

**Figure 21-2** Creating a new Access workgroup

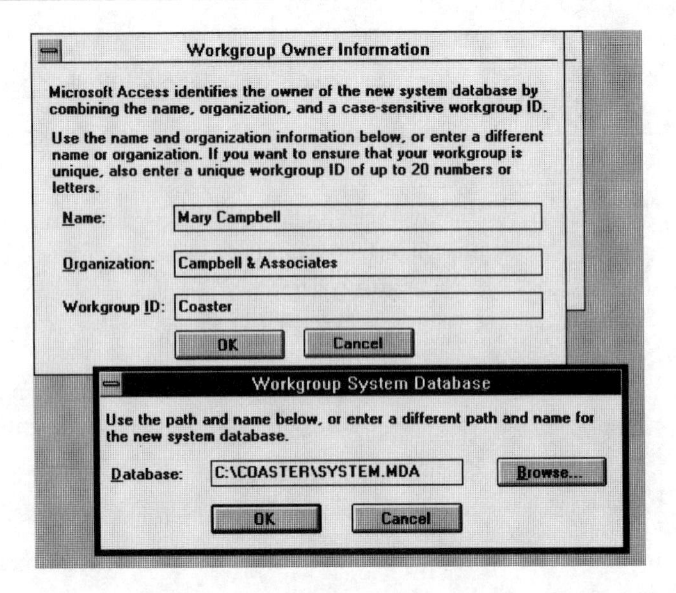

Workgroup Administrator to change which workgroup you are using when you start Access again. After starting the Workgroup Administrator, select Join (Change in Access version 1). The Workgroup Administrator prompts for the location of the workgroup or system database. When you modify the path for the SYSTEM.MDA file of the workgroup you want to use, select OK. After selecting OK again when you see the confirmation that you have changed to the selected workgroup, you can select Exit to leave the Workgroup Administrator. When you start Access, you will be using the workgroup you have just selected.

**tip:** *In addition to storing security information, the SYSTEM.MDA file also stores which files are listed at the bottom of the File menu, the Access customizing options described later in the chapter, and the toolbars. Changing to a different workgroup changes these other settings as well as which databases you are using.*

## Initial Groups and Users

In a secure system, the Admin user is normally reserved for the network administrator, since there are no restrictions on the Admin user. This Admin user is part of the Admins group, and any users that you add to this group also will have full permission to use every object in the database in any way they want. This means that a member of the Admins group can review, create, and modify any object in the database, including objects created by users in any group.

When you first start Access, your system is not secure. You have two additional groups besides Admins: Users and Guests. You also have two defined users: Admin, which belongs to the Admins and Users groups, and Guest, which belongs to the Guests group. Figure 21-3 shows the users and groups that are automatically available when you start using Access. The lines show the groups that the users belong to.

Despite these categorizations, when starting the system, all users begin without the logon procedure and are considered to be Admin users. You can add additional groups. You can add users to the original groups as well as new groups that you add.

You can delete the existing users and remove users from any group except the Users group and the last member of the Admins group, but you cannot delete the existing groups. Adding new users and groups will not have any effect until you make the system secure with passwords. You also must assign permissions for each object to make your databases, as well as your system, secure.

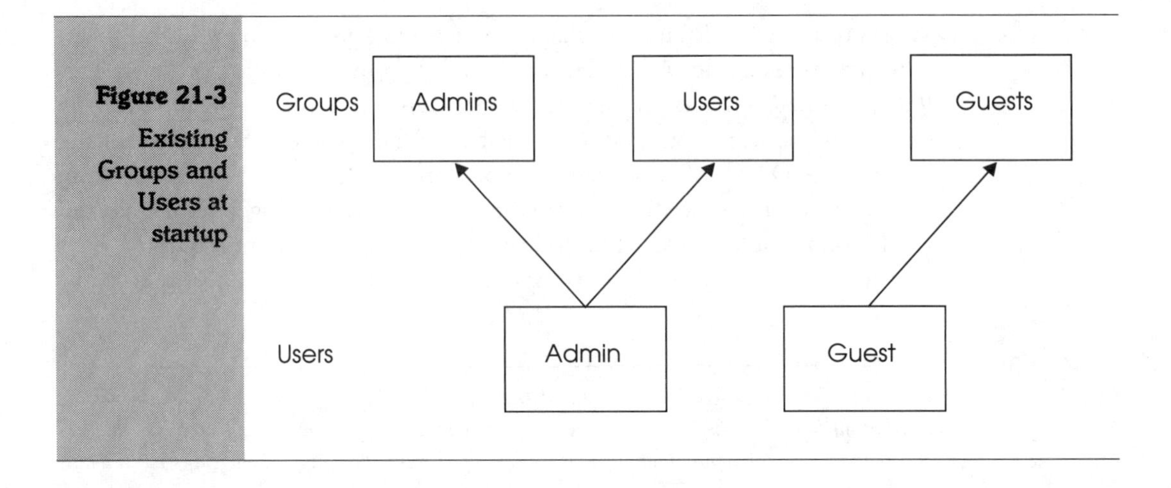


**Figure 21-3** Existing Groups and Users at startup

## Creating Accounts

To secure an application in Access, you need to create several accounts.

The first account you will need is the one for the administrator who will handle assigning security privileges for all other users. You will also need accounts for the owners of applications in the workgroup. Finally, you will need accounts for the people who will use the system. All of these accounts are created the same way.

As an administrator, you want an account belonging to the Admins group. Once you create a new administrator account, you can delete the Admin user account that Access provides just to get you started. You cannot create an administrator account unless you are logged into Access as a user in the Admins group. You automatically log on as Admin before the logon procedure is activated.

To add a user account such as a new administrator account, follow these steps from the Access Database window:

1. Open a database.

   You can open any database in the workgroup, since you only need a database open to have the Security menu available. The security features belong to the workgroup rather than to the database, so Access does not care which database is open when you create these accounts.

2. Choose Users from the Security menu.

3. Type the new user account name in the Users dialog box and press ENTER, or click the New button and enter the account name in the Name text box.

   Account names follow the same rules as passwords and personal IDs (PIDs), which were described earlier in this chapter. Administrator accounts follow the same rules for account names, PIDs, and passwords as other user accounts do.

   Unlike passwords and PIDs, you will find that user account names are not case-sensitive.

4. Type the PID in the Personal ID Number text box.

   A completed New User/Group dialog box might look like this:

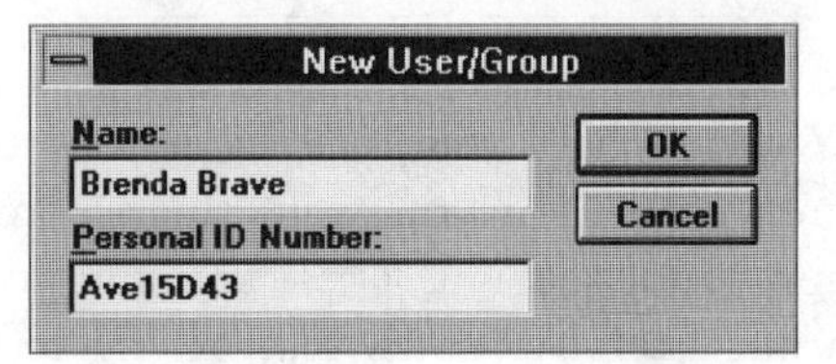


   Access uses the PID combined with the account name to uniquely identify every account. Access version 1 uses four-digit PIN numbers instead of the longer and more flexible PIDs. PIDs for each user should be placed in a safe place, such as a database that only the administrator can access. To communicate across systems, users will need to know the name and PIDs for their recipients.

5. Choose OK to return to the Users dialog box.

6. Choose the groups that the account you are creating belongs to.

   For the administrator, you will select Admins from the Available Groups list box and then choose Add to display Admins in the Member Of list box. You can assign multiple groups to any account you are creating. Access automatically adds the Users group to every account you create. Figure 21-4 shows the completed Users dialog box for a new account.

   If you have more accounts to create at this point, create the account for the next user by starting at step 3. When you create accounts that will be owner accounts, you can assign them to any group.

7. Choose Close.

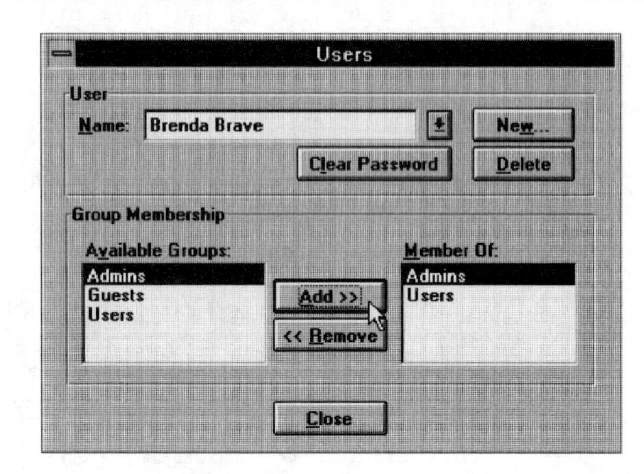


**Figure 21-4** The Users dialog box

You now have your own account in the Admins group. You can delete the Admin account if you want the account you just created to be the only administrator account. These accounts don't have a password yet, but you will add one later. Accounts that belong to the Admins group always have full permissions for all databases in a workgroup. The user accounts that own a database always have full permissions for every object within the database.

## DELETING A USER

Users who leave the company should be removed from the system immediately. You will also want to delete user accounts for accounts that are no longer used. You should delete the accounts rather than just removing them from a group, because you want the accounts to be inoperable.

Follow these steps to delete a user:

1. Log on to an account in the Admins group.
2. Choose Users from the Security menu.
3. Select the user name from the Name box.
4. Select Delete and then select Close.

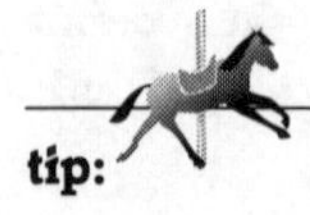

**tip:** *During layoffs or other involuntary terminations, user accounts are normally made inoperable at the time that the user is being informed of termination, to prevent potential malicious damage to the data files by disgruntled employees.*

## Turning on the Logon Procedure

Access provides a logon procedure that does not display when you first install the package, because no password is required to be the Admin user. After assigning a password to this account, a Logon dialog box will display every time you start Access. Since initially starting Access places you in the Admin user account, when you add a password it will be for the Admin user.

Passwords follow different rules than account names do. The password that you enter is case-sensitive, making it especially important to remember not only the word that you use but also its capitalization. The password can be any length from 1 to 14 characters and can include spaces and special characters. The only character that cannot be used is the NULL character represented as an ASCII 0. Since the password is the lock that protects your data, don't share it with others. You should not choose names or numbers that coworkers are likely to guess, and you should never write down your password and place it on your computer or in a desk drawer. Use acronyms instead of words, since they are more difficult to guess. For example, if you took the words "I use Microsoft Access for all my work" and created an acronym such as IuMA4amw, the combination of uppercase and lowercase letters and numbers is not likely to be guessed by coworkers trying to discern your password—yet you are more likely to remember it than you would a random combination of letters.

Here are the steps for adding the password to an account for the first time:

1. Open a database and then choose Change Password from the Security menu.
2. Type a new password in the New Password box, shown here:

   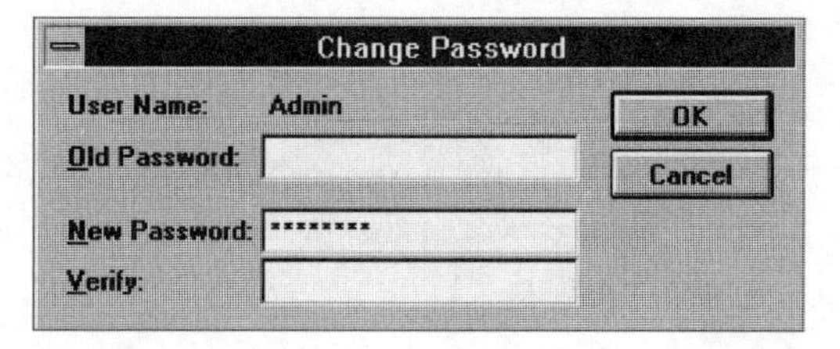
   

   You do not need to type an old password, since none exists. As you type the new password, asterisks appear onscreen so that if anyone happens to glance over your shoulder, they won't see the characters you're typing.
3. Retype the same password in the Verify box and then choose OK.

A Logon dialog box appears when you start Access again; you will need to supply the password that you just assigned.

To see the logon procedure in process, leave Access and start Access again. You will see a Logon dialog box for entering the user account name and password, as shown here:

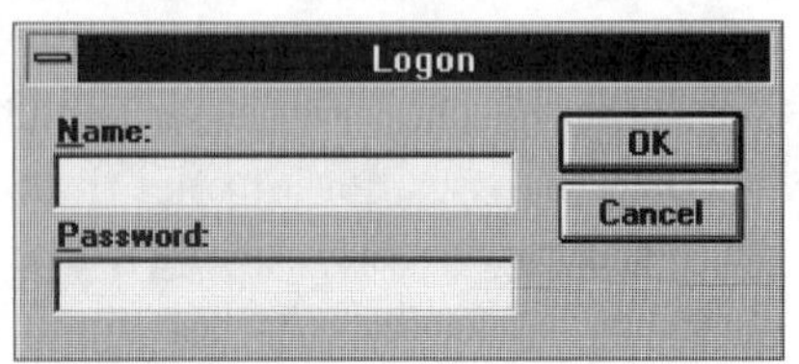


You must supply a correct user name and its matching password to proceed, or else you cannot start Access. You must use a user account rather than a group account to log on to Access. At this point you will have added a basic level of security to the system, which may be adequate if you are the only user. If you operate in a shared environment, the next step is to assign ownership to the database and its objects.

To create passwords for other users, you would follow the same steps as you did to create a password for the Admin user. You must be logged on under the account name for which you want to change the password. If you are logged on as Admin or another user name, you must exit Access and restart the system, supplying the user name for which you want to add a password when the Logon dialog box appears. As a member of the Admins group, you will be called when users cannot remember their password or have other system difficulties. A list of user names and passwords for your reference will help you handle these situations, although as an Admin user, you can remove the passwords to other accounts.

## CHANGING THE PASSWORD

A password is more secure when you change it on a regular basis. You can change the passwords assigned to any user account. To change a password, follow these steps:

1. Log on as the user for which you want to change the password.
2. Choose Change Password from the Security menu.
3. Type the old password in the Old Password box, or leave the box blank if the user does not have a password assigned.
4. Type the new password in the New Password box.

5. Type the new password again in the Verify box.

6. Select OK.

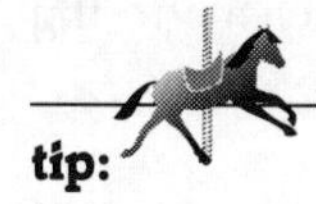

**tip:** *Always change the Guest password after guests have finished using the system. They will not be able to log onto the system without your giving them the new password at a later time.*

To remove a password, choose Change Password from the Security menu and simply type the old password. Then leave the New Password and Verify boxes empty. User accounts without a password can be logged onto by supplying only the account name. A user in the Admins group can remove passwords to other accounts by choosing the Users command in the Security menu, selecting the user name from the Name drop-down list box, and selecting Clear Password. The user in the Admins group does not need to know the user's password to remove it.

## Assigning Owners to Databases and Objects

Owning a database or database object gives a user privileges for the database or database object that cannot be taken away without also taking away ownership to the database or object. Every database in the workgroup has an owner. Before you use Access' security features, the databases are owned by the Admin user. In Access version 2, you can change the user account that owns the databases and objects. Changing the owner lets the owner of the database change the permissions for other users and how the database is used.

Changing the ownership of an existing database requires importing the database into a new database. To change the owner of a database in Access version 2, follow these steps:

1. Log on into Access using the user account for the new database owner.

2. Choose New Database from the File menu, type a new name for the database, and select OK.

   This new database has the user account you used in step 1 as the owner.

3. Select Add-ins from the File menu and select Import Database.

As described in Chapter 19, Import Database imports every object in another database into the current one.

4. Select the database for which you want to change the ownership to the user account selected in step 1, and select OK.

Access requires that you must have Run/Open permissions for the imported database and Read Definitions permissions for its objects. Relationships between the tables and queries are retained when you import a database.

You can also change the owner of an object in the database. For example, if you want to let someone else change a form design in a database that you own, giving them ownership gives them the ability to change the form without giving them permission to change other database objects. Before you can change ownership of database objects, you must have the Administer permission for the database. You will have this permission if you are logged on using an account in the Admins group, if you are given this permission by a user in the Admins group, or if you are the owner of the database. You can change the ownership of a database object by following these steps:

1. Open the database containing the objects for which you want to reassign ownership.
2. Choose Change Owner from the Security menu.
3. Select the type of object for which to reassign ownership from the Object Type drop-down list box, and select the object from the Object list box.
4. Select a new owner in the New Owner drop-down list box and select the Change Owner button.

If you are changing the ownership of a table or query that is related to another table or query, the relationship will be broken and you will have to create it again.

## Setting Up Groups and Users

Before you can give permission to a database and its objects to accounts other than the account owner or accounts in the Admins group, you will want to create the users and groups. You learned earlier how to create user accounts; the steps are the same as those for creating an administrator account. Groups accounts provide shortcuts for giving many users the same sets of permissions. Although you can assign permission for objects at the user level, it is more efficient to create groups of users with similar needs and assign permission to the group of users. You might have a marketing group, a sales group, an accounting group, a management group, and a payroll group within your organization. Each group needs to be able to use different forms, reports, and tables. Assigning permission at the group level also makes it easier when individuals change job responsibilities. You can move them to a group that fits with the new position rather than having to modify the permissions for each of the old and new objects that they need to use.

To create a group, follow these steps:

1. Choose Groups from the Security menu in the Database window.
2. Type a group name in the Name box in the Groups dialog box, as shown here:

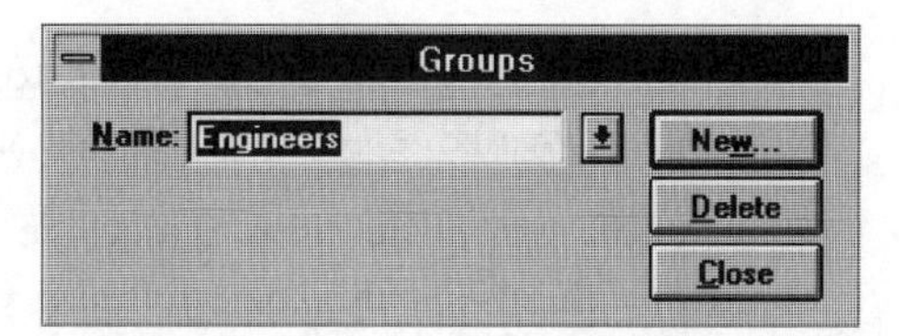


   Group names follow the same rules as account names and PIDs.

3. Choose the New button.

   The New User/Group dialog box appears with the name you entered in the Name box.

4. Type the PID in the Personal ID Number text box.

   Just like user accounts, Access combines the PID and the group name to uniquely identify every account. Access version 1 uses four-digit PIN numbers instead of the longer and more flexible PIDs. PIDs for each user should be placed in a safe place, such as a database that only the administrator can access. To communicate across systems, users will need to know the names and PIDs of their recipients.

5. Select OK to create the group.
6. Continue creating groups until all of the groups are entered, and then choose Close.

Once you have created the group, it appears in the list of groups when you use the Users command in the Security menu to change the groups a user belongs to.

**tip:** *Do not leave old, unused groups in the system. Use the Groups command in the Security menu to remove them. Select a group name after using this command and then select the Delete button.*

### CHANGING A USER'S GROUPS

At a minimum, every user is a part of the group Users. You can add a user to as many other groups as you want. For example, an individual supervising both the accounting and the finance staffs might be part of the groups for accounting, finance, and management.

To add or remove a group for an existing user, follow these steps:

1. Choose Users from the Security menu.
2. Select a user name from the Name drop-down list box.
3. To add the user, select the group to which you want to add the user from the Available Groups list box, and select Add.

   To remove the user, select the group from which you want to remove the user from the Members Of list box, and select Remove.
4. Select Close to leave the dialog box.

## Securing Database Objects

You need to protect the database objects, which consist of tables, forms, reports, macros, and modules. To do this you must establish permissions for each object for each group or user. You can think of permissions as a permission slip like the one shown in Figure 21-5. The recipient of a permission can be a user or a group. The grantor of the permissions can be the owner of the object or a user who logged on using an account in the Admins group.

It is a good idea to establish the permissions for your system as soon as you load Access, since the default is to allow all users to work with any object. You can establish permissions for each database or database object. Users automatically inherit the permissions assigned to any group that they are a part of. For example, every user is part of the group Users, so any user has the permissions assigned to the Users group. When Access checks whether you have permission to do something, Access checks your account's permissions as well as the permissions for all groups that your account belongs to. Permissions are additive, so the most generous permissions among your account and your groups are the ones that you have. This means that you should make the group permissions as

**Figure 21-5** Permission slip for Access objects

**Access Permission Slip**

Account Name: ______________________ *(user or group)*
For: ______________________ *(database or object)*

This user has permission to make the following changes to the database or database object described above.

| | | |
|---|---|---|
| ____ | Open a database, form, or report or run a macro | Open/Run |
| ____ | Exclusively open a database | Open Exclusive |
| ____ | Read designs | Read Design |
| ____ | Modify designs as well as replace and delete | Modify Design |
| ____ | Look at data in a table, query, or form | Read Data |
| ____ | Change data in a table, query, or form | Update Data |
| ____ | Insert records | Insert Data |
| ____ | Delete records | Delete Data |
| ____ | All permissions shown above | Administer |

Permission Given By: ____Member of the Admins group
____Owner of the database or database object

restrictive as necessary and add additional permissions only for users that need them. For example, you will need to remove permissions from the Users group to limit the permissions available to every user.

## SETTING PERMISSIONS

When you first install Access, every user that you add has full permission to all objects. This means that they can read and modify data, read and modify definitions for all objects, and execute macros, reports, and forms. This is because the default permission is set to grant all permissions to all Access users because they are part of the Users group. You can assign permissions for each database object on your own by choosing Permissions from the Security menu and clearing the Administer check box (Full permissions in Access version 1). Access has up to nine permissions that can be assigned for a database or one of its objects. These permissions and the tasks you can do when you have the permissions are shown in the following table:

| Permission | Tasks You Can Do with This Permission |
|---|---|
| Open/Run | Open a database, use a form or report, or run a macro |
| Open Exclusive | Open a database for exclusive use |
| Read Design | View the design of an object |
| Modify Design | Change the design of the object |

| Permission | Tasks You Can Do with This Permission |
|---|---|
| Administer | Have all other permissions available to the object |
| Read Data | Use the table, query, or form to look at data |
| Update Data | Use the table, query, or form to change data |
| Insert Data | Use the table, query, or form to add records |
| Delete Data | Use the table, query, or form to delete records |

All permissions are defined for each object, with some permissions operating on all objects and others restricted to a certain type of object. Table 21-1 shows the objects that are affected by the various permissions. In Access version 1, the Modify Design and Read Design permissions are called Modify Definitions and Read Definitions. The Open/Run permission is called Execute in Access version 1. Access version 1 also combines the Insert Data, Delete Data, and Update Data permissions into the Modify Data permission.

Some permissions imply another permission. For example, if you allow a user to modify the definition of a report, you are implying that he or she can also read the report definition. When you explicitly assign a permission that adds implied permissions, the check boxes for the implied permissions are also selected. However, when you clear the check box of a permission that when added implicitly gives permissions, the implicitly given permissions continue to be given until you explicitly remove them. Look at Table 21-2 to see the permissions that are implied with each explicit permission assignment.

**tip:** *You can set permissions for new objects so that the users can make their own tables, forms, reports, and macros in a database they do not own. New permissions are set by selecting the first option in the Object Name list box and then selecting the permissions.*

| Object | Available Permissions |
|---|---|
| Table | Read Design, Modify Design, Administer, Read Data, Update Data, Insert Data, Delete Data |
| Query | Read Design, Modify Design, Administer, Read Data, Update Data, Insert Data, Delete Data |
| Form | Open/Run, Read Design, Modify Design, Administer |
| Report | Open/Run, Read Design, Modify Design, Administer |
| Macro | Open/Run, Read Design, Modify Design, Administer |
| Module | Read Design, Modify Design, Administer |

**Table 21-1**
**Available Permissions for Objects**

| Explicit Assignment | Implied Permission |
|---|---|
| Read Design | Open/Run (macros only) |
| Modify Design | Read Design<br>Read Data<br>Update Data<br>Delete Data<br>Open/Run (macros only) |
| Administer | All other permissions |
| Read Data | Read Design |
| Update Data | Read Design<br>Read Data |
| Insert Data | Read Design<br>Read Data |
| Delete Data | Read Design<br>Read Data |

**Table 21-2**
**Implied Permissions**

## DEFINING THE PERMISSIONS FOR AN OBJECT

Objects in the database consist of tables, queries, reports, forms, modules, and macros. You can assign permission on an object-by-object basis and specify which users or groups can use them.

To assign permissions, follow these steps:

1. Choose Permissions from the Security menu and the Permissions dialog box appears, as shown in Figure 21-6.
2. Select the type of object from the Object Type drop-down list box (the Type drop-down list box in Access version 1).

   You can also select the first item in the list in Access version 2 when you want to set the permissions for new objects of the selected object type.
3. Select the name of the object from the Object Name list box (the Name drop-down list box in Access version 1).
4. Select the group or user.

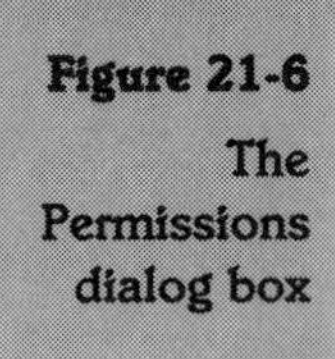

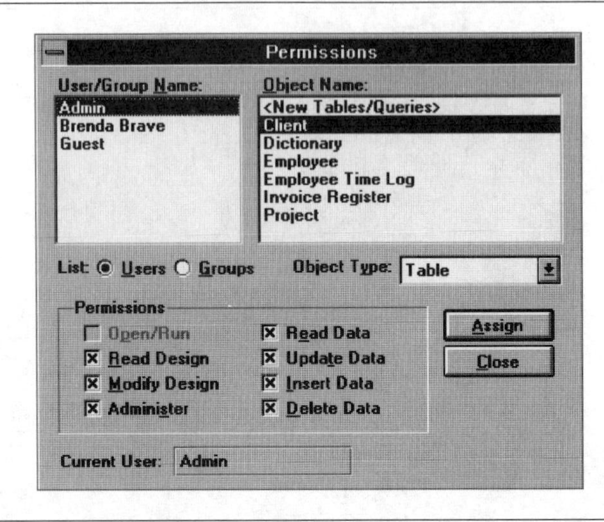


**Figure 21-6** The Permissions dialog box

5. Select the permissions you want to assign to the user or group for the selected object.
6. Select Assign.

   Repeat steps 2 through 6 for each object.

7. Select the Close button to finish assigning permissions for the database and its objects.

**caution:** *If you save a database object to a new object with the Save As command in the File menu, the permissions are not retained in the new object. You will have to assign permissions for the new object.*

***Restricting Access to Less Than a Table*** Field-level security is often desired to more closely control the data that users can see and update. Since Access security is assigned at the object level, the permissions are assigned for an entire table. A solution that fits within the capabilities of the system and effectively provides a more refined security is to define a query or a form that contains only the data elements that a user can see and modify.

Defining a query can allow a staff member to update every field in the Employee table except the pay rate, for example. Since the pay rate is not part of the query, the user who has permission to use the query object will not be able to see or change it. It is important that you do not give this user permission to use the Employee table, or they will be able to read the pay rate field.

### PRINTING SECURITY INFORMATION

You may not remember all of the security settings you make. Access can create a security report that includes information on the established users and groups. To create this report:

1. Select Print Security in the Security menu.
2. From the next dialog box, select whether you want the report to give information on just the users, just the groups, or both.
3. Select OK, and Access displays a preview of the report.
4. Select Print from the File menu or click the Print button in the toolbar.
5. Select OK and Access prints the report.

Figure 21-7 shows the beginning of a report that this command created.

**Figure 21-7** Printed security report

Friday, February 04, 1994 **Security Information** Page: 1

**Users**

| User Name | Groups that User Belongs to |
|---|---|
| admin | Admins, Users |
| BBrave | Testing, Users |
| DDanger | Testing, Users |
| DDare | Admins, Design, Users |
| guest | Guests |
| HHigher | Construction, Users |
| JJump | Construction, Users |
| RRock | Construction, Users |
| RRolling | Design, Users |
| SScary | Design, Users |
| TThrill | Construction, Users |
| WWild | Design, Users |

**Groups**

| Group Name | Users that Belong to Group |
|---|---|
| Admins | admin, DDare |
| Construction | HHigher, JJump, RRock, TThrill |
| Design | DDare, RRolling, SScary, WWild |
| Guests | guest |
| Testing | BBrave, DDanger |
| Users | admin, BBrave, DDanger, DDare, HHigher, JJump, RRock, RRolling, SScary, TThrill, WWild |

## Assign User Account Passwords

To limit the user accounts to the users that these accounts are designed for, you need to protect these accounts with passwords. The users will need to log on to Access using their accounts. When they first log on, their account will not have a password, so they need to supply only their user name. Then use the Change Password command in the Security menu to change their password. This process was described earlier in the chapter for starting the logon procedure by assigning a password to the Admin user.

## Using Encryption to Improve Security

If someone tried to read your database file with a word processor or utility program, the file would not display on the screen as it does from Access. Although the unauthorized user may be able to discern some information, it is not easy to read. However, if the database contains confidential information, even this level of data availability to unauthorized users may be too much. Also, in Access version 2, if a database is not encrypted, users in other workgroups can open the database.

Access can encrypt databases that you do not want accessible to unauthorized users. An encrypted file is one that is not readable if it is displayed on the screen or printer using a utility package or word processor. Everything in the file is represented by secret codes that only Access knows, and this information is transcribed into a readable format only by Access when you look at it from within the Access system or decrypt the file.

Encryption is an important technique if your database contains confidential sales information or salaries. Although encryption does reduce performance slightly, it can be an important technique for protecting your information. This is especially important when you transmit a file over the telephone lines or mail a copy of the information on a disk and are concerned about unauthorized access to its contents.

Encryption is done to an entire database rather than to individual objects. It must be done while the database is closed on your system and the database is not used by any other user. To encrypt your database, follow these steps:

1. Close the database leaving Access open.
2. Choose Encrypt/Decrypt Database from the File menu.

3. Specify a filename, drive, and directory for the database to encrypt in the Encrypt/Decrypt Database dialog box.
4. Select the OK button.
5. Specify a filename, drive, and directory for the encrypted version of the database in the Encrypt Database As dialog box.

   You can use the same name as the database to overwrite it with the encrypted file.
6. Select the OK button.

Access encrypts the database and compacts it at the same time. You can decrypt the database to remove the encryption using the same dialog box.

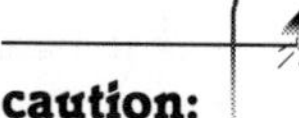

**caution:** *Encryption is best left to the network administrator who has permission for all database objects. If a database is encrypted using the same name as the original file and you do not have permission for these objects, the new file will not contain these objects and will be given a new name by Access. You will not be able to delete the original database, since it is the only location with all of the data.*

### Distributing the Application

Once you have completed the steps for making an Access application secure, described at the beginning of the "Access Security" section earlier in this chapter, you are ready to distribute the files. The files that are distributed include the files for all databases in the workgroup as well as the SYSTEM.MDA file that Access uses for the workgroup system information.

## Additional Database Operations

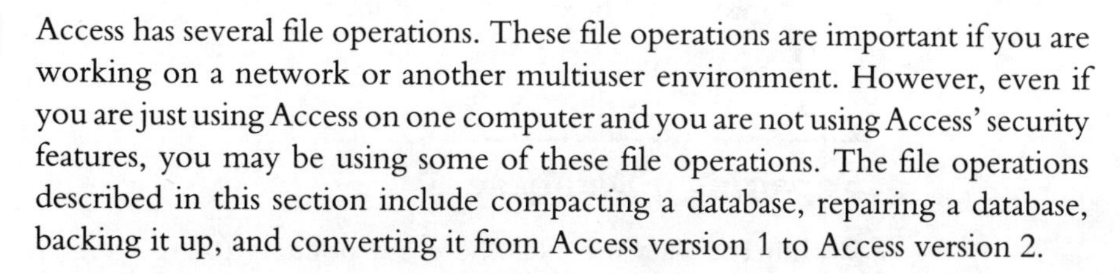

Access has several file operations. These file operations are important if you are working on a network or another multiuser environment. However, even if you are just using Access on one computer and you are not using Access' security features, you may be using some of these file operations. The file operations described in this section include compacting a database, repairing a database, backing it up, and converting it from Access version 1 to Access version 2.

## Compacting a Database

As you continue to add to a database, it becomes impossible for the information to be stored in adjacent locations on your hard disk; data becomes fragmented in many places. When data is subsequently retrieved, performance can be degraded. When you compact the database, you eliminate all of the fragments and make the database more efficient.

How often should a database be compacted in order to run efficiently? There is no one correct answer, since some users will use a database primarily to look up existing information. A database that consists solely of a catalog price list or a list of chemical elements is one example of a database that would not require compacting. Since data is not added, fragmenting doesn't occur; compaction would never be necessary after the initial creation. On the other hand, a database that consists of customer orders and a growing base of other information with many new reports would require compaction just about whenever the database was closed.

A database can only be compacted when it is not open on any system. There also must be adequate storage space for the existing file and the compacted version. You must supply a "from" and "to" database name for the compact operation, but they can be the same. The original file will be replaced after a successful conclusion for the procedure.

Follow these steps to compact a database:

1. Close any open databases.
2. Choose Compact Database from the File menu.
3. From the list of filenames in the Database to Compact From dialog box, select the file that you want to compact, changing the drive and directory if necessary.
4. Select OK.
5. Type the name for the compacted database in the Database to Compact Into dialog box.
6. Select OK.

## Repairing a Database

Within the database file, there are pointers to many interrelated pieces of information. If your system crashes when Access is writing to this file, there is the potential for your database to become corrupted. This could mean that some vital data is missing or the pointers between information are not properly updated. You will not be able to open and use a corrupted database unless you correct the situation. If you experience problems with a database, try closing it and using the Repair Database command. You can start the repair procedure either by choosing Repair Database from the File menu or by clicking OK in response to a prompt when you attempt to open, compact, or encrypt a database. After selecting Repair Database from the File menu, specify the name of the database file to be repaired. Select the drive and directory if the current setting is not the correct one.

## Backups

The network administrator is responsible for backing up all of the shared databases on the network and is expected to advise users about when to back up the databases stored on their own systems.

Backups will protect your organization against data loss and the inevitable down time that occurs when a large database is lost. Databases that are updated infrequently will not require daily backups. If many people update a database each day, then daily backups are essential.

Backup is easy with Access because all tables, reports, forms, macros, and queries are stored in one .MDB file. You may choose to use the DOS Copy command, the Windows File Manager, or backup software. Most organizations will use more efficient backup software to save time when backups must be done on a daily basis, because the database cannot be open and in use during the backup period and it is best to keep this time to a minimum.

You may want to schedule an extra backup immediately following a large, important operation or the creation of numerous macros, reports, or forms to ensure that they are available on the backup copy. Make a backup copy of SYSTEM.MDB along with any databases that you are backing up to ensure that your system configuration changes are also retained. If you have links to OLE objects in your database, backup the files that the OLE objects link to.

A backup copy should be stored offsite in the event that a fire or other major catastrophe strikes the building where the network is installed. Lock up your backups or use encryption, since the value of the data they contain is the same as that of the database. You may want to keep between three to seven backups to be able to restore the database in the event of a backup also being damaged.

## Bringing Access Version 1 Databases into Access Version 2

If you have been using Access version 1, when you switch to Access version 2, you will want to convert the Access version 1 database to an Access version 2 database. Converting the database lets the database take advantage of version 2 features that are not available in Access version 1. Before a database is converted, you can use either Access version 1 or version 2 to work with the database, although you cannot change the design of your database objects using Access version 2. Once you convert the database, you can no longer use the database in Access version 1. If you are using Access' security features, you must be the database owner to make the conversion. Access will make some changes to the design of some of the database objects to match the new features in Access version 2.

To convert the database, use the Convert Database command in the File menu. After choosing this command, select the database by selecting the appropriate drive, directory, and file. Once you select OK, select or type the name for the converted database and select OK. If you use the same database name both times, the converted database replaces the previous version. However, the replacement is not made until the entire database is converted, so you need enough disk space for two versions of your database in order to convert it.

# Customizing Access

Access has many different settings that allow you to customize its operation. These changes are all made by choosing Options from the View menu. It does not matter which database is open when the changes are made, since they will remain in effect for all databases in the system.

Customizing is an important role for the network administrator, becauses all of the individuals who work using the same workgroup use the same options settings.

There are nine different categories of customizing changes that you can make to Access: General, Keyboard, Printing, Form & Report Design, Datasheet, Query Design, Macro Design, Module Design, and Multiuser/ODBC. A brief look at each category lets you focus on which changes can bring the users in different workgroups the best results possible with Access. Figure 21-8 shows the dialog box that appears when you choose Options from the View menu.

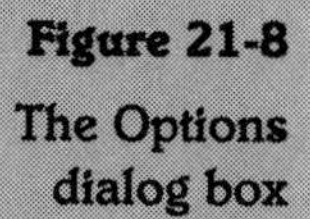

**Figure 21-8**
**The Options dialog box**

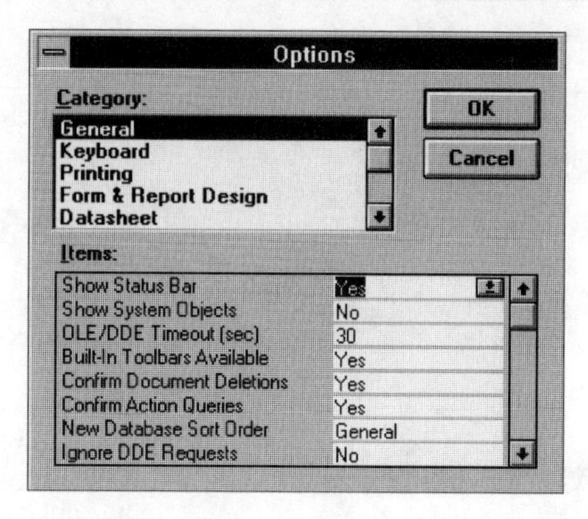


You can choose any category from the Category list box, and the properties list for that category will replace the properties for the General category, which are displayed initially.

## General Options

The General category contains customization options that do not fit into any of the more specific categories. Options in this category allow you to customize the display of the status bar and toolbar, customize the sort order, and provide confirmation of various actions.

Table 21-3 shows each of the General category options and their default settings, and gives a brief explanation of the customizing features that they provide. The settings that do not show a default have the setting from the selections made with the Toolbars command in the View menu.

## Keyboard Options

The keyboard options let you customize the way certain keys on the keyboard work. It is important that you assess this category of changes before users start working with Access and that you leave the settings unchanged, since they are basic to any typing that you do with the package. The Keyboard category also allows you to specify the name of the macro that you will use for definitions of macro tasks assigned to keyboard keys.

| Option | Default Setting | Meaning |
| --- | --- | --- |
| Show Status Bar | Yes | Displays or hides the status bar |
| Show System Objects | No | Displays or hides database objects defined by Access |
| OLE/DDE Timeout (sec) | 30 | Determines how long until Access attempts a failed OLE or DDE task |
| Show Tool Bar (version 1 only) | Yes | Displays or hides the toolbar |
| Built-In Toolbars Available (version 2 only) | Yes | Displays or hides the toolbars that Access provides |
| Confirm Document Deletions | Yes | Determines whether the "Delete object?" prompt displays |
| Confirm Action Queries | Yes | Determines whether a confirmation message box displays when you perform an action query |
| New Database Sort Order | General | Sets the sort order for new databases. Other options are for other languages |
| Ignore DDE Requests | No | Determines whether DDE requests from other applications are serviced |
| Default Find/ Replace Behavior | Fast Search | Determines whether the current field is searched for the whole entry (Fast Search) or whether all fields are searched for any part of the field (General Search) |
| Default Database Directory | . indicating the current Access working directory | Specifies the directory for new database files |
| Confirm Record Changes | No | Determines whether a confirmation message box appears for deleted or pasted records |
| Can Customize Toolbars | Yes | Determines whether you can change the toolbars that Access provides or that you create |
| Enable DDE Refresh | Yes | Enables or disables refreshing DDE links |
| First Weekday | Sunday | Sets the first day of a week |
| First Week | Starts on Jan 1 | Sets when Access considers the first week of a year |
| Show ToolTips (version 2 only) | | Sets the default for whether ToolTips appear |
| Color Buttons on Toolbars (version 2 only) | | Sets the default for whether toolbar buttons use color |
| Large Toolbar Buttons (version 2 only) | | Sets the default for whether Access displays large toolbar buttons |

**Table 21-3**
**General Customizing Options**

Table 21-4 shows the four Keyboard category options and their default settings.

## Printing

The Printing options are all very basic to the print operation, since they establish the default margins on all four sides of the printed output. You can change the default settings to make the printed section of the page either larger or smaller.

## Form & Report Design

The Form & Report Design templates allow you to add standard logos or other changes to the basic forms and reports. This category provides settings that make alignment easier and determines whether or not the grid lines should be displayed. Changes do not affect any existing forms or reports, or those that you may subsequently create with Form Wizards or Report Wizards.

If you want to see all of the options, look at Table 21-5, which contains all of the settings for the Form & Report Design category. The settings that do not show a default have the setting from the last form or report design you used.

## Datasheet

Datasheet category options affect the display of datasheets. This includes new and existing query datasheets and new table and form datasheets. Existing datasheets are not affected. Options include font options, column width, and gridlines. Table 21-6 shows the full set of options.

| Option | Default Setting | Meaning |
|---|---|---|
| Arrow Key Behavior | Next Field | Determines whether the insertion point is moved to the next field or character when the arrow keys are pressed |
| Move After Enter | Next Field | Determines the effect of pressing ENTER on the insertion point. Other choices are No to not move the insertion point and Next Record |
| Cursor Stops at First/ Last Field | No | Determines whether the insertion point stops moving at the first or last field |
| Key Assignment Macro | AutoKeys | Specifies the name of the macro that assigns macros to a key |

**Table 21-4**
**Keyboard Category Options**

| Option | Default Setting | Meaning |
|---|---|---|
| Form Template | Normal | The name of the form in the current database that you want to use as a template when creating forms |
| Report Template | Normal | The name of the report in the current database that you want to use as a template when creating reports |
| Objects Snap to Grid | | Controls whether objects are aligned with the grids |
| Show Grid | | Displays or hides gridlines |
| Selection Behavior | Partially Enclosed | Selects whether controls enclosed or intersected by the selection rectangle are included, or only the ones that are fully enclosed |
| Show Ruler | | Displays or hides the ruler in a new form or report |
| Move Enclosed Controls (version 2 only) | | Selects whether, when you move a control, Access also moves other controls completely inside the control you are moving |
| Control Wizards (version 2 only) | | Selects whether Control Wizards are available when you add certain types of controls |

**Table 21-5**
**Form & Report Design Category Options**

| Option | Default Setting | Meaning |
|---|---|---|
| Default Gridlines Behavior | On | Determines whether gridlines are displayed or hidden |
| Default Column Width | 1 inch | Sets the width of datasheet columns |
| Default Font Name | MS Sans Serif | Selects any installed font for displaying datasheet data |
| Default Font Size | 8 | Sets the font size from available sizes for the font selected |
| Default Font Weight | Normal | Sets the weight with options such as thin, extra light, light, normal, medium, semi-bold, bold, extra bold, or heavy |
| Default Font Italic | No | Displays names and data in italic or non-italic |
| Default Font Underline | No | Displays names and data in underline or non-underline |

**Table 21-6**
**Datasheet Category Options**

## Query Design

The Query Design Category offers options that let you tailor the query design environment to more closely meet your needs. You can control the field names and table names that display and control permissions for running queries. Table 21-7 shows the options that are available.

## Macro Design

The Macro Design category has two customizing options. The Show Macro Names Column determines whether or not new macros display the Macro Name column in a Macro window. The second category option, Show Conditions Column, determines whether new macros display the Condition column within the Macro window. Regardless of these option settings, you can display or hide either column by clicking the Macro Name or Conditions button in the Macro window's toolbar or by making selections from the View menu.

## Module Design

There are two customizing options for the Module Design category. You can turn syntax checking for your Access Basic code on and off. You also can set the tab stops anywhere from 1 to 30 spaces, depending on the level of nesting and indentation you normally use in your programs. Syntax checking is the default, and the default tab setting is 4.

| Option | Default Setting | Meaning |
|---|---|---|
| Output All Fields (Restrict Available Fields in version 1) | Yes | Use only the fields in the QBE grid or all fields when you use the query as the basis for another query, a form, or a report |
| Run Permissions (Run with Owner's Permission in version 1) | Yes | Decides whether users who cannot view a query's underlying tables can view the data in a query or run an action query |
| Show Table Names | No | Sets the default for displaying table names in a QBE grid |

**Table 21-7**
**Query Design Category Options**

| Option | Default Setting | Meaning |
|---|---|---|
| Default Record Locking | No Locks | You can choose locking no records, locking all records, or edited record |
| Default Open Mode for Databases | Exclusive | Selects whether the default open mode for a database is exclusive or shared |
| Refresh Interval (sec) | 60 | Sets the refresh interval from 1 to 32,766 seconds |
| Update Retry Interval (msec) | 250 | Sets the time interval for trying resave on a record locked by someone else from 0 to 1000 milliseconds |
| Number of Update Retries | 2 | Sets the number of retry attempts for saving a changed record from 0 to 10 |
| ODBC Refresh Interval (sec) | 1500 in version 2<br>600 in version 1 | Sets the ODBC refresh rate from 1 to 3600 seconds |

**Table 21-8**
**Multiuser/ODBC Category Options**

## Multiuser/ODBC

The Multiuser/ODBC category provides customizing options that are only of interest in a multiuser environment. You can make changes to features such as record locking, shared versus exclusive access to databases, and refresh intervals. Table 21-8 shows the full set of options and default values.

## Quick Reference

**To Add or Change a Password** Choose Change Password from the Security menu and then type the old password. Type the new password in both the New Password and Verify text boxes and then select OK.

**To Create a New User** Choose Users from the Security menu. Type a user name in the Name text box and then select New. Type a PID or PIN and then choose OK, followed by Close.

**To Create a New Group** Choose Groups from the Security menu. Type a group name and then select New. Type a PID or PIN and then select OK, followed by Close.

**To Add a User to a Group** Choose Users from the Security menu. Select a user name and then select the desired group from the Available Groups list box. Select the Add button and then select Close.

**To Set Permissions for an Object** Select Permissions from the Security menu and then select the type and name of the object. Select the desired permissions, and then select Assign.

**To Encrypt/Decrypt the Database** Choose Encrypt/Decrypt Database from the File menu. Select the desired database and then select OK. Supply a name for the encrypted file and then select OK.

**To Compact the Database** Choose Compact Database from the File menu. Select the file and choose OK. Complete the Database to Compact Into box and supply the name of the compacted file before selecting OK.

**To Change a Custom Setting** Choose Options from the View menu. Choose the category of options that you want to change and then select the particular option and the desired value.

# VI

# Appendixes

# Appendix A

# Installing Access Version 2

THE first step in using Access is to install it on your computer. In order to install all of Access, you should have about 20MB free on your hard disk. If you don't have that much space available, you can install just Access, without all of its features or ancillary applications, with only 5MB free on your hard disk. To install Access version 2, follow these steps:

1. Start Windows by typing **win** at the DOS prompt and pressing ENTER.
2. Select Run from the Program Manager's File menu.
3. Enter **a:\setup** in the Command Line text box, and select OK to start the Microsoft Access Setup application. Make sure to put the Setup disk in drive A.

   If your Access disks are in drive B, you should type **b:\setup** instead.
4. The initial screen includes a warning that all other applications should be closed, so that the Setup application can replace Windows system files that other applications may be using. If you have other applications open, switch to them now and close them.
5. After the initial screen, you are prompted to enter your name and company in the Name and Company text boxes. Select Continue, and then select Yes to confirm that the name and company you have entered are correct. If Access was previously installed on a system using the same disks, you will see a dialog box telling you that this is a copyrighted program, and warning you about copyright liabilities if you are installing it on a second machine. Select OK to continue setting up Access, or select Exit Setup to abort setup.

**tip:** *You can also find the Product ID number if you select About Access from the Help menu.*

6. Now the Setup program displays your Product ID number. This is a serial number identifying your copy of Access. You will want to record this number someplace, to identify yourself as owning a legal copy of the software when you need to request help or upgrades from Microsoft Corporation.

7. Setup now prompts you to select the directory you want Access installed in. By default this is C:\ACCESS\. Enter the name of the directory you want the Access program installed to if it is different, and then select OK to continue installing Access.

   The setup program now examines your hard disk for available space, previously installed Access files, and how much space Access will require.

8. Setup now presents you with three choices for installing Access: Typical, Complete/Custom, and Laptop (Minimum). Select Typical to install the Access and Access help features most often used. This option uses about 15MB of space on your hard disk. Select Laptop (Minimum) if you are short on space. This installs only the Access application itself and uses about 5MB. Select Complete/Custom to install all Access features and ancillary programs, or to install only those elements that you want.

**note:** *If you are installing Access on a network workstation, you will have a fourth option, to install Access for a workstation. If you are installing Access from a network, you should ask your network administrator for instructions.*

   If you select the Complete/Custom installation option, you will see the dialog box listing parts of the Microsoft Access package. Clear the check boxes of those parts that you do not want to install. The amount of space each part requires is listed beside the check boxes. Select specific elements of some of these parts by choosing the Select button. Table A-1 lists the elements you can select.

9. Setup now prompts you to select the program group for the Access icons to be installed in. You can choose one of the existing program groups or create a new one. By default, Setup will add Access to the Microsoft Office program group. Select OK after choosing a program group.

10. Access Setup prompts you for each disk as it finishes installing the preceding one. When prompted, insert the specified disk in the disk drive, and select OK.

| Option | | Hard Disk Space (in KB) | |
|---|---|---|---|
| Access | | 5431 | |
| Help and Cue Cards | | 5064 | |
| | Online Help | | 4248 |
| | Cue Cards | | 816 |
| Wizards | | 2787 | |
| | Table Wizard | | 480 |
| | Query Wizards | | 384 |
| | Form and Report Wizards | | 1121 |
| | Control and Property Wizards | | 801 |
| ISAM Drivers | | 645 | |
| | FoxPro and dBase ISAM | | 299 |
| | Paradox ISAM | | 233 |
| | Btrieve ISAM | | 113 |
| ODBC Support | | 632 | |
| | SQL Server ODBC Driver | | 632 |
| Microsoft Graph | | 2271 | |
| | Microsoft Graph Files | | 1773 |
| | Microsoft Graph Help | | 504 |
| Sample Apps | | 2592 | |
| | Northwind Traders | | 1704 |
| | Orders | | 316 |
| | Solutions | | 672 |
| Tools | | 912 | |
| | Microsoft Access Setup | | 848 |
| | MS Info | | 64 |

**Table A-1**
**Approximate Hard Disk Space Required for Elements of Access**

11. When Setup finishes with the last disk, Setup needs to restart Windows, since it will have made changes to some system files. It may also have made a change to your AUTOEXEC.BAT file, if you did not have SHARE command in that file. Select OK to restart Windows.

 Access will not warn you when it has had to add the SHARE command to your AUTOEXEC.BAT file. However, if your AUTOEXEC.BAT file does not contain this command, you cannot use Access. To have the change in your AUTOEXEC.BAT file take effect, you need to reboot your computer.

# Appendix B

Business

Personal

# Fields in Table Wizards

WHEN you use the Table Wizard, you can select sample fields from the sample tables to create your own table. You can customize your table by mixing and matching fields from the various sample tables. However, since Access offers so many sample tables, it can be difficult to remember which table contains which field. This appendix lists all of the sample tables and their sample fields.

## Business

When you select the Business option button, the Table Wizard displays a list of 26 sample tables that you can use or select fields from.

### Category

| | | |
|---|---|---|
| Category ID | Category Name | Description |

### Classes

| | | |
|---|---|---|
| Class ID | Section Number | Units |
| Class Name | Instructor | Year |
| Department Name | Term | Note |
| Department Number | | |

## Contacts

Contact ID
Prefix
First Name
Last Name
Suffix
Organization Name
Address
City
State
Postal Code
Region
Country
Work Phone
Home Phone
Mobile Phone
Fax Number
Email Name
Birthdate
Contact Type
Last Meeting Date
Action Items
Referred By
Photograph
Note

## Customers

Customer ID
First Name
Last Name
Organization Name
Address
City
State
Region
Postal Code
Country
Contact Name
Contact Title
Phone Number
Fax Number
Note

## Deliveries

Delivery ID
Customer ID
Order ID
Employee ID
Shipped Via
Shipper Tracking Code
Ship Date
Shipper Phone Number
Shipped From
Destination Address
Destination City
Destination State
Destination Postal Code
Destination Country
Arrival DateTime
Package Dimensions
Package Weight
Pick Up Location
Pickup DateTime
Received By
Freight Charge
Note

## Employees

Employee ID
Social Security Number
National Empl Number
First Name
Middle Name
Last Name
Title
Email Name
Extension
Address
City
State
Region
Postal Code
Country
Home Phone
Work Phone
Department Name
Birthdate
Date Hired
Supervisor ID
Spouse Name
Emrgcy Contact Name
Emrgcy Contact Phone
Note
Photograph

## EmployeesAndTasks

- Employee Task ID
- Employee ID
- Task ID

## Events

- Event ID
- Event Name
- Event Type
- Status
- Start Date
- Location
- End Date
- Start Time
- End Time
- Confirmed
- Available Spaces
- Cost Per Person
- Description
- Note

## Expenses

- Expense ID
- Employee ID
- Expense Type
- Purpose of Expense
- Amount Spent
- Description
- Date Purchased
- Date Submitted
- Advance Amount
- Payment Method

## Fixed Assets

- Fixed Asset ID
- Asset Name
- Make
- Model
- Model Number
- Serial Number
- Beginning Value
- Depreciation Method
- Depreciation Rate
- Current Value
- Comments
- Description

## Invoice Details

- Invoice Detail ID
- Invoice ID
- Order ID
- Product ID
- Quantity
- Price Per Unit
- Payment Terms
- Discount

## Invoices

- Invoice ID
- Customer ID
- Employee ID
- Delivery ID
- Status
- Invoice Date
- Salesperson Name
- Ship Date
- Shipped To
- Shipped Via
- Shipping Cost
- Note

## Mailing List

Mailing List ID
Prefix
First Name
Middle Name
Last Name
Suffix
Nickname
Title
Organization Name
Address
City
State
Region
Postal Code
Country
Home Phone
Work Phone
Mobile Phone
Fax Number
Alternative Phone
Email Address
CompuServe ID
Birthdate
Nationality
Emrgcy Contact Name
Emrgcy Contact Phone
Date Updated
Membership Status
Date Joined
Pledge Amount
Pledge Paid Date
Dues Amount
Dues Paid Date
Hobbies
Health Problems
Photograph
Note

## Order Details

Order Detail ID
Order ID
Product ID
Date Sold
Quantity
Unit Price
Discount
Sale Price
Sales Tax
Payment Terms

## Orders

Order ID
Customer ID
Employee ID
Order Date
Required By Date
Promised By Date
Ship Name
Ship Address
Ship City
Ship State
Ship Region
Ship Postal Code
Ship Country
Ship Date
Ship Via
Freight Charge

## Payments

Payment ID
Customer ID
Order ID
Reservation ID
Payment Amount
Payment Date
Payment Method
Check Number
Credit Card Type
Credit Card Number
Credit Card Name
Credit Card Exp Date
Payment Terms
Note

## Products

Product ID
Product Name
Category ID
Supplier ID
Serial Number
Units In Stock
Units On Order
Unit Price
Reorder Level
Discontinued

## Projects

Project ID
Project Name
Customer ID
Project Lead
Project Description
Note

## Reservations

Reservation ID
Customer ID
Event ID
Employee ID
Quantity Reserved
Reservation Date
Deposit Due
Total Due
Amount Paid
Confirmed
Note

## Service Records

Service Record ID
Fixed Asset ID
Service Date
Employee ID
Problem Description
Description
Date Promised
Date Delivered
Received By
Labor Hours
Estimated Cost
Actual Cost
Parts Replaced
Actual Cost
Estimated Cost
Prev Service Date
Next Service Date
Miles Since Last Srvc
Hours Since Last Srvc
Authorized By

## Students

Student ID
First Name
Middle Name
Last Name
Parents Names
Address
City
State
Region
Postal Code
Phone Number
Email Name
Major
Note

### StudentsAndClasses

Student Class ID
Class ID
Student ID
Grade

### Suppliers

Supplier ID
Supplier Name
Contact Name
Contact Title
Address
City
Postal Code
Region
Country
Phone Number
Fax Number
Payment Terms
Note

### Tasks

Task ID
Task Description
Start Date
End Date
Note

### Time Billed

Time Billed ID
Customer ID
Project ID
Employee ID
Billing Date
Hourly Rate
Billable Hours
Note

### Transactions

Transaction ID
Account ID
Payment ID
Transaction Number
Transaction Date
Reference Number
Deposit Amount
Interest Earned
Buy or Sell Date
Buy or Sell Price
Service Charge
Taxable
Note

## Personal

When you select the Personal option button, the Table Wizard presents 19 sample tables that you can use or select fields from to create your new table.

## Accounts

| | | |
|---|---|---|
| Account ID | Account Name | Description |
| Account Number | Account Type | Note |

## Artists

| | | |
|---|---|---|
| Artist ID | Birthdate | Date of Death |
| First Name | Birthplace | Photograph |
| Last Name | Training Location | Note |
| Nationality | | |

## Authors

| | | |
|---|---|---|
| Author ID | Birthdate | Date of Death |
| First Name | Birthplace | Photograph |
| Last Name | Training Location | Note |
| Nationality | Major Influences | |

## Book Collection

| | | |
|---|---|---|
| Book Collection ID | Publisher Name | Date Purchased |
| Author ID | Purchase Price | Pages |
| Title | Edition Number | Shelf Number |
| Copyright Date | Cover Type | Note |
| ISBN Number | | |

## Category

| | | |
|---|---|---|
| Category ID | Category Name | Description |

## Diet Log

| | | |
|---|---|---|
| Diet Log ID | Which Meal | Total Calories |
| Person ID | Grams Carbohydrates | Milligrams Sodium |
| Diet Type | Grams Protein | Vitamins |
| Date Acquired | Grams Fat | Note |

## Exercise Log

Exercise Log ID
Person ID
Activity
Workout Date
Exercise Type
Aerobic or Anaerobic
Time Exercised
Distance Traveled
Resting Pulse
Maximum Pulse
Calories Burned
Hours Sleep
Note

## Friends

Friend ID
First Name
Last Name
Nickname
Spouse Name
Children Names
Address
City
State
Region
Postal Code
Country
Home Phone
Work Phone
Mobile Phone
Fax Number
Alternative Phone
Email Address
CompuServe ID
Birthdate
Date Updated
Date Last Talked To
Hobbies
Health Problems
Photograph
Note

## Guests

Guest ID
Prefix
First Name
Last Name
Spouse Name
Children Names
Address
City
State
Region
Postal Code
Country
Home Phone
Work Phone
Mobile Phone
Fax Number
Alternative Phone
Email Address
Date Updated
Date Last Talked To
Number Attending
Confirmed
Need Daycare
Health Problems
Place Staying
Room Number
Checkin DateTime
Checkout DateTime
Checked In
Gift Given
Thankyou Note Sent
Note

## Household Inventory

Household Inv ID
Item Name
Item Type
Description
Room
Manufacturer
Model
Model Number
Serial Number
Date Purchased
Place Purchased
Purchase Price
Appraised Value
Insured
Note
Photograph

## Investments

Investment ID
Account ID
Security Name
Security Symbol
Security Type
Shares Owned
Action
Type
Clear
Note

## Music Collection

Music Collection ID
Artist ID
Group Name
Title
Recording Label
Year Released
Format
Number of Tracks
Date Purchased
Purchase Price
Note
Photograph
Sample Sound Clip

## Photographs

Photograph ID
Film ID
Date Taken
Time Taken
Place Taken
Subject Name
Subject Address
Subject Phone
Camera
Lens Used
Aperture
Shutter Speed
Filter Used
Flash
Print Size
Note

## Plants

Plant ID
Common Name
Genus
Species
Flowering
Light Preference
Temp Preference
Fertilize Frequency
Watering Frequency
Date Purchased
Place Purchased
Date Planted
Date Repotted
Date Pruned
Date Fertilized
Date Watered
Photograph
Note

## Recipes

Recipe ID
Recipe Name
Recipe Description
Source
Which Meal
Vegetarian
Time To Prepare
Number of Servings
Calories Per Serving
Nutritional Information
Ingredients
Instructions
Quantity On Hand
Note
Photograph

## Rolls Of Film

Film ID
Film Type
Film Speed
Color Film
File Expiration Date
Date Developed
Developed By
Note

## Service Records

Service Record ID
Fixed Asset ID
Service Date
Employee ID
Problem Description
Description
Date Promised
Date Delivered
Received By
Labor Hours
Estimated Cost
Actual Cost
Parts Replaced
Prev Service Date
Next Service Date
Miles Since Last Srvc
Hours Since Last Srvc
Authorized By

## Video Collection

Video Collection ID
Movie Title
Actress ID
Actor ID
Director ID
Producer ID
Year Released
Rating
Subject
Length
Date Acquired
Purchased At
Purchase Price
Review
Sample Video Clip
Note

## Wine List

Wine List ID
Wine Name
Vineyard
Variety
Vintage
Wine Type
Color
Sweet Or Dry
Country Of Origin
Region
Serving Instructions
Percent Alcohol
Note

# Appendix C

# Sample Database Tables

THE examples in this book use the five tables introduced in Chapter 1. If you want to try creating some of these examples yourself, you will want to enter the tables. In the following pages are the tables this book uses. At the beginning of each table is the definition for the table, including field name, data type, description, and other properties that the table and fields use. Following the table definition is the data contained in each table. Field properties not shown are left empty or at their default. The employee pictures were copied from the NWIND sample database included with Access.

## Client Table

### Table Definition

| Field Name | Data Type | Description | Size | Indexed |
|---|---|---|---|---|
| City | Text | | 50 | No |
| Client Id | Counter | Unique client identification number | | Yes |
| Client Name | Text | Name of the amusement park | 50 | No |
| Contact | Text | Contact individual | 50 | No |
| Mailing Address | Text | P.O. Box or other mailing address | 50 | No |
| Park Desc | Memo | Park description and information on other park coasters and planned projects | | No |
| Park Location | Text | Location of park rather than mailing address | 50 | No |
| Phone | Number | | Double | No |
| State | Text | | 50 | No |
| Total Invoices | Currency | | | No |
| Total Payments | Currency | | | No |
| YTD Invoices | Currency | | | No |
| YTD Payments | Currency | | | No |
| Zip Code | Text | | 50 | No |

| Client Id | Client Name<br>Contact<br>Park Location | Mailing Address<br>City, State, Zip Code<br>Phone | YTD Invoices | YTD Payments | Total Invoices | Total Payments |
|---|---|---|---|---|---|---|
| 1 | Family Fun Land<br>Jeff Jackson<br>Isle Royale | P.O. Box 345<br>Houghton, MI 49312<br>6162239999 | $2,500,000 | $2,300,000 | $2,500,000 | $2,300,000 |

**Park Desc:** Large amusement park that has been popular for over 50 years. Only access to the park is by ferry. Three different adult's and two children's coasters are already operational

| Client Id | Client Name<br>Contact<br>Park Location | Mailing Address<br>City, State, Zip Code<br>Phone | YTD Invoices | YTD Payments | Total Invoices | Total Payments |
|---|---|---|---|---|---|---|
| 2 | Teen Land<br>Mary Morris<br>Ashtabula Park | P.O. Box 786<br>Ashtabula, OH 44321<br>2169999090 | $3,900,000 | $1,900,000 | $7,100,900 | $5,100,900 |

**Park Desc:** Turn of the century amusement park with many family riders and some superb coasters

| Client Id | Client Name<br>Contact<br>Park Location | Mailing Address<br>City, State, Zip Code<br>Phone | YTD Invoices | YTD Payments | Total Invoices | Total Payments |
|---|---|---|---|---|---|---|
| 3 | Amusement Technologies<br>Mark Williams<br>Panacea on the Beach | P.O. Box 5346<br>Panacea on the Beach, FL 33012<br>8144444578 | $4,100,000 | $2,000,000 | 11,800,000 | $9,700,000 |

**Park Desc:** This coastal amusement park combines the charm of the Florida landscape with the thrills of its amusement rides.

| Client Id | Client Name<br>Contact<br>Park Location | Mailing Address<br>City, State, Zip Code<br>Phone | YTD Invoices | YTD Payments | Total Invoices | Total Payments |
|---|---|---|---|---|---|---|
| 4 | Arden Entertainment Group<br>Jerry McCellars<br>Indianapolis | 100 Federal Avenue<br>Indianapolis, IN 67821<br>3197777777 | $198,000 | | $198,000 | |

**Park Desc:**

| Client Id | Client Name<br>Contact<br>Park Location | Mailing Address<br>City, State, Zip Code<br>Phone | YTD Invoices | YTD Payments | Total Invoices | Total Payments |
|---|---|---|---|---|---|---|
| 5 | Family Amusements<br>Sally Rogers<br>Stanton | P.O. Box 123548<br>Stanton, PA 78378<br>7173331574 | $1,500,000 | $1,500,000 | $1,500,000 | $1,500,000 |

**Park Desc:**

| Client Id | Client Name<br>Contact<br>Park Location | Mailing Address<br>City, State, Zip Code<br>Phone | YTD Invoices | YTD Payments | Total Invoices | Total Payments |
|---|---|---|---|---|---|---|
| 6 | Playland Consortium<br>Jim Matterson<br>Wheeling | P.O. Box 5839<br>Wheeling, WV 45678<br>3045557824 | $1,800,000 | $1,800,000 | $3,200,000 | $3,200,000 |
| **Park Desc:** | | | | | | |
| 7 | Island Waterplay Inc.<br>Andrea Jacobs<br>Raleigh | 1 Waterplay Lane<br>Raleigh, NC 12378<br>9198881111 | $0 | $0 | $3,100,000 | $2,600,000 |
| **Park Desc:** | | | | | | |
| 8 | Entertainment Plus<br>Charles Winter<br>Jersey City | P.O. Box 4892368<br>Jersey City, NJ 08767<br>7182224444 | | | | |
| **Park Desc:** | | | | | | |

## Employee Table

### Table Definition

| Field Name | Data Type | Description | Size | Format | Caption | Default Value | Indexed |
|---|---|---|---|---|---|---|---|
| Bill Rate | Currency | Hourly client billing rate | | Currency | | | No |
| City | Text | | 20 | | | | No |
| Date of Hire | Date/Time | | | Medium Date | | | No |
| Department | Text | | 12 | | | | No |
| Employee Id | Counter | Employee Identification Number | | | | | Yes |
| Extension | Number | | Double | 000 | Office Ext. | | No |
| First Name | Text | | 15 | > | | | No |
| Home Phone | Text | | 50 | | | | No |
| Job Class | Number | Two digit job class code | Integer | General Number | | | Yes |
| Last Name | Text | | 20 | > | | | No |
| Middle Initial | Text | | 1 | > | | | No |
| Pay Rate | Currency | Hourly pay rate | | Currency | | | No |
| Picture | OLE Object | | | | Photo | | No |
| State | Text | | 2 | | | OH | No |
| Street Address | Text | | 50 | | | | No |
| Zip Code | Text | | 10 | | | | No |

Table Validation Rule: [Bill Rate]>=[Pay Rate]*1.1
Table Validation Text: To make a profit the billing rate must be at least 10% more than the pay rate

**Field Name:** Extension
Validation Rule: [Extension]>0 And [Extension]<3500
Validation Text: Valid Phone extensions are between 1 and 3499

**Field Name:** Job Class
Validation Rule: [Job Class]>9 And [Job Class]<51
Validation Text: Job Class must be between 10 and 50

**Field Name:** Pay Rate
Validation Rule: [Pay Rate]>4.24 And [Pay Rate]<35.01
Validation Text: The pay rate must be between minimum wage and $35 hr.

| Employee Id | First Name, Middle Initial, Last Name<br>Street Address<br>City, State, Zip Code<br>Home Phone | | | Pay Rate | Bill Rate | Date of Hire | Job Class | Department | Office Ext. |
|---|---|---|---|---|---|---|---|---|---|
| 1 | William<br>111 Cedar Ave.<br>Cleveland, OH 44123<br>(216)413-2222 | W. | Wild | $35.00 | $60.00 | 15-Mar-92 | 11 | Design | 234 |
| 2 | Dan<br>51 Mentor Ave.<br>Mentor, OH 44231<br>(216)591-1111 | D. | Danger | $30.00 | $50.00 | 17-Jan-87 | 41 | Testing | 1703 |

| Employee Id | First Name, Middle Initial, Last Name<br>Street Address<br>City, State, Zip Code<br>Home Phone | | | Pay Rate | Bill Rate | Date of Hire | Job Class | Department | Office Ext. |
|---|---|---|---|---|---|---|---|---|---|
| 3 | Rodger<br>886 Larch Street<br>Cleveland, OH 43212<br>(216)765-9999 | R. | Rolling | $33.00 | $55.00 | 15-Apr-90 | 22 | Design | 876 |
| 4 | Sandra<br>1232 Hillside Rd<br>Gates Mills, OH 44040<br>(216)889-8888 | S. | Scary | $31.00 | $50.00 | 01-Feb-92 | 21 | Design | 567 |
| 5 | Harry<br>321 Wood Ave.<br>Mayfield, OH 44120<br>(216)765-7777 | H. | Higher | $6.50 | $10.00 | 16-May-90 | 32 | Construction | 3499 |
| 6 | Tommy<br>213 25th St.<br>Cleveland, OH 44037<br>(216)444-5555 | T. | Thrill | $7.00 | $10.00 | 07-Jun-88 | 33 | Construction | 543 |
| 7 | Richard<br>45 Eagle Lane<br>Solon, OH 44019<br>(216)333-1111 | R. | Rock | $8.00 | $10.00 | 03-Apr-89 | 31 | Construction | 876 |
| 8 | Donna<br>111 Weaver Ave<br>Columbus, OH 43514<br>(614)555-6666 | D. | Dare | $35.00 | $75.00 | 05-Mar-91 | 12 | Design | 321 |
| 9 | Johnny<br>78 Fordham Dri<br>Austinburg, OH 42124<br>(216)777-2222 | J. | Jump | $6.50 | $10.00 | 06-Nov-90 | 31 | Construction | 1098 |
| 10 | Brenda<br>21 Circle Drive<br>Gates Mills, OH 44040<br>(216)999-9999 | B. | Brave | $32.00 | $55.00 | 06-Dec-87 | 41 | Testing | 1230 |

William Wild's picture is a copy of Andrew Fuller's picture in the NWind sample database.
Harry Higher's picture is a copy of Michael Suyama's picture in the NWind sample database.

## Employee Time Log

### Table Definition

| Field Name | Data Type | Description | Size | Indexed |
|---|---|---|---|---|
| Date | Date | First day of the week | | Yes |
| Employee Id | Number | Matches up with Employee Id in the Employee table | Long Integer | Yes |
| Project Number | Number | Matches up with Coaster Id in the Project table | Long Integer | Yes |
| Hours | Number | Number of hours spent on project | Integer | No |

| Date | Employee Id | Project Number | Hours |
|---|---|---|---|
| 6/12/94 | 1 | 1 | 20 |
| 6/12/94 | 1 | 4 | 12 |
| 6/12/94 | 1 | 7 | 8 |
| 6/12/94 | 2 | 2 | 35 |
| 6/12/94 | 2 | 3 | 5 |
| 6/12/94 | 3 | 5 | 40 |
| 6/12/94 | 4 | 5 | 40 |
| 6/12/94 | 5 | 3 | 18 |
| 6/12/94 | 5 | 4 | 6 |
| 6/12/94 | 5 | 8 | 13 |
| 6/12/94 | 6 | 4 | 2 |
| 6/12/94 | 6 | 5 | 38 |
| 6/12/94 | 7 | 2 | 40 |
| 6/12/94 | 8 | 5 | 15 |
| 6/12/94 | 8 | 6 | 25 |
| 6/12/94 | 9 | 2 | 40 |
| 6/12/94 | 10 | 2 | 40 |
| 6/19/94 | 1 | 1 | 4 |
| 6/19/94 | 1 | 5 | 36 |
| 6/19/94 | 2 | 2 | 28 |
| 6/19/94 | 2 | 7 | 12 |
| 6/19/94 | 3 | 5 | 40 |
| 6/19/94 | 4 | 5 | 20 |
| 6/19/94 | 4 | 6 | 20 |
| 6/19/94 | 5 | 2 | 30 |
| 6/19/94 | 5 | 8 | 10 |
| 6/19/94 | 6 | 4 | 40 |
| 6/19/94 | 7 | 2 | 40 |
| 6/19/94 | 8 | 6 | 40 |
| 6/19/94 | 9 | 2 | 40 |
| 6/19/94 | 10 | 2 | 40 |

## Invoice Register Table

### Table Definition

| Field Name | Data Type | Description | Size | Indexed |
|---|---|---|---|---|
| Invoice Amount | Currency | | | No |
| Invoice Date | Date/Time | | | No |
| Invoice Number | Number | | Double | Yes |
| Payment Amount | Currency | | | No |
| Payment Date | Date/Time | | | No |
| Project Id | Number | Matches up with Coaster Id in the Project table | Long Integer | Yes |

| Invoice Number | Invoice Date | Invoice Amount | Payment Amount | Payment Date | Project Id |
|---|---|---|---|---|---|
| 975 | 2/1/91 | $500,000 | $500,000 | 3/13/91 | 9 |
| 986 | 4/1/91 | $2,000,000 | $2,000,000 | 6/2/91 | 9 |
| 1001 | 11/1/91 | $500,000 | $500,000 | 2/19/92 | 9 |
| 1005 | 3/30/92 | $1,500,000 | $1,500,000 | 4/15/92 | 8 |
| 1012 | 6/30/92 | $200,900 | $200,900 | 7/28/92 | 9 |
| 1018 | 10/31/92 | $1,100,000 | $1,100,000 | 3/16/93 | 8 |
| 1021 | 12/31/92 | $250,000 | $250,000 | 2/16/93 | 3 |
| 1030 | 3/31/93 | $400,000 | $400,000 | 5/15/93 | 7 |
| 1056 | 6/30/93 | $500,000 | $0 | | 8 |
| 1057 | 6/30/93 | $500,000 | $500,000 | 7/28/93 | 1 |
| 1058 | 7/30/93 | $2,750,000 | $2,750,000 | 9/7/93 | 3 |
| 1059 | 8/30/93 | $1,000,000 | $1,000,000 | 9/26/93 | 7 |
| 1062 | 10/31/93 | $1,200,000 | $1,200,000 | 12/20/93 | 1 |
| 1063 | 10/31/93 | $3,000,000 | $3,000,000 | 12/21/93 | 3 |
| 1068 | 1/31/94 | $400,000 | $400,000 | 2/13/94 | 4 |
| 1070 | 1/31/94 | $350,000 | $350,000 | 4/5/94 | 6 |
| 1071 | 1/31/94 | $300,000 | $300,000 | 2/20/94 | 4 |
| 1072 | 3/1/94 | $200,000 | $0 | | 4 |
| 1073 | 3/1/94 | $400,000 | $400,000 | 6/2/94 | 2 |
| 1074 | 3/1/94 | $1,600,000 | $1,600,000 | 4/6/94 | 4 |
| 1078 | 4/1/94 | $1,700,000 | $1,700,000 | 5/4/94 | 1 |
| 1085 | 5/1/94 | $1,150,000 | $1,150,000 | 7/19/94 | 6 |
| 1092 | 6/1/94 | $600,000 | $300,000 | 7/16/94 | 1 |
| 1093 | 6/1/94 | $198,000 | $0 | | 5 |
| 1094 | 6/1/94 | $1,500,000 | $1,500,000 | 7/18/94 | 2 |
| 2005 | 7/1/94 | $1,800,000 | $0 | | 3 |
| 2006 | 7/1/94 | $1,800,000 | $1,800,000 | 7/30/94 | 7 |
| 2011 | 8/1/94 | $2,000,000 | $0 | | 2 |

## Project Table

### Table Definition

| Field Name | Data Type | Description | Size | Format | Indexed |
|---|---|---|---|---|---|
| Actual Cost | Currency | Actual labor and material costs | | | No |
| Angle | Number | Greatest angle of descent | Double | | No |
| Capacity | Number | Maximum number of riders in 1 hour | Double | | No |
| Client Id | Number | Number from client table | Long Integer | | Yes |
| Coaster Id | Counter | Unique coaster identification number | | | Yes |
| Coaster Name | Text | Name of coaster ride | 50 | | No |
| Completed | Yes/No | Completed project | | Yes/No | No |
| Drop | Number | Maximum drop | Double | | No |
| Est Cost | Currency | Projected out of pocket cost for labor and material | | | No |
| Features | Memo | Unique features of the ride | | | No |
| Height | Number | Maximum height | Double | | No |
| Operational | Date/Time | Projected or actual operational date | | | No |
| Picture | OLE Object | Picture of model or operational ride | | | No |
| Speed | Number | Greatest speed in mph | Double | | No |
| Time | Number | Length of ride in minutes | Double | | No |
| Track | Number | Length of ride track | Double | | No |
| Vehicles | Number | Total number of vehicles | Double | | No |

**Coaster Id:** 1
**Coaster Name:** Scream Machine
**Client Id:** 3
**Completed:** No
**Operational:** 10/5/95
**Est Cost:** $7,800,000.00
**Actual Cost:** $4,000,000.00

| | | | |
|---|---|---|---|
| **Track:** | 5780 | **Time:** | 2.8 |
| **Height:** | 168 | **Speed:** | 70 |
| **Drop:** | 160 | **Capacity:** | 1800 |
| **Angle:** | 54 | **Vehicles:** | 3 |

**Features:** All wood coaster with steep drops and many curves. Each train holds 28 passengers

**Picture:**

**Coaster Id:** 2
**Coaster Name:** Blue Arrow
**Client Id:** 2
**Completed:** No
**Operational:** 8/21/94
**Est Cost:** $4,000,000.00
**Actual Cost:** $3,900,000.00

**Picture:**

| | | | |
|---|---|---|---|
| **Track:** | 5200 | **Time:** | 2 |
| **Height:** | 205 | **Speed:** | 73 |
| **Drop:** | 182 | **Capacity:** | 2300 |
| **Angle:** | 60 | **Vehicles:** | 6 |

**Features:** Steep 60 degree first hill drop on this steel tubular track coaster with fiberglass cars each holding 36 passengers

**Coaster Id:** 3
**Coaster Name:** Astro Transport
**Client Id:** 3
**Completed:** Yes
**Operational:** 5/22/94
**Est Cost:** $7,500,000.00
**Actual Cost:** $7,800,000.00

**Picture:**

| | | | |
|---|---|---|---|
| **Track:** | 2000 | **Time:** | 2 |
| **Height:** | 68 | **Speed:** | 50 |
| **Drop:** | 30 | **Capacity:** | 1900 |
| **Angle:** | 58 | **Vehicles:** | 5 |

**Features:** Special effects are the highlight of this space age transport

**Coaster Id:** 4
**Coaster Name:** Red Dragon
**Client Id:** 1
**Completed:** No
**Operational:** 4/16/95
**Est Cost:** $4,500,000.00
**Actual Cost:** $2,500,000.00

**Picture:**

| | | | |
|---|---|---|---|
| **Track:** | 2950 | **Time:** | 1.9 |
| **Height:** | 78 | **Speed:** | 42 |
| **Drop:** | 60 | **Capacity:** | 2000 |
| **Angle:** | 48 | **Vehicles:** | 3 |

**Features:** Each suspended train holds 28 passengers. Gravity causes side to side sway. Pretzel loop over the lake is a real thrill.

**Coaster Id:** 5
**Coaster Name:** Taurus
**Client Id:** 4
**Completed:** No
**Operational:** 6/1/96
**Est Cost:** $4,500,000.00
**Actual Cost:** $198,000.00

**Picture:**

| | | | |
|---|---|---|---|
| **Track:** | 4200 | **Time:** | 2.5 |
| **Height:** | 135 | **Speed:** | 65 |
| **Drop:** | 119 | **Capacity:** | 3500 |
| **Angle:** | 56 | **Vehicles:** | 6 |

**Features:** All wood coaster with 30 passenger trains that run continuously

**Coaster Id:** 6
**Coaster Name:** Corker
**Client Id:** 5
**Completed:** No
**Operational:** 7/5/95
**Est Cost:** $2,500,000.00
**Actual Cost:** $1,500,000.00

**Picture:**

| | | | |
|---|---|---|---|
| **Track:** | 1980 | **Time:** | 2 |
| **Height:** | 100 | **Speed:** | 50 |
| **Drop:** | 85 | **Capacity:** | 1800 |
| **Angle:** | 54 | **Vehicles:** | 3 |

**Features:** Triple loop coaster provides an upside thrill at three points in the 360 degree vertical loops and helical curves require riders to wear shoulder straps

**Coaster Id:** 7
**Coaster Name:** Wild One
**Client Id:** 6
**Completed:** No
**Operational:** 9/16/94
**Est Cost:** $3,900,000.00
**Actual Cost:** $3,200,000.00

**Picture:**

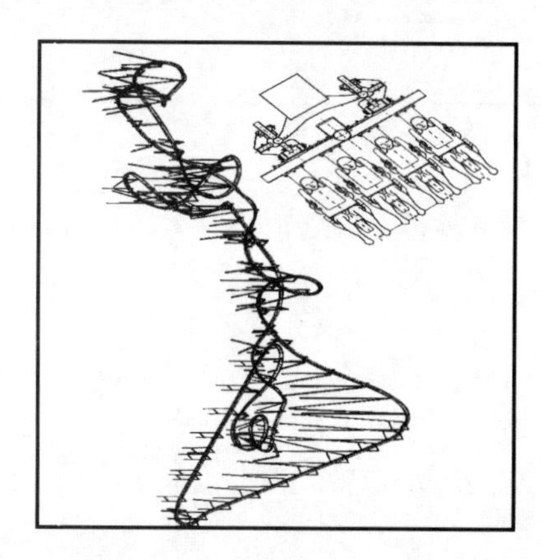

| | | | |
|---|---|---|---|
| **Track:** | 1895 | **Time:** | 1.5 |
| **Height:** | 100 | **Speed:** | 50 |
| **Drop:** | 87 | **Capacity:** | 1000 |
| **Angle:** | 52 | **Vehicles:** | 7 |

**Features:** The four passenger trains can move quickly through sharp turns accentuating speed and turn sensations

**Coaster Id:** 8
**Coaster Name:** White Lightnin
**Client Id:** 7
**Completed:** Yes
**Operational:** 2/15/93
**Est Cost:** $2,800,000.00
**Actual Cost:** $3,100,000.00

**Picture:**

| | | | |
|---|---|---|---|
| **Track:** | 2600 | **Time:** | 2.8 |
| **Height:** | 68 | **Speed:** | 50 |
| **Drop:** | 60 | **Capacity:** | 2500 |
| **Angle:** | 48 | **Vehicles:** | 5 |

**Features:** Sharp spiral turns and splashing water make this ride popular

**Coaster Id:** 9
**Coaster Name:** The Runaway
**Client Id:** 2
**Completed:** Yes
**Operational:** 3/28/92
**Est Cost:** $3,215,000.00
**Actual Cost:** $3,200,900.00

**Picture:**

| | | | |
|---|---|---|---|
| **Track:** | 2675 | **Time:** | 1.75 |
| **Height:** | 120 | **Speed:** | 46 |
| **Drop:** | 100 | **Capacity:** | 1350 |
| **Angle:** | 53 | **Vehicles:** | 2 |

**Features:** Twenty four passengers experience negative G force through exciting dips

# Appendix D

SQL in Access

The SELECT SQL Statement

# Notes for SQL Users

SQL, or Structured Query Language, is a language that is designed to work with relational databases like Access. SQL queries data, updates data, and manages the data in a database. Whether or not you realize it, you have used SQL every time you created a query. Other database management products also can use SQL. Access supports a subset of SQL statements that you will find adequate for many tasks. You can use SQL statements to select the data you want to use.

Microsoft has an SQL server that you can use to store your databases. SQL databases are relational databases that let you access the data over several platforms. You can use the tables you store in the SQL server by attaching the SQL tables to an Access database. For example, you might have an SQL server to store your database and use Microsoft Access to work with the data.

## SQL in Access

Microsoft Access can use SQL statements in several locations. SQL statements are used in queries to describe the data the query presents. SQL statements can select the items that appear in list boxes and combo boxes. You can use SQL statements that choose the data that appears in forms and reports. You can run SQL statements in macros as well as use parts of SQL statements for other actions in a macro. Procedures in modules also use SQL statements, although the features they provide are beyond the introduction to programming presented in Chapter 19.

### SQL Statements in Queries

The SQL statement Microsoft Access uses in a query is a statement that defines the data the query uses and the results this query presents. You do not have to create this SQL statement; Access does it for you. Access takes the query design you create in the query design window and creates an SQL statement that represents the results you want the query to present. You can see this SQL statement by selecting SQL from the View menu or by clicking the SQL View button in Access version 2's toolbar when looking at a query's design. A sample SQL statement might look like this:

```
SELECT DISTINCTROW [Employee Time Log].Date, [Employee Time
Log].[Employee Id], [Employee Time Log].[Project Number],
[Employee Time Log].Hours, Employee.[First Name],
Employee.[Last Name], Employee.[Bill Rate]
FROM Employee, INNER JOIN [Employee Time Log] ON
Employee.[Employee Id] = [Employee Time Log].[Employee Id]
WHERE ((([Employee Time Log].Date)=#06/12/94#))
WITH OWNERACCESS OPTION;
```

This particular SQL statement is for the Employee Names and Hours query shown in Chapter 7 as an example of using two tables in a query. An SQL statement like the one shown here can continue for several lines, since it is the semicolon at the end that indicates the end of the statement. When looking at the SQL query, you can copy it by pressing CTRL+INS just as you would copy other entries that you edit. You may want to copy the SQL statement so that you can use it to select the items that appear in a list or combo box control of a report. You can change the SQL statement, and Access will modify the query design to match any changes you have made. If you are not familiar with SQL, use the query design window to design a query that lets Access make the conversion between the query design and the SQL statement that defines the query.

Most of the queries you create use the SELECT SQL statement, which is described in the last section in this appendix. The append, delete, and update action queries use other SQL statements. These SQL statements are INSERT INTO for append queries, DELETE for delete queries, and UPDATE for update queries.

Access version 2 introduced several features for SQL statements. When you are at a property in the property sheet that can use an SQL statement, clicking the Build button opens a query design window to create the SQL statement to use as the property. When you look at the SQL statement for a query in Access version 2, Access changes the query design window to SQL view, which shows the SQL statement for the query. You can continue to switch to other windows and use the menus. You can add an SQL statement in a Criteria or Field row of a query design to be a subquery. Subqueries in the Criteria row select the records to appear in the query and subqueries in the Field row select the field entries for the query. You can create union queries using the Union Query

Wizard. Union queries use SQL statements to combine tables into one query rather than appending the tables together.

Another new type of query that uses SQL statements is a data definition query. Data definition queries create, change, or delete tables and indexes. You create these queries by choosing SQL Specific from the Query menu and Data Definition, and then typing the SQL statements to perform as the data definition query. You can also pass through SQL statements directly to ODBC databases that improve the connectivity in client-server environments. This lets you send SQL statements that are not normally part of a query to the ODBC database server. Create a pass-through query by choosing SQL Specific from the Query menu and Data Definition, and then typing the SQL statement to perform. You will also need to change the ODBC Connect Str property to the connection string to connect to the SQL database.

## SQL Statements in List and Combo Box Controls

List box and combo box controls can use SQL statements to select the items that Access presents in the list boxes and controls. To use an SQL statement for a list box and combo box control, supply the SQL statement for the Row Source property of the list box and combo box control either by typing the SQL statement directly or by copying the statement from the Clipboard. In Access version 2, you can click the Build button to open a query design window to create the query and SQL statement that selects the data to show in the list box or combo box. Often you will create the SQL statement from a query design window. In Access version 1, you will copy the SQL statement from the query design and then paste it into a form's list box or combo box control's Row Source property. The results of the SQL statement are the contents in the list of the list box or combo box control. An example of an SQL statement provided for the Row Source property is

```
SELECT Client.[Client Name], Client.[Client Id] FROM Client
```

The Row Source Type property is set to Table/Query. This sample SQL statement includes the client names and numbers from the Client table in the list box.

## Using SQL Statements for a Form or Report

Forms and reports can use an SQL statement as the Record Source property of the form or report. When you use an SQL statement as the Record Source property, the form or report includes the records that the SQL statement selects. You can use the SQL statement from a query as the Record Source property, and the results are the same as they would be if you created a query that used the same SQL statement and used that query as the Record Source property of the form or report. Using an SQL statement for a Record Source property means you do not have to create a query that will only be used for one form or report.

## Using SQL Statements in a Macro

Macros can include SQL statements as actions or arguments. To run an SQL statement in a macro, use the RunSQL action. This action has a single argument, the SQL statement that the RunSQL action performs. An example of an SQL statement entered for this purpose is

```
SELECT Client.[Client Name], Client.[Client Id],
Client.Contact INTO [Temporary Client] FROM Client
```

This creates a new table named Temporary Client that contains the values from three fields from each of the records.

Several macro actions use part of SQL statements for their Where Condition action argument. The information for the argument is an expression—the same expression an SQL SELECT statement uses to choose which records the statement chooses. The SQL statement for an ApplyFilter action's Where Condition argument selects the records that the filter displays. An SQL statement for an OpenForm or OpenReport action's Where Condition argument selects the records included in the form or report.

## SQL Statements in Modules

SQL statements in modules usually are for advanced features beyond the basics of modules, which were presented in Chapter 19. Procedures use SQL statements for various reasons. Here are several:

- The CreateSnapshot method for databases, record sets, or QueryDef objects can use SQL statements to choose the data that appears in the snapshot object this method creates.
- The Filter property of dynaset and snapshot objects can be set to part of an SQL statement. This is just like the parts of SQL statements that the Where Condition argument uses for various macro actions. When you use part of an SQL statement for the Filter property of these objects, you are selecting which records in these objects are selected.
- The SQL property of QueryDef objects uses SQL statements to set the records selected by a query definition object.
- You want to use a longer SQL statement than the 256-character limit available to the RUNSQL macro action. SQL statements in procedures can be up to 32,768 characters. The SQL statement from the Employee and Employee Time Log query shown earlier in this chapter is too long to be a macro's argument, but you can include it in a procedure without a problem.

## The SELECT SQL Statement

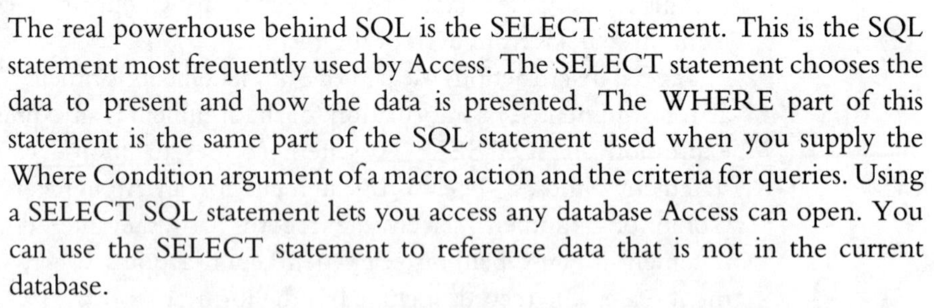

The real powerhouse behind SQL is the SELECT statement. This is the SQL statement most frequently used by Access. The SELECT statement chooses the data to present and how the data is presented. The WHERE part of this statement is the same part of the SQL statement used when you supply the Where Condition argument of a macro action and the criteria for queries. Using a SELECT SQL statement lets you access any database Access can open. You can use the SELECT statement to reference data that is not in the current database.

Like all SQL statements, the SELECT statement ends with a semicolon. Using this character to end statements means you can use multiple lines in a single statement. Access knows that it has reached the end of the statement when it finds the semicolon.

After SELECT is the data you want to return. For each field to appear in the data returned, supply the table or query name (in brackets if the name includes spaces) and a period. Then enter the name of the field, enclosed in brackets if the field name includes spaces. An example is Employee.[First Name]. These field names are separated by commas. If you want a field renamed, follow the field description with the word AS and the new field name, enclosed in brackets if it includes spaces. You can use an asterisk (*) in place of a field name when you want to include all fields from the chosen table. The order of the fields in the SELECT statement is the order of the fields returned by this statement.

You may see DISTINCTROW in the SELECT statements before the field names. DISTINCTROW is a *reserved word,* a word that has a special meaning to SQL and that you cannot use for other purposes. Other reserved words you may see in a SELECT statement include ALL, DISTINCT, and TOP.

Next, the SELECT statement describes the source of the data by the word FROM and the tables or query names that provide the source of data. These table and query names are separated by commas, and the names must be enclosed in brackets when the name includes spaces. If the database containing the tables is not the current database, enter **IN** followed by the database name to include data from the outside database in the results of the SQL statement.

In the example given at the beginning of the chapter, Access included INNER JOIN to link the tables. Following INNER JOIN is the name of one of the tables or queries, and then ON followed by the expression that links the two tables or queries. In the example, the records from the two tables are joined by the Employee ID fields of the Employee table and the Employee Time Log table.

The WHERE part of a SELECT statement selects the records from the tables that appear in the statement's results. WHERE is followed by an expression that chooses the records you want to see. The information after WHERE is similar to the entries in the Criteria rows in the QBE grid. Since everything needed for a query is explicitly provided in the SQL SELECT statement, you will see ANDs to indicate the parts of the criteria that are located on the same line and ORs to indicate the parts of the criteria that are located on separate lines in the QBE grid.

GROUP BY creates groups of records according to the common values of the fields you place after GROUP BY. ORDER BY indicates how the records that the SELECT statement chooses are organized. The ORDER BY clause provides the information that appears in the Sort row of the QBE grid.

# Appendix E

Working with the Toolbars

Access' Built-in Toolbars

# Toolbar Reference

ACCESS version 2 has many toolbars that you will use. This appendix shows the different Access environments and the toolbars that appear for each one. Next to each button is a description of the function that the button performs.

In addition to using the built-in toolbars, you can edit these built-in toolbars or create your own. These steps are also explained.

## Working with the Toolbars

Toolbars are simply sets of buttons that you can select to carry out a command or to use an Access feature. The advantage to toolbars is that they are fast and easy to use.

In Access version 2, the toolbar feature is greatly expanded. You can display several toolbars at once and you can create and modify toolbars. You can also change where toolbars appear on the screen by dragging them.

### Setting Toolbar Display

1. Select Toolbars from the View menu or right-click an empty spot on a toolbar and select Toolbars from the shortcut menu.
2. Highlight a toolbar in the Toolbars list box and select Hide or Show to choose to display or conceal it. Toolbars that will be shown have a check mark in front of them.
3. Clear the Color Buttons check box to have Access display the buttons in shades of gray instead of using color.
4. Select Large Buttons to have Access use a larger button that can be more easily seen. You may need to customize your toolbars if you plan to use this feature, so that you can see all of the buttons on the toolbars. You

won't want to use this feature unless you have a fairly high-resolution monitor.

5. Select Show ToolTips to have Access display a small box with the name of the button when you point the mouse at the button for a few seconds.
6. Select New to create a new toolbar. Access prompts you for the name of the new toolbar. After you select OK, this new toolbar is added to the Toolbars list box. To add buttons to this new toolbar, you need to edit it, as described in the next section, "Editing a Toolbar."

   Access' built-in toolbars, including any changes you make to them, are available to all of your databases. The toolbars you create from scratch are only available in the database that is open when you create it.
7. Select Customize to edit the highlighted toolbar. The steps for editing a toolbar are described under "Editing a Toolbar."
8. Select Rename to rename the highlighted custom toolbar. Type a new name for the toolbar and select OK. You cannot rename the built-in toolbars.
9. Select Delete to remove the highlighted custom toolbar. You cannot delete the built-in toolbars.
10. Select Reset to remove all of your changes from one of the built-in toolbars.
11. Select Close to close the Toolbars dialog box and display only the toolbars selected in the Toolbars list box.

## Editing a Toolbar

1. Display the toolbar you want to modify.
2. Select Toolbars from the View menu or right-click an empty spot on a toolbar and select Toolbars from the shortcut menu.
3. Select Customize.
4. Select the category of buttons or other database objects you want to assign to the toolbar from the Categories list box. The buttons for each category appear in the Buttons box on the right.

**tip:** *If you point the mouse at the displayed buttons, you will see the Status Bar text associated with it in the Description box, and its name in a ToolTip box.*

5. Drag a button or object to the place on the toolbar where you want it to appear.

   When you drag a button to the toolbar, that button appears in that location on the toolbar. You can add buttons for individual database objects such as for opening specific tables, queries, forms, and reports or for running macros. To add these items, select All Tables, All Queries, All Forms, All Reports, or All Macros in the Categories list box and the specific object for the object type in the Objects list box. When you select a database object, the button that appears in the toolbar uses the icon for the object's type.

**tip:** *You can choose different faces for existing buttons by right-clicking the button and selecting Choose Button Face. You can't do this for database objects, but only for pre-created buttons.*

   You can delete a button by dragging it off of the toolbar.

   If you want to create a new toolbar, simply drag a button or database object outside the Customize Toolbars dialog box and release it. Access creates a toolbar named Custom Toolbar #, where # is a sequentially assigned number, to hold the button. You can later rename the toolbar.

6. When the toolbar looks the way you want it, select Close.

## Moving Toolbars

In Access version 2, you can easily move toolbars around on the screen so they fit where you want them. To drag a toolbar, simply point to a blank location on it and drag it to a new location. When you pull the toolbar toward the center of the window, it becomes a window. You have seen the toolbox and Palette toolbars displayed in this fashion. When you drag a toolbar close to one of the edges of the window, it snaps to the window's border, just like it snaps to the top border of the window by default.

# Access' Built-In Toolbars

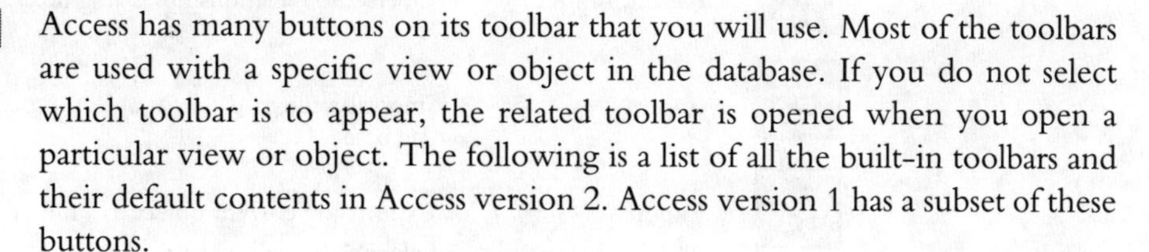

Access has many buttons on its toolbar that you will use. Most of the toolbars are used with a specific view or object in the database. If you do not select which toolbar is to appear, the related toolbar is opened when you open a particular view or object. The following is a list of all the built-in toolbars and their default contents in Access version 2. Access version 1 has a subset of these buttons.

Some of the toolbars are very similar, such as the Table and Query Datasheet view toolbars and the Form and Report Design view toolbars. These toolbars are given together, because there is so little difference between them.

## Database Window

| Button | Button Name | Description |
|---|---|---|
| | New Database | Closes the current database and creates a new one |
| | Open Database | Closes the current database and opens another one |
| | Attach Table | Attaches an external table to the current database |
| | Print | Prints the object currently selected in the Database window |
| | Print Preview | Shows how the currently selected object will appear when printed |
| | Code | Opens the Module window for the currently selected report or form |
| | Cut | Cuts the selected object to the Clipboard |
| | Copy | Copies the selected object to the Clipboard |
| | Paste | Pastes the contents of the Clipboard into the currently selected object |

| Button | Button Name | Description |
|---|---|---|
| 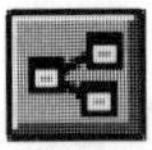 | Relationships | Opens the Relationships dialog box |
|  | Import | Imports a file or database object into the current database |
|  | Export | Exports the current object to a file or another database |
|  | Merge It | Starts the Microsoft Word Mail Merge Wizard, to merge the data in the selected object with a Microsoft Word document |
|  | Analyze It with MS Excel | Starts Excel and displays the data of the current object as an Excel worksheet |
|  | New Query | Creates a new query based on the query or table selected in the Database window, if one is selected |
| 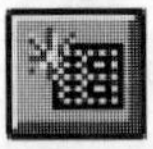 | New Form | Creates a new form based on the query or table selected in the Database window, if one is selected |
| 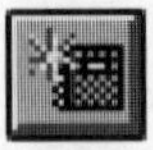 | New Report | Creates a new report based on the query or table selected in the Database window, if one is selected |
|  | Database Window | Restores the Database window |
|  | AutoForm | Creates a simple form based on the selected table or query |
|  | AutoReport | Creates a simple report based on the selected table or query |
|  | Undo | Undoes your most recent action |
|  | Cue Cards | Displays the main menu for the Cue Cards, which coach you through tasks |
|  | Help | Opens Microsoft Access Help showing information based on the next item you click |

## Relationships

| Button | Button Name | Description |
|---|---|---|
| 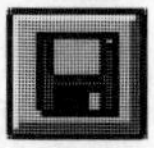 | Save | Saves the layout of elements in the Relationships dialog box |
|  | Add Table | Adds a table to the Relationships window |
|  | Show Direct Relationships | Shows relationships with the currently selected table |
| 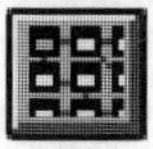 | Show All Relationships | Shows all relationships in the database |
|  | Database Window | Switches back to the Database window |
|  | Cue Cards | Displays the main menu for the Cue Cards, which coach you through tasks |
|  | Help | Opens Microsoft Access Help showing information based on the next item you click |

## Table Design

| Button | Button Name | Description |
|---|---|---|
|  | Design View | Switches you to the Design view of a table, query, or form |
|  | Datasheet View | Switches you to the Datasheet view of a table, query, or form |
| 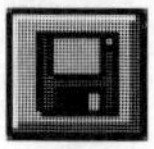 | Save | Saves the current table design |
|  | Properties | Displays or conceals the property sheet for the selected field |
|  | Indexes | Displays or hides the Indexes window, used to index fields in the table |
| 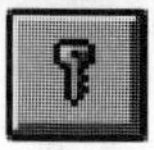 | Set Primary Key | Makes the selected field or fields the primary key for the table |

| Button | Button Name | Description |
|---|---|---|
| | Insert Row | Inserts a row for a new field above the row containing the insertion point |
| | Delete Row | Deletes the row containing the insertion point |
| | New Query | Creates a new query based on the current table |
| | New Form | Creates a new form based on the current table |
| | New Report | Creates a new report based on the current table |
| | Database Window | Restores the Database window |
| ... | Build | Invokes a builder for the current object |
| | Undo | Undoes your most recent action |
| | Cue Cards | Displays the main menu for the Cue Cards, which coach you through tasks |
| | Help | Opens Microsoft Access Help showing information based on the next item you click |

## Table and Query Datasheet View

| Button | Button Name | Description |
|---|---|---|
| | Design View | Switches to the Design view of a table or query |
| SQL | SQL View (Queries Only) | Switches to the SQL view of a query |
| | Datasheet View | Switches to the Datasheet view of a table or query |
| | Print | Prints the datasheet |

| Button | Button Name | Description |
|---|---|---|
|  | Print Preview | Displays the datasheet as it will appear when printed |
|  | New | Moves the insertion point to the blank record at the end of the datasheet |
|  | Cut | Cuts the selection to the Clipboard |
|  | Copy | Copies the selection to the Clipboard |
|  | Paste | Pastes the contents of the Clipboard into the current location |
|  | Find | Opens the Find dialog box, allowing you to search the active table or dynaset for the data you specify |
|  | Sort Ascending (Table only) | Sorts the records according to the current field from lowest to highest values |
|  | Sort Descending (Table only) | Sorts the records according to the current field from highest to lowest values |
|  | Edit Filter/Sort (Table only) | Opens the Filter window used to define how you want Access to sort or select records to appear |
|  | Apply Filter/Sort (Table only) | Applies the currently defined filter |
| 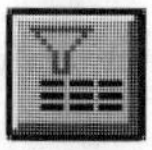 | Show All Records (Table only) | Removes the current filter to display all records |
|  | New Query | Creates a new query based on the current table or query |
| 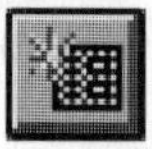 | New Form | Creates a new form based on the current table or query |
| 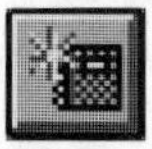 | New Report | Creates a new report based on the current table or query |
|  | Database Window | Switches to the Database window |

| Button | Button Name | Description |
|---|---|---|
|  | AutoForm | Creates a simple form based on the current table or query |
|  | AutoReport | Creates a simple report based on the current table or query |
|  | Undo Current Field/Record | Undoes all changes to the current field or record since you started editing the record |
|  | Undo | Undoes your most recent action |
|  | Cue Cards | Displays the main menu for the Cue Cards, which coach you through tasks |
|  | Help | Opens Microsoft Access Help showing information based on the item you click next |

## Query Design View

| Button | Button Name | Description |
|---|---|---|
|  | Design View | Switches you to the Design view of a table, query, or form |
|  | SQL View | Switches you to the SQL view of a query |
|  | Datasheet View | Switches you to the Datasheet view of a table, query, or form |
|  | Save | Saves the current query design |
|  | Run | Runs a query, or, in a macro window, a macro |
|  | Properties | Displays or conceals the property sheet |
|  | Add Table | Adds a table to the query design |
|  | Totals | Displays or conceals the Totals row in the QBE grid |

| Button | Button Name | Description |
|---|---|---|
|  | Table Names | Adds the Table Names row to the QBE grid |
|  | Select Query | Makes the current query a select query |
| 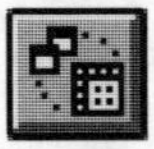 | Crosstab Query | Makes the current query a crosstab query |
|  | Make-Table Query | Makes the current query a make-table action query |
|  | Update Query | Makes the current query an update action query |
| 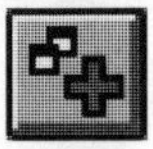 | Append Query | Makes the current query an append action query |
|  | Delete Query | Makes the current query a delete action query |
|  | New Query | Creates a new query based on the current query |
|  | New Form | Creates a new form based on the current query |
| 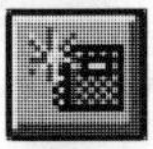 | New Report | Creates a new report based on the current query |
|  | Database Window | Switches back to the Database window |
|  | Build | Invokes a builder for the current selection |
|  | Undo | Undoes your most recent action |
|  | Cue Cards | Displays the main menu for the Cue Cards, which coach you through tasks |
|  | Help | Opens Microsoft Access Help showing information based on the item you click next |

## Form or Report Design View

| Button | Button Name | Description |
|---|---|---|
| | Design View | Switches you to the Design view of a form or report |
| | Form View (Forms only) | Switches you to the Form view of a form |
| | Datasheet View (Forms Only) | Switches you to the Datasheet view of a form |
| | Save | Saves the current form or report design |
| | Print Preview | Shows how the current form or report will appear when printed |
| | Sample Preview (Reports Only) | Displays a sample preview of the report |
| | Sorting and Grouping (Reports Only) | Conceals or displays the Sorting and Grouping window to let you select how you want to sort and group data for your report |
| | Properties | Displays or conceals the property sheet for the selected control or section of the form or report |
| | Field List | Conceals or displays a window listing all fields in the underlying table or query |
| | Code | Opens the Module window for the form or report |
| | Toolbox | Displays the toolbox |
| | Palette | Displays or conceals the Palette |
| MS Sans Serif | Font Name | Selects the font for the selected control |
| 8 | Font Size | Selects the size of the font for the selected control |

| Button | Button Name | Description |
| --- | --- | --- |
|  | Bold | Makes the text in the selected control bold |
|  | Italic | Makes the text in the selected control italic |
|  | Left-Align Text | Left-aligns the text in the selected control |
|  | Center-Align Text | Centers the text in the selected control |
|  | Right-Align Text | Right-aligns the text in the selected control |
|  | Database Window | Switches to the Database window |
|  | Undo | Undoes your most recent action |
|  | Cue Cards | Displays the main menu for the Cue Cards, which coach you through tasks |
|  | Help | Opens Microsoft Access Help showing information based on the next item you click |

## Form View

| Button | Button Name | Description |
| --- | --- | --- |
|  | Design View | Switches you to the Design view of a table, query, or form |
| 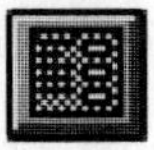 | Form View | Switches you to the Form view of a form |
|  | Datasheet View | Switches you to the Datasheet view of a table, query, or form |
|  | Print | Prints the form |
|  | Print Preview | Displays the form as it will appear when printed |

| Button | Button Name | Description |
|---|---|---|
|  | New | Moves to a blank record for making new entries |
| 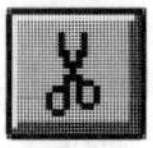 | Cut | Cuts the selection to the Clipboard |
|  | Copy | Copies the selection to the Clipboard |
|  | Paste | Pastes the contents of the Clipboard into the current location |
|  | Find | Opens the Find window, allowing you to search the active table or dynaset for the data you specify |
|  | Sort Ascending | Sorts the records according to the current field from lowest to highest values |
|  | Sort Descending | Sorts the records according to the current field from highest to lowest values |
|  | Edit Filter/Sort | Opens the Filter window to create or edit a filter |
|  | Apply/Sort Filter | Applies the current filter |
|  | Show All Records | Displays all records in the underlying table by removing any applied filters |
|  | Database Window | Switches to the Database window |
|  | Undo Current Field/Record | Restores the field or record contents to the pre-edited state |
|  | Undo | Undoes your most recent action |
|  | Cue Cards | Displays the main menu for the Cue Cards, which coach you through tasks |
|  | Help | Opens Microsoft Access Help showing information based on the next item you click |

## Macro

| Button | Button Name | Description |
|---|---|---|
| | Save | Saves the displayed macro |
| | Macro Names | Displays or conceals the Macro Name column used to designate macro names within a macro group |
| | Conditions | Displays or conceals the Condition column used to enter conditions that determine whether an action is performed in a macro |
| | Run | Executes the displayed macro |
| | Step Into | Executes a macro one step (an action or statement) at a time |
| | Database Window | Switches to the Database window |
| | Build | Opens a builder for the current location |
| | Undo | Undoes your most recent action |
| | Cue Cards | Displays the main menu for the Cue Cards, which coach you through tasks |
| | Help | Opens Microsoft Access Help showing information based on the next item you click |

## Module Window

| Button | Button Name | Description |
|---|---|---|
| | Save | Saves the current module |
| (general) | Object | Selects the object with the event procedures displayed in the Module window |

| Button | Button Name | Description |
|---|---|---|
| (declarations) | Procedure | Selects the procedure or declarations section displayed in the Module window |
| | Previous Procedure | Displays the previous Access Basic procedure in the Module window |
| | Next Procedure | Displays the next Access Basic procedure in the Module window |
| | New Procedure | Creates a new procedure in the Module window |
| | Run | Executes the displayed procedure |
| | Compile Loaded Modules | Compiles all loaded modules in the database |
| | Step Into | Executes the Access Basic procedure one step (an action or statement) at a time |
| | Step Over | Moves you through the Access Basic code one procedure at a time |
| | Reset | Stops execution of Access Basic procedures and clears all variables |
| | Breakpoint | Sets or clears a breakpoint on the current line of code |
| | Build | Opens a builder for the current location |
| | Immediate Window | Displays or hides the Immediate window, used to test or debug code |
| | Calls | View procedure calls |
| | Undo | Undoes your most recent action |
| | Help | Opens Microsoft Access Help showing information based on the next item you click |

## Print Preview

| Button | Button Name | Description |
| --- | --- | --- |
| | Close Window | Closes the Print Preview window |
| | Print | Prints the datasheet, form, or report |
| | Print Setup | Displays the Print Setup dialog box |
| | Zoom | Switches between showing a magnified portion of the page or the entire page |
| | Publish It with MS Word | Saves the object being viewed as a Microsoft Word for Windows document and opens Word to view it |
| | Analyze It with MS Excel | Saves the object being viewed as a Microsoft Excel document and opens Excel to view it |
| | Mail It | Sends the object being viewed as an electronic mail message |
| | Database Window | Switches back to the Database window |
| | Cue Cards | Displays the main menu for the Cue Cards, which coach you through tasks |
| | Help | Opens Microsoft Access Help showing information based on the next item you click |

## Toolbox

| Button | Button Name | Description |
| --- | --- | --- |
| | Select objects | Lets you select controls and objects |
| | Label | Adds a label control |
| | Text Box | Adds a text box control |

| Button | Button Name | Description |
|---|---|---|
|  | Option Group | Adds an option group control |
|  | Toggle Button | Adds a toggle button control |
| 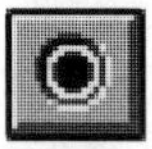 | Option Button | Adds an option button control |
|  | Check Box | Adds a check box control |
|  | Combo Box | Adds a combo box control |
|  | List Box | Adds a list box control |
| 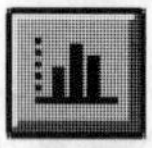 | Graph | Adds a graph control |
|  | Subform/ Subreport | Adds a subform/subreport control |
|  | Object Frame | Adds an unbound object frame control |
|  | Bound Object Frame | Adds a bound object frame control |
|  | Line | Adds a line control |
|  | Rectangle | Adds a rectangle control |
|  | Page Break | Adds a page break control |
|  | Command Button | Adds a command button control |
| 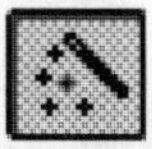 | Control Wizards | Sets Access to start the Option Group, Combo Box, List Box, or Command Button Wizards when you add these controls |
|  | Tool Lock | Keeps the same tool selected after you add a control to the design |

The owner of this business is
WHSmith Limited
Registered number 237811 England
Registered office
Strand House, 7 Holbein Place,
London SW1W 8NR

VAT No. 238 5548 36

Thank You For Shopping At



| Button Name | Description |
|---|---|
| Normal Appearance | Gives the selected control or section a normal appearance |
| Raised Appearance | Gives the selected control or section a raised appearance |
| Sunken Appearance | Gives the selected control or section a sunken appearance |
| Hairline Border Width | Gives the selected control a hairline border |
|  1-pt. Border Width | Gives the selected control a 1-point border |
|  2-pt. Border Width | Gives the selected control a 2-point border |
|  3-pt. Border Width | Gives the selected control a 3-point border |
| 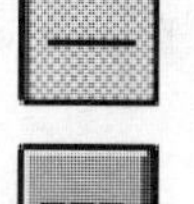 Solid | Gives the selected control a solid border |
| Dashes | Gives the selected control a dashed border |
| 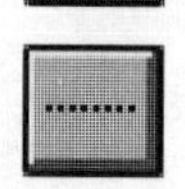 Dots | Gives the selected control a dotted border |
| 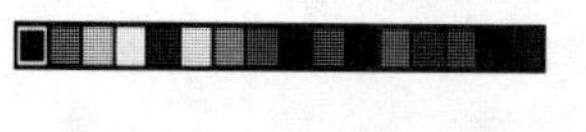 Fore Color | Assigns the color of text and the front color of patterns in the selected control |
| 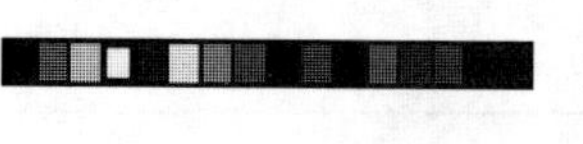 Back Color | Assigns the color for the background of the selected control |
|  Transparent Background | Makes the background transparent |

| Button | Button Name | Description |
|---|---|---|
| | Border Color | Assigns the color for the border of the selected control |
| Clear | Transparent Border | Removes the border from the selected control |

## Microsoft

| Button | Button Name | Description |
|---|---|---|
| | Switch to MS Word | Switches to Microsoft Word for Windows, opening it if necessary |
| | Switch to MS Excel | Switches to Microsoft Excel, opening it if necessary |
| | Switch to MS Mail | Switches to Microsoft Mail, opening it if necessary |
| | Switch to MS PowerPoint | Switches to Microsoft PowerPoint, opening it if necessary |
| | Switch to MS FoxPro | Switches to Microsoft FoxPro, opening it if necessary |
| | Switch to MS Project | Switches to Microsoft Project, opening it if necessary |
| | Switch to MS Schedule+ | Switches to Microsoft Schedule+, opening it if necessary |

## Filter/Sort

| Button | Button Name | Description |
|---|---|---|
| | Save | Saves the currently defined filter as a filter |
| | Apply Filter/Sort | Applies the currently defined filter |
| | Database Window | Switches to the Database window |

| Button | Button Name | Description |
| --- | --- | --- |
| | Undo | Undoes your last action |
| | Cue Cards | Displays the main menu for the Cue Cards, which coach you through tasks |
| | Help | Opens Microsoft Access Help showing information based on the item you click next |

# Appendix F

Databases

Tables

Queries

Forms and Reports

Macros

# Limits in Microsoft Access

As you start creating your database, you may be curious to know the limitations Access places on various features. These limitations are not very restrictive, so usually you won't have to worry about them. For example, the largest possible database file is 1 gigabyte, which is much larger than most hard drives. However, you may need to know that "Snugglebunnies" (14 characters) is the longest possible password you can create, and therefore "JohnLawrenceThird" (17 characters) is too long. These limitations are useful checkpoints while you are designing a new database to make sure that what you are designing is acceptable to Access.

## Databases

| Feature | Maximum |
| --- | --- |
| .MDB file size | 1 gigabyte |
| Characters in object names (tables, queries, forms, reports, modules, or macros) | 64 |
| Characters in passwords | 14 |
| Characters in user or group name | 20 |
| Concurrent users | 255 |
| Database size | As large as available memory capacity, assuming you attach files instead of adding them to the database file |
| Objects in database file | 32,768 |

## Tables

| Feature | Maximum |
|---|---|
| Characters in a field property setting | 255 |
| Characters in a field name | 64 |
| Characters in a Memo data field | 64,000 |
| Characters in a record, not including the Memo and OLE Object data fields | 2,000 |
| Characters in a Text data field | 255 |
| Characters in a validation message | 255 |
| Characters in a validation rule | 2,048 |
| Fields in a table | 255 |
| Fields in an index | 10 |
| Indexes in a table | 32 |
| Number of characters in a table or field description | 255 |
| Size of OLE Object field | 1 gigabyte |
| Table size | 1 gigabyte |

## Queries

| Feature | Maximum |
|---|---|
| AND's in a WHERE or HAVING clause | 40 |
| Characters in a QBE grid cell | 1,024 |
| Characters in an SQL statement | 64,000 |
| Dynaset size | 1 gigabyte |
| Fields in a dynaset | 255 |
| Levels of nested queries | 50 |
| Sorted fields in a query | 10 |
| Tables in a query | 32 |

## Forms and Reports

| Feature | Maximum |
| --- | --- |
| Characters in a label control | 2,048 |
| Characters in a text box control | 64,000 |
| Fields/expressions you can sort or group by | 10 |
| Form or report width | 22 inches (55.87 cm) |
| Height of all sections and headers in Design view | 200 inches (508 cm) |
| Levels of nested forms and reports | 3 |
| Printed pages in a report | 65,536 |
| Report headers and footers | 1 report header/footer<br>1 page header/footer<br>10 group headers/footers |
| Section height | 22 inches (55.87 cm) |

## Macros

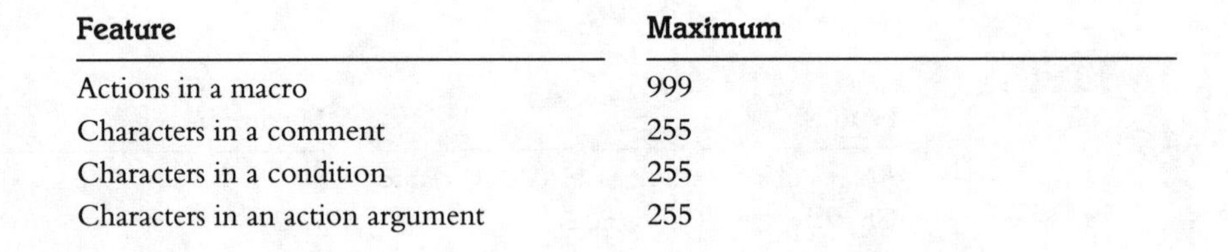

| Feature | Maximum |
| --- | --- |
| Actions in a macro | 999 |
| Characters in a comment | 255 |
| Characters in a condition | 255 |
| Characters in an action argument | 255 |

# Index



## A

## B



## C

## D

## E

## F

## M

## N

## P

## S

# T

## X



## Y



## Z

Some of Access' function key assignments are global, which means that these function keys do the same thing all the time. Other function keys are specific to views or windows. These keys may not be used in all views or windows, or they may have a different purpose in one window than they do in another. Therefore, the function keys are listed in four sections. The first section explains the global function key assignments, the second explains the function keys used in the Design view, the third explains the function keys used in the Datasheet and Form views, and the fourth explains the function keys used in the Module window.

## Global Function Keys

| Press | To |
|---|---|
| F1 | Display Help with information about the selected command, dialog box, property, control, action, Access Basic keyword, or window. |
| F11 | Bring the Database window to the front. |
| F12 | Open the Save As dialog box. |
| SHIFT+F1 | Display the question mark pointer instead of the normal mouse pointer. Click the question mark pointer on a screen object for which you want more information. |
| SHIFT+F12 | Save a database object. |
| CTRL+F4 | Close the active window. |
| CTRL+F6 | Cycle between open windows. |
| ALT+F1 | Bring the Database window to the front. |
| ALT+F2 | Open the Save As dialog box. |
| ALT+F4 | Close a dialog box or quit Access. |
| ALT+SHIFT+F2 | Save a database object. |

## Design View Function Keys

| Press | To |
|---|---|
| F2 | Toggle between showing an insertion point and selecting the field in the Design view of tables, queries, and macros. |
| F6 | Toggle between the top and bottom portions of the window in the Design view of tables and queries and the Filter window. |
| SHIFT+F2 | Open the Zoom box to enter text more conveniently into small input areas. |

## Datasheet and Form View Function Keys

| Press | To |
|---|---|
| F2 | Toggle between showing an insertion point and selecting a field. |
| F4 | Open a combo or list box. |
| F5 | Move to the Record Number box. Enter the record number you want to move to and press ENTER. |
| F6 | In Form view, cycle forward through the header, detail section, and footer of a form. |
| F7 | Open the Find dialog box. |
| F8 | Activate Extend mode. Keep pressing this key to extend the selection to the word, field, record, and all records. Cancel Extend mode by pressing ESC. |
| F9 | Recalculate the fields in the window. |
| SHIFT+F4 | Find the next occurrence of the text you specified without reopening the Find or Replace dialog box. |
| SHIFT+F6 | In Form view, cycle backward through the header, detail, and footer sections of a form. |
| SHIFT+F7 | Open the Replace dialog box. |
| SHIFT+F8 | Reverse the selection made with F8. To cancel Extend mode completely, press ESC. |
| SHIFT+F9 | Requery the underlying tables. In a subform, only the tables underlying the subform are requeried. |

## Module Window Function Keys

| Press | To |
|---|---|
| F2 | View procedures. |
| F3 | Find the next occurrence of the text you specified without reopening the Find or Replace dialog box. |
| F5 | Continue execution. |
| F6 | Toggle between the upper and lower panes when the window has been split. |
| F7 | Open the Find dialog box. |
| F8 | Run in single-step mode. |
| F9 | Toggle a breakpoint at the selected line. |
| SHIFT+F2 | Go to the procedures selected by the insertion point's location. |
| SHIFT+F3 | Find the previous occurrence of the text you specified without reopening the Find or Replace dialog boxes. |
| SHIFT+F7 | Open the Replace dialog box. |
| SHIFT+F8 | Runs the Access Basic code one procedure at a time. |